Handbook of Research on Machine and Deep Learning Applications for Cyber Security

Padmavathi Ganapathi
Avinashilingam Institute for Home Science and Higher Education for Women, India

D. Shanmugapriya
Avinashilingam Institute for Home Science and Higher Education for Women, India

A volume in the Advances in Information Security, Privacy, and Ethics (AISPE) Book Series

Published in the United States of America by
    IGI Global
    Information Science Reference (an imprint of IGI Global)
    701 E. Chocolate Avenue
    Hershey PA, USA 17033
    Tel: 717-533-8845
    Fax: 717-533-8661
    E-mail: cust@igi-global.com
    Web site: http://www.igi-global.com

Library of Congress Cataloging-in-Publication Data

Names: Ganapathi, Padmavathi, 1964- editor. | Shanmugapriya, D., 1978- editor.
Title: Handbook of research on machine and deep learning applications for cyber security / Padmavathi
   Ganapathi and D. Shanmugapriya, editors.
Description: Hershey, PA : Information Science Reference (an imprint of IGI
   Global), [2020] | Includes bibliographical references.
Identifiers: LCCN 2019005217| ISBN 9781522596110 (h/c) | ISBN 9781522596134
   (eISBN) | ISBN 9781522596127 (s/c)
Subjects: LCSH: Computer networks--Security measures. | Computer
   security--Data processing. | Computer crimes--Prevention--Data processing.
   | Machine learning.
Classification: LCC TK5105.59 .M325 2020 | DDC 006.3/1--dc23 LC record available at https://lccn.loc.gov/2019005217

This book is published in the IGI Global book series Advances in Information Security, Privacy, and Ethics (AISPE) (ISSN: 1948-9730; eISSN: 1948-9749)

British Cataloguing in Publication Data
A Cataloguing in Publication record for this book is available from the British Library.

For electronic access to this publication, please contact: eresources@igi-global.com.

Advances in Information Security, Privacy, and Ethics (AISPE) Book Series

Manish Gupta
State University of New York, USA

ISSN:1948-9730
EISSN:1948-9749

MISSION

As digital technologies become more pervasive in everyday life and the Internet is utilized in ever increasing ways by both private and public entities, concern over digital threats becomes more prevalent.

The **Advances in Information Security, Privacy, & Ethics (AISPE) Book Series** provides cutting-edge research on the protection and misuse of information and technology across various industries and settings. Comprised of scholarly research on topics such as identity management, cryptography, system security, authentication, and data protection, this book series is ideal for reference by IT professionals, academicians, and upper-level students.

COVERAGE

- Electronic Mail Security
- Security Classifications
- Cookies
- Tracking Cookies
- Security Information Management
- IT Risk
- Cyberethics
- Internet Governance
- Computer ethics
- Privacy-Enhancing Technologies

IGI Global is currently accepting manuscripts for publication within this series. To submit a proposal for a volume in this series, please contact our Acquisition Editors at Acquisitions@igi-global.com or visit: http://www.igi-global.com/publish/.

Titles in this Series

For a list of additional titles in this series, please visit: www.igi-global.com/book-series

Developments in Information Security and Cybernetic Wars
Muhammad Sarfraz (Kuwait University, Kuwait)
Information Science Reference • ©2019 • 351pp • H/C (ISBN: 9781522583042) • US $225.00

Cybersecurity Education for Awareness and Compliance
Ismini Vasileiou (University of Plymouth, UK) and Steven Furnell (University of Plymouth, UK)
Information Science Reference • ©2019 • 306pp • H/C (ISBN: 9781522578475) • US $195.00

Detection and Mitigation of Insider Attacks in a Cloud Infrastructure Emerging Research and Opportunities
T. Gunasekhar (Koneru Lakshmaiah Education Foundation, India) K. Thirupathi Rao (Koneru Lakshmaiah Education Foundation, India) P. Sai Kiran (Koneru Lakshmaiah Education Foundation, India) V. Krishna Reddy (Koneru Lakshmaiah Education Foundation, India) and B. Thirumala Rao (Koneru Lakshmaiah Education Foundation, India)
Information Science Reference • ©2019 • 113pp • H/C (ISBN: 9781522579243) • US $165.00

Network Security and Its Impact on Business Strategy
Ionica Oncioiu (European Academy of the Regions, Belgium)
Business Science Reference • ©2019 • 289pp • H/C (ISBN: 9781522584551) • US $225.00

Exploring Security in Software Architecture and Design
Michael Felderer (University of Innsbruck, Austria) and Riccardo Scandariato (Chalmers University of Technology, Sweden & University of Gothenburg, Sweden)
Information Science Reference • ©2019 • 349pp • H/C (ISBN: 9781522563136) • US $215.00

Cryptographic Security Solutions for the Internet of Things
Mohammad Tariq Banday (University of Kashmir, India)
Information Science Reference • ©2019 • 367pp • H/C (ISBN: 9781522557425) • US $195.00

Advanced Methodologies and Technologies in System Security, Information Privacy, and Forensics
Mehdi Khosrow-Pour, D.B.A. (Information Resources Management Association, USA)
Information Science Reference • ©2019 • 417pp • H/C (ISBN: 9781522574927) • US $285.00

Handbook of Research on Information and Cyber Security in the Fourth Industrial Revolution
Ziska Fields (University of KwaZulu-Natal, South Africa)
Information Science Reference • ©2018 • 647pp • H/C (ISBN: 9781522547631) • US $345.00

701 East Chocolate Avenue, Hershey, PA 17033, USA
Tel: 717-533-8845 x100 • Fax: 717-533-8661
E-Mail: cust@igi-global.com • www.igi-global.com

List of Contributors

Table of Contents

Detailed Table of Contents

    P. Subashini, Avinshilingam Institute for Home Science and Higher Education for Women,
        India
    M. Krishnaveni, Avinashilingam Institute for Home Science and Higher Education for
        Women, India
    T. T. Dhivyaprabha, Avinashilingam Institute for Home Science and Higher Education for
        Women, India
    R. Shanmugavalli, Avinashilingam Institute for Home Science and Higher Education for
        Women, India

Cyber security comprises of technologies, architecture, infrastructure, and software applications that are designed to protect computational resources against cyber-attacks. Cyber security concentrates on four main areas such as application security, disaster security, information security, and network security. Numerous cyber security algorithms and computational methods are introduced by researchers to protect cyberspace from undesirable invaders and susceptibilities. But, the performance of traditional cyber security algorithms suffers due to different types of offensive actions that target computer infrastructures, architectures and computer networks. The implementation of intelligent algorithms in encountering the wide range of cyber security problems is surveyed, namely, nature-inspired computing (NIC) paradigms, machine learning algorithms, and deep learning algorithms, based on exploratory analyses to identify the advantages of employing in enhancing cyber security techniques.

    Thiyagarajan P., Central University of Tamil Nadu, India

Digitalization is the buzz word today by which every walk of our life has been computerized, and it has made our life more sophisticated. On one side, we are enjoying the privilege of digitalization. On the other side, security of our information in the internet is the most concerning element. A variety of security mechanisms, namely cryptography, algorithms which provide access to protected information, and authentication including biometric and steganography, provide security to our information in the Internet. In spite of the above mechanisms, recently artificial intelligence (AI) also contributes towards strengthening information security by providing machine learning and deep learning-based security mechanisms. The artificial intelligence (AI) contribution to cyber security is important as it serves as a provoked reaction and a response to hackers' malicious actions. The purpose of this chapter is to survey recent papers which are contributing to information security by using machine learning and deep learning techniques.

Chapter 3

Thangavel M., Thiagarajar College of Engineering, India
Abiramie Shree T. G. R., Thiagarajar College of Engineering, India
Priyadharshini P., Thiagarajar College of Engineering, India
Saranya T., Thiagarajar College of Engineering, India

In today's world, everyone is generating a large amount of data on their own. With this amount of data generation, there is a change of security compromise of our data. This leads us to extend the security needs beyond the traditional approach which emerges the field of cyber security. Cyber security's core functionality is to protect all types of information, which includes hardware and software from cyber threats. The number of threats and attacks is increasing each year with a high difference between them. Machine learning and deep learning applications can be done to this attack, reducing the complexity to solve the problem and helping us to recover very easily. The algorithms used by both approaches are support vector machine (SVM), Bayesian algorithm, deep belief network (DBN), and deep random neural network (Deep RNN). These techniques provide better results than that of the traditional approach. The companies which use this approach in the real time scenarios are also covered in this chapter.

Chapter 4

Sailesh Suryanarayan Iyer, R. B. Institute of Management Studies, India
Sridaran Rajagopal, Marwadi University, India

Knowledge revolution is transforming the globe from traditional society to a technology-driven society. Online transactions have compounded, exposing the world to a new demon called cybercrime. Human beings are being replaced by devices and robots, leading to artificial intelligence. Robotics, image processing, machine vision, and machine learning are changing the lifestyle of citizens. Machine learning contains algorithms which are capable of learning from historical occurrences. This chapter discusses the concept of machine learning, cyber security, cybercrime, and applications of machine learning in cyber security domain. Malware detection and network intrusion are a few areas where machine learning and deep learning can be applied. The authors have also elaborated on the research advancements and challenges in machine learning related to cyber security. The last section of this chapter lists the future trends and directions in machine learning and cyber security.

Chapter 5

Charu Virmani, Manav Rachna International Institute of Research and Studies, India
Tanu Choudhary, Manav Rachna International Institute of Research and Studies, India
Anuradha Pillai, J. C. Bose University of Science and Technology YMCA, India
Manisha Rani, D. N. College, India

With the exponential rise in technological awareness in the recent decades, technology has taken over our lives for good, but with the application of computer-aided technological systems in various domains of our day-to-day lives, the potential risks and threats have also come to the fore, aiming at the various security features that include confidentiality, integrity, authentication, authorization, and so on. Computer scientists the world over have tried to come up, time and again, with solutions to these impending problems. With time, attackers have played out complicated attacks on systems that are hard to comprehend and even harder to mitigate. The very fact that a huge amount of data is processed each second in organizations gave birth to the concept of Big Data, thereby making the systems more adept and intelligent in dealing with unprecedented attacks on a real-time basis. This chapter presents a study about applications of machine learning algorithms in cyber security.

Chapter 6

This chapter aims to discuss applications of machine learning in cyber security and explore how machine learning algorithms help to fight cyber-attacks. Cyber-attacks are wide and varied in multiple forms. The key benefit of machine learning algorithms is that it can deep dive and analyze system behavior and identify anomalies which do not correlate with expected behavior. Algorithms can be trained to observe multiple data sets and strategize payload beforehand in detection of malware analysis.

Chapter 7

Cyberspace plays a dominant role in the world of electronic communication. It is a virtual space where the interconnecting network has an independent technology infrastructure. The internet is the baseline for the cyberspace which can be openly accessible. Cyber-security is a set of techniques used to protect network integrity and data from vulnerability. The protection mechanism involves the identification of threats and taking precaution by predicting the vulnerabilities in the environment. The main cause of security violation will be threats, that are caused by the intruder who attacks the network or any electronic devices with the intention to cause damage in the communication network. These threats must be taken into consideration for the mitigation process to improve the system efficiency and performance. Machine learning helps to increase the accuracy level in the detection of threats and their mitigation process in an efficient way. This chapter describes the way in which threats can be detected and mitigated in cyberspace with certain strategies using machine learning.

Chapter 8

In recent years, the field of machine learning grows very fast both on the development of techniques and its application in intrusion detection. The computational complexity of the machine learning algorithms increases rapidly as the number of features in the datasets increases. By choosing the significant features, the number of features in the dataset can be reduced, which is critical to progress the classification accuracy and speed of algorithms. Also, achieving high accuracy and detection rate and lowering false alarm rates are the major challenges in designing an intrusion detection system. The major motivation of this work is to address these issues by hybridizing machine learning and swarm intelligence algorithms for enhancing the performance of intrusion detection system. It also emphasizes applying principal component analysis as feature selection technique on intrusion detection dataset for identifying the most suitable feature subsets which may provide high-quality results in a fast and efficient manner.

>   *Manokaran Newlin Rajkumar, Anna University Coimbatore, India*
>   *Varadhan Venkatesa Kumar, Anna University Coimbatore, India*
>   *Ramachandhiran Vijayabhasker, Anna University Coimbatore, India*

This modern era of technological advancements facilitates the people to possess high-end smart phones with incredible features. With the increase in the number of mobile applications, we are witnessing the humongous increase in the malicious applications. Since most of the Android applications are available open source and used frequently in the smart phones, they are more vulnerable. Statistical and dynamical-based malware detection approaches are available to verify whether the mobile application is a genuine one, but only to a certain extent, as the level of mobile application scanning done by the said approaches are in general routine or a common, pre-specified pattern using the structure of control flow, information flow, API call, etc. A hybrid method based on deep learning methodology is proposed to identify the malicious applications in Android-based smart phones in this chapter, which embeds the possible merits of both the statistical-based malware detection approaches and dynamical-based malware detection approaches and minimizes the demerits of them.

Chapter 10

>   *Jorge Maestre Vidal, Indra, Spain*
>   *Marco Antonio Sotelo Monge, Universidad Complutense de Madrid, Spain*
>   *Sergio Mauricio Martínez Monterrubio, Universidad Complutense de Madrid, Spain*

Anomaly-based intrusion detection has become an indispensable player on the existing cybersecurity landscape, where it enables the identification of suspicious behaviors that significantly differ from normal activities. In this way, it is possible to discover never-seen-before threats and provide zero-day recognition capabilities. But the recent advances on communication technologies are leading to changes in the monitoring scenarios that result in novel challenges to be taken into consideration, as is the case of greater data heterogeneity, adversarial attacks, energy consumption, or lack of up-to-date datasets. With the aim on bringing the reader closer to them, this chapter deepens the following topics: evolution of the anomaly definition, anomaly recognition for network-based intrusion detection, outlier characterizations, knowledge acquisition for usage modelling, distances and similarity measures for decision-making, anomaly recognition and non-stationarity, metrics and evaluation methodologies, and challenges related with the emergent monitorization environments.

Chapter 11

Vanitha N., Avinashilingam Institute for Home Science and Higher Education for Women,
India & Dr. N. G. P. Arts and Science College, India
Padmavathi Ganapathi, Avinashilingam Institute for Home Science and Higher Education
for Women, India

The world is moving to an autonomous era. Autonomous vehicles take a major role in day-to-day activity, helping human personnel do work quickly and independently. Unmanned aerial vehicles (UAVs) are autonomous vehicles controlled using remotes in ground station by human personnel. These UAVs act as a network that plays a vital role in the digital era. There are different architectures of UAV networks available. This chapter concentrates on centralized UAV network. Because of wireless and autonomy characteristics, these networks are prone to various security issues, so it's very important to monitor and analyze the traffic of the UAV network in order to identify the intrusions. This chapter proposes enhanced deep feed forward neural network (EDFFNN) in order to monitor and analyze the traffic of the UAV network to detect the intrusions with maximum detection rate of 94.4%. The results have been compared with the previous method of intrusion detection.

Chapter 12

Sasirekha K., Periyar University, India
Thangavel K., Periyar University, India

For a long time, image enhancement techniques have been widely used to improve the image quality in many image processing applications. Recently, deep learning models have been applied to image enhancement problems with great success. In the domain of biometric, fingerprint and face play a vital role to authenticate a person in the right way. Hence, the enhancement of these images significantly improves the recognition rate. In this chapter, undecimated wavelet transform (UDWT) and deep autoencoder are hybridized to enhance the quality of images. Initially, the images are decomposed with Daubechies wavelet filter. Then, deep autoencoder is trained to minimize the error between reconstructed and actual input. The experiments have been conducted on real-time fingerprint and face images collected from 150 subjects, each with 10 orientations. The signal to noise ratio (SNR), peak signal to noise ratio (PSNR), mean square error (MSE), and root mean square error (RMSE) have been computed and compared. It was observed that the proposed model produced a biometric image with high quality.

Chapter 13

Rosemary Koikara, Kyungpook National University, South Korea
Eun-Joon Yoon, Kyungil Univeristy, South Korea
Anand Paul, Kyungpook National University, South Korea

In secret sharing, a secret is distributed between various participants in a manner that an authorized group of participants in the appropriate access structures can recover this secret. However, a dealer might get corrupted by adversaries and may influence this secret sharing or the reconstruction process. Verifiable secret sharing (VSS) overcomes this issue by adding a verifiability protocol to the original secret sharing scheme. This chapter discusses a computationally secure publicly verifiable secret sharing scheme constructed using the three-dimensional cellular automata (3D CA). The initial configuration of the 3D CA is the secret. The following configurations are devised to be the shares distributed among the participants. Update mechanisms and various rules make it hard for an adversary to corrupt or duplicate a share. To make it even more efficient, the authors added a verifiability layer such that a dealer posts a public share and a private share to each shareholder. The NIST test suite has been used to calculate the randomness of the shares.

Chapter 14

Luis Filipe Dias, Instituto Universitário Militar, Portugal
Miguel Correia, Universidade de Lisboa, Portugal

Intrusion detection has become a problem of big data, with a semantic gap between vast security data sources and real knowledge about threats. The use of machine learning (ML) algorithms on big data has already been successfully applied in other domains. Hence, this approach is promising for dealing with cyber security's big data problem. Rather than relying on human analysts to create signatures or classify huge volumes of data, ML can be used. ML allows the implementation of advanced algorithms to extract information from data using behavioral analysis or to find hidden correlations. However, the adversarial setting and the dynamism of the cyber threat landscape stand as difficult challenges when applying ML. The next generation security information and event management (SIEM) systems should provide security monitoring with the means for automation, orchestration and real-time contextual threat awareness. However, recent research shows that further work is needed to fulfill these requirements. This chapter presents a survey on recent work on big data analytics for intrusion detection.

Chapter 15

Valliammal Narayan, Avinashilingam Institute for Home Science and Higher Education for
Women, India
Shanmugapriya D., Avinashilingam Institute for Home Science and Higher Education for
Women, India

Information is vital for any organization to communicate through any network. The growth of internet utilization and the web users increased the cyber threats. Cyber-attacks in the network change the traffic flow of each system. Anomaly detection techniques have been developed for different types of cyber-attack or anomaly strategies. Conventional ADS protect information transferred through the network or cyber attackers. The stable prevention of anomalies by machine and deep-learning algorithms are applied for cyber-security. Big data solutions handle voluminous data in a short span of time. Big data management is the organization and manipulation of huge volumes of structured data, semi-structured data and unstructured data, but it does not handle a data imbalance problem during the training process. Big data-based machine and deep-learning algorithms for anomaly detection involve the classification of decision boundary between normal traffic flow and anomaly traffic flow. The performance of anomaly detection is efficiently increased by different algorithms.

Chapter 16

Anitha J., Dayananda Sagar Academy of Technology and Management, India
Prasad S. P., Dayananda Sagar Academy of Technology and Management, India

Due to recent technological development, a huge amount of data generated by social networking, sensor networks, internet, etc., adds more challenges when performing data storage and processing tasks. During PPDP, the collected data may contain sensitive information about the data owner. Directly releasing this for further processing may violate the privacy of the data owner, hence data modification is needed so that it does not disclose any personal information. The existing techniques of data anonymization have a fixed scheme with a small number of dimensions. There are various types of attacks on the privacy of data like linkage attack, homogeneity attack, and background knowledge attack. To provide an effective technique in big data to maintain data privacy and prevent linkage attacks, this paper proposes a privacy preserving protocol, UNION, for a multi-party data provider. Experiments show that this technique provides a better data utility to handle high dimensional data, and scalability with respect to the data size compared with existing anonymization techniques.

Chapter 17

Swathy Akshaya M., Avinashilingam Institute for Home Science and Higher Education for
Women, India
Padmavathi Ganapathi, Avinashilingam Institute for Home Science and Higher Education
for Women, India

Cloud computing is an emerging technological paradigm that provides a flexible, scalable, and reliable infrastructure and services for organizations. Services of cloud computing is based on sharing; thus, it is open for attacker to attack on its security. The main thing that grabs the organizations to adapt the cloud computing technology is cost reduction through optimized and efficient computing, but there are various vulnerabilities and threats in cloud computing that affect its security. Providing security in such a system is a major concern as it uses public network to transmit data to a remote server. Therefore, the biggest problem of cloud computing system is its security. The objective of the chapter is to review Machine learning methods that are applied to handle zero-day attacks in a cloud environment.

Chapter 18

Rama Mercy Sam Sigamani, Avinashilingam Institute for Home Science and Higher
Education for Women, India

The cyber physical system safety and security is the major concern on the incorporated components with interface standards, communication protocols, physical operational characteristics, and real-time sensing. The seamless integration of computational and distributed physical components with intelligent mechanisms increases the adaptability, autonomy, efficiency, functionality, reliability, safety, and usability of cyber-physical systems. In IoT-enabled cyber physical systems, cyber security is an essential challenge due to IoT devices in industrial control systems. Computational intelligence algorithms have been proposed to detect and mitigate the cyber-attacks in cyber physical systems, smart grids, power systems. The various machine learning approaches towards securing CPS is observed based on the performance metrics like detection accuracy, average classification rate, false negative rate, false positive rate, processing time per packet. A unique feature of CPS is considered through structural adaptation which facilitates a self-healing CPS.

Chapter 19

Dhamodharavadhani S., Periyar University, India
Rathipriya R., Periyar University, India

Regression model (RM) is an important tool for modeling and analyzing data. It is one of the popular predictive modeling techniques which explore the relationship between a dependent (target) and independent (predictor) variables. The variable selection method is used to form a good and effective regression model. Many variable selection methods existing for regression model such as filter method, wrapper method, embedded methods, forward selection method, Backward Elimination methods, stepwise methods, and so on. In this chapter, computational intelligence-based variable selection method is discussed with respect to the regression model in cybersecurity. Generally, these regression models depend on the set of (predictor) variables. Therefore, variable selection methods are used to select the best subset of predictors from the entire set of variables. Genetic algorithm-based quick-reduct method is proposed to extract optimal predictor subset from the given data to form an optimal regression model.

Foreword

'Cyber security' can be visualized as anassortment of technologies, techniques, processes, and policies to protect the Confidentiality, Integrity, and Availability (CIA) triad of the compute, network, software and data resources. The expeditious technological advancements in each dimension of computing and the popularity of the Internet have resulted in a scenario wherein the people's day-to-day activities heavily rely on the information systems. Since these information systems are open to the Internet, there has been an increasing awareness of the socio-economic impacts associated with the ever-advancing cyberattacks. Many business and academic organizations realize the need for the use of advanced security tools and techniques to protect their information system and networks from the adverse impacts of malicious activities. On the other end, cyber security researchers and professionals put up more efforts to design a powerful and adaptive algorithms to enhance the efficiency of the security tools and techniques in terms of high detection rate and less false alarm rate.

Over the past few decades, cyber security research areas like intrusion detection, spam detection, malware analysis, etc. have been exploiting the complete benefits ofmachine learning and deep learning techniques for the design of a set of efficient, accurate and robust defense in depth security models. Machine learning approaches outperform the traditional rule based security solutions, in turn, the better generalization ability of deep learning approaches enables them to provide significant performance improvements over the machine learning approaches. However, limited domain experts and difficulty in identifying the malicious activities due to impersonation, polymorphism, obfuscation, and compression poses a significant challenge in the field of cybersecurity irrespective of its applications in various domains like social networks, Internet of Things, smart grids, etc.

This book aims to bridge the gap between cybersecurity and machine learning & deep learning techniques by focusing on new, automated, and effective security solutions to replace traditional cyber security mechanisms. Each chapter of this book makes the readers walk through the recent advancements in machine learning and deep learning algorithms and their applications towards the development of intelligent and future-proof security solutions

V. S. Shankar Sriram
SASTRA University (Deemed), India

V. S. Shankar Sriram, *Professor and Associate Dean – Computer Science & Engineering, Chair Professor for TATA Communications – Cyber Security at School of Computing, SASTRA Deemed University, India, has long been associated with research in the area of Machine Learning and Network Security. He has received his Bachelor's degree in Science from Madurai Kamaraj*

University, Madurai, India and obtained his Master's degree in Computer Applications from Madurai Kamaraj University, Madurai, India. Also received Master's degree in Engineering from Thapar University, Punjab, India and conferred Ph.D. in Information and Network Security from Birla Institute of Technology, Mesra, India in 2011. He has been in the Academia for the past 18.5 years and a member of IEEE. He has a significant contribution in carrying out several research projects on the design of the computational models for various applications like Network Security, Bioinformatics, and Cloud Computing. His important research contribution includes design of Hypergraph-based computationally intelligent models for Intrusion Detection System (IDS) paves the way for the Government funded projects (ICPS-DST, MeitY) and received the IBM Shared University Research (SUR) Award' 2017. He has also guided number of research works, in which useful algorithms for Feature Selection, Classification, and Prediction have been developed and implemented. He has significant number of publications in Top-notch SCI/SCIE indexed journals.

Preface

Cyber security plays a predominant role in modern days as advanced technology is the primary concern. Every aspect of day-today routine is highly dependent on Internet which makes the system vulnerable to various advanced and severe cyber attacks which leads to lose of confidential information. Securing the Cyber space from attacks is one of the important research areas in the field of computer science. Various Machine Learning and Deep Learning methods are being applied to address the wide range of problems in cyber security. The book aims to collect quality and recent research findings in the area of cyber security and cyber attack handling mechanisms particularly by applying machine learning and Deep learning techniques which in turn will be beneficial to the people working in this field.

The purpose of editing this book is to provide latest research findings in the area of cyber security which applies Machine learning and deep learning techniques. The book will help the future researchers to identify their area of research in cyber security and narrow down their research. Also, the book will facilitate the researchers and scholars who are working in this area with in-sight knowledge of applying machine learning and deep learning for cyber security challenges. This book is aimed to provide a roadmap to recent research areas, challenges and countermeasures in cyber security research.

There are a total of 19 chapters in this edited book. Chapter 1 investigates the implementation of intelligent algorithms in encountering the wide range of cyber security problems by Nature Inspired Computing (NIC) paradigms, machine learning algorithms and deep learning algorithms based on which exploratory analyses can be done to identify the advantages of employing in enhancing cyber security techniques. Chapter 2 reviews recent papers which are contributing to information security by using machine learning and deep learning techniques. Chapter 3 covers common cyber threats and attacks happening in the world and discusses how these threats can be solved using machine learning and deep learning effectively. The chapter also elaborates the general application of machine learning and deep learning in real-world industrial problems. Chapter 4 discusses the concept of Machine Learning, Cyber Security, Cyber Crime and applications of Machine Learning in Cyber Security domain. It also elaborates on the research advancements, challenges in Machine Learning related to Cyber Security and lists the future trends and directions in Machine Learning and Cyber Security. Chapter 5 discusses the Applications of Machine Learning in cyber security. Chapter 6 discusses on applications of machine learning in cyber security and explore on how machine learning algorithms help in Malware and Anomaly Detection. Machine learning helps to increase the accuracy level in the detection of threats and their mitigation process in an efficient way. Chapter 7 describes the way in which threats can be detected and mitigated in cyberspace with certain strategies using machine learning. Chapter 8 address the issues of achieving high accuracy and detection rate and lowering false alarm rates in designing an intrusion detection system by hybridizing machine learning and swarm intelligence algorithms for enhancing the performance of intrusion detection system. This chapter also emphasis on applying Principal Component Analysis as feature selection technique on intrusion detection dataset for identifying the most suitable feature subsets. Chapter 9 proposes a hybrid method based on Deep learning Methodology to identify the Malicious Applications in Android based Smart Phones. This chapter embeds the possible merits of both the Statistical based Malware Detection Approaches and Dynamical based Malware Detection Approaches and minimizes the demerits of them. Chapter 10 comprehends the evolution of the anomaly definition; anomaly recognition for network-based intrusion detection; outlier characterizations; knowledge acquisition for usage modeling; distances and similarity measures for decision-making; anomaly recognition and non-stationarity; metrics and evaluation methodologies; and challenges related with the emergent monitorization environments. Chapter 11 proposes Enhanced Deep Feed Forward Neural network (EDFFNN) in order to monitor and analyse the traffic of the Unmanned aerial vehicles (UAV) network to detect the intrusions with maximum detection rate. Chapter 12 proposes a Biometric Image Enhancement Approach with the Hybridization of Undecimated Wavelet Transform and Deep Autoencoder. The experiments have been conducted on real-time fingerprint and face images collected from 150 subjects each with ten orientations. Chapter 13 discusses a computationally secure publicly verifiable secret sharing scheme constructed using the three-dimensional cellular automata (3D CA). The chapter added a verifiability layer such that a dealer posts a public share and a private share to each shareholder. The NIST test suite has been used to calculate the randomness of the shares. Chapter 14 presents an overview of recent work on big data analytics for intrusion detection. Chapter 15 presents Big data based machine and deep-learning algorithms for anomaly detection involving the classification of decision boundary between normal traffic flow and anomaly traffic flow. Chapter 16 proposes a privacy preserving protocol - UNION, for integrating distributed person specific data among multiple parties while preserving both privacy and information utility on the final published High dimensional integrated Bigdata. Since the Services of cloud computing is based on sharing which open up the way for attacker to attack on its security and providing security in such a system is a major concern as it uses public network to transmit data to a remote server. Chapter 17 briefs the Machine Learning Methods Applied for Handling Zero-Day Attacks in Cloud Environment. Chapter 18 discusses various machine learning approaches towards securing Cyber Physical System (CPS) based on the performance metrics like detection accuracy, average classification rate, false negative rate, false positive rate, processing time per packet. A unique feature of CPS is considered in this chapter through structural adaptation which facilitates a self-healing CPS. In the Chapter 19, Computational Intelligence based variable selection method is discussed with respect to the regression model in cyber security. The chapter apply variable selection methods to select the best subset of predictors from the entire set of variables. Genetic Algorithm based quick-reduct method is proposed to extract optimal predictor subset from the given data to form an optimal regression model.

Finally, in this book, we have carefully selected and included the chapters by considering their relevancy towards the applications of Machine Learning and Deep Learning in Cyber Security. Various graphical illustrations, images, diagrams, and tables which are included in each chapter will make these chapters easy to understand. We strongly believe that our enormous effort taken to bring these chapters together in the form of valuable book will help the Academicians, Research scholars, Industrial experts, Scientists, post graduate students who are willing to work / working in the field of Cyber Security.

Padmavathi Ganapathi
Avinashilingam Institute for Home Science and Higher Education for Women, India

D. Shanmugapriya
Avinashilingam Institute for Home Science and Higher Education for Women, India

Acknowledgment

We would like to thank IGI Global for offering us the opportunity to edit this book on Machine and Deep Learning Applications for Cyber Security. We are grateful to the Editorial Advisory Board Members for their support, assistance and suggestions. We thank all the valuable contributing authors of this book for their contribution.

Our sincere thanks are extended to all reviewers who provided insightful and constructive feedback on the contributed chapters.

Padmavathi Ganapathi
Avinashilingam Institute for Home Science and Higher Education for Women, India

D. Shanmugapriya
Avinashilingam Institute for Home Science and Higher Education for Women, India

Chapter 1
Review on Intelligent Algorithms for Cyber Security

P. Subashini

https://orcid.org/0000-0002-8603-6826

Avinshilingam Institute for Home Science and Higher Education for Women, India

M. Krishnaveni

Avinashilingam Institute for Home Science and Higher Education for Women, India

T. T. Dhivyaprabha

Avinashilingam Institute for Home Science and Higher Education for Women, India

R. Shanmugavalli

Avinashilingam Institute for Home Science and Higher Education for Women, India

ABSTRACT

Cyber security comprises of technologies, architecture, infrastructure, and software applications that are designed to protect computational resources against cyber-attacks. Cyber security concentrates on four main areas such as application security, disaster security, information security, and network security. Numerous cyber security algorithms and computational methods are introduced by researchers to protect cyberspace from undesirable invaders and susceptibilities. But, the performance of traditional cyber security algorithms suffers due to different types of offensive actions that target computer infrastructures, architectures and computer networks. The implementation of intelligent algorithms in encountering the wide range of cyber security problems is surveyed, namely, nature-inspired computing (NIC) paradigms, machine learning algorithms, and deep learning algorithms, based on exploratory analyses to identify the advantages of employing in enhancing cyber security techniques.

DOI: 10.4018/978-1-5225-9611-0.ch001

INTRODUCTION

In the recent scenarios, there is a significant growth in the usage of digital technologies, such as, Internet of Things (IoT), smart devices, sensors, cloud computing, big data, internet, mobile, wireless technologies and artificial intelligence covers that includes education, healthcare, communication, banking, government sector, armed force and enterprise in the world wide. The usages of digital technologies cause big challenges on the level of security, data protection and regulations followed by organizations to tackle threats in the cyber space. Providing and ensuring security mechanism in cyber space is a highly complex task. In order to meet these challenges, cyber security industry have developed several secured infrastructure, security algorithms, architecture and software applications to protect computational resources that involve software, hardware, electronic data and network from unauthorized access or vulnerability attacks that intended for exploitation. The primary areas covered in cyber security are application security, disaster security, information security and network security which are briefly stated below (Deepa, 2014). Application security focus on developing security measures to protect against threats detected in the application design, application development, deployment and maintenance. Disaster security deals with the development of cyber security processes that include developing risk assessment plans, setting priorities and establishing recovery strategies if any disaster occurred. Network security concentrates on ensuring protection, integrity, usability and reliability in the network connectivity. The components of network security include anti-virus or spyware, firewalls, virtual private network and intrusion prevention system to detect rapidly spreading threats in the computer networks. Finally, information security focuses on providing security to the information from unauthorized access. The statistical report and facts of cyber security in 2017-2018 posted (Dennis Anon on 11 September 2018) website states that Top 10 countries are affected by target attacks in which 303 known attacks present in Figure 1. It is understood that currently India occupies the second place with 133 cyber-attacks.

Cyber Security R & D Center (CSRDC) established by U.S. Department of Homeland Security has introduced several security technologies, infrastructures, operators and algorithms to protect vulnerable threats retrieved from 5 February 2019). Information Security Research Association (ISRA) is a non-profit organization which is focused on developing security technologies for web application security, wireless security, offensive security, malware protection and creates cyber security awareness in the society (retrieved from 5 February 2019). An Annual cyber security report released by Cisco states that mobile phone is the first device targeted by several attackers that are intended for exploitation. Overall, 34% security professionals completely focuses on machine learning and artificial intelligence techniques for developing cyber security algorithms to defend against intruders especially, IoT threats, ransomware, big data, cloud environment, damaging General Data Protection Regulation (GDPR), smart devices, insider attacks, sensors and crypto currency mining (retrieved from 5 February 2019) (retrieved from 5 February 2019). Specifically, NIC paradigms, machine learning algorithms and deep learning algorithms play a vital role to improve the performance of cyber security algorithms and enhanced information technology security protocols in the recent era. Intelligent algorithms are essential to develop strong cyber security strategies that defend against malicious attacks.

Intelligent algorithms have capability to discover hidden patterns and detect threats in the computer information systems. The development of hybrid cyber security methods and building computational systems that integrates with intelligent algorithms is needful to analyze big data, mitigate threats and protect against the new invaders. The implementation of optimization techniques is a continuous evolution process in improving the performance of cyber security algorithms in order to yield promising

Figure 1. Taxonomy of NIC algorithms

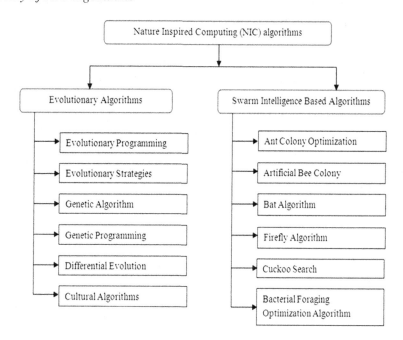

results. Optimization techniques are utilized in diverse perspectives, such as, parameter tuning, satisfy constraints, maximize or minimize objective function, feature selection, weight values optimization, meet multiple criteria, search strategy and finds trade-off solutions. The objective of this chapter is to review the implementation of NIC paradigms, machine learning algorithms and deep learning algorithms that covers a broad spectrum of cyber security problems. The overall aim of this chapter is to identify and summarize the need of aforementioned algorithms in solving cyber security applications. The proposed research work clearly states the need of intelligent algorithms in solving different kinds of cyber security problems and also, it infers the conceptual ideas, significances and implications of these algorithms that improve efficiency and effectiveness for obtaining quantitative and qualitative experimental outcomes. The proposed chapter would be greatly beneficial to different peer groups of people, namely, research scholars, academicians, scientists, industrial experts and post graduate students who are working in the cyber security research area based on intelligent algorithms.

NIC paradigms are partitioned into two categories, namely, Swarm Intelligence (SI) and Evolutionary Algorithm (EA) as shown in Figure 2. Swarm Intelligence includes Ant Colony Optimization (ACO), Artificial Bee Colony (ABC), Particle Swarm Optimization (PSO), Firefly Algorithm (FA), Cuckoo Search (CS) and Bacterial Foraging Optimization (BFO). Evolutionary algorithm includes Genetic

Figure 2. .A simplified view of computational intelligence

Algorithm (GA), Evolutionary Programming (EP), Memetic algorithm, Genetic Programming (GP), Evolutionary strategies, Differential Evolution (DE) and Cultural algorithms. Machine learning techniques is also partitioned into three categories, such as supervised adaptation, reinforcement adaptation and unsupervised adaptation which are described below. Linear regression, Logistic regression, Linear discriminant analysis, classification and regression trees, Naïve bayes, K-Nearest Neighbour (K-NN), K-means clustering Learning Vector Quantization (LVQ), Support Vector Machines (SVM), Random Forest, Monte Carlo, Neural networks and Q-learning are traditional examples of machine learning algorithms.

The abstract view of computational intelligence concept is depicted in Figure 3. It comprises adaptation and self-organization using processed data and embedded knowledge as input and produces predictions, decisions, generalizations and reason as output. Computational intelligence techniques partitioned adaptation characteristics into three categories, such as supervised adaptation, reinforcement adaptation and unsupervised adaptation portrayed in Figure 4and Figure 5through Figure 6 which are described below (Russel Eberhart, and Yuhui Shi, 2011).

Supervised Adaptation: The adaptation is carried out in the execution of system at every iteration. The fine-tuned variables/parameters are subjected to generalize the behavior of a computational model in the dynamic environment, and the performance of the system is consistently improved.

Reinforcement Adaptation: The number of variables/parameters involved in the system is interacted to achieve best fitness solution through heuristic reinforcement approach. It deals with a time series of input vector space, evaluate fitness of the system and produces possible outcomes for each input.

Unsupervised Adaptation: It follows trial and error method. The number of variables/parameters involved in the system performs task. Based on the obtained fitness value, computational model is generalized to achieve better results in an iterative approach.

Figure 3. Supervised adaptation model

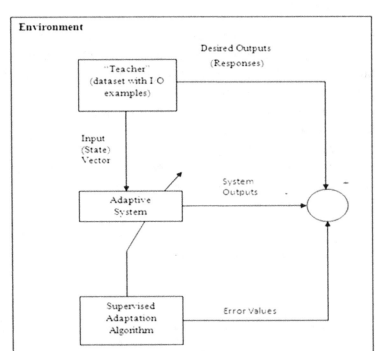

Figure 4. Reinforcement adaptation model

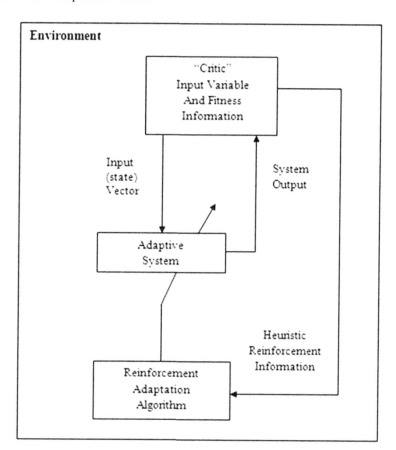

Deep learning algorithms are a part of machine learning algorithms which involves multiple layers of deep learning data architectures, representations and transformations. Convolutional Neural Network (CNN) and Recurrent Neural Network (RNN) are typical examples of deep learning algorithms. Aforementioned three categories of algorithms are utilized to solve a wide range of cyber security problems which are discussed here. Machine learning algorithms are utilized to design and development of a learning based security model. NIC algorithms are applied for fine-tuning parameters involved in the security model in order to improve the efficiency and performance. Deep learning algorithms are generally implemented for solving the complicated cyber security problems that involves huge volume of varied dataset.

The proposed chapter focuses on the implementation of NIC algorithms, machine learning algorithms and deep learning algorithms in cyber security which spans across different applications, such as, network security, information security, secure communication in wireless sensor networks, cryptographic algorithm to reduce threats in data transmission over the network, intrusion detection, phishing detection, machine monitoring, signature verification, virus detection, insider attack detection, profiling network traffic, anomaly detection, malware detection, IoT security, security in web service, ad hoc security, cyber warfare, security in electronic services, biometric security, honeypot security, vulnerability assessment, social applications security, botnet detection, attack detection and sensor network security.

Figure 5. Unsupervised adaptation model

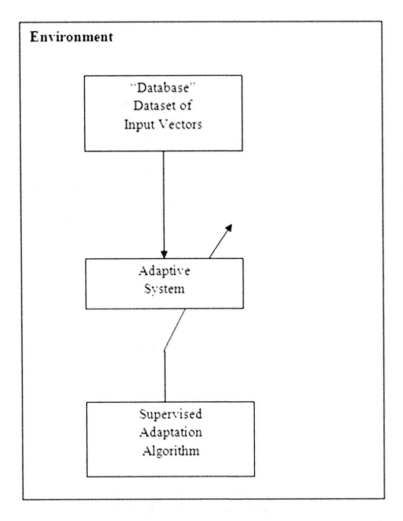

Figure 6. Implementation of intelligent algorithms – cyber security problems

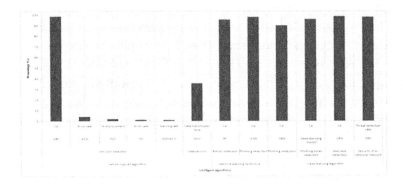

The structure of the remaining chapter is organized as follows. Section 2 describes the implementation of nature inspired computing algorithms in solving cyber security problems. The utilization of machine learning algorithms for resolving cyber security problems are given in Section 3. Section 4 explains the application of deep learning for solving cyber security problems. The research summaries / inferences about the implementation of algorithms are provided in Section 5 and Section 6 draws conclusion and future works.

STUDY ON NIC ALGORITHMS IN CYBER SECURITY

The characteristics of NIC algorithms are partitioned into two segments such as swarm intelligence and evolutionary algorithm. The Swarm Intelligence-based Algorithms (SIA) are developed based on the idea of collective behaviours of insects such as ants, bees, wasps and termites living in colonies. Researchers are interested in the new way of achieving a form of collective intelligence called swarm intelligence. SIAs are also advanced as a computational intelligence technique based around the study of collective behaviour in decentralized and self-organized systems. The development of evolutionary computation techniques is derived from three main observations. First, the selection of most appropriate individuals (parents) is determined by combination (reproduction). Second, randomness (mutation) expands the search space of the diversity. Third, the fittest individuals have a higher probability of surviving to the next generation. The combination of natural selection and self-organization is denoted in equation 1 as follows. The implementation of nature inspired computing algorithms for solving cyber security problems are tabulated in Table 3.

$$Evolution = \left(natural\,selection\right) + \left(self organization\right)$$

(1)

STUDY ON MACHINE LEARNING IN CYBER SECURITY

Machine learning algorithm is defined as a methodology involving computing that provides a system with an ability to learn and deal with new situations, such that the system is perceived to possess one or more attributes of reason, such as, generalization, discovery, association and abstraction. The output of a machine learning model often includes perceptions and/or decisions. It consists of practical adaptation and self-organization concepts, paradigms, algorithms, and implementations that enable or facilitate appropriate actions (intelligent behaviour) in complex and changing environments. Adaptation and self-organization are the two most important characteristics exhibited by intelligent paradigms which are widely applied to develop intelligent system and computational model that provide promising solution for solving the large scale of complicated optimization problems. The implementation of machine learning algorithms for solving cyber security problems are presented in Table 2.

Table 1. Role of NIC algorithms in solving cyber security problems

S. No.	Application	Algorithm	Methodology	Dataset / Tools / Metrics	Description
1.	Network intrusion detection (Changseok, Wei-Chang, Mohd, Yuk, & Tsung-Jung, 2012)	ABC, SVM, Naïves Bayes, Classification tree, K-NN and C4.5 used optimizing control parameter.	Anomaly -Network Intrusion Detection System (NIDS) based on ABC algorithm to choose optimal features for the construction of rule based system.	KDD Cup 1999 dataset	NIDS-ABC method achieved 98.5% classification accuracy.
2.	Network intrusion detection (Monther, Yaser, & Mohammad, 2015)	ABC, SVM, CART, multi-objective genetic fuzzy IDS (MOGF-IDS), K-NN, C4.5, Classifier anomaly intrusion detection using genetic algorithm (GALC) and Bayesian Network and Markov Blanket (BNMB)	Anomaly-based intrusion detection systems using ABC algorithm is proposed. Classical CART and BNMB methods are implemented to choose optimal feature set to develop rule based system.	KDD Cup 99 dataset	ABC based intrusion detection systems gives average accuracy of 97.5% for known attacks and 93.2% accuracy for overall known and unknown attacks.
3.	Security threats in Mobile Adhoc Network (MANET) (Pradeep, & Prasad, 2015)	ACO, PSO and SI	Survey on open issues and different types of attack in MANET are studied. Energy, scalability and Quality of Service (QoS) are three main issues that play a vital role in the management of trust schemes in MANET using SI.	No dataset are available	A novel method comprises of game theory and SI is considered as effective mechanism for providing security in MANET.
4.	Network security (Parul, & Arun. Patel, 2013)	ACO	Detect vulnerabilities and improving performance in the network security management.	Java Nessus ACO API is utilized to detect moving vulnerability in the network host using the following six methods of TCP connect() scan, TCP SYN scans, stealth FIN scans, XMAS tree scans, NULL scans, UDP scans, and ping scans.	Java Nessus ACO API provides better results than conventional methods.
5.	Threat detection in the network (Julio, & Pierre, 2016)	ACO	Morwilog, a hybrid method of Manhill and ACO is proposed for finding multiple modular attacks in the network.	Simulated dataset created by Splunk Event Generator composed by a total of 1038 different types of logs.	ACO based system effectively travels through path to identify the sequence of actions (attacks) in the tree (network) and improve security in a better way.
6.	Data transmission over wireless network (Shankar, & Karthikeyan, 2017).	ACO, Session Initiation Protocol (SIP), Verifiable Secret Sharing (VSS), Shamir Secret Sharing (SS) and Multiplex-Multicast (M-M) scheme and used QoS Parameters.	M-M scheme integrated with VSS is proposed to enhance the quality and reduce the cost of voice transmission in the network. The fitness evaluation of ACO is measured using Mean Opinion Score (MOS) for attaining quality of Voice Over Internet Protocol (VOIP) in Wireless Local Area Network (WLAN).	It is evaluated in the Network simulator(NS-2) to measure packet delay variations, round trip time and jitter. The mobile Wi-MAX IEEE 802.16e is used as standard protocol in the wireless network.	The proposed VSS with M-M method gives Round Trip Time (RTT) of 16.69% and 35.67% better results than VSS and Shamir SS methods respectively.
7.	Intrusion detection system (Farha, & Shailendra, 2017)	Intelligent Water Drops (IWD), ACO, GA, Principal Component Analysis (PCA), Information Gain, Information Gain Ratio SVM and analyzed Number and velocity of water drops.	Combined version of IWD and ACO algorithms.	KDD Cup 99 dataset	IWD+ACO method consumes lowest training time of 0.97 minutes to SVM.
8.	Intrusion detection (Namita, & Vineet, 2012)	SVM, Naïve Bayes and ACO	ACO algorithm is implemented to choose optimal feature space to give training for both SVM and naïve bayes.	KDD Cup 99 dataset	ACO combined with naïve bayes attains 4.81% and 5.32% detection rate better than SVM and naïve bayes respectively.
9.	Improvement of security in physical layer network (Kumarnath, & Batri, 2018)	Bat algorithm, Game Assisted Routing and Spectrum Assignment (GA-RSA)	Multidomain elastic optical networks (MDEONs) are introduced to enhance interoperability, network scalability and service coverage. BAT algorithm is utilized to choose routing wavelength based on echolocation character with varying rate of emission and loudness.	Simulated dataset	Bat algorithm is able to choose best routing path which is proved to produce better spectrum assignment, increase in the delivery ratio and hop count reduction compared to GA-RSA.
10.	Anomaly detection (Arvinder, Saibal & Amrital, 2018)	FA, K-Means, CS, Bat algorithm and Canopy and Farthest First	K-Means with firefly algorithm based anomaly detection method is proposed. K-Means clustering is applied to build training model and metaheuristic algorithm is utilized to validate classification performance on the testing dataset.	NSL-KDD dataset	K-Means with FA and Bat algorithm achieves highest classification accuracy than conventional approaches.

continued on following page

Table 1. Continued

S. No.	Application	Algorithm	Methodology	Dataset / Tools / Metrics	Description
11.	Enhancing security in wireless sensor network (Anbuchelian, Lokesh, & Madhusudhanan, 2016)	FA	Trust based cluster head selection mechanism using firefly algorithm is proposed.	Mica testbed consist of 23nodes	Proposed trust firefly algorithm improves the performance of detecting malicious nodes and energy level compared to weighted clustering algorithm and trust with weighted clustering algorithm.
12.	Improving security in MANET (Mahalakshmi, Vadivel, (2018)	PSO and Dynamic Path Strategy	PSO algorithm is implemented to choose optimal path for transferring packets from source node to destination node.	Simulation environment of Java EE and Java Net beans.	PSO based approach reduces 42.68% execution time and improves 70.27% throughput than dynamic path strategy method.
13.	Network intrusion detection (Xiang, 2018)	PSO and Back Propagation Neural Network (BPNN)	PSO algorithm is applied to choose optimal feature space and it is implemented for training BPNN using trial and error method.	KDD Cup 99 dataset	PSO-BPNN improves 2% accuracy to identify anomaly than GA-BPNN method.
14.	Security in trusted Peer to Peer system (Senthil & Revathi, 2016)	PSO	PSO based optimal selection (PSO-OPS) approach is proposed. PSO algorithm is employed to choose best peer for data transmission in the heterogeneous network.	Simulated dataset	The PSO-OPS achieves better results, in terms of, link stress, average query delay, communication delay, finish time, network cost and success rate.
15.	Prediction of network security situation (Zongming, Guolong, Wenzhongc, & Yanhua, 2008)	PSO, Radial Basis Function (RBF), GA and BPNN	PSO algorithm is utilized to optimize weight value and threshold value incorporated in BPNN to forecast network security situation.	Dataset from HoneyNet	PSO-BPNN method achieves high accuracy, minimize error values and exhibit good performance index than RBF, BPNN and GA-BPNN.
16.	Botnet detection mechanism (Shing-Han, Yu-Cheng, Zong-Cyuan, & David, 2015)	PSO and K-Means clustering algorithm	PSO with K-Means clustering algorithm is proposed to detect botnet in the network.	Real time environment of educational campus network.	Better performance in the detection of some suspicious botnet members than earlier approaches.
17.	Intrusion detection model (Hodashinsky, & Mech, 2018)	DE, Harmony Search (HS) and Fuzzy rule based classifier	HS algorithm is utilized to select optimal (relevant) feature space for the design of rule based classifiers. DE is applied to parameter tuning of Fuzzy rule based classifier.	KDD Cup 99 intrusion detection dataset	Adequacy of 1.21% type I error and a 0.39% type II error compared to other methods.
18.	Study on Differential Evolution for Mobile Ad-hoc networks (Prabha, Yadav, 2018)	DE	Application of DE algorithms in solving mobile ad-hoc networks is surveyed.	No dataset required	The study shows that DE is applied in solving issues such as handling networks (up to 500 nodes) with minimum overhead and strengthening of cryptographic algorithms (up to 9 key size).
19.	Development of security policy in network (Lobo, & Suhas. Chavan, 2012)	GA	This research is focused on identification of the following three types of attack namely active attack, passive attack and brute force attack. Network security policy, framework and analysis are carried out using genetic algorithm to choose best security policy for mitigating attacks.	Real time dataset taken from internet and local area network is used. Open source software consists of Jpcap, winpcap and Colasoft Capsa is used for implementation.	Network security model is hosted on web server. Examined results show that the proposed system is able to detect attack and security policy introduced by GA is more effective.
20.	Information security (Muhammad, Ghula, Noor, Raheel, & Muhammad, 2018)	GA	Genetic algorithm is utilized for random generation of keys which is injected into data for encryption.	The key strength is measured using GRC Interactive Brute Force key Search Space Calculator and compared with Data Encryption Standard (DES) and Advanced Encryption Standard (AES) algorithms.	Less execution time and better key strength.

STUDY ON DEEP LEARNING IN CYBER SECURITY

Deep learning algorithm is precisely an extension of Artificial Neural Network (ANN) constructed with several layers of hidden nodes between input node and output node. Initialization and adjustment of weight factor in the intermediate hidden nodes is greatly improved the learning ability or efficiency of neural network. Activation functions namely, sigmoid, tanh, ReLU, leaky-ReLU and ELU are most

Table 2. Role of machine learning algorithms in solving cyber security problems

S.No	Application	Algorithm	Methodology	Dataset / Tools / Metrics	Description
1.	Anomaly detection (Jerry, 2016)	Neural network	An effective sparse encoder tool is introduced using neural network to indicate anomalies in the health system.	Large dimension healthcare data	The proposed 2D sparse auto encoder system effectively indicates the anomalies. The error threshold for anomaly detection is evaluated and trained error values are incorporated in neural network to produce better results.
2.	Distributed Denial of Service (DDoS) attack detection in cloud environment (Marwane, Said, Noureddine, & Youssef, 2017)	C4.5 algorithm	Using machine learning and signature detection techniques. Decision tree (C4.5) algorithm is adopted to extract features from signature archives to detect DDoS attack in the network layer and transport layer of Open Systems Interconnection(OSI) model.	It is tested in open source Open Stackjuno software to build public, private and hybrid cloud in the simulation environment of virtual machine and virtual LAN.	To detect and mitigate DDoS threat that inflicts serious damage to cloud performance.
3.	Botnet detection (Xuan, & Quynh, 2018)	K-NN, C4.5, Random Forest and Naïve Bayes	To effectively identify botnet measures, namely, honeynet-based and Intrusion Detection Systems (IDS)-based model is proposed.	Domain Name Service (DNA) query data.	Random forest algorithm produces 90% overall classification accuracy
4.	HTTP based botnet detection (Rudy, Faizal, Fahmi & Lee, 2018)	Decision tree, K-NN, Naïve Bayes and Random Forest	Classifier algorithm is implemented to detect HTTP botnet threat in the network traffic.	It is validated in the real time test bed environment consist of five computers installed with windows 7 operating system. There are five types of HTTP botnets used in this study, such as, Dorkbot, Zeus, Citadel, Spy Eye, and Cutwail.	Random Forest algorithm yields classification accuracy of 90% True Positive Rate (TPR) with Dorkbot, Zeus, Spy Eye and Cutwail detection. Moreover, k-NN is able to show good performance, in terms of, average TPR of 95.47% botnet detection accuracy and reduce false alarm rate than other classifiers.
5.	Cyber-attacks detection (Rafał, & Michał, 2014)	Bayesian network and GA	Genetic algorithm is implemented to extract signatures from SQL (Structured Query Language) log files. Injection attack detection system is proposed using bayesian network for identifying intruder attack file.	It used to SQL attack injection methodology and tested with sql map tool and compared with Apache SCALP, SNORT and ICD (Idealized Character Distribution).	The hybrid method combines signature based approach and anomaly-based methods produces promising results in the attack file detection than traditional signature based method.
6.	Role of machine learning in cyber security (Vitaly, & Ambareen, 2014)	Logistic regression, Regression Trees (CART), Bayesian Additive Regression Trees (BART), SVM, Random Forest and NN	To investigate the characteristics namely, adaptability, scalability and potential of machine learning algorithm to solve various of kinds of cyber security problems.	This review encompasses network intrusion detection, phishing detection, spam detection in social network, testing security properties of protocols, authentication with keystroke dynamics, cryptography, human interaction proofs, smart meter energy consumption profiling and limitations of machine learning techniques in solving cyber security problems are addressed.	Machine learning techniques are successfully employed in many areas, for instance, spam detection, virus detection, and surveillance camera robbery detection. In some situations, classifier algorithms itself may cause malicious attacks in the network.
7.	Honeypot detection in web services (Abdallah, Tarek, & Adel, 2013)	SVM,SVM Regression and Apriori algorithm	A model is proposed to detect and classify web services honeypot target attackers.	Data captured from SOAP (Simple Object Access Protocol) messages on the web services have been taken for this study.	Classifier algorithms are able to identify and categorize normal and suspicious web services attacks on the honeyspot.
8.	Honeypot attacks (Philippe, 2014)	Clustering ensemble and sub-space clustering	Unsupervised learning method is applied	It is tested in honeypot traffic traces gathered at the University of Maryland.	The proposed unsupervised techniques perform better in identifying risk analysis of honeypot traffic in the internet.
9.	Honeypot configurations (Marcus, & Christopher, 2017)	Multi-Armed Bandit (MAB) problem and Upper Confidence Bound (UCB)	A set of honeypot selection strategies are framed to configure security model.	The algorithms are tested in the scenario of uniform random, fixed random and pure strategy.	A new model is effective to improve exploit detection by applying learning methods.
10.	Malware detection (Hanaa, Nidaa, & Assmaa, 2017)	K-means algorithm	The smartphone honeypot system is designed and developed.	1260 malicious dataset	It shows that performance counter is used as effective tool for malware detection.
11.	Honeypot detection (Fatna, Nisrine, Younes, & Habiba, 2017)	Feature based strategy	An improved security model is developed for identifying malicious users in social network websites like Facebook, Twitter and LinkedIn.	300 user profiles collected from Twitter using WEKA tool.	The proposed approach is greatly identifying malicious accounts in the online social networks.

continued on following page

Table 2. Continued

S.No	Application	Algorithm	Methodology	Dataset / Tools / Metrics	Description
12.	IoT threat detection (Tayyaba, 2017)	ANN	An IoT threat is classified into Distributed Denial of Service (DDoS), malware, data breaks and weakening perimeters. ANN technique is suggested to detect anomaly and intrusion in the network.	No dataset required	It signifies that the proposed Intrusion Detection System (IDS) could be avoid DDoS attacks in IoT.
13.	Malware detection (Dragos, Mihai, Dan, & Liviu, 2009)	One-sided perceptron, Kernelized One-sided perceptron and Optimized One-sided perceptron	A versatile framework is constructed using machine learning methods to distinguish between malware files and normal files.	Cross validation test is carried out with combinations of 7822 malware unique files and 415 clean unique files.	Optimized one-sided perceptron gives better results for malware detection than other algorithms.
14.	Phishing detection (Basnet, Srinivas, & Andrew, 2008)	SVM, K-Means, ANN and Self Organizing Maps (SOMs)	Phishing detection system using machine learning techniques is proposed. Machine learning algorithm is applied to extract feature subset (HTTP-email, IP-based URL, age of domain name, number of links, URL based image source, matching domains and keywords).	Totally, there are 4000 dataset consist of (3027 – legitimate emails and 973 – phishing emails) have been taken for this study. 2000 samples are used for training and remaining used for testing purpose.	The examined results show that ANN gives classification accuracy of 97.99% than other algorithms.
15.	Phishing website detection (Waleed, 2017)	BPNN, RBFN, KNN, SVM, Naïve bayes, C4.5 algorithm and RF)	In the wrapper based feature selection method, Machine learning technique is applied to extract features from address bar based URLS, abnormal based features, HTML and Javascript based features and domain based features.	UCI machine learning repository dataset	Investigational results show that BPNN, K-NN and RBF achieves better classification results compared to other algorithms.
16.	Review on security threats and defensive techniques using machine learning algorithm (Qiang et al., 2018)	Machine learning algorithm such as Naïve bayes, Logistic regression, Decision tree, SVM, Principal Component Analysis (PCA), clustering algorithm and deep learning algorithm are applied.	A study on application of machine learning techniques for security threat detection and defensive techniques applications are done.	No dataset required	Machine learning algorithms are greatly implemented to identify security threats in the network. Application of defensive techniques are viewed in two perspectives, namely, security assessment mechanisms in the training phase and data security and privacy in the testing or inferring phase.
17.	Signature verification (Harish, Sargur. Srihari, & Matthew, 2006)	Person-independent (General) learning and person-dependent (Special) learning	A generic learning model is developed to classify genuine and forged signatures. Kolmogorov-Smirnov (KS), Kullback-Leibler (KL), Reverse KL, Symmetric KL and Jensen-Shannon KL measures are applied.	It is validated with 1320 genuine signatures and 1320 forgeries to measure error rate of signature authentication.	Features extracted using Gradient, Structural and Concavity (GSC) based hybrid (KL and KS) method deliver promising results than other algorithms.
18.	Vulnerability discovery (Saahil, Ricardo, Alexander, & Pooja, 2018)	Random Forest and Naïve Bayes	A framework is constructed to design and develop predictive model using metaheuristic algorithm in order to discover vulnerability threats in the software's.	The dataset from National Vulnerability Database (NVD) consist of Common Vulnerabilities and Exposures (CVEs)	The empirical study and feedback obtained from experts of secure software development are ultimately utilized to improve effectiveness of predictive model.
19.	Intrusion detection (Yi, & Myat. 2018)	K-Means clustering and Random forest algorithm	Intrusion Detection System (IDS) is developed using machine learning algorithm to detect various attacks namely, DoS attacks, Probing attacks (information gathering attacks), user-to-root (U2R) attacks (unauthorized access to local super-user) and remote local attacks.	KDD 99 Cup intrusion detection benchmark dataset	Random forest algorithm produces better results to categorize normal and attack connections.
20.	Intrusion detection in fog computing (Kai, Victor, Shangguang, Chao, & Tao, 2018)	Decision tree, BernoulliNB and K-NN	String replace algorithm is applied and, data normalization technique is utilized to normalize the whole dataset. Then, Decision tree algorithm is employed to classify normal attack, DoS attack, probing attack, Remote to User (R2L) Attack and User to Root (U2R) attack.	KDD 99 Cup intrusion detection benchmark dataset	Machine learning approach is considered as effective mechanism to detect intrusion in the fog environment.

widely used in the neural network. Convolutional Neural Network (CNN) and Recurrent Neural Network (RNN) are classical examples of deep learning algorithm. Implementation of deep learning algorithm in solving cyber security problems is still in the progressing stage and few contributions have been done so far. The primary challenges involved in the utilization of deep learning algorithm is that, it requires huge processing power, large volume of data, overfitting (model could not be easily generalize) and vanishing gradients. Table 3.given below illustrates the application of deep learning algorithm for solving cyber security problems.

INFERENCES

To summarize it, the inferential analysis on the implementation of intelligent algorithms is portrayed in Figure 7 It illustrates that nature inspired algorithms are frequently applied to further improve the performance of classical cyber security algorithms. It is also utilized to choose fine-tuned parameters and enhance learning rate in order to yield better results. From the figure, it is understood that, in solving intrusion detection problems, nature inspired algorithms are employed to choose optimal features which are feed into learning model to categorize normal attack and abnormal attack. It leads to improve classification accuracy, learning rate and reduce error rate. ACO algorithm is utilized to choose optimal protocols to configure network model for data transmission. Machine learning algorithms are utilized to train learning models for feature analysis and pattern recognition. It demonstrates that machine learning techniques are significantly improves the classification accuracy in botnet detection, phishing detection and intrusion detection. It shows that deep learning algorithms are ultimately enhanced the efficiency of decision model to detect vulnerable threats in the cyber space.

Figure 7. Application of intelligent algorithms in cyber security problems

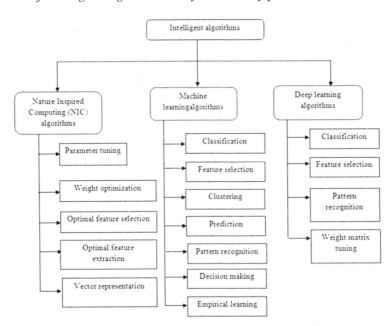

Table 3. Role of deep learning algorithms in solving cyber security problems

S.No.	Application	Algorithm	Methodology	Dataset / Tools / Metrics	Description
1.	Network anomaly detection (Donghwoon et al., 2017)	Restricted Bolzmann Machine (RBM), deep belief network (DBN), Deep Neural Network (DNN), and RNN, SVM, random forest and Adaboosting.	In the classification, RBM, DNN, RNN, SVM, random forest and Adaboosting techniques are utilized to categorize DoS attack, User to Root attack, Remote to local attack and probing attack.	NSL-KDD dataset	Deep learning algorithms deliver promising results with improved accuracy compared to conventional machine learning techniques.
2.	Anomaly detection in 5G network (Lorenzo, Angel, Félix, Manuel, & Gregorio, 2018)	Virtualized Infrastructure (VI), Virtualized Network Functions (VNF), Management and Orchestration (MANO) and Operations and Business Support Systems (OSS/BSS), Anomaly Symptom Detection (ASD), Long Short-Term Memory Recurrent Networks (LSTM), Deep Learning Neural Network (DLNN), Network Anomaly Detection (NAD) and Radio Access Network (RAN).	Network Anomaly Detection (NAD) learning model is constructed to analyze complex symbolic patterns by extracting features from network traffic. Improved learning model is efficiently trained to find intrusion in the 5G mobile network.	CTU dataset	The proposed two-level deep learning model has achieved high classification accuracy and effective resource utilization to attain highest performance in the 5G network.
3.	Multi-biometric secure system (Veeru, Matthew, & Nasser, 2017)	CNN and DNN	DNN is proposed to develop multi-biometric secure system. Bilinear architecture model of CNN is employed to extract features from archives of face and iris data samples. Reed-Solomon code is implemented to provide error correcting capabilities of multi-biometric secure system.	Face-CNN and Iris-CNN 2012-2013 subsets of the West Virginia University (WVU) multimodal dataset	The classification performance of DNN based two fusion architecture maintains good security and robustness.
4.	Cyber threat detection (Glenn Monroe Lambert II, 2017)	K-Means clustering and DNN	K-means algorithm is implemented to group outliers present in the dataset and preprocessed data is applied to deep learning model to detect intrusion found in the network.	Sanitized set of log files provided by The University of North Florida Information Technology Security Department is used for this experiment.	The examined results show that Deep learning algorithm is able to exactly detect and classify starvation attack, malware attack, denial of service attack and reconnaissance attack.
5.	Intrusion detection, malware detection, spam and phishing detection (Giovanni, Michele, Luca, Alessandro & Mirco, 2018)	RNN, Deep Belief Networks, Fully Forward Neural Network (FNN), Stacked Auto Encoders (SAE), Domain Generation Algorithms (DGA), Naïve Bayes (NB), SVM, K-NN, Random Forest (RF), Logistic Regression (LR), Shallow Neural Network (SNN), Deep Learning (DL) algorithm and Hidden Markov Model (HMM)	Machine Learning (ML) algorithms for solving various kinds of cyber security applications is analyzed.	Random forest algorithm is used for give training using features extracted from 20,000 DGC domain contributed by real enterprise systems to do classification. FNN and Deep learning algorithms are trained using ReLU and sigmoid activation function to detect malware and benign network flows collected from large organization of nearly 10,000 hosts.	Machine learning algorithm solve three relevant cyber security problems such as intrusion detection, malware analysis and spam detection have been performed. The experimental results show that right selection of ML algorithms and cyber security problems determines its effectiveness. But still, continuous training and parameter tuning are required to make ML and DL algorithms to produce promising required are also need to be considered.
6.	Deep learning based IoT/Fog network attack detection system (Abebe, & Naveen, 2017)	Deep Learning Model and Shallow Learning Model	Deep learning and traditional machine learning algorithms are implemented to detect threats in social IoT/Fog ecosystem consist of various category of attacks namely, probe, Remote to Local (R2L), User to Root (U2R) and Denial of Service (DoS). Tanh, Rectified Linear and Maxout are used as activation functions for give training to proposed Deep learning based Intrusion Detection System (IDS).	KDDCUP99, ISCX and NSL-KDD dataset	Deep learning model is greatly identify normal/attack data and it has shown excellent performance than traditional machine learning algorithms, such as, SVM, decision trees and other neural networks.

continued on following page

Table 3. Continued

S.No.	Application	Algorithm	Methodology	Dataset / Tools / Metrics	Description
7.	Intrusion detection (Chuanlong, Yuefei, Jinlong, & Xinzheng, 2017)	RNN	RNN algorithm is introduced to construct intrusion detection learning model for finding normal and anomaly attacks in the network.	NSL-KDD dataset	Compared with traditional algorithms, namely, J48, Naïve Bayesian and Random forest, RNN-IDS has achieved high accuracy rate and reduce detection with false positive rate.
8.	Intrusion detection (Zheng, 2018)	Fast Gradient Sign Method (FGSM), Jacobian-Based Saliency Map attack (JSMA), DeepFool and CW attack	State-of-the-art attack algorithms are utilized to construct Deep learning model for finding distinctive threats, namely, Denial of Service (DoS), probe, R2L and U2R.	NSL-KDD dataset	JSMA attack in the construction of deep learning model causes less vulnerability and deliver better protection and defense effort compared to other conventional algorithms.
9.	Web phishing detection (Ping et al., 2018)	Deep Belief Networks (DBN)	DBN model is developed to find website security threats in the Internet. The learning model is trained by using two set of features: original feature and interaction feature extracted from SVM.	Real time Internet Service Provider (ISP) data	DBN model is able to approximately achieve 90% true positive rate and minimize 0.6% false positive rate.
10.	Intelligent malware detection (William Lingwei and Xin Li, 2016)	Stacked Auto Encoders (SAEs), SVM,Naïve Bayes, Decision Tree (DT) and ANN	Deep learning model is constructed using SAE for identifying malware threats. Analysis on the Windows Application Programming Interface (API) is generated from Portable Executable (PE) files to extract features for giving training to the learning model.	Real time data samples collected from Comodo Cloud Security Center industry.	Results proved that the proposed method outperforms than conventional shallow learning architectures.
11.	Malware detection (Felix et al., 2018)	CNN	A novel approach is formulated to find injected malware in the binary files. Fast Gradient Sign Method (FGSM) is proposed to collect features from adversarial examples which are utilized for give training to CNN model.	There are two set of data samples are used. The first dataset consist of exe/dll with size of 32 KB benign binary files collected from 50 different vendors. Second dataset taken from Kaggle 2015 dataset.	The proposed model is able to detect normal files and attack files effectively.
12.	Phishing e-mail detection (Reza, Erdogan, Roya, Onur, & Nazli, 2018)	Deep Learning Network algorithm	Deep learning architecture is modelled to detect fraudulent e-mails that try to steal individual personal information like username, password, credit card number and so on. E-mails represented in vector format is utilized to develop a neural network model.	Benchmark dataset	The validation of results shows that learning model achieves 96% classification accuracy than standard machine learning algorithms.
13.	Malware signature generation and classification (Eli, & Nathan, 2015)	Deep Belief Network (DBN)	Invariants of signatures consist of 300 variants in each category and totally 1,800 samples are fed into DBN model for finding categories of malware families such as Zeus, Carberp, Spy-Eye, Cidox, Andromeda, and Dark Comet in Internet logged from API calls and their parameters, registry entries, websites and ports accessed.	Totally, 1,800 vectors size of over 20,000 data samples converted into 30-sized Representations are conducted in this study.	Experimental results portray that DBN model obtained 98.6% classification of signature detection than SVM classifier.
14.	Secured middleware in Wireless Sensor Network (WSN) (Remah, & Khaled, 2018)	SVM, DT, Adaboost and CNN	Convolutional neural network based Secure Wireless Sensor Network Middleware (SWSNM)is framed and trained using features extracted from generative adversarial network algorithm. It consists of two networks: a generator (G) network and a discriminator (D) network. The G network combines fake data with real dataset generated from sensors are feed into confuse the attacker. The D network is trained to find distinction between real data and fake data.	NSL-KDD benchmark dataset	Results signify that the proposed SWSNM provides more stronger mechanism, consumes less energy, reduce delay time and attains high throughput compared to counterpart algorithms.
15.	Security of in-vehicular network (Min-Joo, & Je-Won, 2016)	DBN and ANN	Features extracted from DBN are fed into model a deep neural network to detect intrusion of in-vehicular network.	Simulated data	The proposed model produces 98% average detection accuracy rate to classify normal packets and hacking packets than ANN architecture.

Table 4. Role of algorithms for security in Mobile Ad-hoc Network (MANET) applications

S.No.	Application	Algorithm / Parameter Selection	Methodology	Dataset / Tools / Metrics	Description
1.	Detection of malicious attacks in real time basis	Logistic Regression (LR) and Support Vector Machine (SVM) Packet Delivery Ratio (PDER) and Packet Modification and Misroute Rate (PMMR)	LR and SVM are applied to classify normal packets and abnormal packets	Anderson's Iris dataset	LR outperforms than SVM in differentiating between normal and abnormal MANET packets.
2.	Intrusion detection in MANET	ANN Setdest and Cbrgen	ANN is applied to attack detection, isolation and reconfiguration in varied network traffic condition.	Weka Tool / Simulated 16 nodes in network	Achieved highest classification accuracy.
3.	Anomaly detection in MANET	C4.5, K-NN, Multilayer Perceptron (MLP) and SVM	Machine learning techniques are applied to detect normal and attacked behaviour of the system.	Black hole and Gray hole attacks	MLP is better than other classification models.

Figure 8. Rastrigin function

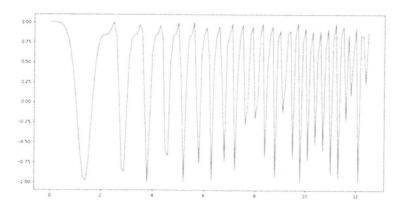

Moreover, most of the organizations are investing huge amount in building AI based cyber-security model to protect computer system against vulnerable threats. The tool developed by Symantec called Symantec's Targeted attack analytics (TAA) tool which integrates machine learning and AI techniques for building expert systems to discover targeted attacks. Intercept X tool is developed by Sophos which is a British security hardware and software company. It applies deep learning network to develop learning model which works in a same way like human brain to detect threats. US Defense Advanced Research Projects Agency (DARPA) developed Cyber Genome program to discover malware threats in 2010. Darktrace's Enterprise Immune System introduced Darktrace Antigena software product based on machine learning techniques which is able to detect viruses, human intervention, malicious attacks, pattern identification and respond to the real world environment based on the severity of threats. IBM developed IBM's QRadar Advisor tool based on Artificial Intelligence that uses IBM Watson technology. It is able to deliver brilliant reasoning by identifying malicious attacks based on cognitive analysis. Vectra's Cognito platform uses AI techniques to find real time attackers and threats in IoT devices (https://www.vectra.ai/solutions/use-cases/attack-detection). Aforementioned potential cyber security research works progressing in industries / organizations proved that intelligent algorithms are significantly encountered in the large scale of cyber security problems / applications.

RESEARCH SUMMARY

An elaborative study on the implementation of intelligent algorithms, namely, nature inspired computing paradigms, machine learning techniques and deep learning algorithms for solving the large scale of cyber security problems, such as, network security, information security, secure communication in wireless sensor networks, cryptographic algorithm to reduce threats in data transmission over the network, intrusion detection, phishing detection, signature verification, anomaly detection, malware detection, IoT security, security in web service, ad hoc security, biometric security, honeypot security, vulnerability assessment, social applications security, botnet detection, attack detection and sensor network security are successfully analyzed. The potential study exemplify that the application of intelligent algorithms play a vital role in improving the performance, in terms of, security, threat detection, throughput, end-to-to delay, less energy consumption, packets delivery, vulnerability detection in IoT and social networking sites of cyber security applications. Figure 8 portrays the skeleton of intelligent algorithms utilization areas in solving cyber security problems. In this research work, intelligent algorithms are broadly categorized into three types, such as, NIC algorithms, machine learning algorithms and deep learning algorithms.

This study illustrates that all these three intelligent classification algorithms are significantly utilized to solve a wide variety of cyber security problems. The major difference that exists in the selection of intelligent algorithms is discussed as follows. Machine learning technique involves supervised adaptation, unsupervised adaptation and reinforcement adaptation which are primarily employed to categorize dataset, such as normal attack and abnormal attack, grouping similar data patterns namely outlier detection, dimensionality reduction and transformation namely feature subset extraction involved in the learning model. Nature inspired computing paradigms are employed to enhance the performance of machine learning techniques for solving the specific cyber security problems. That is, NIC algorithms are applied to optimize weight values and parameters tuning involved in the learning model, extraction of optimal feature subset and selection of optimal features that improves the efficiency and accuracy of learning model. Deep learning algorithms exhibit better performance than standard shallow learning architectures. Because, Deep learning model consist of large number of hidden layers encompasses distinct hidden nodes that ultimately enhances the learning ability which leads to produce promising results, in terms of, throughput, packets delivery, end to-end delay, less energy consumption and learning approach. The construction of Deep learning model is a more appropriate method where it involves large volume of dataset, GPU system acceleration and requires complex activation function to perform computation.

An exploratory analysis of Rastrigin benchmark function for finding the global optimum is analysed and portrayed in Figure 9 (Monther Aldwairi et al. (2012).

Rastrigin's function (Continuous, Differentiable, Partially-Separable, Scalable, Multimodal)

$$f\left(x\right) = 10.n\sum_{i=0}^{n} x_i^2 - 10.\cos\left(2\pi x_i\right) \tag{1}$$

CONCLUSION AND FUTURE WORKS

In this work, the implementation of intelligent algorithms, namely, nature inspired computing paradigms, machine learning techniques and deep learning algorithms involved in cyber security problems to obtain betterment results are summarized. The requirements of employing intelligent algorithms in developing cyber security models to detect various types of attacks and its significance make traditional cyber security algorithms to exhibit better performance are investigated. The most prominent AI based cyber security tools developed by several organizations are studied. It emphasizes the efficiency of intelligent algorithms for constructing powerful cyber security models to detect threats or any vulnerability. This study could be extended to focus on fitness function evaluation, selection of activation function and performance metrics incorporated in the intelligent algorithms to produce highly quantitative and qualitative results that improves the performance of cyber security problems/applications in the future.

REFERENCES

Ahmed, H. M., Hassan, N. F., & Fahad, A. (2017). Designing a smartphone honeypot system using performance counters. *Karbala International Journal of Modern Science*, 3(1), 46–52. doi:10.1016/j.kijoms.2017.02.004

Aldwairi, M., Khamayseh, Y., & Al-Masri, M. (2015). Application of artificial bee colony for intrusion detection systems. *Security and Communication Networks*, 8(16), 2730–2740. doi:10.1002ec.588

Ali, W. (2017). Phishing website detection based on supervised machine learning with wrapper features selection. *International Journal of Advanced Computer Science and Applications*, 8(9), 72–78. doi:10.14569/IJACSA.2017.080910

Alshinina, A. R., & Elleithy, M. K. (2018). A highly accurate deep learning based approach for developing wireless sensor network middleware. *IEEE Access: Practical Innovations, Open Solutions*, 6, 29885–29898. doi:10.1109/ACCESS.2018.2844255

Anbuchelian, S., & Lokesh, S., & Baskaran, M. (2016). Improving security in wireless sensor network using trust and metaheuristic algorithms. *International Conference on Computer and Information Sciences*, 233-241. 10.1109/ICCOINS.2016.7783220

Apruzzese, G., Colajanni, M., Ferretti, L., Guido, A., & Marchetti, M. (2018). On the effectiveness of machine and deep learning for cyber security. In T. Minárik, R. Jakschis, & L. Lindstrom (Eds.), *International Conference on Cyber Conflict* (pp. 371-390), Tallinn, Estonia: Academic Press. 10.23919/CYCON.2018.8405026

Aung, Y. Y., & Min, M. M. (2018). An analysis of k-means algorithm based network intrusion detection system. *Advances in Science. Technology and Engineering Systems Journal*, *3*(1), 496–501. doi:10.25046/aj030160

Bae, C., Yeh, W.-C., Mohd, A. M. S., Chung, Y. Y., & Hsieh, T.-J. (2012). A novel anomaly-network intrusion detection system using ABC algorithms. *International Journal of Innovative Computing, Information, & Control*, *8*(12), 8231–8248.

Basnet, R., Mukkamala, S., & Sung, A. H. (2008). Detection of phishing attacks: A machine learning approach. In B. Prasad (Ed.), Soft Computing Applications in Industry (pp. 373-383). Berlin, Germany: Springer-Verlag.

Chhikara, PPatel, K. A. (2013). Enhancing network security using Ant Colony Optimization. *Global Journal of Computer Science and Technology Network. Web & Security*, *13*(4), 1–5.

David, O. E., & Netanyahu, S. N. (2015). Deepsign: Deep learning for automatic malware signature generation and classification. In *International Joint Conference on Neural Networks* (pp. 1-8). Killarney, Ireland: Academic Press.

Deepa, T. P. (2014). *Survey on need for cyber security in India.* doi:10.13140/2.1.4555.7768

Diro, A. A., & Chilamkurti, N. (2017). Distributed attack detection scheme using deep learning approach for Internet of Things. *Future Generation Computer Systems*, *82*, 761–768. doi:10.1016/j.future.2017.08.043

Dollah, R. F. M., Faizal, M. A., Arif, F., Mas'ud, M. Z., & Xin, L. K. (2018). Machine learning for http botnet detection using classifier algorithms. *Journal of Telecommunication, Electronic and Computer Engineering*, *10*(1-7), 27-30.

Eberhart, R., & Shi, Y. (2011). *Computational Intelligence: Concepts to Implementations*. Elsevier Morgan Kaufmann Publications.

Elmendili, F., Maqran, N., Idrissi, Y. E. B. E., & Chaoui, H. (2017). A security approach based on honeypots: Protecting online social network from malicious profiles. *Advances in Science. Technology and Engineering Systems Journal*, *2*(3), 198–204. doi:10.25046/aj020326

Ford, V., & Siraj, A. (2014). Applications of machine learning in cyber security. In *International Conference on Computer Applications in Industry and Engineering* (pp. 1-7). Academic Press.

Gavrilut, D., Cimpoesu, M., Anton, D., & Ciortuz, L. (2009). Malware detection using machine learning. In *Proceedings of the International Multiconference on Computer Science and Information Technology* (pp. 735–741). Mragowo, Poland: Academic Press.

Ghourabi, A., Abbes, T., & Bouhoula, A. (2013). Automatic analysis of web service honeypot data using machine learning techniques. In *International Joint Conference CISIS'12-ICEUTE'12-SOCO'12 Special Sessions* (pp. 1-11). Berlin, Germany: Springer-Verlag. 10.1007/978-3-642-33018-6_1

Glenn, M., & Lambert, I. I. (2017). *Security Analytics: Using deep learning to detect cyber attacks.* University of North Florida.

Gutierrez, M., & Kiekintveld, C. (2017). Adapting with honeypot Configurations to detect evolving exploits. In *Conference on Autonomous Agents and MultiAgent Systems* (pp. 1565-1567). Sao Paulo, Brazil: Academic Press.

Haneef, F., & Singh, S. (2017). Selection technique for intrusion detection system based on IWD and ACO. *International Journal of Advanced Research in Computer Science, 8*(9), 270–275. doi:10.26483/ijarcs.v8i9.4857

Hardy, W., Chen, L., Hou, S., Ye, Y., & Li, X. (2016). DL 4 MD: A deep learning framework for intelligent malware detection. In *Int'l Conf. Data Mining* (pp. 61-67). CSREA Press.

Hassanpour, R., Dogdu, E., Choupani, R., Goker, O., & Nazli, N. (2018). Phishing E-mail Detection By Using Deep Learning Algorithms. *ACMSE Conference*, New York. NY. 10.1145/3190645.3190719

Hoang, X. D., & Nguyen, Q. C. (2018). Botnet detection based on machine learning techniques using DNS query data. *Future Internet, 10*(43), 1–11.

Hodashinsky, I. A., & Mech, M. A. (2018). Constructing a fuzzy network intrusion classifier based on differential evolution and harmonic search. *International Journal of Computer Networks & Communications, 10*(2), 85–91. doi:10.5121/ijcnc.2018.10208

Kang, M. J., & Kang, J.-W. (2016). Intrusion detection system using deep neural network for in-vehicle network security. *PLoS ONE, 11*(6).

Kaur, A., Pal, S., & Singh, A. P. (2018). Hybridization of k-means and firefly algorithm for intrusion detection system. *International Journal of System Assurance Engineering and Management, 9*(4), 901–910. doi:10.100713198-017-0683-8

Khalil, T. (2017). IoT security against DDoS attacks using machine learning algorithms. *International Journal of Scientific and Research Publications, 7*(6), 739–741.

Kozik, R., & Choraś, M. (2014). Machine learning techniques for cyber attacks detection. In R. S. Choraś (Ed.), *Image Processing and Communications Challenges 5* (pp. 391–398). Springer International Publishing. doi:10.1007/978-3-319-01622-1_44

Kreuk, F., Barak, A., Aviv, S., Baruch, M., Pinkas, B., & Keshet, J. (2018). Deceiving End-to-End Deep Learning Malware Detectors using Adversarial Examples. In *Conference on Neural Information Processing Systems* (pp. 1-6), Montreal, Canada: Academic Press.

Kumar, K. P., & Prasad, B, B. R. (2015). Investigating open issues in swarm intelligence for mitigating security threats in MANET. *Iranian Journal of Electrical and Computer Engineering, 5*(5), 1194–1201.

Kumarnath, J., & Batri, K. (2018). A BAT algorithm based enhancement of physical layer security in a multi domain-elastic optical network. *International Journal of Pure and Applied Mathematics, 119*(15), 2519–2525.

Kwon, D., Kim, H., Kim, J., Suh, S. C., Kim, I., & Kim, K. J. (2017). A survey of deep learning-based network anomaly detection. In Cluster Computing (pp 1-13). Springer Science+Business Media.

Li, S.-H., Kao, Y.-C., Zhang, Z.-C., Chuang, Y.-P., & Yen, D. C. (2015). A network behavior-based botnet detection mechanism using PSO and k-means. *ACM Transactions on Management Information Systems*, *6*(1), 1–30. doi:10.1145/2676869

Lin, Z., Chen, G., Guo, W., & Liu, Y. (2008). PSO-BPNN-based prediction of network security situation. In *International Conference on Innovative Computing Information and Control* (pp. 1-5). Dalian, Liaoning, China. IEEE.

Liu, Q., Li, P., Zhao, W., Cai, W., Yu, S., & Leung, C. M. V. (2018). A survey on security threats and defensive techniques of machine learning: A data driven view. IEEE. *IEEE Access: Practical Innovations, Open Solutions*, *6*, 12103–12117. doi:10.1109/ACCESS.2018.2805680

Lobo, L. M. R. J., & Chavan, S. B. (2012). Use of genetic algorithm in network security. International Journal of Computers and Applications, 53(8), 1–7. doi:10.5120/8438-2221 doi:10.5120/8438-2221

Mahalakshmi, S., & Vadivel, R. (2018). Particle Swarm Optimization algorithm (PSO) used for security enhancement in MANET. *International Journal of Advanced Research in Computer Science*, *9*(2), 233–241. doi:10.26483/ijarcs.v9i2.5643

Maimo, L. F., Angel, L. P. G., Clemente, F. G. J., Pérez, M. G., & Pérez, G. M. (2018). A self-adaptive deep learning-based system for anomaly detection in 5G networks. In Special on Cyber-Physical-Social Computing and Networking (pp. 7700 – 7712). Academic Press.

Murphree, J. (2016). *Machine learning anomaly detection in large systems*. Anaheim, CA: IEEE Autotestcon. doi:10.1109/AUTEST.2016.7589589

Nallakannu, S. M., & Thiagarajan, R. (2016). PSO-based optimal peer selection approach for highly secure and trusted P2P system. *Security and Communication Networks*, *9*(13), 2186–2199.

Navarro-Lara, J., Deruyver, A., & Parrend, P. (2016). Morwilog: An ACO-based System for Outlining Multi-Step Attacks. In *IEEE Symposium Series on Computational Intelligence* (pp. 1-9). Athens, Greece: IEEE. 10.1109/SSCI.2016.7849902

Nazeer, M. I., Mallah, G. A., Bhatra, N. R., & Memon, R. A. (2018). Implication of genetic algorithm in cryptography to enhance security. *International Journal of Advanced Computer Science and Applications*, *9*(6), 375–379. doi:10.14569/IJACSA.2018.090651

Ognawala, S., Amato, R. N., Pretschner, A., & Kulkarni, P. (2018). Automatically assessing vulnerabilities discovered by compositional analysis. In *International Workshop on Machine Learning and Software Engineering in Symbiosis* (pp. 16-25). New York, NY: Academic Press. 10.1145/3243127.3243130

Owezarski, P. (2014). Unsupervised classification and characterization of honeypot attacks. In *International Conference on Network and Service Management* (pp. 1-10). Rio de Janeiro, Brazil: Academic Press. 10.1109/CNSM.2014.7014136

Pavani, K., & Damodaram, A. (2014). Anomaly detection system for routing attacks in mobile ad hoc networks. *International Journal of Network Security*, *6*, 13–24.

Peng, K., & Leung, V., Zheng, LWang, S., Huang, C., & Lin, T. (2018). Intrusion Detection System Based on Decision Tree over Big Data in Fog Environment. *Wireless Communications and Mobile Computing*, 1–10.

Prabha, S., & Yadav, R. (2018). Differential evolution for mobile ad-hoc networks: A review. *International Journal on Computer Science and Engineering*, 6(6), 1459–1467.

Ramasamy, S., & Eswaramoorthy, K. (2017). Ant colony optimization based handoff scheme and verifiable secret sharing security with M-M scheme for VoIP. *International Journal of Intelligent Engineering and Systems*, 10(5), 267–277. doi:10.22266/ijies2017.1031.29

Sebopelo, R., Isong, B., & Gasela, N. (2019). Identification of compromised nodes in MANETs using machine learning technique. *International Journal of Computer Network and Information Security*, 1(1), 1–10. doi:10.5815/ijcnis.2019.01.01

Shrivastava, N., & Richariya, V. (2012). Ant colony optimization with classification algorithms used for intrusion detection. *International Journal of Computational Engineering & Management*, 15(1), 54–63.

Sowah, A. R., Ofori-Amanfo, K. B., Mills, G. A., & Koumadi, M. K. (2019). Detection and prevention of man-in-the-middle spoofing attacks in MANETs using predictive techniques in Artificial Neural Networks (ANN). *Journal of Computer Networks and Communications*, 1-14.

Srinivasan, H., Srihari, S. N., & Beal, J. M. (2006). Machine learning for signature verification. In P. Kalra, & S. Peleg (Eds.), Computer Vision, Graphics and Image Processing (pp. 761-775). Berlin, Germany: Springer-Verlag.

Talreja, V., Valenti, M. C., & Nasrabadi, M. N. (2017). Multibiometric secure system based on deep learning. In *IEEE Global Conference on Signal and Information Processing* (pp. 298-302). West Virginia University. 10.1109/GlobalSIP.2017.8308652

Wang, Z. (2018). Deep learning-based intrusion detection with adversaries. *IEEE Access. Challenges and Opportunities of Big Data Against Cyber Crime*, 6, 38367–38384.

Xiang, C. (2018). Network intrusion detection by using particle swarm optimization and neural network. *Journal of Networking Technology*, 9(1), 22–30.

Yi, P., Guan, Y., Zou, F., Yao, Y., Wang, W., & Zhu, T. (2018). Web phishing Detection Using a Deep Learning Framework. *Wireless Communications and Mobile Computing*, 2018, 1–9. doi:10.1155/2018/4678746

Yin, C., Zhu, Y., Fei, J., & He, X. (2017). A deep learning approach for intrusion detection using recurrent neural networks. *IEEE Access: Practical Innovations, Open Solutions*, 5, 21954–21961. doi:10.1109/ACCESS.2017.2762418

Zekri, M., El Kafhali, S., Aboutabit, N., & Saadi, Y. (2017). DDoS attack detection using machine learning techniques in cloud computing environments. In *International Conference of Cloud Computing Technologies and Applications* (pp. 1-8). Rabat, Morocco: Academic Press. 10.1109/CloudTech.2017.8284731

KEY TERMS AND DEFINITIONS

Cyber Security: A set of information and computer technologies (ICT) are employed to protect computational resources from unauthorized access.

Deep Learning Algorithm: It is a kind of machine learning algorithm which involves multiple layers of neural network architecture, large set of dataset and highly powerful computer system for execution.

Machine Learning Algorithm: A set of mathematical approaches are utilized to give training, make computer system to learn and perform set of actions or tasks autonomously.

Nature-Inspired Computing (NIC) Paradigms: Global optimization algorithm is developed by inspiring natural phenomena such as foraging behavior, evolution, cell and molecular phenomena, reproduction, cognition and neuro systems, alignment phenomena in microscopes, non-biological systems and geo-science based techniques as source of metaphor for problem solving.

Chapter 2
A Review on Cyber Security Mechanisms Using Machine and Deep Learning Algorithms

Thiyagarajan P.
Central University of Tamil Nadu, India

ABSTRACT

Digitalization is the buzz word today by which every walk of our life has been computerized, and it has made our life more sophisticated. On one side, we are enjoying the privilege of digitalization. On the other side, security of our information in the internet is the most concerning element. A variety of security mechanisms, namely cryptography, algorithms which provide access to protected information, and authentication including biometric and steganography, provide security to our information in the Internet. In spite of the above mechanisms, recently artificial intelligence (AI) also contributes towards strengthening information security by providing machine learning and deep learning-based security mechanisms. The artificial intelligence (AI) contribution to cyber security is important as it serves as a provoked reaction and a response to hackers' malicious actions. The purpose of this chapter is to survey recent papers which are contributing to information security by using machine learning and deep learning techniques.

INTRODUCTION

Today is the era of Internet where everything become digitalized including purchasing items in mall, bank transactions, ticket reservations, online shopping, top secrets in government organisation especially in military and defence. On one hand we are enjoying the privilege of digitalization which results on accumulating data in terabytes, but on the other hand the accumulated data need to be converted to information and the information need to be mined to get knowledge to enhance user experience in usage of Internet.

DOI: 10.4018/978-1-5225-9611-0.ch002

While the users are enjoying the advantage of Internet, the most concerning thing about Internet is the safety our data. The technique of protecting computers, networks, programs and data from unauthorized access or attacks that are aimed for exploitation is called Cyber Security.

The digital world is replacing the physical, the more realistic view is that the two worlds are coming together. Organizations are not really prepared to face the challenges which is the result of the amalgamation of digital and physical world. In the case of cybercrime, it states that it isn't displacing physical acts of crime, they are occurring in concert. Criminals who might once have used explosives to cripple critical infrastructure, such as transportation, power grids or water systems, for example, may be now able to achieve their goals remotely by attacking the computers that operate those systems, incurring less risk in the process.

Cyber Security is broadly categorised into four major areas, they are:

1. Application Security
2. Information Security
3. Disaster Recovery
4. Network Security

Approach to Cyber Security

In the case of Cyber Security, securing the data is a very big challenge. The attacks are increasing at a very high speed and the tools which can break the security are becoming popular. Nowadays, it is possible even for the layman without any technical knowledge to use different types of tools to break the security.

In the current context, it is not only necessary for us to protect the data but also is highly necessary for us to protect whole information system. The unexpected and drastic increase of attackers makes the security of data in Internet a major concern. In addition to the various security mechanism available now artificial intelligence and machine learning also contributes in strengthening the Information Security.

Cyber Threats in US from 2010-2018 Statistics

Annual number of data breaches and exposed records in the United States from 2010 to 2018 (in millions) in shown in Figure.1.

Impact of Various Threats in Cyber World (Present and Future):

With a serious lack of digital security mechanisms and experts to battle progressively refined invaders combined with a developing reliance on innovation, the cybercrime pose a potential threat in forthcoming years in Internet. Here are a few of the numerous digital dangers anticipated to cause hurt in the year ahead.

Automated Cars with Connection: We are in the digital age of making driverless cars and vehicles. To optimize the performance and make the customers zone comfortable the driverless cars are associated with inbuilt sensors. This is done by embedding and integrating the devices by the smartphone. As the advancement of the technology, the security can be breached as it is connected with the sensors.

Insider support Attacks: Beyond hackers hoping to make a benefit through taking individual and corporate information, whole country states are presently utilizing their digital aptitudes to invade dif-

Figure 1. Annual number of data breaches and exposed records in U.S.

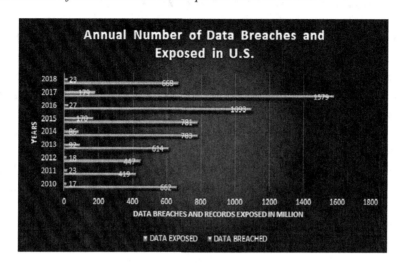

ferent governments and perform assaults on basic framework. Digital world today is a noteworthy risk not only for the private division and for people however for the administration and the country in general.

IoT Attacks: The Internet of Things is one of the progressively growing fields. The IoT is becoming easier for the hackers to breach the security of the connected devices available. By using a botnet toolkit, hackers can access any device with quick and ease.

Cryptocurrency Attacks: As the ransomware attacks makes the biggest threat in present digital world, the growth of bitcoin and the cryptocurrency is also increasing. The hackers making the money by cryptocurrency as it is not get tracked by anyone. "Mining is a computationally intensive process that computers comprising a cryptocurrency network complete to verify the transaction record, called the blockchain, and receive digital coins in return," explained the MIT Technology Review. In 2020, the threat won't just be the mining but the theft of computer processing power (Lilian Weng, 2017).

Smart Medical Devices and Smart Healthcare: The role of digitalizing network is making a revolution in the healthcare field. By using IoT, we can easily access the patient records online and medical specialists can better use the innovation and advancement of the technology by adapting to the smart medical devices. However, as the healthcare industry adapts to digital, there are a number of concerns around privacy, safety and cyber security threats.

Outside Parties: Outside parties such as vendors and contractors positioning a huge risk to corporations, as the majority does not have a secure system or steadfast team in place to manage these third-party employees. According to a Ponemon Institute Research Report, "there is no clear accountability for the correct handling of the third-party risk management program" (Lilian Weng, 2017).

A few common types of cyber security threats remain pervasive are:

1. Phishing attacks
2. DoS attacks
3. Insider threats
4. Malware
5. Weak credentials

Various Kinds of Approach to Cyber Security

The Internet has become a significant feature for any business movement. In spite of so many security features available, Cyber Crimes in Internet is something which cannot be avoided. Some crimes preceding to the Internet, such as theft and scams, have now found the perfect tool for developing these attacks in the Internet. The internet allows criminals to hide their original identity and allows to make the fake identity and to execute several kinds of offenses (e.g. to sell drugs, to sell privacy information, etc.)

In recent years, Internet Crime (e-Crime) has changed its business model, becoming more professional. The most skilled criminals offer their services to other criminals with less IT skills. This is known as CaaS (Crime-as-a-Service). Criminals often offer their skills in forums and markets of the Deep Web and the Dark Net, where advanced anonymization techniques are used to allow users to communicate freely without being traced. In these sites, potential clients can find many types of solutions for cyber illegal activities. For instance, they find software kits, which allow less skilled criminals to infect thousands of computers to steal sensitive information, such as online bank credentials and credit card details (JT Gaietto 2018).

Some of the approaches to strengthen cyber security are:

1. Computational and artificial intelligence
2. Internet of Things (IoT)
3. Big Data
4. Social implications of technology
5. Incident Response and Malware Analysis
6. Machine Learning
7. Deep Learning

From among the above listed approaches, here we are going to discuss about how the two emerging approaches called as Machine Learning and Deep Learning are used in strengthening cyber security.

Diagrammatic Representation for Machine Learning, Deep Learning and Artificial Intelligence

The relationship between machine learning, deep learning and artificial intelligence is shown in Figure 2.
Let us briefly discuss about the Cyber Security by using Machine Learning.

Machine Learning Towards Cyber Security

Machine learning is a system which automatically improve itself with its experience. This machine learning is quite different from software, which doesn't improve itself how many ever time it is executed to perform the same task. For example, if a user launch a browser and browse the same exact website, a traditional browser will not learn that it should load the website on launch which you are frequently accessing. With machine learning, the browser can gain the ability to learn from previous observations to make inference about future behaviour and predict what you want to do in extremely new situations.

To understand how machine learning works it is necessary for us to understand "Data" the back bone of Machine Learning. Consider an email spam detection algorithm, in which ordinary spam filters will

Figure 2. Relationship between machine learning, deep learning and artificial intelligence

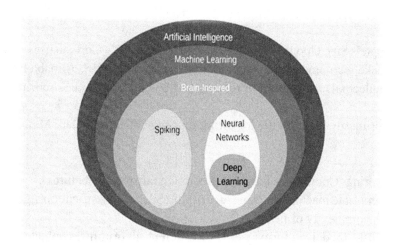

simply blacklist certain addresses and allow other email to inbox. Where as in Machine Learning this approach is improved by comparing verified spam emails with verified legitimate email. By comparing the common features between spam and legitimate emails, which features were more frequently present in spam and legitimate emails were found out. Using the features the process will automatically infer a label (Spam or Legitimate) and it is called as classification. Another important technique in Machine Learning is forecasting which predicts the future with the help of past data.

Machine learning is the subset of Artificial Intelligence (AI). Artificial Intelligence is a way of making a computer to think intelligently like human. The human intelligence is created in machines based on how human brain thinks, how human brain learn, decide and work on solving a problem in efficient way. The usage of artificial intelligence was started way back in 1923 when "Rossum's Universal Robots" were came into exist. After which there were so many revolutions in the field of artificial intelligence some of the major breakthrough are listed below:

In 1964, Danny Bobrow from MIT proved that computers can understand natural language which were used to solve algebra. In 1969, Scientist at Stanford developed a robot with locomotion, perception and problem solving.

In 1979, first computer-controlled vehicle was built. In 1997, artificial intelligence was used to develop program called "Deep Blue Chess Program" which beats the then world chess champion Garry Kasparov. In 1998, Furby, the first artificial intelligence player, was driven to the market.

In 2000, Kismet named robot which can use gesture and mimic movements in communication is introduced. In 2000, The Nomad robot explores remote regions of Antarctica looking for meteorite samples.

In 2000, iRobot's Roomba autonomously vacuums the floor while navigating and avoiding obstacles. In 2004, OWL Web Ontology Language was introduced. In 2004, DARPA introduces the DARPA Grand Challenge requiring competitors to produce autonomous vehicles for prize money.

In 2004, NASA's robotic exploration rovers Spirit and Opportunity autonomously navigate the surface of Mars. In 2005, Asimo, the closest robot to artificial intelligence and human ability and skill, is introduced and at the same time Blue Brain is born, a project to simulate the brain at molecular detail.

In 2007, DARPA launches the Urban Challenge for autonomous cars to obey traffic rules and operate in an urban environment. In 2009, Google builds an autonomous car. In 2010: Asimo is made to act using mind power.

In 2011-2014 Apple's Siri, Google's Google now and Microsoft's Cortana uses natural languages to answer questions, make recommendations and perform actions. In 2018, Alibaba language processing AI outscores top intellectuals at Stanford in reading and comprehension test scoring 82.5 on 1,00,000 questions.

An ML method primarily includes the following four steps (Ciresan, Dan; Meier, U.; Schmidhuber, J. 2012):

1. Feature Engineering. Choice as a basis for prediction (attributes, features).
2. Choose the appropriate machine learning algorithm. (Such as classification algorithm or regression algorithm, high complexity or fast)
3. Train and evaluate model performance. (For different algorithms, evaluate and select the best performing model.)
4. Use the trained model to classify or predict the unknown data.

Application of AI

AI has placed its finger prints in almost all fields, some of them are discussed here:

1. Natural Language Processing (NLP): Artificial Intelligence makes the computer to understand the natural language spoken by humans. NLP is broadly defined as the automatic manipulation of natural language (Speech and text) by computer software.
2. Expert Systems: There are some applications which integrate machine, software and special information to impart reasoning and advising. Expert Systems also provides advice to the users.

Concepts of Learning

Learning is the process of converting experience into expertise or knowledge. Learning can be broadly classified into three categories

Supervised Learning

Supervised learning as the name indicates a presence of supervisor as teacher. Basically supervised learning is a learning in which we teach or train the machine using data (training data test) which is well labelled that means some data is already tagged with correct answer. After that, machine is provided with new set of examples (testing data) so that supervised learning algorithm analyses the training data (set of training examples) and produces a correct outcome from labelled data.

Supervised learning classified into two categories of algorithms:

Classification: The classification algorithm is used when the output variable is a category, such as "Red" or "blue" or "disease" and "no disease".

Regression: The regression algorithm is used when the output variable is a real value, such as "dollars" or "weight".

Unsupervised Learning

Unsupervised learning is the training of machine using information that is neither classified nor labelled and allowing the algorithm to act on that information without guidance. Here the task of machine is to group unsorted information according to similarities, patterns and differences without any prior training of data.

Unlike supervised learning, no teacher is provided that means no training will be given to the machine. Therefore machine is restricted to find the hidden structure in unlabelled data by itself.

Unsupervised learning classified into two categories of algorithms:

Clustering: A clustering problem is where you want to discover the inherent groupings in the data, such as grouping customers by purchasing behaviour.

Association: An association rule learning problem is where you want to discover rules that describe large portions of your data, such as people that buy X also tend to buy Y.

Reinforcement Learning

Reinforcement learning is an area of Machine Learning. Reinforcement is taking about suitable action to maximize reward in a particular situation. It is employed by various software and machines to find the best possible behaviour or path it should take in a specific situation. Reinforcement learning differs from the supervised learning in a way that in supervised learning the training data has the answer key with it so the model is trained with the correct answer itself whereas in reinforcement learning, there is no answer but the reinforcement agent decides what to do with the given task. In the absence of training dataset, it is bound to learn from its experience.

Various Kinds of Machine Learning Algorithms in General

The machine learning algorithms are classified into seven major categories, they are:

1. Deep learning
2. Neural Networks
3. Regularization
4. Rule system
5. Regression
6. Ensemble
7. Bayesian Networks
8. Decision Tree
9. Dimensionality reduction
10. Instance based
11. Clustering

The above categories is further classified and it is represented in Figure.3.

Figure 3. Classification of machine learning

CYBER SECURITY SOLUTIONS USING MACHINE LEARNING AND ARTIFICIAL INTELLIGENCE IN LITERATURE:

Problems in cyber security and the solutions using artificial intelligence and machine learning which are reported in various articles are summarised and tabulated below in Table 1.

Some of the Machine Learning Algorithms Used in Strengthening Cyber Security

Among the available machine learning algorithm, the majority of machine learning algorithms which are used in strengthening cyber security are shown in Figure.4.

Deep Learning

Deep Learning is about learning multiple levels of representation and abstraction that help to make sense of data such as images, sound, and text.

Deep learning architectures such as deep neural networks, deep belief networks and recurrent neural networks (Alex Graves, Abdel-rahman Mohamed,Geoffrey Hinton 2013) have been applied to fields including computer vision, speech recognition, natural language processing, audio recognition, social network filtering, machine translation, bioinformatics, drug design, medical image analysis, material inspection and board game programs where they have produced results comparable to and in some cases superior to human experts (Krizhevsky, Alex; Sutskever, Ilya; Hinton, Geoffry 2012) (R. Pascanu, J. W. Stokes, H. Sanossian, M. Marinescu, and A. Thomas 2015).

Deep learning is subset of machine learning in Artificial Intelligence (AI) that imitates the working of human brain in processing data and creating patterns for use in decision making. Deep learning utilizes a hierarchical level of artificial neural networks to carry out process of machine learning. This hierarchical function of deep learning enables machines to process data in a nonlinear approach.

Table 1. Summarization of various research articles which uses machine learning in strengthening cyber security

S.No	References	Proposed Method	Algorithm Used	Dataset Used	Solutions
1.	(Sherif, S., Issa, T., Ali A., Ghorbani, B. S., David, Z., Wei Lu, John Felix, Payman Hakimian. 2011)	DDoS attack detection system	SVM with RBF (Gaussian) kernel	Three training and test datasets were used	Evaluating success of system, precision, recall, negative predictive value was calculated and achieved 85% accuracy.
2.	(Nguyen, H. T., FRANKE, K. 2012)	Novel method for cyberattacks targeting web application	Naïve Bayes AdaBoost Part J48 (Best solution given)	CSIC 2010 HTTP dataset	Higher detection percentage while having low positive rate
3.	(Hoque, M. S., Mukit, M., Bikas, M., Naser, A. 2012)	Models for detecting intrusion	Genetic algorithms and fuzzy logic	Decision tree algorithm (best results)	Effective on Different features of CI models
4.	(Zamani, M., Mahnush M. 2013)	Short sequence model for detecting anomalies	Support Vector Machine (SVM) ADFA-LD for conducting experiments	k values used (k=3,5,8,10) when k=5 provides best solution	Satisfactory achievement with decrease of computational cost largely.
5.	(Neethu, B., 2013)	Bio inspired computing technique	Two clustering algorithms: 1. ATTA-C 2. K-means for comparison	ISOT dataset (huge volume)	Exploring botnets quickly and precisely
6.	(Kato, K., Vitaly K. 2014)	Feature-Feature Score (FFSc)- A Novel statistical methodology to analyse DDoS attacks from normal traffic.	Entropy form source IP, Variation of source IP, packet rate.	CAIDA DDoS 2007, MIT DARPA datasets.	Detection of accuracy yields 98%.
7.	(Xie, M., Jiankun, H., Jill, S. 2014)	Adaptive Intrusion Detection System (A-IDS)	Naïve Bayes, Bayes Network, Decision Stump, RBF Network for comparison	ECML -PKKD 2007 HTTP dataset, CISIC 2010 HTTP dataset	For detecting heterogeneous and adversarial network environments with 10%(first dataset) and 8% (second dataset) higher accuracy
8.	(Kozik, R., Choras, M., Renk, R., Hołubowicz, W. 2015)	PCA framework for network intrusion detection system	Naïve Bayes	KDDCup 1999 dataset	Higher Detection rate, Less time consuming, with 94% accuracy.
9.	(Bhuyan, M. H., Dhruba K. B., Jugal K. K. 2015)	Novel approach with two stages	Empirical distribution: 1.Flow based approach 2. Graph based approach Social Network Community	CTU 13 datset	To detect the presence of botnet and identifying botnet.
10.	(Wijesinghe, U., Udaya T.,Vijay V. 2015)	Creating unbiased full feature real-life network intrusion datasets	Six different attack scenarios were created and discussed.	Intrusion dataset	For compensating crucial lack of available datasets, development and validation operation of detection systems.
11.	(Haddadi, F., Le L., D., Porter, Zincir-Heywood L. 2015)	Detecting wide range of botnet families by analysing network traffic flows.	IP flow data in unlabelled traffic.	IPFIX dataset, Dataset templates in first part.	New methodology in contributing available IP flow based botnet detection studies.
12.	(Bhuyan, M. H., Bhattacharyya, D. K., Jugal K. Kalita. 2015)	Analyzing various botnet detection approaches based on model used and type of data employed. (BotHunter and Snort)	C4.5, Knn (k nearset neighbor), SVM, Bayesian Networks. Data Mining Techniques used: Packet payload based, Traffic flow based.	CAIDA, ISOT, five publicly available botnet dataset.	Performance of the flow based system is higher or similar to the results shown.
13.	(Bhamare, D., Salman, T., Samaka, M., Erbad, A., Jain, R. 2016)	Detecting P2P bots that is newest and most challenging types of botnets currently available.	Nearest neighbour, Linear support vector machine, Artificial neural network, Nearest neighbour classifiers, Naïve Bayes.	P2P botnet C&C phase.	True detection rate of 90% for SVM, Nearest neighbour, Artificial neural network.
14.	(Hoque, N,, Dhruba K. B,, Jugal K. Kalita. 2016)	Empirical study using different information metrics for detection DDoS attacks.	Entropy measures: Hartley entropy, Shannon entropy, Renyin++s entropy, Renyin++s generalised entropy.	CAIDA, TUIDS, DDoS datasets.	Handling important security problems of detecting high-rate and low-rate DDoS attacks.
15.	(Chowdhury, S. 2017)	New botnet detection method	Unsupervised algorithm: Self Organizing Map (SOM) clustering. Detection algorithm: Support Vector Machine (SVM) for comparison.	CTU13: The largest dataset	Detecting bot within limited no. of nodes with accepted accuracy.
16.	(Wang, J., Ioannis Ch Paschalidis. 2017)	IDS using genetic algorithms	Evolution theory for information evolution	KDD99 benchmark dataset	To Efficiently detect various types of network intrusions in order to filter the traffic data and decreasing complexity.

Figure 4. Machine learning algorithm used in strengthening cyber security

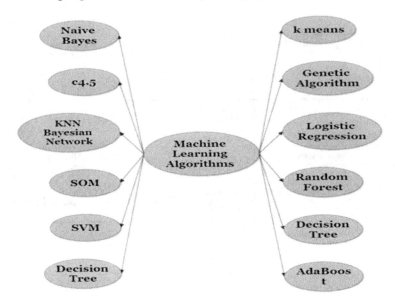

Various Kinds of Approach in Deep Learning

Deep learning is not a solution that can solve all the Information Security problems because it needs extensive labelled datasets. Unfortunately, no such labelled datasets are readily available. However, there are several Information Security use cases where the deep learning networks are making significant improvements to the existing solutions. Malware detection and network intrusion detection are two such areas where deep learning has shown significant improvements over the rule-based and classic machine learning-based solutions.

Network intrusion detection systems are typically rule-based and signature-based controls that are deployed at the perimeter to detect known threats. The primary goal of cyber-attacks is to steal the enterprise customer data, sales data, intellectual property documents, source codes and software keys. The adversaries exfiltrate the stolen data to remote servers in encrypted traffic along with the regular traffic.

Most often adversaries use an anonymous network that makes it difficult for the security defenders to trace the traffic. Moreover, the exfiltrated data is typically encrypted, rendering rule-based network intrusion tools and firewalls to be ineffective. Recently, anonymous networks have also been used for C&C by specific variants of ransomware/malware.

Deep Learning in Cyber Security Algorithms

Almost both the machine learning and deep learning uses similar types of algorithms and datasets. However, SVM (Support Vector Machine) and K-nearest neighbour are the most frequently used algorithm in the Deep Learning and it is discussed in this chapter.

SVM- Support Vector Machine

SVM is an exciting algorithm and the concepts are relatively simple. SVM is explained in simple terms through Maximal-Margin Classifier.

Maximal-Margin Classifier

The Maximal-Margin Classifier is a hypothetical classifier that best explains how SVM works in practice. The numeric input variables (x) in your data (the columns) form an n-dimensional space. For example, if you had two input variables, this would form a two-dimensional space.

A hyperplane is a line that splits the input variable space. In SVM, a hyperplane is selected to best separate the points in the input variable space by their class, either class 0 or class 1. In two-dimensions you can visualize this as a line and let's assume that all of input points can be completely separated by this line. For example:

$$B_0 + (B_1 * X_1) + (B_2 * X_2) = 0$$

where the coefficients (B_1 and B_2) that determine the slope of the line and the intercept (B_0) are found by the learning algorithm, and X_1 and X_2 are the two input variables. We can make classifications using this line. By plugging in input values into the line equation, we can calculate whether a new point is above or below the line.

Above the line, the equation returns a value greater than 0 and the point belongs to the first class (class 0). Below the line, the equation returns a value less than 0 and the point belongs to the second class (class 1). A value close to the line returns a value close to zero and the point may be difficult to classify. If the magnitude of the value is large, the model may have more confidence in the prediction.

The distance between the line and the closest data points is referred to as the margin. The best or optimal line that can separate the two classes is the line that as the largest margin. This is called the Maximal-Margin hyperplane.

The margin is calculated as the perpendicular distance from the line to only the closest points. Only these points are relevant in defining the line and in the construction of the classifier. These points are called the support vectors. They support or define the hyperplane. The hyperplane is learned from training data using an optimization procedure that maximizes the margin.

K Nearest Neighbour

The k-Nearest-Neighbors (kNN) method of classification is one of the simplest methods in machine learning, and is a great way to introduce to machine learning and classification in general. At its most basic level, it is essentially classification by finding the most similar data points in the training data, and making an educated guess based on their classifications. Although very simple to understand and implement, this method has seen wide application in many domains, such as in recommendation systems, semantic searching, and anomaly detection.

As we would need in any machine learning problem, we must first find a way to represent data points as feature vectors. A feature vector is our mathematical representation of data, and since the desired characteristics of our data may not be inherently numerical, pre-processing and feature-engineering may be required in order to create these vectors. Given data with N unique features, the feature vector would be a vector of length N, where entry I of the vector represents that data point's value for feature I. Each feature vector can thus be thought of as a point in R^N.

The gist of the kNN method is, for each classification query, to:

1. Compute a distance value between the item to be classified and every item in the training data-set
2. Pick the k closest data points (the items with the k lowest distances)
3. Conduct a "majority vote" among those data points — the dominating classification in that pool is decided as the final classification.

The datasets like DARPA 1998, HTTP CSIC, ISOT are some of the important datasets used for kNN in machine learning.

Dataset and its Need

The term **dataset** refers to the file which contains one or more records similar to database. It may have hospital patient records, insurance policy records, like anything that is recorded as a group that is used to run an application.

It is also used to store information needed by applications of the Operating Systems, source programs, macro functions, system libraries or parameters. In Machine learning- a sort of AI that uses massive datasets to show computers a way to reply to and act like humans – permits businesses to optimize operations, deliver higher client experiences, enhance security and additional operations.

There are two important types of datasets.

1. Training dEODtasets
2. Testing datasets

Separating knowledge into training and testing sets is a very important a part of data processing models. Typically, after we separate an information set into a training set and testing set, most of the information is employed for training, and a smaller portion of the information is employed for testing.

After a model has been developed with the help of training set, the developed model can be tested with testing data. In supervised algorithms we know all the data are labelled including the testing data, hence the output from the developed model can be validated with the label and its accuracy can be determined.

Cyber Security Datasets Using Machine Learning

There are various cyber security data sets out of which some of them are discussed below:

KDD Cup 1999 Dataset (DARPA 1998)

Intrusion Detection Evaluation Dataset. There were two parts to the 1998 DARPA Intrusion Detection Evaluation: an off-line evaluation and a real-time evaluation. Intrusion detection systems were tested in the off-line evaluation using network traffic and audit logs collected on a simulation network.

It is the first standard data by MIT Lincoln Laboratory under Défense Advanced Research Project Agency (DARPA) and Air Force Research Laboratory (AFRL) sponsorship to evaluate the network intrusion detection systems.

This DARPA evaluation dataset is used for the purpose of training as well as testing the intrusion detectors. These evaluations contributed significantly to the intrusion detection research by providing direction for research efforts and an objective calibration of the technical state-of-the-art. (DARPA Intrusion Detection Evaluation Dataset, 1998)

The attacks fall into five main classes namely, **Probe, Denial of Service (DoS), Remote to Local(R2L), User to Remote(U2R) and the Data attacks.** The Probe or Scan attacks automatically scan a network of computers or a DNS server to find valid IP addresses, active ports, host operating system types and known vulnerabilities. The DoS attacks are designed to disrupt a host or network service, TCP connections to a specific host, corruption of ARP cache entries. The Data attack is to exfiltrate special files which the security policy specifies should remain on the victim hosts.

ECML-PKKD 2007 Dataset

The ECML/PKDD 2007 Discovery Challenge was a data mining competition held in conjunction with the 18th European Conference on Machine Learning (ECML) and the 11th European Conference on Principles and Practice of Knowledge Discovery in Databases (PKDD) (Analyzing Web Traffic ECML/PKDD, 2007)

The Discovery Challenge outlined two tasks related to HTTP attack detection:

1. Classification of HTTP requests into attack types.Submissions were to be judged on runtime performance as well as classification performance.
2. Isolation of attack patterns. The goal of this task was to identify (within an attack) the shortest string that conveys the attack.

Dataset Format

The dataset will be defined in XML (portable and standard format). Each sample will be identified by a unique id, and will contain three major parts: Context (describes the environment in which the query is run), Class (describes how an expert will classify this sample) and the description of the query itself.

Context: It contains the following attributes:

1. Operating system running on the Web Server (UNIX, WINDOWS, UNKNOWN).
2. HTTP Server targeted by the request (APACHE, MIIS, UNKNOWN).
3. Is the XPATH technology understood by the server? (TRUE, FALSE, UNKNOWN)
4. Is there an LDAP database on the Web Server? (TRUE, FALSE, UNKNOWN)
5. Is there an SQL database on the Web Server? (TRUE, FALSE, UNKNOWN)

Classes

Classes lists the different subdivision levels of HTTP query categorization (and how they are represented in the context part of the dataset).

The "type" element indicate which class this request belongs to:

1.   Normal query (Valid)
2.   Cross-Site Scripting (XSS)
3.   SQL Injection (SqlInjection)
4.   LDAP Injection (LdapInjection)
5.   XPATH Injection (XPathInjection)
6.   Path traversal (PathTransversal)
7.   Command execution (OsCommanding)

Information Security and Object Technology (ISOT) Dataset

There are eight types of datasets in ISOT:

1.   ISOT Botnet Dataset
2.   ISOT Mouse Dynamics Dataset
3.   ISOT Stylometry Dataset
4.   ISOT Twitter Dataset
5.   ISOT Web Interactions Dataset
6.   ISOT Mouse gesture Dataset
7.   ISOT Fake news Dataset
8.   ISOT HTTP Botnet Dataset

The ISOT Botnet dataset is the combination of several existing publicly available malicious and non-malicious datasets. Unlike Storm using over net as a communication channel, Waledac utilizes HTTP communication and a fast-flux based DNS network exclusively. To represent non-malicious, everyday usage traffic, there are two different datasets, one from the Traffic Lab at Ericsson Research in Hungary and the other from the Lawrence Berkeley National Lab (LBNL) (Sherif Saad, Issa Traore et.al., 2011) The Ericsson Lab dataset contains a large number of general traffic from a variety of applications, including HTTP web browsing behaviour (Torrano-Gimenez, C,2009) World of Warcraft gaming packets, and packets from popular bittorrent clients such as Azureus. The recording of the network trace happened over three months period, from October 2004 to January 2005 covering 22 subnets (Dataset,2010) The dataset contains trace data for a variety of network activities spanning from web and email to backup and streaming media. This variety of traffic serves as a good example of day-to-day use of enterprise networks (Galllagher, B., Eliassırad, T. 2009).

HTTP CSIC 2010 DATASET

The HTTP dataset CSIC 2010 contains thousands of web requests automatically generated. It can be used for the testing of web attack protection systems. It was developed at the "Information Security Institute" of CSIC (Spanish Research National Council).

A current problem in web attack detection is the lack of publicly available data sets to test WAFs (Web Application Firewalls). The DARPA data set (ISOT Dataset Overview 2011) (Galllagher, B., Eliassırad, T. 2009) has been widely used for intrusion detection.

The HTTP dataset CSIC 2010 contains the generated traffic targeted to an e-Commerce web application. In this web application, users can buy items using a shopping cart and register by providing some personal information. As it is a web application in Spanish, the data set contains some Latin characters (Carmen Torrano Giménez, 2010).

The dataset is generated automatically and contains 36,000 normal requests and more than 25,000 anomalous requests. The HTTP requests are labelled as normal or anomalous and the dataset includes attacks such as SQL injection, buffer overflow, information gathering, files disclosure, CRLF injection, XSS, server side include, parameter tampering and so on. This dataset has been successfully used for web detection in previous works (C. Torrano-Gimenez,2009), (DARPA Intrusion Detection Evaluation Dataset 1998), (Sherif Saad,2011), Dataset (2010), Analyzing Web Traffic ECML/PKDD (2007), (Carmen Torrano Giménez,2010).

The dataset is divided into three different subsets. One subset for the training phase, which has only normal traffic. And two subsets for the test phase, one with normal traffic and the other one with malicious traffic.

Most Commonly Referred Dataset for Developing Cyber Security Machine Learning Model

The most commonly used Dataset for Cyber Security machine learning is summarised in the Table 2.

Acquisition of relevant data is the major challenge in Machine learning and Deep learning. Based on algorithms, data need to be processed before providing as input to respective algorithms. This has significant impact on results to be achieved or obtained. The dataset listed in table 2 are frequently used in Machine and Deep learning algorithms to provide solution to IDS (Intrusion Detection System) and Botnets.

In the paper authored by Neethu B, which detect Intrusion Detection attacks resulted in 94% of accuracy. In the paper authored by Nguyen and Franke, two datasets has been used namely

Table 2. Dataset for developing cyber security machine learning model

S. No	Dataset Name	Referred By	Analyzation
1.	KDD Cup 1999 Dataset (DARPA1998)	Neethu B	For detecting IDS Intrusion Detection System and for DDoS attacks
2.	ECML – PKDD 2007	Nguyen and Franke	Advanced -IDS (Intrusion Detection System)
3.	HTTP CSIC 2010 Dataset	Nguyen and Franke	Advanced -IDS (Intrusion Detection System)
4.	ISOT Dataset	Huseynov Haddadi et al	For detecting Botnets
5.	CTU13	Chowdhury et al	For detecting botnets

ECML – PKDD 2007 and HTTP CSIC 2010. The following machine learning algorithms has been used in the two data sets: Naive Bayes, Bayes Network, Decision Stump, RBF Network, Majority Voting, Hedge/Boosting, A-IDS and A-ExIDS. Among these algorithms for the dataset CSIC 2010, RBF Networks results in 72.46 which is the lowest accuracy and A-ExIDS provides 90.98 of accuracy results in detecting attacks in heterogeneous and adversarial environments. For the HTTP CSIC 2010 Dataset, decision stump algorithm provide 84.27 accuracy of results which is the minimum among the algorithm listed above and A-ExIDS algorithm provided 92.56 accuracy in detecting attacks in heterogeneous and adversarial environments.

ISOT Dataset was used by Haddadi et.al. and it was experimented by four algorithms namely C4.5, KNN, SVM and Bayesian Networks. All these algorithms in the ISOT Dataset provides 99% (approximately) of accurate results.

In the paper authored by Chowdhury et.al., CTU-13 datasets is being used. CTU-13 is the largest dataset that consists of bot-labelled nodes. Numerical results in the paper portrays that it is capable of detecting the bots by searching limited number of nodes (less than 0.1% of all nodes).

Tools using Artificial Intelligence for Cyber Security:

Some of the tools that uses Artificial Intelligence for Cyber Security are discussed below:

Symantec's Targeted Attack Analytics (TAA) Tool

This tool was developed by Symantec and it is used to uncover stealthy and targeted attacks. It applies AI and machine learning on the processes, knowledge, and capabilities of the Symantec's security experts and researchers. The TAA tool was used by Symantec to counter the Dragonfly 2.0 attack last year. This attack targeted multiple energy companies and tried to gain access to operational networks.

Sophos' Intercept X Tool

Sophos is a British security software and hardware company. Its tool, Intercept X, uses a deep learning neural network that works similar to a human brain. In 2010, the US Defense Advanced Research Projects Agency (DARPA) created their first Cyber Genome Program to uncover the 'DNA' of malware and other cyber threats, which led to the creation of algorithm present in the Intercept X.

Darktrace Antigena

Darktrace Antigena is Darktrace's active self-defense product. Antigena expands Darktrace's core capabilities to detect and replicate the function of digital antibodies that identify and neutralize threats and viruses. Antigena makes use of Darktrace's Enterprise Immune System to identify suspicious activity and responds to them in real-time, depending on the severity of the threat.

IBM QRadar Advisor

IBM's QRadar Advisor uses the IBM Watson technology to fight against cyber-attacks. It uses AI to auto-investigate indicators of any compromise or exploit. QRadar Advisor uses cognitive reasoning to give critical insights and further accelerates the response cycle. With the help of IBM's QRadar Advisor, security analysts can assess threat incidents and reduce the risk of missing them (Savia Lobo 2018)

Vectra's Cognito

Vectra's Cognito platform uses AI to detect attackers in real-time. It automates threat detection and hunts for covert attackers. Cognito uses behavioural detection algorithms to collect network metadata, logs and cloud events. It further analyses these events and stores them to reveal hidden attackers in workloads and user/ IoT devices.

CONCLUSION

Artificial Intelligence is one of the indispensable area in computer science which is placing its foot prints in all walks of life. Artificial Intelligence is a way of making a computer to think intelligently in a way an intelligent human think. With the advancement in AI, Machine learning and Deep learning which are branches of AI are now being used as powerful weapon against the cyber attacks. AI allows to automate the detection of cyber threat and battle with hackers even without involvement of humans. This chapter summaries some of the major research articles which uses AI to prevent cyber attacks. The various datasets used in machine and deep learning algorithms along with the tools which uses AI in strengthening cyber security mechanisms are also discussed in this chapter.

REFERENCES

Analyzing Web Traffic ECML/PKDD. (2007). *Discovery Challenge*. Retrieved from http://www.lirmm.fr/pkdd2007-challenge/

Bhamare, D., Salman, T., Samaka, M., Erbad, A., & Jain, R. (2016). Feasibility of Supervised Machine Learning for Cloud Security. In *2016 International Conference on Information Science and Security (ICISS)*, (pp. 1- 5). Academic Press.

Bhuyan, M. H., Bhattacharyya, D. K., & Jugal, K. (2015). An empirical evaluation of information metrics for low-rate and high-rate DDoS attack detection. *Pattern Recognition Letters, 51*, 1–7. doi:10.1016/j.patrec.2014.07.019

Bhuyan, M. H., Dhruba, K. B., & Jugal, K. K. (2015). *Towards Generating Real- life Datasets for Network Intrusion Detection. IJ Network Security*.

Chowdhury, S. (2017). Botnet detection using graph-based feature clustering. *Journal of Big Data*, 1-13.

Ciresan, D., Meier, U. & Schmidhuber, J. (2012). Multi-column deep neural networks for image classification. *IEEE Conference on Computer Vision and Pattern Recognition*, 3642–3649. doi:. doi:10.1109/cvpr.2012.6248110

DARPA Intrusion Detection Evaluation Dataset. (1998). Retrieved from https://www.ll.mit.edu/r-d/datasets/1998-darpa-intrusion-detection-evaluation-dataset

Dataset. (2010). *ISOT Research lab.* Retrieved from https://www.uvic.ca/engineering/ece/isot/datasets/

Gaietto, J. T. (2018). *Three emerging cyber security trends to focus on in 2018.* Retrieved from https://www.housingwire.com/blogs/1-rewired/post/43827-three-emerging-cybersecurity-trends-to-focus-on-in-2018

Galllagher, B., & Eliassırad, T. (2009). *Classification of http attacks: a study on the ECML/PKDD 2007 discovery challenge. Lawrence Livermore National Laboratory.* Livermore, CA: LLNL.

Giménez, C. T., Villegas, A. P., & Marañón, G. Á. (2010). *HTTP dataset CSIC.* Retrieved from http://www.isi.csic.es/dataset/

Graves, A., Abdel-rahman, M., & Hinton, G. (2013). Speech Recognition with Deep recurrent neural networks. *IEEE International Conference on Acoustics, Speech and Signal Processing*, 26-31. 10.1109/ICASSP.2013.6638947

Haddadi, F., Le Cong, D., Porter, L., & Zincir-Heywood, A. N. (2015, May). On the effectiveness of different botnet detection approaches. In ISPEC (pp. 121–135). Cham, Switzerland: Springer.

Hoque, M. S., Mukit, M., Bikas, M., & Naser, A. (2012). *An implementation of intrusion detection system using genetic algorithm.* arXiv preprint arXiv:1204.1336

Hoque, N., Dhruba, K. B., & Jugal, K. K. (2016). A novel measure for low-rate and high-rate DDoS attack detection using multivariate data analysis, In *8th International Conference on Communication Systems and Networks (COMSNETS).* IEEE.

ISOT Dataset Overview. (2011). Retrieved from https://www.uvic.ca/engineering/ece/isot/assets/docs/isot-datase.pdf

Kato, K., Vitaly, K. (2014). An Intelligent DDoS Attack Detection System Using Packet Analysis and Support Vector Machine. *IJICR*, 478-485.

Kozik, R., Choras, M., Renk, R., & Hołubowicz, W. (2015). A Proposal of Algorithm for Web Applications Cyber Attack Detection. In *IFIP International Conference on Computer Information Systems and Industrial Management* (pp. 680-687). Berlin, Germany: Springer.

Krizhevsky, A., Sutskever, I., & Hinton, G. (2012). ImageNet Classification with Deep Convolutional Neural Networks. NIPS 2012: Neural Information Processing Systems, Lake Tahoe, NV.

Lobo, S. (2018). *Six artificial intelligence cyber security tools you need to know.* Retrieved from https://hub.packtpub.com/6-artificial-intelligence-cybersecurity-tools-you-need-to-know/

Neethu, B. (2013). Adaptive Intrusion Detection Using Machine Learning. *International Journal of Computer Science and Network Security*, *13*(3), 118.

Nguyen, H. T., & Franke, K. (2012). Adaptive Intrusion Detection System via online machine learning. In *12th International Conference on Hybrid Intelligent Systems.* IEEE.

Pascanu, R., Stokes, J. W., Sanossian, H., Marinescu, M., & Thomas, A. (2015). Malware classification with Recurrent networks. *IEEE International Conference on Acoustics, Speech and Signal Processing (ICASSP).*

Saad, S., Traore, I., Ghorbani, A., Sayed, B., Zhao, D., Lu, W., ... Hakimian, P. (2011). Detecting P2P botnets through network behavior analysis and machine learning. In *Proceedings of 9th Annual International Conference on Privacy, Security and Trust (PST2011)*. Montreal, Quebec, Canada: Academic Press.

Saad, S., Traore, I., Ghorbani, A. A., Sayed, B., Zhao, D., Lu, W., Felix, J., & Hakimian, P. (2011). Detecting P2P botnets through network behaviour analysis and machine learning. In *Proceedings of 9th Annual Conference on Privacy, Security and Trust (PST2011)*. Montreal, Quebec, Canada: Academic Press.

Torrano-Gimenez, C., Perez-Villegas, A., & Alvarez, G. (2009, July). An Anomaly-based Web Application Firewall, In *Proc. of International Conference on Security and Cryptography (SECRYPT 2009)* (pp. 23-28). INSTICC Press.

Wang, J., & Paschalidis, I. C. (2017). Botnet detection based on anomaly and community detection. *IEEE Transactions on Control of Network Systems*.

Weng, L. (2017). *An Overview of Deep Learning for Curious People*. Retrieved from https://lilianweng. github.io/lil-log/2017/06/21/an-overview-of-deep-learning.html

Wijesinghe, U., Udaya, T., & Vijay, V. (2015). An enhanced model for network flow based botnet detection. *Proceedings of the 38th Australasian Computer Science Conference (ACSC 2015)*, 27.

Xie, M., Jiankun, H., & Jill, S. (2014). Evaluating host-based anomaly detection systems: Application of the one-class svm algorithm to adfa-ld. In *11th International Conference on Fuzzy Systems and Knowledge Discovery*. IEEE.

Zamani, M., & Mahnush, M. (2013). *Machine learning techniques for intrusion detection*. arXiv preprint arXiv:1312.2177

Chapter 3
Review on Machine and Deep Learning Applications for Cyber Security

Thangavel M.
Thiagarajar College of Engineering, India

Abiramie Shree T. G. R.
Thiagarajar College of Engineering, India

Priyadharshini P.
Thiagarajar College of Engineering, India

Saranya T.
Thiagarajar College of Engineering, India

ABSTRACT

In today's world, everyone is generating a large amount of data on their own. With this amount of data generation, there is a change of security compromise of our data. This leads us to extend the security needs beyond the traditional approach which emerges the field of cyber security. Cyber security's core functionality is to protect all types of information, which includes hardware and software from cyber threats. The number of threats and attacks is increasing each year with a high difference between them. Machine learning and deep learning applications can be done to this attack, reducing the complexity to solve the problem and helping us to recover very easily. The algorithms used by both approaches are support vector machine (SVM), Bayesian algorithm, deep belief network (DBN), and deep random neural network (Deep RNN). These techniques provide better results than that of the traditional approach. The companies which use this approach in the real time scenarios are also covered in this chapter.

DOI: 10.4018/978-1-5225-9611-0.ch003

INTRODUCTION

In today's world, information is one of the most important aspects in almost every part of our life; the information is valuable for individual, organization, and country. Privacy is needed for such valuable information. Due to invention and innovation, is widespread use of device and technology, which makes people communication and industrial productions more sophisticated. This technology is not only providing sophistication to the information holders and users but also to the attackers. This same technology also ensures the attacker in many ways to launch attacks in a more creative way. Cybersecurity/information system security is the technique consists of protecting the systems, computer programs, data, and networks form attackers or unauthorized user, which are aimed for exploitation. The cybersecurity reduces the risk of cyber attacks; the cyber attacks are usually concentrating on accessing, destroying, changing the most sensitive information in order to create a risk to individual or organization. The Deep Learning and Machine Learning concept to break these constraints. The birth of Machine learning is started in conjunction with other technologies like virtual machines, test simulators, etc. This ML algorithm quickly scales the analysis process of information collected by the Sec Intel. The basic principle of the ML algorithm is it will improve its response by learning and learning. Nearly it will take 2-3 days for the security group to analyze the information provided by the Sec Intel, but the ML will take 1day at first learning, then reduce it slowly by learning and the next day it will take 12hours, and the next time it will take 8hours and so on., The effective scale analysis by ML is more times greater than the security group especially for the automated task so this is what the wonder of ML. But, Machine Learning can perform efficiently in small scale data and lower configured systems. This emerges the Deep Learning which is a subfield of the Machine learning approach. Deep Learning can perform well only in a tremendous amount of data and high configured systems. The main advantage of Deep Learning on cybersecurity is the deep neutral network process. This process deeply examines the data and for this study, the deep learning algorithm requires a vast amount of data. As we already know today's world generating googol of data than what about the future! yes, obviously it will become too large. For handling cyber security for this much amount of data the deep learning is the precise answer. Deep Learning algorithm is categorized into supervised deep learning and unsupervised deep learning. Supervised deep learning approach will predict only the targeted values from a set of data but in unsupervised approach, there are no such target values and it simply predicts all the possible values from the dataset. The usage of these two categories depends on the implementation of cybersecurity needs. The approach of deep learning to the field of cybersecurity ranges from the intrusion detection system for sensor networks and transport layer, Malicious Code Detection, Hybrid malware classification, Behaviour detection of Botnet, traffic identification and anomaly detection. Although, the application of deep learning for cybersecurity isn't easy. A report last week stated that a recent attack happened in a private organization. It was hacked during the midterms and that attack compromised access to their email accounts of their company, where they had been watched and spied by the hackers over a long time which included the details of their client. Even for an organization like this took a long time and a large amount of money to detect the intrusion and recover from the attack. A yet another report stated by Forbes, a major cyber-attack was traced in tax software which impacted people who belong to 64 countries. The attackers made an offer of 300 dollars of bitcoin for the retrieval of their hacked data as an initial payment. It gave lots of uneasiness to the government of the country as well as the individual victims who and all affected by this massive attack. So, these real-time attacks which clearly proves that the effort which we put on the safeness of our system will easily make us pay a lot of amount and time when it gets compromised.

Here, these learning techniques such as machine learning and deep learning will automatically allow our system to take necessary actions before these attacks will lead us to a critical situation. This book chapter, will tour you from the basic features of cyber security that we can offer to our data and the limitation of cybersecurity prone to the huge set of attacks that can't be handled by us within a short period of time, which enables us to use the vast use of machine learning and deep learning approach. It also helps to identify the machine learning algorithms as well as the deep learning algorithms which are also used for the real-time datasets. It also helps to identify the use of these approaches in the real-time industry problems which are taking more time to solve the problem in normal methods. It again states the application of these algorithms in all types of attacks possible in cybersecurity. These applications in cyber security will facilitate an attack-free world which we are hoping for a long period of time. This chapter covers from common cyber threats and attacks happening in the world and how these threats can be solved using machine learning and deep learning effectively and the general application of these machine learning and deep learning in real-world industrial problems and along with the conclusion.

COMMON CYBERSECURITY THREATS AND ATTACKS

The important principles of securities are confidentiality, integrity, and availability (CIA) triad. All types of information security measures should address any one of the above principles. It is a model with policy and procedure to guide information security within an organization. Confidentiality will deal with the secrecy of the information assets. It is an ability to conceal the information from the unauthorized user so the information will become senseless to the attacker. Confidentiality can be ensured by encryptions. Integrity is responsible for to maintain trustworthiness, assurance, consistency, and completeness over an entire life cycle of data. This also ensures that the data can be only modified by the legitimate user. The availability will ensure that the network is always readily available to its users, for this, the network admin will maintain bandwidth, hardware, upgrades regularly. The attacks like DOS and DDOS will affect the availability of access to the user.

Denial of Service and Distributed Denial of Service Attacks

Denial of Service attack is a cyber attack in which the attacker seeks to make a network resource unavailable to the legitimate user. The primary goal of a dos attack is not to steal the information but to slow or take down a website. The categories of resources which can be attacked by denial of service are network bandwidth, system resources, and application resources. In DDOS attacks, many computers start performing DOS attacks on the same target server. As the DOS attack is distributed over a large group of computers, it is known as a distributed denial of service attack. The DDOS attacks can take place by volume based, application based, and protocol based. In a volume-based attack, the flooding attacks can take place in a variety of forms based on which network protocol is being used to implement the attack. Floods may be through ICMP, UDP, and TCP. The application based attack will make use of the vulnerability in application to crash the server. The protocol based attack will utilize the server resource by targeting the intermediates like a firewall. The attacker may use a zombie network, which is a collection of affected or infected computers on which the attacker has silently installed the dos attacking tool. The common tool which is used by the attackers to launch dos attacks is hulk, xoic, loic, davoset ddosim-layer7 DDOS simulator, etc.

Man in the Middle Attack

Man in the Middle attack is the cyber attack where the cybercriminals launch this type of attack in two ways such as interception and decryption. The attacker will simply intercept the communication of a legitimate user. A man in the middle attack is similar to the eavesdropping where communication between two users is monitored and modified by the attacker or an unauthorized user in order to achieve some specific goals of attackers in sense of stealing or accessing the privileges of the authorized user. This is mainly done by intercepting a public key message exchange and by retransmits the message while replacing the requested key with their own. The attackers launch any one of the attacks such as IP spoofing, ARP spoofing, and DNS spoofing. The attacker may use sniffing techniques, packet injection techniques, session hijacking, SSL was stripping and many more to launch a man in the middle attacks.

Phishing Attack

Pronounced "fishing", the word origin from two words "password harvesting" or fishing for passwords. A phishing attack is also called as brand spoofing. A phishing attack is a type of attack in which the attacker can do some fraudulent attempt to obtain sensitive information of users such as user names, passwords, and credit card details. The phishing attack is a cyber-attack that uses email as a weapon. This attack is often carried out by email spoofing and instant messaging or text message. Link manipulation, website forgery; phone phishing is some of the phishing techniques. Phishing takes place by sending deceptive email, running malicious software on the user's machine, DNS based phishing, for example, host file poisoning, man-in-the-middle phishing, and ect., The causes of phishing are misleading e-mails, a vulnerability in browsers and application, limited use of digital signatures, no check of the source address and lack of user's awareness. One of the most phishing attacks happened in 2016 is the phishing email sent to the Clinton campaign chairman John Podesta's Gmail account.

Drive-by Attack

The drive-by downloads are a common method of spreading malware. A drive-by download is a program that is automatically downloaded to the user machine without any consent or user's knowledge. The drive-by downloads can be initiated by simply visiting a website or viewing HTML email messages. The attackers look for the insecure website and plant a malicious script into HTTP or PHP code on one of the pages. This script may install malware directly onto the machine of someone who visits the site, or it may take the form on an IFRAME that re-directs the victims to a site controlled by the attackers.

Password Attack

For the illegal purpose, the attackers try to obtain users password and also try to decrypt a user's password with the help of cracking programs, dictionary attacks, and password sniffers in password attacks. The password attack is the illegal purpose to gain unauthorized access. Brutus, Rainbow crack, Wfuzz, Cain and Abel, Lophtcrack, Ophcrack are some of the password cracking tools used by hackers.

Types of Password Attack

- Brute force attack.
- Rainbow table attack.
- Malware.
- Offline cracking.
- Phishing.
- Dictionary attack.
- Hash Guessing.

Dictionary Attack

Most of the passwords are chosen by the users, it is always containing a common word. The dictionary attack makes use simple file containing words that can be found in a dictionary, the attacker uses exactly the kind of words that many people use as their password.

Brute force Attack

Brute force attack is similar to that of a dictionary attack, this attack makes use of every possible letter, number, and character combination or alpha-numeric combination to guess the password. The brute force attacks involve repeated login attempts by using various numbers of tries. These attacks can take several minutes to several hours or several years depending upon the system used and also depend on the length of the password. The attacker may use a brute force attack to obtain access to a website and account in order to steal sensitive data.

Rainbow Table Attack

In a rainbow, table cryptanalysis is done very fast and effectively by calculating the hash function of every string and compares it with the system at every step. Creating a table and cracking the password is the main role of a rainbow table attack. The beauty of rainbow table needs not to know the exact string password, if the hash is matched then it will not bother about the password string matching and it will move on to the next step then is it will get authenticated.

SQL Injection Attack

SQL injection attack is one of the most serious security vulnerabilities in a web application system, mainly caused by a lack of input validation and SQL parameters. SQL injection attack will take place by executing malicious SQL statements /malicious payload by the attacker, which will control web application servers. The vulnerabilities in the web application will loss data confidentiality and data integrity. The attackers trick the SQL engine into executing unintended commands by supplying specially crafted string input, thereby gaining unauthorized access to a database so that the attacker can easily use or access the restricted data of the legitimate user. When an application uses entrusted data then SQL injection weakness will occur such as data entered into web form fields, as a part of a database query. The SQL injection utilizes weakness of applications to misguide the application into running a database backend query or command usually an application has a menu, which is used for searching personal information such as age, telephone number, sex... The application will execute an SQL query in the database backend.

```
SELECT patient_name, patient_medicine, patient_disease
WHERE patient_number = 12345.
If the user enters the number "123 or 1=1", then the SQL query passes to the
database as follows:
SELECT patient_name, patient_medicine, patient_disease
WHERE patient_number = 12345 or 1=1.
```

Cross-Site Scripting Attack

In this cross-site scripting attack, the attacker will insert the client-side code into the web pages that is executing the malicious script into a legitimate website or web application. This attack enhances hacker by utilizing greater access. The effect of a cross-site scripting attack is to redirecting the websites, stealing of cookies, showing ads in hidden IFRAMES and pop-ups. The cross-site scripting attack can take place by three types such as non-persistent, persistent, DOM-based.

Malware Attack

Malware attack is a type of cyber attack which is nothing but software is built to create damage to the target computer called malicious software. This was implanted into the target system to damage the system or to steal the information system of client, server and computer network. The growth of malware attack is increasing more nowadays and people use the word virus in the past decades but now ransomware, malware, spyware is playing more. This attack has to be taken as a serious way to solve. To launch a variety of attack the malware uses different types of delivery mechanism like Trojans, Virus, Worm. "In India usage of aadhaar cards is becoming ubiquitous and the danger is that only this mask the hackers easier to identify online, once the malware codes come into the open market, it can be repurposed by hacker anywhere in the world", Narayanan said

MACHINE LEARNING FOR CYBER SECURITY

Cyber Security's core functionality is to protect all types of information which includes hardware and software from cyber threats. These attacks are usually aimed at accessing, changing, or destroying sensitive information of any private or government sectors. In 2014, more than 60% of business networks suffer from these types of cyber-attacks which results in the decrease of the customer trust and even loss of personal details. There range a large number of cyber-attacks such as ransomware, malware, social engineering, phishing from which we can get protected using cybersecurity. The SECINTEL exchange is started to exchange between the collaboration of largest security infrastructure firms like Symantec, MacAfee, Palo Alto, etc, this exchange is dealing only about their attacks, not their solution. The idea behind this exchange is to understand how the attacks are done and what type of attacks is there so this will help the others to be aware of attack before they did. The analysis of sec Intel exchange is a time-consuming process, so Cybersecurity is influenced by the data dependencies, hardware dependencies and the problem-solving techniques that we used. Machine learning includes techniques such as Support Vector Machines and Bayesian Algorithm. These algorithms provide extra ordinal results that the normal level use of the cyber solution for those threats. The effective scale analysis by ML is more times greater than the security group especially for the automated task so this is what the wonder of ML. But Machine Learning can perform efficiently in small scale data and lower configured systems. The Machine learning helps to verify the spam mail, valid mail and seeing the features one or more frequent difference. This process automatically reduce a label and it is the major application of machine learning ML classification techniques was two types one is supervised another one is semi-supervised.

Supervised Learning

Supervised learning provides a set of label training data. They are a different type of many labels are used to verification.

Unsupervised Learning

Unsupervised learning provides a set of unlabeled training data. Labelled data is sometimes rare. The Unlabeled data set is covert to labelling data set in this process to be difficult so introduced.

Semi-supervised learning

Semi-supervised learning is both supervised and unsupervised learning. Semi-supervised learning is unlabeled data so unlabeled data as an alternative using signature generation.

Reinforcement Learning

It is full power by the artificial intelligence. The neural network used for implement reinforcement learning. It is followed by a specific type of cyber attack.

LITERATURE REVIEW OF USING MACHINE LEARNING IN CYBER SECURITY

Machine Learning in IDS

Intrusion Detection System is one of the traditional cyber security solutions. Machine Learning approach can be effectively used in Intrusion Detection System to improve its detection mechanism because in IDS the detection of intrusion events is mostly misinterpreted by the behavior or activities of the normal user. Here, it generates a large number of false positives, which complicates the process of detecting the actual attack from normal events. So, the researchers (Stroeh 2013) proposed a machine learning solution to these IDS problems. The solutions are intrusion as well as the normal events are collected, normalized and then it is fused together to form meta events. These meta events are classified based on the attributes present in them to detect the actual attacks from the normal work of the authorized users.

In the Figure1 Collection and Normalization phase, it takes sources to form the logs files of the system, network and firewalls to categorize them into two elements such as active and passive elements. The passive element is done by simply observing the above source file to detect the events but the active elements interact with the source events or element states. On observing the alert events from the source files, it brings three types. They are action against an object, a condition of an object and a suspicion of the state. The second phase is the fusion phase which helps to generate the meta alerts from the previous phrase. In the third phase that is the classification of the intrusion is done by the Support Vector Machine which is the latest classification technique in machine learning and Bayesian algorithm to differentiate the actual attack from the normal actions of the user. Therefore, machine learning can overcome the traditional perimeter defence in the IDS by providing quick and accurate responses to the intrusion in the system.

Machine Learning in Denial of Service Attacks

One of the popular network attacks in a cyber attack is the Denial of Service attack. This attack prevents the access of the service for the authorized users, which is done by the unauthorized person of the system. (Mukkamala, 2013) concerns the detection and prevention of Dos attack with the help of special machine learning technique Support Vector Machine. The main role is to detect the Dos attack and issues involved in identifying important input features in which Support Vector Machine classifiers reduce the input size which enhances the faster training and supports the more accurate result. Here, the log data is classified into two varieties of patterns in which one is a normal pattern and other is Dos pattern. Dos patterns cover the six different attacks possible in the system namely back, Neptune, ping of death, land, smurf, and teardrop. With the help of SVM, the normal patterns are differentiated from the Dos patterns. The authors' works on the DARPA dataset in which the input vector data is extracted from the TCP/IP dump and it is pre-processed to produce a single value data which the Dos attack pattern. The SVM in Intrusion Detection System is based on three categories such as Pre-processing, Training, and Testing.

Figure 1 Phases of the machine learning in IDS

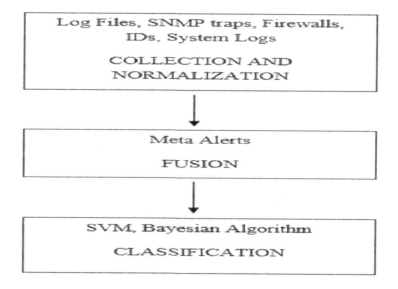

Pre-processing is focused on the process of raw data into actual patterns. In the Training phase, the SVM is trained to differentiate the normal pattern from the Dos attack patterns. Here, this differentiation is identified by two classes where one class denotes the normal data and another class denotes the data of Denial of Service attacks. The last phase which is the Testing phase and it is responsible for the detection of the Denial of Service attack accurately. From this technique, we acquired higher accuracy in a short period of time than that of the neural network techniques.

Improving Intrusion Detection System Based on Bayesian Algorithm

An IDS is a very important security mechanism to secure the information system. It should be designed in such a way to prevent unauthorized access to resources and data. A lot of machine learning algorithm has been applied to the Intrusion Detection System to enhance the efficiency and accuracy of the detection and prevention. (Dewan, 2008) proposed an intrusion detection system based on an adaptive Bayesian algorithm. These machine learning algorithms work well with a large volume of complex and dynamic audit data and make the classification of different types of attack of KDD99 benchmark intrusion detection dataset. For each attribute value, the class conditional probabilities are evaluated which is based on the occurrence of each attribute value present in the training dataset. All training dataset have unit weight, the authors first calculated the sum of weights for each attribute value in the same class. Then the authors calculated the last conditional probabilities for each attribute values by the sum of weight for each class and then the classification of test dataset took place. If the calculated value is wrong then it has to be updated with the weight of training dataset. Each test example is compared with every training example and finding out the similarity between them. If the classification is done on test example correctly then the training set weight will be unchanged again the class conditional probabilities for each attribute values are calculated for the updated training dataset. If the classification is done on test examples for the new set perfectly then the algorithm comes to an end else the algorithm takes places until it produces perfect classification from this it produces accurate and absolute classification. The naive Bayesian algorithm takes 106.7 m training time and the testing time as 26.4m but for the proposed adaptive Bayesian algorithm consumes 52.8 m as training time and 13.2 as a testing time. With this approach, the possibility of applying the machine learning based intrusion detection system commercially.

Detecting P2P Botnets Using Machine Learning

A botnet is the collection of infected devices and internet of things devices which were connected through the internet such as personal computer, servers, mobile devices, and other internet devices. These devices are controlled by the common type of malware. Even no one knows that their system is infected and controlled by malware. Detection of P2P Botnet is an uncovered area but here the authors (Garg 2013) used some machine learning techniques to detect the peer to peer [P2P] botnets. This algorithm analyses the detection rate of the classifiers which helps to detect the botnet malfunctions in the real-time environment. This method of machine learning algorithm also analyses the true positives and false positive in each class which are all advanced that of the traditional botnet detection systems.

Machine Learning Solutions to Bitcoin Threats and Attacks

The Cryptocurrency is the emerging field in which the transaction is possible between the peer to peer is possible without the intervention of any third party between them. This popular technology is also called a Blockchain. Here, the attackers can be a part of this network by creating or initiating a transaction process which appears to be a reliable person in the peer environment. This attack can also be detected with the help of machine learning algorithms. Another problem in the double spending problem where the transactions between the two peers are not either in acceptance or in rejection stage because of the presence of the lengthy blockchain. Here, this leads to the possibility of an attack by any third peer who leads to false acceptance or rejection of the transaction. Another most common attack at this point of time is the Denial of Service attack. It can also be eradicated with the help of the machine learning process at both the ends of the peer networks. Another type of attack is that the pool hoping attack, in this attack the attackers present in the place where the individual code miners are presented. The authors (Rahouti 2018) stated that these attackers get benefited due to the reward stealing from the miners who work to solve an unsolved problem. This can also be eradicated with the machine learning approach. Other possible attacks are gold finger attack and feather forking attack which are also used to cause damages to the miners as well as the peers present in the field. These attacks can also be suppressed with the help of the machine learning approach.

Machine Learning for the Internet of Things Security

This type of security can be efficiently applied with the help of the deep learning algorithm. But the working Machine Learning is combined with the Big Data can also be used to provide better results than that of the machine learning algorithm. This approach is introduced by (Kotenko 2018) where the handling of the massive amount of data generated by the IoT devices can be done with the Big Data approach. Here, the Mapper and Reducer can also be used along with the Hadoop Framework. It also includes the Hadoop Distributed File System where the handling and storing of data is possible. Then after this Machine Learning approach Support Vector Machine (SVM) is used to classify the data present in the IoT environment which reduces the possibility of threats to them. The classifier is the main role of the SVM where the normal activity of the environment is separated from the attack's intrusion data. This provides the best results also compared to the normal IDS based detection system. All possible attacks are identified with the use of the machine learning approach. But the classifier works well only in the presence of big data handling is done prior to them. Combination of the two advanced technology helps to solve all the attacks possible in the IoT environment.

Machine Learning for Security and Privacy of Data

Privacy is needed in all types of communication for the transfer or exchange of sensitive data between the source and destination. Privacy can also be achieved through the use of a machine learning approach. The researchers (Liu 2018) proposed that without the use of the data mining along with the Support Vector Machine privacy cannot be achieved precisely. Here, the sensitive data are first separated from that of the normal flow of data. These data are then fine-tuned by the use of the SVM classifiers which also helps to separate the higher priority data to provide the security along with the privacy to the data. Again, the results are massively correct than that of the traditional approach and provide better results.

Malware Classification using Self Organizing FeatureMaps and Machine Activity Data

Cyber attacks became large in recent years. These questions the liability of the authorized access too. Here, the malware classification is done which helps to differentiate the normal activities from the malicious one. The researchers (Niyaz 2014) proposed that this type of automated classification can be done with the help of Weka machine learning libraries. It helps to create a number of supervised classifiers that are tested and trained with the help of behavioral features which are CPU User Use, CPU System Use, RAM use, SWAP use, received packets, received bytes, sent packets, sent bytes, number of processes running. For doing these behavioral features, the authors produce two datasets which are clean and malicious files. Using this the feature is extracted from the classifier which is showing better classification of the malicious files from the legitimate ones.

APPLICATION OF MACHINE LEARNING

Machine learning is to collect gathering and process of data so cybersecurity can be used to detect the cyber-attack prevention to be automated. Machine learning techniques apply to many areas. Cybersecurity is a recent growing technique. The machine learning method is deploying to a wide range of problem in cybersecurity. The application of machine learning in cybersecurity like network intrusion detection system, spam detection in social network, keystrokes dynamic, smart meter energy consumption profiling.

Network Instruction Detection

Network intrusion detection system is identified as a malicious attack. This is one of the harmful attacks. Attackers must be changing tools and techniques. However, the intrusion detection system always changing in order to the attacks happening in the system which also changes the task to handle the detection of intrusion. Network instruction detection dataset is classified to the various machines learning performance. These are sequentially monitored to false negative and false positive performance.

Pros

- Response capabilities.
- Visibility.
- Defence.
- Evidence.
- Tracking of virus transmission.

Cons

- More maintenance.
- False positive.
- False negative.

Phishing Detection

One of the applications of machine learning in cybersecurity is phishing detection. Phishing is only focused on sensitive personal data to be taken. They have three types of anti-phishing methods. It is a detective, preventive and corrective. Detective solution is a continuously watch control life cycling and band monitoring. The preventive solution is Email authentication and web application security. Corrective is a forensic and investigation. Machine learning algorithm gives the solution to identifying the pattern which reveals malicious mails. The malicious content which splits into various behavior to detect whether the email is malicious or not. A cybersecurity provider named Barracuda network in which they found a machine learning technique to analyse unique pattern without human interaction. In real time this engine studies patterns for anomalous signals and gives notification to the administrator with details of phishing attack.

Pros

- User basic level trained to Bayesian filtering contents.
- It avoids a false negative statement.

Cons

- It should be the only filter for database contents so easily words are transformed.

Watering Hole

Hackers track the site in which users visit frequently. This concept is called a watering hole let us consider one example for a watering hole. Take a popular coffee shop where a number of people place their orders through the coffee shop URL. Now hackers will not attack the shop's network but they will access the coffee shop web site. Next, they will easily access the credential. Machine learning algorithms will ensure the security for the web application services. These algorithms will detect whether users are directed to malicious web sites when they are traveling to their destination path. These algorithms detect the malicious domain which helps to further solve the problem present in the URL. These methods are very effective in the watering hole attack of the system.

Webshell

Web shell is a piece of malicious code which is loaded into the web sites. This is the path for the attacker to make a modification of the directories of the server. So, the attacker can easily gain the database of the system. The e-commerce web sites might be attackers monitor to frequently in order to collect customer credit card information. Most of the attackers are from backend e-commerce platform. E-Commerce platforms mostly get affected by online payments these are expected to be more secure and confidential. So, in this process, a machine learning goal is to be wanted to detect the normal behavior of the credit card. Next, it Needs to train a machine learning model to identify normal behavior from malicious behavior. Web shell attack is noted as file less attack that relay of traditional malware.

Remote Exploitation

Remote exploitation is a final list of machine learning and cybersecurity. They are only referring to a remote attack is a malicious action. That they are focused on one or more network of computers. Their remote attacks are a target to take sensitive data and damage the machine. They can happen in various ways like denial of service, DNS poisoning, port scanning. Machine learning analyses to the behavior of system and abnormal network behavior can be identified. These algorithms trained for many data sets and it's detecting the remote exploitation attack.

Pros

- It can be managed to the thousands of cyber-attacks for at a time.
- Customer shift to after the three or four testing process.

Cons

- The main cons are mirror images of the attack.
- Distributed the malware code to be embedded.

Machine Learning for Cyber Securing in IOT

Internet of things (IOT) is a network connected object. IOT object is able to collect data from physical and virtual sensor nodes continuously and transfer to sensitive data. In this data transfer over the internet without needing human to human or human to computer interaction. Data transmitted from the communication device to remotely control device. The most possible ways of attacking are Computer attacks, data interception, and software vulnerabilities. IOT security is safeguarding for IOT device. Some of the IOT security prevent and detect the malicious attack. The security requirements are data authentication, access control, and resilience attack.

Some of the IDS algorithms applies to the detect cyber attack IOT. The author (Elrawy 2018) used a machine learning technique called Principle component analysis for detection of a cyber attack. IDS system depends on the least and most significant component. IDS based PCA used for data mining, machine learning, and statistical modelling. Misuse-based intrusion detection to detect well-known attacks. Disadvantages are network overloading and large numbers of false alarms. So, they are continuously updated to pattern and signature.

DEEP LEARNING FOR CYBER SECURITY

Machine Learning can perform efficiently in small scale data and lower configured systems. This emerges the Deep Learning which is a subfield of the Machine learning approach. Deep Learning can perform well only in a tremendous amount of data and high configured systems. The main advantage of Deep Learning on cybersecurity is the deep neural network process. This process deeply examines the data and for this study, the deep learning algorithm requires a vast amount of data. In industry, government sector, peoples and organization generating a large amount of data. For handling cyber security for this much amount of data the deep learning is the precise answer. The big companies like Google, Amazon, Microsoft, and salesforceman.com to follow deep learning technology now cybersecurity institute takes and follow them in this algorithm but deep learning is a challenging field for full helpfulness. Deep Learning algorithm is categorized into supervised deep learning and unsupervised deep learning. Supervised deep learning approach will predict only the targeted values from a set of data but in unsupervised approach, there are no such target values and it simply predicts all the possible values from the dataset. The usage of these two categories depends on the implementation of cybersecurity needs. The approach of deep learning to the field of cybersecurity ranges from the intrusion detection system for sensor networks, transport layer, Malicious Code Detection, Hybrid malware classification, Behaviour detection of Botnet, traffic identification and anomaly detection. Benefits deep learning for cybersecurity protects the plenty of data and the data are hybrid categories. It only focuses on the multivariate categorical distributions.

The Current Stage for Deep Learning in Cybersecurity

It is difficult to solve the information security problem in which need to extensive dataset labelled and if they are sometimes no such that dataset labelled. However, most of information security problem solved or significant improvement of deep learning techniques. Two areas such as improved in these techniques like malware detection and intrusion detection. Network intrusion detection system is evaluating to detect threat based on signature and rule. It is controlled to deploy at the known threat. Now, detecting the types of many anomalies using the deep learning-based system.

LITERATURE SURVEY OF USING DEEP LEARNING IN CYBER SECURITY

Deep Learning in Network Intrusion Detection System

Network Intrusion Detection System is used to detect the security compromises in any type of organization. It is the first line of defensive mechanism which can be very useful for the detection of the intrusion in the system. Here, it will also produce false results due to the time consuming and low latency of the audition of files. But it can be improved with the help of the deep learning approach which produces better results than that of the normal approach. The authors (Niyaz 2014) stated that the Network Intrusion Detection System (NIDS) can be improved with the Self-taught Learning (STL), a deep learning-based method to automate the detection system with high precise results. STL contains two stages which are used as classifiers. The first method is used to the unlabelled data which are learned the good representation of the data. Another stage is to present the data in a related form where the learning is done on the previous stage. These stages are applied to the NIDS which easily provides better results and also helps to do things well in future too. The STL classification achieves an accuracy of up to 98% than the all other classifications. In the future, this can also be used for the observation of the raw network traffic of the system which is very much advanced than that of the NIDS.

Deep Learning in Sensor Network Security

In sensor networks, a vast number of cyber attacks is possible for the malfunction of the sensor devices. Here, the intrusion or threats are also screened and monitored with the help of the IDS. (Wang 2015) proposed a deep learning-based approach to these problems. SCDNN which the combination of both Spectral Clustering and Deep Neural Network algorithms that are the clustering of data and ink subsets and the distances are calculated with the help of deep neural approach. These algorithms are applied to both the training data and the testing dataset. The sensed data are classified using DNN classifier after the clustering the data. The results of this approach not only better than that of the traditional approach but also advances the Support Vector Machine and Bayesian algorithm which are all the machine learning approaches. It also provides the facility to work for a large amount of dataset which is considerably larger than the machine learning. So, Deep learning approach is widely used for the vast dataset or project which yields best results than that of the smaller project work.

Deep Learning Approach in Detecting Threats to the IoT Environment

Internet of Things is the communication between devices to devices with human intervention. Here, a large number of attacks is possible at the gateway of the network. Most common attacks in the IoT environment are Denial of Service attacks and Denial of Sleep attacks. Denial of Service is simply the host devices are denied with flooding of requests from the attackers which restricts the host to connect with the intended devices. In Denial of Sleep attack which mostly drains the power of the sensor nodes where the sensor device lost its ability to connect with the IoT environment. Using the traffic of this environment the attackers can also read the packets and send false responses to the devices. Here, the authors (Brun 2018) used the deep random neural networks (Deep RNN) which help to understand the network attacks more precisely. The processing of this approach comparatively helps to reduce the disabling of nodes in the network with an early prediction of the attack happening in the environment. In the future, this approach can also be applicable to the Zigbee and Bluetooth devices to reduce the network attack of the ad-hoc network. Here, the attacks and intrusions are prevented with the Deep RNN technique which provides a unique solution to the core problem present in real time. The results are far best than that of the traditional machine learning approach where the Support Vector Machine is very difficult to be used in the IOT environment which is normally a large system which provides vast data with high amount of security issues. Instead of SVM, the Deep RNN approach is used to generate the efficiency of the system.

Deep Learning in Android Malware Detection

In the Android platform, large numbers of applications are developed and deployed everyday which also leads a large number of malware application with causes serious troubles to the Android OS and corrupts the data of our smartphone devices. Each malware effects are different from each other. The detection and prevention of this malware are a tedious process in cyber forensics. It can be easily done with the help of a deep learning approach. Here the researchers (Yuan 2014) proposed a model for this malware detection for Android environment which is Deep Belief Network (DBN). It consists of two phases namely Pre-training phase and propagation phase. In the pre-training phase, the learning space is given to the DBN whereas in the propagation phase the trained pre-training phases are again finely improved with supervision. The dataset which contains both normal applications as well as the malware containing applications which are fed into this DBN framework to detect the malware software's present in it. It provides a result of up to 96.4% better than that of the machine learning approach which includes SVM, Naive Bayesian algorithm and LR. So, deep learning plays a major role in now a day's challenges to eradicating the intrusion or malware in the system.

Hybrid Malicious Code Detection Using Deep Learning

A hybrid malicious code detection using deep learning algorithm based on AutoEncoder and DBN. The autoencoder deep learning method is applied which is responsible for to reduce the dimensionality of data with nonlinear mapping, and extracting the main features of the data. The authors (Li 2013) used a Deep Belief Networks learning methods to detect malicious code. This deep belief network is consisting of multilayer restricted Boltzmann machines and a layer of BP neural network. This algorithm is based on both supervised and unsupervised learning. First, every layer of RBM is learned under unsupervised training then the output vector of the last layer of RBM is given as an input vector of BP neural network which undergoes supervised training. The outcome shows accurate detection performance and reduces the time complexity. The autoencoder consists of two parts encoder and decoder and three layers (input, output, hidden layers) here the data dimensionality reduction is defined when the hidden layer neurons are less than the number of input layer neurons and output layer neurons. The autoencoder takes place by three steps which are pretraining, unrolling and fine-tuning. The pretraining process is nothing but the output vector of each RBM hidden layer neuron is given to the input for next RBM. Connecting these independent RBM into a multilayered autoencoder is done in the unrolling process. After the pretraining process to get optimal weights the adjustment is done on initial weights further is called a Fine-tuning process. The hybrid detection algorithm will take care of digitizing and normalizing the input data, reducing the dimensionality of the data, feature mapping, DBM classifier, through the RBM learning rules the network layer is trained layer by layer, and finally the input test samples into the trained classifier to detect the malicious code and the normal code. The result of this algorithm shows greater accuracy of detecting hybrid malicious code by using the combination of AutoEncoder and DBM and this ensure the best time complexity for this model.

Deep Learning Network Based Malware Detection

Malware are increasing day by day parallel along with the evolution of technology. The detection of malware is a complex process which requires a large amount of time and works in the modern period whereas a new approach this problem is Stacked Auto-Encoders (SAEs) framework. It is used for the intelligent detection of the malware present in the network. The authors (Hardy 2015) proposed this method which contains two phases which are having both unsupervised and supervised learning a feature of SAE framework. This model is specially designed to detect the presence of malware in Windows API calls. By performing this type of detection, helps to improve the systems which are free from all the general attacks that will affect the sensitive data and also improve the performance of the system. Staked Auto-Encoders provides a wide range of classification with deep learning impact leads to the three layers in the input layer, Hidden layer, and Output layer. Each layer helps to extract the features from the data which is useful for the future application of classifier. This method also provides better results than that of the other approaches to cybersecurity.

Deep Learning Approach for Flash Malware Detection

Adobe Flash is a platform-independent software where all the multimedia is supported by them. It can also subject to a large number of attacks in recent years due to the development of technology. This software is widely used by all the users who operate on the computer. So, this can be an easy target by the attacks who all try to hack the system of the users. Recently, Casper malware which affects a large number of host systems leads to a large amount of data loss and also gives the opportunity to the hacker to earn money through this mode of attacks. To avoid this type of malware the use deep learning approach SWF is used. This method is better than that of machine learning because of the complex nature of the malware data present in today's environment. The data are first extracted as static and dynamic analysis and then the SWF classifier is applied to the system. This classifier is proposed by the authors (Jung 2015) to detect this malware in the present-day flash. This approach can also be used to detect the intrusions in the other independent platforms also. It is the additional advantage of using deep learning approach where the same classifier is used to detect the problems.

Applications for Deep Learning

The most of deep learning application apply to market, sales and finance field. Deep learning technique protects sensitive data and product from malicious code and hacker attack.

Learning-Based Detection

JavaScript code analysis is done for generating detection model. These models to be consist of deep learning techniques.

Evaluation

The malicious Java code applicable for a larger dataset which is consists of 2700 samples.

Zero-Day Attacks Detection

A zero-day attack is an ability to identify malicious code and analysis of unknown attacks.

Malware, Zero Day, and APT Detection

Deep learning is classified as malicious code without any rules. The neural network learns to identify the malicious code once identify the unknown files. In real time apply to in this process need for high accuracy. They are trained in malware detection neural network must analyse the millions of accurate malicious code classification. These are trained neural network deploy to the endpoint of the device. For example, a trained neural network would be deployed in mobile device endpoint. It is access to without network connection. So, in which that detect the malicious attacks.

Advanced Intrusion Detection and Network Anomaly Detection

Now intrusion detection system work through the grouping of anomaly detection and misuse detection techniques. These techniques are deploying to particular system network and host level. System guesses of intrusion based on deep learning techniques. Deep learning techniques analyse and filter to unknown codes. Packet analysis techniques include deep learning. These are preventing distributed denial of service, ransomware, spam, and phishing and botnet attack. It can find unusual behavior for network communication. In this method find the network communication likelihood. Network communication also selects as low likelihood.

Phishing Detection

Phishing attack already discussed previously. It is sensitive to personal data gathering techniques. Cyber-attack mostly injected to these types of method. Machine learning and deep learning is performed to pattern recognition so attack to be detected. Deep insight is a graph analysis algorithm. Deep insight text used to analyse email pattern identification and harmless mail. These are the best tool for identifying phishing attack.

Identification of Insider Threats

The pattern could be gritty to the device, user individual and network let use to deep learning techniques. Those threats in progress to be indicated are correlated data let's identify subtitles. They are modelled for application, key business system and, user behavior. The incorporate data to be a loss to deploy the file dropbox and any other cloud service. APT identification is the main added benefit for the system. It is intrusion detection, firewall, and server log and information security management event. It is could not just insider. Training material needed for the neural network could be providing an important resource.

Traffic Detection Using Deep Learning

Cyber-attack is mostly taking for source code, consumer data, important document, and software keys. Anomaly network is used to trace traffic in which that security is difficult to in this method. Now anomaly network used for communication by specific of malware based on rule-based intrusion network tools. They are transmitted of stolen encrypt with remote server traffic to occur. It is detecting the TOR traffic and analysis to traffic package. In this analyse done by a single flow of packet. Source address, source port, destination address, and destination port are involved in each flow constitutes. TOR is a safeguard for the user. TOR transfer to information hacker get access to information. The IP address cannot directly predict the in this attack. A landscape sends alert for distill network. Let us apply to deep learning method easy to detect the attack and increase the security.

CYBERSECURITY SOLUTION -INDUSTRIAL APPROACH WITH ML AND DL

HDFC Bank

Sameer ratolikar, chief information security officer of HDFC bank stated that current security technology is coupled with the power of AI which includes machine learning and deep learning in a way to move HDFC security to the next level. HDFC Bank has completed a pilot for AI-based Cyber Security Operations Centre (CSOC). The log data generated from the CSOC is then sending for processing on the AI for 8months on a cloud platform. This helps the bank to monitor insider threats. The major components of AI are machine learning and deep learning with a well-established algorithm. There are two teams, one team will manage the CSOC and the second team will focus threat hunting by writing rules for machine learning.

LogRhythm

LogRhythm is a security intelligence company (located in Boulder, Colo) that unifies SIEM security information and event management, log management, network endpoint monitoring, and forensics, and security analytics. This helps the worldwide customers to detect cyber threats before it gets breach and answers it fast. The case study on logarithm shows that regional bank required a matured security system. The logarithm will eradicate the time consumed in consolidating different data logs and points, this is done by the company by using a machine learning algorithm to profile and detect the threats, compromised accounts, misuses, and anomalies. By using machine learning it will reduce the detection time and response time for the security teams.

DarkTrace

Darktrace is located in San Francisco it is a global intelligence company in the field of cyber defence. Industry impact is that the DirectTV needed a system to provide proactive defences against data breaches and leaks of customer information. Darktrace AI platform analyses data in order to make calculations and identify patterns. The deviation from the behavior and identifying the threats is done with the use of data by machine learning technology. It helps thousands of companies across the industry to detect and fight cyber threats so that the companies use Darktraces AI-powered technology to make a detection in a better accuracy

Versive

Versive is the company founded in 2012 based on machine learning start-up and provide on-premises software, cloud service, and professional service solution. Versive is now a part of the entire company and the versive security engine is focusing on the threats that matter by identifies the bad actor, automatically understand core activities, finds the few threats. The industrial impact is the host had not to exchange the information before so, VSE alerted a bank who sent an odd volume of data from an internal to another internal host. Therefore, the backed-up on an internet-accessible server is more vulnerable to attacks. Versive helps the business team member who wasting time in identifying the threats to reducing the time or saving time by using machine learning to sort out the critical risk forms normal network activities. The machine learning also consists of a well-planned algorithm to provide the effective and appropriate result to the team and keeps the business team greatly away from the work.

Fortinet

Fortinet is an American multinational corporation headquartered. The Fortinet will develop cybersecurity software, application, and service. Industry impact of furniture manufacturer use two cloud center for hosting, they are Microsoft Azure and Amazon Web Services by making using the Fortinet security service. The Fortinet is a web application firewall that uses two layers of statistical probabilities and Machine learning to accurately detect threats.

Perimeter

PerimeterX is a cybersecurity company that prevents the automated web and mobile application from attackers. PerimeterX provides botnet detection solution for e-commerce, hospitality, media, and enterprise SaaS customer through implementing Machine learning technology. This machine learning technology analyses the sensor data to produce the risk score that identifies and tells whether a client is under risk or not.

PROBLEMS TO BE ADDRESSED

Remote Exploitation

Machine learning and deep learning in cybersecurity is remote exploitation, in which the malicious action of remote attack targets one or an entire network of the system. Due to system vulnerability, the hacker can easily exploit or steal sensitive system information with the help of malicious software. The Machine learning algorithm can be used to analyse system behavior and identifies the normal and abnormal instances which are not related to the network behavior. This machine learning algorithm trained for multiple data sets so, by self-learning from more data set it has a capability to trace before damage. The network device and management software producing company Juniper Networks using machine learning to analyse mountains of data gathered automatically. This algorithm ensures automation by learning from a huge data set and generates an appropriate prediction solution.

Predication of Unknown Ransomware

Ransomware is a type of malicious software. Mainly used to open the locked files of the user to utilize the data of the user or damage the data. The deep learning algorithm can be used to detect the unknown ransomware, for this, the data set is trained properly to provide better analyse minute behavior of ransomware. The deep learning algorithm will use both normal clean data files and a large set of ransom files for their training purpose after training, the algorithm finds out the key features of each file present in the data set. When it attacks the system, the file is checked in the trained model and the actions are implemented before it works. The cloud data protecting firm, Acronis developed their security with the aim of zero attack day by implementing machine learning to analyses the detection fast and effective.

CONCLUSION AND FUTURE WORK

As we know the technology is booming every day with new features along with an attractive name. We cannot predict the data that are in the movement and we also cannot manage the issues that rise along with them. In any field of innovation, there needs the security of data. In cybersecurity, large numbers of attacks, malware, ransom wares, viruses and trojans which are embedded along with our applications in our day to day activities. These attacks can be handled by the Intrusion Detection System and also along with the use of Intrusion Prevention System. But the time and cost spent on this process are large when compared to the use of the modern advanced domain. The Machine Learning and Deep Learning approach to the field of cyber security help to automate the process of detecting and preventing the attacks. So, this chapter covers the need for the Machine Learning and Deep Learning approach along with the effects that cause the identification of false data. Then, the survey of both fields in the cybersecurity is done by the researchers is covered which helps to identify the methods used and also helps to view the results produced by the applying of the proposed methods in the real-time dataset. Again, the approaches can also be used in the real-time application such as phishing detection, watering hole, malware detection, anomalies identification, remote exploitation and also identifying the threats. After that, the use of both machine learning and deep learning in the industrial point of view is also analysed which helps us to realize the visual use of the fields to the current cyber attacks. In the future, everything is going to be automated which does not require human interactions with them. This type of self-learning along with the solution producing strategies is delivered by both the machine learning and deep learning approach. With this, the advancement of threats will require the advancement of the technique used to handle the threats and need to recover from them.

REFERENCES

Brun, O., Yin, Y., & Gelenbe, E. (2018). *Deep learning with dense random neural network for detecting attacks against IoT-connected home environments.* Science Direct.

Elrawy, M. F., Awad, A. I., & Hamed, H. F. A. (2018). *Intrusion detection systems for IoT-based smart environments.* Springer.

Farid, D. M., & Rahman, M. Z. (2008). *Learning Intrusion Detection Based on Adaptive Bayesian Algorithm.* IEEE.

Garg, S., Singh, A. K., Sarje, A. K., & Peddoju, S. K. (2013). *Behaviour Analysis of Machine Learning Algorithms for detecting P2P Botnets.* IEEE. doi:10.1109/ICACT.2013.6710523

Hardy, W., & Chen, L., Hou, S., & Ye, Y. (2015). *A Deep Learning Framework for Intelligent Malware Detection.* Springer.

Javaid, A., Niyaz, Q., Sun, W., & Alam M. (2014). *A Deep Learning Approach for Network Intrusion Detection System*. Science Direct.

Jung, W., Kim, S., & Choi, S. (2015). *Deep Learning for Zero-day Flash Malware Detection*. IEEE.

Kotenko, I., Saenko, I., & Branitskiy, A. (2018). *Framework for Mobile Internet of Things Security Monitoring Based on Big Data Processing and Machine Learning*. IEEE. doi:10.1109/ACCESS.2018.2881998

Li, Y., Ma, R., & Jiao, R. (2013). *A hybrid malicious code detection method based on deep learning*. Springer.

Liu, Q., Li, P., & Zhao, W. (2018). *A Survey on Security Threats and defensive techniques of Machine Learning: A Data-Driven View*. IEEE.

Rahouti, M., *Kaiqi, X., & Ghani, N. (2018). Bitcoin Concepts, Threats, and Machine-Learning Security Solutions*. IEEE.

Srinivas, M. & Sung, A. H. (2013). *Detecting Denial of Service Attacks Using Support Vector Machines*. IEEE.

Stroeh, K., *Madeira, E. R. M., & Goldenstein, S. K. (2013). An approach to the correlation of security events based on machine learning techniques*. Springer Open Journal.

Wang, F., Cheng, J., & Yu, Y. (2015). *A Hybrid Spectral Clustering and Deep Neural Network Ensemble Algorithm for Intrusion Detection in Sensor Networks*. Science Direct.

Yuan, Z., Lu, Y., Wang, Z., & Xue, Y. (2014). *Droid-sec: Deep learning in android malware detection*. ACM.

Chapter 4
Applications of Machine Learning in Cyber Security Domain

Sailesh Suryanarayan Iyer
R. B. Institute of Management Studies, India

Sridaran Rajagopal
Marwadi University, India

ABSTRACT

Knowledge revolution is transforming the globe from traditional society to a technology-driven society. Online transactions have compounded, exposing the world to a new demon called cybercrime. Human beings are being replaced by devices and robots, leading to artificial intelligence. Robotics, image processing, machine vision, and machine learning are changing the lifestyle of citizens. Machine learning contains algorithms which are capable of learning from historical occurrences. This chapter discusses the concept of machine learning, cyber security, cybercrime, and applications of machine learning in cyber security domain. Malware detection and network intrusion are a few areas where machine learning and deep learning can be applied. The authors have also elaborated on the research advancements and challenges in machine learning related to cyber security. The last section of this chapter lists the future trends and directions in machine learning and cyber security.

INTRODUCTION

The digital revolution is transforming the global scenario. Desktop are being replaced by Laptops and Laptops by Mobiles and Tablets. Internet which was considered a luxury before a few decades has become the necessity of the hour. Social Media and online transactions are transforming ordinary people to smart people through Smart devices. The Information Technology is touching the life of the urban as well as rural population. Digi-Farming has become a reality with Companies and Government implementing Sensors to help identify type of Soil, Soil moisture, temperature, humidity and leaf wetness.

DOI: 10.4018/978-1-5225-9611-0.ch004

Figure 1. Artificial intelligence/machine learning classification

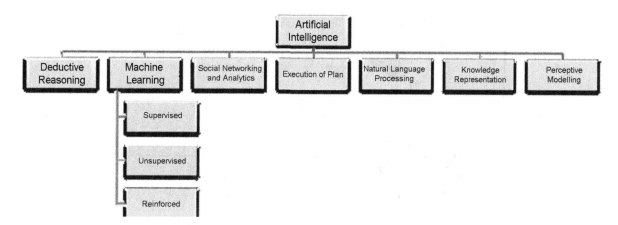

Water Conservation can be increased by spraying water only where required. Smart Devices are replacing mundane tasks bringing about a 360° transformation in the way business and social networking is done. Technical concepts like Cyber Crime, Cyber Security, Artificial Intelligence, Machine Learning and Deep Learning are soon invading workplaces. Artificial Intelligence is the ability of machine to behave like a human being, Machine Learning can be considered an AI variant wherein learning and improving from previous experience takes place.

Figure 1 shows the classification of AI and Machine Learning. AI can be classified into Deductive Reasoning, Machine Learning, Social Analysis, Natural Language Processing (NLP), Knowledge Representation and Perceptive Modeling (Sanjeevi, 2017).

Intelligent people can be defined as those possessing important qualities as knowing, learning, understanding, communicate, judge, think etc. Artificial Intelligence is the application of human qualities to solve real life problems which previously only humans solved. Artificial Intelligence is used for solving problems like Computer Vision and Image Processing, Robotics, etc. to name a few. AI's goal is to make computers/computer programs smart enough to imitate the human mind behavior. Vertical Artificial Intelligence concentrates on one job only. Horizontal Artificial Intelligence concentrates on many tasks at the same time (Maruti Tech Labs, 2019).

Machine Learning (Maruti Tech Labs, 2019) can be considered as a subset of Artificial Intelligence. Machine Learning consists of designing and applying algorithms capable of learning from historical occurrences. Some of the major applications of Machine Learning are Self Driving Cars, face detection and recognition, Marketing Campaigns, Credit card or banking fraud detection. The world's finest player of Chess Gary Kasparov was defeated in his own turf by IBM's product Deep Blue. Machine Learning also has various applications in product recommendations e.g. Book recommendations.

Figure 2. represents the classification of machine learning (InfoTechLead, n.d.)

Machine Learning can further be classified into three (3) categories:

1. **Supervised Learning:** In Supervised Learning, rules are provided to the system. The Supervised algorithm analyzes the data and produce inferences. e.g. Credit Card fraud detection is Supervised Learning application. Trained data is required for Supervised Learning. Some of the examples of Supervised Learning include Speech automated system in mobile captures voice and trains to

Figure 2. Machine learning classification

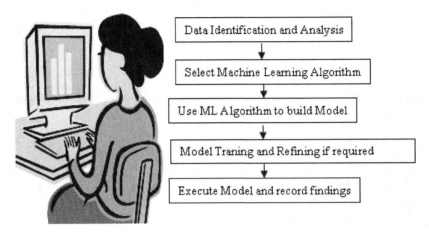

recognize the voice, Biometric identity of a person is captured and based on the training data identification of the person is done, Classification or filtering of mail into spam or junk folder based on trained characteristics of mail, Weather prediction based on trained data of humidity, temperature and other characteristics, Handwriting identification using trained details of group of people's handwriting, Team victory prediction based on trained toss details and other characteristics.

2. **Unsupervised Learning:** In Unsupervised Learning, rules are not predefined or provided in advance. Clustering is performed based on pattern identified or similar characteristics. e.g. Recommendations of books on Amazon site, Friend suggestions on social media, classification of groups based on similar characteristics without any trained data are some of the applications of Unsupervised Learning. Unsupervised Learning can be assumed to be that type of learning where no Professor is present but students do self-learning (Stack Overflow, 2018).

3. **Reinforcement Learning:** This Machine Learning algorithm allows software agents and machines to automatically determine the ideal behavior within a specific context, to maximize its performance. Reinforcement learning is defined by characterizing a learning problem and not by characterizing learning methods. Any method which is well suited to solve the problem, we consider it to be the reinforcement learning method. Reinforcement learning assumes that a software agent i.e. a robot, or a computer program or a BOT, connect with a dynamic environment to attain a definite goal. Just imagine a small child operating a mobile or remote (Drinkwater, 2017). The child will first try to operate mobile or remote and see or analyze the response. Depending upon the response, the child will react.

Figure 2 provides Machine Learning classification into Supervised Learning, Unsupervised Learning and Reinforcement Learning.

Figure 3 gives an insight into Machine Learning process. It starts with preparing data sets for analysis, choosing the Machine Learning Algorithm, building an Analytical model based on chosen algorithm, training the model based on test data and generate findings or results based on the implementation of the model. The challenge starts from preparing data for analysis and when to use which Algorithm. Analytical model preparation requires the domain knowledge and hence commercial domain knowledge is required if not high level of technical know-how. The step following the analytical model preparation is the Model training, executing model and then finally recording findings.

Figure 3. Machine learning process

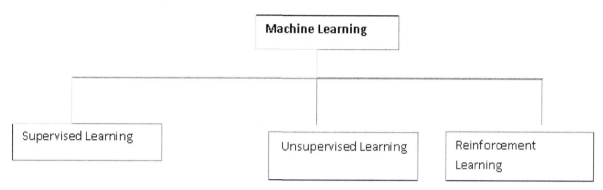

CYBER SECURITY AND CYBER CRIME

Cyber Crime has been on the rise in the last few years and so-called Hackers have devised new techniques and technologies to penetrate and commit crime ranging from simple privacy invasion to terrorist attack. Information Technology has been increasing by leaps and bounds acting as boon as well as curse for the society.

There has been a lot of work done in area of Artificial Intelligence/Machine Learning/Deep Learning in the area of Sales, Retail, and Business Intelligence etc but very less initiative has been taken to use them in Cyber Security or security of data. The primary goal of cyber-attacks is to steal the enterprise customer data, sales data, intellectual property documents, source codes and software keys (Revett, 2007).

Figure 4 depicts the types of Cyber Crime which can provide some useful information regarding Cyber Crime and help prevent Cybercrime by providing Cyber Security mechanism. These mechanisms to be developed require knowledge of cyber crime classification and develop scenarios where such crimes can be prevented or at least the impact of cyber crime considerably reduced. Cyber Crime needs to be countered and an effective way of mitigating it is to provide Cyber Security. Cyber Security Cells are being set up in India to deal with menace of Cyber Crime. Siphoning off funds through mobile or e-commerce related deals is on the rise. Cyber Crime classification deals with various crimes whether big or small and classifies them. These crimes are then reported to concern Cyber Cell department and Investigation conducted. Many Cyber Security Tools are available which can help to find out and steps taken to mitigate them. The Cyber Security tools are very popular and can give accurate results and help in nabbing the person committing Cyber Crime (Ajeet, 2014).

Corporate Companies are doing their best to safeguard data. They are concerned with data availability, security or secrecy of data and Integrity of data. Secrecy of data involves secure exchange of data such that sensitive information is not leaked to unauthorized personnel. Audit trails lead to advanced level of Computer Security as the person involved in manipulation of data can be traced. Spam Filtering is an example of distinguishing between Regular and Spam mails. This allows those unwanted mails to be classified as spam and filtered so that we receive only regular mails.

Malware Detection, Intrusion Detection, Spam Mitigation etc. are some of the Cyber Security Information Detection. Honey tokens involve faked digital data in the genuine database. Many other security authentication measures like Biometric, Identity theft, Trojans etc. are used to counter different security related problems.

Figure 4. Classification of cyber crime

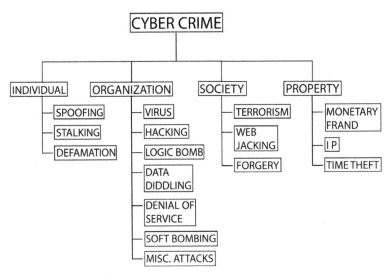

Malware can also prove costly as they can have harmful effects like stealing data, displaying irritating messages, giving hackers control over your system or can even lock system until certain amount or ransom is paid. Cyber stalking uses online platform to stalk, blackmail or harass any individual or group which may lead to violence, murder or rape. Online fraud consists of posing as a charity or social organization and asking for funds. People donate and these funds can be siphoned off. Other types of Cyber crimes are where the email may seem to be from a legitimate sender but may end up in transmitting secret information without the knowledge of the person comprising his/her privacy. False mail is received confirming it to be from some foreign bank and informing you that you have won 1 million dollars in a lucky draw. They then ask you to pay an amount of Rs. 51000/- to 1 Lakh as exchange or commission charges to transfer the amount from overseas bank account to your local account. After you pay the amount, these criminals don't contact you and look for another prey. The best way to confirm is to get in touch with any nationalized bank overseas dealing branch who will guide regarding the procedure to be followed or report it to Cyber Crime cell.

Physical Layer attacks like Jamming, Eavesdropping etc. lead to compromising confidentiality of Information. Data Link layer attacks like malicious behavior of nodes leads to misdirected traffic. Network attack includes Black Hole, Phishing attack result in loss of confidential information on packet. Cyber Criminals are involved in Information Collection which remains the first step of planning an attack. Just like a robber who surveys the house surroundings few times before executing a robbery, the Cyber criminal does a background check before attacking. The next step involves acting like a related person trying to gain unauthorized access to some important resources. The actual attack happens later through malware or Denial of Service Attack. Once attack is done, it can be automated and executed frequently on the target.

Cyber Crime is primarily classified based on its application into four categories:

1. **Individual:** The Cyber crime affecting individuals can be further divided into following types:
    ◦   **Spoofing:** Spoofing can be defined as such a cyber crime which is committed using guise of an unknown source. It can take place through emails, websites, phone calls etc. Spoofing

mainly takes place in guise of email. Spoofed mail consists of same header which looks like original mail sender but is originating from an unknown source and hence is not credible. This may contain attachments which can ask for personal data which can then be used to compromise the individual's account.

- ○ **Stalking:** This involves following or observing the activities of the Individual. All activities of the person on Internet is critically watched without the knowledge of the individual which can make the person vulnerable. This can also lead to harrasement of the individual in form of blackmail, monetary or personal damage.
- ○ **Defamation:** Defamation refers to the image or character assination of a person or individual by publishing objectionable content on the Internet. Someone may publish some material, photo or article on the website which may tarnish the image of the Individual. This occurs mainly with a personal vengenence or enimity to tarnish the reputation and hence bring disrepute to the targetted individual or his/her families.
- ○ **Spamming:** This is the most common type of communication where multiple copies or large quantity of emails such as chain letters are posted. Normally the most common way of Social media communication of religion, political or superstition targetted towards a mass audience. Credibility of this communication received through such emails are negligible yet client or target audience are not aware about the fake intentions of such emails.

2. **Organization:** Organizations have been the epicentre where Cyber crimes take place and most of them go unreported. The primary reason why organizations are targetted may be due to Ex-employee revenge mentality, compromising secret data, crashing of server so that services are disrupted, Changing or modifing data before processing etc. The Cyber crimes affecting Organization can be listed as below:

- ○ **Virus:** This attack is aimed at disrupting the services of the organization. Virus attack can affect the systems and lead to the organization operations being disrupted for few hours which affects the credibility and customer support system of the organisation. Virus are also spread by anti-virus companies to promote their products. They first release the virus and then approach the companies with solution providing anti-virus.
- ○ **Hacking:** The most common form of attack is the unauthorised access into the organization computer system and compromising of data. The data can also be manipulated which can lead to big loss and affect the transactions of the company. The data may not be changed but just accessed without the organization knowing about the unauthorized access.
- ○ **Logic Bomb:** This is specialized way of committing the crime where whenever a particular event occurs the system crashes or a certain virus is released or some program activated which damages the entire system or particular major functions of certain software are affected.
- ○ **Data Diddling:** Just imagine, someone has a vital information about some event. The person or related stakeholder changes the data to provide some sort of benefit to the data diddler, generally financial. Data diddling happens at possible points where data changes hands or data entry takes place which normally cannot be detected. It can be something as small as a time clerk substituting his own name or employee number for another employee's name or number. It can be combated by ensuring that all information is identical, whether it is a hard copy or the data within a digital system (Legistify, 2018).

- **Denial of Service:** This happens in organization where lot of users or client request for service. They are flooded with innumerable fake requests or messages which are generated to slow or crash the server. The ultimate result is that the genuine users request for service is disturbed and they are starved of the services which may lead to Customers shifting loyalty.
- **Software Bomb:** This is also known as e-mail bombing. In this type of attack, large number of emails are send to organization resulting in heavy traffic and crashing of the server.
- **Miscellaneous Attacks:** Such attacks include Salaami Attack which happen in Banks etc. where a negligible small amount like 0.40 paise are siphoned off from every account. This may result in truncation of the amount for which a small program may be run. Account holders do not notice small amount of less than 1 Rupee and at the same time since there are many crores of bank accounts, the amount siphoned off is to the tune of crores of Rupees.

3. **Society:** Cyber crimes against Society is a new trend and this is practiced to inflict maximum losses to Society. These crimes include:

- **Terrorism:** They use Information Technology to target a large number of people or community and spread hatred in the name of religion or other preferences. Use of technology to identify target and execute plan has seen many innovative modus operandi in the last few years.
- **Web Jacking:** Web Jacking refers to hacking of website, changing content and making illegal entry or modifyind data of the website. This is mainly done to earn money, political gains, to show the vulnerability of website and provide safeguards thereby creating clout and expanding business.
- **Forgery:** This is more of a cyber crime which has been committed since many years. Marksheet forgery, revenue stamp, currency note printing etc. are some of such crimes. These activiites involve the use of high end technology like 3D printing technology which gives exceptional quality of output.

4. **Property:** Most of the Cyber crimes are targetted towards property related transactions. They include:

- **Monetary Fraud:** This involves banking fraud, credit card fraud and related financial crimes. There may be some mails or social media contact claiming that you have won 1 Million US $ lottery or your name has been selected in lucky draw. You may be asked to pay some thousand rupees to claim the amount as transfer fees. Once the fees are paid, you will not get any reply leaving such people cheated to the tune of Crores of Rupees in India itself. Other monetary fraud includes asking for OTP pin or stealing passwords and siphoning off a huge amount from unsuspecting account holders. Greed of money is the primary reason for getting trapped in such crimes. Online banking safeguards are very much required to prevent such crimes. RBI and banks have been issuing guidelines to this effect preventing or educating the Account holder not to share personal identification information like PIN, CVV and OTP to anyone.
- **Intellectual Property:** Theft of Source code is not reported as Cyber Crime. Intellectual Property violations like Patent, Copyright, Trademarks etc. are serious Cyber crimes and still occur frequently. Many people are not aware of their rights regarding Intellectual Property and hence fail to register with the appropriate authority like Patent office.
- **Time Theft:** Usage of Internet or Wi-Fi without authorisation is time theft. Computer or Internet resource usage without permission can lead to inflated bills and illegal activities. Proper security mechanisms should be in place to avoid such thefts.

MACHINE LEARNING IN CYBER SECURITY

Machine Learning can be used in innumerable ways to control Cybercrime and assist in providing Cyber Security. Some of the primary applications of Machine Learning (Jordan, 2015) in Cyber Security are listed below:

- Detect malicious activity and stop attacks.
- Analyze mobile points using Machine Learning.
- Enhancing Human Analysis.
- To automate repeated Security tasks.
- To counter and close zero-day vulnerabilities.

Figure 5 shows the integration between Machine Learning and Cyber Security and how Machine Learning being an active AI component can help in various use-cases.

Malware detection and network intrusion detection are two such areas where Deep learning has shown significant improvements over the rule-based and classic machine learning-based solutions (Xiao, 2017). The primary difference between Machine Learning and Artificial Intelligence is that AI deals with Machines which carry out the work in a smarter way whereas ML refers to application of AI which learns from previous data.

Machine Learning applications can distinguish between whether text written is in complaint form or compliment.

Machine Learning can protect against many crimes such as Spear Phishing, Watering Hole, Webshell, Ransomware and Remote Exploitation.

- **Spear Phishing:** The attacks through Phishing have taken new dimensions. The old techniques used for Phishing detection (Wu, 2006) are not capable enough as they lack speed and accuracy. Predictive URL Classification models using Machine Learning Algorithms that identify patterns that reveal malicious sender's mails. Cybersecurity provider Barracuda Network, Inc. developed an engine based on machine learning to analyze unique communication patterns without human interference, depending on the customer's nature of business and requirements (Abu, 2007).

Figure 5. Machine learning in cyber security

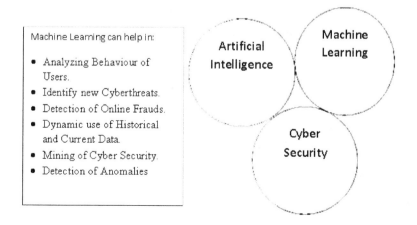

- **Watering Hole:** Hackers track the sites that are frequently visited external to the client's network which is called Watering Hole. The cyber defence service provider, Paladion, developed a proprietary RisqVU platform to effectively counter watering hole attacks. It's a combination between Artificial Intelligence and big data analytics. A watering hole attack requires simultaneous analysis of data from proxy, email traffic, and pocket. RisqVU is a big data analytics platform applying analysis from multiple sources, such an AI-based study helps to visualize a single view of an attack. (Cranor, 2006).

- **Webshell:** This can be described as a portion of code loaded on the website without proper authorization and permits the hacker access to web root directory. The server access results in complete database access allowing hacker all the monetary card information of customer. M-Commerce or e-portals are the frequent targets as they have confidential information of clients like payment mechanism information. Machine Learning models can be modeled to identify difference between normal and malicious activity. Cybersecurity firm Crowd Strike developed Falcon to detect files less Webshell attacks that relay on advanced vulnerabilities instead of traditional malwares.

- **Ransomware:** Software demanding some compensation for sharing the encryption keys of User's files. Cloud data protection firm, Acronis, developed a new level Cybersecurity solution with the aim of a zero attack day. Acronis uses machine learning study to analyze scripts.

- **Remote Exploitation:** This includes such attacks which are done on a set or network of computers. This includes Denial of Service attack, DNS Poisoning and Port Scanning. Machine learning algorithms can be used to analyze system behavior and identify abnormal instances which do not correlate with the typical network behavior. Algorithms can be trained for multiple data sets so that it can track down an exploitation payload beforehand.

RELATED RESEARCH WORK ON MACHINE LEARNING IN CYBER SECURITY

The loss due to Cyber Security breaches are more than 500 billion dollars per year. The domains most affected are Banking and Finance followed remotely by Information Technology, Defence, Telecommunications and manufacturing organizations like Oil & Gas, etc.

1200+ companies surveyed as per KPMG report for Cyber Security, almost 97% reported serious security breaches and 24% attacks generated resembled pattern of targeted attack (KPMG, 2017). This survey is a conservative study and real facts may lead to an incremental statistic of the projections.

Machine Learning can play an important part in Cyber Security by preventing or detecting cyber crimes. Literature study of related areas in Machine Learning, Cyber Security and Artificial Intelligence in a broad prespective has been presented below.

Benaicha et. al. proposed a model based on Intrusion detection using Genetic Algorithm to maximize the detections and minimize the time taken for the detections. The time taken to detect the intrusion is negligible and increases the penetration detection rate (Benaicha, 2014).

Ojugo et. al. has proposed Genetic Algorithm rule based Intrusion Detection System for optimizing the parameters using classification resulting in increased quality of Information Security. The parameters considered are confidentiality, similarity measure, resource usage, time taken for detection and hit rate (Ojugo, 2012).

Sekeh et. al. has implemented a model using data mining in a simulated network for intrusion detection. The primary concerns are robustness of database, size and complexity and detection time. The efficiency of the mining technique is also an important takeaway and can be a major factor in improving the performance of the model (Sekeh, 2009).

Pei et. al. implements a mixed model modifying existing algorithm to enhance the intrusion detection process. This process increases the accuracy rate and hit ratio of the model compared to existing models of similar nature (Pei, 2008).

Ferreira et al. have proposed a model using Artificial Neural Network and results show exemplary detection rate close to over 90% which is considered to be above acceptable standards. This model uses data mining process to summarize and visualize the data related to intrusion detection (Ferreira, 2011).

Chaudhary et al. designed and developed a model using various characteristics to form a graph using nodes. This model used unsupervised learning to generate a map using datasets and was popularly known as bot detection. The proposed methodology is able to detect anomaly by searching a limited number of nodes. The comparison of this model with another model using Support Vector Machine resulted in more accurate results for bot detection model (Chaudhary, 2014).

Various research studies have suggested different models using variants of Support Vector Machine, Genetic Algorithm, Fuzzy Logic, K-Means, Knowledge discovery in databases, Naïve Bayes Classifier, Clustering methods, Nearest neighbor method, Swarm Particle optimization etc. to just name a few.

Liang Xiao et. al. has suggested an integrated version of Internet of things (IoT) to detect cyber breaches. The devices like sensors are used to detect and filter the packets using basic protocol features (Li, 2011). The features are selected and classified after which they are stored in database. The trained data is then classified through Machine Learning Classifier utilizing K-means nearest neighbor (KNN) and random forest to identify deviations and detect malware. Results indicate that this model provides an accuracy of more than 99%. (Xiao, 2016). Sheng et. al. has discussed IoT as an effective mechanism

Table 1. Comparative study of various machine learning methods on predefined criteria

Machine Learning Method	PERFORMANCE CRITERIA			
	Types of Attacks	Accuracy	Detection Rate	Robust
Statistical Method	DDos Attack	Perfect	Positive Rate	Yes
KNN	Bot Net and Anomaly Detection	Perfect	False Positive Rate	Partially
Naïve Bayesian	Web Attack, Intrusion Detection	Average	False Positive Rate	Yes
Support Vector Machine	DDoS and Bot Net Detection	Perfect	Positive Rate	Yes
Genetic Algorithm	Intrusion Detection	Perfect	Positive Rate	Yes
Decision Tree	HTTP Attacks	Perfect	Positive Rate	Yes
Random Forest	Web Detection	Average	Positive Rate	Yes
Swarm Particle Optimization	Anomaly Detection	Perfect	False Positive Rate	Yes
Clustering	Intrusion and Outlier Detection	Perfect	Positive Rate	Yes
Logistic Regression	Cloud Security	Perfect	Positive Rate	Yes
Information Metrics	DDoS Attack	Average	Positive Rate	No

and suggested IoT model to help in Machine Learning (Sheng, 2013). Liu et. al. has discussed IoT architecture and the challenges involved in implementing IoT (Liu, 2017). Andrea et. al. has also discussed IoT architecture from a different prespective and provided solutions to existing problems (Andrea, 2015).

Shu et. al. has discussed Machine Learning Security Protocols and given a comparative study of available protocols (Shu, 2007). Subbulakshmi et. al. has discussed at length DDOS in Machine Learning Domain and given an insight into challenges and possible applications (Subbulakshmi, 2010).

Liang Xiao et. al. has also proposed Dyna-Q malware detection model which learns from existing data and provides real time and virtual experience resulting in greater efficiency. A comparative study made with Q-Learning model suggests that Dyna-Q provides around 20% increase in precision and provides reduction in intrusion detection time (Xiao, 2017).

Table 1 shows a comparative study on various Machine Learning Methods based on predefined Performance criteria.

APPLICATIONS OF MACHINE LEARNING ALGORITHMS TO CYBER SECURITY

Machine Learning can be classified into two main categories:

1. **Shallow Learning:** In Shallow Learning, subject domain expert is required to classify and evaluate performance and characteristics of data related to the particular domain. Suppose if Shallow learning is being applied to financial domain, the Financial expert is required to critically name and evaluate the characteristics related to data before execution of the Shallow Learning Algorithm. This is also classified into Supervised Shallow Learning and Unsupervised Shallow Learning.
2. **Deep Learning:** Deep Learning uses representation learning based on historical data and can perform feature selection without any help from domain expert. Deep Learning can also be classified into Supervised and Unsupervised Deep Learning (Guest Blog, 2018)

Figure 6. Machine learning overview

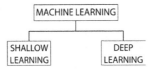

Shallow Learning Supervised Algorithms

Table 2 shows or depicts the classification of Shallow Learning Supervised Algorithms. These algorithms mainly consist of Naive Bayes, Support Vector Machine (SVM), Random Forest, Logistic Regression, Shallow Neural Network, Hidden Markov Models and KNN just to name a few.

Table 2. Shallow learning supervised algorithm overview

Sr. No.	Name of Algorithm	Characteristics
1	Naïve Bayes	• Probabilistic Classifier • Features of dataset independent. • Scalable. • Can work on small datasets to produce accurate results.
2	Support Vector Machines	• Non-probabilistic Classifiers. • Maximize distance between clusters. • No assumptions made. • Less scalability.
3	Logistic Regression	• Categorical classifiers. • Size of data important. • Performance based on size of training data. • Features of dataset important.
4	Shallow Neural Network	• Neural Network related. • Consists of Neurons and Layers. • Classification tasks. • More communicating layers.
5	Random Forest	• Set of Decision Trees. • Conditional Classifier. • Better for large datasets. • Can lead to over fitting.
6	Hidden Markov Models	• Find out sequence of states. • Preferable with labeled datasets. • Useful for predicting sequence of events.
7	K-Nearesst neighbor (KNN)	• Classification. • Training and Test data both required. • Application for problems having multiple classes.

Shallow Learning Unsupervised Algorithms

Table 3 shows or depicts the classification of Shallow Learning Unsupervised Algorithms. These algorithms mainly consist of Clustering and Association.

Table 3. Shallow learning unsupervised algorithms overview

Sr. No.	Name of Algorithm	Characteristics	Remarks
1	Clustering	• Distance between elements placed in same cluster. • Less scalability. • Used for Anomaly detection.	k-Means, H-Clustering
2	Association	• Detect hidden patterns. • Used in Prediction. • Human Intervention needed. • Algorithm may produce more relations leading to wrong results.	Apriori Algorithm

Deep Learning Supervised Algorithms

Table 4 shows or depicts the classification of Deep Learning Supervised Algorithms. These algorithms mainly consist of Fully Connected Feed Forward Deep Neural Networks, Convolutional Feed Forward Deep Neural Networks and Recurrent Deep Neural Networks (Lecun, 2015).

Table 4. Deep learning supervised algorithms overview

Sr. No.	Name of Algorithm	Characteristics	Remarks
1	Fully connected Feed Forward Deep Neural Networks	• Each Neuron connected to all other neurons. • No assumption on input data. • Classification. • Expensive for data calculations.	Costly
2	Convolutional Feedforward Deep Neural Networks (CNN)	• Good at Spatial Data Analysis. • Less performance if applied to non-spatial data. • Lower computational cost.	Excellent results for Spatial Data Analysis.
3	Recurrent Deep Neural Networks (RNN)	• Difficult to train, • Sequence Generators. • Long short-term memory.	

Deep Learning Unsupervised Algorithms

Table 5 shows or depicts the classification of Deep Learning Unsupervised Algorithms. These algorithms mainly consist of Deep Belief Networks and Stacked Auto Encoders.

Table 5. Deep learning unsupervised algorithms overview

Sr. No.	Name of Algorithm	Characteristics	Remarks
1	Deep Belief Networks (DBN)	• No output layer. • Good for pre-training tasks. • Feature Extraction. • Training phase. • Unlabelled datasets.	
2	Stacked Autoencoders (SAE)	• Multiple AutoEncoders. • Pre-defined tasks. • Good for tiny datasets	

APPLICATIONS OF MACHINE LEARNING IN CYBER SECURITY DOMAIN

Artificial Intelligence can be effectively used to combat Cyber Crimes. Some Cybercrimes like Shoulder surfing, Phishing, Network Intrusion, Protocol testing, Human Intervention, Smart Energy profiling, Social Network related, Cryptography, Malware etc. are very much prevalent in this digital society. The shocking aspect is that previously Hacking used to be handiwork of very few intelligent, juvenile male, very sharp in computers whereas recent cases coming to the forefront are hackers in the age group starting from 12 to retirement with varying skill levels, unknown history and coming from affluent families.

Figure 7. Web classification

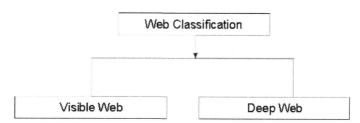

Cyber crimes are directed from various sources and such intrusion is very hard to detect as they are not localized. Artificial Intelligence uses deductive reasoning, perception, natural language processing, creativity, social intelligence, multi-agent planning, motion and manipulation. An agent tries to understand the environment and reacts to decision making. Artificial Intelligence has an advanced technique called Genetic Algorithm which deals with the process of natural selection (Recorded Future Team, 2018).

The Visible Web is where the outer surface in terms of transactions and information exchange take place. Deep Web is where all the process of Hacking and Cyber Crime take place. The objective of Machine Learning is to prevent Cyber Crime from spreading to the different regions of the globe.

Important applications of Machine Learning are Phishing Detection, Network Intrusion Detection, Malware Analysis, Spam Detection, Keystroke Dynamic authentication, Breaking Human Interaction proofs, Smart meter profiling etc (Koppula, 2018)

- **Phishing Detection:** Phishing means accessing unauthorized information by disguising as someone else. Phishing is equivalent to robbing any valuable object or accessing data without knowledge of the owner. Phishing can be stopped using three effective methods such as Detection, Prevention and Correction. Phishing Detection techniques like Logistic Regression (LR), Classification and Regression Trees (CART), Bayesian Additive Regression Trees (BART), Support Vector Machines (SVM), Random Forests (RF), and Neural Networks (NNets) have been used effectively to counter cybercrime of Phishing. Vitaly Ford et. al. has made a comparative study of Machine Learning techniques listed above on the criteria of Precision, Recall and F-measure. Logistic Regression (LR) had the greatest precision and low recall. LR is more used for Phishing Detection as it has low false positive rate which means that there are few chances that actual mails are classified as junk. Phishing using Machine Learning involves identifying different customer behavior without human interference to generate patterns and promote related businesses.
- **Network Intrusion Detection:** Network Intrusion is performing illegal activities using a network. BOTNET is a group of machines controlled by hackers and is widely misused to conduct shady activites. Major threat to the organization as sensitive and confidential information may be leaked or even modified. Decision Trees, Pruning Algorithm, Support Vector Machines (SVM), Genetic Programming etc. are used for Network Intrusion Detection. Results have proved that Support Vector Machines are found to be more accuracy in classification compared to other methods (Giovanni, 2018).
- **Malware Analysis:** Normally Malware are capable of duplicating but appear as completely different executable files. Supervised Deep Learning Tools are FNN, CNN and RNN and unsupervised tools like DBN and SAE are used for Malware Analysis. Shallow Learning Supervised

Machine Learning uses Naïve Bayes, Random Forest, SVM, Logistic Regression, KNN etc. for Malware Analysis. Unsupervised ML consists of Clustering and Associate Rule Mining is used for Malware Analysis.

- **Spam Detection:** Lot of unnecessary mails are circulated which get accumulated in Inbox. Detection of Spam mails will ensure that such mails land in Spam and not Inbox. This reduces the burden of the User as he/she can ignore such mails or not fall prey to such unsolicited mails. Unsupervised Deep Learning methods like SAE and DBN are used for Spam Detection. Shallow Learning Supervised Machine Learning uses Naïve Bayes, Random Forest, SVM, Logistic Regression, KNN etc. and Unsupervised Shallow Learning uses Clustering and Association for Spam Detection.

- **Keystroke Dynamics Authentication:** Neural Networks are used for Keystroke dynamics. The behavioral characteristics are recorded and accordingly Neural network is used to authenticate if the login process is genuine or not (Revett, 2017).

- **Breaking Human Interaction Proof:** Captcha's can be broken by using Machine Learning. Chellapila (2005) have conducted primary testing and proved that Captcha can be easily tracked using Machine Learning (Chellapila, 2005).

- **Social Network Spam Detection:** Social Networking sites were scanned for months and based on the data collected, separation into spam was conducted using Support Vector Machine (SVM). Average Spam Detection efficiency on Social Network is found to be approximately 76% (Pei, 2008).

- **Smart Meter Data Profiling:** Smart Grid related data pertaining to electricity and energy consumption is stored. If such data is compromised and distributed according to consumption statistics, it can be dangerous as privacy of consumer is invaded. The safe hours for such operations can be when customer is not at residence or out of station. Any unusual usage of energy can be tracked by Energy corporation so that energy can be saved and secure data exchange can take place (Ford, 2013).

CHALLENGES IN MACHINE LEARNING

The more promising Machine Learning seems to be, the more challenges are being faced. Slowly and steadily the base of people using Machine Learning is on the rise and it is soon catching the imagination of one and all with so many applications all over the world. However, there are some grey areas or challenges which are required to be addressed:

- **Large Data Size:** Data size is a great challenge. Most of the applications of Machine Learning is in such a domain where there is tremendous magnitude of data. The data cleaning, preprocessing etc. takes long time. Some of the Machine Learning methods are giving excellent results when applied for small data.

- **Multi Dimensional:** Data despite being huge in size also consist of lot of dimensions. All these dimensions have to be analyzed and then the algorithm applied.

- **Data is Temporal:** Many of the data are not permanent in nature but have to be stored and accessed for a shorter duration. This also leads to lots of issues like identification of data, what is the duration of data accessibility, the links to various other data etc.

- **Skewed Distribution of Data:** The data is not properly distributed and may contain lot of variance which can lead to ambiguity in data. So, data needs to be properly distributed into related frequency table and then the future process will commence.
- **Data Preprocessing:** Missing values need to be removed or detected, noise should be removed and certain records need to be understood. This process should be carried out with due understanding of topic or training data should be present. Many companies have a repository where data related to previous transactions are stored in archive.
- **Speed of Computing:** It includes online transactions, capacity of portal to cater to customers. This also leads to high efficiency service, computing capabilities, ability to match the hacker in terms of computing speed and tools.
- **Affordability:** Machine Learning jobs involve high packages and all companies cannot provide such package. Data Scientist, Cyber Analyst, Networking Engineer in Cyber Security etc. are job profiles which are most sought after jobs.
- **Business Models:** Agile Business models are the need of the hour. Company needs to change physical setup, mindset and skillset of employees and hence it is not possible for all companies to press for this change. Management of Agile Business models is also difficult and requires Staff with a self motivated vision.
- **Wrong Content Detection:** The algorithm or methods are for specific task. So if wrong method is used for classification, it can result in waste of time and energy.
- **Implementing IoT solutions in Cyber Security:** Certain domains involve multidisciplinary approach. The biggest challenge is to bring about IoT and its awareness integrating data mining.
  - **Cost:** Some solutions provided are very costly to develop, deploy and test solutions. The costing and budgeting aspect needs to be verified.
  - **Miscellaneous Issues:** Oversampling, Insufficient Training and Bad feature identification are some of the reasons for detection resulting in failure to detecting the attacks.
  - **Web Based Knowledge:** Lot of teens or college students has great knowledge at their disposal. It becomes difficult to keep pace with the cyber crime methods and suggest appropriate corrections to prevent cybercrime.

Microsoft, Google, Amazon etc are coming up with Cloud Machine Learning Platforms. Some of the very common applications of Machine Learning in daily life are image tagging @Facebook, providing email spam detectors. Additional scope for Machine Learning is in the field of Financial Analysis, Computer Vision, Medical Diagnosis, Customer Segmentation, Data entry Manually, Product Recommendation for books etc..

FUTURE TRENDS

The trend for 2020 is the era of Smart Cities. This requires the knowledge of IoT, Big Data, Behavioral Sciences, Data Analytics, Machine Learning, Robotics, Image Processing etc. just to name of few. The trend of Machine Learning would be multi disciplinary requiring domain knowledge spread across various faculties. Mundane or Clerical jobs would be performed by Robots, precision and accuracy would be the need of the hour.

Cyber Crime would also grow at a rapid pace as more and more people are becoming net-savvy. This is disturbing the Emotional Quotient and the future generations would be lacking skills and manpower. A robust mechanism in terms of Cyber Security, Government Policy Implementations and Machine Learning Advancements –this triangle would change the dimensions of doing business. Corporate companies would be spending more on Information Security and investing into Machine Learning solutions making the domain of Machine Learning very attractive.

REFERENCES

Abu-Nimeh, S., Nappa, D., Wang, X., & Nair, S. (2007). A comparison of machine learning techniques for phishing detection. *APWG eCrime Researchers Summit*. 10.1145/1299015.1299021

Andrea, I., Chrysostomou, C., & Hadjichristofi, G. (2015, February). Internet of Things: Security vulnerabilities and challenges. In *Proc. IEEE Symposium on Computers and Commun*, (pp. 180–187). Larnaca, Cyprus: IEEE. 10.1109/ISCC.2015.7405513

Anti-Phishing Working Group. (n.d.). *Phishing and Fraud solutions*. Available at http://www.antiphishing.org

Apruzzese, G., & Colajanni, M. (2018). On the Effectiveness of Machine and Deep Learning for Cyber Security. *2018 10th International Conference on Cyber Conflict*, 371-390.

Benaicha, S. E., Saoudi, L., Bouhouita Guermeche, S. E., & Lounis, O. (2014). Intrusion detection system using genetic algorithm. *Science and Information Conference (SAI)*, 564-568.

Buczak, A., & Guven, E. (2015). A survey of data mining and machine learning methods for cyber security intrusion detection, *IEEE Communications Surveys and Tutorials*.

Chaudhary, A., Tiwari, V. N., & Kumar, A. (2014). Design an anomaly based fuzzy intrusion detection system for packet dropping attack in mobile ad hoc networks. *IEEE International Conference on Advance Computing (IACC)*, 256-261. 10.1109/IAdCC.2014.6779330

Chellapilla, K., & Simard, P. Y. (2005). Using Machine Learning to Break Visual Human Interaction Proofs (HIPs). In Advances in neural information processing systems (pp. 265–272). Academic Press.

Cranor, L. F., Egelman, S., Hong, J., & Zhang, Y. (2006). *Phinding phish: An evaluation of anti-phishing toolbars*. Technical Report CMU-CyLab-06-018. CMU.

Drinkwater, D. (2017). *5 Top Machine Learning Use Cases for Security*. Retrieved from https://www.computerworld.com.au/article/631162/5-top-machine-learning-use-cases-security

Ferreira, E. W. T., Carrijo, G. A., de Oliveira, R., & de Souza Araujo, N. V. (2011). Intrusion Detection System with Wavelet and Neural Artificial Network Approach for Networks Computers. *IEEE Latin America Transactions, 9*(5), 832-837.

Ford, V., & Siraj, A. (2013, December). Clustering of smart meter data for disaggregation. *Proceedings of IEEE Global Conference on Signal and Information Processing*. 10.1109/GlobalSIP.2013.6736926

Guest Blog. (2018). *Using the Power of Deep Learning for Cyber Security (Part 1)*. Retrieved from https://www.analyticsvidhya.com/blog/2018/07/using-power-deep-learning-cyber-security/

InfoTechLead. (n.d.). *What can Machine Learning do for Cyber Security*. Retrieved from www.infotechlead.com/security /can-machine-learning-cybersecurity-50357/attachment/what-can-do-machine-learning-fo-cyber-security

Jordan, M. I., & Mitchell, T. M. (2015). Machine learning: Trends, perspectives, and prospects. *Science*, *349*(6245), 255–260. doi:10.1126cience.aaa8415 PMID:26185243

Koppula, R. (2018). *Applications of Machine Learning in Cyber Security You Need to Know About*. Retrieved from https://apiumhub.com/tech-blog-barcelona/applications-machine-learning-cyber-security/

KPMG. (2017). *Cybercrime Survey Report 2017*. Retrieved from https://home.kpmg/in/en/home/insights/2017/12/cybercrime-cybersecurity-law-enforcement-agencies.html

LeCun, Y., Bengio, Y., & Hinton, G. (2015). Deep learning. *Nature*, *521*(7553), 436–444. doi:10.1038/nature14539 PMID:26017442

Legistify. (2018). *What Is Data Diddling*. Retrieved from www.legistify.com/qna/answer/1920-what-is-data-diddling

Li, X., Lu, R., Liang, X., Shen, X., Chen, J., & Lin, X. (2011, November). Smart community: An Internet of Things application. *IEEE Communications Magazine*, *49*(11), 68–75. doi:10.1109/MCOM.2011.6069711

Liu, X., Zhao, M., Li, S., Zhang, F., & Trappe, W. (2017, June). A security framework for the Internet of Things in the future Internet architecture. *Future Internet*, *9*(3), 1–28. doi:10.3390/fi9030027

Maruti Tech Labs. (2019). *Artificial Intelligence and Machine Learning Made Simple*. Retrieved from https://www.marutitech.com/artificial-intelligence-and-machine-learning/

Ojugo, A. AEboka, A. OOkonta, O. EYoro, R. E., & Aghware, F. O. (2012). Genetic Algorithm Rule-Based Intrusion Detection System (GAIDS). *Journal of Emerging Trends in Computing and Information Sciences*, *3*(8), 1182–1194.

Pei, Z., & Song, J. (2008). Application of Immune Algorithm to Generate Fuzzy-detector in Intrusion detection. *Fourth International Conference on Natural Computation (ICNC)*, 5, 183-186. 10.1109/ICNC.2008.840

Recorded Future Team. (2018). *Machine Learning: Practical Applications for Cybersecurity*. Retrieved from https://www.recordedfuture.com/machine-learning-cybersecurity-applications/

Revett, K., Gorunescu, F., Gorunescu, M., Ene, M., Magalhaes, S. T., & Santos, H. M. D. (2007). A machine learning approach to keystroke dynamics based user authentication. *International Journal of Electronic Security and Digital Forensics*, *1*(1), 55. doi:10.1504/IJESDF.2007.013592

Sekeh, M. A., & Bin Maarof, M. A. (2009). Fuzzy Intrusion Detection System via Data Mining Technique with Sequences of System Calls. *Fifth International Conference on Information Assurance and Security (IAS '09)*, 1, 154-157. 10.1109/IAS.2009.32

Sheng, Z., Yang, S., Yu, Y., Vasilakos, A., Mccann, J., & Leung, K. (2013, December). A survey on the IETF protocol suite for the Internet of Things: Standards, challenges, and opportunities. *IEEE Wireless Communications*, *20*(6), 91–98. doi:10.1109/MWC.2013.6704479

Shu, G., & Lee, D. (2007). Testing Security Properties of Protocol Implementations – a Machine Learning Based Approach. *Proceedings of 27th International Conference on Distributed Computing Systems (ICDCS'07)*. 10.1109/ICDCS.2007.147

Stack Overflow. (2018). *Can Anyone Give a Real Life Example of Supervised Learning and Unsupervised Learning?* Retrieved from https://stackoverflow.com/questions/26182980/can-anyone-give-a-real-life-example-of-supervised-learning-and-unsupervised-learn

Stiennon, R. (2016). *Chief Research Analyst*. IT-Harvest, National Fintech Cybersecurity Summit.

Subbulakshmi, T., Shalinie, S. M., & Ramamoorthi, A. (2010). Detection and Classification of DDoS Attacks using Machine Learning Algorithms. *European Journal of Scientific Research, 47*(3), 334 – 346.

Wu, M., Miller, R. C., & Garnkel, S. L. (2006). Do security toolbars actually prevent phishing attacks? *Proceedings of the SIGCHI conference on Human Factors in computing systems*. 10.1145/1124772.1124863

Xiao, L., Li, Y., Han, G., Liu, G., & Zhuang, W. (2016, December). PHY-layer spoofing detection with reinforcement learning in wireless networks. *IEEE Transactions on Vehicular Technology*, *65*(12), 10037–10047. doi:10.1109/TVT.2016.2524258

Xiao, L., Li, Y., Huang, X., & Du, X. J. (2017, October). Cloud-based malware detection game for mobile devices with offloading. *IEEE Transactions on Mobile Computing*, *16*(10), 2742–2750. doi:10.1109/TMC.2017.2687918

Yavanoglu, O., & Aydos, M. (2017, December). A review on cyber security datasets for machine learning algorithms. In *2017 IEEE International Conference on Big Data* (pp. 2186-2193). IEEE.

Chapter 5
Applications of Machine Learning in Cyber Security

Charu Virmani
Manav Rachna International Institute of Research and Studies, India

Tanu Choudhary
Manav Rachna International Institute of Research and Studies, India

Anuradha Pillai
J. C. Bose University of Science and Technology YMCA, India

Manisha Rani
D. N. College, India

ABSTRACT

With the exponential rise in technological awareness in the recent decades, technology has taken over our lives for good, but with the application of computer-aided technological systems in various domains of our day-to-day lives, the potential risks and threats have also come to the fore, aiming at the various security features that include confidentiality, integrity, authentication, authorization, and so on. Computer scientists the world over have tried to come up, time and again, with solutions to these impending problems. With time, attackers have played out complicated attacks on systems that are hard to comprehend and even harder to mitigate. The very fact that a huge amount of data is processed each second in organizations gave birth to the concept of Big Data, thereby making the systems more adept and intelligent in dealing with unprecedented attacks on a real-time basis. This chapter presents a study about applications of machine learning algorithms in cyber security.

INTRODUCTION

With the exponential rise in technological awareness in the recent decades, technology has taken over our lives for good but with the application of computer aided technological systems in various domains of our day to day lives, the potential risks and threats have also come to the fore aiming at the various security features that include confidentiality, integrity, authentication, authorization and so on. Computer

DOI: 10.4018/978-1-5225-9611-0.ch005

scientists, the world over have tried to come up, time and again with solutions to these impending problems. With time, attackers have played out complicated attacks on systems that are hard to comprehend and even harder to mitigate. Even upon recognition, responding in real time remained a problem. The capability of the system was hence extended using artificial intelligence and machine learning techniques. The very fact that a huge of data is processed each second in organizations gave birth to the concept of Big Data, thereby making the systems more and adept and intelligent in dealing with unprecedented attacks on a real time basis. Various authors having worked on the problem, devised a host of algorithms that may be used for purposes such as image processing, speech recognition, biomedical area, and of course cyber security domain.

The chapter primarily presents a survey about the role of machine learning when applied in the domain of cyber security. The chapter aims at introducing the reader to the basics of machine learning along with its various components and tasks associated with it. The chapter presents in detail a set of approaches to classify the various Machine Learning algorithms and goes on to recount the application of Machine Learning in our day-to-day lives. Having introduced the reader to the basics, a detailed description of the cyber security tasks in machine learning aided with examples are narrated in the later sections.

WHAT IS MACHINE LEARNING?

As the scientists focused more on solving the issues related with the computer systems including the security aspect, they drove themselves closer to a technology that acted like humans. This was the beginning of AI (Artificial Intelligence) applications that surpassed their detection as computer systems by users. Initially generated, AI applications aimed at clearing the Turing Test which is a test of a machine's ability to showcase intelligent behavior that is tantamount to or indiscernible from that of a human intelligence. But since AI was initiated with the very purpose of specific application domains such as face recognition, object recognition, it was soon realized that creating an AI that worked in terms of the human brain completely was an arduous task. Hence, the concept of Machine Learning was evolved.

Machine Learning is essentially an approach to Artificial intelligence that makes use of any system that is adept in learning like humans, i.e., from experience (Al-Jarrah et al., 2015; Buczak & Guven eta l, 2016). Just like a human brain, it aims at recognizing the patterns and upgrades itself to apply them in the future decisions. Thus, it defies the old traditions of feeding data into the systems through programming and learns by examples. The decisions in Machine Learning are driven by data rather than algorithms and also change its behavior, upon accommodating new information, that sets' it apart from the lot of technologies aiming to achieve cyber security (Michalski, 2013). Simply put, Machine Learning is a type of Artificial intelligence that allows the system to learn without being explicitly programmed wherein computer programs are developed in such a way that they change whenever exposed to new data (Cavelty, 2010).

The ultimate aim of Machine Learning techniques can be thought of as enabling software's to be able to make decisions much like humans do in cases of cyber attacks that have been previously encountered by the system and also those not encountered before. The breach of data in big organizations has incurred a huge loss, with the average cost being over $3 million. Since cyber crimes have become rhetoric in the current scenario, it is the most researched field today and the scientists have been struggling to devise techniques that could reduce the cost factor while dealing with the attacks.

Though the buzz around Machine Learning technology has just gained momentum, but the concept is as old as the computer history itself. Data produced from computer systems and sensors were processed and were derived some meaning from since the first computers were in use. The discussion has caught up pace today because of the huge amount of data available to us today, thus giving it a name, Big Data.

Big data is being created day in and day out by everything that surrounds us. Each and every digital process and information across online social media networks produces data. The various Systems, sensors and mobile devices play a role in transmitting the data. Big data is generally characterized by the 3Vs: the volume of data, the variety of data types and the velocity at which the data must be processed (Chapelle et al., 2009). Although there isn't any specific volume of data defined, the term is referred to describe terabytes, petabytes and even exabytes of data captured over time across different platforms. The data available for processing would continue to be on the rise in the future as well due to the widespread use of IoT technology. Thus, the opportunity to develop some intelligence systems using machine learning to analyze big data more easily has grown because it is technically impossible for humans to analyze the data at this big scale (Kim et al., 2007). Big Data and Machine Learning can be thought of as two components which are complementary to each other. Marrying the two concepts comes naturally to develop an intelligent system using Machine Learning that uses a lot of data. Also, to analyze Big Data, Machine learning is the only viable option. The Machine Learning technique may be thought of as an intersection of various entities that are illustrated in figure 1.

- **Data:** These are the various facts and statistics collected together, which may or may not make sense and can be used for future reference or analysis.
- **Features:** A pattern recognition or feature is an important metrics in defining the characteristics of Machine Learning.
- **Data Science:** It is a field that makes use of scientific methods, processes, algorithms and systems to get an insight from structured and unstructured data in various forms.
- **Algorithms:** A set of protocols that need to be followed in any calculations or other problem solving operations especially in computer related fields.

Figure 1. Components of machine learning

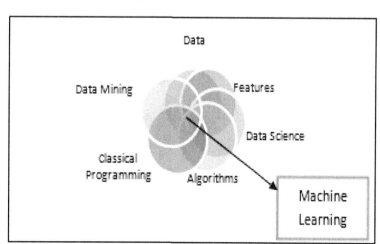

- **Classical Programming:** Involves the use of various programming languages that have been ousted from Machine Learning and replaced with data to recognize and evaluate patterns.
- **Data Mining:** When a huge amount of information in database repositories is analyzed with the aim of creating new information using it, this constitutes the practice of data mining.

Machine Learning is an approach of many similar ones to AI that utilizes a system which learns from experience and not meant to focus on AI goals such as copying human behavior. On the same hand, it efficiently reduces times and effectively utilizes efforts in both simple and complex scenarios such as stock prediction. A system will said to be Machine Learning when it changes its behavior while making its decision from its own learning using data rather than algorithms (Dua et al., 2016). The technique involves solving certain tasks with the use of data available at hand and also the tasks are not human-related. Some of the tasks are shown in figure 2.

- **Regression:** It is a task that involves the prediction of next value based upon the previous values.
- **Classification:** It involves the segregation of things into various different categories.
- **Clustering:** This task is much similar to classification but here, the classes are unknown and things are grouped on their perceived similarity.
- **Association Rule Learning:** It is involved in recommendation task. Based upon previous experiences, a thing is recommended in the future.
- **Dimensionality Reduction:** Also known as generalization, it involves the task of searching common and most important features in multiple examples.
- **Generative Models:** This task deals with the creation of something new based on the previous knowledge of distribution.

Figure 2. Tasks in machine learning

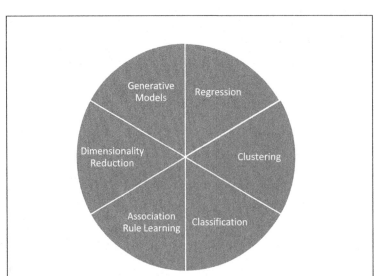

With the above listed tasks in machine learning, there are different approaches to implement the tasks in machine learning which can be classified on different variations as discussed in next section.

APPROACHES TO CLASSIFY MACHINE LEARNING ALGORITHMS

Machine learning Algorithms can be classified on varying views and classification models depending upon variety of paradigms for weak boundaries and cross relationships. The detailed study of literature among the myriad of algorithms which is applied to cyber detection is represented in figure 3. It is broadly classified into shallow learning and deep learning algorithms (Huang & Stokes, 2016; Kasun et al., 2013; Kotsiants et al., 2007; LeCun et al., 2015). A domain expert who can identify the relevant data attribute before the execution of the algorithm is the primary requirement of shallow learning whereas autonomous identification of feature selection using multi-layered representation of the input data is the beauty of Deep Learning.

Shallow Learning and Deep Learning may be further categorized under Supervised and Unsupervised Algorithms. The former techniques are dependent on a large set of data that is pre-requisite of a training process while the latter function without a required pre-labeled training dataset (LeCun et al., 2015). This section mainly deals with the discussions of the various categorizations of ML algorithms.

SHALLOW LEARNING

1.   Supervised SL algorithms

The various algorithms that fall under this sub-category have been discussed briefly:

Figure 3. Classification of machine learning

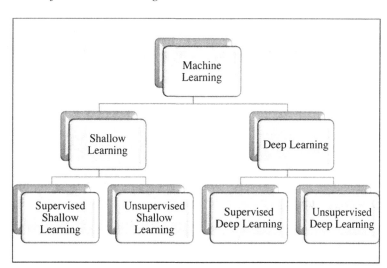

a. **Naive Bayes Algorithm (NB):** Based upon a prior assumption that the input dataset features are independent of one another, they are generally probabilistic classifiers which are scalable and not dependent on huge training datasets to create appreciable outputs (Linda et la, 2011).

b. **Logistic Regression (LR):** These algorithms make use of a discriminative model as unlike Naïve Bayes, these are categorical classifiers. Similar to the above algorithm, this also includes a prior assumption considering the input dataset features as independent. The size of the training data has a huge role to play in assessing its performance (Marsland, 2011).

c. **Support Vector Machine (SVM):** These are the non-probabilistic classifiers used for the purpose of mapping data samples in a feature space with the aim of optimizing the distance between each available category of samples (Wang, 2005). It does not involve any assumption on the input data and perform miserably in case of multi-class classification. Long processing time may be a down-point due to their restricted scalability (Nasrabadi, 2007).

d. **Random Forest (RF):** It can be reckoned as a set of decision trees, wherein the output of each tree is taken into consideration before proposing a final response. Each of the trees has to be a conditional classifier. The tree is approached from the top to each and every node where a given condition is juxtaposed against one or more feature of the data so analyzed. Random forest algorithms fir right for large datasets and are much efficient in dealing with multiclass problems. However, greater depth of the tree may lead to over-fitting.

e. **Hidden Markov Models (HMM):** Outputs with different probabilities are achieved in this case, as the system is made to behave as a set of states. The ultimate objective thus lies in identifying the states sequence for which the output was produced. The model enables us to calculate the probable chances of an event's sequence occurrence and also aids in the understanding of the temporal behavior of the observations. The model may be trained on labeled as well as unlabeled datasets, generally for their applications into security; they are deployed with labeled datasets only (Dua et al., 2016).

f. **K-Nearest model (KNM):** These can be used for classification and also for multi-class problems. The training as well as the training part can be computationally arduous however as it involves the comparisons against all available test samples and along the classification of each of the test sample (Uma & Padmavathi, 2013).

g. **Shallow Neural Networks (SNN):** It involves a corpus of processing entities known as neurons that are organized in two or more communication networks. Though based upon neural networks, it has a very constrained amount of neurons and layers involved. The SNN is deployed in the domain of cyber-security mostly for the task of classification (Xin et al., 2018).

2. Unsupervised SL Algorithms

There are basically two categorizations under this topic which are as mentioned below:

a. **Clustering:** These are clustered group of data points that depict similar features. There are two famous classifications under clustering, known as K-means and Hierarchical Clustering. They have a very restricted scalability but offer a pliable solution that are generally deployed in the prefatory phase before selecting a supervised algorithm or moving on to the anomaly detection procedure.

b. **Association:** Its task is to identify the unknown patterns amongst available data in order to make them viable for the task of prediction. The only downpoint is the excess of data produced which does not necessarily comply with the given rules, thus making it impertinent to combine the procedure with expert and accurate human inspections .

DEEP LEARNING

Deep Neural Networks (DNN) is the very foundation upon which all Deep Learning Algorithms are based (Zhang et al., 2018) The neural networks are organized in different layers wherein each layer is proficient in autonomous representation learning.

1. Supervised DL Algorithms
    a. **Fully-Connected Feedforward Deep Neural Networks (FNN):** These are the derivates of DNN wherein each neuron is connected to the neurons in the prior layers. There are no assumptions involved regarding the input data and stands as an epitome of economically viable and flexible general-purpose solutions for the task of classification.
    b. **Convolutional Feedforward Deep Neural Networks (CNN):** This variant of DNN involves neurons that receive inputs from the subsets of neurons of the previous layers. It is much effective in analysis of spatial data but the performance seems to go downhill with the very application of algorithm to non-spatial data. The computational cost is also much less as compared with FNN.
    c. **Recurrent Deep Neural Networks (RNN):** The architectural design of RNN makes its training a hard task as it involves the neurons sending their outputs to the previous layers as well. They are excellent sequence- generators especially the long short-term memory.
2. Unsupervised DL Algorithms
    a. **Deep Belief Networks (DBN):** A composition of Restricted Boltzmann Machines is involves its modeling which is a class of neural networks that consist of no outer layers. It can be effectively deployed for the pre-training tasks they are standout in the function extraction feature. Though a training phase is required, it involves unlabeled datasets for that purpose.
    b. **Stack Autoencoders (SAE):** They are a composition of multiple Autoencoders which are neural networks having the same number of input and output neurons. Much like DBN, they are excellent at the pre-training tasks but the results are far more better when deployed for small datasets.

The next section throws light on the applications of machine learning in cyber security.

APPLICATIONS OF MACHINE LAERNING

Machine Learning techniques are deployed for an enormous range of application area across the globe. To permit users to use countless intelligent systems which are created with the aid of machine learning techniques, umpteen numbers of times in the span of a single day. While making use of mobile phones, surfing the internet or doing online shopping across commercial sites on the internet we are faced with a whole lot of intelligent systems. Organizations that develop technologies have spent huge amount of money for creating more intelligent systems (Domingos,2012). Since intelligent systems make lives easier for people, almost all machines will be intelligent in the future and there is huge demand in the market for any such technology that easies life of people. Following are the applications of Machine Learning in day-to-day life as illustrated in figure 4.

- **Virtual Personal Assistant:** Some common examples such as Siri, Alexa help the user in accessing/finding information with the use of voice. To respond to the commands, information is collected from related queries and from other resources such as phones. Based upon past involvements, the information is collected and refined and accordingly utilized to respond to the users' requests.
- **Predictions While Travelling:** The technology could be deployed for estimating congested areas based on the daily experiences. Though, GPS system may be used for navigation purposes but not all cars come equipped with it.
- **Online Customer Support:** It is a common scenario today that websites offer customers with an option to chat with a representative from the organization but they are not always live executives. To respond to user queries on a real-time basis, a bot is used. This bot tends to understand the user queries and serve them with the best possible response which is only a result of machine learning techniques.
- **Social Media Services:** While navigating across social networking sites, many of these web based sites notify about the people that "we may know" based on frequent profile visits, places and things of interest via a continuous and comprehensive analysis of user data. There is also an added feature of face recognition that recognizes the person whenever or wherever his/her picture is posted.
- **Surveillance:** Rids a single person loaded with the work of monitoring a number of video cameras which is also subject to human error. In case of Machine Learning, the crimes may be detected even before they occur by analyzing the unusual behavior of employees and giving them an alert in order to prevent any mishap.

Figure 4. Machine learning applications in daily lives

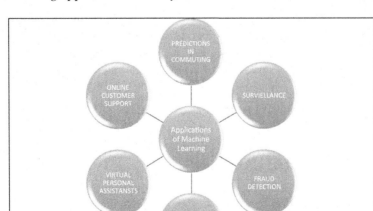

- **Fraud Detection:** In order to make cyberspaces more secure for information exchanges, monetary transfers organizations have started to deploy Machine Learning solutions to discern between legitimate and illegitimate transactions between two parties across a network.

MACHINE LEARNING TASKS AND CYBER-SECURITY

Here are some examples of different techniques that can be deployed to solve machine learning tasks and how they are connected with cyber-security tasks.

Regression

Regression (or prediction) is the simplest task of all. The knowledge regarding the existing data is used in such a manner to have an idea about the new data. Houses is an example of price prediction of various entities. In terms of cyber-security application, it could be extremely effective in fraud detection. The various features such as the total amount of suspicious transaction, location, etc. can be helpful in determining a probability and possibility of fraudulent actions occurrence (Zhang et al., 2019). Figure 5 depicts methods of machine learning that can be used for regression tasks.

Classification

Classification is also a very straightforward task. It deals with categorization of entities or things, for instance two stacks of pictures classified by their respective types. In terms of cyber-security, a spam filter separating spams from other messages can be an efficient example. Spam filters are probably the first Machine Learning approach applied to Cyber-security tasks. The supervised learning approach mentioned above is commonly applied for classification where instances of certain groups are known. All classes need to be defined in the beginning (Uma & Padmavathi, 2013). Figure 6 depicts machine learning algorithms for classification.

Figure 5. Machine learning techniques for regression tasks

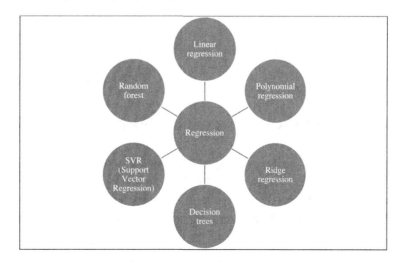

Figure 6. Machine learning techniques for classification

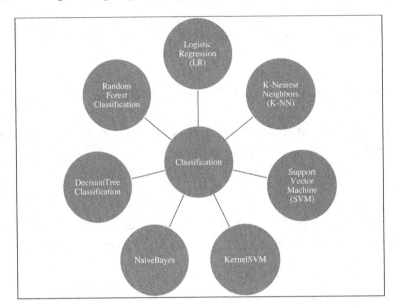

It is reckoned that methods like SVM and random forests work the best. Keeping in mind the fact that there are no one-size-fits-all rules, and they probably won't operate properly for all tasks.

Clustering

Clustering is very much similar to classification with the only but major difference being that the information about the classes of the data is unknown. There is no clue as to whether this data can be classified. This is called "unsupervised learning". Perceivably, the best task for clustering is analysis in forensics. The reasons, of course, and outcomes of an incident are obsolete. It is very much required to classify all the activities to find some anomalies. Solutions to malware analysis such as malware protection and secure email gateways may be used to implement it to separate the legitimate files from outliers (Yousefi-Azar et al., 2017).

Another intriguing area where clustering can be deployed is "user behavior analytics". In this instance, application users are clustered together so that it is possible to comprehend if they should belong to a particular group or not. Usually clustering is not applied to solving a particular task in cyber-security as it is more like one of the subtasks in a pipeline such as grouping users into separate groups to adjust the risk values. Figure 7 depicts machine learning algorithms for clustering.

Association Rule Learning (Recommendation Systems)

There are certain applications such as Netflix and SoundCloud that are able to understand user preferences in movies and films respectively and recommend them accordingly. In cyber-security, this principle can be used primarily for incident response purposes. If a company is faced with a tide of incidents and offers various types of responses, a system learns a type of response for a particular incident such as mark it as a false positive, change a risk value and then run the investigation. Risk management solu-

Figure 7. Machine learning techniques for clustering

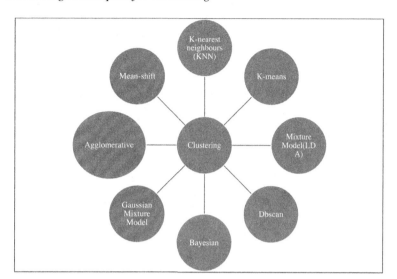

tions can also have an upper hand if they automatically assign risk values for new vulnerabilities or mis-configuration built on their descriptions. Following is the list of machine learning algorithms for solving recommendation tasks:

- Apriori
- Euclat
- FP-Growth.

Dimensionality Reduction

Dimensionality reduction or generalization is not as much popular as the task of classification, but very much necessary if you deal with complex systems with unlabeled data and many other potential features. clustering cannot be just applied because typical methods restrict the number of features or they simply do not work. Dimensionality reduction can help us in handling it and cutting out unnecessary features.Just like clustering, dimensionality reduction is also usually one of the tasks in a more complex model. As for the cyber-security tasks, dimensionality reduction is common for face detection solutions—similar to the ones that is used in Iphone. Figure 8 depicts machine learning algorithms for dimensionality reduction.

Generative Models

The task of the generative models differs much from the above-mentioned tasks. While the above tasks deal with the existing information and associated decisions, generative models are basically designed to simulate the actual data and not the decisions based upon the previous evaluated decisions. The easy task of offensive cyber-security is to generate a list of input metrics or parameters so as to test a particular application for the various Injection vulnerabilities.

Figure 8. Machine learning techniques for dimension reality

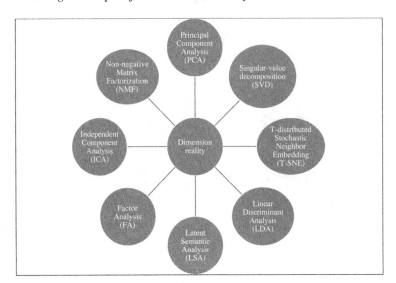

An alternative to this, vulnerability scanning tool is also an option for a host of web applications. One of its modules is testing files for any unauthorized access. These tests are able to copy the existing file names to identify the new ones. For an instance, if a crawler is detected a file called "login.php", it is always recommended to check the existence of any backup or test its copies by trying different names such login_1.php, login_backup.php, login.php.2017. Generative models are very adept in doing this. Machine learning generative models are:

- Markov Chains
- Genetic algorithms

PROPOSED CYBER-SECURITY TASKS AND MACHINE LEARNING

Instead of looking at the various ML tasks mentioned above and trying to apply them to cybersecurity, let us try and have a view at the common cyber-security tasks and machine learning opportunities. There are three dimensions as to Why, What, and How. The first dimension defines the very goal, or a task like detecting threats, predicting the cyber-attacks, etc. Also, according to the Gartner's PPDRM model, all security tasks can be divided into five categories:

- Prediction
- Prevention
- Detection
- Response and
- MONITORING.

The second dimension is a technical layer and an answer to the question "What" .For example, it deals with the level at which to monitor the cyber-security issues. Following is the list of layers for this dimension:

- Network (network traffic analysis and intrusion detection);
- Endpoint (anti-malware);
- Application (WAF or database firewalls);
- User (UBA);and
- Process (anti-fraud).

Each layer also has its different subcategories. For example, network security can be Wired, Wireless or Cloud. It is to be assured of the fact that one simply cannot apply the same algorithms with the same hyper parameters to both areas, at least in the near future. The reason is the scarcity of data and algorithms to search for better dependencies of the three areas so that it becomes possible to change one algorithm to different ones. The third dimension is a question of "How" .For instance,how to check security of a specific area or region:

- In transit in real time;
- At rest;
- Historically; and so on.

For instance, if endpoint protection is a point of concern, looking for the intrusions, monitoring processes of an executable file, static binary analysis, analyzing the history of actions in this endpoint among others can be an option. There are certain tasks that need be solved in three dimensions only. At times,there are no values in some dimensions for certain tasks. Approaches may be the same in one dimension under consideration. Nonetheless, each particular point of this three-dimensional space of cybersecurity tasks has its intricacies. It is an arduous task to detail them all hence let's shift our focus on the most imperative dimension—thetechnology layers that are detailed in Table 1.

Machine learning for Network Protection

Network protection is not merely a single area but it encompasses a whole set of different solutions that focus on various protocols such as Ethernet, wireless, SCADA, or even virtual networks like SDNs.

Mostly the theme of network protection deals with Intrusion Detection System (IDS) solutions (Zhang et al., 2018). A whole lot of them used a kind of Machine Learning technique years ago and mostly dealt with signature-based approaches of security.Machine Learning in the networks security presses on the new solutions commonly referred to as "Network Traffic Analytics" (NTA) which is generally aimed at in-depth analysis of all the traffic at each layer and also to detect the attacks and anomalies. Following are the examples of machine learning that can help in achieving network protection.

1. Regression to predict the network packet parameters and compare them with the normal ones;
2. Classification to identify different classes of network attacks such as scanning and spoofing; and
3. Clustering for forensic analysis.

Table 1. Examples of cyber security tasks achieved via machine learning

Cyber-security tasks in Machine Learning	Regression	Classification	Clustering
1. Network Protection	To predict the network packet parameters	To identify different classes of network attacks	For forensic analysis
2. Endpoint Security	To predict the next system call for executable process	To demarcate the programs under various category heads such as malware, spyware and ransom ware	For malware protection on secure email gateways
3. Application Security	To detect anomalies in HTTP requests	Detect known types of attacks like injections	To detect DDOS attacks and mass exploitation
4. User Behavior	To detect anomalies in User actions	To group different users for peer-group analysis	To separate groups of users and detect outliers
5. Process Behavior	To predict the next user action and detect outliers	To detect known types of fraud	To compare business processes and detect outliers

There could also be an evaluation of various machine learning algorithms to derive solutions for Intrusion Detection Systems. Big Data may also be involved in the approaches for Intrusion Detection System Solutions.

Machine learning for Endpoint Protection

The new generation of anti-viruses being rolled out is dependent much on Endpoint Detection and Responses. It always comes in handy to learn the various features in executable files or in the process behavior. However, need to reckon the fact that while dealing with machine learning at endpoint layer, our solution may differ depending upon the type of endpoint (Dua et al., 2016). For example: workstation, server, and container, cloud instance, mobile, PLC, IoT device and so on. Every endpoint has its own set of specific characteristics but the tasks are almost common that includes:

1. Regression to predict the next system call for executable process and compare it with the real ones;
2. To classify the programs under various category heads such as malware, spyware and ransomware;
3. Clustering for malware protection on secure email gateways.For example:, to separate legal file attachments from outliers.

Academic papers about endpoint protection and malware specifically are gaining popularity. A wide range of them dealing with the elimination of experimental biasing in the the classification of malwares across different parameters of time and space.

Machine learning for Application Security

Application security is an intriguing area, with much scope for protection especially by means of ERP Security.Machine Learning in application security may be applied to —WAFs or Code analysis, both static and dynamic. It should always be reckoned that Application security can differ. There are web applications, databases, ERP systems, SaaS applications, micro services, and so on to talk about variation in Application Security. It is nearly impossible to build a universal Machine Learning model to deal with all threats effectively and efficiently in the near future. However, one can try and aim at solving some of tasks. Following are instances of what one can do with machine learning for application security:

1. Regression to detect anomalies in HTTP requests (for example, XXE and SSRF attacks and auth bypass);
2. Classification to detect known types of attacks like injections (SQLi, XSS, RCE, etc.);and
3. Clustering user activity to detect DDOS attacks and mass exploitation.

The techniques may involve the detection of malicious queries while dealing with Web based attacks, the classification of the malicious scripts may also be included along with the malicious URL detection.

Machine Learning for User Behavior

The whole concept of User Behaviour started with the "Security Information and Event Management" (SIEM). Security Information And Event Management was capable of solving a number of tasks if they are configured properly including user behavior search and Machine Learning. Then the UEBA solutions declared that SIEM could not handle effectively new, more advanced types of attacks and constant behavior change.The market has come to terms with the fact that a special solution is required if the threats are regarded from the user level.However, even the UEBA tools do not necessarily cover all things connected or associated with different user behaviors. There are domain users, application users, SaaS users, social networks, messengers, and other accounts that need to be monitored.

Unlike conventional malware detection techniques that focus mainly on common attacks and the possibility to train a classifier, user behavior is one of the complex layers and unsupervised learning problem. As a rule, there is no labeled dataset as well as any idea of what to search for. Therefore, the task of generation of a universal algorithm for all types of users is tricky in the user behavior area. Below are some of the tasks that organizations try and solve with the help of Machine Learning:

1. Regression to detect anomalies in User actions (e.g., login in unusual time);
2. Classification to group different users for peer-group analysis;
3. Clustering to separate groups of users and detect outliers.

The other tasks may also include the detection of Anomalous user behaviour with the help of specifically devised algorithms and also to deal with threat detection in Cyber-security data streams among many others.

Machine Learning for Process Behavior

The process area is the last but definitely not the least. While dealing with it, it is important to know a business process in order to fulfill the purpose of finding something anomalous. Business processes can differ significantly. For instance, one can look for frauds in banking and retail systems or a plant floor in manufacturing. The two are completely unrelated, and they demand a lot of domain knowledge. In machine learning feature engineering (the way you represent data to your algorithm) is essential to achieve results. Similarly, features are different in all processes. Following are the examples of tasks in the process area:

1. Regression to predict the next user action and detect outliers such as credit card fraud.
2. Classification to detect known types of fraud.
3. Clustering to compare business processes and detect outliers.

With the rapid exponential evolution in the Artificial Intelligence and Machine Learning technologies and also the wide spectrum of cyber-security threats haunting the cyber world, Machine Learning can be of imperative importance in the coming decades to tackle the problems at hand regarding security.

Adversarial Machine Learning

It's a technique employed with the aid of malicious inputs to fool the models. The adversarial is a burgeoning menace in the field of cyber security as it can cause malfunctioning in the standard models of machine learning (Zhu et al., 2017). A sample of input data is modified in the slightest sense to make the machine learning classifiers misclassify it. The severity of it lies in the fact that the adversarial can launch attacks without even having access to the underlying model. Researches across the globe in eminent institutions hint at machine learning systems being vulnerable to the adversarial. By surreptitiously manipulating the input data, sometimes the changes are so subtle that they bypass the human eye; the malicious adversary is able to exploit a set of vulnerabilities of the machine learning algorithms and hence compromising the security. A few examples such as attacks in spam filtering, confounding of the malware code inside the network packets, fake biometric traits to masquerade a legitimate individual etc.

FRONTIERS OF CYBER SECURITY

Over the decades, cyber security threats have evolved essentially in three important ways:

Intent: Over the past years, viruses were deployed on systems by inquisitive programmers to explore the dimensions of computer systems. Today the attacks have changed humungously as cyberattacks these daya are a result of well executed plan by trained comrades in lieu of cyber warfare.

Momentum: The potential rate at which the attack spreads has also improved significantly and can affect computer systems connected via a network all over the globe in a matter of seconds.

Impact: The potential impact has increased manifold due to the immense penetration of internet across the globe and having surpassed the boundaries of traditional computer systems to have a role in our day-to-day lives.

It is a perceived notion that it is next to impossible to keep up with the momentum and rate of cyber attacks. Thus, this explanation renders Machine Learning as more of a necessity rather than a mere choice available before us. Computers are experts at redundancy unlike the human nature and can go on repeating the same task million times over without much hassle. This can prove to a demerit if the wrong action is being repaeted at such a rate. Though, it is pertinent to underscore that it is good to increase the use of ML/AI, but due diligence should also be given to bad entities that these algorithms have at their disposal. Researchers have been able to address six different facets of intersection of Machine Learning techniques with cybersecurity.

Legal and Policy Issues

AI and Machine learning is a buzz word today with its implementations found in almost every field. The results has been promising leading to a belief that Machine Learning application would invariably lead to success.While there is no denying of the fact that Machine Learning promises to improve some of the aspects of defence techniques through automation, a great amount of caution is required for the deployment of such systems. A small glitch or error may invariably jeopardize the national security and the whole national social structure. Mirai botnet in the year 2016 set the trend of botnet attacks. It involved multiple distributed denial-of-service attacks (DDoS attacks) that targeted the systems operated by Domain Name System (DNS) provider Dyn. This led the major Internet platforms and services to be unavailable to large groups of users in Europe and North America. and one can only imagine the disaster that could be impended via the use of high level and sophisticated Machine Learning programs across the world.

The other demerit that can be thought of is that if a developer loses control of his Artificial Intelligence program and causes people's faith in the application of Artificial Intelligence and Machine Learning would be gone, once and for all. Therefore, the use of Machine Learning for cyber safety should have some legal binding and adequate care should be taken in its the creation, deployment, and use by some global authority as well as local authorities entrusted with the task at national levels.

Human Factors

History has it that Stanislav Petrov, a Soviet officer, with his agile mind and experience had been able to averte a nuclear war in 1983. Petrov had been assigned to the Serpukhov-15 secret command centre outside Moscow. It was then that the attack detection algorithms warned that the United States had launched five intercontinental ballistic missiles at the Soviet Union. A normal tendency for any body in that situation would be to panic and report the situation to superior. Petrov did just the opposite. Petrov had years of experience and he knew exactly about the loopholes of the system. Hence, he could not trust the system completely which proved correct eventually. The predictive algorithms miscalculated and the alarm had been falsely triggered by sun's reflection from clouds, a data input the system's programmers had apparently not adequately anticipated (Khanna & Singh,2017).

This incident clearly highlights the future of security through Machine Learning will not only require Technical trust but Human trust as well. Even the most sophisticated computer systems can fail. But the question is whether they will 'fail well' i.e with minimum damage.Indeed, it will be these human trust factors in the operationalization of Machine Learning systems that will dictate their adoption rates.

Data: New Information Frontiers

Data is a indeed a very critical feature. Security of Machine Learning algorithms will actually help us in reckoning their true potential when trained on large, diverse training data sets. Here not only the quantity matters but quality also is a key player. Even though large volumes of data are available today which is doubling every second, most of the data lack in completeness. This is because:

1. Most of the devices which are used were not primarily designed with instrumentation and measurement as an integral feature; data available from them is not able to capture critical points.

2. Most of the times individuals and companies do not disclose data pertaining to cybersecurity events either due to reputational concerns(as this reduces stakeholder's confidence)or legal and privacy concerns.

Others concerns associated with data are Integrity and relevance. It is easy to generate simulated data sets but they do not imbibe the reality. Also regular updating of data in terms of all recent attacks should be done regularly. Data collection techniques, by their very nature, often include unintended human and technical biases. Understanding, documenting, and sharing those biases are important to ensure AI/ML effectiveness and operation. Data integrity also affects human confidence in AI/ML. If the AI/ML training data set is incomplete, includes questionable biases, or is, in general, not fully understood, then confidence in the entire system is diminished. Preprocessing of the data prior to use for training can also alter data integrity and reduce confidence.

Hardware for AI/ML and Cybersecurity

Today, a network implies human users connected by smart devices all over the globe. Network is not merely defined by electronic equipment in a room or building. Due to such vastness, it becomes an easy target for cyberattacks aided by AI bots. Many leading CISOs admit that cyberattacks is no more viewed as question that whether they will be hacked but when .Hardware holds the key in more than one way.

By incorporating security into hardware designs

- By creating hardware network architectures that can intelligently monitor the network's security state
- Creating hardware that allows AI/ML systems to solve more complex problems by eliminating existing compute barriers

AI requires a great deal of computer hardware for training purposes. This prevents the real time threat assessment and response required by cybersecurity for new threats. The only solution to this problem is by allowing computer hardware engineers to change their approach towards the concept of computing. Emphasis should be given on how data flows through a processor rather than how computations are done. Academia, funded by government agencies and industry, can lead the way by experimenting with new and novel outside-the-box architectures. Innovative approaches are the only way to shake up a field that hasn't effectively changed in the last 50 years. Without a new architecture, AI/ML will be unable to solve large-scale problems such as those in the cybersecurity application.AI/Ml can also be utilized to design and implement better hardware. AI can be incorporated into current design tools. Even if one is able to plug few of the hardware bugs, this will go a long way in making the network secure because hardware faults and design errors are among the most reliable targets for exploits. .

Software and Algorithms for AI/ML and Cyber Security

As the typical cyber security data sets are extremely large, networks for data delivery and the processing of Machine Learning models must be capable of efficiently handling staggering amounts of diverse data. The scarcity of such networks today is a major hindrance to progress in the field. Achieving such networks for real-time analytics requires even more careful software design and algorithms. Natural language processing (NLP) makes it possible to derive actionable insights from previously inaccessible data. Analyzing unstructured text with NLP enables the extraction of key actors from past cyber incidents, news stories, analysis reports, and many other similar text sources.

Cyber-security is highly dynamic due to rapid evolution in the underlying technologies and the because the offense and defense are locked in a threat–response–threat co-evolution. This dynamic and constantly evolving landscape requires constant vigilance and upgradation to threat classification, identification, and response. The adversarial characteristic nature of the cyber domain presents a modeling challenge that can be perceived as an opportunity. Cyber competitions, in which teams act and react to others, are valuable laboratories to explore interactions. The goal of these experiments is to imitate processes by which an adversary learns of defensive measures and then preempts evasive measures. Understanding an adversary's strategy, then, helps refine the models.

CONCLUSION

This chapter details the applications of machine learning in cyber security. The world has finite resources that it can dedicate to improve upon the Cyber-security issues, a fact that will inevitably lead to issues of resource allocation. A properly developed and deployed Machine Learning would be highly desirable to give the good intended crowd an overwhelming advantage over the bad intended ones. But every possibility holds an opportunity. Through hardware and Software improvements, over the time, the organisations will be better able to integrate the Machine Learning systems in their Cyber-security framework, which was next to impossible even few years ago. Machine Learning will also help in creating the integrated meaning from hundreds and thousands of disparate data streams; support automated, real-time prevention platforms; and augment humans' decision- making ability.

Repairing or mitigating vulnerabilities will remain a challenge. Most users either do not know or do not have a way to report discovered vulnerabilities. Current use cases, such as fraud detection in the banking industry and diagnosis in the health-care industry, serve as enablers for the future operationalization of AI/ML in the cybersecurity domain. Although not all use cases and current AI/ML algorithms are designed to be employed in real-time environments, they serve as foundations for real-time detect–defend or defend–attack situations in cybersecurity. For certain domains, the ability to consciously disable AI/ML actions or disregard recommendations is an enabler of AI/ML operationalization for cybersecurity. In such cases, it is important to have the ability to disable or alter specific system aspects without necessarily turning everything off while, at the same time, comprehending any repercussions.

The chapter emphasizes on Various approaches that uses machine learning to enhance the traditional security mechanisms.

REFERENCES

Al-Jarrah, O. Y., Yoo, P. D., Muhaidat, S., Karagiannidis, G. K., & Taha, K. (2015). Efficient machine learning for big data: A review. *Big Data Research, 2*(3), 87–93. doi:10.1016/j.bdr.2015.04.001

Buczak, A. L., & Guven, E. (2016). A survey of data mining and machine learning methods for cyber security intrusion detection. *IEEE Communications Surveys and Tutorials, 18*(2), 1153–1176. doi:10.1109/COMST.2015.2494502

Cavelty, M. D. (2010). Cyber-security. *The Routledge Handbook of New Security Studies*, 154-162. Retrieved from https://www.researchgate.net/profile/Myriam_Dunn_Cavelty/publication/281631032_Cyber-security/links/55f1426408ae199d47c243b1/Cyber-security.pdf

Chapelle, O., Scholkopf, B., & Zien, A. (2009). Semi-supervised learning (O. Chapelle et al., Eds.; 2006) [book review]. IEEE Transactions on Neural Networks, 20(3), 542-542.

Do Hoon Kim, T. L., Jung, S. O. D., In, H. P., & Lee, H. J. (2007, August). Cyber threat trend analysis model using HMM. In *Proceedings of the Third International Symposium on Information Assurance and Security* (pp. 177-182). Academic Press.

Domingos, P. M. (2012). A few useful things to know about machine learning. *Communications of the ACM, 55*(10), 78–87.

Dua, S., & Du, X. (2016). *Data mining and machine learning in cybersecurity*. Auerbach Publications. doi:10.1201/b10867

Dua, S., & Du, X. (2016). *Data mining and machine learning in cybersecurity*. Auerbach Publications. doi:10.1201/b10867

Huang, W., & Stokes, J. W. (2016, July). MtNet: a multi-task neural network for dynamic malware classification. In *International Conference on Detection of Intrusions and Malware, and Vulnerability Assessment* (pp. 399-418). Cham, Switzerland: Springer. 10.1007/978-3-319-40667-1_20

Kasun, L. L. C., Zhou, H., Huang, G. B., & Vong, C. M. (2013). Representational learning with extreme learning machine for big data. *IEEE Intelligent Systems, 28*(6), 31–34.

Khanna, U., & Singh, P. (2017). *Hybrid Approach of KNN+ Euclidean Distance to Detect Intrusion within Cloud Based Systems*. Retrieved from http://www.irjaes.com/pdf/V2N3Y17-IRJAES/IRJAES-V2N2P325Y17.pdf

Kotsiantis, S. B., Zaharakis, I., & Pintelas, P. (2007). Supervised machine learning: A review of classification techniques. *Emerging Artificial Intelligence Applications in Computer Engineering, 160*, 3-24.

LeCun, Y., Bengio, Y., & Hinton, G. (2015). Deep learning. *Nature, 521*(7553), 436.

Linda, O., Manic, M., Vollmer, T., & Wright, J. (2011, April). Fuzzy logic based anomaly detection for embedded network security cyber sensor. In *2011 IEEE Symposium on Computational Intelligence in Cyber Security (CICS),* (pp. 202-209). IEEE. 10.1109/CICYBS.2011.5949392

Marsland, S. (2011). *Machine learning: an algorithmic perspective*. Chapman and Hall. Retrieved from http://dspace.fue.edu.eg/xmlui/bitstream/handle/123456789/3667/10501.pdf?sequence=1

Michalski, R. S., Carbonell, J. G., & Mitchell, T. M. (Eds.). (2013). *Machine learning: An artificial intelligence approach*. Springer Science & Business Media.

Nasrabadi, N. M. (2007). Pattern recognition and machine learning. *Journal of Electronic Imaging*, *16*(4), 049901. doi:10.1117/1.2819119

Uma, M., & Padmavathi, G. (2013). A Survey on Various Cyber Attacks and their Classification. *IJ Network Security, 15*(5), 390-396.

Wang, L. (Ed.). (2005). *Support vector machines: theory and applications* (Vol. 177). Springer Science & Business Media.

Woon, I., Tan, G. W., & Low, R. (2005). A protection motivation theory approach to home wireless security. *ICIS 2005 Proceedings*, 31.

Xin, Y., Kong, L., Liu, Z., Chen, Y., Li, Y., Zhu, H., & Wang, C. (2018). Machine learning and deep learning methods for cybersecurity. *IEEE Access: Practical Innovations, Open Solutions*, *6*, 35365–35381. doi:10.1109/ACCESS.2018.2836950

Yavanoglu, O., & Aydos, M. (2017, December). A review on cyber security datasets for machine learning algorithms. In *2017 IEEE International Conference on Big Data (Big Data)* (pp. 2186-2193). IEEE. 10.1109/BigData.2017.8258167

Yousefi-Azar, M., Varadharajan, V., Hamey, L., & Tupakula, U. (2017, May). Autoencoder-based feature learning for cyber security applications. In *2017 International joint conference on neural networks (IJCNN)* (pp. 3854-3861). IEEE. 10.1109/IJCNN.2017.7966342

Zhang, C., Patras, P., & Haddadi, H. (2019). Deep learning in mobile and wireless networking: A survey. *IEEE Communications Surveys and Tutorials*, 1. doi:10.1109/COMST.2019.2904897

Zhang, T., & Zhu, Q. (2018). Distributed privacy-preserving collaborative intrusion detection systems for VANETs. IEEE Transactions on Signal and Information Processing over. *Networks*, *4*(1), 148–161.

Zhu, J. Y., Park, T., Isola, P., & Efros, A. A. (2017). Unpaired image-to-image translation using cycle-consistent adversarial networks. In *Proceedings of the IEEE international conference on computer vision* (pp. 2223-2232). IEEE. 10.1109/ICCV.2017.244

Chapter 6
Malware and Anomaly Detection Using Machine Learning and Deep Learning Methods

Valliammal Narayan
Avinashilingam Institute for Home Science and Higher Education for Women, India

Barani Shaju
Avinashilingam Institute for Home Science and Higher Education for Women, India

ABSTRACT

This chapter aims to discuss applications of machine learning in cyber security and explore how machine learning algorithms help to fight cyber-attacks. Cyber-attacks are wide and varied in multiple forms. The key benefit of machine learning algorithms is that it can deep dive and analyze system behavior and identify anomalies which do not correlate with expected behavior. Algorithms can be trained to observe multiple data sets and strategize payload beforehand in detection of malware analysis.

INTRODUCTION

Today, technology has become most essential part of our life. Internet usage has grown rapidly for the past years. Internet has brought about a new revolution in the fields of computing and communicating technology as it connects billions of infinitesimal devices. Potential intelligent support is provided by internet and the limitations of workplace is exempted using the wireless network providing excess mobility and flexibility over the conventional networks (Altaher. A, 2016). The sensitive information can be exposed by the transactions which were performed using the internet. Apart from the benefits of internet there are some drawbacks too like all our records, personal as well as professional, banking, medical, passwords, communication etc. can be made easily available to the antagonists using various illegal techniques and can finally receive our complete information, misuse our records imprecating the transactions which are online.

In the year 2018, the number of internet users has significantly increased. There are about 55.1% internet users as compared to the world population in table as Figure 1.

DOI: 10.4018/978-1-5225-9611-0.ch006

Figure 1. Tabulation and graph on malware statistics

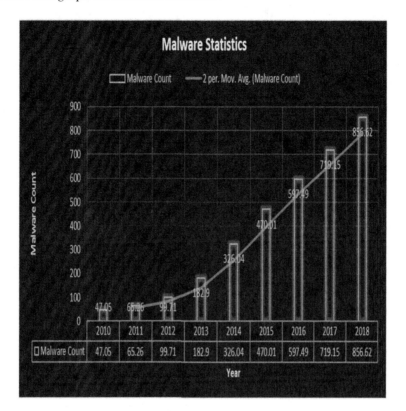

Definition

Malware: It is a term used to describe malicious software, including spyware, ransomware, viruses, and worms. Malware breaches a network through vulnerability, typically when a user clicks a dangerous link or email attachment that then installs risky software (Bhattacharya A, 2017). Inside the system, malware can do the following access:

Malvertising: This is the usage of web-based exposing to stretch malware. It ordinarily includes infusing malware-loaded commercials into genuine web-based publicizing systems and website links.

The number of cyber attacks has grown gradually during the last few years. In Figure 2, upshots shown that the malware attack have the highest percentage rate compared to other attacks. The increase of malware has presented a long-lasting and serious threat to the security of computer systems and

Box 1.

- Blocks access to key components of the network (ransomware)

- Installs malware or additional harmful software

- Covertly obtains information by transmitting data from the hard drive (spyware)

- Disrupts certain components and renders the system inoperable

Figure 2. Distribution of attacks in cyber security

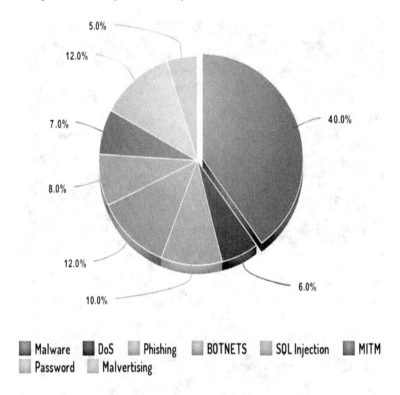

internet. For example, the well-known WannaCry ransomware attack has affected millions of devices and caused billions of dollars damage. The number of malware has increased greatly every year, and it is reported that every 4.6 seconds a new malware specimen emerged in 2018.

Major Consequence

- More attacks are launched from the web - and not from executable files (PE-files)
- Overall numbers are decreasing, as attacks are more targeted
- Illegal hidden crypto mining (Crypto jacking) is on the rise
- Attackers make use of novel standards such as Web assembly for better efficiency

KNOW-HOW: UNDERSTANDING ABOUT MALWARE IN ITS DEPTH AND BREADTH

Malware is deployed by cyber attackers to concession computer systems by developing their security vulnerabilities. This software is utilized to change the PC settings, delete software, cause errors, watch browsing habits, or open computer to attacks without user knowledge. It uses deceptive and unethical tactics to install itself on your computer without user consent. For instance, they may visit a website and receive an unrequested download, and mistakenly run this software on their computer (F. Alotaibi,2016). It may also use vulnerabilities in the operating system or web browser to install itself without requiring the user to manually run the software. Malware access can be disastrous consequences include data theft, extortion or the crippling of network systems.

The journey of malware started around 1982 when the first virus with replicating features and malicious intent was written by a high-school student called Rich Skrenta for the Apple II systems. The virus was named "The Elk Cloner". It used to infect a computer when the machine was booted from an infected floppy disk, copying itself to the new machine. When an uninfected floppy disk was inserted in an infected machine, it copied itself to the floppy, thus spreading itself. Even though its behavior was relatively harmless but it displayed a small poem on every 50th boot, however, it also had the unintended effect of overwriting code on particular systems.

A system can be affected by malware by clicking an infected website, downloading/ installing infected software. Antivirus and anti-spyware software are used to prevent, detect and remove the malware from the computer. Most antivirus software can clean malware but at the same time, it's a smart thought to run an anti-malware. An example of malware infecting a PC is shown in Figure 3,

To create countermeasures to malware contagions, investigate has been dynamic in innovation for recognizing infections and deciding their basis and innovation for dissecting malware.

Makers of Malware

Malware customers go by a collection of names. Presumably the most outstanding names are dark caps, programmers, and saltines. The real individuals or affiliations that go up against the previously mentioned names could be an outer/interior risk, an outside government, or a mechanical covert operative.

Figure 3. Ways of spread on PC

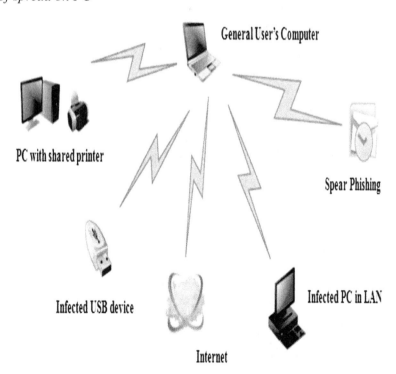

There are basically two stages in the lifecycle of programming amid which malware are embedded. These phases are alluded to as the pre-discharge stage and the post-discharge stage. An inward threat is commonly the main kind of programmer equipped for embeddings malware into programming before its discharge to the end-clients. An insider is a confided in the developer, regularly inside an association, of some product to be conveyed to its end clients. Every single other individual or associations that go up against the programmer job embed malware amid the post-discharge stage, which is the point at which the product is accessible for its target group.

In making new malware, black hats, by and large, utilize either of the accompanying systems: muddling and conduct expansion/adjustment so as to go around malware identifiers. Muddling endeavors to conceal the genuine goals of pernicious code without expanding the practices displayed by the malware. Conduct expansion/adjustment viably makes new malware, in spite of the fact that the substance of the malware probably won't have changed.

Types of Malware

Malware is classified into multiple points of view. Sometimes they are classified on the basis of behavior, on the basis of their target platform or on the basis of their attack directive. In this section classifies the malware randomly by mixing all the categories (Kai Huang, 2009).

The different classes and terms related to malware are shown in Figure 4.

Figure 4. Types of malware

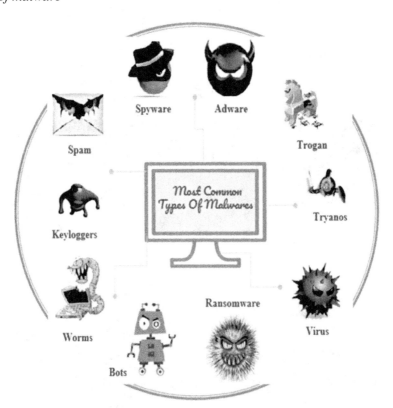

Each of the above-mentioned classes causes a massive amount of damage to the system or software (Boukhtouta A, 2016). The details of the given malware classes are as follows:

- **Virus:** Virus is a category of malware that, when executed, tries to replicate itself into other executable code, when it succeeds, the code is said to be infected. At the point when the tainted code is executed, the infection likewise executes. A computer virus is a kind of bad software code (malware) that, when runs, multiplies by reproducing itself (copying its own program code) or tainting other computer programs by editing them. Corrupting the computer programs also includes data files or the "boot" sector of the hard disk.
  - ○ **Boot Infectors**
    - ▪ A virus can contaminate a framework as an occupant infection by introducing itself as a component of the working framework with the goal that it stays in the RAM from the time a PC is booted up to when shutdown. These kinds of infections are exceptionally uncommon nowadays, what with the approach of the Internet, and security methods incorporated with current working frameworks like Windows 10.
  - ○ **File Infectors**
    - ▪ Numerous viruses creep up into common executable records like.EXE and.COM so as to up their odds of being controlled by a client. Any program that documents type that Windows can call for execution is vulnerable, including clump and content records like. BAT, .JS. .VB and considerably screensaver records with the.SCR extension.
  - ○ **Macro Viruses**
    - ▪ These sorts of infections are the ones that kept running inside explicit applications that enable full-scale programs so as to broaden the capacities of given programming. Infections that focused Microsoft Office were across the board a couple of years back, however, the risk of large scale infections has additionally declined as of late as unsigned macros are consequently incapacitated in Office and are not permitted to run.
- **Worm:** A worm is a computer program that can run without any support that means it runs independently and can propagate a complete working version of itself onto other hosts on a network. A computer worm may also be thought of as an independent vindictive computer program that creates copies of itself in order to spread to other machines. Most of the times, it uses a distributed environment to spread itself, depending on vulnerabilities or weaknesses on the target computer to access it. Unlike a computer virus, it does not require to attach itself to an existing program.
- **Logic Bomb:** It is a program inserted into System or Software by an intruder. It remains in the dormant state until a predefined condition is met. On meeting the condition an unauthorized action is performed. Software that is intrinsically vindictive, such as viruses and worms, mostly consist of logic bombs that run a certain consignment at a pre-decided time or when some other criteria are fulfilled. This method can be used by a virus or worm to attain impulse and spread before being caught. Some viruses attack their host systems on particular dates only, such as Friday the 13th or April Fools' Day. Trojans that attack particular dates are frequently called time bombs.
- **Trojan Horse:** It is a computer program which appears harmless but is actually a harmful program. It has a hidden and potentially malicious function which evades the security process, sometimes by exploiting legitimate authorizations of a system entity that invokes the Trojan horse program. Trojans are most of the times propagated by some form of social engineering, for example where a user is lured into running an e-mail attachment disguised to be harmless. Although their

consignment can be anything, many new forms act as a backdoor, communicating with a controller which can then have illegitimate access to the smitten computer system. This corruption allows an attacker to access system owner's personal details such as banking credentials, passwords, or personal identification details.

- **Backdoor:** A backdoor virus is a software program that makes entry into a computer system without being notices and caught and executes in the background to open ports. It allows third parties to control the computer surreptitiously. These harmful backdoor programs can pass themselves off as legitimate ones. It is a type of program that bypasses a normal security check; it may allow the unauthorized access to the crucial information.

- **Mobile Code:** It is software which may be a script, macro or any other type of portable instruction that can be moved unaltered to different types of platforms and get executed with similar semantics. Mobile code is any software program, application, or data content that is able to perform movement while existing in an email, document or website. Mobile code uses distributed environment or storage media, such as a Universal Serial Bus (USB) thumb drive, to execute local program execution from another machine.

- **Exploits:** These are the kind of codes which are specific to a particular type of vulnerability or a set of vulnerabilities. Exploits attack on the system on finding certain type of weakness. An exploit is a part of software program, a piece of data, or a serial arrangement of commands that takes benefit of an error or weakness in order to cause unintentional or unanticipated demeanor to exist in computer software, hardware, or anything electronic. Such behavior mostly includes acts like gaining control of a computer system, allowing privilege rise, or a denial-of-service (DoS or related DDoS) attack.

- **Downloader's:** It is a kind of program which if gets executed on a machine installs other program or items on a machine. Normally downloader's are sent through emails. On opening the email, the user is lured to download a program which in turn downloads other malicious items. Downloader's are harmful programs with the intention to seditious download and install malware on a victim's machine. Once executed, a downloader communicates with its command-and-control (C&C) server(s) through C&C channels. After receiving download guidelines, it then directs at least one download channel to load malware through the network.

- **Auto Rooter:** Auto rooters are the harmful program or software's that act as tools that are used to break into new machines lying at different locations through network. The phrase "auto rooter" is based on security jargon for successfully breaking and obtaining privileged access to a Computer system. Auto rooters can be designed to scan a network for weak machines in terms of security or attack everything they encounter. Once a computer system is successfully captured or compromised, or rooted, some type of harmful code can be installed and configured: data might be caught using a software component known as sniffer, Web pages defaced, servers installed. Some autorooters are destroyed after sending the results back to the cracker, others may install bots that wait for further directions from the attacker.

- **Kit (Virus Generator):** These are the set of programs or software's which act as tools and have capability to generate new viruses on their own. These work through an automated system. It is a program that creates a virus or worm on its own with any role of the user. They make it possible for those people who have very small knowledge of viruses or even computers to develop viruses. As early viruses were almost entirely coded in Assembly language, it was nearly impossible for anyone to create a virus or worm without having good experience with computers.

- **Spammer:** These are the software programs used to send large volumes of unwanted emails which fill the mailbox of person under attack. These mails are sometimes called junk mails or spam mails. These are sometimes a list of individuals and organizations noteworthy for engaging in bulk electronic spamming using the spamming software program, either on their own behalf or on behalf of others.
- **Flooders:** These are the types of malware form or software programs that are used to attack the networked computers with a massive amount of data traffic to carry out a DOS (Denial of Service) attack.
- **Keyloggers:** These are the programs which capture keystrokes and log them. These are the types of information stealers which record keypresses and store them locally for later retrieval or pass them to a server lying at remote location that the attacker has access to. Keystroke logging, mostly referred to as keylogging or keyboard capturing, is the process of recording the keys pressed on a keyboard, usually secretly, so that the person typing on the keyboard is ignorant of the fact that their events are being recorded. Keylogging may also be used for studying human–computer communication. Large number of keylogging techniques exist, they range from hardware and software-based methodology to auditory investigation.
- **Zombie or Bot:** Zombie is a program stored or activated on a compromised machine used to launch different types of attacks on other machines. "Robot" is otherwise called as "Bot", which is another type of malware as well as is a sort of machine-driven undertaking that connects with other disseminated administrations. An exemplary use of bots is to collect information (such as web crawlers), or communicate on its own with instant messaging (IM), Internet Relay Chat (IRC), or other web based interactive tools. A typical bot software allows an operator to remotely control each machine and group them together to form what is commonly referred to as a bot army or botnet.
- **Spyware:** Spyware is a software program that collects information without the victim's knowledge and transmits it to another system. It is software that aims to collect information about an individual or a company without their awareness and that may send such information to another entity without the owner's permission, or that claim control over a computer without the consumer's consent. Whenever spyware is used for harmful reasons, its presence is normally hidden from the user and can be intricate to detect. Some spyware, such as keyloggers, may be sent by the owner of a shared, commercial, or public computer deliberately in order to monitor users.
- **Adware:** It is a kind of badware that displays pop up commercial ads or it redirects the browsers to other business websites. The term adware is frequently used to describe a form of malevolent software which presents unwanted ads to the user of a computer. The advertisements produced by adware are sometimes in the form of pop-ups or sometimes in a Window that cannot be closed. Adware, or advertising-supported software, is any software packages that automatically deliver commercials in order to produce monetary gain for its developer. The advertisements may be in the user interface of the software program or on a screen shown to the user during the installation procedure.
- **Ransomware:** It is a kind of malicious software program that takes control of data files and keep them as hostage and asks for the ransom amount from the owner in lieu of making such files are held by the ransomware, the user or owner of such files is unable to access them. Ransomware is a computer malware that installs secretly on a one's computer, executes an attack by encrypting all the document files that badly affects it, and demands a ransom payment to decrypt it or not publish

it. Simple ransomware programs may freeze the system in such a way which is not difficult for an experienced person to overturn, and display a message asking for a payment to unlock the system. Highly developed and superior malware encrypts the victim's computer's useful files, making them unapproachable, and insists a ransom amount to decrypt them or unlock them. The ransomware may also encode the computer's Master File Table (MFT) or the entire contents hard drive. Thus, ransomware is a kind of denial-of-access attack that avoids computer users from accessing files since it is difficult to decrypt the files without the decryption key. Ransomware attacks are normally carried out using a Trojan that has a consignment concealed as a genuine file.

- **Grayware**: It is a recently coined term that came into use around 2004. It is utilized to depict undesirable applications and records that however are not named malware, can exacerbate the execution of PCs and lead to security threats. At the base, these projects carry on in an irritating or unwanted way, and even from a pessimistic standpoint, they screen a framework and telephone home with data. Grayware suggests both adware and spyware. Practically all financially accessible antivirus programming can identify these possibly undesirable projects, and offer separate modules to distinguish, isolate and expel malware that shows commercials.

  ◦ **Adware**

Albeit advertisement bolstered programming is currently substantially more typical and known as adware in a few circles, the word has been connected to malware for a long while. While adware can refer to any program that is supported by advertising, malicious adware usually shows ads in the form of pop-ups and windows that cannot be closed.

It is the maybe the most rewarding and least unsafe malware, planned with the particular reason for showing promotions on your PC. Adware usage is on the rise on mobile, in particular, with some Chinese firms bundling in adware by default in certain low-cost Android smart phones.

- **Spyware**

Spyware is programming that continually keeps a spies on you its principle intention is to monitor your Internet exercises so as to send adware. Spyware is likewise used to accumulate data around an association without their insight, and send that data to another substance, without the assent of the person in question.

- **Rootkits:** It is a collection of software specifically designed to permit malware that gathers information, into your system. These work out of sight with the goal that a client may not see anything suspicious. Be that as it may, out of sight, a rootkit will allow a few kinds of malware to get into the framework. These product work like a secondary passage for malware to enter and unleash devastation, and are presently being utilized broadly by programmers to contaminate frameworks. A rootkit establishment can either be programmed, or an assailant can introduce it once they have gotten overseer benefits.

Malwares at Recent Years

- **Kovter:** It is a Trojan, which has been observed acting as click fraud malware or an ansomware downloader. It is spread through malspam email connections containing noxious office macros. Kovter is lifeless malware that sidesteps discovery by covering up in vault keys. A few reports demonstrate that Kovter diseases have gotten refreshed directions from order and control framework to fill in as a remote access indirect access.

- **Emotet:** It is a modular Trojan that downloads or drops banking Trojans. Introductory contamination happens by means of malspam messages that contain malevolent download joins, a PDF with installed connections, or a large scale empowered Word connection. Emotet joins spreader modules so as to engender all through a system. Emotet is known to download/drop the Pinkslipbot and Dridex managing an account Trojans. Presently, there are 4 known spreader elements: Outlook scraper, WebBrowserPassView, Mail PassView, and a credential enumerator.

    ○ **Outlook Scraper:** This is a device that rub names and email addresses from the injured individual's Outlook records and uses that data to convey phishing messages from the traded off record.

    ○ **WebBrowserPassView:** This is a password recovery tool that captures passwords stored by Internet Explorer, Mozilla Firefox, Google Chrome, Safari, and Opera and passes them to the credential enumerator module.

    ○ **Mail PassView:** It is a password recovery tool that reveals passwords and account details for various email clients such as Microsoft Outlook, Windows Mail, Mozilla Thunderbird, Hotmail and so on;

    ○ **Credential Enumerator:** It is a self-extracting RAR file containing a bypass and a service component. The detour part is utilized for specification of system assets and either fined writable offer drives or attempts to animal power client accounts, including the director account. When an accessible framework is found, Emotet then composes the administration segment on the framework, which composes Emotet onto the plate.

- **WannaCry:** It is a ransomware worm that utilizes the EternalBlue endeavor to spread. Adaptation 1.0 is known to have a "killswitch" space, which stops the encryption procedure. Later forms are not known to have a "killswitch" space. WannaCry is dispersed by means of malspam.

- **ZeuS/Zbot:** A Trojan malware that has affected thousands of devices for a long time, Zbot has been labeled as one of the ruthless malicious attacks in the recent era. It is a modular banking Trojan which uses keystroke logging to compromise victim credentials when the user visits a banking website.

- **CoinMiner:** It is a cryptocurrency miner that was initially disseminated via malvertising. When a machine is tainted, CoinMiner utilizes Windows Management Instrument (WMI) and EternalBlue to misuse SMB and spread over a system. CoinMiner utilizes the WMI Standard Event Consumer scripting to execute contents for diligence.

- **Gh0st:** It is a RAT used to control infected endpoints. Gh0st is dropped by other malware to make a secondary passage into a gadget, enabling an assailant to completely control the tainted gadget.

- **NanoCore:** It is a Remote Access Trojan (RAT) spread via malspam as a malicious Excel XLS spreadsheet. As a RAT, NanoCore can acknowledge directions to download and execute records, visit sites, and include library keys for steadiness.

- **Ursnif:** Ursnif and its variant Dreambot, are banking trojans known for weaponizing documents. Ursnif as of late overhauled its web infusion assaults to incorporate TLS callbacks so as to muddle against hostile to malware programming. Ursnif gathers unfortunate casualty data from login pages and web shapes.

- **Mirai:** It is a malware botnet known to compromise Internet of Things (IoT) devices in order to conduct large-scale distributed denial of service (DDoS) attacks.

- **Redyms:** It is a click-fraud Trojan that is primarily downloaded via exploit kit.
- **Loyphish:** This is fundamentally a phishing page which camouflages as a real saving money site. These site pages are very advanced in structure, which influences you to trust that you're interfacing with the first site of your bank. These pages are astutely worked with all the first pictures, logos, and content. These assaults are focused against essentially everybody. In this way, on the off chance that you ever enter your managing an account data into any of these pages, you may lose generous measures of cash. More often than not, malware phishing pages can be maintained a strategic distance from by twofold checking the URL of the page in your program's location bar. Likewise, utilizing an Internet Security apparatus can help you significantly in keeping away from such dangers.
- **Sirefef:** This is a standout amongst the most progressive malware dangers out there. Numerous gadgets have been influenced by this in the ongoing occasions. Otherwise called ZeroAccess, this malevolent danger works in total stealth mode, leaving practically no hint of its reality in your gadget. Besides, it additionally has the capacity of crippling the security resistances of your PC. This document normally gets into your gadget when you're downloading pilfered records, programming, and comparative others. In this way, in case you're downloading split programming or keygens, you could be making your PC powerless. Sirefef likewise transmits your private data to remote servers. Moreover, it can likewise cripple your Windows Firewall and Windows Defender too.
- **Suspicious.Emit:** It is a Trojan malware that can complete a genuine mischief to your PC. Typically, Trojan steeds are truly malignant documents that camouflage themselves as valuable applications, for example, utility apparatuses. Suspicious. Radiate is among such Trojan dangers, which could display unfortunate harm to your gadget. It works through code infusion procedure, where it picks up invulnerability from location. Alongside that, it additionally makes an autorun. inf document and places it in the root catalog of the injured individual's gadget. This kind of risk is normally conveyed through removable gadgets, for example, USB drives. Suspicious. Emit additionally can take your data and transmits to different gadgets and servers.
- **FBI Virus:** An exceedingly perilous malware, FBI infection which is on the other hand known as FBI Money pack Scam, is an astutely planned pernicious record. At the point when assaulted by this risk, your PC will show a ready which expresses that your PC has been secured because of infringement of copyrights. This alarm attempts to swindle you that you've been hindered because of an illicit access or downloads of documents, for example, music, programming, motion pictures, and numerous others. So as to get your PC unblocked, you would need to pay two hundred dollars. Numerous ordinary citizens have succumbed to this trick, making it one of the dangerous assaults in the ongoing past.

MALWARE ANALYSIS AND DETECTION TECHNIQUES

Malware Analysis

Malware examination considering malicious records with the point of having improved comprehension around a few parts of malware like malware conduct, development after some time, and their chose targets. The result of malware investigation ought to permit security firms to fortify their resistance procedures against malware assaults. It is important to create successful malware recognition system. Procedures utilized for malware investigation for the most part classified into three sections: Static, Dynamic, and Hybrid examination. Figure 5 demonstrates malware analysis methods as well as their general features,

Static Analysis

It is additionally called as code examination. It is the way toward dissecting the code by analyzing it for example programming code of malware is seen to pick up the learning of how malware's capacities function. In this strategy figuring out is performed by utilizing dismantle apparatus, decompile device, debugger, source code analyzer devices, for example, IDA Pro and Ollydbg so as to comprehend structure of malware. Before program is executed, static data is found in the executable including header information and the grouping of bytes is utilized to decide if it is vindictive. Dismantling system is one of the strategies of static examination. With static examination executable record is dismantled utilizing dismantling instruments like XXD, Hexdump, NetWide direction, to get the low level computing construct program document. From this record the opcode is separated as a component to statically dissect the application conduct to recognize the malware (Nikolopoulos SD, 2016).

This procedure alludes to examining the PE records without executing code. Malware ordinarily utilizes binary packer, for example, UPX and ASP Pack Shell, to abstain from being examined. A PE records should be unloaded and decompressed before being examined. To decompile windows executable document a dismantle apparatus can be utilized, for example, IDA Pro and OlleyDbg that show get together directions, give data about the malware, and concentrate example to distinguish the assailant.

Figure 5. Types of malware analysis with features

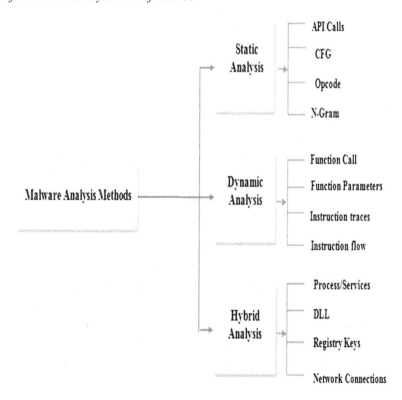

The recognition example can be separated in static investigation like Windows API calls, string mark, control stream diagram, opcode recurrence and byte grouping n-grams (Siddiqui M, 2008).

Application Programming Interface (API)

Practically all projects use Windows API calls to converse with the working framework. For instance, the "OpenFileW" is a Windows API in "Kernel32.dll" that makes another record or opens a current one. Thusly, API calls uncover the conduct of projects and could be considered as a fundamental stamp in malware discovery. For example, the Windows API calls "WriteProcessMemory", "LoadLibrary" and "CreateRemoteThread" are a presumed conduct utilized by malware for DLL infusion into a procedure, while infrequently met up in an authentic set. DLL infusion is examined in the memory investigation area. Strings are a decent pointer of malignant presence.

Control Flow Graph (CFG)

A CFG is a coordinated diagram that shows the control flow of a code, where squares of code are exhibited by hubs and control flow sends through edges. In malware identification, CFG can be utilized to catch the conduct of a PE record as well as concentrate the program formation.

Opcodes(Operation Codes)

It is the initial segment of a machine language guidance that distinguishes what task to be executed by the CPU. Full machine dialect guidance made out of opcode and, alternatively, at least one operands. Opcode can be utilized as a component in malware recognition by testing opcode frequency or computing the similitude between opcode arrangements.

N-grams

N-grams are the majority of the coterminous subsequences of a grouping of a length N. For instance, "MALWARE" is a grouping of letters of length 7, it very well may be divided into 3-grams as: "MAL", "ALW", "LWA", "WAR" and "ARE". N-Grams have been connected with different discovery highlights like API calls as well as opcodes. Adjacent to the past features, there are different highlights that have been utilized in static assessment like size and capacity length of the file. Networking elements such as TCP/ UDP ports, destination IP as well as HTTP request are also features in static analysis.

Dynamic Analysis

It is additionally called a behavioral investigation. Assessment of tainted code amid its execution is known as unique investigation. After that malware scientists use SysAnalyzer, Process Explorer, ProcMon, Reg-Shot, and different apparatuses to recognize the general conduct of record. In the dynamic investigation, the record is recognized in the wake of executing it in a genuine domain, amid the execution of document its framework association, its conduct and impact on the machine are checked. The upside of dynamic investigation is that it precisely dissects the referred to just as obscure, new malware.

Hybrid Analysis

Hybrid method accumulates data about malware from static and dynamic method. By utilizing half and half examination, security scientists gain the advantages of the two investigations, static and dynamic. In this manner, expanding the capacity to identify vindictive projects accurately. The two examinations have their very own points of interest and constraints. Static examination is shabby, quick and more secure contrasted with dynamic investigation. Be that as it may, malware dodges it by utilizing confusion strategies. Then again, dynamic examination is dependable and can beat jumbling methods. Besides, it can perceive malware variations and obscure malware families. In any case, it is time escalated and assets expending.

Malware Detection Framework

Malware identification methods are utilized to distinguish the malware and keep the PC framework from being tainted, shielding it from potential data misfortune and framework trade off. Malware identification has to do with the speedy recognition and approval of any occurrence of malware so as to avert further harm to the framework. The last piece of the activity is control of the malware, which includes exertion at halting the heightening and forestalling further harms to the framework (Wuechner T, 2017). Malware recognition strategies are in a general sense gathered in various classes from various perspectives. The following figure Figure 6 illustrates the general framework of malware detection system:

The general framework for malware detection using machine learning exhibits three distinct stages: Feature extraction, feature selection sometimes followed by dimensionality reduction techniques, and then classification using machine learning algorithm. This flow of malware detection process is as shown in Figure 6. Each stage demonstrates diverse measure and strategies utilized in already existing techniques. Initially the dataset is readied which comprises of malware and generous executables. These files are preprocessed depending on the FE method and next feature selection is done to quantify the correlation of feature for improving performance and reducing number of computations to attain the learning speed. Further after generalizing the feature capability, classifier is trained on the basis of the filtered results of feature selection. Researchers have adopted supervised machine learning approach which uses classifiers Decision trees, Support vector machine, Nave bayes, Bayesian network, KNN algorithm, etc. The best classifier is chosen which gives the clear margin, and reduces interference and misclassification between maliciousness and benignancy of executables. The dataset is tested corresponding to the trained classifier and results are generated as malicious or benign software. The obtained outcomes are evaluated with consequent performance metrics (Wu S, 2016).

Feature Extraction

Feature extraction is a dimension reduction method that reduces the number of random variables being considered. This extraction process is performed through either static or dynamic analysis, or a combination of both, while examination and correlation are carried out by using machine learning techniques. Approaches based on static analysis look at the content of samples without requiring their execution, while dynamic analysis works by running samples to examine their behavior.

Debuggers are used for instruction level analysis. Simulators model and show a behavior similar to the environment expected by the malware, while emulators replicate the behavior of a system with higher

Figure 6. General framework of malware detection system

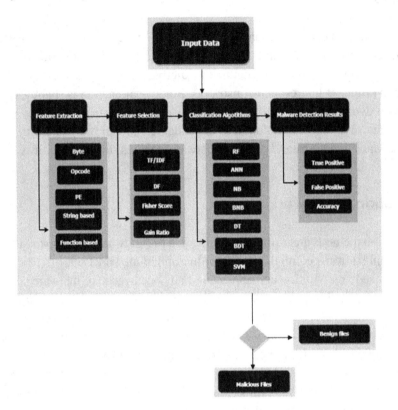

accuracy but require more resources. Sandboxes are virtualized operating systems providing an isolated and reliable environment where to detonate malware.

Byte n-Gram Features

Byte n-gram highlights are successions of n bytes removed from malware utilized as the mark for perceiving malware. Despite the fact that this kind of highlight does not give important data, it yields high exactness in identifying new malware.

Opcode n-Gram Features

Previous studies represented that opcodes feature extraction was more efficient and successful for classification. They reveal statistical diversities between malicious and legitimate software. Some rare opcodes are better predictor's of malicious behavior. First all dataset executable files are disassembled and opcodes are extracted. Opcodes are capable to statistically derive the variability between malicious and legitimate software.

Portable Executables (PE)

These features are extracted from certain parts of EXE files. PE features are extracted by static analysis by using structural data of PE. These meaningful features indicate that the file was manipulated or infected to perform malicious activity. These features may incorporate piece of the snippets of data given as pursues:

- **File Pointer:** Pointer denotes the position within the file as it is stored on disk, CPU type.
- **Import Section:** Functions from which DLLs were used and Object files, list of DLLs of the executable can be imported.
- **Exports Section:** Describes which functions were exported.
- **Resource Directory:** Indexed by a multiple-level binary-sorted tree structure, resources like dialogs and cursors used by a given file.

String Features

These features are based on plain text which is encoded in executables like windows, get version, get start up info, get module filename, message box, library, etc.

Function Based Features

Function based features are extracted over the runtime behavior of the program file. Function based features functions that reside in a file for execution and utilize them to produce various attributes representing the file. Dynamically analyzed function calls including system calls, windows application programming interface (API) calls, their parameter passing, information flow tracking, instruction sets, etc. These functions increase the code reusability and maintenance. It is semantically richer representation. In this system, addressed automatic behavior analysis using Windows API calls, instruction set, control flow graph, function parameter analysis and system calls are used as features.

Hybrid Analysis Features

These features are obtained by combining both techniques static analysis as well as dynamic analysis. It decreases the impact of countermeasures of every static and dynamic procedure for breaking down malware and enhances the execution and identification rates.

Feature Selection

Feature selection is an important step for this process. The main objective is to select the smallest number of features that keep the detection rate as high as possible to allow using the minimum quantity of resources for the malware detection task. Besides, include determination and decrease is now realize that can diminish the clamor, enhance the exactness, and obviously enhance speed for preparing the arrangement calculations as given that time increased in $O(n^2)$ with respect to the number of features as state by Kolter and Maloof. The stages of feature selection methods are listed as follows,

- TF/IDF (term frequency/ inverse document frequency)
- DF (document frequency)
- Fisher Schore
- Gain Ration

Many researchers are developing malware detection, analysis, classification and antidote technologies in a four-phase manner to solve the malware attacks. These phases are described below.

- In the primary stage, identification method is being produced to gather information about attacks, which is a mystery framework for pulling in assaults and gathering malware. It also collects access destinations and communication patterns at time of malware infection.
- In the second stage, analysis method is being created to break down the gathered malware. The fact of the matter is to understand the malware's abilities and choose the hazard that it presents, and all around, to acquire distinct information about the attack
- After that, the classification of malware is carried out. It is a difficult process. Software that allows unauthorized control of a system is obviously malicious. Malware comes in various forms and categories. These are usually classified according to their propagation method and their actions that are performed on the infected machine using the designed malicious program.
- The characterization of malware is completed. It is a troublesome procedure. Programming that permits unapproved control of a framework is clearly pernicious. Malware comes in different structures and classes. These are generally grouped by their proliferation strategy and their activities that are performed on the contaminated machine utilizing the structured malevolent program.
- At last, in the third stage, cure innovation is being created to utilize the data acquired by the above identification and investigation advancements to produce boycotts in an arrangement that can be utilized by administrations. Addresses of access goals showing up at the season of a malware contamination extricated by discovery innovation can be utilized to create boycotts comprising of URL records, IP address records, and so forth.

Malware Classification Methodology

Methodologies towards characterization of malware can be gotten from Machine Learning, information mining, and content order. The most common way is to use the n-grams approaches which are extracted from executables to form training examples. Then after extracting these ngrams we can apply several learning methods such as

- Instance Based Learner
- Naïve Bayes (NB)
- Support Vector Machines (SVM)
- Decision Tree (DT)
- RF(Rain)
- J48
- ANN
- BN
- Boosted Classifiers

Malware Detection Approach

This chapter strategizes Malware Detection approaches are classified into signature-based and behavior-based. Malware Family Attribution technique of binding a malicious element as a "family" associated to its "Ancestors". Machine learning algorithm provides defensive support with varied guards and provisions as provided by Swiss Army Knife to disseminate and decode the resources found in binaries (Sheen S, 2015). Three types of malware detection methods are illustrated in Figure 7.

Signature-Based Detection

This method is used to checking the substance of PC files and cross-referencing their substance with the "code marks" having a place with known infections. A library of known code marks is refreshed and revived continually by the counter infection programming merchant. On the off chance that a viral mark is distinguished, the product demonstrations to shield the client's framework from harm. Suspected files are typically quarantined or encrypted in order to render them inoperable and useless. Unmistakably, there will dependably be new and rising infections with their very own special code marks. So by and by, the counter infection programming merchant works continually to survey and absorb new mark based identification information as it ends up accessible, frequently progressively so updates can be

Figure 7. Types of malware detection techniques

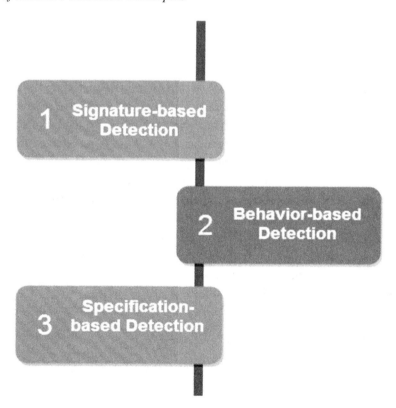

pushed out to clients quickly and zero-day vulnerabilities can be evaded. However, this technique has certain disadvantages:

Susceptible to Evasion: Since the check byte plans are gotten from known malware, these byte structures are in like manner normally known. From now on they can be viably avoided by software engineers using fundamental confusing frameworks, for example, embeddings no-operations and code re-requesting. Thus malware code can be altered and signature-based recognition can be equivocated.

Zero-Day Attacks: While the check-based adversary of malware structures are created dependent on known malware, they can't recognize darken malware or even varieties of known malware. Hence, without exact marks, they can't successfully distinguish polymorphic malware. Subsequently, signature-based location does not give zero-day security. What's more, since a stamp-based pointer uses an alternate check for each malware variety, the database of imprints creates at an exponential rate (Norouzi M, 2016).

Behavioral-Based Detection

This malware detection method is made out of a few applications, which together give the assets and components expected to recognize malware on the Android stage. Each program has its own particular usefulness and reason in the framework and the blend of every one of them makes the Behavior-Based malware discovery framework. The Android information mining contents and applications referenced in are the in charge of gathering information from Android applications, and the content running on the server will be the in charge of parsing and putting away all gathered information. Besides, the content will be in charge of making the framework call vectors for the k-implies grouping calculation (Ming J, 2016).

Specification-Based Malware Detection

Specification based discovery makes utilization of a specific principle set of what is considered as would be expected so as to choose the malevolence of the program disregarding the predefined rule set. Therefore programs damaging the standard set are considered as a vindictive program. In detail-based malware identification, where a discovery calculation that tends to the inadequacy of example coordinating was produced. This calculation consolidates guidance semantics to recognize malware occurrences. The methodology is high strength to basic jumbling systems. It utilized format T to depict the noxious practices of malware, which are the arrangement of directions spoken to by factors and representative constants. The impediment of this methodology is that the property of a program can't be precisely indicated. Particular based recognition is the derivate of oddity-based discovery (Mohaisen A, 2015).

Flexibility: It monitoring decouples strategy production from enforcement. For instance, one can think about having a plan in a specification-based monitoring system that is derived using anomaly detection.

Lower False-Positives: While methodologies in an overall structured, specific based watching system can be viably tuned, it can effect in low false positives.

A COMPARISON OF THE REVIEWED MALWARE CLASSIFICATION ALGORITHMS

In this part, a measurable investigation of surveyed methodologies of malware elucidation utilizing different systems is displayed. Beneath figure demonstrates the measurable graph for the majority of the order strategies in the chose malware discovery approaches.

According to the various author's researches, the comparison of the existing classification methods has illustrated in Table 1. Additionally, Table 1 demonstrates a specialized correlation of the order factors in each article.

From Figure 8, the SVM strategy has the most rates for malware classification approach with 29%, j48 has 17%, NB has 10%, RF has 5%, ANN has 3% and alternate techniques have fewer than 2% utilization in existing research results. In this way, this investigation finds that the SVM strategy simply has the best precision in the malware order approaches among different procedures.

Machine Learning (MI)

ML has developed from the investigation of computational learning hypothesis and example acknowledgment. It is the most effective method used in the field of classification in order to predict something by developing algorithms (N. Srivastava, 2014). These algorithms allow researchers to produce reliable and valid results and decisions. It also helps to discover some hidden features through historical learning's and trends in data. Feature selection is the mainly imperative mission of ML. Algorithm is

Figure 8. An analysis of classification algorithms

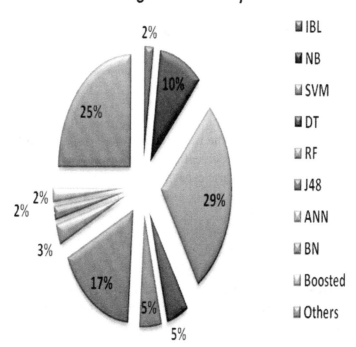

123

Table 1. Comparison of the reviewed malware classification algorithms

S.NO	Author (Year)	Classification approach	Data analysis method	Usage	Total dataset	Accuracy %
1	Bhattacharya et al., (2017)	Random forest	Dynamic	Android malware detection	170	86
2	Mohaisen A et al.,(2015)	Decision trees	Dynamic	Automated malware analysis	2086	98
3	Altaher A (2016)	Neuro fuzzy inference system	Dynamic	Android malware detection	500	90
4	BoukhtoutaA et al.,(2016)	Naïve Bayesian	Dynamic	Deep Packet Inspection for Malware	4560	99
5	Sheen S et al.,(2015)	SVM	Static	Android based malware	2000	98.91
6	Norouzi M et al., (2016)	J48	Dynamic	Behavioral Malware	7000	98.3
7	Siddiqui M et al.,(2008)	Boosted Classifiers	Static	Malware Feature extraction method in cloud	15,000	99.69
8	Wu S et al., (2016)	BN	Static	Data flow android malware detection	2200	97.66
9	Wuechner T et al., (2017)	Compression based malware detection	Dynamic	ANN	7507	99.3
10	Dali Z et al., (2017)	Deep-learning malware detection	Hybrid	Hybrid (Naive Bayes, PART, Logistic Regression, SVM and MLP)	11,000	95.05
11	Yuan Z, et al.,(2016)	Deep belief networks	Hybrid	Android malware characterization and detection	1860	96.76
12	Nikolopoulos et al., (2016)	SaMe-NP	Dynamic	System-call malware	2667	95.9
14	Y. Ye et al., (2010)	Adapting Post processing Techniques	Dynamic	API calls and function calls of malware	15,000	88
15	Kai Huang et al., (2009)	ISMCS	Dynamic	Automated malware (e.g., viruses, backdoors, spyware, Trojans and worms) categorization	2029	79

created based on the results gathered from the training data that is why machine-learning algorithms are non-interactive. It thinks about the past perceptions to make exact expectations. It is an exceptionally troublesome undertaking to make a precise expectation rule dependent on which calculation can be produced. Fundamentally machine learning can be assembled into three classifications:

The figure Figure 9 shows the categories.

Machine Learning in Cyber Security

ML systems have been connected in numerous territories of science because of their one of kind properties like versatility, adaptability, and potential to quickly change in accordance with new and obscure difficulties. Digital security is a quickly developing field requesting a lot of consideration on account of astounding advances in informal communities, cloud and web innovations, and web-based saving money, versatile condition, brilliant matrix, malware grouping and so forth (Y. Ye, 2010). Diverse machine learning methods have been successfully deployed to address such wide-ranging problems in cyber security.

A variety of approaches have been attempted to tackle the problem of Malware detection and classification. According to the fundamental principles, machine learning approaches can be broadly used into malware classification system. These approaches try to analyze the information of a malware and by extracting good feature representations of malware, and training a prediction model on training data of both malicious and benign. The three phases such as data collection, feature extraction and machine learning classification are outlined in Figure 10.

DEEP LEARNING (DL)

It is an almost human personification of knowledge given to computer systems. The whole system is relied on the way that the mind can absorb learning at a fast rate, and this information can be effectively changed over for various employments. Individuals regularly underestimate a great deal of things, and the capacity of the cerebrum is downplayed. When the human cerebrum absorbs data, it nearly turns out to be second nature for it to spread this data. For instance, if the human cerebrum recognizes a type of a puppy, it has normally engraved on the brain. On the off chance that the human is, demonstrated a

Figure 9. Categorization of machine learning algorithms

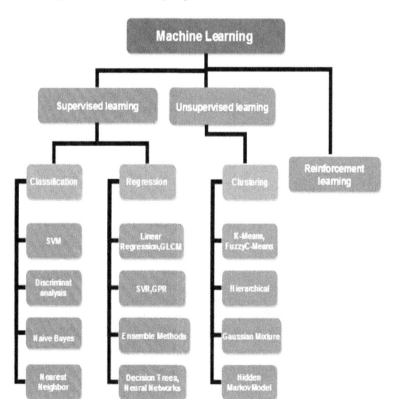

Box 2.

- *Supervised learning:* The majority of practical machine learning uses supervised learning. All data is labeled and the algorithms learn to predict the output from the input data.

- *Unsupervised learning:* All data is unlabeled and the algorithms learn to inherent structure from the input data.

- *Semi-supervised:* Some data is labeled but most of it is unlabeled and a mixture of supervised and unsupervised techniques can be used.

- *Reinforcement learning:* Reinforcement learning is an area of Machine Learning. It is all about making decisions sequentially. In simple words, it can define that the out depends on the state of the current input and the next input depends on the output of the previous input. In Reinforcement learning decision is dependent, so user gives labels to sequences of dependent decisions.

Figure 10. Malware classification approach by using machine learning system

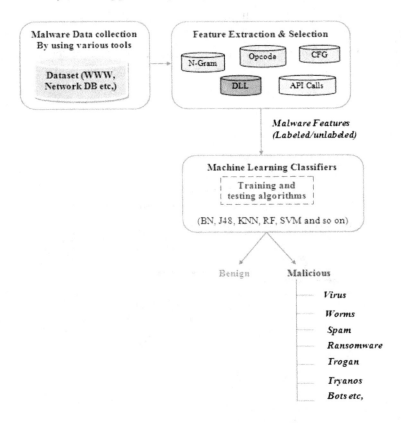

very pixilated type of a canine, the cerebrum is as yet ready to recognize this shape as a pooch. This is somewhat how Deep Learning functions for digital security and malware recognition. It is compared to a cerebrum that is always learning and developing. It is along these lines ready to distinguish these illnesses and malware absent much exertion in light of its capacity to absorb data at a fast rate (Dali Z, 2017).

DL is a propelled model of conventional machine learning. This has the capacity to extricate ideal component portrayal from crude info tests. This method is been employed by researchers in recent days. This has been connected to different use cases in digital security, for example, interruption recognition, malware order, android malware identification, spam and phishing location and binary investigation as shown in Figure 11 There are many other classification algorithms like MLP and J48 that can be used for different problem statements.

- A class of machine learning techniques that exploit many layers of non-linear information processing for supervised or unsupervised feature extraction and transformation, and for pattern analysis and classification.
- Deep learning is a set of algorithms in machine learning that attempt to learn in multiple levels, corresponding to different levels of abstraction. It typically uses artificial neural networks.
- The levels in these learned statistical models correspond to distinct levels of concepts, where higher-level concepts are defined from lower-level ones, and the same lower-level concepts can help to define many higher-level concepts.

The key concept within deep learning is the notion of layers, where each layer recognizes progressively more complex features and learns from the previous layer (Yuan Z, 2016). The following graphic illustrates the types of deep learning techniques

Figure 11. Perception of deep learning

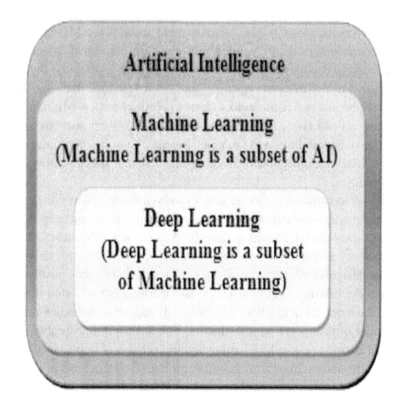

Box 3.

- *Deep convolutional network* is a special category the feed-forward multilayer neural network. It involves convolutional multiple layers followed by a few fully-connected layers.

- *Deep neural network* represents a multilayer perceptron with several hidden layers. The weights are entirely linked and are initialized using supervised/unsupervised pre-training method.

- *Boltzmann machine* represents a symmetrically linked network, where the stochastic decisions are determined based on the neuron.

- *Deep belief network* represents a probabilistic generative scheme consists of multiple stochastic layers of hidden variables. The first (top) two layers have symmetric/undirected connections.

Deep Learning in Cyber Security

The DL is sub-field of AI that is gaining an ever increasing extent of concentration. It holds the promise of attaining many of the long-standing goals for AI. Over the coming years, advances in unsupervised deep learning (interpreting unlabeled data) will propel AI's success in cyber security. While the promise of DL is amazing, the current state of the art is still complex.

MACHINE LEARNING(ML) VS DEEP LEARNING(DL)

In the course of the most recent couple of years' ML in has moved from the research center to the cutting edge of operational frameworks. Google, Amazon, and Facebook use ML each day to show signs of improvement customer encounters, recommended buys/associate individuals socially with new applications and encourage individual associations. ML's amazing capacity is likewise there for cyber security. Cyber security is situated to use machine learning out how to enhance malware identification, triage occasions, and perceive breaks and ready associations to security issues. ML can be used to perceive advanced concentrating on and risks, for instance, affiliation profiling, establishment vulnerabilities, and potential dependent vulnerabilities and attempts. Machine learning can fundamentally change the digital security scene. Malware independent from anyone else can speak to upwards of three million new examples sixty minutes.

Conventional malware identification and malware examination can't pace with new assaults and variations. New assaults and modern malware have possessed the capacity to sidestep system and end-direct identification toward convey digital assaults at disturbing rates. New procedures like profound learning must be utilized to address the developing malware issue. As opposed to progressively ordinary machine learning and highlight designing calculations, Deep Learning has favorable position of possibly giving an answer for location the information investigation and learning issues found in gigantic volumes of info information. All the more explicitly, it helps in naturally separating complex information portrayals from expansive volumes of unsupervised information. This makes it a profitable apparatus for digital security. The profound learning answer for learning highlight chains of importance is to illuminate an arrangement of basic shallow issues. In each progression, profound strategies become familiar with another dimension highlights increasing new bits of knowledge into the info information circulation in transit.

Table 2. Features of learning paradigms

Features	Machine Learning	Deep Learning
Accuracy	Moderate, with a false positive rate at up to 5%	Extremely high with a false positive rate at nearly zero
Domain Expert	Required for feature engineering & extraction	Not required
Analysis of Data Set	Only 2.5-5% of available data	Processes 100% of available raw data
Correlations	Only simple, linear correlations	Non-linear correlations, i.e. correlations that exist in complex patterns, rather than simple 1-1 correlations.

Table 2 represents the features of two learning paradigms.

The recent development in learning deep representations has demonstrated its wide applications in traditional vision tasks like classification and detection. Deep learning is a prominent algorithm employed in several malware classifications. Considering several traditional methods and machine learning methods deep learning algorithms considered as a robust way to solve problems. It is clear that most of the deep learning algorithms come up with better accuracy rate, which will be helpful in building a real time application for analyzing malware activities.

CONCLUSION

The growth and assortment of malware tests intensifies the requirement for development in programmed discovery and characterization of the malware variations. Machine learning is a characteristic decision to adapt to this expansion, since it tends to the need of finding hidden examples in vast scale datasets. These days, neural system procedure has been developed to the express that can outperform impediments of past machine learning strategies, for example, Hidden Markov Models and Support Vector Machines. As an outcome, neural systems would now be able to offer unrivaled arrangement precision in numerous areas, for example, PC vision or natural language processing. This enhancement originates from the likelihood of building neural systems with a higher number of conceivably various layers and is known as Deep Learning.

During the past few years, deep learning has achieved a 20-30% improvement in most of application in computer vision. The domain of deep learning has a multitude of powerful algorithms that may be applied to almost any problem in cyber security. In view of the rising demand for responses and solutions to malware classification, applying other deep learning techniques onto cyber security problems holds an extremely large prospect for future work.

REFERENCES

Alotaibi, F., Furelli, S., Stengeli, I., & Papadakii, M. (2016). A Survey of Cyber-Security Awareness in Saudi Arabia. *11th International Conference for Internet Technology and Secured Transactions (ICITST-2016)*. 10.1109/ICITST.2016.7856687

Altaher, A. (2016). An improved Android malware detection scheme based on an evolving hybrid neuro-fuzzy classifier (EHNFC) and permission-based features. *Neural Computing & Applications*, *28*(12), 4147–4157. doi:10.100700521-016-2708-7

Bhattacharya, A., & Goswami, R. T. (2017). DMDAM: data mining based detection of android malware. *Proceedings of the first international conference on intelligent computing and communication*, 187–194. 10.1007/978-981-10-2035-3_20

Boukhtouta, A., Mokhov, S. A., Lakhdari, N.-E., Debbabi, M., & Paquet, J. (2016). Network malware classifcation comparison using DPI and fow packet headers. *J Computer Virol Hacking Tech*, *12*(2), 69–100. doi:10.100711416-015-0247-x

Dali, Z., Hao, J., Ying, Y., Wu, D., & Weiyi, C. (2017). Deep Flow: deep learning-based malware detection by mining Android application for abnormal usage of sensitive data. In 2017 IEEE symposium on computers and communications (ISCC), (pp. 438–443). IEEE.

Huang, K., Ye, Y., & Jiang, Q. (2009). Ismcs: an intelligent instruction sequence based malware categorization system. In *ASID'09: Proceedings of the 3rd international conference on Anti-Counterfeiting, security, and identification in communication*, (pp. 509–512). Piscataway, NJ: IEEE Press. 10.1109/ICASID.2009.5276989

Ming, J., Xin, Z., Lan, P., Wu, D., Liu, P., & Mao, B. (2016). Impeding behavior-based malware analysis via replacement attacks to malware specifications. *J Computer Virol Hacking Tech*, *13*(3), 193–207. doi:10.100711416-016-0281-3

Mohaisen A., Alrawi O., & Mohaisen M. (2015). *AMAL: high-fidelity, behavior-based automated malware analysis and classification.* Academic Press.

Nikolopoulos, S.D., & Polenakis, I. (2016) A graph-based model for malware detection and classification using system-call groups. *J Comput Virol Hacking Tech, 13,* 29–46.

Norouzi, M., Souri, A., & Samad Zamini, M. (2016). A data mining classification approach for behavioral malware detection. *J Comput Netw Commun, 2016,* 9.

Sheen, S., Anitha, R., & Natarajan, V. (2015). Android based malware detection using a multi feature collaborative decision fusion approach. *Neurocomputing, 151*(2), 905–912. doi:10.1016/j.neucom.2014.10.004

Siddiqui, M., Wang, M. C., & Lee, J. (2008). A survey of data mining techniques for malware detection using fle features. In *Proceedings of the 46th annual southeast regional conference on xx*. ACM. 10.1145/1593105.1593239

Srivastava, N., Hinton, G., Krizhevsky, A., Sutskever, I., & Salakhutdinov, R. (2014). Dropout: A Simple Way to Prevent Neural Networks From Over fitting. *Journal of Machine Learning Research, 15*(1), 1929-1958.

World Internet, . (2010, May). *World internet users and 2016 population stats*. World Internet.

Wu, S., Wang, P., Li, X., & Zhang, Y. (2016). Effective detection of android malware based on the usage of data fow APIs and machine learning. *Information and Software Technology, 75*, 17–25. doi:10.1016/j.infsof.2016.03.004

Wuechner, T., Cislak, A., Ochoa, M., & Pretschner, A. (2017). Leveraging compression-based graph mining for behavior-based malware detection. *IEEE Trans Dependable Secur Comput.*

Ye, Y., Li, T., Jiang, Q., & Wang, Y. (2010). CIMDS: Adapting postprocessing techniques of associative classification for malware detection. *IEEE Transactions on Systems, Man, and Cybernetics, Part C (Applications and Reviews), 40*(3), 298–307.

Yuan, Z., Lu, Y., & Xue, Y. (2016). Droid detector: Android malware characterization and detection using deep learning. *Tsinghua Science and Technology, 21*(1), 114–123. doi:10.1109/TST.2016.7399288

Chapter 7
Cyber Threats Detection and Mitigation Using Machine Learning

Vaishnavi Ambalavanan
Pondicherry University, India

Shanthi Bala P.
Pondicherry University, India

ABSTRACT

Cyberspace plays a dominant role in the world of electronic communication. It is a virtual space where the interconnecting network has an independent technology infrastructure. The internet is the baseline for the cyberspace which can be openly accessible. Cyber-security is a set of techniques used to protect network integrity and data from vulnerability. The protection mechanism involves the identification of threats and taking precaution by predicting the vulnerabilities in the environment. The main cause of security violation will be threats, that are caused by the intruder who attacks the network or any electronic devices with the intention to cause damage in the communication network. These threats must be taken into consideration for the mitigation process to improve the system efficiency and performance. Machine learning helps to increase the accuracy level in the detection of threats and their mitigation process in an efficient way. This chapter describes the way in which threats can be detected and mitigated in cyberspace with certain strategies using machine learning.

INTRODUCTION

Cyberspace plays a major role in the today modern world. It is a place where the technologies are integrated to create an interactive illusion irrespective of the geographical location and time. This virtual environment has become a semi-conscious entity in our lifestyle like net banking, video conferencing, e-shopping, etc. The usage of electronic devices has reached millions of mobile units in both public and private sectors for a different purpose. This gradual growth is possible through technologies like Internet of things (IoT), Cloud Computing, Big Data, and Artificial Intelligence. Another important part is

DOI: 10.4018/978-1-5225-9611-0.ch007

the information storage, where the data is stored either in client or server side based on the application and the system has to maintain integrity. It can be achieved through some of the standardized security mechanisms in order to protect the resources from cyber threats like malware, ransomware, phishing, exploit-kit and application attack (Colorossi, 2015). The threats are elevated due to the technology enrichment, which creates a path to the sophisticated attackers at lower cost and thus makes the security more challenging one.

Cybersecurity deals with issues like the way in which the information is handled and delivered to the end users by holding the principle of Confidentiality, Integrity, and Availability(CIA). These destructive acts of accessing the information with malicious intention lead to cyber threats. The threats initially start with the system vulnerability, which increases the attacking rate by loopholes and back doors that are available in it. The security mechanism involves a protection scheme for the user information and the network environment in which the hacker observes the vulnerability of the systems and may attack the victim. Generally, the user information contains both personal and professional details that are more sensitive. The fact of being exposed to risk is more which are directly proportional to the confidentiality of the data. The possibility of attacks is started when the data is transferring through the public network. The network helps to route the data from source to destination. So, the intruder analyzes the network set-up to identify the possibilities of penetrations method with least time and effort to gain a higher success rate. This penetration process is often carried out by means of the weak authentication system that are maintained by the administrator. As a result, the developer can provide safeguard measures for the existing threats. But it is not easy in case of emerging threats on a daily basis. Thus, the detection techniques require an adaptive learning method to increases the performance level that is possible through machine learning.

Machine learning is based on artificial intelligence, which uses the mathematical method of statistical analysis to predict the desired output. It has the ability to learn from the data sets without explicit programming. The method used for implementing the required needs and applications is based on the type of learning approach. The main agenda is "to learn and improve" system performance with maximum efficiency. The learning mechanism is incorporated by training the system to learn from the datasets by themselves. This includes different stages like the extraction of the pattern from data sets to provide an optimized result in the adaptive environment. The use of machine learning in threat detection helps to identify the occurrence of threats with higher accuracy. It also effectively deals with the detection and mitigation of threats.

CYBER THREATS

In the digital revolution, everything is exercised through mobile devices and other electronic gadgets for sharing and accessing of resources with anonymous hazards. The scaling of valuable resources is calibrated based on the information prioritized by the user on their own standard. Even the lowest scaling data must be secured from the malicious act of penetration. The attack can be either active or passive which is used to obtain the desired information from the victim. To avoid such problems, a defensing mechanism is needed to safeguard the resources from invaders.

In order to provide security, a certain validation measure is necessary to protect the user data from the intruder. This includes the penetration process like detecting the vulnerable spots by various attacking techniques in order to get a higher success rate. They target initially at the network set up to analyze to identify the devices that are connected through the network. Then, the transmission channel through which information can be sent. In the transmission medium, the possibility of sniffing and spoofing can be done while moving from one end to another. The intrusion is occurred due to the poor encryption standards.

Attacking Poles in Cyber Space

In this online world, the most crucial part is to minimize intrusion through the backdoor or vulnerable ports. It will not only affect the principle of CIA but also could cause tedious effects in the social well-being. At least to some extent, it should resist those resources that are being accessed by the outsiders. Therefore, some basic preventive measures are needed to protect the resources from the invader without any expertized knowledge and technical skills. Thus the user needs to know about the attacking poles and the possibility of attacks to avoid human negligence. The probability of securing data in digital life is more challenging. Some of the attacking strategies are discovered once they lost many and even that is unknown the data loss. Even the threats in the devices can't be nullified but it can be reduced. If they could be able to distinguish between the data and the information that is supposed to be protected by providing a certain security measure. This helps in prioritizing the type of attacks and their counter-measures. This can be categorized as per-attack, post-attack, and on-attack to find the attacking stages. Thus the defender only needs to concentrate among the three situations and to choose one method in prevention, precaution, and avoidance. The method for mitigating the threats differ based on the priority and their technical support.

Information security is purely based on the priority whereas providing high security for low standard data and vice versa leads to the worthless effort, time and money. Hence, considering the end user, it must be preached well to avoid the careless handling of resources and their impacts. In addition to understanding the invader attacks, the main focus must be given by providing security for three major areas which include network, communication link and end user involved in the entire setup. The baseline for the security must be drawn to reduces possible intrusion. All three attacking poles are inter-related to each other is shown in figure 1.

Figure 1.Attacking pole

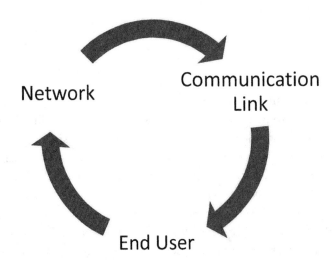

Network

The network is the backbone of the cyberspace for communication. It consists of policies and assignments which is being adapted to monitor the malicious act of unauthorized user access and prevent them. They mainly deal with both hardware and software resource protection through the authentication process, where the network administrator can assign priority to access data in a network. The administrator targets all kind of threats which affects the basic principle. It can be revised periodically based on the evolutionary update in the upcoming techniques and technologies. The authentication process is classified into three categories based on the priority of information. The one with least category of information but still need to be protected, in that case, developer use one-factor authentication. The one-factor authentication consists of only the user name or user id with the password to pass through the network. If the network holds some more sensitive information which requires more security then they use additional features like mobile number, ATM card number, security token, etc. which is known as two-factor authentication.

Finally, if the network holds highly confidential information with the highest priority of securing the data then three-factor authentication is used. In this, they are not only deal with the security tokens with user id and password but they also use the biometric way of securing the information like retina scanning or fingerprint recognition for safeguarding the resources. After the successful authentication process based on the priority level, the users are grouped by a range of accessing the resources which indeed helps in accessing their information.

Communication Link

The communication link acts as a transmission medium where the information can be transferred within the cyberspace. The logical connection is established between two or more devices that are connected in a network. The connecting nodes are linked with each other either through a physical link or the logical link for the delivery of data from one end to another end. There are various types of link such as unicast, multicast, broadcast are used which entirely depends on the type of services required by the user.

The integrity of the entire network system for communication must be well guarded to provide a high level of security. It ignited the concept of cryptography to avoid manipulation. The user data is concealed with a certain encryption algorithm from the sender side to the receiver side. This workflow involves the conversion of plain-text (original message) to the cipher-text (encrypted message) and then transferred via a communication medium. The recipient receives the data via the communication channel and converts the information from cipher-text to the plain-text using decryption process. The cryptographic concept uses standard keys for the encryption and decryption among the communication group. Here, the key acts as a password between the sender and receiver to avoid eavesdropper to get the actual message. The sender encrypts the message using a particular key and receiver decrypt using the key shared between them. The key can be either symmetric or asymmetric key which is chosen based on the user's requirement.

In symmetric key encryption, the sender and the receiver use the same key for both encryption and decryption. The private key is mutually shared between the two users to increase the confidentiality in the communication group and kept as a secret key among them. In asymmetric key encryption, they use different keys for encryption and decryption. The use of public key and private key are preferred for the encryption which is based on the type of communication. If the sender uses the public key to encrypt the message and the receiver decrypt the message using a private key to get the original message. Then the public-private key encryption process is mainly used to provide both confidentiality and integrity of the communication. If a public key is used on the receiver side and private key in the sender side during communication. It helps to validate the sender authentication so that the malicious user identity can be easily detected and helps to maintain the authorization of the system which boosts the defending system.

End-User

In the cyberspace, network and communication link plays a predominant role in expelling the level of security from the intruders. The intruder is provoked for a more successful possibility of finding a vulnerable point from the user side. The end user is comparatively considered as weakest spot in the attacking hole. They use an active method and attacking skills to the user using certain things like social engineering. This helps to gain the trustworthiness of the victim and use it to gain the resources from them. In this case, if it's encountered as a weak defense system in the user side then the confidentiality is completely drained.

Although authenticity is increased with a high level of security, attackers use authorized access during the intrusion. At this point, even the high-end security system can't react to it. The main cause of this sort of attacks is due to the fact that the user shares their security pins, password or the storing them as a written script to sustain it in the memory. In this case, even the electronic devices can't provide efficiency of the ideal devices. But the more reliable error like carelessness, malicious intention, personal vengeance, can happen to spot and enjoy the beneficiary(Mrabet, Kaabouch, Ghazi, & Ghazi, 2018). Some of the attacking poles are shown in figure 2.

Figure 2. Attacks in cyberspace

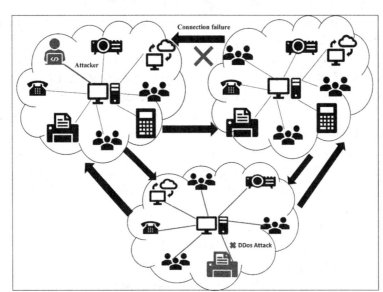

CYBER ATTACKS

Cyber-attacks can be in many forms which include the style, technologies control and the hacking knowledge. It can be divided into broader categories as hackers based attack, location-based attack, method based attack(Uma & Padmavathi, 2013). The classification of cyber attacks is shown in figure 3.

Hackers Based Attack

The hackers with expertized knowledge in programming, who break through the security wall for some cause. These people hold colored hats based on their knowledge, tool usage and the cause of the attacks. In a basic level, a hacker without any knowledge towards the hacking field relying on the procedure of how its made on the demos and just try to implement it blindly. They will try more explore the software and watch videos to make the hacking as possible. These type of hackers who are framed as script kiddies or amateur hackers.

The hacking can be done in an acceptable manner by the white hat hacker or ethical hacker. Those hackers generally find the vulnerable spots or the way in which penetration is possible ie., the possibility that intruder can approach the victim's resources. Then by testing the level of penetration helps to find the withstanding capacity of a particular system. In case if the system is in the weaker side then the system protection are taken into account which is to exposed to attacks. This kind of hacker use certification like Certified Ethical Hacker (CEH) from the EC-Council to pursue their hacking career. The Black hat hackers are also known as Crackers who use their own pattern of hacking from what they learned. These hackers gather information like the company which has higher penetration and the effort and cost required to pass through it. Hence, poor defensing of resources with the minimal security level is chosen as a target company to accomplish their needs.

Figure 3. Classification of cyber attacks

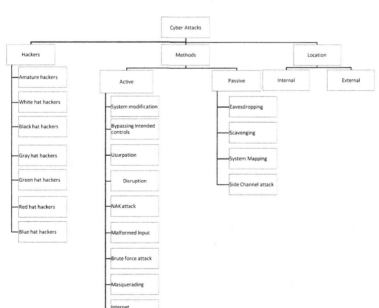

The hackers with both intention and skills of the ethical hackers to find the vulnerable point in the system out of curiosity. But these hacker doesn't follow the legal approach for finding the security lack and suggest the administrator that there are some flaws for the defense. Gray hat hackers are the one who barley violates the laws. Unlike amateur hacker, Green hat hackers have less knowledge or even doesn't have any idea about it. This hacker wants to train themselves to obtain excellence. Due to the low knowledge, they don't know the impact on the work and don't know how to roll back to the previous state.

The Red hat hackers are the aggressive hacker, who is kind of white hat hacker for finding malicious hackers. They are called as "avengers" in the hacking world, who act without a second thought and penetrate into the intruder system and spread virus, worm or perform some sort of shutdown acts. They put their whole effort to collapse the intruder system. Revenge with the negative intention and lack of technical skills are termed as Blue hat hacker. This hacker doesn't have any idea for learning or upgrading their skills rather harming the target will be their main agenda.

Method Based Attack

An attacker uses certain methods like active and passive method. In the active attack, the trespasser can be detected easily and mitigated. In a passive attack, it is difficult to find whether integrity is maintained or not. In an active attack, the attacker breaks down the integrity by altering the original information sent to recipient this happens more often in the communication flow. In this intruder alters the message then sent to the recipient. The intruder acts as a sender and the one who originally sent the message is unaware of the altered message. The active attack can be done in different ways. System modification deals with the altering of user data and changes the privileges based on the hacker's requirements. Bypassing Intended control attacks to completely tear down the authentication process of the target. Usurpation is a form of attacking where the delay of the delivery will be the main goal, ie., the message delivering time from the source to destination will be increased. This attacking style focuses on interrupting the availability of a specific service or a device to perform any other task. In Disruption attacking, they acquire all the available state of services and interrupt other user services. In NAK attack, the intruder use strategies by keeping the sender in a blindfold that the sender messages are sent in a proper way without any error or alteration in it.

In the Malformed Input attack, the security setup will be more vulnerable that is even the hacker corrupts the data slightly might impact in a larger way. The security mechanism is programmed in a way that the prediction is more complex to detect the error rate in a message. If the message is slightly affected by the attacker, it shows a larger impact on communication. Brute force attack is the master for all the attacking style, the intensity to break through the security barriers will be higher. They still focus on finding a way to crack into it even though it is tough for penetration. If the attack made in the routing path in the communication link and the link acts as a target for the hackers which is named as Internet infrastructure attack.

The router decides the path through which the data should be sent. If the routing mechanism is altered, then the entire network gets isolated in a linked chain for the transfer of information. On another hand Masquerading attack, where the attacker is authorized to access the resources and they are freely exposed to resources. Thus the integrity of the communication is dropped down but the user is clueless of what is happening around them.

Location Based Attack

An attack occurs either intentionally or accidentally by human-being, technologies, and environmental causes. The hackers first decide the victim then they gather information about the environment and their workflow. They collect the information and analyze it to find the benefits and fulfill their needs. The attacking location is a key factor in the cyber threats which can be decomposed as external threat and internal threat

External Threat

These threats are caused by hackers who don't have any relation with the targeted people. These crackers goal is to collapse or misuse the resources by neglecting the social status of the suffering people.

Internal Threat

Internal threats are caused by the intruder who already knows the behavior of the victim. Due to some personal vengeance attacker drag down the victim image in society. They are aware of every move of the target which reduces their time for analyzing the victim workflow and can easily fix the vulnerable spot for the intrusion. In comparison, internal attacks are more challenging than the external attack. But from the designer side, internal threat detection and mitigation is the most difficult task.

In-depth knowledge about the victim increases the threat level. The intruder has authenticated access to the resources of the victim and could harm them. The traceability of this attack is the most crucial part and some prevention is required in this problematic situation. This is shown in figure 4.

The above classification in cyber threats intensively shows the situation of how user assets are exposed to attacks. These attacks are broken into infinite causes either intentionally or accidentally, but the goal is to overcome the threats and attacks. They need some sort of prevention mechanism to overcome such issues so that resources can be guarded against any malicious objective of the hackers.

Figure 4. Location based attack

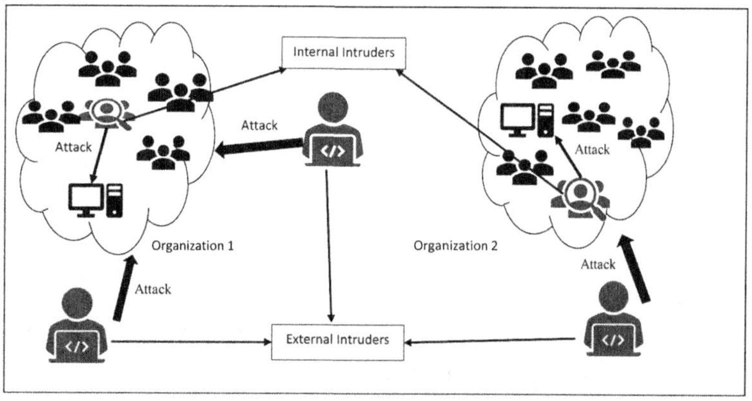

Threat Detection and Mitigation Techniques

The cause and effects are triggered due to technological development that leads to the threat exists. It cannot be avoided in today scenario because of the advancement in techniques and it may have both merits and demerits. This problem can be minimized by taking precautions that could help to sustain the secrecy and integrity of information. Even though they have a higher performance rate in overcoming threats but it can't nullify the threats like an ideal system. The user needs a common knowledge about the consequences of threats in their well being in society. In order to organize a network in a considerable manner, one should understand the circumstances and the attacking strategies to make a counter attack and to protect the resources. The personal interests of the user are learned from their social network and it can be used against them by the attackers. In this process flow, the victim is unaware of the attacker motive and reveal the information that is supposed to be concealed from other knowledge. There are a number of ways to detect the attack and some countermeasures can be done based on the attacking style. The defender must be prepared for three phases of attacks which includes

1. Pre-attack
2. Post-attack
3. On-attack.

In the pre-attack phase, they monitor and analyze the workflow of the network to detect malicious activity in the attacking poles. They have to focus on the network, communication link and the user device for the anomaly detection.

In on-attacking phase, attack detection and attack mitigation are two important part. In the threat detection phase, they include various algorithm and techniques are used based on accuracy in threat detection, the execution time for computation and memory consumption. Eradication process is the next step, which contains a survey of attacks their effects in a summarised format so that the mitigation process is easily carried out.

In post attack, If the attack is not detected then Post-attack phase plays the major role, at first the entity that is involved in the attack must be detected. The upgraded version of security policies, antivirus decreases the vulnerability and minimize the probability of getting attacked. The use of forensic analysis in identifying the motivation and the entities involved in an attack is the preliminary step.

The fundamental steps should be taken by the user by familiarizing certain knowledge about the loophole that can be used against them because technology plays a major part in human life. Due to the lack of knowledge about the cause and effects of using technology, the victim resources are used by the malevolent. Some of the prevention mechanism must be known to the user are

1. The firewall acts a potential barrier between the public and the private world of the user which helps in safeguarding the resource against the unauthorized users with malicious intention.
2. The user should periodically update the software like anti-virus software, security policies due to technological development.
3. Social engineering is one of the common threat causing factor where the victim is unaware of the intention of the attacker and reveals the information that supposed to be concealed. Thus one should be aware of the environment before revealing the information that might cause harm to them.

4. The knowledge about the usage of the technology and their pros and cons must be analyzed before and should take precaution if the vulnerability is high.

The end user should adopt these precaution measures. Experts should have focused more on flaws so that, the resources can be safeguarded in the technical aspects either through hardware or software.

Confidentiality is one of the security principles in the information security which plays a predominant role in the organization particularly with the information that cloud drag their market share and their social status. Some of the factors that affect confidentiality are social engineering, traffic analysis, Man-in-the-middle attack(MITM), privacy violation, backdoor, masquerade attack, etc., which can be retrieved by the possible countermeasures like Secure DNP3(Distributed Network Protocol) highly reliable on by using cyclic redundancy check to detect the error. For secure transferring of data through the communication channel is made possible by public key infrastructure(PKI) which uses heavy-handed authentication proof to break through the links. Secure Socket Layer (SSL) which is used for the encryption process and provide a unique encryption channel. SSL is used for safeguarding the communication link in the network setup. They provide a private channel for communication over the public internet to maintain confidentiality and integrity. Similarly, Transport Layer Security (TLS) provides secure communication process to overcome security flaws like eavesdropping, tampering, etc.

In a network, if an anonymous user is detected with the malicious intent and it can be detected by the protocol called intrusion detection system(IDS). This detection is mainly used for the monitoring the user and their logs are audited regularly if anyone intended to harm the system then it alert the system administrator, who has the authority to take action further regarding this issues and try to solve it. It has multiple layers of intrusion that occurs in the network side or the effects which are caused by the host. In the detection mechanism majority of them deals with one of the following methods for the prevention processing. The system found a certain malicious pattern which is being injected into it and left undetected. Thus when the system went through a periodical scan about the existence of certain unrelated pattern one needs to be checked by the past logs from recorded pattern to know whether it harms the user resources.

The attacker follows particular attacking style which exhibits a certain pre-defined pattern in attacking style as a signature move. The attacking pattern is captured for recognizing the feasible intrusion which requires knowledge about the vulnerability that becomes a threat to the system. This type of detection is termed as knowledge-based detection. In statistical anomaly based detection, a baseline is drawn out based on the reference of the past history of how the resources are used by the user. This reference attributes can be the bandwidth usage, the protocol used, etc, which completely depends on the behavior of the human being or the user who is using it. However, even in case of making base-line to some extent is quite challenging and there is a possibility of having the False positive alarm for the legitimate user and True positive for the illegitimate user in the case of bandwidth. Thus the designer should be more careful enough while drawing those baselines with multiple attributes.

The study of user profile has a variance at the different situation which includes the number of the message being sent and received, usage of the processor, etc. This type of detection is based on the behavior of the user so it also called the behavior-based detection system. If this is done in the generalized format of analyzing the process by tracing the protocol and knowing them are termed as Stateful protocol analysis detection. The key difference is anomaly deals with the network or user specific in a preloaded format whereas in stateful protocol based analysis deals with the specific protocol for general profiles (Liao, Richard Lin, Lin, & Tung, 2013). The prevention mechanism involves the four different types based on circumstances are Network-based intrusion prevention system (NIPS), Wireless intrusion prevention system (WIPS), Network behavior analysis (NBA) and Host-based intrusion prevention system (HIPS).

The availability is one of the basic parameters in information security because of the usage of a resource at the correct time and in a precise format. In an organization, they check for the resources that are required for their employee to get the desired outcomes. Thus they try to make it available for those who need but due to some employees with malicious intent, it becomes more challenging to acquire the resources. The use of Whitelist-based intrusion detection (WBID) helps in identifying issues but they require training and standardization. This requires time for identifying the correct and normal behavior of the user if the training data set is not available. So this approach is quite complex in nature. It can be resolved using Heimdall which increases the scalability, reduced overhead and provide centralized architecture. It also provides higher reliability with remarkable effectiveness in its throughput (Habibi, Midi, Mudgerikar, & Bertino, 2017).

In an organization, the intruder will be more because of its competitor. Therefore the chance of attacking will be relatively more from both inside and outside the organization. A survey shows that insider threats will be more dangerous than the outside threats because these intruders have legitimate access to the resources. These people might have some conflicts against the organization or may be due to personal vengeance within the people an organization. This attacker bypasses the security violation easily through their authentication accessibility as a legitimate user. Hence in order to increase, the defending system of the organization use some precaution. The intruder in an organization can be anyone like an auditor, ex-employee, customers, vendors, etc.

A detection technique called Corporate Insider threats Detection (CITD) used a role-based profile to maintain the pattern log performed by the individuals. The use of Anomaly-based metric for the detection of the malicious users in which the level of deviation occurred from the pattern, that leads a path to an anomaly. The detection mechanism uses anomaly metric is defined based on the individual user behavior. This includes the user acting on certain circumstances and their behavioral change observed for different activities. Based on the observation a report is generated for each and everyone based on the workflow exhibited by the person on multiple tasks are noted. The mean rate of anomaly could be found in the attack pattern. But still the intruder can delete the log history and they can delete the sensitive information, thus they didn't consider multiple anomalies on different data set.

Some of the counter-measures for insider attack includes

1. Role Based Access Control
2. Attribute-Based Access Control
3. Bi-Layer Access Control

Role Based Access Control

RBAC is an extended version of access control and integrated the risk assessment by considering the threshold value. It is an adaptive framework that checks the malicious behavior and reduces the privileges of the user when they fall from the range of the threshold value. Risk assessment has been used for calculating the threshold value. In specific, a detection interface called as Coloured-Petri net had been used for reducing the level of risk exposure (Baracaldo & Joshi, 2013).On another hand, the novel automated anomaly method based on Gaussian mixture model is used for threat detection based on their behavioral changes. This model is used for the detection process by monitoring normal behavior and their malicious changes. The use of expert knowledge helps to reduce the false positive rate and improves the false negative rate of the system. The highly confidential informative files used the threshold templates where they can increase or decrease the level of privileges by which the profile sensitivity will be maintained. In order to enhance the performance, they prioritize the user behavior only for needed features. Thus the designer used Situational Crime Prevention Theory (SCPT) for minimizing the opportunity of intrusion occurrence by Delphi technique. They used virtual space for processing rather than the physical landscape.

The mitigation process is made possible by increasing the priority of the information and the administrator redefines the security policies as a precaution. The Delphi technique deals with smaller data values and designed a product based on assumptions given to them without direct contact with the environment. According to Ambre, Insider threat required continuous monitoring for the detection of intrusion occurrence. The author used log management for finding the root cause by analyzing the log file and correlated the events. The author used four criteria to maintain the level of accuracy that includes the ability to handle any formatted file and as platform independent, event correlation doesn't follow batch processing within the network across the devices, rules are easy for creating, read and modify for correlation processing(Ambre & Shekokar, 2015)

Padayachee et al used several theories for detection and mitigation process which includes two theory namely

1. Social Bound Theory (SBT)
2. Situational Crime Prevention Theory (SCPT).

In Social Bound Theory, the underlying motivation for malicious activity can be found (Ambre & Shekokar, 2015). SCPT used opportunity reduction mechanism for detection and mitigation process. They reduced the crime by making it difficult in any period. This is achieved by increasing the effort and risk to break the security system. Thus due to reduced rewards and provocations, the attacker discards the intention for an attack. In SBT, the attacker is involved towards the attachments social image, commitments, work, personal norms of an individual suppress the intention for an attack(Safa, Maple, Watson, & Von Solms, 2018).

Attribute-Based Access Control

Granularity for the level accessing the data to the right user is not defined in the Role-Based model. Attribute-Based Access Control (ABAC) provides fine granular access control to the user. But it is difficult to process a large data set. In order to overcome this issue Bilayer Access Control(BLAC) is used.

Bilayer Access Control

In this access control, the concept of pseudo role is used instead of the static subject attributes which exhibit lower complexity than ABAC (Alshehri et al., 2016). They used Bayesian knowledge bases (BKB) that represents the random variables. The specific behavior of the insider is taken as a component which is represented in terms of random variables. They also used characteristics like Predictability, Susceptibility, awareness (PSA) to determine the prediction. Along with the prediction of an insider, it should react for a particular event. Hence, they have used three manipulation strategies such as Specifically Trust-Based Manipulation(STBM), Empathy-Based Manipulation(EBM) and False Identity-Based Manipulation (FIBM). Threats in masquerader include port scan, network vulnerability scan, web application vulnerability scan, database vulnerability scan, social engineering, email spam, etc.

In the above methods, even though it provides high-performance rate due to the technological development every day new threat is rising and even become more challenging one to handle so machine learning makes the problem little easier. This is explained in the tabular form as table1

MACHINE LEARNING

Machine learning uses the statistical technique and mathematical format which enable the computer to learn by itself using the past datasets to improve the performance. It is a branch of science which deals with the field of artificial intelligence in which the computer explicitly programmed to predict the outcome. They use the casual variable which is gained from the given data set and process them to identify the underlying model. The reference model is used as an input for problem-solving scenarios. Machine learning overlap with the statical analysis where they use the prediction process in which the number of possible outcome for mathematical computation. The main agenda is to learn and improve system performance. This is feasible by giving machines the ability to access data from which they can learn by themselves. The learning flow includes the extraction of the pattern from data sets to provide an optimized result in the adaptive environment. The learning process can be categorized into three as supervised learning, unsupervised learning and reinforcement learning.

Supervised Learning

Supervised learning is performed by predicting algorithm by means of analyzing the input data for which the precise output is obtained. It helps in finding the appropriate algorithm from the training datasets which is governed to find accurate results. The input data from the training data are considered as a

Table 1. Threat detection and mitigation

Attacking pole	Security Parameters	Attacks	Counter-measures
Network	Confidentiality	Scanning IP, Port, Services, Vulnerabilities	SIEM, IDS, security compliance checks.
Communication link	Confidentiality	Traffic analysis, Social engineering, Man-in-the-middle attack	Secure DNP3, PKI, TLS, SSL
End-user	Confidentiality	Privacy violation, Back door	Authentication, Anti-virus
Communication link	Availability	Jamming attack	Anti-jamming
Network	Availability	DDOS	Whitelist-based intrusion detection
End-user	Integrity	Insider attack	Role-based access control, Attribute-Based Access Control, Bi-Layer Access Control model

feature vector and output as a supervisory signal. They analyze the procedure of the training data and derive the inferred functionality and mapped to the new problem. The learning method undergoes the following steps

1. Determine the type of training dataset – based on the attacking style designer must choose the type of dataset required for training.
2. Gathering of resources - the dataset should be chosen in such a way that should be similar to the input features of the current threat.
3. Input feature for learned function- Choose the input features properly because those input features are converted into a feature vector for the similar attacks for problem-solving. If the input feature becomes ambiguous then the accuracy of the output decreases.
4. Define structure and algorithm- The proper learned function and appropriate algorithm should be identified.
5. Validation- After identifying the algorithm and input features output must be validated to check the correctness of the output.
6. Accuracy Evaluation – After adjusting the parameter, exactness of the output is verified.

With the proper analyses and prediction of correct training data sets and algorithm, there will be an increase in throughput. The predictability of complex problem will have high accuracy if the dataset is trained in a proper way.

Issues in Supervised learning

There are four major issues in supervised learning Bias-variance trade-off, training data cost and function complexity, the dimensionality of input space and noise in the output.

1. Bias-variance trade-off

In Bias-variance, data sets are trained based on one set of input which generated higher accuracy rate whereas, if they are used in similar problems then accuracy drops to a greater extent due to the biased input. This problem leads to the wrong prediction of output for a different problem with similar issues.

2. Training data cost and Function complexity

In smaller issues which have a minimal budget size then training a dataset cost must be considered. Even if they provide a higher output accuracy there will be lack of training data. The training data set is directly proportional to the outcome of the result accuracy. The feature vector should be low biased and high variance in nature to increase the predictability of the output. If an algorithm is flexible enough then with a minimal amount of training data set, maximum throughput can be achieved.

3.   Dimensionality of input space

For a proper outcome with less fuzziness in learning functionality, then dimensionality of the input space must be considered. Even if they provide high accuracy through prediction process the excess of input value increases the space in dimensionality. This measure can be mitigated through the dimensionality reduction algorithm where it can reduce by neglecting the irrelevant features in it.

4.   Noise in output value

If supervisory target variables (output variables) cause error rate due to human error or sensor error then the designer should try high biased and low variance method to overcome this issue. If they try to fit carefully with the input, then it leads to overfitting problem.

Unsupervised Learning

They concentrate on identifying the underlying structure. It uses a concept of clustering where they deal with the grouping based on similarities. This type of machine doesn't have a classification, categorizing or labeling. Instead, they react based on the feedback they gain from the outcome. They use a trial and error method for finding the presence and absence of the outcome positivity. In this, the level of accuracy is comparatively less because there is no governing is performed for the level of arrogation. In supervised learning, they deal with the statistical concept of conditional probability distribution whereas in Unsupervised learning inference is made from a prior probability distribution.

Reinforcement Learning

In the reinforcement, software agents and machines automatically determine the ideal working. They use rewards to maximize the outcome where the learning agent is trained in such a way to predict the output by increasing or decreasing the grade point to it. In this way, an optimized output can be obtained. Reinforcement learning differs from supervised learning in terms of known answer key and having the input data for training to achieve the required outcome. Whereas, In reinforcement training the answer key is unknown and the data set for training is not available. The agent decides every move and outcome are taken in the database. Thus the learning process is made through experience.

ANALYSIS OF MACHINE LEARNING APPROACHES IN THREATS DETECTION

In the rapid development of technology, sophisticated tools are used for breaking the defending system become much easier. Thus defencing system should be designed in such a way to get adapted with the environment and should learn to perform preventive action through self-learning which is made possible by machine learning. Threat detection and mitigation process using machine learning for different application are shown in Table 2.

In Anomaly-based intrusion detection system, data set are trained and monitored for the specified output. Supervised learning technique is used in a detection process where the outcome is inferred using an appropriate algorithm. Intrusion detection systems provide higher accuracy by using an algorithm like

Table 2. Threat detection in machine learning

Machine Learning Technique	Algorithm	Application
Supervised Learning	Genetic algorithm, Bayesian network, Markov models, Neural network, fuzzy logic, Clustering and Outlier detection	An anomaly-based intrusion detection system.
Semi-Supervised Multi-Layered Clustering	K-means clustering	Network Intrusion Detection
Supervised Learning	Adversarial learning, Classifier resilience	Adversarial resilience detection
Supervised Learning	Naïve Bayes, Bayesian network, Decision tree classifier	Malicious Email detection
Supervised Learning (Extreme Learning machine)	Neural Network	Attack detection in Edge computing
Supervised Learning	AB, CART, KNN, LDA, LR, MLP, NB, RF	Attack detection in Robots and Autonomous system

Bayesian Network, Markov model, Neural Network, Genetic algorithm, Clustering and outlier detection (García-Teodoro, Díaz-Verdejo, Maciá-Fernández, & Vázquez, 2009).

In semi-supervised learning, the feature vector is non-labeled or partially labeled because of the critical importance of the data. The use of K-means clustering is used for grouping similar datasets and process the training phase for the desired outcome. This type of machine learning used for a diversified application among the basic classifiers to increase the level of accuracy for Network Intrusion Detection system based application(Al-Jarrah, Al-Hammdi, Yoo, Muhaidat, & Al-Qutayri, 2018).

In the Role-Based module, only specific part is analyzed and even adding Signature-based module for detection, they provide poor efficiency in detecting new malicious threats from a different domain. Thus by using supervised learning new threat detection, an application like emails can be detected with more accuracy. They used three algorithms for the detection process such as asNaïve Bayes, Bayesian and decision tree. Naïve Bayes is used for finding the maximum likelihood with the independence assumption of the relationship between feature vectors. Bayesian network is used for finding a mutual relationship between the feature vector for deriving the probability distribution. Finally, the Decision tree classifier helps to break a large set of input features into smaller part and maintained in the tree structure in an incremental manner (Cohen, Nissim, & Elovici, 2018). Neural Network consists of multiple hidden layers for analyzing and learning the feature vector. In this algorithm, accuracy depends on the number of neurons available in the network ie., the number of neurons is directly proportional to the performance of the system. In a neural network when the processing is made the neurons calculate attribute weight connected to each other and learn from the result generated. Thus by the use of Extreme Learning machine(ELM) in supervised learning increases the detection of attack in the field of edge computing(Kozik, Choraś, Ficco, & Palmieri, 2018).

Identifying the vector attack of an indoor real-time Localization System for autonomous system and robots in cyberspace uses a supervised learning technique. They use Ultra Wideband beacons to pinpoint the user location with high accuracy. In the learning process, they deal with the attacks like Denial of Service, Spoofing and Real-Time Localization System. The detection method uses multilayer perceptron to minimize the error rate with maximum output accuracy. The use of eight algorithms such as Adaptive Boosting (AB), Classification And Regression Tree (CART), K-Nearest Neighbors (KNN),

Linear Discriminant Analysis (LDA), Logistic Regression (LR), Multi-Layer Perceptron (MLP), Naive Bayes (NB), and Random Forest (RF) helps to gain the lowest validation error (Guerrero-Higueras, DeCastro-García, & Matellán, 2018).

CONCLUSION

In cyberspace, due to the varying nature and expertise stage of technology brought the need for cybersecurity. The attackers use sophisticated tools and other resources for the penetration process to get desired resources from the end user and use against them. The security mechanism used for identifying the type of attack and provide precaution for them. The threats can be created either internally or externally. The usage of a mitigation mechanism yields an efficient output only for the detected attacks because of the evolving world and rapid development in technology. This induced the use of machine learning to improve the mitigation process by detecting threats with high accuracy. Machine Learning uses the concept of prediction through statistical analysis to produce a higher success rate. This chapter provided a detail description of various attacks, detection techniques, and the mitigation process using various machine learning algorithms. Machine learning not only increases the efficiency of the system but also helps in identifying the new threats with higher accuracy.

REFERENCES

Al-Jarrah, O. Y., Al-Hammdi, Y., Yoo, P. D., Muhaidat, S., & Al-Qutayri, M. (2018). Semi-supervised multi-layered clustering model for intrusion detection. *Digital Communications and Networks*, *4*(4), 277–286. doi:10.1016/j.dcan.2017.09.009

Alshehri, S., Mishra, S., & Raj, R. K. (2016). Using Access Control to Mitigate Insider Threats to Healthcare Systems. In *2016 IEEE International Conference on Healthcare Informatics (ICHI)* (pp. 55–60). Chicago, IL: IEEE. 10.1109/ICHI.2016.11

Ambre, A., & Shekokar, N. (2015). Insider Threat Detection Using Log Analysis and Event Correlation. *Procedia Computer Science*, *45*, 436–445. doi:10.1016/j.procs.2015.03.175

Baracaldo, N., & Joshi, J. (2013). An adaptive risk management and access control framework to mitigate insider threats. *Computers & Security*, *39*, 237–254. doi:10.1016/j.cose.2013.08.001

Cohen, A., Nissim, N., & Elovici, Y. (2018). Novel set of general descriptive features for enhanced detection of malicious emails using machine learning methods. *Expert Systems with Applications*, *110*, 143–169. doi:10.1016/j.eswa.2018.05.031

Colorossi, J. L. (2015). Cyber Security. In *Security Supervision and Management* (pp. 501–525). Elsevier. doi:10.1016/B978-0-12-800113-4.00038-9

García-Teodoro, P., Díaz-Verdejo, J., Maciá-Fernández, G., & Vázquez, E. (2009). Anomaly-based network intrusion detection: Techniques, systems and challenges. *Computers & Security*, *28*(1–2), 18–28. doi:10.1016/j.cose.2008.08.003

Guerrero-Higueras, Á. M., DeCastro-García, N., & Matellán, V. (2018). Detection of Cyber-attacks to indoor real time localization systems for autonomous robots. *Robotics and Autonomous Systems*, *99*, 75–83. doi:10.1016/j.robot.2017.10.006

Habibi, J., Midi, D., Mudgerikar, A., & Bertino, E. (2017). Heimdall: Mitigating the Internet of Insecure Things. *IEEE Internet of Things Journal*, *4*(4), 968–978. doi:10.1109/JIOT.2017.2704093

Kozik, R., Choraś, M., Ficco, M., & Palmieri, F. (2018). A scalable distributed machine learning approach for attack detection in edge computing environments. *Journal of Parallel and Distributed Computing*, *119*, 18–26. doi:10.1016/j.jpdc.2018.03.006

Liao, H.-J., Richard Lin, C.-H., Lin, Y.-C., & Tung, K.-Y. (2013). Intrusion detection system: A comprehensive review. *Journal of Network and Computer Applications*, *36*(1), 16–24. doi:10.1016/j.jnca.2012.09.004

Mrabet, Z. E., Kaabouch, N., Ghazi, H. E., & Ghazi, H. E. (2018). Cyber-security in smart grid: Survey and challenges. *Computers & Electrical Engineering*, *67*, 469–482. doi:10.1016/j.compeleceng.2018.01.015

Safa, N. S., Maple, C., Watson, T., & Von Solms, R. (2018). Motivation and opportunity based model to reduce information security insider threats in organisations. *Journal of Information Security and Applications*, *40*, 247–257. doi:10.1016/j.jisa.2017.11.001

Uma, M., & Padmavathi, G. (2013). *A Survey on Various Cyber Attacks and Their Classification*. Academic Press.

Chapter 8
Hybridization of Machine Learning Algorithm in Intrusion Detection System

Amudha P.
Avinashilingam Institute for Home Science and Higher Education for Women, India

Sivakumari S.
Avinashilingam Institute for Home Science and Higher Education for Women, India

ABSTRACT

In recent years, the field of machine learning grows very fast both on the development of techniques and its application in intrusion detection. The computational complexity of the machine learning algorithms increases rapidly as the number of features in the datasets increases. By choosing the significant features, the number of features in the dataset can be reduced, which is critical to progress the classification accuracy and speed of algorithms. Also, achieving high accuracy and detection rate and lowering false alarm rates are the major challenges in designing an intrusion detection system. The major motivation of this work is to address these issues by hybridizing machine learning and swarm intelligence algorithms for enhancing the performance of intrusion detection system. It also emphasizes applying principal component analysis as feature selection technique on intrusion detection dataset for identifying the most suitable feature subsets which may provide high-quality results in a fast and efficient manner.

INTRODUCTION

Network security has become a vital aspect of computer technology as there is great improvement in usage of internet. There is a tremendous growth in the field of information technology due to which, network security is also facing significant challenges. As traditional intrusion prevention techniques have failed to protect the computer systems from various attacks and intruders, the concept of Intrusion Detection System (IDS) proposed by Denning (1987) has become an essential component of security infrastructure for the networks connected to the internet and is useful to detect, identify and track the intruders.

DOI: 10.4018/978-1-5225-9611-0.ch008

Intrusion Detection System

An Intrusion Detection System (IDS) is a software application that continuously perceives computer network looking for malicious actions or strategy defilements and generates reports. According to recent studies, an average of twenty to forty new vulnerabilities in commonly used networking and computer products are discovered every month. These wide-ranging vulnerabilities in software enlarge or increase today's insecure computing/networking environment. Hence, such insecure environment has paved way to the ever evolving field of intrusion detection and prevention. The cyberspace's equivalent to the burglar alarm, intrusion detection systems complement the beleaguered firewall.

Intrusion Detection System is a security mechanism which has been acknowledged by the researchers from all over the world because of their capability to keep track of the network behaviour, so that abnormal behaviour can be detected quickly. The traditional IDS is unable to handle the recent attacks and malwares. Hence, IDS which is a vital element of the network needs to be safeguarded.

Steps of IDS are

- Monitoring and analysing traffic.
- Identifying abnormal activities.
- Assessing severity and raising alarm.

Figure 1 shows the basic architecture of intrusion detection system.

The Major Components of IDS Include

- Knowledge Base which encompasses pre-processed information provided by network experts and collected by the sensors.
- Configuration Device which provides data related to the present state of the IDS.
- Detector – ID Engine which identifies intrusive actions based on the data collected from sensors and sends an alarm to response component if intrusion occurs.
- Response Component which initiates response if an intrusion is detected.
- Data Gathering Device which is responsible for collecting data from monitored system.

The packets that are received are transmitted over the computer network and captured. Data are collected and pre-processed to remove the noise and irrelevant attributes. Then the pre-processed data are analysed and classified based on their severity actions. If the record is found normal, then it does not need any change in the action, otherwise, it is sent for report generation. Depending on the state of the data, alarms are raised to alert the administrator to handle the state in advance. The attack is modelled in order to facilitate the classification of network data.

Intrusion Detection Methods

In IDS, detection method is categorized into misuse detection and anomaly detection (Endler 1998) which are also known as knowledge based and behaviour based intrusion detection (Debar 2000) respectively. Patterns of well-known attacks are used to identify intrusions in misuse detection, whereas, anomaly

Figure 1. Basic architecture of intrusion detection system

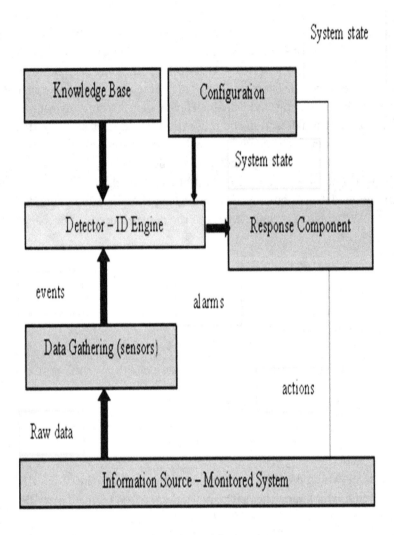

detection determines the deviation from the normal usage patterns which can be flagged as intrusions. Some IDSs combine the capabilities of both the methods by hybridization of techniques.

Misuse detection technique is also known as Signature-based detection and a database is usually used to store the signatures of known attacks which may be constantly updated. The limitation of this type of detection technique is that, if any new type of threat comes, which is not already known to the IDS, the system becomes vulnerable to that attack. Anomaly detection is also known as Profile detection, which monitors network traffic and compares it against an established baseline for normal use bandwidth, protocols, ports and devices generally connecting to each other. The administrator is given 'alerts' when the traffic is sensed as anomalous, or if the attack types are unknown. In the case of detecting a data target, intrusion detecting system can be classified as host-based and network-based (Debar 2000).

1. **Host-based Intrusion Detection System (HIDS):** It consists of a representative of a host that detects interventions by examining system calls, application logs, file-system modifications and other host activities.
2. **Network-based Intrusion Detection System (NIDS):** It detects intrusions by monitoring network traffic and observing multiple hosts. Also NIDS can obtain the means to access network traffic by linking to a network hub, network switch configured for port mirroring, or network taps.

The characteristics of intrusion detection system are shown in Figure 2.

Features of Intrusion Detection System

The features of intrusion detection system are:

*   The IDS must be able to detect any modifications forced by an attacker.

Figure 2. Characteristics of Intrusion Detection System

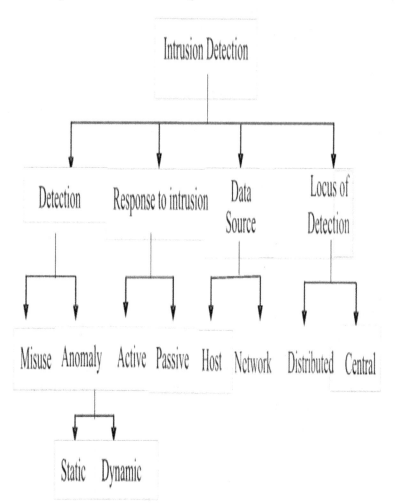

- Impose minimal overhead on the system.
- Be easy to deploy.
- Detects different types of attacks.
- The IDS must be able to recover from system crashes, either accidental or caused by malicious activity.

Goals of Intrusion Detection System

- Identify varied type of intrusions
  - Known and unknown attacks.
  - Detect intrusions in a timely manner.
  - Analysis to be presented in simple and understandable format.
- Be accurate
  - Reduce false positives, false negatives where, false positive is an event, incorrectly identified by the IDS as an intrusion, and false negative is an event that the IDS fails to identify an intrusion.
  - Minimize the time spent on verifying attacks.

Importance of Intrusion Detection System

Intrusion Detection Systems are implemented in order to detect malicious activities and it functions behind the firewall, observing for patterns in network traffic that might indicate malicious action. The extreme development of the internet, the high occurrence of the threats over the internet has been the cause in recognizing the need for both IDS and firewall to help in securing a network. Thus, the IDSs along with the firewall form the important technologies for network security. Joshi & Pimprale (2013) discussed that with the rapid development in communication technology, the security of computer network is one of the challenging issues and so as an Intrusion Detection system.

IDS methodologies which are currently in use require human intervention to generate attack signatures or to determine effective models for normal behavior. In order to provide a potential alternative to expensive human input, we are in need of learning algorithms. The predominant task of such learning algorithm is to discover appropriate behavior of IDS as normal and abnormal (system is under attack). The algorithm should be accurate and it should process the information in quick successions which is one of the major drawbacks in IDS because of the large amount of features.

Recently several researchers have exposed a great interest in intrusion detection based on machine learning and swarm intelligence techniques. These techniques provide improved performance in intrusion detection process with good detection rate (Dokas et al 2002). Also, to improve the performance of classifiers, currently researchers focus more on combining the techniques to exploit the advantages of individual techniques. Hence, this work focuses on hybrid swarm based intrusion detection system in which the performance of swarm intelligence algorithms and machine learning algorithms are analysed with the feature subsets formed and to classify the data and detect intrusions.

Applications of Intrusion Detection System

The application of IDS in various fields is described:

IDS in Mobile Adhoc Network

IDS are used in MANET to find the intruder when transmitting the series of packets to the destination through mobile network.

IDS in Cloud Computing

Cloud computing is the most vulnerable targets for intruder due to their distributed environment. Hence, IDS are used in the cloud to detect malicious action and improve the security measures (Shelke et al 2012).

IDS in Machine Learning

To deal with the new arising attacks in networks, machine learning can help improve intrusion detection by distinguishing attack from common traffic on the network.

MACHINE LEARNING IN INTRUSION DETECTION SYSTEM

Intrusion detection using machine learning has gained prominence among the research community in recent years. Applying machine learning techniques on network traffic data is a promising solution that helps to develop better intrusion detection systems.

Machine Learning explores algorithms that can,

- learn from data / build a model from data
- use the model for prediction, decision making or solving some tasks

The broad types of machine learning are shown in Figure 3.

Supervised Learning

The training data based on observation, measurement are accompanied by the labels indicating the class of the observation. New data is classified based on the training. In this method user has to provide training examples.

Unsupervised Learning

Unsupervised learning refers to the process of finding the hidden structure in unlabelled data. Unsupervised learning also encompasses many other techniques that seek to summarize and explain key attributes of the data.

Figure 3. Types of machine learning

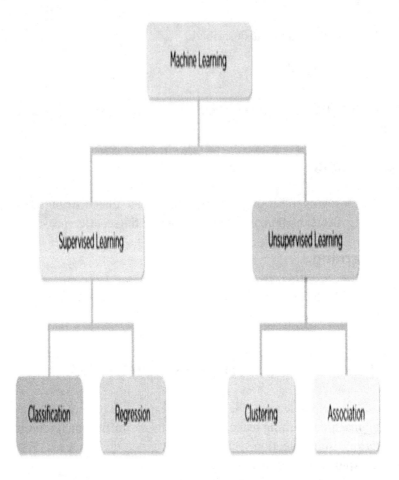

Need of Machine Learning in Intrusion Detection

The use of machine learning techniques is important in an intrusion detection system due to the following:

- Analyze large volumes of network data.
- Perform data summarization and visualization.
- Manage firewall rules for anomaly detection.
- Differentiate data that can be used for deviation analysis.

When machine learning is introduced into intrusion detection, it focuses on two main problems: 1) to establish the adaptive feature dataset; 2) to improve the detection rate.

Feature Selection

In machine learning and statistics, feature selection (Kira & Rendell 1992) is the method of choosing a subset of significant features for constructing robust learning models. It is also known as variable selection, feature reduction, attribute selection or variable subset selection. Feature selection also helps to acquire a better understanding about the significant features and how they are associated with each other.

In general, the feature selection process consists of three steps:

- Selects a subset of original features and evaluates each feature's worth in the subset.
- Using this evaluation, some features in the subset may be eliminated or enumerated to the existing subset.
- It checks whether the final subset is good enough using certain evaluation criterion.

The main aim is to reduce the great burden of inspecting huge volumes of audit data and realizing performance optimization of detection rules. One of the major challenges in this area is the poor detection rate, due to the large amount of features in the data set. In IDS, the amount of data is huge that contains traffic data with various features such as the length of the connection, the protocol type, and other information. Certain features may be irrelevant with very low prediction capability to the target patterns, and certain other features may be redundant due to that they are highly inter-correlated with one or more of the other features.

Due to the presence of irrelevant and redundant features in the analysis, the detection speed becomes slow and also the detection accuracy possibly decreases. Hence, irrelevant and redundant features must be eliminated from the original feature set to attain a better overall detection performance. Therefore, selecting significant set of features from the network traffic data becomes a vital task in the intrusion detection process.

As the volume of data to be processed is reduced using feature selection method, the performance of detector may be improved. Feature selection contributes to improve the overall accuracy, reduces the number of false alarms and improves the detection of instances in the training data. As there are number of feature selection approaches, it is a challenging problem to know which method perform the best, especially under what classification techniques for intrusion detection.

Classification Techniques

Classification or supervised learning models are the most widely used of all machine learning approaches, which arranges the data into predefined groups. A classification task begins with training data for which the target values are known where the classification algorithm can construct a predictive model to classify the data. Intrusion detection can also be considered as a classification problem where, each record can be classified under the category, normal or intrusion. As it is very challenging to detect new attacks, constructing a classifier model is also a challenge for an efficient intrusion detection system. The main disadvantages of using single classifier are:

- If the classifier produces wrong output, then the final result may be incorrect.
- The classifier may not be proficient to tackle the problem.

Hence, Hybrid classifiers which combine number of trained classifiers overcome the defects of single classifiers and can lead to a better performance than any single classifier. Hence, in this work, to improve the accuracy of an individual classifier, the classifiers are combined which is the prevalent approach and analyzed the performance of algorithms to detect intrusions with the feature subsets formed.

SWARM INTELLIGENCE

Evolutionary computation and swarm intelligence techniques are great examples of nature which has been a continuous source of inspiration. A swarm can be considered as a group of cooperating agents to achieve some purposeful behaviour and task. It links to artificial life, in general, there are several collective behaviours like birds flocking, ant colonies, social insects and swarm theory, which have inspired swarm intelligence researchers to devise new optimization algorithms.

The term Swarm Intelligence (SI) introduced by Beni & Wang (1993) has received extensive attention in the research community, mostly as Particle Swarm Optimization (PSO), Ant Colony Optimization (ACO), Bee Colony Optimization (BCO) and Cuckoo Search algorithm. Swarm intelligence is an artificial intelligence technique involving the study of collective behaviour in decentralized systems. Such systems are made up by a population of simple individual, interacting locally one another and with their environment. The local interaction among the individual cause a global pattern to emerge.

Researchers in the field of computer science have constructed swarm-based systems based on the efficiency of swarms to solve difficult problems. The swarm intelligence algorithms, inspired by animal behaviour in nature have been successfully applied to optimization, robotics and military applications (Grosan et al 2006).

Swarm Intelligence in Intrusion Detection System

In the last decade, there have been successful applications of nature inspired computing techniques in engineering applications and various optimization problems, such as travelling salesman problem, scheduling, robotics, network security and data mining. Swarm Intelligence (SI) approaches intend to solve complicated problems by multiple simple agents without centralized control or the provision of a global model. Use of Swarm intelligence techniques in intrusion detection problem would decompose into several simpler ones, making IDSs autonomous and cost efficient. The capability of swarm intelligence makes it as a suitable aspirant for IDS to differentiate normal and abnormal connections from huge volume of data. The unique features of SI make it perfect for intrusion detection and hence this work uses swarm intelligence algorithms in the intrusion detection for classification purpose.

RELATED STUDIES

Over the years, many researchers have done some substantial work on the development of intrusion detection system. Shrivastava presented Pulse Coupled Neural Networks (PCNN) to identify important input features and Gaussian kernel of support vector machine was integrated for classification which detected known attack types with high accuracy and low false positive rate (less than 1%). Modified

Mutual Information-based Feature Selection algorithm (MMIFS) was proposed by Song et al for intrusion detection in which C4.5 classification method was used which improved most of the performance indicators. Eesa et al applied bee algorithm to select the optimal subset of features and ID3 algorithm as a classifier which obtained higher accuracy and detection rate with a lower false alarming rate for IDS.

In literature, several researchers have benchmarked a range of machine learning algorithms such as Naïve Bayes (NB), Support Vector Machine (SVM), Decision tree, Neural Networks (NN) as a single classifier to address the problem of intrusion detection, investigating that different algorithms perform better at detecting different classes of intrusions (Sabhnani and Serpen). Panda and Patra found that NB was effective in identifying network intrusion and generated detection rate of 95% whereas, false positive was high. SVM has been applied increasingly to misuse detection and anomaly detection in the last decade. The research on single classifier has been slowly replaced by the hybrid classifier which offers much promising results. Hence, combining a number of trained classifiers lead to a better performance than any single classifier.

Li and Wang established a hybrid classifier algorithm (HCA) which is composed of Kernel Principal Component Analysis (KPCA), Core Vector Machine (CVM) and Particle Swarm Optimization (PSO). The system based on HCA had better performance in reducing the classifier errors, producing low false positive rate, but the false negative rate was high. Gan et al combined CVM and Partial Least Square (PLS) algorithms to increase the ability of identifying abnormality intrusions. Chandrashekhar and Raghuveer presented K-Means clustering algorithm which were trained with neural network and classified by support vector machine. The results indicated that there was an improvement in the accuracy rate of 97.5%, 98.7%, 98.8% and 98.8% for DoS, Probe, R2L and U2R attacks respectively. Laftah Al-Yaseen et al presented Hybrid modified K-Means with C4.5 algorithm which improved the the detection accuracy with highest accuracy (90.67%) and detection rate (84.80%) in a Multi Agent System (MAS-IDS).

Mohammad Almseidin et al demonstrated that the decision table classifier achieved the lowest value of false negative while the random forest classifier achieved the highest average accuracy rate. Suad Mohammed Othman et al compared the performance of Chi-SVM classifier and Chi-Logistic Regression classifier using intrusion detection data and showed that SparkChi-SVM model produced high performance with reduced the training time. Peng et al proposed a clustering method for IDS based on Mini Batch K-means with principal component analysis (PCA). Tchakoucht TA and Ezziyyani M proposed a lightweight intrusion detection system, for probe and DoS attacks detection, used Information Gain (IG), and Correlation-based Feature (CFS) selection filters for feature selection, and employed four machine learning methods, namely C4.5, NB, Random Forest (RF) and REPTree and achieved good detection and false positive rates, of around 99.6%, and 0.3% for DoS attacks, and 99.8% and 2.7% for Probe attacks.

Kanaka Vardhini and Sitamahalakshmi proposed ACO with new heuristic function enhanced the accuracy in finding the patterns which are useful for intruder detection. The usage of performance metrics as heuristic function increased the accuracy with less time complexity. Pengyuan Pei proposed a model of fish swarm optimization algorithm based on neural network for IDS, and the detection effect of fish swarm optimization algorithm model based on neural network was stronger, detection efficiency was higher, with supreme application value. Chie-Hong et al applied the equality constrained-optimization-based extreme learning machine to network intrusion detection and the experimental results showed that the approach was effective in building models with good attack detection rates and fast learning speed. Saroj Kr. Biswas used CFS, IGR, PCA, for feature selection and k-NN, DT, NN, SVM and NB classifiers for intrusion detection and highest accuracy was obtained in all the combinations for IGR feature selection with k-NN. Bahram Hajimirzaei and Nima Jafari Navimipour proposed a new intrusion detection system (IDS) based on a combination of a multilayer perceptron (MLP) network, and artificial bee colony (ABC) and fuzzy clustering algorithms and the proposed method outperformed other IDSs with respect to the evaluation criteria in terms of MAE and RMSE.

DATASET DESCRIPTION AND VALIDATION

This section provides the description of dataset considered in this study and pre-processing of data which is carried out for data cleaning and data selection. The validation method and the performance metrics that are used for validating IDS in this work are elaborated.

Data Source

The benchmark datasets commonly used by the researchers in both misuse and anomaly detection are: DARPA 1998 TCPDump Files (DARPA98), DARPA 1999 TCPDump Files (DARPA99), KDDCup'99 dataset (KDDCUP99), 10% KDDCup'99 dataset (KDDCUP99-10), UNIX User dataset (UNIXDS), University of New Mexico dataset (UNM). In this work, as an experimental study for evaluating the performance of classification algorithms, the benchmark KDDCup'99 intrusion detection dataset is used.

The dataset description of KDDCup'99 which is derived from UCI Machine Learning Repository (Lichman 2013) is provided. In 1998, DARPA intrusion detection, evaluation program, to perform a comparison of various intrusion detection methods, a simulated environment was setup by the Massachusetts Institute of Technology (MIT) Lincoln Laboratory to obtain raw TCP/IP dump data for a Local Area Network (LAN). The functioning of the environment was like a real one which included both background network traffic and wide variety of attacks. A version of 1998 DARPA dataset, KD-DCup'99, is now widely accepted as a standard benchmark dataset and received much attention in the research community of intrusion detection. This dataset is publicly available and labelled; hence, most of the researchers make use of it as network intrusion dataset. As it is a time-consuming process for generating accurate labels for custom datasets, this dataset is still used, despite its age.

Dataset Description

The KDDCup'99 dataset is a collection of simulated raw TCP/IP dump data over a period of nine weeks of simulating a U.S. Air Force Local Area Network. The seven weeks of network traffic of about four gigabytes of compressed training data were processed into five million connection records. Similarly, two weeks of test data yielded about two million connection records. There are 4,898,430 labelled and 311,029 unlabelled connection records in the dataset. The labelled connection records consist of 41 attributes.

Feature Information

The complete listing of the set of features in the dataset is given in Table 1.

In KDDCup'99 dataset, each example represents attribute values of a class in the network data flow, and each class is labelled either normal or attack. The dataset consists of one type of normal data and 22

Table 1. Set of features of KDDCup'99 dataset

Feature No.	Name of the feature	Feature No.	Name of the feature
1	duration	22	is_guest_login
2	protocol_type	23	count
3	service	24	srv_count
4	flag	25	serror_rate
5	src_bytes	26	srv_serror_rate
6	dst_bytes	27	rerror_rate
7	land	28	srv_rerror_rate
8	wrong_fragment	29	same_srv_rate
9	urgent	30	diff_srv_rate
10	hot	31	srv_diff_host_rate
11	num_failed_logins	32	dst_host_count
12	logged_in	33	dst_host_srv_count
13	num_compromised	34	dst_host_same_srv_rate
14	root_shell	35	dst_host_diff_srv-rate
15	su_attempted	36	dst_host_same_srv_port_ rate
16	num_root	37	dst_host_srv_diff_host_rate
17	num_file_creations	38	dst_host_serror_rate
18	num_shells	39	dst_host_srv_serror_rate
19	num_access_files	40	dst_host_rerror_rate
20	num_outbound_cmd	41	dst_host_srv_rerror_rate
21	is_host_login		

different attack types categorized into 4 classes, namely: Denial of Service (DoS), Probe, User-to-Root (U2R) and Remote-to-Login (R2L).

- Normal connections are generated by simulated daily user behaviour such as downloading files and visiting web pages.
- Denial of Service (DoS): Attacker tries to prevent legitimate users from using a service, e.g., syn flood.
- Probe: Attacker tries to gain information about the target host, e.g., port scanning.
- User-to-Root (U2R): Attacker has local access to the victim machine and tries to gain super user privileges, e.g., various ``buffer overflow'' attacks.
- Remote-to-Login (R2L): Attackers try to gain access to the victim machine that does not have an account, e.g., guessing passwords.

Details of 10% KDDCup'99 Dataset

The KDDCup'99 dataset consists of three components, namely: 10% KDD, Corrected KDD, Whole KDD as shown in Table 2.

Table 2. Number of attacks in training KDDCup'99 dataset

Dataset	Normal	DoS	U2R	R2L	Probe
10% KDD	97277	391458	52	1126	4107
Corrected KDD	60593	229853	70	11347	4106
Whole KDD	972780	3883370	50	1126	41102

In this work, 10% KDDCup'99 dataset which is a more concise version of the Whole KDD dataset is used for experimentation.

DATA PRE-PROCESSING

Data pre-processing is an essential task in network-based intrusion detection, which tries to classify network traffic as normal or abnormal. It is a time-consuming task which transforms the network data into proper form for further analysis as per the requirement of the intrusion detection system model. Pre-processing converts network traffic into a series of observations, where each observation is represented as a feature vector and are labelled with its class, such as "normal" or "attack". The main deficiency in KDDCup'99 dataset is the large number of duplicate/redundant instances. This large amount of redundant instances will make learning algorithms, to be partial towards the frequently occurring instances, and inhibiting it from learning infrequent instances which are generally more unsafe to networks. Also, the existence of these redundant instances will cause the evaluation results to be biased by the methods which have better detection rates on the frequently occurring instances. Eliminating redundant instances helps in reducing false positive rates for intrusion detection. Moreover, irrelevant attributes of dataset may lead to complex intrusion detection model which will reduce the detection accuracy. Hence, redundant instances are removed, so the classifiers will not be partial towards more frequently occurring instances.

The numbers of instances after removing duplicates in each attack are detailed in Table 3. It is noted that there are no duplicate instances in R2L class but DoS class contains large number of duplicates in Neptune and Smurf attack (55381 and 280149 respectively).

EXPERIMENTAL SETUP

After pre-processing, random sample of 10% normal data and 10% Neptune attack in DoS class are selected and they include 8783 normal instances, 7935 DoS instances, 2131 Probe instances, 52 U2R instances and 999 R2L instances. Four new sets of data are generated with the normal class and four categories of attack: DoS+10%normal, Probe+10%normal, R2L+10%normal and U2R+10%normal. In each data set, instances with the same attack category and 10% normal instances are included, where each dataset has its own distribution of categories of instances. The composition of dataset generated is given in Table 4.

VALIDATION METHOD

Cross-validation (Diamantidis et al 2000) is a technique for assessing how the results of a statistical analysis will generalize to an independent dataset. It is the standard way of measuring the accuracy of a learning scheme and it is used to estimate how accurately a predictive model will perform in practice. In this work, 10-fold cross-validation method (Refaeilzadeh et al 2009) is used for improving the classifier reliability. In 10-fold cross-validation, the original data is divided randomly into 10 parts. During each run, one of the partitions is chosen for testing, while the remaining nine-tenths are used for training. This process is repeated 10 times so that each partition is used for training exactly once. The average results from the 10-fold gives the test accuracy of the algorithm.

Table 3. Number of instances after removing duplicates

Category of attack	Attack Name (no. of instances after removing duplicates)	After removing duplicates	No. of duplicates
Normal	Normal (87832)	87832	9445
DoS	Neptune (51820), Smurf (641), Pod (206), Teardrop (918), Land (19), Back (968)	54572	336886
Probe	Portsweep (416),IPsweep (651), Nmap (158), Satan(906)	2131	1976
U2R	Bufferoverflow (30), LoadModule (9), Perl (3), Rootkit (10)	52	0
R2L	Guesspassword (53), Ftpwrite (8), Imap (12), Phf(4), Multihop(7), Warezmaster(20), Warezclient (893)	999	127
Total Examples		145586	348434

Table 4. Composition of dataset generated

Dataset	Number of Instances
DoS+10%normal	16718
Probe+10%normal	10914
U2R+10%normal	8835
R2L+10%normal	10782

Table 5. Confusion matrix

Confusion Matrix		Predicted Class	
		Class = Normal	Class = Attack
Actual Class	Class = Normal	TP	FN
	Class = Attack	FP	TN

Validation Parameters

A confusion matrix (Freitas 2003) contains information about the number of instances predicted correctly and incorrectly by a classification model and is given in Table 5. It is used to evaluate the performance of a classifier.

When referring to the performance of IDSs, the following terms from the confusion matrix are often used with respect to their capabilities:

- **True Positive (TP):** The number of attacks that are correctly identified.
- **False Positive (FP):** The number of normal records incorrectly classified.
- **False Negative (FN):** The number of attacks incorrectly classified.
- **True Negative (TN):** The number of normal records that are correctly classified.

The Performance metrics calculated from the above terms are: Classification Accuracy, Detection Rate (DR), False Alarm Rate (FAR) and Specificity.

The classification accuracy is the percentage of the overall number of connections correctly classified and is calculated using Equation (1).

$$Classification\,accuracy = \frac{\left(TP + TN\right)}{\left(TP + FP + TN + FN\right)} \tag{1}$$

Detection Rate (True Positive Rate) is the percentage of the number of attack connections correctly classified and is calculated using Equation (2). The term is synonymous with sensitivity and recall.

$$Detection\,Rate\left(DR\right) = \frac{TP}{\left(TP + FN\right)} \tag{2}$$

False Alarm Rate (False Positive Rate) is the percentage of the number of normal connections incorrectly classified and is calculated using Equation (3).

$$False\,Alarm\,Rate\left(FAR\right) = \frac{FP}{\left(TN + FP\right)} \tag{3}$$

METHODOLOGY

In addition to the popular and well-accepted algorithms such as genetic algorithms, ant colony optimization, and particle swarm optimization, the algorithms which appeared in the last five years include bat algorithm, cuckoo search and others. Different algorithms have different sources of inspiration, and they can also perform differently. However, some efficient approaches can be based on the combination of different algorithms. This section presents a hybrid approach which combines Cuckoo Search Algorithm (CSA) with Core Vector Machine (CVM) using principal component analysis to select the most informative features to obtain more quality results.

Cuckoo Search Algorithm

Cuckoo Search Algorithm (CSA), which is proposed by Yang & Deb (2009), is an optimization technique which imitates the breeding strategy of the cuckoos and has been employed in diverse domains. The Cuckoo search was inspired by the obligate brood parasitism of some cuckoo species which lay their eggs in the nest of host bird. Some host birds will have direct conflict with intruding cuckoos. In this case, if host birds find that the eggs are not their own, they will either throw them away or simply destroy their nests and build new ones in a different place. Parasitic cuckoos often choose a nest where the host bird just laid its own eggs. It is assumed that, each nest has one egg and it represents a solution, and a cuckoo egg represents a new solution. The objective is to employ the new and better solutions (cuckoos) to replace the existing solutions in the nests. The Cuckoo search is based on three idealized rules:

1. Each cuckoo lays one egg in a random manner by selecting the host nest at a time, where the egg represents the possible solution to the problem under study;
2. the CSA follows the survival of the fittest principle. Only the fittest among all the host nests with high quality eggs will be passed on to the next generation;
3. the number of host nests in the CSA is fixed beforehand. The host bird spots the intruder egg with a probability $pa \in [0, 1]$. In that case, the host bird will either evict the parasitic egg or abandon the nest totally and seek for a new site to rebuild the nest.

The algorithm for cuckoo search (Deb & Yang 2009) is as follows:

Algorithm: Cuckoo Search

```
begin
Generate initial population of q host nest x_i, = 1, 2, . . ., q
for all x_i do
Evaluate the fitness function F_i = (x_i)
end for
while (iter < MaxGeneration) or (stopping criterion)
Generate a cuckoo egg x_j from random host nest by using Levy flight
Calculate the fitness function F_j = (x_j)
Get a random nest i among q host nest
if (F_j > F_i) then
Replace x_i with x_j
Replace F_i with F_j
end if
Abandon a fraction p_a of the worst nests
Build new nests randomly to replace nests lost
```

```
Evaluate the fitness of new nests
end while
```

```
Core Vector Machine
```

Core Vector Machine (CVM) (Tsang et al 2005) algorithm is an optimization technique which applies kernel methods for data intensive applications involving large data sets. The classification problem using SVM is formulated as Quadratic Programming (QP) problem. In CVM, the quadratic optimization problem involved in SVM is formulated as an equivalent Minimum Enclosing Ball (MEB) problem. It is much faster and can handle very larger data sets than existing SVM algorithms. It produces fewer support vectors on very large data sets. Core vector Machine (CVM) is suitable for efficient large-scale pattern classification. CVM has proven to produce a very good experimental result in performing classification task. The training time of CVM is independent of the sample size and obtains similar accuracies compared to the other SVM approaches (Tsang et al 2005).

It can improve the algorithm complexity defects of SVM algorithm and it also significantly reduces the space and time complexities compared to SVM. The time complexity of CVM is O(n) and space complexity does not depend on n, where n is the size of samples set. But whereas, in SVM, the time complexity is O(n3) and space complexity is O(n2).

CVM divides the da'abase between useless and useful points. The useful points are designated as the core set and correspond to all the points that are candidates to be support vectors. As there is no removing step involved, this set can only grow. Among the points of the core set, all are not vectors in the end. Figure 4 illustrates the inner circle of MEB. The inner circle of MEB contains the set of squares and the outer circle, which covers all the points, which is $(1 + \epsilon)$ expansion of the inner circle, where ϵ is the stopping tolerance (user defined parameter) and R is the radius. The set of squares is a core set.

The steps in CVM algorithm are:

Algorithm: Core Vector Machine

1 Initialize the first center of the ball, the first radius in the core set
2 If no point in the remaining points falls outside the ϵ-ball then
3 Stop
4 End If
5 Take the furthest point from the center of the current ball, add it to the Core set
7 Solve the QP problem on the points contained in the core set
8 Update the ball (center and radius)
9 Go to 2nd step.

Principal Component Analysis

Principal Components Analysis (PCA) is a statistical method for analysing the data to identify patterns and to reduce the dimensions of the dataset with minimal loss of information (Han & Kamber 2006). The preferred outcome of the PCA is to form a dataset consisting of n x d-dimensional samples onto a smaller subspace that represents the data "well". A promising application is pattern classification, to

Figure 4. Minimum enclosing ball

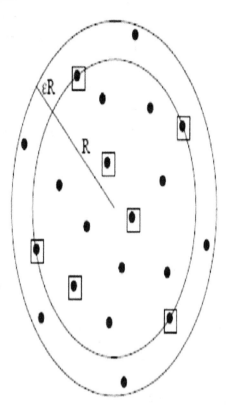

reduce the computational costs and reducing the number of dimensions of the dataset by extracting a subspace that describes the data "best". The method generates a set of variables called Principal Components (PC), which are calculated using the Eigen value decomposition of the data covariance matrix or correlation matrix.

Algorithm: Principal Component Analysis

Input: Dataset consisting of n x d-dimensional samples
    Output: **Datas**et with reduced features

1. Compute the d-dimensional mean vector
2. Calculate the covariance/correlation matrix of the data set
3. Calculate eigenvectors and corresponding eigenvalues
4. Arrange the eigenvectors by decreasing eigenvalues
5. Choose k eigenvectors with the largest eigenvalues to form a d x k eigenvector matrix

Tables 6 show the list of reduced features and the number of features selected using principal component analysis.

Table 6. Reduced features using principal component analysis

Data sets	Reduced features	# of features
DoS+10%normal	1,2,3,4,7,8,9,10,13,14,32,33	12
Probe+10%normal	1,3,4,8,9,12,13,14,15,17,18,19,24,26, 28,31,32,33,36,37	20
R2l+10%normal	1,2,3,4,6,7,18,22,23,25,26	11
U2R+10%normal	1,2,3,4,5,6,7,12,21,23	10

Hybrid CVM-CSA Model

CVM procedure is simple, and does not require sophisticated heuristics as in other decomposition methods and CSA is able to converge faster in less iteration. Thus, by combining these two recent and effective methods, it is possible to achieve better performance by combining advantages of both the methods. The CVM performs the training based on different training data sets and it finds the coreset between the entire training data points. In this model, data points from each class are chosen randomly. CVM classifier is built which locates support vectors among the chosen points. The clustering technique is needed for data selection process in CVM. Hence, the optimal cluster centroids are achieved through the cuckoo search algorithm. The points in the clusters are added to the training set and using the updated training set, CVM is trained again. The pseudocode of the hybrid approach is given below:

Algorithm: Hybrid CVM-CSA approach

Given a training data set as input;

```
Let acc be set as 0 initially
Begin
    Let acc be the accuracy rate during execution initially 0;
    While acc < ACC do                      //ACC is the accuracy rate thresh-
old
            For k = 1 . . ., n do           // n is the number of itera-
tions
                Perform training using CVM classifier
                Perform clustering using Cuckoo Search algorithm
        End
    Construct classifiers;
    Update acc
End While
End
```

Moreover, in this hybrid approach, two profiles for normal data are obtained by CVM and CSA. Hence, to reduce the number of false negatives, the data item is confirmed as normal, only when both the classifiers, classify it as normal. If both classifiers confirm that the data is abnormal, then category of the intrusion is determined by the CSA classifier. If the classified results are not consistent by the classifiers, then it is considered as a new type of intrusion in the network traffic which helps IDS to enhance the performance.

ANALYSIS ON CVM-CSA APPROACH

The experimental results of the proposed hybrid classification algorithm using PCA are depicted in Figures 5 to 8. The accuracy rate obtained by the hybrid approach using PCA technique is 99.01% and a highest accuracy (99.12%) is obtained for U2R dataset. It also indicated that CVM and CSA illustrate a competitive performance by obtaining accuracy of 98.51% and 98.26% respectively.

Figure 5. Comparison on accuracy rate of CVM-CSA

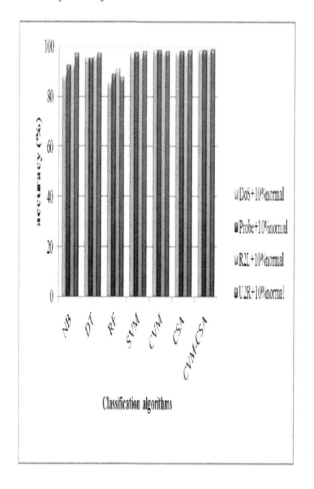

Figure 6. Comparison on detection rate of CVM-CSA

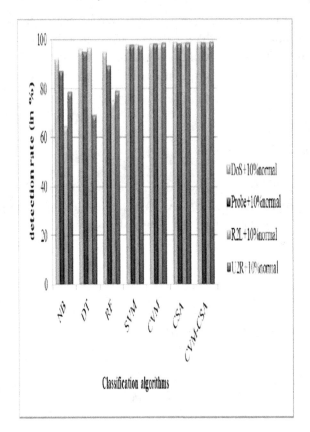

The hybrid approach, CVM-CSA using PCA obtains a detection rate of 98.76% which is comparatively higher than other methods and it is specified in Figure 6. Also the classifiers, CVM and CSA show an equivalent result (98.2% and 98.44% respectively).

The false alarm rate of the classifiers: CVM, CSA and hybrid CVM-CSA is very low and it shows a competitive performance in Figure 7. Comparatively, the false alarm rate of naïve bayes and random forest is high. It is noted from Figure 7 that, false alarm rate of the classification algorithms, CVM, CSA and CVM-CSA is very low, ranging from 0.001 to 0.003. The computation time of various classifiers is compared and is shown in Figure 8 and it indicates that the time required by CVM, CSA and hybrid CVM-CSA classifier is relatively lesser than other methods.

CONCLUSION

The major objective of this work is to provide a promising solution to address the intrusion detection problem and it focuses on classification algorithms and feature selection methods to improve the detection performance and to reduce the time required to carry out the computations for intrusion detection

Figure 7. Comparison on false alarm rate of CVM-CSA

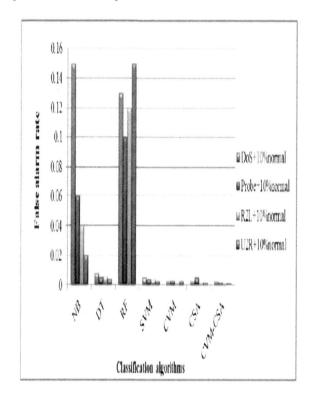

systems. To improve the accuracy rate of the detection system, this work refers predominantly on a hybrid approach using core vector machine and cuckoo search algorithm (CVM-CSA) and its performance is investigated on benchmark intrusion detection dataset, KDDCup'99 using a subset of features chosen using principal component analysis (PCA) algorithm. The proposed hybrid CVM-CSA approach using bat algorithm achieves an accuracy rate of 99.44%, detection rate of 99.85% and false alarm rate ranging from 0.001 to 0.002. Hence, the comparison of the metrics shows that the proposed hybrid algorithms provide an efficient Intrusion Detection System. Moreover, the results determine that, selecting appropriate algorithm for the intrusion detection problem depends on the working condition and the features involved. Future work can be extended using bio-inspired algorithms for feature selection and classification with real-time network datasets. The effectiveness of IDS can be still improved to handle newly rising attacks for achieving 100% detection rate. The privacy preserving Online Analytical Processing (OLAP) can be integrated with the proposed framework to enhance and improve the effectiveness and the flexibility of the IDS system.

Figure 8. Training time of classifiers

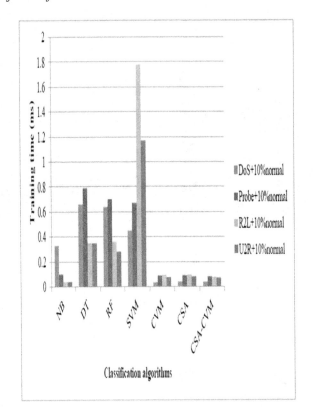

REFERENCES

Almseidin, M., Alzubi, M., Kovacs, S., & Alkasassbeh, M. (2018). Evaluation of Machine Learning Algorithms for Intrusion Detection System. In *IEEE 15th International Symposium on Intelligent Systems and Informatics* (pp.1-12). IEEE.

Amor, N. B., Benferhat, S., & Elouedi, Z. (2004). Naive bayes vs decision trees in intrusion detection systems. In *Proceedings of the 2004 ACM symposium on Applied computing* (pp. 420-424). ACM. 10.1145/967900.967989

Amudha, P., Karthik, S., & Sivakumari, S. (2015). A hybrid swarm intelligence algorithm for intrusion detection using significant features. *The Scientific World Journal*, 2015. PMID:26221625

Araújo, N., de Oliveira, R., Shinoda, A. A., & Bhargava, B. (2010). Identifying important characteristics in the KDD99 intrusion detection dataset by feature selection using a hybrid approach. In *2010 IEEE 17th International Conference on Telecommunications (ICT),* (pp. 552-558). IEEE. 10.1109/ICTEL.2010.5478852

Bache, K., & Lichman, M. (2013). *UCI Machine Learning Repository*. Irvine, CA: University of California, School of Information and Computer Science. Retrieved from http://archive. ics. uci. edu/ml

Beni, G., & Wang, J. (1993). Swarm intelligence in cellular robotic systems. In *Robots and Biological Systems: Towards a New Bionics?* (pp. 703–712). Berlin, Germany: Springer. doi:10.1007/978-3-642-58069-7_38

Bouzida, Y., & Cuppens, F. (2006, September). Neural networks vs. decision trees for intrusion detection. In *IEEE/IST Workshop on Monitoring, Attack Detection and Mitigation (MonAM)* (pp. 81-88). IEEE.

Cortes, C., & Vapnik, V. (1995). Support-vector networks. *Machine Learning, 20*(3), 273–297. doi:10.1007/BF00994018

Data Mining with Open Source Machine Learning. (n.d.). Available from www.cs.waikato.ac.nz/ml/weka/

Debar, H. (2000). An introduction to intrusion-detection systems. *Proceedings of Connect, 2000.*

Denning, D. E. (1987). An intrusion-detection model. *IEEE Transactions on Software Engineering, SE-13*(2), 222–232. doi:10.1109/TSE.1987.232894

Diamantidis, N. A., Karlis, D., & Giakoumakis, E. A. (2000). Unsupervised stratification of cross-validation for accuracy estimation. *Artificial Intelligence, 116*(1-2), 1–16. doi:10.1016/S0004-3702(99)00094-6

Dokas, P., Ertoz, L., Kumar, V., Lazarevic, A., Srivastava, J., & Tan, P. N. (2002, November). Data mining for network intrusion detection. In *Proc. NSF Workshop on Next Generation Data Mining* (pp. 21-30). Academic Press.

Eesa, A. S., Orman, Z., & Brifcani, A. M. A. (2015). A new feature selection model based on ID3 and Bees algorithm for intrusion detection system. *Turkish Journal of Electrical Engineering and Computer Sciences, 23*(2), 615–622. doi:10.3906/elk-1302-53

Endler, D. (1998, December). Intrusion detection. Applying machine learning to Solaris audit data. In *Proceedings of the 14th Annual Computer Security Applications Conference, 1998* (pp. 268-279). IEEE.

Freitas, A. A. (2003). A survey of evolutionary algorithms for data mining and knowledge discovery. In *Advances in evolutionary computing* (pp. 819–845). Berlin, Germany: Springer. doi:10.1007/978-3-642-18965-4_33

Gan, X. S., Duanmu, J. S., Wang, J. F., & Cong, W. (2013). Anomaly intrusion detection based on PLS feature extraction and core vector machine. *Knowledge-Based Systems, 40*, 1–6. doi:10.1016/j.knosys.2012.09.004

Gandomi, A. H., Yang, X. S., & Alavi, A. H. (2013). Cuckoo search algorithm: A metaheuristic approach to solve structural optimization problems. *Engineering with Computers, 29*(1), 17–35. doi:10.100700366-011-0241-y

Gholipour Goodarzi, B., Jazayeri, H., & Fateri, S. (2014). Intrusion detection system in computer network using hybrid algorithms (SVM and ABC). *Journal of Advances in Computer Research, 5*(4), 43–52.

Grosan, C., Abraham, A., & Chis, M. (2006). Swarm intelligence in data mining. In *Swarm Intelligence in Data Mining* (pp. 1–20). Berlin, Germany: Springer. doi:10.1007/978-3-540-34956-3_1

Hajimirzaei, B., & Navimipour, N. J. (2019). Intrusion detection for cloud computing using neural networks and artificial bee colony optimization algorithm. *ICT Express*, *5*(1), 56–59. doi:10.1016/j.icte.2018.01.014

Han, J., Pei, J., & Kamber, M. (2012). Data mining: concepts and techniques. Amsterdam, The Netherlands: Elsevier.

Biswas, S. K. (2018). Intrusion Detection Using Machine Learning: A Comparison Study. *International Journal of Pure and Applied Mathematics*, *118*(19), 101–114.

Joshi, S. A., & Pimprale, V. S. (2013). Network Intrusion Detection System (NIDS) based on data mining. *International Journal of Engineering Science and Innovative Technology*, *2*(1), 95–98.

Kantardzic, M. (2011). *Data mining: concepts, models, methods, and algorithms*. Hoboken, NJ: John Wiley & Sons. doi:10.1002/9781118029145

Kira, K., & Rendell, L. A. (1992, July). The feature selection problem: Traditional methods and a new algorithm. In AAA (vol. 2, pp. 129-134). Academic Press.

Kohavi, R., & Quinlan, J. R. (2002, January). Data mining tasks and methods: Classification: decision-tree discovery. In Handbook of data mining and knowledge discovery (pp. 267-276). Oxford, UK: Oxford University Press.

Laftah Al-Yaseen, W., Ali Othman, Z., & Ahmad Nazri, M. Z. (2015). Hybrid Modified-Means with C4. 5 for Intrusion Detection Systems in Multiagent Systems. *The Scientific World Journal*, *2015*, 1–14. doi:10.1155/2015/294761 PMID:26161437

Lee, C.-H., Su, Y.-Y., Lin, Y.-C., & Lee, S.-J. (2017). Machine learning based network intrusion detection. *2nd IEEE International Conference on Computational Intelligence and Applications*. doi:10.1109/CIAPP.2017.8167184

Li, X., & Yin, M. (2015). Modified cuckoo search algorithm with self-adaptive parameter method. *Information Sciences*, *298*, 80–97. doi:10.1016/j.ins.2014.11.042

Li, Y., & Wang, Y. (2012). A misuse intrusion detection model based on hybrid classifier algorithm. *International Journal of Digital Content Technology and its Applications, 6*(5).

Lichman, M. (2013). *UCI Machine Learning Repository*. Irvine, CA: University of California, School of Information and Computer Science.

Nguyen, H. A., & Choi, D. (2008, October). Application of data mining to network intrusion detection: classifier selection model. In *Asia-Pacific Network Operations and Management Symposium* (pp. 399-408). Berlin, Germany: Springer. 10.1007/978-3-540-88623-5_41

Ong, P. (2014). Adaptive cuckoo search algorithm for unconstrained optimization. *The Scientific World Journal*, 2014. PMID:25298971

Othman, S. M., Fadl, M. B. A., Alsohybe, N. T., & Al Hashida, A. Y. (2018). Intrusion detection model using machine learning algorithm on Big Data environment. *Journal of Big Data*, *5*(34).

Pengyuan, P. (2017). Studies on the Network Anomaly Intrusion Detection of a Fish Swarm Optimization Algorithm Based on Neural Network. *Revista de la Facultad de Ingeniería U.C.V., 32*(13), 585-589.

Panda, M., & Patra, M. R. (2007). Network intrusion detection using naive Bayes. *International Journal of Computer Science and Network Security, 7*(12), 258-263.

Peng, K., Leung, V. C., & Huang, Q. (2018). Clustering approach based on mini batch K-means for intrusion detection system over Big Data. *IEEE Access: Practical Innovations, Open Solutions.*

Refaeilzadeh, P., Tang, L., & Liu, H. (2009). Cross-validation. In *Encyclopedia of database systems* (pp. 532–538). Boston, MA: Springer.

Sabhnani, M., & Serpen, G. (2003). *Application of Machine Learning Algorithms to KDD Intrusion Detection Dataset within Misuse Detection Context.* MLMTA.

Shelke, M. P. K., Sontakke, M. S., & Gawande, A. D. (2012). Intrusion detection system for cloud computing. *International Journal of Scientific & Technology Research, 1*(4), 67–71.

Shen, X. J., Wang, L., & Han, D. J. (2016). Application of artificial bee colony optimized BP neural network in intrusion detection. *Computer Engineering, 42*(2), 190–194.

Shrivastava, A., Baghel, M., & Gupta, H. (2013). A Novel Hybrid Feature Selection and Intrusion Detection Based on PCNN and Support Vector Machine. *International Journal of Computer Technology and Applications., 4*(6), 922–927.

Tchakoucht, T. A., & Ezziyyani, M. (2018). Building a fast intrusion detection system for high-speed networks: Probe and DoS attacks detection. *Procedia Computer Science, 127*, 521–530. doi:10.1016/j.procs.2018.01.151

Tsang, I. W., Kwok, J. T., & Cheung, P. M. (2005). Core vector machines: Fast SVM training on very large data sets. *Journal of Machine Learning Research, 6*(Apr), 363–392.

UCI Machine Learning Archive. (2009). Available from http://www.kdd.ics.uci.edu/databases/kddcup99/task.html

Vardhini, K., & Sitamahalakshmi, T. (2017). Enhanced Intrusion Detection System Using Data Reduction: An Ant Colony Optimization Approach. International. *Journal of Applied Engineering Research, 12*(9), 1844–1847.

Witten, I. H., Frank, E., Hall, M. A., & Pal, C. J. (2016). *Data Mining: Practical machine learning tools and techniques.* Burlington, MA: Morgan Kaufmann.

Yang, X. S., & Deb, S. (2009, December). Cuckoo search via Lévy flights. In *World Congress on Nature & Biologically Inspired Computing, 2009. NaBIC 2009* (pp. 210-214). IEEE.

Zhu, X. H. (2017). Application of artificial neural network based on artificial fish swarm algorithm in network intrusion detection. *Modern Electronic Technology, 40*(1), 80-82.

Chapter 9

A Hybrid Approach to Detect the Malicious Applications in Android–Based Smartphones Using Deep Learning

Manokaran Newlin Rajkumar
Anna University Coimbatore, India

Varadhan Venkatesa Kumar
Anna University Coimbatore, India

Ramachandhiran Vijayabhasker
Anna University Coimbatore, India

ABSTRACT

This modern era of technological advancements facilitates the people to possess high-end smart phones with incredible features. With the increase in the number of mobile applications, we are witnessing the humongous increase in the malicious applications. Since most of the Android applications are available open source and used frequently in the smart phones, they are more vulnerable. Statistical and dynamical-based malware detection approaches are available to verify whether the mobile application is a genuine one, but only to a certain extent, as the level of mobile application scanning done by the said approaches are in general routine or a common, pre-specified pattern using the structure of control flow, information flow, API call, etc. A hybrid method based on deep learning methodology is proposed to identify the malicious applications in Android-based smart phones in this chapter, which embeds the possible merits of both the statistical-based malware detection approaches and dynamical-based malware detection approaches and minimizes the demerits of them.

DOI: 10.4018/978-1-5225-9611-0.ch009

INTRODUCTION

Revolution of Smart Phones and Its Features

With the growing pace of innovative development, Smartphones have changed into the inevitable gadget of our everyday life. Smartphones are cell phones which are developed with highly advanced technologies that makes them to function more like a PC. In the past, mobile phones were used for making phone calls and sending SMS. Now, Smartphones offers much more services. They are fully facilitated to serve like a computer that is compact enough to be in the pocket. Smartphones can make voice or video calls, provide access to the internet and browse the web, take photos, upload data to the web, Navigational information can be retrieved with GPS if the phone has GPS built-in, Play back music and video stored on the phone or from the internet, store and manage your contacts and appointments, send emails, Play games, run new applications and games downloaded from the internet. The Operating System is the key feature of the smart phones that enables it to provide all expected sophistications. ("Introduction to Smart Phones," 2008). There are number of mobile Operating systems like Symbian OS, Android OS, Apple iOS, Windows OS, Blackberry OS, BADA, Maemo, MeeGo, Palm OS, Open WebOS, verdict and even more.Android, the popular smart phone OS was introduced by Google in 2008. The popularity of Android OS is because of its advanced and attractive features. The key features includes Messaging, Auto Correction and Dictionary, Web browser, Voice-based features, Multi-touch, Multitasking, Screen capture, TV recording, Video calling, Multiple language support, Android supports multiple languages, Accessibility, Bluetooth Connectivity, Tethering, various media support, Streaming media support, External storage, Hardware support, Java support, Handset layouts, Native Apps, Instant Apps. (Lekies, 2015).

The more advanced features renders more sophistication such as Battery Saver, text to speech, mobile remote which controls other devices, Screen Magnification, Guest mode access for the other users like password protected PCs, Controlling using facial movements, sharing internet access using hotspot access, fast switching between apps, Screen pinning, Dual chrome viewing options, Do not Disturb rules for having smoother meeting sessions, Notification channels for notifying the received mails, messages, updates etc, Locking the apps in foreground, One swipe for quick settings, Unlocking the phones with Bluetooth device, Zoom in with one finger, rotating maps with two fingers, taking pctures with volume rocker, actions with long press etc. (Hersey, 2017). The list extends with a numerous number of features which are very useful to the users and provides a highly sophisticated technical service anywhere in the world that one can do maximum computer oriented needs just by carrying a Smartphone. The Ability of the android OS are not restricted and are not the destiny as it is an open source and more new features will keep emerging to make it more powerful and more useful.

MOBILE APPS

Mobile phones became a part of our routine life and people feel uncomfortable to lead a normal day without a mobile. Earlier mobile phones had only few restricted functions that enabled people to make calls and send text messages. The later generation mobile phones are multifunctional that enables usage of internet, browsing, sending emails, accessing books online, sending medias over internet, playing games etc. This was possible with the help of mobile application. (Rashedul & Rofiqul, 2010). A Mobile application is shortly referred as mobile App, which is a software application developed to run in a mobile device. This doesn't means mobile apps are for smart phones alone. ("Protection form Malware," 2009). The imprint of mobile apps came along with mobile devices which provided functions like calculator, alarm manager, ringtone maker and etc. Now it became more popular as the functional fields are vast and are more useful to the user. There are a number of operating system for smartphones developed by various manufacturers for their own manufacturing and collaborative manufacturing like Symbian OS, Android OS, Mac iOS, Windows OS, Blackberry OS etc.

All the Operating systems allows the third party software i.e. Mobile Apps unlike the conventional standard mobile phones as the mobile users expect more customized functionalities, the app developer needs freedom to design more powerful and reachable applications and also the service providers want to provide more value added services on the demand to the users. ("Android OS," 2008). Mobile apps are classified as Native Apps (developed for targeted platform), Hybrid apps (web based apps that can act as native apps) and Web-based apps(developed to work in the presence of strong internet). ("Malware," 2006). Development of mobile apps considers various factors like platforms, device hardware specifications and configurations, IDEs and emulators for testing, User Interface requirements, back-end support that facilitates data routing, security, authentication, authorization, working off-line, and service orchestration, and middleware needs also. ("How do APIs work," 2016). Distribution of apps to the users is done through app stores like google play store, App Store, Microsoft Store, Amazon Appstore, Samsung Apps, mi store, blackberry world etc. ("Malicious Code," 2009). There are a numerous number of mobile application under various categories like education, entertainment, games, mobile tools etc. a few examples are facebook, skype, line for communication, BYJU's, Elevate for education, camscanner, QR code reader, digital locker, ringtone maker, WPS office, Foxit reader, Navigator etc are used as effective tools. Flipkart, Amazon etc for shopping. ("Features of Android OS," 2008). Apps like Raksha, red eye, Kavalan are used for individual safety. There are a hundreds of gaming apps like PUBG, racer, word finder, candy crush etc which are extreme time killers. ("Malware Detection," 2013). Still the various apps are emerging to provide a enriched mobile usage to the customer.(Salama & Bach, 2013).

MALWARE APPS: BACKGROUND STUDY

Zheng, Lui, & Sun (2013) explained about the impact of Malware and the methods used for analyzing it. Based on their study, Malware is the short form of Malicious Software that gets installed into our system without our consent and causes damage to the system, server, or the network. It is a spyware. Smartphones usage is growing up progressively and are more innovatively propelled, making them focuses for advanced lawbreakers who try to plant noxious programming, Trojans, or infections onto your cell phones. (Malware Identification, 2009). Smartphone clients are at the most serious hazard contrasted with different suppliers like Apple and have as of late been the subject of advanced assaults. For the most part, any information transmission and correspondence channel can fill in as an assault and malware dispersion vector. ("Advanced Persistent Threat," 2019). Channels which are not implied for transmitting programming may at present be taken control of by run of the mill strategies for expecting command over any application's or administration's control stream because of incorrect programming. (Clark, 2009). These vectors incorporate USB, bluetooth, and NFC associations, standardized identifications, QR codes, unbound remote associations which can be misused to infuse information, incorrect GSM/UMTS/LTE radio bundle taking care of, and some more. Regular correspondence channels which are intended to convey programming are the official Google Play Store and outsider application markets.

Rooting a process of making the root account on their phone always accessible where root access is normally not given to for endusers or enduser software. In order to grant root access to apps, this utility is often installed on rooted devices which can be used by malware, which at that point does never again need to run benefit acceleration abuses alone to obtain root benefits. ("Mobile Security Threats," 2010).

Blasing, Schmidt, Batyuk, Albayrak, & Camtepe (2010) explained the basic principles of Malware and the detection of it. In this manner, establishing one's own gadget, much the same as utilizing outsider application markets, can present higher dangers. Similar to this connecting with cross platforms may be taken as path of spreading malware. ("Study of Malware," (2009). A procedure progressively sent by malware because of its favorable circumstances in identification avoidance is the dynamic downloading of code. There are a numerous number of malware application flows in the internet. ("Android Malware," 2008). AccuTrack is an application turns an Android Smartphone into a GPS tracker. ("Malicious Mobile Apps," 2009). Ackposts is a Trojan that steals contact information from the compromised device and uploads them to a remote server. Acnetdoor is opens a backdoor on the infected device and sends the IP address to aremote server. Adsms is a Trojan type malware which is allowed to send SMS messages. The distribution channel is through a SMS message containing the download link. ("Mobile Malware Detection," 2015).

BankBot is a malware tries to steal users' confidential information and money from bank andmobile accounts associated with infected devices. Like this there a number of malwares DroidKungFu, plankton, Droid Dream, Android. Pjapps, Hong TouTou, Geinimi, scavir, Selfmit, Rufraud, Saiva, Spambot. Each have different vulnerabilities. Effective malware detection software have to be installed to track and remove the harmful infections at the earliest. Malware is a harmful application code which can damage System OS and track personal information from the system. It is created by attackers in any language. ("Dynamic Malware Detection," 2014). As it seems like a normal program code, differentiation is difficult. Malicious software, malcode, malicious code are the other names. Bots, viruses, adware, bugs, rootkits, Trojan horses, spyware and worms are different types of malwares with different characteristics. Bots can be operated from a remote system to control the infected system. Viruses are infectious code that spread from one system to other when get connected by some means. Adware is a malware which are spreads through ads shown in the internet. Bug is compliable source code with errors created by programmers by mistake. Rootkit accesses remote computers. Trojan Horses steals the financial information and creates backdoor access to malicious owners. Spyware spies the activities of the user without their knowledge. Worms runs independently and gets propagated. The malware existence can be identified by monitoring certain activities like seeing unwanted ads in the sites, changes in the settings of the system, unwanted components in the browsers, reduction in the system speed, unnecessary modification in file system, behavioral changes in the system, emails send automatically without the knowledge of the users. Signature based technique, Anomaly based technique, Emulation based technique, Obfuscation based technique, Heuristics based technique, CBR based technique, Bioinformatics based technique, KNN algorithm technique are detection techniques used to find malwares. There are three basic types in malware signature like basic(Entry point of program), polymorphic(changes encrypted code by adding an additional component) and metamorphic(capable of changing its code). This is based on the signature of the malware i.e. sequence of bytes in the code. Signature based technique is used to find such malwares. Anomaly based detection Technique is used to find the malware by observing any abnormal activity that occurs in the program it can be arise. Emulation based detection Technique is used to detect the polymorphic malware as well as metamorphic malware. Heuristics based detection technique has 2 approaches: static approach (Pattern matching) and dynamic approach(vulnerable exe files). Obfuscation

Technique is used as a dead code which transforms the functionality of malware. The bioinformatics techniques effectively used to find Metamorphic malware which mutates its code on each replication. Case Based Reasoning (CBR) Technique uses knowledge reuse technique to find the malwares. All the techniques finds the existence of malware by pattern matching with previously detected patterns.

PATTERN RECOGNITION

A Pattern is an object or data or an event. Pattern recognition is an automated algorithm to find the common patterns and regularities in objects. (Zhang, 2015). It is a sub part of machine learning. The recognition may be supervised or unsupervised. Krizhevsky & Hinton (2009) explained the principles of identifying the layers of pattern from tiny images. In supervised recognition the pre found patterns may be checked whereas in unsupervised patterns the new data patterns may be recorded. ("Pattern Recognition," 2016). Pattern recognition is concentrated about the structure and improvement of frameworks that perceive patterns in information. ("Introduction to Pattern recognition system," 2012). The reason for a pattern recognition program is to dissect a scene in reality and to touch base at a portrayal of the scene which is valuable for the achievement of some errand. This present reality perceptions are assembled through sensors and pattern recognition framework characterizes or portrays these perceptions. A feature extraction procedure processes numeric or representative data from these perceptions. These removed highlights are then characterized or portrayed utilizing a classifier. The procedure utilized for pattern recognition comprises of numerous systems that guarantee proficient portrayal of the patterns. (Goyal–He et.al, 2017).

Pattern recognition involves two phases where the first phase is training or learning the pattern and the second phase involves detection/ classification. ("Pattern Recognition: An Overview," 2012). The pattern recognition generally follows the approaches like Template matching (comparison with expected prototype), Statistical classification(classification is based on statistical model generated by considering the pattern as a random variable), Syntactic matching(primitives and their relationship representation) and Neural networks (parametric models) to identify the pattern. Feature extraction is the process in which the inputs are selected for the pattern recognition system. Pattern recognition algorithms depends on the factors like type of label output, supervised or unsupervised, and statistical or non-statistical in nature. Statistical algorithms are dub classified into generative or discriminative. ("Android App," 2008), A number of predefined algorithms like clustering algorithms, Ensemble algorithms, Bayesian networks, Markov random fields, Multilinear subspace learning algorithms regression algorithms are used to improve the performance (Shams, Platania, Lee & Park 2017). The applications of the pattern recognition are computer aided Diagnosis in medical sciences speech recognition, email categorization (e.g., spam/ non-spam email messages), the automatic recognition of handwritten postal codes on postal envelopes, automatic human faces recognition from images, or handwriting image extraction from medical forms, OCR recognition and more. (Coleman-Zaharia et.al, 2017). In its broadest sense pattern recognition is the core of all logical request, including understanding ourselves and this present reality around us. Furthermore, the creating of pattern recognition is expanding quick, the related fields and the use of pattern recognition ended up more and more extensive (He, Zhang, Ren & Sun, 2016).

APPLICATION PROGRAMMING INTERFACE (API) CALLS

API (Application Programming Interface) is a software that enables two applications to communicate to each other.API sends the request to the server and retrieves the response back.API helps in developing a computer program, by giving all the basic building blocks that can be combined by the programmer. ("API Calls," (2016). There are a numerous types of APIs like Webservice API(services through the World Wide Web), WebSocket API, Library based API(reference a library of code and use the functions/ routines from that library to perform actions and exchange information), class based API(functionality organized around classes), OS functions and routines, object remoting API, Hardware API(access the hardware level of devices), etc. Li *et al.* (2015) explained the purpose of API calls and their importance. They are used to perform specific operations that your client applications can request at runtime to do tasks.API Calls have the characteristics like Service Requests and Responses, Synchronous and Committed Automatically Versus Rollback on Error.

API needs following factors to be favour to provide a hassle free service that the applications has to support API access, permission based login for users, permission to share the data externally, ID based access to provide referential integrity.API also provides error handling mechanism. API sends a SOAP fault message with an associated Exception Code when errors like badly formed messages, failed authentication, or similar problems occurs. For query related problems API returns error (Carlini & Wagner, 2017). The API call is made by considering the following parameters API end point(unique URL that contains the objects), Method(functions that perform corresponding operations), Rest Endpoint(endpoint for all the API calls), Headers(information about variables in the request), Params(user specifications), Data(Payload). these parameters can vary depending on call required. The main advantages of API are Internet-based connectivity, Two-way Communication, reliable transactions sets, user-friendly experiences, evolving functionality improves the performance. The disadvantages of API are implementation cost and time, maintenance support, extensive programming knowledge needed and Security concern APIs. The main benefits of API are Efficiency (data can be distributed between different systems), Wider Reach, Automation (machine to machine interaction) and Partnership. (Tamada, Okamoto, Nakamura, Monden & Matsumoto, 2007).

DEEP LEARNING

Deep Learning, is a part of Machine Learning, utilizes calculations to process information and mirror the reasoning procedure, or to create deliberations. Wu, Liu, Pu & Wei (2018) presented a general overview of Deep Learning Frameworks. Deep Learning (DL) utilizes layers of algorithms to process information, comprehend human discourse, and outwardly perceive objects. ("Deep learning," 2009). Data is gone through each layer, with the yield of the past layer giving contribution to the following layer. The primary layer in a system is known as the input layer, while the last is called a output layer. ("Applications of Deep Learning," 2016). Every one of the layers between the two are alluded to as concealed layers. Each layer is ordinarily a straightforward, uniform calculation containing one sort of enactment work. Learning can be supervised, semi-supervised or unsupervised (Chetlur-Shelhamer et.al, 2014). Artificial neural networks are the base for Deep learning models. In deep learning, the inputs in each layer turned into a abstract and composite representation. For example, image recognition application, the inputs are pixels. The primary layer abstracts the pixels and encodes edges. The next layer encodes the arrangements of edges and likewise follows the constitutive layers. The name deep learning is coined to represent deep into the layers the data is being processed (Ioffe & Szegedy 2015). Credit Assignment path (CAP) depth describes the connections from input layer to Output layer. The depth of the CAP for a feed forward network is number of hidden layers plus one. Whereas in a recurrent neural network the same is unlimited as it may pass through the same layer more than once. Deep models with CAP > 2 are capable of extracting better features. Therefore, it is understood that more number of layers and features are learned deeply. (Wei – Wu et.al, 2018).

Deep learning unravels these reflections and choose which highlights enhance execution (Xu, Shi & Chu, 2017). For supervised learning tasks, deep learning methods obviate feature engineering, by translating the data into compact intermediate representations akin to principal components, and derive layered structures that remove redundancy in representation. For Supervised learning assignments, profound learning techniques block include building, by making an interpretation of the information into reduced middle portrayals much the same as important parts, and determine layered structures that expel repetition in portrayal. (Madry, Makelov, Schmidt, Tsipras, & Vladu, 2017).

Unsupervised learning tasks can also use deep learning algorithms as raw data are more than identified data. The main challenges in deep learning are overfitting and time taken for data computation. Deep Learning is still evolving as processing of Big Data and the evolution of Artificial Intelligence are both dependent on it. The main advantages of deep learning are More consistent, Designed for hard-to-solve applications, Requires less data and computing power, More reliable, Easier to configure, Simple training interface, Faster, Tolerates variations, Global support. (Bahrampour, Ramakrishnan, Schott & Shah, 2015). There are a numerous number of application for deep learning for example Colorization of Black and White Images, Voice automated translations, Adding Sounds to Silent Movies, Self-driving cars, Automatic Machine Translation, Object Classification in Photographs, Automatic Handwriting Generation, Character Text Generation, Advertising, Image Caption Generation, Predicting earth quakes, Automatic Game Playing. (Szegedy – Fergus et.al., 2013)

BUSTER SANDBOX ANALYZER

Buster Sandbox Analyzer is a software tool that has been intended to examine the behavior of processes and its reflection on the system and then checks for suspicious malware. The process may make changes the file system, registry and port. By monitoring the changes the necessary information are collected to calculate the "risk" of a portion of the change made by sandboxed applications. Buster Sandbox Analyzer is an efficient tool which is capable of detecting changes made in the file system such as creation, modification and deletion of files and detects the modification made in registry, network connections and also has lots of facilities to ease the analysis. The analysis can be either manual or automatic; It can perform multiple tests simultaneously. This tool also monitors the actions like keyboard logging; sudden end of the Windows session, loading a driver, starting a service, connecting to Internet, etc. when such actions are happening in unexpected time, the software will evaluate the reason for malfunctioning. ("Buster Sandbox Analyzer," 2011).

The main advantage of the Buster Sandbox Analyzer is that can run in any system along with installed sandboxie. The software can be used as web based service also which requires internet connection whereas direct software doesn't needs internet connection. It is capable of analysing all types of executable files. The other advantage is that the other required accomplishment software can be added just by copying or installing. Buster Sandbox Analyzer also allows the program to do the required actions. It provides detailed information to the user. Buster Sandbox Analyzer is free software which works well with paid and licensed Sandboxie. Buster Sandbox Analyzer can be customized while configuration. Buster Sandbox Analyzer for Windows version is independent of platforms. It can analyse process of batch of files in automatic mode. It can be incorporated with automatic mode that enables on demand service from command line. It can analyse multiple samples simultaneously. It can also evaluate single or list of URLs. The switch time over between consecutive process is none. It is very fast and light software. It is able to analyse 64 bit applications also. The main demerit of the software is that it cannot watch all system changes performed by programs which install a driver. Codes running out of the sandbox cannot be analysed. On automated mode Buster Sandbox Analyzer will neglect to dissect legitimately a few examples requiring human mediation to be introduced. The limitations of software are driver installation are not allowed by sandboxie and system hooks, Code injection may not work in certain conditions. Sandboxie fails to sandbox compressed executable files. Buster Sandbox Analyzer is a valuable, adaptable and useful asset proposed for individuals that need to know whether a program has a malware conduct or for individuals that need to have a quick and general thought of what a malware does. A major preferred standpoint of Buster Sandbox Analyzer contrasted with different frameworks doing likewise undertaking is that BSA can be better, increasingly exact and report pretty much data depending of the client, in the mean time different analyzers will be as great or as terrible as their creators did it.

SCOPE OF BUSTER SANDBOX ANALYZER

Buster Sandbox Analyzer will run on any computer where Sandboxie is installed and working. An Internet connection is not required but it is recommended. Web-based malware analyzers require an Internet connection to be able to submit the sample to analyze and retrieve analysis results. Buster Sandbox Analyzer will be able to analyze any kind of file type (EXE, BAT, VBS, PDF, XLS, DOC, ...). If the file can be executed Buster Sandbox Analyzer will be able to analyze it. Usually malware analyzers just process PE files (Win32 executables). With Buster Sandbox Analyzer if a library (DLL, OCX, ...) or other software is required you can accomplish the requirement just copying or installing whatever it´s necessary to get the application working properly. Some other malware analyzers just run a program at a time. If a library or anything else is required the analysis will fail and there is nothing could be done about this. With Buster Sandbox Analyzer if a program requires to click any button to continue or whatever, e.g. installations and setups, the user will be able to do it. Other malware analyzers are "automatic" (unattended) and can only analyze programs that perform actions directly, without human intervention. The analysis will stop if the program waits for the user to click "Next" or click in "Accept the agreement" checkbox e.g. Buster Sandbox Analyzer shows information that can be clearly understood even by non advanced users. Other malware analyzers usually show a big amount of information when the analysis finishes.

A never ending list of used APIs can be a scaring thing for non advanced users and probably they will not be able to understand what they are seeing. Web-based malware analyzers are free of charge but the service can be discontinued at any time. Norman Sandbox, GFI Sandbox or ValidEDGE are really expensive. Buster Sandbox Analyzer can be configured. The user can define what file types to watch, what registry entries must be considered as AutoStart locations, etc. The user can configure BSA to save network traffic. Other malware analyzers can not be configured by the user. With Buster Sandbox Analyzer advanced users can enhance the analysis running additional software inside the sandbox to retrieve more information, like Mark Russinovich´s Process Monitor, Process Explorer, etc. In other malware analyzers the analysis can not be improved at all.

Buster Sandbox Analyzer is Windows version independant. It can be used in Windows 2000, Windows XP, Windows Vista, Windows 7 or Windows 8. Other malware analyzer will analyze the malware only under Windows XP, Windows Vista or Windows 7. If the malware is version dependant or crashes on a specified operating system this will be a problem. Buster Sandbox Analyzer can be configured to work in automatic mode, therefore it can process a batch of files. Other malware analyzers, like online analyzers, don´t analyze batch of files. Buster Sandbox Analyzer can run on-demand in automatic mode from command line. That means it can be incorporated to batch processes. Other malware analyzer can not work in this way. Buster Sandbox Analyzer can automate the execution of most setups when running in automatic mode. Other malware analyzers will be unable to analyze properly setups because they stop when the setup requests the user to press "Next" or other button. Buster Sandbox Analyzer is a Windows native software, therefore it´s the right solution for analyzing Windows programs. Other malware analyzers are Linux based applications, therefore Windows support must be emulated. In that cases Windows compatilibitycan not be garanteeed to 100%, so certain files may fail to be analyzed properly.

Buster Sandbox Analyzer can analyze multiple samples at the same time. Other malware analyzers can only process one sample at a time. Buster Sandbox Analyzer can be translated to the user's language and the user can do it by his own. Other malware analyzers only support one language. Buster Sandbox Analyze can analyze a single URL or a list of them loaded from a file in automatic mode. Other malware analyzer does not support analyzing URLs. With Buster Sandbox Analyzer the required time between an analysis and the next one is near to none. Other malware analyzers must shutdown the virtual machine, restore the snapshot, etc., which are time and resource consuming tasks. Sandboxie, the framework used by Buster Sandbox Analyzer to perform malware analysis, is very fast and light, so it almost does not take system resources. Other malware analyzers use as framework for malware analysis a virtual machine like VirtualBox, VMWare, …, which take many system resources and it is slow. Buster Sandbox Analyzer is able to analyze 64-bit applications. Other malware analyzers only analyze 32-bit applications. ("Scope of Buster Sandbox Analyzer," 2011).

TECHNIQUES FOR MALWARE DETECTION

Statistical Method

Basic schemes in Malware Detection were clearly explained by Amin *et al.* (2016). Two novel approaches were discussed. In this method before running the source code it is dissembled and analyzed for the possibilities of malware existence. This method is classified as Signature Based Detection, Permission Based Detection, Byte code Analysis, Collaborative Malware Detection and Drebin Method of Malware Detection. Moreover, Baskaran & Ralescu (2016) explained some schemes as a general study, related to the detection of Malware.

Merits

1. Malwares at opcode level could be detected
2. Malwares generated by Data Obfuscation and Repackaging could be identified.
3. Accuracy
4. Scalable
5. Lightweight
6. Dynamic simulation is not needed
7. API calls of sensitive nature could be identified easily
8. Performing Data flow analysis is easier
9. Detection of repackaged apps is done at ease
10. Security at the time of installation is achieved
11. Notification about the threat to the user instantly
12. Variety of classifiers are used to classify the apps
13. Downloaded apps could be checked for authenticity.

Demerits

1. Availability of signature databases is inadequate
2. Comparatively false rates are high
3. Handling Complex API calls of reflective nature is not possible
4. Entire codes are not scrutinized
5. When a malware is identified it is not possible to do second screening without using Machine Learning or Deep Learning techniques.
6. Higher rates of False positive
7. Not easy to classify the threats of all nature
8. Sometimes the genuine apps could be considered as malicious apps.
9. Detection of adware samples is not easy
10. Malwares using reflection leaking the data could not be identified.
11. Concurrency handling is not possible directly.
12. Data based are limited
13. Users should check the warning messages manually and periodically.
14. Proper use of Data obfuscation could possible break this method.
15. Mimicry attacks and poisoning attacks could not be identified as the analysis is not dynamic

Dynamic Method In this method, run time detection of malwares and their variants could be done effectively. This method is classified as Anomaly Based Detection, Taint analysis and Emulation Based Detection.

Merits

1. Detection of evolving malwares and their features is possible
2. Since the analysis is done in real time tracking of data from different sources could be done easily.
3. Data leakage could be identified at ease.

4. Supervising the entire Operating system is possible.
5. (v) Attacks based on certain privileges could be identified.
6. (vi) Data Obfuscation could be handled in an easier mode.
7. (vii) Could automatically detect the Malicious app.

Demerits

- If many API calls are invoked simultaneously then it is difficult to be handled.
- Issues arising due to the drainage of batteries is possible.
- While detecting evolving malware the detection time could be comparatively higher.
- Track of the Data Flow and its control is not maintained in this method.
- Coverage of code is shortened.
- When the code loading is dynamic in some cases the detection is not possible.
- Properties of user reflection could not be identified.
- Malwares which are transformational in nature could not be detected.
- Malware identification accuracy could be minimized when some benign features are included.
- Malware identification accuracy entirely depends on the availability of training data and its reliability.

PROPOSED SYSTEM

Objective

1. Combining the Merits and Demerits of Statistical Method and Dynamic Method thereby acquiring the best features of both the methods and provide an Enhanced version of the Malware Detection Methods
2. Providing a robust solution in terms of usage, a user-friendly mechanism.

Liu, Li, & Chen (2016) presented a Highly efficient Hybrid scheme for detecting Malware Applications. Understanding the Merits and Demerits of both the methods, a Hybrid Architecture is proposed (in Fig.1) which tries to embed the Merits of both the methods and possibly eliminate the Demerits. Both Deep learning and usage of Busty Sandbox Analyzer tool was the prime combination in this proposed work. In this method previous Malware Application patterns and their features of them are learnt based on API calls and gathered using Deep Learning, and based on those patterns a data set is formed. This data set is compared with the upcoming Malware Application's patterns using a pattern recognition algorithm and based on the outcome of the comparison, the Malware Application could be judged for its reliability. The pattern recognition algorithm could be explored and modified as per the requirements of the administrator to defend the network from the timely intrusions by Malicious users. In the proposed Hybrid Architecture, ptrace is included, which is an effective tool in linux operating system, which helps to capture and record API calls. Along with function, this tool checks all the calls which are running already with the process ID. Every process posses its own process id. In order to obtain this ID an application should be launched. Fastboost tool is a powerful command line tool which helps to communicate with an android device. This tool is used to start an android application based on the name of the package on the app. When the ID of an app is identified, the app could be started using Busty Sandbox Analyzer (BSA) tool which could run on a device and has the ability to develop pseudo random streams based on the user events. Under isolated conditions on an Android Virtual Machine, each app is executed using BSA tool. The time taken 1482 events was 3 minutes and a delay of 600ms was allowed in between each event. Then the ptrace tool is started and in parallel the BSA tool is also initiated. All the API calls were traced until the apps stopped running. Finally the process was closed. Then, the ptrace output was retrieved to the server and the program was uninstalled from the Android Virtual Machine. Later, the ptrace output was combined for all the applications used and finally one dataset was formed for further classifications and analysis.

Figure 1 depicts the Control Flow Diagram of the Proposed Hybrid Architecture.

For the purpose of Data Collection (API calls) Google Play Store was the source from its 1482 benign android apps. Moreover, 1482 Malwares was also obtained from the Android Malware Genome Project to detect and perform behavioural analysis using Deep Learning method.

Testing Process

Sandboxie and Busty Sand Box Analyzer was used to test the performance of the proposed system. Figure 2 explains the ptrace output for an application followed by Figure 3which shows the Embedded API calls of all applications put together in a single sleeve.

Figure 1.

Figure 2.

Fig.2 Ptrace output for an Application

	time	seconds	usecs/call	calls	errors	syscall
1	60.00	0.002000	38	40	1	writev
2	60.00	0.002000	36	38		loct1
3.	50.00	0.001000	28	02		read
4.	00.00	0.000000	00	04	1	dup
5.	00.00	0.000000	00	08		mmap2
6.	00.00	0.000000	00	12	10	close
7.	00.00	0.000000	00	01		madvise
8.	00.00	0.000000	00	03		fcnt164
9.	00.00	0.000000	00	02		epoll_ctl
10.	00.00	0.000000	00	01		clone
11.	00.00	0.000000	00	03		fcnt164
12.	00.00	0.000000	00	02		mprotect
13.	00.00	0.000000	00	01		write
14.	00.00	0.000000	00	03		fcnt164
15.	00.00	0.000000	00	02		epoll_ctl
16.	00.00	0.000000	00	11		getuid21
17.	00.00	0.000000	00	03		fcnt164
18.	00.00	0.000000	00	02		epoll_ctl
19.	00.00	0.000000	00	01		write
20.	00.00	0.000000	00	03		fcnt164
21.	00.00	0.000000	00	03		clone
22.	00.00	0.000000	00	03		pread64
23.	00.00	0.000000	00	03		write
24.	00.00	0.000000	00	03	10	epoll_pwait
25	170.00	0.005000	00	154	22	total

Performance Evaluation

The performance of the proposed system was analyzed based on the metrics which we considered for evaluation. They are listed below:

1. True Positive
2. True Negative
3. False Positive
4. False Negative
5. Sensitivity
6. Accuracy
7. Specificity
8. Confusion Matrix
9. Precision
10. Recall

True Positive: It is defined as the total number of instances that are considered as positive and really they are positive.

True Negative: It is defined as the total number of instances that are considered as negative and really they are negative.

False Positive: It is defined as the total number of instances that are considered as positive but really they are negative.

Figure 3.

Fig.3 Embedded API calls of all Applications

	A	B	C	D	E	F	G	H
1	Application Name	Clone	Close	Connect	Dup	Clock_gettime	llseek	Epoll_pwait
2	2daovnon094t52vmvds421dt	23	616	1	1	56	61	6
3	Vamp030t40mkbq043hmgejrr	4	4	4	1	0	125	24
4	234m4bkbtrtntnntjk356h4nmr	35	532	6	3	0	1	22
5	Kvf34g-3g3gkgggkgkgk3g0k	36	6	234	5	0	21	2
6	43kvgbkgg3kbkgg95k4k569g	63	5	5	3	0	55	24
7	342gk0mfugjgjkghgt4mgkmm	1	525	6	5	0	22	45
8	Urunfhkrh32rtyernemymhyyeg	234	6	5	4	0	24	51
9	Uehdnfy49gfk9btdgnstndhdjeu	1	5	4	3	0	26	21
10	Yehhhhdgtebgdte7483483fhjer	41	4	45	3	0	258	23
11	Fnmuytrgfhyerdbstehdn37846	14	24	4	21	10	22	21
12	Tebdg45hydndyekifmfur47dhg	134	5	412	3	0	2	84
13	Tmnghutiyrhuftrnhytregstd432hy	14	5	5	3	0	85	26
14	Uhrnfhtdgetrusyen563mdfhyfr	74	4124	3	31	0	61	26
15	Oijuktihgyhrye64h63njd78dfaa	7690	5	6	1	11	62	69
16	Rr3gjoipnbhepwgw45663ggegh	14	5	6256	3	0	26	62
17	Gineho0inhepinhpnheerhrw4364	267	5	6	4	10	18	1
18	Bebe40hnhe93mgo752389negn	4378	532	16	5	0	62	1
19	Gnwobnobgw65ewomh3ahahjtrj	53	5	60	33	0	26	2
20	Yabgohbanineraohanth346743t	362	6	26	2	0	35	4
21	Gainjihoaeh349hme3936yh56hh	257	5	66	2	0	30	0
22	tyweohreobhreherheh0hjeh346g	78	5	64	1	0	3	52
23	G4nmh44hjmqy5hj45mjq4j4qm4	253	5	6	3	0	31	33
24	Hh34qj4qaehpmnhjtqthjmu59y5	5	5	2	3	0	30	56

False Negative: It is defined as the total number of instances that are considered as negative but really they are positive.

Sensitivity: It is defined as the ratio between True Positive and the sum of True Positive and False Negative.

Specificity: It is defined as the ratio between True Negative and the sum of True Negative and False Positive.

Accuracy: It is defined as the ratio between the sum of True Positive and False Positive with the sum of True Positive and False Positive and True Negative and False Negative.

Confusion Matrix: This matrix is a two dimensional square matrix in which each element predicts the total number of instances in which the real class is the row and the predicted class signifies column.

Precision: It is defined as the ratio between True Positive and the sum of True Positive and False Positive

Recall: It is defined as the ratio between True Positive and the sum of True Positive and False Negative

Results

Considering 1482 benign applications and 1482 Malware applications this work was constructed. Random Prism algorithm was utilized. Initially the testing was done using Random Forest algorithm but due to the high number of sample sets the accuracy of this algorithm was not upto the level. Hence, we concentrated on the Random Prism algorithm which is a advanced version of Random Forest Algorithm. Along with this algorithm the Incremental version of J48 Random tree algorithm was also employed. Both these algorithms were utilized as the classifiers on the embedded dataset. The results proved that the accuracy of this hybrid system was 88% when the test was performed with 2964 instances. In spite of the huge number of instances this method proved the accuracy. As a whole, while classifying the malicious applications the accuracy obtained was 90%. On the other hand while classifying the benign applications the accuracy obtained was 86%. Finally, based on the test results performed with 2964 instances in which 1482 was malicious applications and 1482 was benign applications. The classification helped to identify the top priority system calls and listed as the first 100 system calls among the 1482 malicious applications and in the same way the top priority system calls were identified and listed as the first 100 system calls among the 1482 benign applications. These API calls could be formed as a feature set inorder to analyse the characteristics of the evolving malware applications in the future.

CONCLUSION

In this chapter, we have proposed a hybrid architecture which combines the merits of both statistical and dynamic based anomaly detection of malware applications and verify the analyse the characteristics of the API calls that are made by the malicious applications each time. Through this hybrid method an accuracy level of 88% was obtained in a overall manner. In particular while testing the 1482 malicious applications the accuracy level obtained was 90% and while testing the benign applications the accuracy level was 86%. These levels are comparatively higher while compared to the number of malicious applications and benign applications. Hence, we conclude that this hybrid approach will be suitable for handling huge number of API calls, aiding in keeping a track of data flow, overcoming user reflection, evolving malwares could be identified, accuracy of malware identification could be increased, even though the false rates are high the function of testing will be authentic, complex API calls could be handled quickly, scrutinising can be done again if the results are not satisfied, minimizing the higher rates of false positive, threats of all natures could be undertaken, genuine applications will not be treated as malicious applications, any type of adware sample could be tested, malwares using reflection could be identified, handling concurrency testing is easier, Data obfuscation challenge could be handled in an effective manner and attacks could be identified easily.

REFERENCES

Advanced Persistent Threat. (2019). Retrieved from https://www.hackread.com/hackers-abusing-google-app-engine-to-spread-pdf-malware/

Amin, M. R. (2016) Behavioral malware detection ap- proaches for Android. *IEEE International Conference on Communications (ICC)*.

Android OS. (2008). Retrieved from https://en.wikipedia.org/wiki/Android_(operating_system)

Android Malware. (2008). Retrieved from https://forensics.spreitzenbarth.de/android-malware/

AppA. (2008). Retrieved from https://play.google.com/store/

Applications of Deep Learning. (2016). Retrieved from https://machinelearningmastery.com/inspirational-applications-deep-learning/

Bahrampour, S., Ramakrishnan, N., Schott, L., & Shah, M. (2015). Comparative study of caffe, neon, theano, and torch for deep learning. CoRR, vol. abs/1511.06435

Baskaran B & Ralescu A (2016), A Study of Android Malware Detection Techniques and Machine Learning, *MAICS2016*, 15-23.

Blasing, T., Schmidt, A.-D., Batyuk, L., Albayrak, S., & Camtepe, S. A. (2010), An android application sandbox system for suspicious software detection. *5th international conference on Malicious and unwanted software (MALWARE)*, 55–62.

Buster Sandbox Analyzer. (2011). Retrieved from http://bsa.isoftware.nl/

Carlini, N., & Wagner, D. (2017). Towards evaluating the robustness of neural networks. *IEEE Symposium on Security and Privacy (SP)*, 39–57. 10.1109/SP.2017.49

Chetlur, S., Woolley, C., Vandermersch, P., Cohen, J., Tran, J., Catanzaro, B., & Shelhamer, E. (2014). *DNN: Efficient Primitives for Deep Learning.* ArXiv e-prints.

Clark. (2009). *History of Mobile Apps.* Retrieved from http://www.uky.edu/~jclark/mas490apps/History%20of%20Mobile%20Apps.pdf

Coleman, C., Narayanan, D., Kang, D., Zhao, T., Zhang, J., Nardi, L., ... Zaharia, M. (2017). Dawnbench: An end-to-end deep learning benchmark and competition. *NIPS ML Systems Workshop.*

Deep Learning. (2009). Retrieved from https://en.wikipedia.org/wiki/Deep_learning

Dynamic Malware Detection. (2014). Retrieved from https://www.iit.cnr.it/sites/default/files/dynamic-malware-detection.pdf

Features of Android OS. (2008). Retrieved from https://en.wikipedia.org/wiki/List_of_features_in_Android

Goyal, P., Doll´ar, P., Girshick, R., Noordhuis, P., Wesolowski, L., Kyrola, A., Tulloch, A., Jia, Y., & He, K.,(2017). *Accurate, Large Minibatch SGD: Training ImageNet in 1 Hour.* ArXiv e-prints.

He, K., Zhang, X., Ren, S., & Sun, J. (2016). Deep residual learning for image recognition. *Proceedings of the IEEE conference on computer vision and pattern recognition*, 770–778.

Hersey. (2017). *Smart Phones*. Retrieved from https://en.wikipedia.org/wiki/Smartphone

How Do APIs Work. (2016). Retrieved from https://blogs.mulesoft.com/biz/tech-ramblings-biz/what-are-apis-how-do-apis-work/

Introduction to Pattern Recognition System. (2012). Retrieved from http://shodhganga.inflibnet.ac.in/bitstream/10603/25143/7/07_chapter%201.pdf

Introduction to Smart Phones. (2008). Retrieved from https://www.telstra.com.au/content/dam/tcom/seniors/pdf/beginners-intro-smartphones.pdf

Ioffe, S., & Szegedy, C. (2015). *Batch Normalization: Accelerating Deep Network Training by Reducing Internal Covariate Shift*. ArXiv e-prints.

Krizhevsky, A., & Hinton, G. (2009). *Learning multiple layers of features from tiny images*. University of Toronto.

Lecun, Y., Bottou, L., Bengio, Y., & Haffner, P. (1998). Gradient-based learning applied to document recognition. *Proceedings of the IEEE*, *86*(11), 2278–2324. doi:10.1109/5.726791

Lekies. (2015). *Dangers of Scripting*. Retrieved from https://www.usenix.org/system/files/conference/cset17/cset17-paper-gagnon.pdf

Li, Y. (2015). Detection, Classification and Characterization of Android Malware Using API Data Dependency. In *International Conference on Security and Privacy in Communication Systems*. Springer International Publishing. 10.1007/978-3-319-28865-9_2

Liu, Y. Z. Y., Li, H., & Chen, X. (2016). A hybrid malware detecting scheme for mobile Android applications. IEEE.

Madry, A., Makelov, A., Schmidt, L., Tsipras, D., & Vladu, A. (2017). *Towards deep learning models resistant to adversarial attacks*. arXiv preprint arXiv:1706.06083

Malicious Code. (2009). Retrieved from https://www.veracode.com/security/rise-malicious-mobile-applications

Malicious Mobile Apps. (2009). Retrieved from https://searchsecurity.techtarget.com/securityschool/How-best-to-find-and-fend-off-malicious-mobile-apps

Malware. (2006). Retrieved from https://en.wikipedia.org/wiki/Malware

Malware Detection. (2013). Retrieved from https://www.researchgate.net/publication/258820759_Malware_detection_by_behavioural_sequential_patterns

Malware Identification. (2009). Retrieved from https://www.consumer.ftc.gov/articles/0011-malware

Mobile App. (2008. Retrieved from https://en.wikipedia.org/wiki/Mobile_app

Mobile Malware Detection. (2015). Retrieved from https://www.ijcsmc.com/docs/papers/December2015/V4I12201556.pdf

Mobile Security Threats. (2010). Retrieved from https://www.google.com/search?q=10+high+risk+mobile+malware+apps&spell=1&sa=X&ved=0ahUKEwils4OV36PgAhUKY48KHaT9BuUQBQgrKAA&biw=1536&bih=754

Pattern Recognition. (2016). Retrieved from https://en.wikipedia.org/wiki/Pattern_recognition

Pattern Recognition: An Overview. (2012). Retrieved from http://article.sapub.org/pdf/10.5923.j.ajis.20120201.04.pdf

Protection from Malware. (2009). Retrieved from https://www.consumer.ftc.gov/media/video-0056-protect-your-computer-malware

Rashedul & Rofiqul. (2010). *Mobile Applications*. Retrieved from http://www.ijens.org/107506-0909%20ijet-ijens.pdf

Salama & Bach. (2013). *Smart Phones*. Retrieved from https://www.researchgate.net/publication/256703317_Introduction_of_6th_Generation_Smart_Phone_combining_the_features_of_both_Apple_and_Android_smart_phone

Scope of Buster Sandbox Analyzer. (2011). Retrieved from https://www.securityartwork.es/2012/12/12/buster-sandbox-analyzer/

Shams, S., Platania, R., Lee, K., & Park, S. J. (2017). Evaluation of deep learning frameworks over different hpc architectures. *IEEE 37th International Conference on Distributed Computing Systems (ICDCS)*, 1389–1396.

Study of Malware. (2009). Retrieved from https://pdfs.semanticscholar.org/4265/8775f329f2544c268c23c0375f60845b2ac6.pdf

Szegedy, C., Zaremba, W., Sutskever, I., Bruna, J., Erhan, D., Goodfellow, I., & Fergus, R. (2013). *Intriguing properties of neural networks*. arXiv preprint arXiv:1312.6199

Tamada, H., Okamoto, K., Nakamura, M., Monden, A., & Matsumoto, K. (2007). Design and Evaluation of Dynamic Software Birthmarks based on API calls. Nara Institute of Science and Technology, Technical Report.

Wei, W., Liu, L., Truex, S., Yu, L., Gursoy, E., & Wu, Y. (2018). *Demystifying Adversarial Behaviors in Deep Learning*. Georgia Institute of Technology, School of Computer Science.

Wu, Y., Liu, L., Pu, C., & Wei, W. (2018). GIT DLBench: A Benchmark Suite for Deep Learning Frameworks: Characterizing Performance, Accuracy and Adversarial Robustness. Georgia Institute of Technology, School of Computer Science, Tech. Rep.

Xu, P., Shi, S., & Chu, X. (2017). *Performance Evaluation of Deep Learning Tools in Docker Containers*. ArXiv e-prints.

Zhang. (2015). *Pattern Recognition Techniques*. Retrieved from https://fredfeng.github.io/papers/de-mobile14.pdf

Zheng, Lui, & Sun. (2013). Droid analytics: a signature based analytic system to collect, extract, analyze and associate android malware. *Trust, Security and Privacy in Computing and Communications (TrustCom), 2013 12th IEEE International Conference*, 163–171.

Chapter 10
Anomaly–Based Intrusion Detection:
Adapting to Present and Forthcoming Communication Environments

Jorge Maestre Vidal

ⓘ https://orcid.org/0000-0002-4131-5100

Indra, Spain

Marco Antonio Sotelo Monge

Universidad Complutense de Madrid, Spain

Sergio Mauricio Martínez Monterrubio

ⓘ https://orcid.org/0000-0002-1520-1249

Universidad Complutense de Madrid, Spain

ABSTRACT

Anomaly-based intrusion detection has become an indispensable player on the existing cybersecurity landscape, where it enables the identification of suspicious behaviors that significantly differ from normal activities. In this way, it is possible to discover never-seen-before threats and provide zero-day recognition capabilities. But the recent advances on communication technologies are leading to changes in the monitoring scenarios that result in novel challenges to be taken into consideration, as is the case of greater data heterogeneity, adversarial attacks, energy consumption, or lack of up-to-date datasets. With the aim on bringing the reader closer to them, this chapter deepens the following topics: evolution of the anomaly definition, anomaly recognition for network-based intrusion detection, outlier characterizations, knowledge acquisition for usage modelling, distances and similarity measures for decision-making, anomaly recognition and non-stationarity, metrics and evaluation methodologies, and challenges related with the emergent monitorization environments.

DOI: 10.4018/978-1-5225-9611-0.ch010

INTRODUCTION

The preliminary research in the Intrusion Detection Systems (IDS) field focused on monitoring and analyzing the protected environment looking for previously known patterns of malicious actions, which was typified as Signature-Based (SB) intrusion detection. But although nowadays this paradigm still playing an essential role in the cybersecurity landscape, the rapid proliferation of malware and related threats eventually encouraged the design of novel approaches, which were able to deal with never-seen-before threats (Maestre Vidal, Sandoval Orozco, & García Villalba, November 2017). This resulted in a wide variety of Anomaly-Based (ABS) Intrusion Detection Systems, that typically attained to recognize attacks by distinguishing the normal and habitual protected system usage (hypothesized as legitimate) form discordant (hypothesized as malicious). This modus operandi involves the adoption of knowledge acquisition and modelling capabilities that for the sake of effectiveness, should be adapted to the evolution over the years of the monitoring environments.

Consequently, the emergent communication ecosystem entails a brand-new change for researchers on anomaly-based intrusion detection, where environments like Internet of Things (IoT), Edge computing, the fifth generation of cellular mobile communications (5G), smart cities or Software-Defined Networks (SDN), lead to multiple and dynamic data sources, and more heterogeneous traffic with non-stationary features (Sotelo Monge, Maestre Vidal, & García Villalba, 2017). Another difficulty inherent to the new communication enablers is the constraint of computing resources, which is particularly present in ubiquitous computing and wearable devices. Due to this, the anomaly-based detection algorithms should not only be effective, but efficient.

With the aim on bringing the reader closer to these concerns, this chapter has the main objectives of reviewing and discussing the principal aspects of anomaly-based detection applied to intrusion detection and deepening in the challenges posed by the emerging communication technologies. The chapter is organizing into nine sections, being the first of them the present introduction. The second section defines the anomaly conceptualization and introduces the main lines of research related to this term; the third section reviews the different anomaly characterizations; the fourth section provides an overview of the knowledge acquisition strategies applied to the identification of anomalies; the fifth section introduces the different measures of similarity that are usually taken into account for their identification; the sixth section discusses the problem of detecting anomalies in non-stationary scenarios; the seventh section outlines their evaluation criteria; the eighth section describes the challenges faced by anomaly-based intrusion detection at the forthcoming communication scene; and the last section presents the conclusions and future research trends.

Anomalies and Conceptualization

The problem of identifying anomalies has been object of study for decades, as it can be observed in publications like (Edgeworth, 1887), where instead of the term "anomaly" the expression "discordant observation" was considered. As pointed out by (Chandola, Banerjee, & Kumar, 2009), the word anomaly has been replaced by equivalent concepts over the years, being also referred to as: outliers, isolated parts, exceptions, aberrations, surprises, peculiarities or polluting elements. The use of each of these tags usually varied according to the domain in which it has been used, just as it happened with their definition. In order to familiarize the reader with the evolution of this concept, the following discusses some of the most popular anomaly conceptualizations and the research topics directly related with their study.

Definitions of Anomaly

Among the classical definitions of the term anomaly with greatest repercussion at present, it is worth mentioning that proposed by (Hawkings, 1980), referring to anomalies as "observations that deviate so much from other observations as to arouse suspicion that they were generated by a different mechanism". Other highly resorted definitions were proposed by (Grubbs, 1969), where the term anomalies indicated "observations that seem to deviate in a representative way from the rest of the elements of the sample in which they are", the description of (Barnett & Lewis, February 1994), in which they refer to "observations that appear to deviate markedly from other members of the sample in which they occurs", or that of (Aggarwal & Yu, May 2001), where anomalies are "background noise points that are outside the previously established clusters of information, or points that remain outside these clusters and are also distinguished from noise". In a perspective much closer to information security, (Chandola, Banerjee, & Kumar, 2009) defined anomalies as "patterns in data that do not conform to expected behavior". This latter acceptance has been adapted to different monitoring scenarios, such as the modification of (Savage, Zhang, Yu, Chou, & Wang, 2014) for its application in the analysis of social networks, being anomalies the "regions of the network whose structure differs from that expected at the normal model".

More recently, (Zimek, Campello, & Sander, 2013) analyzed the problem of the generalization of this definition. They concluded that regardless of the nature of the observations, whether network traffic, credit card data, information captured by weather sensors, etc., they pose characteristics that may be predicted if their behavior has been properly understood. The presence of unpredictable observations demonstrates a partial or total lack of awareness about the monitoring environment, which probably entails the need to further investigate suspicious discovered events. They denominated these unpredictable situations anomalies. The approach of (Zimek, Campello, & Sander, 2013) is completely independent of the context in which it is applied. However, it keeps in mind the ideas about perception of the monitoring environment and the projection of acquired knowledge, which are aligned intuitively with the model of situational awareness published by (Endsley, January 1988). This model establishes the bases of the current identification, evaluation and incident management systems, by constructing a cognitive model of the environment divided into three great levels of assimilation: perception, comprehension and projection; where perception is the stage of monitoring, collection evidence and acquisition of basic knowledge; comprehension is the correlation, pattern recognition, evaluation and interpretation of the data obtained; and projection is the anticipation and simulation of their evaluation (Barona López et al.,2017).

To improve the performance of accurate flow traffic classification, several models have been proposed. For example, port-based and payload-based techniques are the most known traditional ones. The port-based technique uses well known port numbers for internet traffic identification such as for SMTP is 25, DNS is 53 and HTTP uses port number 80. Moreover, using port-based techniques we cannot identify and classify several applications as they use encryption methods to avoid from being detected. Payload-based also known as deep packet inspection (DPI) technique was proposed to mitigate security restraints over ports. (Shafiq, Yu, Kashif Bashir, Chaudrhry, & Wang, 2018).

Homomorphic encryption, used in cloud computing, receives and executes computation all in encrypted data, called ciphertext, and generates an encrypted result that can then be decrypted by a user. When applied to neural networks, this technique is particularly fast and efficient at computing linear algebra (Juvekar, 2018).

RELATED RESEARCH TOPICS

As pointed in (Chandola, Banerjee, & Kumar, 2009), it is important to take into account the presence of areas of research strongly related to the anomaly concept and their identification, which have risen to discussions about whether they should be considered as subtopics of the outlier detection field. Among the lines of research related to the object of study of this document, it is possible to highlight those that focus on the elimination and accommodation of noise, novelty detection, identification of points of change, and trend detection. They are briefly described below:

- **Noise Elimination and Accommodation:** The noise is a frequent phenomenon in collections of samples and data, which unlike anomalies, has slightly interest from the analytical point, but it can alter the results obtained at their study.
- **Novelty Detection:** According to the definition of (Chandola, Banerjee, & Kumar, 2009), novelty detection addresses the problem of recognizing patterns that have not been previously observed in the monitoring environment. Therefore, novelties are anomalies that often require specific strategies for their identification. In addition, they play a very important role in pattern recognition methods adapted to non-stationary monitoring scenarios (O'Reilly, Gluhak, Imran, & Rajasegarar, 2014).
- **Identification of Change Points:** As described in (Takeuchi & Yamanishi, 2006), the problem of identifying change points focuses on determining when a significant statistical change has occurred in the monitoring environment, as well as any other unusual behavior. This definition highlights the important connection between the study of anomalies and this field, which often share and/or complement analysis and processing techniques (Chandola, Banerjee, & Kumar, 2009).
- **Trend Discovery:** Detecting trends and identifying new topics are two common problems related with text mining. As it is discussed in (Schubert, Weiler, & Zimek, 2015), their objective is to discover changes in data flow distributions that denote the beginning of new events, which essentially is termed as anomaly recognition in text flows.

CHARACTERIZATIONS OF ANOMALIES

Bearing in mind the current disagreement of the research community on how the term anomaly and its scope were defined, it is difficult to generalize a classification of anomalies that facilitates their distinction. From the different ontologies presented in the bibliography, it is worth mentioning the approach of (Chandola, Banerjee, & Kumar, 2009) for being one of the most referenced. It establishes three large sets of outliers: point anomalies, contextual anomalies and collective anomalies. An illustrative example of their application is observed in (Ahmed, Mahmood, & Hu, 2016), where the most common attacks against communication networks are mapped according to these definitions. As an alternative to this classification, they are usually generalized into two bigger groups: global and local anomalies. The term global anomaly encompasses the point anomalies of the taxonomy of (Chandola, Banerjee, & Kumar, 2009). But local anomalies refer to contextual anomalies, which is a well-known term from the research field on outlier recognition detection based on the analysis of densities. In this taxonomy, the collective anomalies described by (Chandola, Banerjee, & Kumar, 2009) became cases within any of these two groups, hence offering a much more general view of their nature. Note that these types of discordances have been raised for general purpose, which often leads to the need for distinguishing anomalies in a much more specific way within each monitoring scenario. This encourages the publication of new classifications adapted to each use case, as can be observed in (Savage et al., 2014), where specific anomalies framed in the analysis of communication networks represented by graph-shaped data structures are defined.

Point Anomalies

Point categories bring together all those particular instances of discordance with respect to the rest of the monitored data. An example of this kind of discordances is illustrated in Figure 1 by taking the Euclidean space as a reference. As it can be seen, two different regions of similarity (C_1, C_2) and two divergences (A_1, A_2) can be distinguished from the samples taken, which can be labeled as point anomalies within such data set.

But even though point anomalies are the most simple and intuitive set of discordances, their detection poses different challenges, such as the problem of identifying the optimal measure of similarity of their deviation (Han, Kamber, & Pei, 2011). In addition, (Kriegel, Kröger, & Zimek, 2010) emphasized other important aspects to be taken into account, such as the fact that the set of reference samples considered at sensor training and/or modeling stages may contain other point anomalies, which may involve results that potentially do not match to reality.

Contextual Anomalies

As indicated by (Song, Wu, Jermaine, & Ranka, 2007), if a data instance is anomalous in a specific context, but not otherwise, it is termed contextual anomaly (also referred to as conditional anomaly). An example of this group of discordances is illustrated in the bandwidth consumption of a Hotel local

Figure 1. Example of point anomalies in the euclidean space

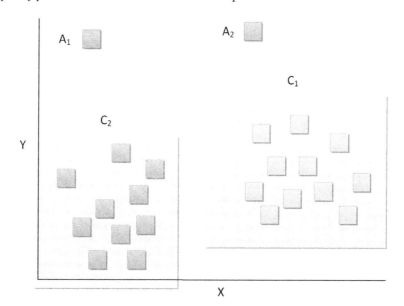

network at different seasonal movements: although a record of 14 Gbit/s can be considered normal when measured at tourism season, the reading of this same value in the same hotel at another period, can be considered a contextual anomaly (i.e. 4 Gbit/s at non-tourism season). Another example is illustrated in Figure 2, where normal seasonal variations are shown at various time intervals (D_1, D_2), as well as three observations with the same value in Y, which may be contextual discordances (A_1, A_2) or not (P_1) depending on the observation date.

In order to facilitate the study of this kind of observations, it is usual their complementation by two types of attributes: contextual and behavioral. Contextual attributes determine the circumstances in which the observation is framed; for example, in the case of the Hotel bandwidth, a good contextual attribute may be the month of the year in which it was measured. On the other hand, the behavioral attributes are the characteristics of the observation itself, being in the previous case bandwidth measurements in Gbit/s.

Collective Anomalies

When a set of observations presents divergence regarding the expected behavior, it is termed as collective anomaly (Han, Kamber, & Pei, 2011). They are clearly illustrated in the example of the denial of service attacks. These intrusions are based on depleting computational resources, generally by injecting a large volume of information that must be processed by the victim. Recent advances toward mitigating denial of service attacks on communication networks include the description of a great variety of metrics and measurements of relationships between data observations (Bhuyan, Bhattacharyya, & Kalita, 2015). But there is an idea that is common in all of them: if only the malicious packets that the attacker addresses to the individual victim are analyzed, it is very difficult to discover these attacks. To determine if there are malicious intentions, it is important to consider the complete set of packets, where collective anomalies entail significant variations of the relationships between them. Figure 3 illustrates an example of collective anomalies, where the set of points (A_1, A_2, A_3, A_4) suspiciously differs from the cluster C_1 that represents a network normal usage.

Figure 2. Examples of contextual anomalies

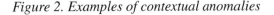
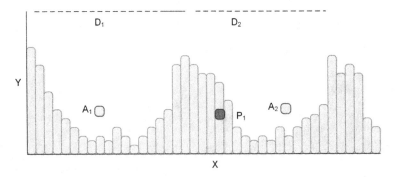

Figure 3. Example of point anomalies in the Euclidean space

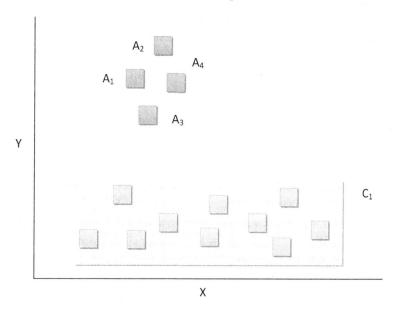

KNOWLEDGE ACQUISITION AND MODELING

The nature of the data that anomaly recognition methods analyze for defining what is normal and what is discordant, restraints the selection of the strategies to be implemented and affects their behavior. According to (Chandola, Banerjee, & Kumar, 2009), in the scope of intrusion detection the greater distinction can be identified from sample labeling, where normal is legitimate, and anomalous is potentially malicious, being these the most frequent classifications in the previous publications. Bearing this in mind, (Laskov, Düssel, Schäfer, & Rieck, September 2005) realized two essential observation necessary to understand the different strategies for acquiring knowledge and to decide the most appropriate for each use case: firstly, it must be taken into account that labeled samples are very difficult to obtain and, on the other hand, there is no way of collecting malicious samples that cover every possible attack. Anomaly detection methods are often classified based on the nature of the reference samples, which correspond to the principal paradigms on machine learning: supervised, semi-supervised, unsupervised, reinforcement and transduction learning. Some examples of these methods and their impact on anomaly recognition are briefly described below.

Supervised Learning

Anomaly detection systems that implement supervised learning techniques assume both, normal and malicious datasets for constructing the use models of the protected system. They consider labeled inputs and outputs. Given the great amount of reference information this entails, they tend to build accurate approximations with less tendency to emit false positives than other solutions. Their main drawbacks are the difficulty of obtaining reliable samples properly labeled, and the fact that the reference datasets usually contain fewer abnormal samples than normal, which leads to risks related with imbalance between classes (Han, Kamber, & Pei, 2011). But alongside that, it is one of the most popular knowledge acquisition methods on the intrusion detection field, where it is applied in malware detection in networks (Bhuyan, Bhattacharyya, & Kalita, 2014), identification of internal threats (Maestre Vidal, Sandoval Orozco, & García Villalba, 2016), analysis of applications for mobile devices (Faruki, Bharmal, & Laxmi, 2015), and many other use cases.

Semi-Supervised Learning

Unlike supervised learning, semi-supervised anomaly detection considers labeled and unlabeled samples, being typically applied for models build from one class of reference data, which is often a representation of the normal observations. As described in (Chandola, Banerjee, & Kumar, 2009), the typical approach for semi-supervised detection is to build a model of the usual and legitimate usage of the protected environment, and then analyze the new observations looking for significant discordances. Therefore, this leads to the development of IDS that are usually easier to train but that are more sensitive, generally offering an improvement in the ability to identify unknown anomalies at the cost of penalizing the false positive rate (Maestre Vidal, Sotelo Monge, & García Villabla, 2018). Note that in the field of intrusion detection, semi-supervised knowledge acquisition is used in similar contexts than supervised learning, but allowing the implementation of alternative algorithms, such as Support Vector Machines (SVM), autoencoders or Gaussian mixture model (Goldstein & Uchida, 2016).

Unsupervised Learning

The anomaly recognition approaches that acquire knowledge by unsupervised schemes do not consider categories a priori, or in other words, they do not use labeled datasets. Instead they manage the monitored data as a set of random samples, from which it is possible to build density models and defining groups. As indicated by (Han, Kamber, & Pei, 2011), in order to minimize labeling errors, the anomaly detection systems that adopt this paradigm must take into account the following assumption: the normal observations conform to certain patterns or distributions much more frequently than discordances. As the monitored information moves away from this premise, the detection systems will tend to increase the emission of labeling errors, which makes them their main vulnerabilities. In practice, unsupervised learning is specially exploited in complex monitoring environments where data acquisition is difficult and expensive. The growing of the research community interest in unsupervised Deep learning solutions resulted in a plethora of Network-based Intrusion Detection Systems (NIDS) (Mohammadi, Al-Fuqaha, Sorour, & Guizani, 2018), that under the assumption of a large training dataset, are able to differentiate network situations without preliminary knowledge about them.

Reinforcement Learning

The principal target of the reinforcement learning paradigm is to facilitate that anomaly recognition systems and actuators make better decisions. In systems that implement this paradigm, each time an agent decides, its impact on the quality of service is monitored to be considered for future reasoning.

This has been used in order to improve different characteristics of the conventional anomaly recognition approaches, for example when deciding what data must be analyzed when the sensor operates in real-time, optimization of pattern prediction in local environments or at the dynamic reconfiguration of intrusion detection systems depending on the characteristics of the discovered anomalies (He, Dai, Ning, & Dutta, December 2015).

Transduction

Transduction reasoning allows inferring knowledge by assuming a set of tagged observations as a reference, and by previously knowing the specific samples to be analyzed, i.e. it is reasoning from observed specific training cases to specific test cases. Unlike inductive schemes (supervised, semi-supervised, etc.), transduction does not construct rules or a generic model of the monitoring environment and applies them to concrete predictions; instead it poses a specific solution to a set of concrete and finite objects to be analyzed. The main advantage of this method is that it is more accurate than inductive algorithms in cases where the set of reference samples is smaller. However, given the lack of reference models/rules, the transduction process must be repeated for each new set of elements to be labeled, which involves a greater consumption of computational resources (Sotelo Monge, Maestre Vidal, & García Villalba, 2017).

DISTANCES AND SIMILARITY MEASURES

Anomaly detection systems often must compare the perception of "normal" elements made during their knowledge acquisition stage with the observations being analyzed. Therefore, the characteristics of the distances and measures of similarity that are taken into consideration affect directly to their effectiveness. According to (Weller-Fahy, Borghetti, & Sodemann, 2014), the definition of distance measure entails the fulfillment of three great requirements: non-negativity, identity of indiscernible and symmetry. Those distance measures which also satisfy the triangle inequality are also qualified as distance metrics. Weller-Fahy et al. defined these properties base on the function : $A \times B \rightarrow \mathbb{R}$, wich takes two generic input positions A and B, and returns the value of their distance. The previously described properties are defined as follows:

- Non-Negativity. The distance between A and B is always a value greater than or equal to zero:

$$dist\left(A, B\right) \geq 0$$

- Identity of indiscernible. The distance between A and B is equal to zero if and only if A is equal to B:

$$dist\left(A, B\right) = 0 \leftrightarrow A = B$$

- Symmetry. The distance between A and B is equal to the distance between B and A:

$$dist\left(A,B\right) = dist\left(B,A\right)$$

Triangle inequality. Considering the presence of a third point C, the distance between A and B is always less than or equal to the sum of the distance between A and C and the distance between B and C: $dist\left(A,B\right) \le \left(dist\left(A,C\right) + dist\left(B,C\right)\right)$.

At present, there are hundreds of distances and measures of similarity, which are adapted to the nature of the data to be analyzed. In the context of anomaly-based intrusion detection three groups of general-purpose approaches predominate: those that compare quantitative, qualitative and mixed data. The following describes each of them.

Similarity Distances in quantitative Data

The distances of similarity for quantitative data are centered in the study of variables represented in the domain of the real numbers, i.e., where the A, B observations to correlate satisfy $\left\{A,B\right\} \epsilon \mathbb{R}$. Quantitative data may be discrete or continuous; in the case of discrete variables, the domain is limited to a previously known range of values, whereas in continuous data any value can be observed. A case on discrete data is when the variables are binary, which assume $\left\{A,B\right\} \epsilon \left\{0,1\right\}$. As indicated by (Cha, 2007), the calculation of similarity distances in quantitative data has an important resemblance to the comparison of the nominal data represented in histograms. In (Bhuyan, Bhattacharyya, & Kalita, 2014) the most common distances of similarity related with the study of quantitative data are reviewed. Among them, Euclidean, squared X^2, Canberra, Bhattacharyya, Mahalanobis and Divergence are the most frequently used.

Similarity Distances in Qualitative Data

From a statistical point of view, categorical variables (also known as qualitative or attribute variables) are those that represent categories or values. For example, a network end-point may provide different qualitative characteristics, such as location (IP Address, MAC Address, Network, Tenant, etc.) or Type (Firewall, Personal Computer, DNS server, etc.). The greatest challenge in processing this class of information lies in the fact that its attributes do not present any explicit notion of order, which makes the effectiveness of the distances directly dependent on the nature of the data. Some of the most frequent similarity measures referred in the literature (Boriah, Chandola, & Kumar, April 2008) are: Overlap, Eskin, IOF, OF, Lin, Gambaryan, Burnaby, among others.

Similarity Distances in Mixed Data

Mixed variables contain both numerical and qualitative values, being very frequent in distributed anomaly detection systems with different sources of information. The most frequent approach to the comparison of this category of data is the application of clustering algorithms, which requires the identification of the number of groups to be defined and the selection of the attributes that will be considered within each of them. As indicated by (Foss, Markatou, Ray, & Heching, 2016), recent publications related to this problem focused on the construction of groups that consider a single attribute, being usual the conversion of the categorical values to numerical or vice versa. At present, there is a great variety of measures of proximity for mixed data. According to (Bhuyan, Bhattacharyya, & Kalita, 2015), the two most common approaches are the general similarity coefficient and the general distance coefficient, followed closely by the Minkowski generalized distance (Gan, Ma, & Wu, 2007).

NON-STATIONARITY

Most of the machine learning and datamining methods, those that involve anomaly recognition, hypothesize that reference datasets present stationary distributions. They also assume that the information to be analyzed is gathered from a monitoring environment with static characteristics, a situation that is not always satisfied in their deployment at real use cases, and event less at the emerging communication environments. Consequently, and as discussed in (Zait & Messatfa, 1997), this can lead to unrealistic and incoherent results. With the aim of introducing the reader to the challenges posed by these varying scenarios, this section describes the causes that lead to representative changes in the monitored data regarding reference datasets, as well as their consequences on anomaly-based intrusion detection. Finally, the most frequent strategies for their mitigation are reviewed.

Causes and Impact of Non-Stationary

According to (Holte, 1993), the traditional approach to pattern recognition assumes that the reference samples are representative of the observations that will be made in the future, highlighting the possibility that from a specific event, the relationship between the variables to be studied will considerably change. (Kelly, Hand, & Adams, August 1999) described the three most probable fluctuations on these features supported by Bayes theorem: let the observation x and the class w, the probability of distribution changes in the monitoring environment is defined from the following expression:

$$P\left(w|x\right) = \frac{P\left(x \mid w\right) P\left(w\right)}{P\left(x\right)}$$

where 1) $P\left(w\right)$ is susceptible to change over time; 2) the distribution at w may vary; 3) $P\left(w|x\right)$ also may vary on future.

Another problem that could impair the quality of the classifications, is the presence of gradual changes over time in the statistical characteristics of the class to which an observation belongs, so that: $P_t\left(w|x\right) \neq P_{t+1}\left(w|x\right)$. In the bibliography, this issue is well-known as *concept drift*. Accordingly, when changes occur in a short period of time, they are termed *concept shift*. In (Schubert, Wojdanowski, Zimek, & Kriegel, 2012) the characteristics of these fluctuations in different monitoring environments are discussed. Note that some scenarios are especially susceptible to this kind of inconsistencies, such as communication networks or economic data. Consequently, a network usage model previously tagged as "normal" may become "anomalous" over time and vice versa, resulting in the need for adapt the deployed anomaly-based intrusion detection capabilities to the current environment characterization.

Adapting IDS to Non-Stationary

In order to adapt the conventional detection strategies to the challenges posed by anomaly recognition on non-stationary monitoring scenarios, the research community has developed different proposals. As pointed by (O'Reilly, Gluhak, Imran, & Rajasegarar, 2014), the most appropriate way of grouping these publications is to select as classification axis the features of the stages involved in the analytic processes. The first of these steps is the detection of relevant changes in the distribution of monitored data. It is achieved by combining techniques for novelty and change point detection. The next step is to update the models associated with the classes to be recognized. Finally, there are approaches that skip this stage by allowing the constant updating of the reference data over time. (O´Reilly et al., 2014) divided these strategies into two large groups: active and passive response methods. Each of them is briefly described below.

1. Active Response Methods

Active responses are characterized by encompassing modeling and machine learning methods that act after identifying changes in the monitoring environment, or when considering that errors derived from the identification of outliers depend in a representative way of the modeling process. In (Alippi, 2014) this strategy is refereed as *detection and response*; once a significant change is discovered, the system discards the obsolete knowledge and adapts to the new environment. These mechanisms are usually grouped into three great families: windowing, weighting and random sampling. The first one is the most frequent in the bibliography, and it is based on the application of a sliding window that allows selecting the most recent samples of a reference dataset and discarding the old ones. The model is rebuilt assuming the new knowledge. Unlike methods based on sliding windows, weighted proposals consider the entire collection of reference samples. If a change at the monitoring environment is discovered, the samples with better weights have greater relevance in the construction of the new model. Finally, proposals based on random sampling consider a subset of the reference dataset with elements that have been previously random selected.

2. Passive Response Methods

Anomaly detection strategies based on passive responses do not require identifying certain events to trigger countermeasures. Instead, they assume that the monitored environment varies steadily over time. To accommodate to these fluctuations, these schemes continuously perform small changes on the reference models/regressions, thus maintaining updated information about the context in which the information is observed. The different contributions to this area can be divided into two major categories: those that focus on updating a single detection system, and those that affect classifiers that integrate different sensors. The first ones are often more efficient, and therefore more recommended for systems that operate at real-time. This is clearly illustrated in (Ye, Squartini, & Piazza, 2013), where Extreme Learning Machines (ELM) are applied on neural networks which adjustment varies over time.

On the other hand, the ensembles of sensors demonstrated to behave more stable than individual sensors in stationary monitoring environments. This is because they tend to compensate the error of the worst-performing classifiers of each use case. They also facilitate the incorporation of new data in the previously built models and provide strategies to discard the less relevant information (Zimek, Campello, & Sander, 2013). Therefore, at seasonal contexts the diversity of sensors in an ensemble beneficially affects their results.

EVALUATION AND METRICS

In the last decades, different methodologies for the evaluation of anomaly recognition systems have been published. They do not only consider their ability to identify discordances, but also measure other parameters that facilitate the decision of which detection strategies are best suited for each use case. Note that as indicated by (Bhuyan, Bhattacharyya, & Kalita, 2015), the evaluation of an anomaly-based intrusion detection system only considering accuracy, provides a snapshot of its effectiveness in a concrete instant of time. Therefore, as changes occur in the monitoring scenario, this comparison with future proposals tends to lose relevance. Because of this, the research community has also been provided by other criteria for estimating their impact on a monitoring environment. The most popular in the bibliography are: accuracy, efficiency, response time, ease of updating, scalability and resistance to evasion attacks. With the aim of introduce the reader into this problem, throughout this section the main evaluation criteria of anomaly recognition systems are reviewed.

Accuracy

The accuracy of an anomaly-based IDS is its capability for detecting attacks and distinguishing them from the legitimate usage of the system. These systems classify events observed in the monitored system, labeling them as positives or negatives. The evaluation of the labels is usually divided into four sub-categories: true positives, true negatives, false positives and false negatives. Figure 4 illustrates the different labeling evaluations issued by a two-class anomaly-based IDS (classes "Anomalous" and "Normal"). Alerts in green boxes (true positives and true negatives) are correct labels and the others correspond to detection errors. The following describes each of them:

- **True Positives (TP):** Let the class C, true positives are observed when the classifier indicates that the analyzed samples belongs to C and it is correct. In the example, they indicate the normal observations properly labeled as normal. The true positive rate is often refereed as hit rate.
- **True Negatives (TN):** Let the class C, true negatives are observed when the classifier indicates that the analyzed samples do not belong to C, and it is correct. In the example, they are discordant observations properly labeled as anomalous.
- **False positives (FPs).** Let the class C, false positives are observed when the classifier indicates that the analyzed samples belongs to C, but the correct is that they belong to different ones. In the example, they are normal observations wrongly labeled as anomalous. Besides posing a problem

Figure 4. Labeling evaluation

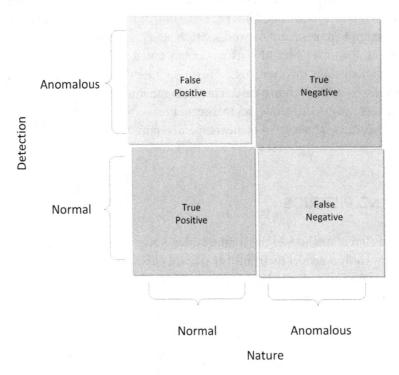

for the system quality of service, such errors can be exploited by attackers by inducing the IDS to issuing large amounts of alerts, in addition causing computing resources depletion.

- **False negatives (FN):** Let the class C, false negatives are observed when the classifier indicates that the analyzed samples do not belong to C, but the correct is that they belong to a different one. In the example, they are discordant observations wrongly labeled as normal. In the context of information security and binary classification, this is the worst case, because FNs are instances of the opposite of that an IDS intends to do. The false positive rate is also known as specificity.

Based on this classification, (Bhuyan, Bhattacharyya, & Kalita, 2015) concluded that the target of an intrusion detection system must be achieving the highest true positive and true negative rates, as well as the lowest false positive and false negative rates. In the last decades, several schemes for evaluate the quality of the labeling of anomaly recognition systems have been published, highlighting among them for their relevance in the bibliography the ROC curve analysis and the study of metrics derived from confusion matrix. Both are described below.

Receiver Operating Characteristic Analysis

The Receiver Operating Characteristic, also known as ROC curve is a graphical representation of the sensitivity of the system and its specificity. From them, the statistic Area Under the Curve (AUC) is calculated with the purpose of compare sensors operating in a similar context, but with different calibration. It is expressed as follows:

$$AUC = \int\limits_{-\infty}^{\infty} TPR\big(X\big)FPR'\big(X\big)dX$$

Figure 5 illustrates an example of ROC curve where in the upper left axis the best settings are grouped, i.e. those closest to the optimal calibration $TP = 1$ and $FP = 0$. The worst calibrations display results closest to the lower right corner, i.e. where $TP = 0$ and $FP = 1$. At this example, the AUC approximates 0.9.

An exhaustive study on the use of the ROC curve and the AUC applied to anomaly recognition is described in (Schubert, Wojdanowski, Zimek, & Kriegel, 2012). This publication also reviews the problematic on their implementation, pointing as main difficult the fact that the ROC analysis does not consider the degree of discordance of each performed classification. To mitigate this problem, they propose the use of metrics based on the detected degree of discordance. But despite the drawbacks, the analysis of ROC curves entails the most commonly evaluation scheme in the bibliography.

Confusion Matrix

In contrast to the ROC curve analysis it is usual considering confusion matrix, also known as error matrix or contingency matrix. These data structures have nxn dimension, where n is the number of classes considered, columns contain the reference data and rows are the labeled observations belonging to each class. Therefore, the diagonal displays the correct classification. An example of confusion matrix

Figure 5. Example of ROC curve

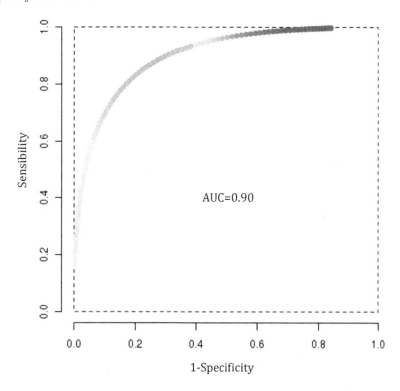

is illustrated in Table 1, where the classes $Legi1$ and $Legi2$ group normal observations, and the class $Anomaly$ contains discordances.

Note that anomaly recognition rarely adopts $n > 2$, where the classes use to be: "anomalous data" and "normal data". Once the confusion matrix is built, it is possible to deduce different indices related with the sensor behavior, highlighting among them ACC (Accuracy), Pre (precision), Re (Recall) and Fa (Fall-Out) (Bhuyan, Bhattacharyya, & Kalita, 2015). They are defined by the following expressions:

$$ACC = \frac{\sum TP + \sum TN}{\sum TP + \sum TN + \sum FP + \sum FN}$$

$$\mathrm{Pr}e = \frac{\sum TP}{\sum TP + \sum FP}$$

$$Re = \frac{\sum TP}{\sum TP + \sum FN}$$

$$Fa = \frac{\sum FP}{\sum TP + \sum FP}$$

In the example of Table IV, the global accuracy of the sensor is $ACC = 0.34$; the precision of each class separately are $Pre\left(Legi1\right) = 0.47$, $Pre\left(Legi2\right) = 0.42$ and $Pre\left(Anomaly\right) = 0.09$; the recalls per class are $Re\left(Legi1\right) = 0.31$, $Re\left(Legi2\right) = 0.35$, $Re\left(Anomaly\right) = 0.41$. Finally, the fall-outs are $Fa\left(Legi1\right) = 0.53$, $Fa\left(Legi2\right) = 0.58$ and $Fa\left(Anomaly\right) = 0.91$. In view of these results it is possible deduce that the sensor is not very effective.

Efficiency

The efficiency of an anomaly-based IDS determines its ability to process information in function of time. This parameter usually depends on the detection strategy and its processing capacity on the monitoring environment. Note that if the data processing capabilities of the sensor are lower than the performance of the protected system, ensuring their real-time operability implies to limit the data processing rate of the

Table 1. Example of 3-class confusion matrix

	Legi1	Legi2	Anomaly
Legi1	900	860	123
Legi2	1070	893	126
Anomaly	875	753	175

monitoring environment, which usually led to an important penalty in terms of quality of service. Nowadays there are different metrics for evaluating the efficiency of an anomaly recognition system. Some of them are of general scope, as is the case of the system memory consumption or processing time by unit of information; others adapt to the characteristics of the use case, as it common when analyzing traffic on communication networks by studying their packet loss rate (Bhuyan, Bhattacharyya, & Kalita, 2015).

Response Time

The response time criteria evaluate the speed of the anomaly-based IDS for being able to report the presence of an anomaly from the moment it occurs in the monitoring environment. Unlike in efficiency estimation metrics, the response time considers that certain processes require a previous observation interval prior to the analysis of the collected data. Therefore, the time invested in processing the information is added to the delay on the data acquisition. An example that clearly illustrates this idea is observed in (Ozcelik & Brooks, 2015), where with the aim on detecting Denial of Service attacks against communication networks, the impact of the variation of the size of the basic units of information to be analyzed (observations) is studied. From the monitored data, at each period of observation the fundamental metric for the analysis process is extracted, which is the entropy on the number of received packets. According to (Ozcelik & Brooks, 2015), observations can be defined as predefined d dimension data sets (at this use case, observations are packets) extracted sequentially from the monitoring environment, or as the set of data (packets) monitored in a particular T time interval. The impact of making decisions on the efficiency of the sensor depends on the characteristics of the monitoring environment (Maestre Vidal, Sandoval Orozco, & García Villalba, 2018). The parameters to be considered for evaluating the response time in anomaly-based recognition are deeply reviewed in (Bhuyan, Bhattacharyya, & Kalita, 2015).

Updating

Given the non-stationary nature of most of the current monitoring scenarios, when assessing an anomaly-based IDS it is convenient to consider the cost of modifying the reference factual and procedural knowledge required for building normal and anomalous usage models. Therefore, the upgradeability of a system has direct impact on its response time (Ozcelik & Brooks, 2015) and the QoE of users. The latter is clearly observed in certain use cases, among them proposals related with access control and dynamic authentication grounded on biometrics. As demonstrated in (Djioua & Plamondon, 2009), some biometric traits tend to vary over time, so for the proper behavior of the anomaly recognition methods the registered users should periodically update their reference data. If this process requires the insertion of many samples or their processing is especially sluggish, the QoE is penalized. Note that the ease of updating of a sensor can also be measured by considering the observation of its impact on the response time.

Scalability

The scalability of an anomaly-based IDS is its ability to adapt to the growth of the monitoring scenario on which it operates. This situation often has direct impact on its data processing capacity, so a scalable system must be able to adapt to these changes without significant consequences in terms of effectiveness. Scalability can be measured in different dimensions, such as ability to include additional functionality or ease of adaptation to brand new rates of workload. Consequently, the criteria to be considered when evaluating scalability directly depends on the sensor implementation and the use case for which it was developed. For example, the scalability of the sensor at logical level may consider to what extent new kinds of information corresponding to new profiles of normal behavior can be admitted. Many of the metrics traditionally employed with this purpose are compiled in (Jogalekar & Woodside, 2000). But despite their great variety, at present there is no a unified criterion for their application; instead each proposal analyzes the scalability from a specific point of view and focused on a specific use case.

Straightening Against Adversarial Attacks

As reviewed in the previous sections, strategies for anomaly recognition are often part of intrusion detection systems that analyze and authorize access to sensitive information. Because of this, over the years many attackers have developed methods to attempt to diminish their effectiveness, which range from Denial of Service attempts (Minku, White, & Yao, 2010), to altering the sequences of the intrusion actions in order to simulate patterns related with legitimate use (Maestre Vidal, Sandoval Orozco, & García Villalba, 2016). Many of these techniques are compiled in (Coronoa, Giacinto, & Roli, 2013), where their most relevant countermeasures and the new challenges to their mitigation are discussed. Hence, for an anomaly recognition system to be effective, it must be robust to these threats. But despite the importance of this premise, at present there are no unified criteria for robustness valuation; it used to be estimated by comparing their accuracy with results at similar approaches.

DIFFICULTIES AND CHALLENGES

The evolution of the communication landscape has been propitiated by technological advances. This has led to the emergence of much more sophisticated computing systems, with greater processing capabilities and which are able to handle the information provided by a wide variety of sources. Consequently, the new proposals in the field of anomaly-based intrusion detection must deal with a greater amount of information of much more heterogeneous characteristics. In order to facilitate the design and development of novel detection tools, this section describes and reviews the main difficulties and challenges posed by anomaly-based intrusion detection on current monitoring scenarios, highlighting the following issues: high false positive rates, lack of general purpose strategies, adversarial attacks, monitoring scenarios with variable features, availability of training/validation datasets, difficulties in selecting distances or similarity measures and resource consumption.

High False Positive Rates

The difficulty of establishing metrics and confidence intervals that distinguish the set of normal observations from those that are discordant is not a recent problem. (Chandola, Banerjee, & Kumar, 2009) already warned that it is frequent that in anomaly-based IDS normal observations are confused with anomalous and vice versa; this happens even in approaches capable of adapting to changes in the monitoring environment (i.e. data flowing through communication networks (Bhuyan, Bhattacharyya, & Kalita, 2015).

The trends on recent monitoring scenarios leads to the need of analyzing a greater amount of information with much more heterogeneous traits, which in general terms not only implies the perseverance of this problem; also amplifies it. Consequently, researchers have initiated lines of study focused on reducing false positive rates and mitigating their impact on the system

Lack of a Universal Detection Strategy

As highlighted in (Ahmed, Mahmood, & Hu, 2016), currently there is not a unified anomaly-based detection strategy capable of operating effectively in any monitoring scenario. This is due, among other issues, to the fact that the characteristics of each use case raise too specific requirements and limitations, which often hampers the interoperability of the proposals. Consequently, the efforts made in this field have tended towards specifying rather than unifying; a situation that leads that in many approaches, the previous advances towards discordance identification were overlooked.

Adversarial Attacks

The recent increase in the popularity of the new technologies, as well as the great growth of the information society, has led to that targeted attacks against these systems become more profitable. This also empowered the raise of a series of evasion methods capable of rendering even the most effective anomaly detection strategies useless, which has alerted the different public and private organizations for information security (Police, 2016). The direct consequence of these threats is the need to develop robust detection schemes, among others capable of withstanding denial-of-service attempts or identifying malicious activities obfuscated by imitation observations of legitimate behaviors (Minku, White, & Yao, 2010) (Coronoa, Giacinto, & Roli, 2013).

Monitoring Scenarios with Variable Features

As the level of heterogeneity on monitoring scenarios grows, they become more susceptible to changes, which imply the presence of inconsistencies between feature distributions in the reference data and the information to be analyzed. According to (Ahmed, Mahmood, & Hu, 2016), this entails changes in the behaviors considered normal, so they are no longer considered legitimate in future observations. By contrast, initially discordant observations may become patterns of normal activities. Therefore, the adaptation of the anomaly recognition methods to these non-stationary scenarios is necessary in most real use cases, being a hot topic in research lines related to intrusion detection in communication networks.

Availability of Training/Validation Datasets

The difficulty in acquiring datasets for training and validation on anomaly recognition strategies is a classic problem in many of their applications (Chandola, Banerjee, & Kumar, 2009). As indicated in (Bhuyan, Bhattacharyya, & Kalita, 2015), capturing and gathering information enough representative to train a sensor is already a complicated task. In addition, datasets of public domain samples often contain more normal than discordant samples, a situation that for some researchers may call into question the false-negative rates that some proposals presumed to reach, that may entail the problems related with class unbalancing. (Zimmermann, 2014) studied this problem in depth, highlighting among other aspects to be considered, the antiquity of the public collections of samples assumed as public benchmarks, and the existence of labeling errors within them. The latter leads to the observation of important differences between the accuracy obtained by detection systems in functional evaluation standards, and the accuracy displayed in real use cases. An extensive review of the most relevant datasets considered in the bibliography is illustrated in (Milenkoski, Vieira, Kounev, Avritzer, & Payne, 2015).

Difficulties in selecting distances and similarity measures

As described in Section Distances and similarity measures", the decision of the most suitable distances and similarity measures to recognize anomalies on a particular context may not be a trivial task. Although certain adjustment parameters are easily configured from a learning process, the choice of appropriate distances will condition the behavior of the sensor even from its knowledge acquisition stage. In (Weller-Fahy, Borghetti, & Sodemann, 2014) four typical errors related to the use of distances and similarity measures in the current proposals are identified: 1) selection of inappropriate distances and measures, 2) non optimal distance configuration parameters, 3) improper justification of the decision of distances and similarity measures implemented, 4) errors when dealing with distances and similarity measures as other relevant factors to take bear in mind at the experimentation, so it is possible to state that they are not properly evaluated.

Resource/Energy Consumption

The need to analyze a greater amount of information usually implies the requirement of deploying more complex algorithms, and therefore more computationally expensive. The current monitoring scenarios have high impact on the data processing capacity of sensors, which directly impacts on their efficiency and memory consumption. At the same time, these new use cases increasingly require the emission of real-time responses (Bhuyan, Bhattacharyya, & Kalita, 2014), being their high resource consumption a major limitation. Note that it is important to stress that the recent trends towards implement anomaly-based IDS in ubiquitous and wearable devices also demand the development of strategies that cause a smaller impact on the device battery (Polakis, Diamantaris, Petsas, Maggi, & Ioannidis, July 2015). The energy consumption metrics can also be considered as pattern recognition features for intrusion detection.

CONCLUSION

Thorough this chapter the anomaly-based intrusion detection paradigm has been reviewed in detail, deepening into the evolution of the anomaly concept, related research topics, outlier characterizations or the most frequent knowledge acquisition strategies for modeling "normal" and "suspicious" network usage models. This included the study of the most outstanding families of distances and similarity features applied for distinguishing how discordant are the analyzed observations. From the analysis of the existing/forthcoming challenges and open topics, among them the rising of non-stationarity scenarios, limitation of computing resources or need for additional interoperability/scalability, it was possible to draw lines for being taken into consideration at future anomaly-based IDS designs, which are expected to guide future researchers. It is important to highlight that as demonstrated in some of the reviewed publications, if they are not implemented, the deployment of the resultant sensors may be unviable and/or ineffective at real or emerging scenarios. Consequently, they comprise a set of actions that every researcher in the anomaly-based intrusion detection field must assume.

ACKNOWLEDGMENT

This work has been possible by the support of the Under Secretary of Science, Technology and Innovation of Mexico City in the postdoctoral scholarship of Sergio Mauricio Martínez Monterrubio.

REFERENCES

Aggarwal, C., & Yu, P. (May 2001). Outlier detection for high dimensional data. In *Proc. of the 2001 ACM SIGMOD international conference on Management of data* (pp. 37-46). Santa Barbara, CA: ACM.

Ahmed, M., Mahmood, A., & Hu, J. (2016, January). A survey of network anomaly detection techniques. *Journal of Network and Computer Applications, 60*, 19-31.

Alippi, C. (2014). Intelligence for Embedded Systems. Springer-Verlag.

Barnett, V., & Lewis, T. (1994, February). Outliers in Statistical Data (3rd ed.). Hoboken, NJ: John Wiley & Sons.

Barona López, L., Valdivieso Caraguay, L., Maestre Vidal, J., Sotelo Monge, M., & García Villalba, L. (2017, January). *Towards Incidence Management in 5G Based on Situational Awareness*. Academic Press.

Bhuyan, M., Bhattacharyya, D., & Kalita, J. (2014). Network Anomaly Detection: Methods, Systems and Tools. IEEE Communications Surveys & Tutorials, 16(1), 303-336.

Bhuyan, M., Bhattacharyya, D., & Kalita, J. (2014, June). Network Anomaly Detection: Methods, Systems and Tools. *IEEE Communications Surveys & Tutorials, 16*(1), 303-336.

Bhuyan, M., Bhattacharyya, D., & Kalita, J. (2015). An empirical evaluation of information metrics for low-rate and high-rate DDoS attack detection. *Pattern Recognition Letters, 51*(1), 1–7. doi:10.1016/j.patrec.2014.07.019

Boriah, S., Chandola, V., & Kumar, V. (2008, April). Similarity Measures for Categorical Data: A Comparative Evaluation. In *International SIAM Conference of Data Mining*, (pp. 243-254). Atlanta, GA: Academic Press. 10.1137/1.9781611972788.22

Cha, S. (2007, January). Comprehensive Survey on Distance/Similarity Measures between Probability Density Functions. *International Journal of Mathematical Models and Methods in Applied Sciences, 1*(4), 300-307.

Chandola, V., Banerjee, A., & Kumar, V. (2009, July). Anomaly Detection: A Survey. *ACM Computing Surveys, 41*(3).

Coronoa, I., Giacinto, G., & Roli, F. (2013, August). Adversarial attacks against intrusion detection systems: Taxonomy, solutions and open issues. *Information Sciences, 239*, 201-225.

Djioua, M., & Plamondon, R. (2009, October). Studying the variability of handwriting patterns using the Kinematic Theory. *Human Movement Science, 28*(5), 588-601.

Edgeworth, F. (1887). On discordant observations. *Philosophical Magazine, 23*(5).

Endsley, M. (1988, January). Design and evaluation for situation awareness enhancement. In *Proc. of the 32nd Annual Meeting on Human Factors Society*, (pp. 97–101). Santa Monica, CA: Academic Press.

Faruki, P., Bharmal, A., & Laxmi, V. (2015, May). Android Security: A Survey of Issues, Malware Penetration, and Defenses. *IEEE Communications Surveys & Tutorials, 17*(2), 998-1022.

Foss, A., Markatou, M., Ray, B., & Heching, A. (2016, July). A semiparametric method for clustering mixed data. *Machine Learning*, 1-40. doi:10.100710994-016-5575-7

Gan, G., Ma, C., & Wu, J. (2007, July). Data Clustering: Theory, Algorithms, and Applications. SIAM, 20.

Goldstein, M., & Uchida, S. (2016, April). A Comparative Evaluation of Unsupervised Anomaly Detection Algorithms for Multivariate Data. *PLoS One*. doi:10.1371/journal.pone.0152173

Grubbs, F. (1969, February). Procedures for Detecting Outlying Observations in Samples. *Technometrics, 11*(1), 1-21.

Han, J., Kamber, M., & Pei, J. (2011, July). Data Mining: Concepts and Techniques. Elsevier.

Hawkings, D. (1980). *Identification of Outliers*. Monographs on Applied Probability and Statistics. doi:10.1007/978-94-015-3994-4

He, X., Dai, H., Ning, P., & Dutta, R. (2015, December). Dynamic IDS Configuration in the Presence of Intruder Type Uncertainty. In *Proc. IEEE Global Communications Conference* (pp. 1-6). San Diego, CA: IEEE.

Holte, R. (1993, April). Very simple classification rules perform well on most commonly used datasets. *Machine Learning, 11*(1), 63-90.

Jogalekar, P., & Woodside, M. (2000, June). Evaluating the scalability of distributed systems. *IEEE Transactions on Parallel and Distributed Systems, 11*(6), 589-603.

Juvekar, C. (2018, August). *More Efficient Security for Cloud-Based Machine Learning*. Retrieved from http://0-search.proquest.com.cisne.sim.ucm.es/docview/2090233415?accountid=14514

Kelly, M., Hand, D., & Adams, N. (1999, August). The impact of changing populations on classifier performance. In *5th ACM SIGKDD international conference on Knowledge discovery and data mining* (pp. 36-371). San Diego, CA: ACM.

Kriegel, H., Kröger, P., & Zimek, A. (2010). Outlier Detection Techniques. *16th ACM SIGKDD Conference on Knowledge Discovery and Data Mining*, Washington, DC.

Laskov, P., Düssel, P., Schäfer, C., & Rieck, K. (2005, September). Learning Intrusion Detection: Supervised or Unsupervised? In *Proc. of the 13th International Conference on Image Analysis and Processing*, (pp. 50-57). Cagliari, Italy: Academic Press.

Maestre Vidal, J., Sandoval Orozco, A., & García Villalba, L. (2016, November). Online masquerade detection resistant to mimicry. *Expert Systems with Applications, 61*, 162-180.

Maestre Vidal, J., Sandoval Orozco, A., & García Villalba, L. (2017, November). Alert Correlation Framework for Malware Detection by Anomaly-based Packet Payload Analysis. *Journal of Network and Computer Applications, 29*, 11–22. doi:10.1016/j.jnca.2017.08.010

Maestre Vidal, J., Sandoval Orozco, A., & García Villalba, L. (2018). Adaptive Artificial Immune Networks for Mitigating DoS flooding Attacks. *Swarm and Evolutionary Computation, 38*, 94–108. doi:10.1016/j.swevo.2017.07.002

Maestre Vidal, J., Sotelo Monge, M., & García Villabla, L. (2018). A Novel Pattern Recognition System for Detecting Android Malware by Analyzing Suspicious Boot Sequences. *Knowledge-Based Systems, 150*, 198–217. doi:10.1016/j.knosys.2018.03.018

Milenkoski, A., Vieira, M., Kounev, S., Avritzer, A., & Payne, B. (2015, September). Evaluating Computer Intrusion Detection Systems: A Survey of Common Practices. *ACM Computing Surveys, 48*(12), 1-41.

Minku, L., White, A., & Yao, X. (2010, May). The impact of diversity on online ensemble learning in the presence of concept drift. *IEEE Transactions on Knowledge and Data Engineering, 22*(5), 731-742.

Mohammadi, M., Al-Fuqaha, A., Sorour, S., & Guizani, M. (2018). Deep Learning for IoT Big Data and Streaming Analytics: A Survey. *IEEE Communications Surveys and Tutorials, 20*(4), 2923–2960. doi:10.1109/COMST.2018.2844341

O'Reilly, C., Gluhak, A., Imran, M., & Rajasegarar, S. (2014). Anomaly Detection in Wireless Sensor Networks in a Non-Stationary Environment. *IEEE Communications Surveys and Tutorials, 16*(3), 1413–1432. doi:10.1109/SURV.2013.112813.00168

Ozcelik, I., & Brooks, R. (2015, February). Deceiving entropy based DoS detection. *Computers & Security, 48*(1), 234-245.

Polakis, I., Diamantaris, M., Petsas, T., Maggi, F., & Ioannidis, S. (2015, July). Powerslave: Analyzing the Energy Consumption of Mobile Antivirus Software. In *12th International Conference on Detection of Intrusions and Malware, and Vulnerability Assessment*, (pp. 165-184). Milan, Italy: Academic Press. 10.1007/978-3-319-20550-2_9

Police, E. (2016). *The Internet Organised Crime Threat Assessment (iOCTA)*. Retrieved from https://www.europol.europa.eu/activities-services/main-reports/internet-organised-crime-threat-assessment-iocta-2016

Savage, D., Zhang, X., Yu, X., Chou, P., & Wang, Q. (2014, October). Anomaly detection in online social networks. *Social Networks, 39*, 62-70.

Schubert, E., Weiler, M., & Zimek, A. (2015). Outlier Detection and Trend Detection: Two Sides of the Same Coin. *IEEE International Conference on Data Mining Workshop*, (pp. 40-46). Atlantic City, NJ: IEEE. 10.1109/ICDMW.2015.79

Schubert, E., Wojdanowski, R., Zimek, A., & Kriegel, H. (2012). On Evaluation of Outlier Rankings and Outlier Scores. In 12th SIAM International Conference on Data Mining (SDM), (pp. 1047-1058). Anaheim, CA: Academic Press.

Shafiq, M., Yu, X., Kashif Bashir, A., Chaudrhry, H., & Wang, D. (2018). A machine learning approach for feature selection traffic classification using security analysis. *The Journal of Supercomputing, 74*(10), 4867–4892. doi:10.100711227-018-2263-3

Song, X., Wu, M., Jermaine, C., & Ranka, S. (2007, May). Conditional Anomaly Detection. *IEEE Transactions on Knowledge and Data Engineering, 19*(5), 631-645.

Sotelo Monge, M., Maestre Vidal, J., & García Villalba, L. (2017). Entropy-Based Economic Denial of Sustainability Detection. *Entropy (Basel, Switzerland)*, 2.

Sotelo Monge, M., Maestre Vidal, J., & García Villalba, L. (2017). Reasoning and Knowledge Acquisition Framework for 5G Network Analytics. *Sensors (Basel)*, 17. PMID:29065473

Takeuchi, J., & Yamanishi, K. (2006, April). A unifying framework for detecting outliers and change points from time series. *IEEE Transactions on Knowledge and Data Engineering, 18*(4), 482-492.

Weller-Fahy, D., Borghetti, B., & Sodemann, A. (2014, March). A Survey of Distance and Similarity Measures Used Within Network Intrusion Anomaly Detection. IEEE Communications Surveys & Tutorials, 17(1), 70-91.

Ye, Y., Squartini, S., & Piazza, F. (2013, September). Online sequential extreme learning machine in nonstationary environments. *Neurocomputing, 116*, 94–101.

Zait, M., & Messatfa, H. (1997, November). A comparative study of clustering methods. *Future Generation Computer Systems, 13*(1), 149-159.

Zimek, A., Campello, R., & Sander, J. (2013, June). Ensembles for unsupervised outlier detection: challenges and research questions. *ACM SIGKDD Explorations Newsletter, 15*(1), 11-22.

Zimmermann, A. (2014, December). The Data Problem in Data Mining. *ACM SIGKDD Explorations Newsletter, 16*(2), 38-45.

Chapter 11
Traffic Analysis of UAV Networks Using Enhanced Deep Feed Forward Neural Networks (EDFFNN)

Vanitha N.
Avinashilingam Institute for Home Science and Higher Education for Women, India & Dr. N. G. P. Arts and Science College, India

Padmavathi Ganapathi
Avinashilingam Institute for Home Science and Higher Education for Women, India

ABSTRACT

The world is moving to an autonomous era. Autonomous vehicles take a major role in day-to-day activity, helping human personnel do work quickly and independently. Unmanned aerial vehicles (UAVs) are autonomous vehicles controlled using remotes in ground station by human personnel. These UAVs act as a network that plays a vital role in the digital era. There are different architectures of UAV networks available. This chapter concentrates on centralized UAV network. Because of wireless and autonomy characteristics, these networks are prone to various security issues, so it's very important to monitor and analyze the traffic of the UAV network in order to identify the intrusions. This chapter proposes enhanced deep feed forward neural network (EDFFNN) in order to monitor and analyze the traffic of the UAV network to detect the intrusions with maximum detection rate of 94.4%. The results have been compared with the previous method of intrusion detection.

INTRODUCTION

Unmanned Aerial Vehicles (UAV) systems or drones plays a vital role in recent days, which can fly autonomously or it can be functioned remotely. Due to the high mobility of drones they have been widely used for a lot of applications like military, search and rescue operations, health care, delivery, monitoring etc. Ad-hoc networking between UAVs or drones (FANET- Flying Ad-hoc Networks) can solve the

DOI: 10.4018/978-1-5225-9611-0.ch011

problems that arising from the infrastructure-based UAV network. Because of lot of applications the communication between UAVs are very important, so it is vital to have the communication architecture for creating a UAV networks. These Communication architectures prone to various cyber-attacks, it is mandatory to have an Intrusion detection systems (IDS) to detect the cyber- attacks on those architectures. IDS performances are essential in cyber security. This paper aims to introduce the Intrusion detection systems (IDS) for centralized Unmanned Arial Vehicle (UAV) assisted Vehicular ad-hoc network (VANET) architecture having U2V/V2U communication. This chapter concentrates on the Centralized UAV networks assisted VANET architecture. Network Intrusion Detection System (NIDS) shields a network from nasty software attacks. Traditionally, there are two forms of NIDS according to the strategies to detect network attacks. At first, signature-based detection, compares new data with a knowledge base of known intrusions. Regardless of the state of affairs that, this method cannot spot new attacks, this ruins the most widespread tactic in commercial intrusion detection systems. Latter, anomaly-based detection, compares new data with a model of standard user behavior and marks a significant deviation from this model as an anomaly using machine learning. As a result, this approach can detect anomaly-based attacks that have never been seen before. The anomaly-based detection approach is usually combined with flow-based traffic monitoring in NIDS. Flow based monitoring is based on the information which is existing in the packet headers, so flow-based NIDS have to handle a lower amount of data compared to a payload-based NIDS. This exertion builds a Deep Neural Network (DNN) model for an Intrusion detection system and train the model with simulated dataset. (Hichem Sedjelmaci, 2017)

Applications

UAVs or drones have a countless imminent to build abundant applications in military and civilian domains. Applications include,

Military

- Military men and women are protected by drone anytime; they will be armed with live video remote communications to ground troops, essential gear, or weapons.
- The main drone use overseas in war zones is reconnaissance of unknown areas/buildings, adversary tracing, and force defense (making sure our crowds are safe and no one is approaching them).
- Drones are a very good searching tool for lost or injured soldiers as well as a real-time view of various situations and missions, allowing for commanders to make better decisions in resource allocations.

Civilian

Applications of Civilian contains, Healthcare, Filmmaking, Archaeology, Cargo transport, Conservation, Hobby and recreational use, Journalism, Law enforcement, Scientific research, Search and rescue and Surveillance.

Traffic Monitoring

The traffic on a road in a city monitored by UAVs, they are in charge for collecting and sending, in real time, vehicle data to a traffic processing centre for traffic regulation purposes.

Government

This UAV's are more mutual and used for safety, research, and a gathering of tailored uses for federal activities from the Department of Interior, National Park Service, Intelligence Communities, Local Law Enforcement, Fire Departments and much more.

Disaster Monitoring

Disaster monitoring comprises Search and Rescue, Marine Search and Rescue
Flooding, Emergency Uses (delivery of equipment e.g. Deregulator), Wildfire, Damage assessment, Rapid response, Surf Lifesaving (launch delivery)
Fire Detection (e.g. fire towers).

Delivery

Amazon's Prime Air service would see unmanned aerial vehicles (UAVs), or drones, install parcels under five pounds (2.3 kg) to clients within a 10-mile (16 km) radius of Amazon self-actualization centers. In other words, it will drop off your latest desire buying right at your doorstep.

Types of UAV Networks

UAV networks are classified into two types based on Communication between node they are:
Centralised UAV network architecture and Decentralised Network architecture. Again, the Decentralised UAV Network architecture is classified into three types namely, UAV ad-hoc network architecture, Multi-group UAV ad-hoc network architecture and Multi-layer UAV ad-hoc network architecture.

Centralized UAV Network Architecture

A centralized UAV communication architecture has a ground station, to which all UAVs are connected. In such a network, each UAV is directly connected to the ground station transmitting and receiving scheduling command and control data, and the UAVs are not directly connected to each other. The complete network is controlled by the ground station, and communications between two UAV are need to be routed via the ground station acting as a relay. A small information delay is expected for scheduling command and control data transmitted between the ground troop and a UAV, because all UAVs are directly connected to the ground station. Though the data transmitted between two UAVs will experience a longer delay since the data needs to be directed through the ground station. Long distance communications are often conducted between the ground station and UAVs, advanced radio transmission devices with a high transmission power are essential in the UAVs, which may not be practical for medium or small UAVs due to their size and payload constraints. In addition, in the centralized UAV communication architecture,

Figure 1. Types of UAV network based on communication between UAV's

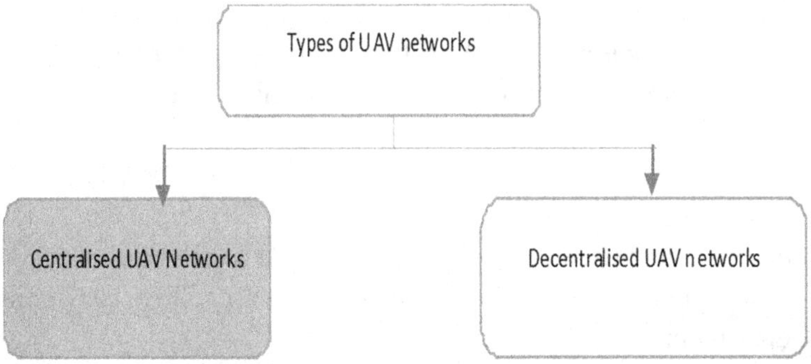

the ground station represents vulnerability of the UAV network by rendering the possible of single-point of failure. Thus, this communication architecture is not robust. Figure 2. shows the centralized UAV communication architecture. (Jun Li, Yifeng Zhou, 2013).

Decentralized UAV Network Architecture

In decentralized communication architecture, a central node is not required, and two UAVs can communicate with each other either directly or indirectly. That is the information that are not intended to the ground station can be routed through a UAV instead of the ground station. In the following, three decentralized communication architectures are conferred. They are UAV ad-hoc Network, which is an ad-hoc network formed by UAV's in air layer with one backbone UAV, that is connected to the ground station, Multi group UAV network, which is group of backbone UAV's connected to the ground station, here the each and every backbone UAV's form an ad-hoc group, Multilayer UAV ad-hoc network, her the backbone UAV's linked together and one backbone UAV connected to the ground station.. (Jun Li, Yifeng Zhou, 2013).

Challenges in UAV networks

There are lot of contests related with UAV, cracking which are critical for safe and consistent employment of such systems in civilian and military scenarios. The following challenges have been identified as being threats to the use of UAV in VANET.

- Unreliable.
- Traffic density and inadequate data rate.
- Scheduling and Channel modelling.
- Vulnerable to interference and performance analysis.
- Communication among nodes.
- Conserving energy of a node and energy limitations.
- Visual line of sight (LoS) action and path planning.
- Tough for real monitoring and administration.
- Security and privacy issues.

Figure 2. Centralised UAV network Architecture
(Jun Li, Yifeng Zhou, 2013).

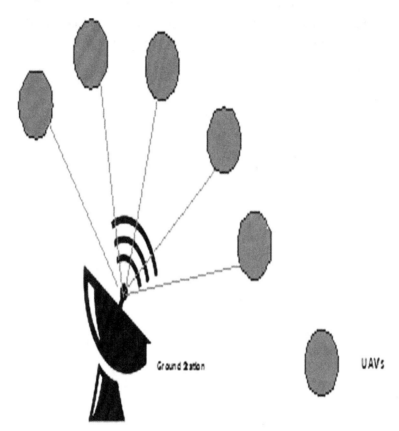

Security plays a major role in UAV to VANET communication.

Objectives

The primary objective of this chapter is to analyze the traffic in order to identify the attacker UAV in Centralized UAV aided Vehicular ad-hoc networks using enhanced feed forward neural networks.

Attacks Classification

Network traffic analysis detects the malicious node's actions once they have penetrated the network and are presently trying to snip data. It helps to realize the threats quicker, thus lessening the time between contamination and resolution, and dropping the cost of data breach for most companies. Thus, instinctive research has been conducted to spread over the Deep Learning practices to the computer security and the network traffic with anomaly detection problems.

Security plays a major role in UAV to VANET communication. This work particularly focuses on cyber-attacks classifications based on their nature specific to UAV assisted Vehicular ad-hoc networks, refer Figure 3. Attack classification. False data dissemination attack is most dangerous attack specific to UAV that comes under application logic attacks, which is a cyber-attack that affects the UAV network tremendously.

False Data Dissemination

A nasty UAV might program a dissimilar physical noticeable fact like some natural situations (storm or forest fires) to its neighbours.

These attacks can be classified into following sub types,

- Wrong Bandwidth Injection
- Automatic Dependent Surveillance – Broadcast (ADS-B)
- Good/Bad Mouthing Attack

Figure 3. Attack classification

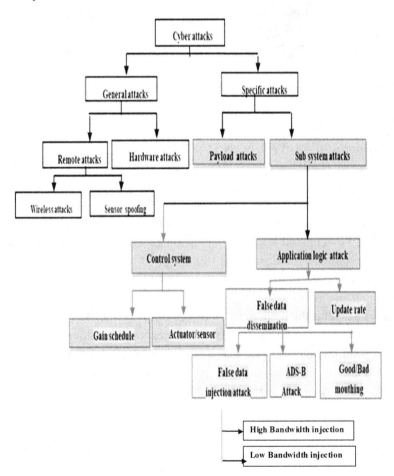

Wrong Bandwidth Injection Attack

The attacker injects forged bandwidth information measure data into UAV network routing protocol. The bandwidth misleading attack is outlined as an interruption, within which the resister injects forged bandwidth data into UAV network routing protocol. The goal of this attack is to disrupt the routing method of knowledge transmission. Two types of wrong bandwidth injections attacks are shown in Fig 2. This work concentrates on high bandwidth injection attack.

High Bandwidth Injection Attack

The adversary forges and claims a higher bandwidth than the link can truly provide. The data transmission process will be interrupted, once the UAV or ground stations obtain the worked bandwidth information. As a result, the link with the manipulated bandwidth information will be assigned more traffic, which will result in congestion and high delay times.

Low Bandwidth Injection Attack

Low bandwidth deceiving attack, the challenger falsifies and privileges a lower bandwidth than the link can really deliver. Whenever the data communication progression begins, the connection with the calculated bandwidth information will cause underutilization in the affected connection and the throughput will decrease in the UAV network (Sixiao Weiy,2014).

The Automatic Dependent Surveillance – Broadcast (ADS-B) Attack (Spoofing GPS Co-Ordinates)

The ADS-B attack tries to disseminate fake data. ADS-B is an on-board element of the UAV structure that televise information's like position and collision evading. From the authors of an ADS-B attacker also tries to broadcast a fake position or take off the GPS coordinates (i.e., GPS spoofing) of a board UAV. Because of that, the lifetime of honest drones is exaggerated (Hichem Sedjelmaci, 2017). The GPS spoofing attack makes a high signal strength intensity (SSI) to get control of the drone, and this SSI is higher than that from satellites as showed by Shepard et al. (D. P. Shepard et al, 2012).

The Bad/Good Mouthing Attack

A nasty intrusion detection agent will give the false discovery information to corrupt the network performance.

1. Bad-Mouthing

UAV Detection Agent (UDA) declares the good UAV as malicious UAV. Authors created an UAV Detection Agent, that is employed in each and every UAV's in order to monitor the UAV's that is performing incorrect bandwidth injection and send the report to ground station. (N. Vanitha & G. Padmavathi,2017), (Z.Bankovic. et al, 2014).

2.   Good-Mouthing

UAV Detection Agent (UDA) recommends a malicious UAV as a good UAV and sends report to the ground station. (N. Vanitha & G. Padmavathi,2017).

In this chapter the researchers focused on incorrect bandwidth injection, the planned intrusion detection system considers a general type of an attack situation where nasty bandwidth information is vaccinated into an TCP data packet header of UAV network. The proposed intrusion detection system monitors broadcasting TCP data packet in the UAV network. (Hichem Sedjelmaci, 2017)

BACKGROUND

Jun Li, Yifeng Zhou, and Louise Lamont presented four Communication Architectures that is One Centralized architecture and Three Decentralized architectures along with its Protocols for Networking Unmanned Aerial Vehicles and conferred pros and cons for those architectures.

Alan Kim, Brandon Wampler, James Goppert and Inseok Hwang, analyzed Cyber Attack Suscepti-bilities and Analysis for Unmanned Aerial Vehicles, they have tracked a study on possible cyber threats and susceptibilities of the current autopilot systems in way to examine the post-attack performance of the autopilot system through simulation.

Hichem Sedjelmaci, and Sidi Mohammed Senouci published a paper for Intrusion detection and response system for spotting intrusion by means of SVM based scheme against Cyber – Attacks in UAV networks with high detection rate of 93.01% and low false positives rates in overall UAV networks.

Hichem Sedjelmaci, and Sidi Mohammed Senouci once more published an intrusion detection and ejection frame work against cyber-attacks by means of A Bayesian Game-Theoretic Methodology a Bayesian Game-Theoretic Model to detect attacks with high detection, low false positive rates and low communication overhead in General UAV aided networks.

N. Vanitha and G. Padmavathi has published a Study on Various Cyber-Attacks and their Classifica-tion in UAV Assisted Vehicular Ad-Hoc Networks, and they have identified the most vulnerable cyber attack that effects the UAV networks namely false data dissemination attacks through security analysis against security principles, confidentiality, integrity and availability. They have studied the causes of the False data dissemination attacks namely, False Data Injection, GPS Spoofing and Good Mouthing /Bad Mouthing attack.

N. Vanitha and G. Padmavathi has published a paper on comparative study on UAV network architec-tures and proposed a new unified architecture. Researchers had made a brief study on centralized UAV network architecture and decentralized UAV network architectures, and conducted a security analysis against security principles.

Sixiao Wei et al, have conducted a simulation study for evaluating the network performance of multi UAV networks using Network Simulator 2(NS-2). And also, they have simulated the erroneous data injection attacks against UAV communication networks in ns-2 and proved the influence of erroneous data injection attacks on network performance.

E. Kesavulu Reddy, used Artificial neural networks (ANN) for detecting network intrusion detection. ANN offers the possibility to recognize and categorizes the network movement grounded on restricted, inadequate, and nonlinear data bases.

Rashmi Amardeep and Dr.K Thippe Swamy, trained Feed forward neural network with back propagation algorithm until the error is minimized. Back propagation (BP) is important algorithm for network that has been recognized for its correctness because it permits itself to pick up and educating itself thus it can reach higher correctness. Deep Neural Network be trained by back propagation algorithm to achieve any recording among the input and the output. Here the researchers discussed merits and demerits of BP algorithm assisted DFFNN training the data set.

Tuan A Tang, Lotfi Mhamdi build a Deep neural network model for network intrusion detection. Authors taken 6 features form 41 features of KDD-NSL dataset for flow-based anomaly detection in SDN environment.

Lot of researchers have been used Feed Forward Neural Network (FFNN) for intrusion detection with highest accuracy in wireless networks, this chapter uses EDFFNN that is Deep Feed Forward Neural Network with Back Propagation algorithm for training and detecting the intrusions in the data set got from the simulation environment. Here Centralized UAV network and the threat model were simulated using Network simulator 3.

Security Challenges and Attacks in UAV Network Architecture

Significance of the UAV network and traffic Analysis

- Traffic analysis of network helps in monitoring all events inside the network. Traffic analysis extracts recognizable traffic structures, such as packet size, frequency of a packet and the packet interarrival time, from traffic movements, and then links the features with certain proofs or secrets.
- Understanding and evaluating the network utilization.
- Analyse the origin, destination type, size, and content/data of packets.
- Provides overall network design of Centralised UAV assisted VANET.
- Simulated the environment in Network Simulator 3(NS - 3).
- Compare the Deep learning-based IDS with the previous SVM based IDS technique.

METHODOLOGY

Centralised UAV Network Model

Figure 2 shows the network model of the centralised UAV communication network, where each and every UAV communicates through the Ground station. Ground station deployment is based on the Random Graph-Based Network Model. All UAV's that is U={u1,u2,u3.....}. Set of UAV's, arrival of UAV's traversing the edge is Poisson, all UAV's follows the shortest path to the ground station. Control and scheduling information sent to UAV's via ground station. Here the authors simulated this network model using NS-3. Due to the wireless nature of multi-UAV systems causes security risks since speedily moving UAVs are installed in the exposed arena. Exactly, the wireless communication makes the information available to anybody, especially those who may actively interrupt, disturb, or operate the information. To protect the multi-UAVs, authors study the subsequent qualities: availability, confidentiality, and integrity. (N.Vanitha et al.,2018)

Threat Model

Integrity refers to defending communicated data from alteration, removal, and/or injection. UAVs are designed for plentiful applications. Cyber-attacks such as message exploitation, false data injection, and others can cause serious penalties and interrupt the assignments maintained by UAVs. Here the authors created a threat model node that injects the false window size in the packet format of tcp header window size in the TCP protocol. Figure 4 and 5 shows the TCP Packet format and header format.

TCP Packet Format

TCP permits clients to run simultaneous submissions using different port numbers and at full-duplex thereby giving a multiplexing capability. TCP labels each octet of data with a Sequence Number and a sequence of octets form a Segment, the sequence number of the first octet in the segment is called the Segment Sequence Number. Figure 4 and 5 shows the TCP packet format. TCP offers depend ability with ACK packets and Flow Control using the method of a Sliding Window. Through the setup of a TCP connection the extreme segment size is determined constructed on the lowest MTU across the network (Min-Joo Kang,2017).

The TCP header looks like this:

Deep Learning Approach

Deep networks that appearance like the multilayer perceptron (MLP) but have a different construction. The difference between the MLP that is feed forward neural network and the deep networks is their training measures. The classification is conducted by training data with many layers in hierarchical networks with unsupervised learning.

Important features of an input are manually designed and the system automatically learns to map the features to an output in classical machine learning. There are multiple levels of features in deep learning. These features are repeatedly revealed and they are collected in various levels to produce outputs. Each level represents intangible features that are revealed from the features offered in the prior level.

Generative Architecture

Generative models are also denoted to as graphical model since they show independence/dependence for supply. They are visualised as graphs that have nodes representing random variables and arcs show the relationship between random variables that represent the given system with millions of parameters graphically. The joint statistical distribution of the variables can be written as products of the nodes and

Figure 4. TCP Packer header format

	16	16	32	32	4	6	6	16	16	16	0 or 32 bits
	Source Port	Dest. Port	SEQ No.	ACK No.	HLEN	Res.	Code Bits	Window	Checksum	Urgent Pointer	IP Options

Figure 5. TCP Packet format

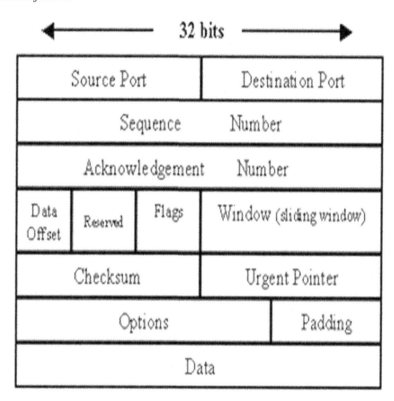

their associated variables. The graphical models have hidden variables that cannot be detected. since their training does not depend on the labels of the data, the generative models are associated with supervised learning. The models go through a pre-training stage (unsupervised learning) for purpose of classification. Through this process, each of the lower layers are trained separately from the other layers which allows the other layers to be trained in a greedily layer by layer from bottom to up. After pre-training all other layers are trained. The sub-classes of generative models are Recurrent Neural Network (RNN), Deep Auto-Encoder, Deep Boltzmann Machine (DBM) and Deep Believe networks (DBN).

Recurrent Neural Network (RNN)

RNN is a session of deep networks that are either measured supervised or unsupervised learning with an input consecutive data whose span could be as large as its depth. A feedback loop linking layer by layer with the ability to store data of previous input increasing the reliability of the model is the RNN model architecture. There are two types architecture in RNN: Elman and Jordan RNNs. The simple feedback looping layer by layer is the Elman model. The feedback looping all neurons within a layer to the next layer is the Jordan model. There exists also a response linking a neuron to itself. The skill of the Jordan RNN to stock data in the neurons permits it to train less input vector for classification of normal and abnormal forms with high correctness.

Figure 6. Classification of deep learning IDS

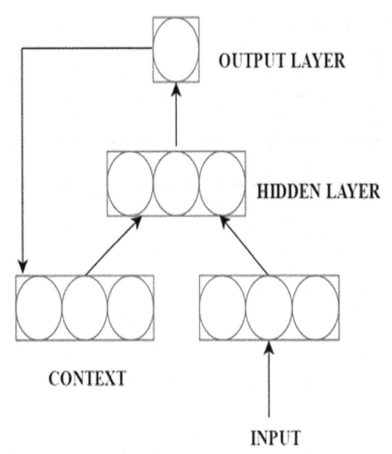

Deep Auto-Encoder

Deep Auto-Encoder is an energy based deep models classified as reproductive models in their original form. It comes in dissimilar forms mostly also generative models. Other methods are stacked auto encoder and de noising auto encoder.

An Auto-Encoder develops deep when it has numerous hidden layers. It is made up of an input layer unit representing the model data, one or two hidden layer units where the features are transformed and then mapped to the output layer unit for renovation. Training the auto-encoder gives it a "bottleneck" structure where the hidden layer becomes narrower than the input layer to prevent the model from learning its uniqueness function.

Unfortunately, the deep auto encoder when trained with back propagation has not been a success the evaluation gets stuck in local minima with a minimal gradient signal when trained with back propagation. Pre-training a deep auto encoder using the greedy layer wise approach by training each of the layers in turns has proven to alleviate the backpropagation problems.

Figure 7. Jordan network

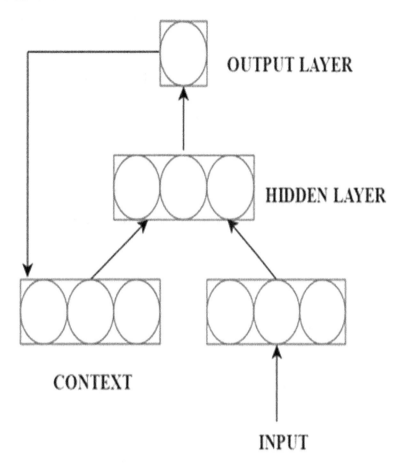

Deep Boltzmann Machine (DBM)

DBM follows a unidirectional graphical model. Presently there exist no connection between units on the same layer but between the input units and the hidden units. DBM when trained with a large source of unlabelled data and fine-tuned with labelled data acts as a respectable classifier. Its structure is an offspring of a general Boltzmann machine (BM) which is a network of units created on stochastic decisions to determine their on and off states. BM algorithm is simple to train but turns to be leisurely in the procedure. A decrease in the number of hidden layers of a DBM to one form a Restricted Boltzmann Machine (RBM). DBM when trained with a large supply of unlabelled data and fine-tuned with labelled data performances a good classifier. Training a stack of RBM with many hidden layers using the feature activation on one RBM as the input for the next layer leads to the creation of Deep Believe Network (DBN).

Deep Belief Networks (DBN)

To construct the models, DBN uses both unsupervised pre-training and supervised fine-tuning techniques. Figure 11 shows a DBN which is made up of a stack of Restricted Boltzmann Machines (RBMs) and one or more additional layers for discrimination mission. RBMs are probabilistic generative models that

Figure 8. Elman network

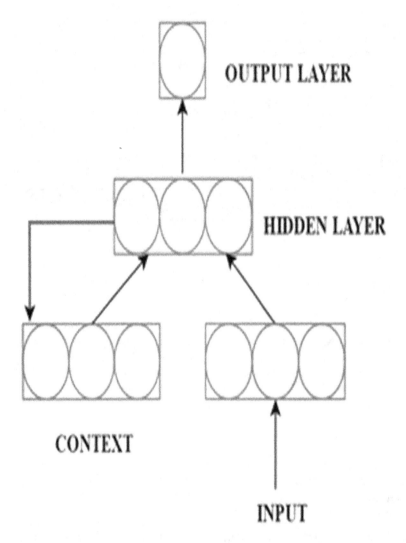

study a combined probability distribution of detected (training) data without using data labels. Once the structure of a DBN is determined the goal for training is to learn the weights w between layers. Each node is autonomous of other nodes in the similar layer given all nodes which gives it the characteristic allowing us to train the reproductive weights of each RBM. Then the DBN goes through a greedy layer by layer learning algorithm which learns each stack of RBM's layer at a time. In Figure 9 left, the top layers in red form a RBM and the lower layers in blue form directed sigmoid believe network.

DBN has been skilled as a classifier by N. Gao *et al*. to detect intrusion by comparing the performance with SVM and ANN. The classifiers were trained on KDD data set. The authors proved that deep learning of DBN can effectively be used as a real ID. They concluded the greedy layer by layer learning algorithm when used to pre-train and fine-tune a DBN gives a high accuracy in classification. The results showed that DBN recorded the best accuracy of 93.49%, a TP value of 92.33 and FP of 0.76% (N. Gao,2014).

Figure 9. Deep auto encoder

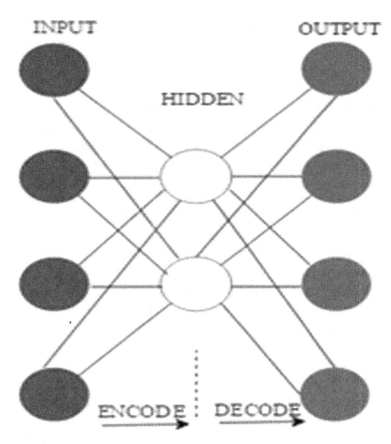

Figure 10. A Boltzmann machine with stochastic on and off hidden features and a variable layer representing a vector of stochastic on and off states. Right: An RBM with no visible to visible units connected and no hidden to hidden units connected.

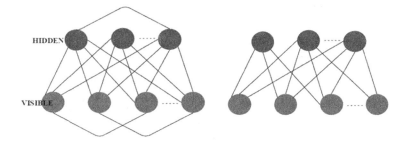

Discriminative Architecture

The discriminative architecture practices discriminative control for classification by characterising the following distributions of classes trained on the input data. There are two types of discriminative architectures, Recurrent neural network and convolutional neural network.

Figure 11. Three-layer deep belief network and three layers deep Boltzmann machine

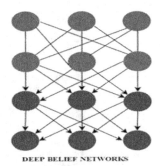 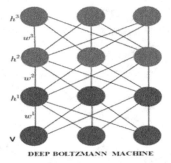

- **Recurrent Neural Network (RNN):** RNN uses discriminative control for classification when the model's output is an explicit labelled data in sequence with the input data sequence. Training data needs to be pre-segmented and a post-processing to transform the output to a labelled data, to train RNN as a discriminative model
- **Convolutional Neural Network (CNN):** A convolutional neural network (CNN) is a type of discrimination deep architecture with one or more convolutional and combining layers in an array to form a multilayer neural network (Li Deng, 2014). Convolutional layers share many weights followed by sampling of the convolutional layer's output by the pooling layer which results in some form of translational invariant properties.

CNN has less parameter as compared to other connected networks with the same number of hidden units which gives it a benefit of easier training. CNN architecture is that of multi-layer perceptron, and are variant of MLP which are encouraged biologically. The series of layers building up a CNN architecture are the convolutional layer, max pooling layer and the completely connected layer. The convolutional layer is finished up of neurons forming a rectangular grid where preceding layers are made of neuros designed as a rectangular grid. The rectangular grid neurons are linked to each other with the inputs from preceding rectangular units through a set of weights recognized as filter banks. These weights for the rectangular units do not alter for every rectangular grid of neuron to form convolutional layers. In architectures where the convolutional layer is completed up of different grids, each grid uses a dissimilar filter bank. Each convolutional layer is followed by a pooling layer which combines subsets of the convolutional layer's rectangular block by taking sub-samples to give an output of the block. Several ways of pooling can be done, such as computing the maximum or average or a learned linear summing of neurons in the blocks. Some blocks turn to be shifted more than a column or a row in turn feed in an s input to neighbouring pooling units. This cause a decrease in the dimension of the system design and thus causing differences to the input. The final stage which has several convolutional and max-pooling layers non-linearly stacked in the neural network form a fully connected layer of network. The connectivity which allows the set of weights of the filter banks to be trained easily (L. Lab, 2016).

PROPOSED TECHNIQUE

Proposed Intrusion Detection System with Recurrent Neural Network (RNN)

In this work, researcher constructed a simple deep Recurrent neural network with an input layer, three hidden layers and an output layer as described in Figure 12. The input and output dimension will be six and two respectively. The hidden layers encompass twelve, six and three neurons correspondingly. Our model beginning parameters are arrangement with 10 for the group size and 100 for the epoch. The learning rate will be 0.1.

Deep Feed Forward Neural network is trained with back propagation algorithm to work like a RNN. The monitoring module checks the incoming packet with the profiling module, if it matches with the profile in profiling module the system carries the attack detection process else stores the new profile in profiling module.

Algorithm for Training DFFNN with Backpropagation

Step1: Determine the architecture Number of input and output neurons Hidden neurons and layers
Step 2: Initialize all weights and biases to small random values, typically $\in$ [-1, 1], choose a learning rate η .
Step 3: Repeat until expiry criteria fulfilled Present a training example and proliferate it through the network (Forward pass) Calculate the actual output
  ◦ Inputs applied
  ◦ Multiplied by weights
  ◦ Summed
  ◦ Squashed by sigmoid activation function
  ◦ Output passed to each neuron in next layer, adapt weights starting from the output layer and working backwards (backward pass). (Rashmi Amardeep, 2017).

Overview of Proposed Intrusion Detection System

In training phase, the anomalous packet is trained with backpropagation algorithm with FFNN and put that profile in the profiling module for future reference. Proposed algorithm extracted 6 features from

Figure 12. Proposed deep recurrent neural network (6-12-6-3-2) (Min-Joo Kang,2017).

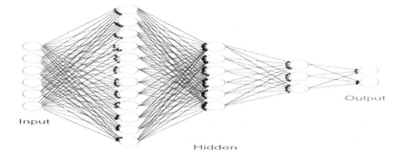

Figure 13. Architecture of IDS based on deep learning techniques

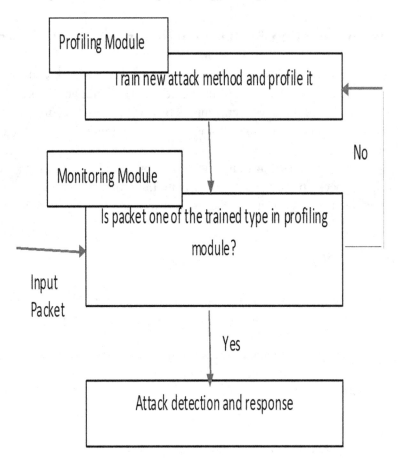

the 34 features of Transmission Control Protocol (TCP) Protocol in the feature extraction process, then the proposed method classifies the node as an attacker or normal node.

Proposed IDS design contains of two phases, i.e., the training phase and the detection phase as in the conventional machine-learning based IDS. The training segment is achieved off-line as the training is time-consuming. In the training phase a TCP packet is processed to extract a feature that represents a statistical behaviour of the network. Individually training TCP packet has its own binary label, i.e., either a normal packet or an attack packet in supervised learning. Therefore, the matching features are anticipated to denote the label information. Authors implement the DNN structure to train the features, in which the weight parameters on the edges linking the nodes are attained. The detection phase is also shown in the figure 14.

The same feature is extracted from an incoming packet through a TCP bus, and the DNN structure computes with the trained parameters to make the binary decision. For the supervised learning as the DBN model, the learning structure should be arranged.

The concluding classification layer together with label information is added to the top layer of the DBN model to construct the discriminative deep learning structure. Parameters are fine-tuned by means of the gradient descent method in the deep feed-forward ANN structure later, however the parameters are used only for initializing the weights.

Figure 14. Proposed IDS Steps

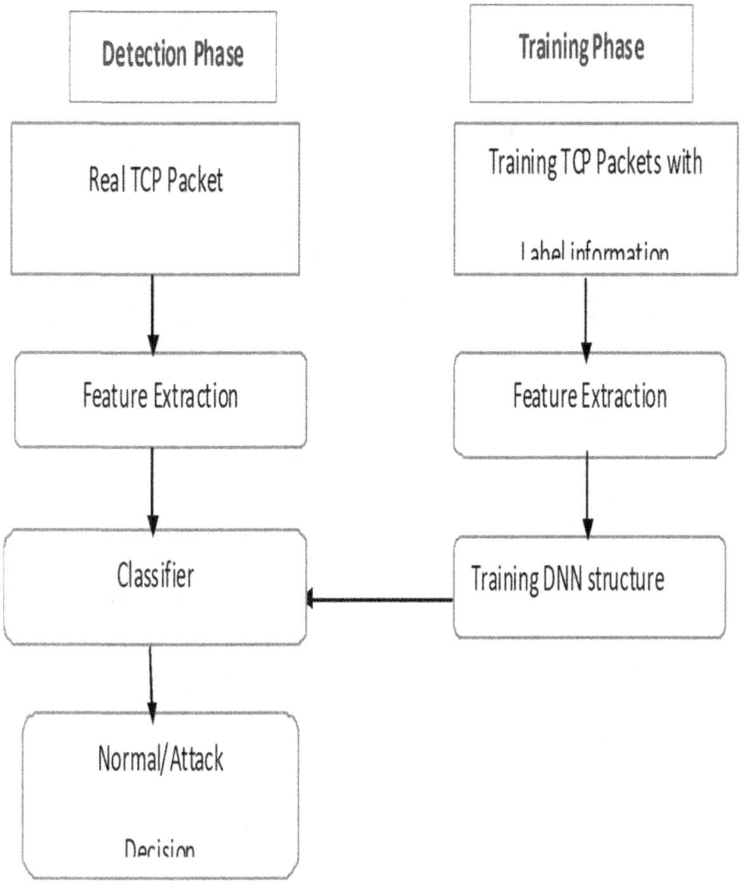

Attack Detection

The class of a testing TCP packet is predicted in the detection phase. The output is computed with the trained weight parameters and the feature set extracted from the testing TCP packet as in the training. The classifier offers the logistic rate 0 or 1, telling if the sample is normal packet or the attack packet, respectively refer figure 15.

There can be a number of attack scenarios considered in a Profiling module, and the weight vectors can be trained fitted to each scenario. The mode of information is used for classifying the situation in the proposed method, because of that the proper training set can be applied. For this purpose, profile matching is established in the projected technique. The profiling unit contains the mode information refers to the data along with the training samples used for the precise scenario. If profiling is matching between the training sample, TCP packet will be tested, the detector uses the corresponding trained parameters obtained from the value information.

Figure 15. Deep neural network in the proposed method

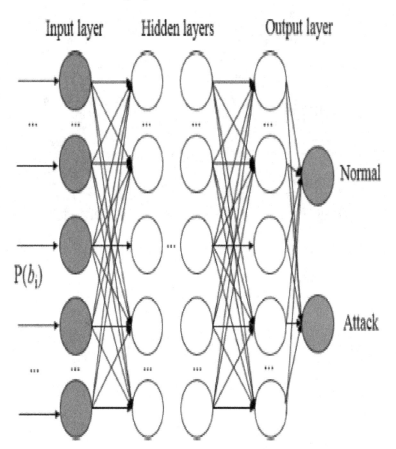

SIMULATION ENVIRONMENT

Simulation and Results

Network simulator 3 (NS3) is used to simulate the Centralised UAV assisted VANET network architecture. The parameter for simulation in NS3 is displayed in the Table 2. The Authors compared the current Deep learning-based Intrusion Detection System with SVM based Intrusion Detection System. Here authors compute the False Positive Rate, True Positive Rate, Efficacy and Detection Rate. The number of anomalous network instances detected are termed as True Positives (TP) and the number of anomalous networks instanced not detected are termed as False Negatives (FN). True Negatives (TN) are the number of normal network instances not detected and False Negatives (FN) are the number of normal network instances detected as anomalous.

To investigate the risk of a potential attack, authors simulated these High bandwidth deceiving attacks using ns-3 based on the Centralised UAV network model, With the packet size fixed at 1000 bytes, reducing the packet arrival interval can achieve a similar effect to increasing the number of users. As time elapses, more users will connect to the UAV network attacks and the normal scenario, in which no attack is launched.

In our simulations for the high bandwidth deceiving attack, authors assume that the true available link bandwidth is 1.5 Mbps and that the adversary advertises a false available link bandwidth of 1.8 Mbps. As the high bandwidth deceiving attack has no obvious impact on the link throughput and the throughput will increase as the number of users increases. Authors note that when 15 users are connected to the network, the link throughput becomes stable.

When the number of users is larger than 15, the communication link will become saturated. Because a portion of the available bandwidth is not utilized, the throughput in this scenario (1.0 Mbps) will be less than that of the normal scenario (1.5 Mbps). Similarly, authors measured the average end-to-end delay when the high bandwidth deceiving attack is launched, before the network bandwidth saturates, the end-to-end delay will not be affected by the attack. When the link becomes saturated after 15 users are included, the attack will cause the end-to-end delay to increase rapidly. Performance equations for Accuracy, Detection Rate (DR), False Negative Rate (FNR), True Negative Rate (TNR) and False Positive Rate (FPR) are as follows,

$$Efficiency = \frac{TP + TN}{TP + TN + FP + FN} * 100$$

$$DR = \frac{TP}{TP + FN} * 100$$

$$TPR = \frac{TP}{TN + FP} * 100$$

$$FPR = \frac{FP}{TN + FP} * 100$$

A deterministic mobility model is used to simulate the mobility of an UAV, here the UAV follows a well- defined path and selects a random speed. During simulation authors insert wrong bandwidth injection in the routing protocol of UAV that provides false information. (Ons Bouachir et al, 2014). Detection through Deep learning technique is good and they provide good results in detection rate, true positive rate and true negative rate. Further details of simulation parameters are shown in the table 1.

Table 2. Provides the TPR, FPR and Detection rate using SVM and EDFFNN methods for Intrusion detection against different number of UAV's. This table shows EDFFNN method is good for TPR than SVM method; SVM method is good in FPR than EDFFNN method and EDFFNN is good in detecting Intrusion better than SVM method of Detection for more number of UAV's (Hichem Sedjelmaci et al., 2018).

Results of the simulation are given in Fig. 16,17,18. It gives the comparison of True positives rate, false positive rates and Detection rates between the SVM and EDFFNN of Intrusion detection against different number of UAV's.

Fig. 16 shows when SVM gives good TPR than EDFFNN for low number of UAVs, when the number of UAV's gets increased EDFFNN method performs better than SVM. (Hichem Sedjelmaci et al, 2017).

Figure 17. Shows EDFFNN method has lower FPR than SVM method for any number of UAV's.

Table 1. Simulation parameters

Parameter name	Value
Simulation area	5000*5000 m²
Simulation time	1000 seconds
Mobility model	Paparazzi deterministic
UAV number	5,10,15
Speed	60 to 150 km/h
Link Layer	802.11 b
Protocol type	TCP
Routing algorithm	DTN routing
Transmission range	20 meters
Packet Size	1000 bytes
Bandwidth	1.5 Mbps

Table 2. TPR and FPR for SVM and DFFNN

Method/No of UAVs	TPR		FPR		Detection Rate	
	SVM	EDFFNN	SVM	EDFFNN	SVM	EDFFNN
5	94.6%	93.3%	0.8%	0.6%	93.78%	94.93%
10	95.1%	96.8%	0.8%	0.7%	92.82%	93.93%
15	90.1%	90.7%	1.1%	1.0%	90.87%	94.94%

Figure 16. True positive rate

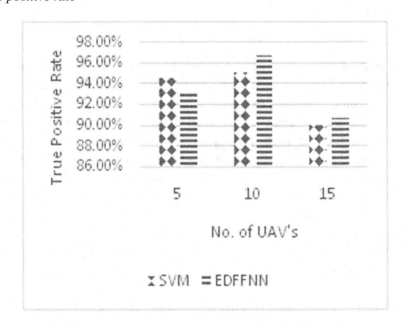

Figure 17. False positive rate

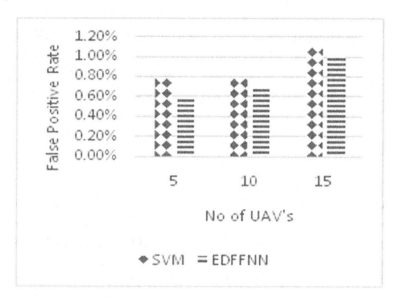

Figure 18 shows EDFFNN method provides the good detection rate than the Support Vector Machine (SVM) method of Detecting Intrusion against any number of UAV's that is for low number of UAV's it provides better detection rate and also for maximum number UAVs it provides better detection rate. From the simulation results Deep Feed Forward Neural Network with back propagation algorithm (EDFFNN) methods outperforms the Support Vector Machine (SVM) method of Intrusion detection in Multi-Layer UAV Ad Hoc Network assisted Vehicular ad hoc networks namely wrong bandwidth injection attack.

Figure 18. Detection rate

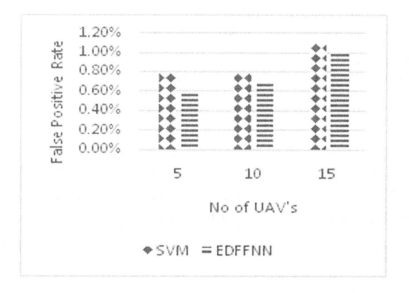

FUTURE RESEARCH DIRECTIONS

This chapter concentrates on traffic analysis and intrusion detection in Centralised Unmanned Aerial Vehicle (UAV) Networks with only false bandwidth injection attacks detection. In future researchers planning to extend their work for other communication architecture of UAV networks and incorporate all the false data dissemination attacks. At present the work concentrates on intrusion detection later it can extend with intrusion detection with response, to provide highest detection rate with prevention.

CONCLUSION

Traffic analysis is an important effort to analyse and identify the intrusions in the network. In this chapter the authors used Enhanced Deep Feed Forward Neural Network (EDFFNN) for training and detecting the Centralised Network traffic data with traffic monitoring. Feed Forward Neural Network is trained with Back propagation algorithm to work like the Recurrent Neural Network (RNN). The EDFFNN works well in the case of intrusion detection which provides 94% of detection rate. Simulation results disclose that the projected Intrusion Detection System is capable and accurate in detecting different kinds of simulated attacks. Compared to previous intrusion detection method of Support Vector Machine (SVM) the EDFFNN provides better detection rate.

REFERENCES

Amardeep, R., & Swamy, K. T. (2017). Training Feed forward Neural Network with Back propogation Algorithm. *International Journal of Engineering And Computer Science*, 6(1), 19860–19866.

Anyanwu, L. O., Keengwe, J., & Arome, G. A. (2010). Scalable Intrusion Detection with Recurrent Neural Networks. *IEEE 2010 Seventh International Conference on Information Technology: New Generations*, 919–923.

Bankovic, Z., Vallejo, J. C., Fraga, D., & Moya, J. M. (2014, December). *Detecting Bad-Mouthing Attacks on Reputation Systems Using Self-Organising Maps*. Researchgate.net.

Bouachir, O., Abrassart, A., Garcia, F., Larrieu, N. (2014, May). A Mobility Model For UAV Ad hoc Network. *International Conference on Unmanned Aircraft Systems*, 383-388.

Deng, L. (2014). A tutorial survey of architectures, algorithms, and applications for deep learning. *APSIPA Trans. Signal Inf. Process.*, 3(e2), 1–29.

Gao, N., Gao, L., Gao, Q., & Wang, H. (2014). An Intrusion Detection Model Based on Deep Belief Networks. *Second International Conference on Advanced Cloud and Big Data*, 247–252.

Kang, M.-J., & Kang, J.-W. (2017). Intrusion Detection System Using Deep Neural Network for In-Vehicle Network Security. *PLOS One*, 1-17. doi:.Pone.0155781 doi:10.1371/journal

Lab, L. (2015). *Deep Learning Tutorial*. Available at http: //deeplearning.net /tutorial / deeplearning.pdf

Li, J., Zhou, Y., & Lamont, L. (2013). Communication Architectures and Protocols for Networking Unmanned Aerial Vehicles. *Globecom 2013 Workshop - Wireless Networking and Control for Unmanned Autonomous Vehicles, 13,* 1415-1420.

Sedjelmaci, H., Senouci, S. M., & Ansari, N. (2017). Intrusion Detection and Ejection Framework Against Lethal Attacks in UAV-Aided Networks: A Bayesian Game-Theoretic Methodology. *IEEE Transactions on Intelligent Transportation Systems, 18*(5), 1143–1153. doi:10.1109/TITS.2016.2600370

Sedjelmaci, H., Senouci, S. M., & Ansari, N. (2018). A Hierarchical Detection and Response System to Enhance Security Against Lethal Cyber-Attacks in UAV Networks, IEEE Transactions on Systems, Man, and Cybernetics. *Systems, 48*(9), 1594–1606.

Shepard, D. P., Bhatti, J. A., Humphreys, T. E., & Fansler, A. A. (2012). Evaluation of smart grid and civilian UAV vulnerability to GPS spoofing attacks. *Proc. ION GNSS Meeting*, 1–15.

Tang, T. A., Mhamdi, L., McLernon, D., Zaidi, S. A. R., & Ghogho, M. (2016). Deep Learning Approach for Network Intrusion Detection in Software Defined Networking. IEEE.

Vanitha, N., & Padmavathi, G. (2017). A Study on Various Cyber-Attacks and their Classification in UAV Assisted Vehicular Ad-Hoc Networks. *Springer Nature, 844,* 124-132.

Vanitha, N., & Padmavathi, G. (2018). A Comparative Study on Communication Architecture of Unmanned Aerial Vehicles and Security Analysis of False Data Dissemination Attacks. In *International Conference on Current Trends towards Converging Technologies (ICCTCT)*. IEEE.

Wei, S., Ge, L., Yu, W., & Chen, G. (2014). Simulation Study of Unmanned Aerial Vehicle Communication Networks Addressing Bandwidth Disruptions. In *Sensors and Systems for Space Applications VII* (Vol. 9085). Academic Press.

ADDITIONAL READING

Bilal, R., & Khan, B. M. (2017). Analysis of Mobility Models and Routing Schemes for Flying Ad-Hoc Networks (FANETS). *International Journal of Applied Engineering Research, 12,* 3263–3269.

Josep Lluis Berral-García. (2018), *When and How to Apply Statistics, Machine Learning and Deep Learning Techniques*, 2018 20th International Conference on Transparent Optical Networks (ICTON), IEEE explore.

Khan, M. A., Safi, A., Qureshi, I. M., & Khan, I. U. (2017). *Flying Ad-Hoc Networks (FANETs): A Review of Communication architectures, and Routing protocols*. IEEE.

Loukas, G., Vuong, T., Heartfield, R., Sakellari, G., Yoon, Y., & Gan, D. (2018). Cloud-Based Cyber-Physical Intrusion Detection for Vehicles Using Deep Learning. *IEEE Access: Practical Innovations, Open Solutions, 6,* 3491–3508. doi:10.1109/ACCESS.2017.2782159

Ivan Maza, Anibal Ollero, Enrique Casado and David Scarlatti, *Classification of multi-UAV Architectures,* Boeing Research & Technology Europe, pp. 1-24.

Xin, Y., Kong, L., Liu, Z., Chen, Y., Li, Y., Zhu, H., ... Wang, C. (2018). *Machine Learning and Deep Learning Methods for Cybersecurity,* Vol. 6. *IEEE Access: Practical Innovations, Open Solutions, 6,* 35365–35381. doi:10.1109/ACCESS.2018.2836950

KEY TERMS AND DEFINITIONS

ADS-B: Automatic dependent surveillance-broadcast; it is a hardware part of UAV holding the GPS co-ordinates of neighboring UAVs.

ANN: Artificial neural network. ANN are considered as a nonlinear arithmetical data modelling tool.

CNN: Convolutional neural network. A convolutional neural network (CNN) is a kind of artificial neural network used in image recognition and processing.

DBN: Deep belief networks. A deep belief network (DBN) is a cultured type of multiplicative neural network that practices an unsupervised machine learning model to yield outcomes.

DR: Detection rate.

FANET: Flying ad-hoc network; these networks formed by UAV's in the air layer.

FNR: False negative rate.

FPR: False positive rate.

IDS: Intrusion detection system. IDS is active in shielding the network in contradiction of both inside and outside intruders.

MLP: Multi-layer perceptron. A multilayer perceptron (MLP) is supposed to be a feedforward artificial neural network that produces a set of yields from a set of contributions.

NIDS: Network intrusion detection system. NIDS is a framework used to detect intrusions in the network.

NS-3: Network Simulator – 3. It is a simulator used to simulate the wired and wireless networks.

RNN: Recurrent neural network. A recurrent neural network (RNN) is an advanced artificial neural network (ANN) that contains directed cycles in memory.

SVM: Support vector machine. A support vector machine (SVM) is a supervised machine learning algorithm that examines data aimed at classification and regression study.

TCP: Transmission control protocol.

TNR: True negative rate.

U2V: UAV-to-vehicle communication.

UAV: Unmanned aerial vehicle. UAVs are termed as drones that fly in the air layer without human being and it is controlled by human being using remote.

UDA: UAV detection agent; it is seated in each and every UAV in the network and monitors the traffic of the UAV network.

V2U: Vehicle-to-UAV communication.

VANET: Vehicular ad-hoc network. Vehicles in the ground form an ad-hoc network in order to communicate between vehicles.

Chapter 12
A Novel Biometric Image Enhancement Approach With the Hybridization of Undecimated Wavelet Transform and Deep Autoencoder

Sasirekha K.
Periyar University, India

Thangavel K.
Periyar University, India

ABSTRACT

For a long time, image enhancement techniques have been widely used to improve the image quality in many image processing applications. Recently, deep learning models have been applied to image enhancement problems with great success. In the domain of biometric, fingerprint and face play a vital role to authenticate a person in the right way. Hence, the enhancement of these images significantly improves the recognition rate. In this chapter, undecimated wavelet transform (UDWT) and deep autoencoder are hybridized to enhance the quality of images. Initially, the images are decomposed with Daubechies wavelet filter. Then, deep autoencoder is trained to minimize the error between reconstructed and actual input. The experiments have been conducted on real-time fingerprint and face images collected from 150 subjects, each with 10 orientations. The signal to noise ratio (SNR), peak signal to noise ratio (PSNR), mean square error (MSE), and root mean square error (RMSE) have been computed and compared. It was observed that the proposed model produced a biometric image with high quality.

DOI: 10.4018/978-1-5225-9611-0.ch012

INTRODUCTION

As our society has become electronically connected and more portable, surrogate representations of identity such as passwords and tokens cannot be trusted to recognize a person. Besides, the token may be lost or stolen and passwords can be guessed easily. Recent researches were evident that the biometric methods provide a more elevated amount of security and are more appropriate than the conventional methods of personal authentication (Jain, Ross, & Nandakumar, 2011) (Sasirekha & Thangavel, 2014). With the rapid technological advancements in the field of biometric authentication, it has been widely exploited for various security purposes. In particular, biometric authentication supports the facet of identification, verification, and non-repudiation in the domain of information security. It is used to identify the identity of a person when compared to a template in the database by certain unique characteristics (Chauhana, Arorab, A.S., & Kaula, 2010).

Furthermore, biometrics recognition is a growing and controversial field in which civil liberties groups express concern over privacy and identity issues. In the recent years, biometric laws and regulations are in process and biometric industry standards are being tested widely.

The biometric traits are broadly classified into two categories: physiological and behavioral. Recently, most of the applications are developed with the avail of physiological traits such as fingerprint, face, hand geometry, iris, retina, etc. On the other hand, the behavioral traits such as voice, dynamic signature, keystroke, gait, etc. are used but paid poor attention. In general, a person can be identified by any of the available biometric traits. The biometric modals possess some of the desirable properties which include universality, uniqueness, permanence, measurability, performance, and acceptability which propels the growth of biometric-based authentication (Jain, Ross, & Prabhakar, 2004).

Among all the biometric traits, the fingerprint and face biometric are the widely employed and cost-efficient method of authentication (Khan & Zhang, 2008) (W. Yu, 2009) (Wu, Lian, & Lu, 2012).

Fingerprint biometric has been used in Forensic Science for a long time for personal identification. This is because the fingerprints of an individual are distinctive and do not change for the duration of one's life. This makes it an ideal signature of a person. In the current scenario, the face is the next widely focused biometric after fingerprint as it plays a vital role to authenticate a right person. The face recognition is employed for identifying an individual by authenticating the input image with the digital images which are already stored in the database.

Generally, a good database of sample patterns is very much crucial for any pattern recognition or classification problem. Hence, image acquisition is the first step in any biometric authentication system. It is concerned with capturing the biometric image using a camera or scanner. In this paper, the fingerprint images are collected using eSSL ZK7500 fingerprint sensor. This device utilizes optical fingerprint scanning technology for superior quality and reliability. And the biometric face images are collected using 2 Mega Pixel Logitech web camera. The images are captured with the resolution of 1280x960. The captured biometric images are poor in quality during acquisition due to illumination, sensor, storage, and many more. It is highly difficult to fetch objects from the dark background of a low contrast biometric image.

In the digital era, biometric image enhancement has become increasingly important for the successful authentication of a person. Specifically, it improves the quality of images for further analysis. In general, image enhancement is the method to improve the visibility of higher and lower frequency values of an image. The objective is to enhance the visual representation of the image or to provide an improved transform representation for appropriate usage in image processing applications. In the literature, many image enhancement techniques are explored to improve the visibility of the images such as Histogram Equalization (HE), Adaptive Histogram Equalization (AHE), Bi-Histogram Equalization (BHE), and many more (Wang, Chen, & Zhang, 1999).

Nowadays, a new machine learning model called deep learning is widely adopted for image enhancement (LeCun, Bengio, & Hinton, 2015) (Druzhkov & Kustikova, 2016) (Bishop & Christopher, 2006). They are more effectual in learning data representation. A salient feature of deep learning is that it allows a machine to be fed with raw image and to automatically discover the unique patterns requisite for enhancement (Hinton & Osindero, 2006). More specifically, the deep model has the generalization ability to solve the real world problems. Empirical studies have explored that data representations attained from deep models often yield better performance (Wang G., 2016) (Yosinski, Clune, Bengio, & Lipson, 2014) (Bengio, Courville, & Vincent, 2013). Before 2006, the neural network with more than one hidden layers was considered to be hard to train efficiently and gained popularity among the researchers when it was shown that training Stacked AutoEncoders (SAEs) layer-by-layer in an unsupervised manner, followed by supervised fine-tuning of the network in pattern recognition problems (Golovko, Kroshchanka, & Treadwell, 2016) (Singh & Om, 2017). In reality, deep learning models are essentially built by stacking multiple consecutive layers. Each layer applies a nonlinear transformation function on its raw input and provides a particular representation in its output. The intention is to learn a more complex and abstract representation of the input data in a hierarchical manner by passing the data through multiple hidden layers.

With Wavelet Transform gaining popularity in the last two decades various algorithms for image enhancement were introduced (David L., 1995) (Mohideen, Perumal, Krishnan, Sathik, & Kumar, 2008) (Grace Chang & Bin Yu, 2000). Additionally, wavelets are mathematical functions that analyze data according to scale or resolution. Wavelet transforms have become one of the most important and powerful tools for image enhancement. Basically, it works on the principle of manipulating the coefficients in the transform domain.

The frequency spectrum generated with the Short Time Fourier Transform (STFT) contains inappropriate frequencies and ill-defined peaks. As a consequence, these frequencies appear noise around the actual frequency peaks. The wavelets provide an alternative way to the Short Time Fourier Transform for representing the data with localized events. On the other hand, they can solve the difficulty of frequency resolution in non-stationary segments. In the wavelet domain, a two-dimensional representation of the data (scale with translation) is created which works similar to STFT (Othman & Stambouli, 2016).

Motivation

Recently, in the domain of image processing, deep learning models and wavelets are the promising avenues of research. The deep learning model automatically extracts complex representations from the raw image, and the wavelets capture both frequency and location of information. Such models develop a layered, hierarchical architecture of learning, where more abstract features are defined in terms of lower-level features. Moreover, the hierarchical learning of deep learning algorithms is motivated by artificial intelligence emulating the deep, layered learning process of human brain, which automatically extracts features and abstractions for further analysis from the underlying data. In particular, the deep learning algorithms are quite beneficial when dealing with learning from large amounts of unsupervised data, and typically learn data representations in a greedy layer-wise manner. Deep learning has become one of the predominant research areas in developing intelligent machine learning applications. In particular, the deep autoencoder model has been applied to a wide variety of enhancement problems with great success.

Major Contribution

In this work, a deep autoencoder with multiple hidden layers is trained layer by layer to minimize the reconstruction error between the original input and reconstructed biometric image in wavelet domain is introduced.

Section 2 elaborately discusses the related work of image enhancement. In section 3, the proposed image enhancement method using deep autoencoder and UDWT is presented. The experimental results are discussed in section 4. Finally, this paper concludes with some future perspectives in section 5.

Background

Enhancement of a biometric image is quite essential to improve the contrast or to emphasize the potential information contained in the image while retaining the intrinsic structure. In particular, when a biometric image is transferred, scanned or compressed, automatically noise will be added and the quality of image will be degraded.

For decades, constructing a machine learning model required careful design of a feature extractor that transformed the raw data into a suitable internal representation or feature vector from which the learning subsystem, often a classifier, could predict or classify patterns in the input. Conventional machine learning algorithms focuses on constructing features and data representations. More conventionally, the feature engineering consumes a large portion of the effort in a machine learning task, and is typically quite domain-specific and involves considerable human effort. Generally, they were limited in their ability to process image in their raw form to extract some useful representation from it. Deep learning would be a major breakthrough in machine learning as this would allow researchers to automatically extract such features without direct human input (Schmidhuber, 2015).

In the current scenario, deep learning models are extensively used in processing biometric images for efficient authentication. Gondara et al. (Gondara, 2016) presented a deep autoencoder with convolutional layers to enhance the medical image. Structural similarity of Convolution autoencoder is compared with the Median filter for mini-MIAS and dental radiography database. Experimental results showed that the constructed deep Convolution autoencoder has achieved the state-of-the-art performance. (Lore, Akintayo, & Sarkar, 2016) Lore et al. have presented a deep autoencoder model to extract more discriminate signal features from images. Also, the lighter parts of images are brightened by utilizing the deep autoencoder model. A variant of the stacked-sparse denoising autoencoder was learned to adaptively enhance the darkened training images. It has been fruitfully applied to low-light environment and hardware degraded images. Results showed the significant credibility of deep autoencoder both visually and by quantitative comparison with many standard techniques. Hui implemented deep autoencoder to enhance images of CIFAR dataset. This method outperformed when compared to the standard algorithms such as KSVD, BM3D in terms of PSNR (Li, 2014).

The wavelet algorithms can process data at various scales or resolutions. In particular, it uses a function called mother wavelet. The most significant properties of wavelet transforms are the admissibility and the regularity conditions. The wavelet provides an appropriate basis for separating noisy coefficient from the image than spatial and frequency based methods. Thangavel et al. have studied UDWT over the conventional Discrete Wavelet Transform (DWT) as it is not a time-invariant transform (Thangavel & Sasirekha, 2016). The biometric image was denoised using a modified universal threshold based on the Golden Ratio and Weighted Median. Tsai et al. have improved the image quality in medical images by utilizing a wavelet-based approach. The wavelet coefficient mapping function was applied to enhance the contrast of images (Tsai, Matsuyama, & Chen, 2013). Cho et al. have presented a computationally efficient framework for image enhancement in the wavelet domain (Cho & Bui, 2014). The developed approach enhanced the contrast of image both globally and locally.

Gondara et al. (Gondara, 2016) showed that denoising autoencoder constructed using convolutional layers can be used for efficient denoising the medical images. SSIM of Convolution AE is compared with Median filter for mini-MIAS and dental radiography database. Experimental results showed that the Convolution AE has achieved the state-of-the-art performance. Lefkimmiatis (Lefkimmiatis, 2016) presented deep network architecture for image denoising which is based on a non-local image model. The experiments have been conducted on the Berkeley segmentation dataset which expound that the developed image model produced better performance for grayscale as well as color image with various noise levels. It makes use of Graphical Processing Unit computing to reduce the computational time through parallel processing. Michael Gharbi et al. (Michael Gharbi, 2016)introduced a deep neural network architecture which has been trained on a huge volume of images instead of using hand-designed filters. It has shown great success with existing datasets when compared with conventional algorithms. Additionally, some metrics were introduced to identify difficult patches for mining photographs.

In general, photo retouching enables the photographers to invoke dramatic visual impressions by artistically improving their photos through stylistic color and tone adjustments. However, it is a time-consuming and difficult task that requires advanced skills beyond the abilities of normal photographers. Automated algorithm was introduced as an alternative solution to this problem. It also faces problems such as subtle adjustments that depend on the image content and spatial variation of these adjustments. Recently, deep learning models have shown unique abilities to solve these problems. This motivated Zhicheng Yan et al. (Zhicheng Yan, 2016) to explore the use of deep learning model in the context of photo editing. In their work, the automatic photo adjustment problem was explained in a suitable manner. They also introduced an image descriptor that accounts for the local semantics of an image. The experimental results expound that the developed deep learning model successfully captured the sophisticated photographic styles in a well defined and organized way.

Junyuan Xie et al. (Junyuan Xie, 2012) described a training scheme that successfully adapts DA which was originally designed for unsupervised feature learning, to the tasks of image denoising and blind inpainting. The performance of this method in the image denoising is comparable to that of KSVD which is a widely used sparse coding technique. More importantly, in blind image inpainting task, it provides solutions to some complex problems that have not been tackled before. Specifically, complex patterns like superimposed text from an image was removed automatically, rather than simple patterns like pixels missing at random. Moreover, this method does not need the information regarding the region that requires inpainting to be given a priori. Experimental results demonstrated the effectiveness of this method in the tasks of image denoising and blind inpainting. It was also showed that the new training scheme for DA is more effective and can improve the performance of unsupervised feature learning. Even though the Boltzmann Machines were successful at unsupervised learning and density modeling of images and speech data, it is very sensitive to noise in the data.

IMAGE ENHANCEMENT WITH DEEP AUTOENCODER AND UNDECIMATED WAVELET TRANSFORM

Undecimated Wavelet Transform

In the wavelet domain, decimation is a challenging issue which generates a shift variant transformation. In the literature undecimated wavelet transforms has been introduced to overcome this problem. The UDWT is studied over the conventional DWT as it is not a time-invariant transform (Sasirekha & Thangavel, 2014). During the wavelet transformation, low-frequency components in the image will be filtered out as approximations and high-frequency components will be filtered out as details. Figure 1 depicts one level filter bank implementation of UDWT. It applies high and low pass filters to the data at each level.

The UDWT produces four subbands at each level of decomposition. They are approximation and detail coefficients such as horizontal, vertical and diagonal as shown in figure 2.

Here, H and L denote high and low-pass filters respectively. The LL subband is the low-resolution residual consisting of low-frequency components and this subband which is further split at higher levels of decomposition (Alsaidi Altaher & Mohd Ismail, 2010) (Demirel & Anbarjafari, 2011).

These four output subbands at $k+1$ are derived from the baseband $X_{k,ll}$ at $k=1$ (first level) as,

Figure 1. One level filter bank implementation of UDWT (a) Forward Pass (b) Backward Pass

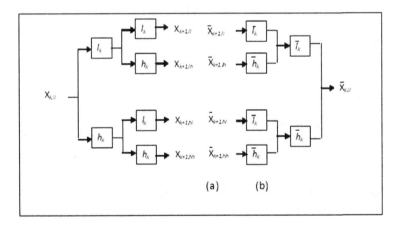

Figure 2. Decomposition of an image using UDWT

LL (Approximation)	HL (Horizontal)
LH (Vertical)	HH (Diagonal)

$$X_{k+1,ll}\left(i,j\right) = \sum_{m=0}^{N_{k,l}-1}\sum_{n=0}^{N_{k,l}-1} l_k\left(m\right) l_k\left(n\right) X_{k,ll}\left(i+m,j+n\right) \qquad (1)$$

$$X_{k+1,lh}\left(i,j\right) = \sum_{m=0}^{N_{k,l}-1}\sum_{n=0}^{N_{k,h}-1} l_k\left(m\right) h_k\left(n\right) X_{k,ll}\left(i+m,j+n\right) \qquad (2)$$

$$X_{k+1,hl}\left(i,j\right) = \sum_{m=0}^{N_{k,h}-1}\sum_{n=0}^{N_{k,l}-1} h_k\left(m\right) l_k\left(n\right) X_{k,ll}\left(i+m,j+n\right) \qquad (3)$$

$$X_{k+1,hh}\left(i,j\right) = \sum_{m=0}^{N_{k,h}-1}\sum_{n=0}^{N_{k,h}-1} h_k\left(m\right) h_k\left(n\right) X_{k,ll}\left(i+m,j+n\right) \qquad (4)$$

Here, $N_{k,l}$ and $N_{k,h}$ are the length of the lowpass and highpass filters respectively. In contrast, the reconstruction (ISWT) is obtained by applying the above procedure in reverse order as,

$$\tilde{X}_{k,ll}\left(i,j\right) = \sum_{m=0}^{N_l^k-1}\sum_{n=0}^{N_l^k-1} \tilde{l}_k\left(m\right) \tilde{l}_k\left(n\right) \tilde{X}_{k+1,ll}\left(i+m,j+n\right)$$

$$+\sum_{m=0}^{N_l^k-1}\sum_{n=0}^{N_{\tilde{h}}^k-1} \tilde{l}_k\left(m\right) \tilde{h}_k\left(n\right) \tilde{X}_{k+1,ll}\left(i+m,j+n\right)$$

$$+\sum_{m=0}^{N_{\tilde{h}}^k-1}\sum_{n=0}^{N_l^k-1} \tilde{h}_k\left(m\right) \tilde{l}_k\left(n\right) \tilde{X}_{k+1,ll}\left(i+m,j+n\right)$$

$$+\sum_{m=0}^{N_{\tilde{h}}^k-1}\sum_{n=0}^{N_{\tilde{h}}^k-1} \tilde{h}_k\left(m\right) \tilde{h}_k\left(n\right) \tilde{X}_{k+1,ll}\left(i+m,j+n\right) \qquad (5)$$

Here, $N_{\tilde{l}}^k$ and $N_{\tilde{h}}^k$ are the lengths of the lowpass and highpass filters respectively (Sasirekha & Thangavel, 2016).

Deep Autoencoder

Generally, at the core of all deep learning models is the domain-independent idea of utilizing hierarchical layers of learned abstraction to effectively accomplish high-level tasks. Among all the deep models, autoencoders are essential for constructing deep architectures such as Deep Belief Networks (DBNs) and Stacked autoencoders (Alain & Bengio, 2012) (Chen, Xu, Winberger, & Sha, 2012). Deep neural networks are trained to avoid the poor convergence with some random initialization of hyperparameters. In this architecture, each layer is trained to produce a higher level representation of data from the observed patterns obtained from the lower layers. Here, each successive layer produces a more abstract representation of data than the previous layer.

An autoencoder neural network with multiple layers can be used as a deep network to learn more complex representation in the input data. While training a multiple layer autoencoder neural network is time-consuming, a pre-training step has been employed to initialize the weights of a deep network to speed up the training process. In the pre-training step, each successive layer is trained individually and the output of each layer is fed to the input of the successive layers. Finally, all the layers are stacked together to form the deep neural network. More specifically, they are trained to encode the input x into some representation r(x) so that the input could be reconstructed from that representation. Hence the target output of the autoencoder is same as the input itself (Swersky, Ranzato, Buchman, Marlin, & de Freitas, 2011) (Vincent, 2011). It consists of two parts, the encoder, and the decoder as shown in figure 3.

The encoder part takes the raw input of the image I(x, y) ∈ Rd and maps it into a hidden representation H (x, y) ∈ R' through a deterministic mapping as,

$$H\left(x,y\right) = \sigma\left(W * I\left(x,y\right)+b\right), \tag{6}$$

Figure 3. An autoencoder with 3 fully-connected hidden layers

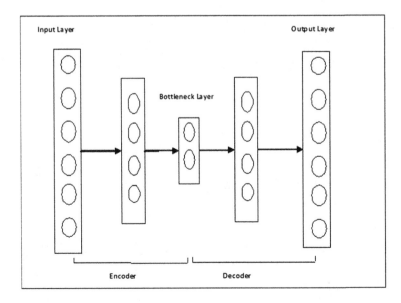

where σ is the transformation function used. Here, W represents the weight matrix and b is the bias value. The latent representation H (x, y), or code is then mapped back into a reconstruction R of the same shape as I(x, y). The mapping happens through a similar transformation as given in (2).

$$R\big(x,y\big) = \sigma\Big(W' * H\big(x,y\big) + b'\Big),$$ (7)

Here, R should be seen as a prediction of I (x, y), given the encode H (x, y). Autoencoders are trained to minimize reconstruction error between the raw input and reconstructed one (Vincent, Larochelle, Bengio, & Manzagol, 2008) (Rifai, Bengio, Dauphin, & Vincent, 2012). The reconstruction error can be measured in many ways, depending on the appropriate distributional assumptions on the input given the code. The conventional squared error is given as,

$$L\Big(I\big(x,y\big), R\big(x,y\big)\Big) = \parallel I\big(x,y\big) - R\big(x,y\big)\parallel^2,$$ (8)

If the input I (x, y) is interpreted as either binary or vector of bit probabilities, then cross-entropy of the reconstruction can be used and is given as,

$$L\Big(I\big(x,y\big), R\big(x,y\big)\Big) = -\sum_{k=1}^{d}[I\big(x,y\big)_k \, log R\big(x,y\big)_k + \Big(1 - I\big(x,y\big)_k\Big) log\Big(1 - R\big(x,y\big)r_k\Big)]$$ (9)

The architecture of deep autoencoder neural network can be thought of as a multi-layer feed forward artificial neural network. Hence the training procedure of deep autoencoder is the same as a multi-layer neural network (Haykin, 2005). Typically the training of the network is done by a method called back-propagation algorithm.

Error Backpropagation

Generally, backpropagation is used to compute the gradient and propagate the error backward throughout the network. Using this error value (E = Desired – Actual), the updating of weight is performed as:

$$' = ES_2\big(1 - S_2\big)$$ (10)

The weights assigned between input and hidden layer, the hidden and output layer are updated as:

$$W_{ho} = W_{ho} + \big(n.'.S_1\big)$$ (11)

$$W_{ih} = W_{ih} + \big(n.'.K_i\big)$$ (12)

where n is the learning rate, δ is the weight and k is the input value to the network. Again the output is calculated for the hidden and output neurons. Then the error value (E) is checked, and the weights are updated. The above procedure is repeated till the target output is equal to the desired output.

Image Enhancement with UDWT and Deep Autoencoder

Initially, the biometric image is decomposed in wavelet domain by utilizing the undecimated wavelet transform with Daubechies wavelet filter. After decomposition, the coefficients in the approximation subbands are reconstructed using deep autoencoder with multiple hidden layers. The block diagram of the proposed method is presented in figure 4 and the image reconstruction with deep autoencoder is shown in figure 5.

The steps involved in image enhancement with undecimated wavelet transform and deep autoencoder are as follows:

- Decompose the biometric image using UDWT with Daubechies wavelet filter
- Encode the decomposed image to a hidden representations with successive autoencoders
- Reconstruct the biometric image using deep autoencoder to get the enhanced image

Figure 4. Block diagram of the proposed method

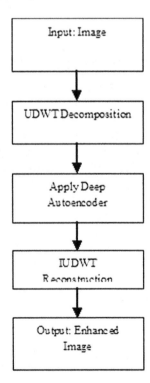

Figure 5. Image Reconstruction using Deep Autoencoder

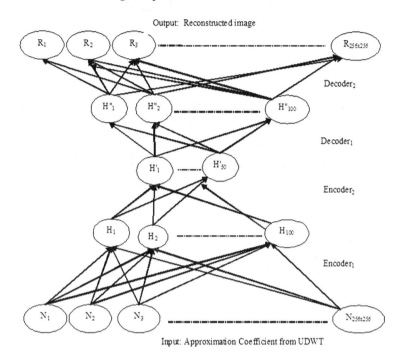

The approximation coefficient obtained from the decomposition of the biometric image using undecimated discrete wavelet transform with Daubechies filter is given as an input to deep autoencoder with multiple hidden layers. The decomposed image is encoded to a hidden representation with an autoencoder through a deterministic mapping,

$$Encode\_1 = \sigma\left(W * i + b\right) \tag{13}$$

The encoded image from the first autoencoder is then given as an input to the second autoencoder for further compression through a deterministic mapping,

$$Encode\_2 = \sigma\left(W * Encode\_1 + b\right) \tag{14}$$

The latent representation $Encode\_2$, or the code is then mapped back into a reconstruction r of the same shape as i using the decoder function

$$r = \sigma\left(W' * Encode\_2 + b'\right) \tag{15}$$

The squared error is computed to minimize the reconstruction error between the actual input image and reconstructed one

$$L\left(i,r\right) = \| \, i - r \, \|^2 \tag{16}$$

Finally, the enhanced image is reconstructed with the decoder function of deep autoencoder. The complete procedure for image enhancement is given in algorithm 1.

Algorithm 1: Image Enhancement Using Deep Autoencoder with UDWT

Input: Original Image (i); **Output:** Enhanced Image (r)

Step 1: Decompose the input image with Undecimated Discrete Wavelet Transform
Step 2: Encode the decomposed image to a hidden representation with an autoencoder through a deterministic mapping,

$$Encode\_1 = \sigma\left(W * i + b\right)$$

Step 3: The encoded image from step 2 is then given as an input to the second autoencoder for further compression through a deterministic mapping,

$$Encode\_2 = \sigma\left(W * Encode\_1 + b\right)$$

Step 4: The latent representation $Encode\_2$, or the code is then mapped back into a reconstruction r of the same shape as n using the decoder function

$$r = \sigma\left(W' * Encode\_2 + b'\right)$$

Step 5: The squared error is computed to minimize the reconstruction error between the actual input image and reconstructed one

$$L\left(i,r\right) = \| \, i - r \, \|^2$$

Step 6: Reconstruct the enhanced image with the decoder function of deep autoencoder
Step 7: Evaluate the performance using image quality metrics such as SNR, PSNR, MSE, and RMSE

Experimental Results and Discussion

The performance of the proposed image enhancement method with Undecimated Wavelet Transform and deep autoencoder for biometric fingerprint and face image has been computed and compared in this section. The proposed method has been compared with existing benchmark image enhancement methods such as Histogram Equalization (HE), Adaptive Histogram Equalization (AHE), and Adaptive Gamma Correction with Weighting Distribution.

Dataset

The proposed method is tested on real-time fingerprint and face images which have been created from 150 subjects each with ten samples using eSSL ZK7500 fingerprint sensor and Logitech WebCam respectively. Additionally, the standard FVC2004 fingerprint (The fingerprint database FVC2004,http://bias.csr.unibo.it/fvc2004/download.asp) and ORL face dataset (The ORL Database of Faces,http://www.cl.cam.ac.uk/research/dtg/attarchive/facedatabase.html) have also been utilized to conclude the efficacy of the proposed approach. The sample fingerprint and face images from the real-time biometric image dataset are given in figure 6 and figure 7 respectively.

Performance Measures

The image quality metrics such as Signal to Noise Ratio (SNR) and Peak Signal to Noise Ratio (PSNR), Mean Square Error (MSE), and Root Mean Square Error (RMSE) (Wang, Bovik, Sheikh, & Simoncelli, 2004) are used to evaluate the performance of the proposed approach. The metrics are shown in table 1.where I_1 indicates the input image, I_2 is the enhanced image, m and n are the number of rows and columns in the image respectively, and R is the maximum fluctuation in the input image data type. In this research work, R is set as 255 since the image data type is an 8-bit unsigned integer.

Figure 6. Fingerprint dataset

Figure 7. Face dataset

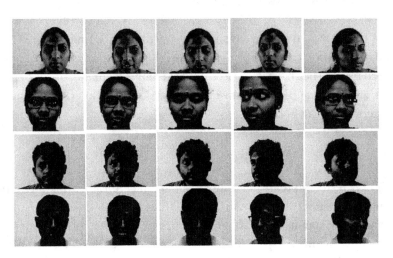

Table 1. Quantitative metrics

Metric	Formula
SNR	$10\log_{10}\left(\dfrac{\mathrm{Var}\left(\mathrm{I}_1\right)}{\mathrm{Var}\left(\mathrm{I}_2\right)}\right)$
PSNR	$10\log_{10}\left(\dfrac{\mathrm{R}^2}{\mathrm{MSE}}\right)$
MSE	$\dfrac{\sum_{\mathrm{m,n}}\left[\mathrm{I}_1\left(\mathrm{m,n}\right)-\mathrm{I}_2\left(\mathrm{m,n}\right)\right]^2}{\mathrm{m}*\mathrm{n}}$
RMSE	$\sqrt{\dfrac{\sum_{\mathrm{m,n}}\left[\mathrm{I}_1\left(\mathrm{m,n}\right)-\mathrm{I}_2\left(\mathrm{m,n}\right)\right]^2}{\mathrm{m}*\mathrm{n}}}$

The signal to noise ratio and peak signal to noise ratio are mathematical measure for image quality assessment between original image and reconstructed image. It shows the measure of peak error. It is the cumulative squared error between the original image and the noise added image. Moreover, mean square error and root mean square error are the cumulative squared error between the original image and the reconstructed image.

Existing Enhancement Methods

Histogram Equalization

The Histogram Equalization is an image enhancement method for adjusting the image intensities to improve contrast. It depicts the frequency of a specific gray or intensity value appears in an image. In the literature, this method is explored in diverse applications such as medical imaging, object tracking, speech recognition, and biometric authentication to pre-process the images in order to obtain better results. (Wang, Chen, & Zhang, 1999) Many research works has been using multiple histograms called sub-histograms to enhance the contrast locally. The objective is to enhance the contrast without producing brightness mean-shift and detail loss artifacts by modifying the conventional histogram equalization method. The Cumulative Distribution Function corresponding to p_x is defined as

$$cdf_x\left(i\right) = \sum_{i=0}^{i} p_x\left(j\right) \tag{17}$$

which represents the image's accumulated normalized histogram.

Adaptive Histogram Equalization

Generally, Adaptive Histogram Equalization is an image pre-processing method which is used to improve the contrast in images. In contrast to conventional histogram equalization method, the adaptive histogram equalization method computes several histograms each corresponding to a separate division of the image and uses them to redistribute the intensity values of the image. It improves the pixel quality by transforming each pixel with a transformation function derived from a neighborhood region (Stark, 2000).

Adaptive Gamma Correction with Weighting Distribution

Recently, the gamma encoding is the technique which is widely employed to optimize the bits required when an image is encoded. It is a non-linear method which follows an approximate gamma or power function (Divya, Thangavel, & Sasirekha, 2016). The adaptive gamma correction is represented as follows

$$T\left(l\right) = l_{max}\left(l | l_{max}\right)^{3} = l_{max}\left(l | l_{max}\right)^{1-cdf\left(l\right)} \tag{18}$$

Experimental Results

The performance results of biometric image enhancement on biometric databases using histogram equalization is presented in table 2.

The PSNR of realtime fingerprint, realtime face, FVC2004, and ORL datasets are 35.79, 30.26, 31.86, and 26.72 respectively. Similarly, the MSEs are 17.11, 61.75, 42.36, 139.61. The performance results of biometric image enhancement on biometric databases using adaptive histogram equalization

Table 2. Performance of image enhancement with histogram equalization

Datasets	SNR	PSNR	MSE	RMSE
Real-time fingerprint	0.0054	35.7981	17.1110	4.1365
Real-time face	0.0177	30.2699	61.7512	7.8529
FVC2004	0.0394	31.8605	42.3676	6.5090
ORL	0.0653	26.7200	139.6193	11.8128

is presented in table 3. The PSNR of realtime fingerprint, realtime face, FVC2004, and ORL datasets are 41.41, 30.46, 36.13, and 29.73 respectively. Similarly, the MSEs are 5.43, 58.97, 15.82, and 69.81.

The performance results of biometric image enhancement on biometric databases using adaptive gamma correction is presented in table 4. The PSNR of realtime fingerprint, realtime face, FVC2004, and ORL datasets are 43.94, 35.81, 41.41, and 30.69 respectively. Similarly, the RMSE values are 1.62, 4.44, 2.24, and 7.64.

The resultant biometric fingerprint and face image after enhancement using deep autoencoder in wavelet domain is presented in figure 8. The contrast of enhanced biometric images is improved than the original images. To train the deep autoencoder, various transfer functions such as Logsig, Satlin, and Purelin are utilized in this work as presented in table 5. The logsig is a logistic function which is given as,

$$f(z) = \frac{1}{1 + e^{-z}} \tag{19}$$

The Satlin is a linear transfer function which is given as,

$$\tag{20}$$

Table 3. Performance of image enhancement with adaptive histogram equalization

Datasets	SNR	PSNR	MSE	RMSE
Real-time fingerprint	0.1983	41.4190	5.4369	2.2498
Real-time face	0.0327	30.4696	58.9702	7.6742
FVC2004	0.0044	36.1381	15.8223	3.9777
ORL	0.0659	29.7306	69.8193	8.3530

Table 4. Performance of image enhancement with adaptive gamma correction

Datasets	SNR	PSNR	MSE	RMSE
Real-time fingerprint	0.1403	43.9408	2.6453	1.6263
Real-time face	0.0543	35.1821	19.7185	4.4406
FVC2004	0.1983	41.4190	5.4369	2.2498
ORL	0.0718	30.6985	58.5981	7.6494

Figure 8. Enhancement using deep autoencoder in wavelet domain: (a) Input fingerprint image; (b) Enhanced fingerprint image; (c) Input face image ; (d) Enhanced face image

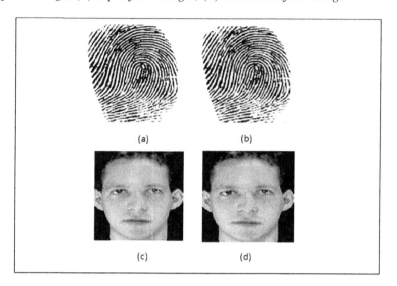

Table 5. Transfer Functions for Autoencoder

TRANSFER FUNCTION	FORMULA
Logsig	$f(z) = \dfrac{1}{1 + e^{-z}}$
Satlin	$f(z) = \begin{cases} 0, & if\, 0 \leq 0 \\ z, & if\, 0 < z < 1 \\ 1, & if\, z \geq 1 \end{cases}$
Purelin	$f(z) = z$

Furthermore, the Purelin is a linear transfer function which is given as,

$$f(z) = z \tag{21}$$

The image quantitative measures such as SNR, PSNR, MSE, and RMSE for real-time fingerprint dataset with various encoder and decoder functions such as Logsig, Satlin, and Purelin has been computed and compared in table 6.

The quantitative measures such as SNR, PSNR, MSE, and RMSE for FVC2004 fingerprint dataset with various encoder and decoder functions such as Logsig, Satlin, and Purelin have been computed and presented in table 7 for comparative analysis.

Table 6. Performance of image enhancement with real-time fingerprint dataset

Encoder Transfer Function	Decoder Transfer Function	SNR	PSNR	MSE	RMSE
Logsig	Logsig	0.0146	46.0033	1.6449	1.2825
	Satlin	0.0198	44.6264	2.2585	1.5028
	Purelin	0.01227	38.9960	8.2579	2.8736
Satlin	Logsig	0.0197	36.6210	14.2682	3.7773
	Satlin	0.0175	30.6080	57.0699	7.5513
	Purelin	0.0659	29.7306	69.8193	8.3530

Table 7. Performance of image enhancement with FVC2004 fingerprint dataset

Encoder Transfer Function	Decoder Transfer Function	SNR	PSNR	MSE	RMSE
Logsig	Logsig	0.0049	44.4888	2.3313	1.5268
	Satlin	0.0023	43.5452	2.8971	1.7020
	Purelin	0.1983	41.4190	5.4369	2.2498
Satlin	Logsig	0.05430	35.1821	19.7185	4.4406
	Satlin	0.0327	30.4723	58.9347	7.6719
	Purelin	0.0201	28.8386	85.9065	9.2610

The quantitative measures such as SNR, PSNR, MSE, and RMSE for real-time face dataset with various encoder and decoder functions such as Logsig, Satlin, and Purelin have been computed and presented in table 8 for comparative analysis. The quantitative measures such as SNR, PSNR, MSE, and RMSE for ORL face dataset with various encoder and decoder functions such as Logsig, Satlin and Purelin has been computed and compared in table 9.

The quantitative results of the proposed method have been compared with various encoder/decoder functions and the results are given in tables 6-9. The measures such Signal to Noise Ratio, Peak Signal to Noise Ratio, Mean Square Error, and Root Mean Square Error is utilized to validate the proposed image enhancement method discussed. From tables 2-9 and from figures 8-12, it is clearly understood that the proposed method in wavelet domain enhances the biometric fingerprint and face image efficiently.

It is observed that highest PSNR of real-time fingerprint dataset is 46.00 with logsig encoder/decoder function. The SNR, PSNR, MSE, and RMSE of real-time fingerprint dataset with logsig encoder/decoder function are 0.01, 46.00, 1.64, and 1.28 respectively. The MSE of logsig encoder with decoder function such as logsig, satlin, purelin are 1.64, 2.25, and 8.25 respectively. The highest and lowest PSNR of FVC2004 fingerprint dataset are 44.48 and 41.41. The SNR, PSNR, MSE, and RMSE of FVC2004 fingerprint dataset with logsig encoder/decoder function are 0.01, 44.48, 2.33, and 1.52 respectively. The RMSE of logsig encoder with decoder function such as logsig, satlin, purelin are 1.52, 1.70, and 2.24 respectively.

Table 8. Performance of image enhancement with real-time face dataset

En coder Transfer Function	Decoder Transfer Function	SNR	PSNR	MSE	RMSE
Logsig	Logsig	0.0164	45.4753	1.8575	1.3629
	Satlin	0.1403	43.9408	2.6453	1.6263
	Purelin	0.0383	36.4598	14.8079	3.8481
Satlin	Logsig	0.0543	35.1821	19.7185	4.4406
	Satlin	0.0394	31.8605	42.3676	6.5090
	Purelin	-0.1136	29.8151	68.3863	8.2696

Table 9. Performance of image enhancement with ORL face dataset

En coder Transfer Function	Decoder Transfer Function	SNR	PSNR	MSE	RMSE
Logsig	Logsig	0.1272	46.0079	1.6627	1.2857
	Satlin	0.0029	43.6994	2.7961	1.6721
	Purelin	0.0044	36.1381	15.8223	3.9777
Satlin	Logsig	0.0249	30.7162	55.6684	7.4579
	Satlin	0.0659	29.7306	69.8193	8.3530
	Purelin	0.0299	26.6269	142.6349	11.9399

Figure 9. Performance of image enhancement with real-time fingerprint dataset

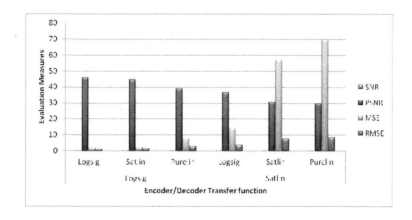

The MSE of logsig encoder with decoder function such as logsig, satlin, purelin on real-time face dataset is 1.85, 2.64, and 14.80 respectively; and the MSE of satlin encoder with various decoder functions such as logsig, satlin, purelin on real-time face dataset is 19.71, 42.36, and 68.38 respectively. The RMSE of logsig encoder with decoder function such as logsig, satlin, purelin on ORL face dataset is 1.28, 1.67, and 3.97 respectively; and the RMSE of satlin encoder with various decoder functions such

Figure 10. Performance of image enhancement with FVC2004 fingerprint dataset

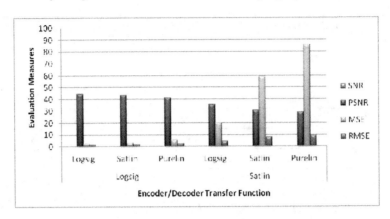

Figure 11. Performance PSNR and MSE of image enhancement with real-time face dataset

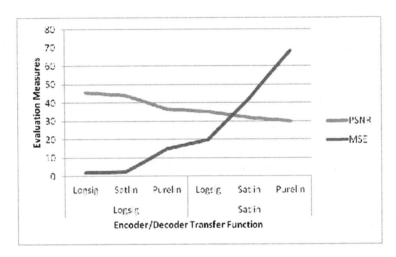

Figure 12. Performance PSNR and MSE of image enhancement with ORL face dataset

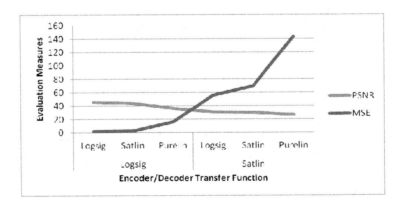

as logsig, satlin, purelin on ORL face dataset is 7.45, 8.35, and 11.93 respectively. The logsig transfer function produced better results than stalin and purelin functions for all the four datasets. The proposed biometric image enhancement method attained improved performance than existing methods such as histogram equalization, adaptive histogram equalization and adaptive gamma correction.

FUTURE RESEARCH DIRECTIONS

However, research in this area can still go a long way further investigating the complex difficulties and hurdles exists. Deep Learning algorithms are trained to learn progressively using raw image data. To validate the efficacy of the built model, enormous data sets are required. Increasingly, huge corpus of parameters is needed to extract powerful abstraction. As a consequence, it increases the complexity of the network. Moreover, these hyper-parameters have to be optimized which have a significant impact on the model performance. To handle a real-world pattern recognition problem, the machine needs to be equipped with adequate processing power. Nowadays, the researchers exploit multi-core GPUs which are expensive. In order to realize the full potential of Deep Learning in the context of image processing, the aforementioned challenges are need to be optimized.

CONCLUSION

Deep Learning is taking over the world; in the day to day life or high-end innovations. In contrast to the conventional machine learning methods, deep learning has gained significant attention in the field of artificial intelligence recently. The efficiency of a biometric authentication system depends on the quality of the image. In this work, deep autoencoder with Undecimated Wavelet Transform is exploited to enhance the biometric fingerprint and face images. The images are decomposed in wavelet domain using UDWT with Daubechies filter. Then, deep autoencoder is trained with various transfer functions to enhance the biometric image. Among all the transfer functions, logsig outperformed the others. To conclude the efficacy of the proposed method, experiments have been conducted on real-time fingerprint, real-time face, FVC2004 fingerprint, and ORL face datasets. The acquired results expound that the proposed method reveals better results in terms of SNR, PSNR, MSE, and RMSE. Hence, the proposed method is effectual in image enhancement of other domains.

ACKNOWLEDGMENT

Authors would like to thank UGC, New Delhi for the financial support received under UGC Major Research Project [Grant No. 43-274/2014(SR)] and SAP DRS [No. F. 5-6/2018/ DRS-II (SAP-II)].

REFERENCES

Alain, G., & Bengio, Y. (2012). *What regularized auto-encoders learn from the data generating distribution.* Technical Report.

Alsaidi Altaher, M., & Mohd Ismail, T. (2010). A Comparison of Some Thresholding Selection Methods for Wavelet Regression. *World Academy of Science, Engineering and Technology, 4*, 105–111.

Bengio, Y., Courville, A., & Vincent, P. (2013). Representation Learning: A Review and New Perspectives. *IEEE Transactions on Pattern Analysis and Machine Intelligence, 35*(8), 1798–1828. doi:10.1109/TPAMI.2013.50 PMID:23787338

Bishop, C. M. (2006). *Pattern recognition and machine learning.* Springer.

Chang, S. G., & Bin Yu, M. V. (2000). Adaptive Wavelet Thresholding for Image Denoising and Compression. *IEEE International transactions on Image Processing*, 1532 -1546.

Chauhana, S., Arorab, A. S., & Kaula, A. (2010). A survey of emerging biometric modalities. *Procedia Computer Science, 2*, 213–218. doi:10.1016/j.procs.2010.11.027

Chen, M., Xu, Z., Winberger, K., & Sha, F. (2012). *Marginalized denoising autoencoders for domain adaptation.* ICML.

Cho, D., & Bui, T. D. (2014). Fast image enhancement in compressed wavelet domain. *Signal Processing, 98*, 295–307. doi:10.1016/j.sigpro.2013.11.007

David, L. D. (1995). Denoising by soft-thresholding. *IEEE Transactions on Information Theory, 41*(3), 613–627. doi:10.1109/18.382009

Demirel, H., & Anbarjafari, G. (2011). Image resolution enhancement by using discrete and stationary wavelet decomposition. *IEEE Transactions on Image Processing, 20*(5), 1458–1460. doi:10.1109/TIP.2010.2087767 PMID:20959267

Divya, K., Thangavel, K., & Sasirekha, K. (2016). Fingerprint image enhancement using DWT domain with adaptive gamma parameter. *The International Journal of Scientific Research in Science Engineering and Technology, 2*(4), 2395–1990.

Druzhkov, P., & Kustikova, V. (2016). A survey of deep learning methods and software tools for image classification and object detection. *Pattern Recognition and Image Analysis, 26*(1), 9–15. doi:10.1134/S1054661816010065

El-leithy, I. M., Salama, G. I., & Mahmoud, T. A. (2017). Fingerprint representation and matching for secure smartcard authentication. *International Journal of Biometrics, 9*(2), 81–95. doi:10.1504/IJBM.2017.085671

Gharbi, M., Chaurasia, G., Paris, S., & Durand, F. (2016). Deep joint demosaicking and denoising. *ACM Transactions on Graphics, 35*(6).

Golovko, V., Kroshchanka, A., & Treadwell, D. (2016). The nature of unsupervised learning in deep neural networks: A new understanding and novel approach. *Optical Memory and Neural Networks*, 127–141.

Gondara, L. (2016). *Medical image denoising using convolutional denoising autoencoders. Data Mining Workshops*. ICDMW.

Haykin, S. (2005). Neural Networks (2nd ed.). Prentice Hall of India.

Hinton, G. E., Osindero, S., & Teh, Y.-W. (2006). A fast learning algorithm for deep belief nets. *Neural Computation, 18*(7), 1527–1554. doi:10.1162/neco.2006.18.7.1527 PMID:16764513

Jain, A., Ross, A. A., & Prabhakar, S. (2004). An introduction to biometric recognition. *IEEE Transactions on Circuits and Systems for Video Technology, 14*(1), 4–20. doi:10.1109/TCSVT.2003.818349

Jain, A. K., Ross, A., & Nandakumar, K. (2011). Introduction. In Introduction to Biometrics. Springer.

Khan, M. K., & Zhang, J. (2008). Multimodal face and fingerprint biometrics authentication on space-limited tokens. *Neurocomputing, 71*(13), 3026–3031. doi:10.1016/j.neucom.2007.12.017

LeCun, Y., Bengio, Y., & Hinton, G. (2015). Deep learning. *Nature, 521*(7553), 436–444. doi:10.1038/nature14539 PMID:26017442

Lefkimmiatis, S. (2016). *Non-local color image denoising with convolutional neural networks.* arXiv:1611.06757

Li, H. (2014). Deep Learning for Image Denoising. *International Journal of Signal Processing, Image Processing and Pattern Recognition*, 171-180.

Lore, K. G., Akintayo, A., & Sarkar, S. (2016). Llnet: A deep autoencoder approach to natural lowlight image enhancement. *Pattern Recognition*, 1–13.

Mohideen, S. K., Perumal, S., Krishnan, N., Sathik, M., & Kumar, T. (2008). Image denoising multi-wavelet and threshold. *IEEE International conference on Computing, Communication and Networking*, 1-5.

Othman, S. A., & Stambouli, T. B. (2016). Undecimated discrete wavelet transform for touchless 2D fingerprint identification. *International Journal of Biometrics, 8*(3-4), 202–215. doi:10.1504/IJBM.2016.082595

Rifai, S., Bengio, Y., Dauphin, Y., & Vincent, P. (2012). *A generative process for sampling contractive auto-encoders.* ICML.

Rifai, S., Vincent, P., Muller, X., Glorot, X., & Bengio, Y. (2011). Contractive auto-encoders: explicit invariance during feature extraction. In *Proceedings of ICML*, (pp. 833–840). Academic Press.

Sasirekha, K., & Thangavel, K. (2014). A Comparative Analysis on Fingerprint Binarization Techniques. *International Journal of Computational Intelligence and Informatics, 4*(3).

Sasirekha, K., & Thangavel, K. (2014). A Novel Wavelet based Thresholding for Denoising Fingerprint Image. In *IEEE International Conference on Electronics, Communication and Computational Engineering*, (pp. 119-124). IEEE. 10.1109/ICECCE.2014.7086644

Sasirekha, K., & Thangavel, K. (2016). *A Novel Feature Extraction Algorithm from Fingerprint Image in Wavelet Domain. Springer.*

Schmidhuber, J. (2015). Deep learning in neural networks: An overview. *Neural Networks, 61*, 85–117. doi:10.1016/j.neunet.2014.09.003 PMID:25462637

Singh, R., & Om, H. (2017). Newborn face recognition using deep convolutional neural network. *Multimedia Tools and Applications*, 1–11.

Sokolova, M., & Lapalme, G. (2009). A systematic analysis of performance measures for classification tasks. *Information Processing & Management*, *45*(4), 427–437. doi:10.1016/j.ipm.2009.03.002

Stark, J. A. (2000). Adaptive image contrast enhancement using generalizations of histogram equalization. *IEEE Transactions on Image Processing*, *9*(5), 889–896. doi:10.1109/83.841534 PMID:18255459

Swersky, K., Ranzato, M., Buchman, D., Marlin, B., & de Freitas, N. (2011). On score matching for energy based models: Generalizing autoencoders and simplifying deep learning. In *International Conference on Machine Learning ICML-11*, (p. 1201). Academic Press.

Thangavel, K., & Sasirekha, K. (2016). *Denoising Iris Image Using a Novel Wavelet Based Threshold*. Digital Connectivity–Social Impact. doi:10.1007/978-981-10-3274-5_5

The fingerprint database FVC2004. (n.d.). Retrieved from http://bias.csr.unibo.it/fvc2004/download.asp

The ORL Database of Faces. (n.d.). Retrieved from http://www.cl.cam.ac.uk/research/dtg/attarchive/facedatabase.html

Tsai, D. Y., Matsuyama, E., & Chen, H. M. (2013). Improving image quality in medical images using a combined method of undecimated wavelet transform and wavelet coefficient mapping. *International Journal of Biomedical Imaging*, *2013*, 1–11. doi:10.1155/2013/797924 PMID:24382951

Vincent, P. (2011). A connection between score matching and denoising autoencoders. *Neural Computation*, *23*(7), 1661–1674. doi:10.1162/NECO_a_00142 PMID:21492012

Vincent, P., Larochelle, H., Bengio, Y., & Manzagol, P. A. (2008). *Extracting and composing robust features with denoising autoencoders*. ICML. doi:10.1145/1390156.1390294

Wang, G. (2016). A perspective on deep imaging. *IEEE Access: Practical Innovations, Open Solutions*, *4*, 8914–8924. doi:10.1109/ACCESS.2016.2624938

Wang, Y., Chen, Q., & Zhang, B. (1999). Image enhancement based on equal area dualistic sub-image histogram equalization method. *IEEE Transactions on Consumer Electronics*, *45*(1), 68–75. doi:10.1109/30.754419

Wang, Z., Bovik, A., Sheikh, H., & Simoncelli, E. (2004). Image quality assessment: From error visibility to structural similarity. *IEEE Transactions on Image Processing*, *13*(6). PMID:15376593

Wu, T.-X., Lian, X.-C., & Lu, B. L. (2012). Multi-view gender classification using symmetry of facial images. *Neural Computing & Applications*, *21*(4), 661–669. doi:10.100700521-011-0647-x

Xie, J., & Xu, L. (2012). Image denoising and inpainting with deep neural networks. In *International Conference on Neural Information Processing Systems*, (pp. 341-349). Academic Press.

Yao, Y., Marcialis, G. L., Pontil, M., Frasconi, P., & Roli, F. (2003). Combining flat and structured representations for fingerprint classification with recursive neural networks and support vector machines. *Pattern Recognition*, *36*(2), 397–406. doi:10.1016/S0031-3203(02)00039-0

Yosinski, J., Clune, J., Bengio, Y., & Lipson, H. (2014). How transferable are features in deep neural networks? *Advances in Neural Information Processing Systems*, 3320–3328.

Yu, W., Jiang, X., & Xiong, B. (2009). Data preparation for sample-based face detection. *International Journal of Computer Applications in Technology*, 35(1), 10–22. doi:10.1504/IJCAT.2009.024591

Zhicheng Yan, H. Z. (2016). Automatic Photo Adjustment Using Deep Neural Networks. *ACM Transactions on Graphics*, 35(2).

Chapter 13
A 3D–Cellular Automata–Based Publicly–Verifiable Threshold Secret Sharing

Rosemary Koikara
Kyungpook National University, South Korea

Eun-Joon Yoon
Kyungil Univeristy, South Korea

Anand Paul
Kyungpook National University, South Korea

ABSTRACT

In secret sharing, a secret is distributed between various participants in a manner that an authorized group of participants in the appropriate access structures can recover this secret. However, a dealer might get corrupted by adversaries and may influence this secret sharing or the reconstruction process. Verifiable secret sharing (VSS) overcomes this issue by adding a verifiability protocol to the original secret sharing scheme. This chapter discusses a computationally secure publicly verifiable secret sharing scheme constructed using the three-dimensional cellular automata (3D CA). The initial configuration of the 3D CA is the secret. The following configurations are devised to be the shares distributed among the participants. Update mechanisms and various rules make it hard for an adversary to corrupt or duplicate a share. To make it even more efficient, the authors added a verifiability layer such that a dealer posts a public share and a private share to each shareholder. The NIST test suite has been used to calculate the randomness of the shares.

INTRODUCTION

Securing information that is flowing on the Internet has become crucial in the past few years. There has been an escalation in the amount of cyber-crime when it comes to an organization's privacy or an individual's privacy. Cryptographic algorithms like DES (Diffie, & Hellman, 1977) and RSA (Rivest,

DOI: 10.4018/978-1-5225-9611-0.ch013

Shamir, & Adleman, 1978) have been used for encrypting data using keys. However, here the security of information lies in the safety of the keys. Key-management techniques were developed to solve this issue. Secret sharing was one of the techniques that emerged mainly for key management though it has many other applications.

Secret sharing (SS) is composed of two algorithms – the secret sharing algorithm and the reconstruction algorithm. In SS, a dealer generates shares and then distributes them to various participants who then become shareholders. The shares generated are then used to reconstruct the secret. The concept of secret sharing was first formulated independent of each other by Shamir (1979) and Blakley (1979) in 1979. The SS scheme developed were (k, n)-threshold SS schemes in which a secret S is divided among n shareholders such that at least k or more shareholders are required to reconstruct the secret correctly. It is not feasible to reconstruct the secret if $k - 1$ or fewer shares are present. Polynomial arithmetic operations and interpolation form the basis of Shamir's Scheme. The goal was to take k points and guarantee that a unique polynomial with those points exists. The interpolation of the missing points corresponding to the polynomial is made possible. Blakley's scheme, on the other hand, was based on hyperplane intersections instead of polynomial interpolation.

The shareholders in SS belong to various subsets of participants called the access structure. Suppose, $\mathcal{A}$ is the access structure, then $\mathcal{A}$ determines the mechanism to share and reconstruct the secret. "Any subset in $\mathcal{A}$ can reconstruct the secret from its shares, and any subset not in $\mathcal{A}$ cannot reveal any information about the secret" (Beimel, 2011). Depending upon the access structure, there can be many SS schemes. A hierarchical threshold SS scheme that had a hierarchical access structure was proposed by Tassa (2007). This scheme was based on Birkhoff interpolation and could share one secret.

Shamir's SS scheme among other commonly used SS mechanisms can be used to distribute only one secret. However, the secret messages are not always small, and they may be huge on certain occasions (Capocelli, Santis, Gargano, & Vaccaro, 1991). There has to be a technique to share more than one secret message among shareholders. In ref. (He, & Dawson, 1994; Blundo, De Santis, Di Crescenzo, Gaggia, &Vaccaro, 1994), multi-secret sharing schemes were proposed. These schemes as mentioned earlier use were based on Shamir's schemes.

Numerous research has been carried out in the field of SS (Benalo, & Leichter, 1990; Ito, Saito, & Nishizeki, 1989; Simmons, 1991; Brickell, 1989; Karchmer, &Wigderson, 1993; Bertilsson, & Ingemarsson, 1992). Shamir's SS scheme is the most widely researched SS technique. Researchers have also proposed different techniques. Mignotte (1982) and Asmuth and Bloom (1983) proposed to use the Chinese Remainder Theorem (CRT) to share the secret. It was later pointed out by Kaya and Selçuk (2008) that Mignotte's and Asmuth-Bloom's schemes are not safe against dishonest dealers. A dealer can distribute inconsistent shares to the shareholders, and the schemes cannot prevent that. Kaya et al. proposed a Verifiable Secret Sharing (VSS) scheme based on the CRT and the RSA assumption. Goyal and Kumar (2018) introduced an SS scheme for general access structures such that if an adversary tampers with any or all of the shares, either the original secret is reconstructed or lost.

Cellular automata (CA) have also been used to design SS algorithms. A CA is an arrangement of cells. The state of each cell depends on the states of neighboring cells and is updated with time. An update mechanism and rules govern the approach used to make the change in the state of each cell. The same update rule is used to synchronously modify the states of the cells across the CA. A CA may be of various dimensions: one dimensional (1D), two dimensional (2D) or three dimensional (3D). The use of 3D-CA in a SS scheme increases the complexity of a third party to attack the system.

A new (t,n)-threshold SS scheme based on a memory CA was proposed such that the secret is reconstructed successfully if at least t consecutive subsets are available (del Rey, Mateus, & Sánchez, 2005). Though this scheme was proved to be perfect and ideal, a malicious participant can disrupt the secrecy of the message by providing fake shares to other participants. The scheme is not designed to prevent the participants from behaving maliciously. Later, Martin del Rey et al. proposed an SS scheme that used Boolean functions for digital images such that cellular automata were used to enhance the secret image (del Rey, & Sáchez, 2009). Two-dimensional cellular automata were used to propose an (n,n)-threshold multi-SS scheme (Eslami, Razzaghi, & Ahmadabadi, 2010) such that n secret images were shared and all the secrets were required to reconstruct the secret images. In (Eslami, & Ahmadabadi, 2010) 1D CA was used for a (t,n)-threshold SS scheme to share k secrets. Eslami, Pakniat & Noroozi (2015) used CA to improve the hierarchical threshold SS scheme proposed by Tassa (2007). This scheme could share multiple secrets. In 2016, Lu et al. (2016) proposed a threshold SS scheme that used linear memory CA and the Chinese Remainder Theorem. Li, Yu, and Hao (2017) proposed a VSS scheme that shares multiple secrets, Yu, and Hao (2017). In this scheme CA is used for SS and we assume that the dealer is not necessarily trusted. Hence, the assistance of a dealer is not required. Fan et al. (2019) used 1D CA for transforming medical images as part of the watermarking process. In this process distinct initial values and rules have been used to achieve CA transformation across 3 levels.

VSS schemes are conventional SS schemes with an additional layer of verifiability over it. Ref. (Cramer, Damgård, & Maurer, 2000) assumes that the communication channel is secure and proposes a VSS method with perfect security under a detailed access structure. Suppose a channel is not secure and there is a possibility of there being an adaptive adversary that corrupts any of the un-authorized shareholders, then it is possible to convert an ordinary SS scheme to a secure VSS up to a polynomial black-box reduction. However, this does not apply to multiparty computation. Stadler (1996) introduced the notion of publicly VSS scheme. A publicly verifiable secret sharing (PVSS) scheme is an extension of non-interactive VSS where anyone outside the access structure can verify a share. In this chapter, a PVSS scheme based on 3D CA is discussed at length.

The issues of previous research that has been tackled in this chapter are:

- The dealer is not assumed to be trusted.
- This scheme uses three-dimensional CA, contrary to 1D CA used previously.
- This scheme is publicly verifiable in contrast to some schemes that are susceptible to fake shares.

This chapter is organized as follows.

- **Background:** In this section, the basic terminology, notation, and concepts used throughout the paper are introduced.
- **Verifiable 3D Cellular Automata based Secret Sharing:** A verifiable threshold secret sharing scheme that uses 3D CA is explained in detail.
- **Analysis:** The verifiable 3D CA based SS discussed in this chapter is analyzed and compared with other forms of SS.

Background

Notation

Let $\{i, i+1, \ldots, j-1, j\}$ be represented as $[i, j]$, $[1, i]$ as [i] and $\{r_i, r_{i+1}, \ldots, r_{j-1}, r_j\}$ as $[r_i, r_j]$. Suppose S is a set then $s \leftarrow S$ is a random element from S. If M is a method then $u \leftarrow M(x)$ is the result when M is performed on the input y. In this chapter,

3D-CA: Three-dimensional cellular automata.
GF: The Galois Field
SS: Secret sharing
VSS: Verifiable secret sharing
PVSS: Publicly verifiable secret sharing

(k, n)-Threshold Secret Sharing

The threshold secret sharing scheme discussed in this paper is not derived from Shamir's SS scheme (Shamir, 1979). However, understanding Shamir's scheme will help in visualizing the proposed PVSS scheme. The (k, n)-threshold SS scheme proposed by Adi Shamir is as follows. Let, S be the secret that has to be kept secure. This S is divided into n shares, $[S_1, S_n]$ in such a way that:

1. Of the n shares, any k or more shares are needed to compute S.
2. The availability of $k-1$ or fewer shares result in failure to compute S.

The dealer, $\mathcal{D}$, generates a polynomial $f(x)$ using Equation (1) to divide S into shares.

$$f(x) = S + a_1 x + a_1 x^2 + \cdots + a_{k-1} x^{k-1} \ (mod \ p) \tag{1}$$

where, p is a prime number, and x is each participant's ID. The dealer assigns the polynomial $f(x)$ into the participant's share y_j, where $j = \{1, 2 \ldots, n\}$, and distributes the shares to n participants. When the participants wish to reconstruct the secret message, the dealer collects k or more shares from the participants and conducts the reconstruction using Lagrange's interpolation as given in Equation (2).

$$x = \sum_{j=1}^{k} y_i \prod_{i=1, k \neq j}^{k} \frac{x - x_k}{x_j - x_k} \ (mod \ p) \tag{2}$$

This scheme satisfies privacy and correctness property. The privacy parameter of this scheme lies in the guarantee that in Lagrange's interpolation no less than k shares can yield the original secret message. Also, the privacy assures that any combination of $Y_T = \{y_{i_j} \mid y_i \in Y, j \geq k\}$ produces the same secret polynomial.

Publicly Verifiable Secret Sharing

In SS, the dealer or a subset of shareholders may get corrupted due to some third party. In the basic SS schemes (Shamir, 1979; Blakley, 1979), the participants are assumed, to be honest. To avoid disruptions caused by malicious participants a VSS scheme was proposed by Feldman (1987). In this scheme, the dealer checks the correctness of the shares during the distribution phase and verifies the shares supplied by the shareholders during the reconstruction phase. In VSS, shareholders can verify only their shares. Stadler (1996) proposed a PVSS such that anybody could verify shares. PVSS has large applications in verifiable elections and electronic cash.

PVSS schemes generally use discrete logarithmic problems or integer factoring problem. Stadler (1997) noted that the two criteria for PVSS were that the shares could be publicly verified and this could be dealt with implicitly. In Ref. (Schoenmakers, 1999) it is pointed out that for a proper PVSS the shares also show proof of correctness. Schoenmakers proposed a PVSS scheme that depended on the hardness of the discrete logarithm problem. The concepts used in traditional public-key systems were applied to SS to obtain PVSS schemes (Chien, Jan, & Tseng, 2000; Chien, Jan, & Tseng, 20002; Yu, Kong, & Hao, 2007). The Diffie-Hellman assumption has been the central assumption on which the verifiability of PVSS stood. Then in 1993, Menezes, Okamoto, and Vanstone (1993) proposed the Weil pairing that lead to the solution of the Diffie-Hellman problem. As a result of this many pairing-based PVSS schemes have been proposed (Boneh, & Franklin, 2001; Tian, & Peng, 2009; Tian, Peng, & Ma, 2012; Wu, & Tseng, 2011).

VSS (VSS) is an extension of an SS, where some corrupt adversaries may exploit the dealer that generates the share and a subset of participating shareholders. The shares now have to be verified for corruption. The dealer sends the shares to the shareholders to verify them. For the sharing to be effective, the honest players must produce a share, or else all the shares are rejected. Once verification is complete, the authorized subset of shareholders can reconstruct the secret together. The following properties have to be satisfied:

1. If the dealer is compromised and the sharing phase is successful, then any authorized shareholders that belong to the accurate access structure should be able to reconstruct the secret.
2. If the dealer is honest, the sharing phase is always successful, and the secret is accurately reconstructed.
3. An un-authorized subset of players, i.e., an adversary has no information on the secret.

The above three arguments show that in this type of VSS, the presence of the dealer is not crucial for detecting discrepancies in shares. Using VSS ensures that a dealer cannot influence the outcome of an SS scheme. An ideal VSS scheme would be one in which there is as little interaction between shareholders as possible.

The goal of VSS is to handle situations where a dealer sends inconsistent shares to one or all of the shareholders, and also when a shareholder submits fake shares during the reconstruction protocol. A VSS enables shareholders to ensure that their shares are consistently generated by the dealer. This has to be done without disclosing the secret and the shares. Several schemes that use provable security have been proposed. Heidarvand and Villar (2008) proposed a PVSS scheme which used the Decisional Bilinear Square (DBS) assumption to make it publicly verifiable. DBS is a variant of the Diffie Hellman Assumption. Another PVSS scheme was proposed by Wu and Tseng (2011) which uses the pairing-based cryptography to secure the data. A PVSS scheme that can verify shares without the zero-knowledge proofs was implemented Jhanwar (2011).

Cellular Automata

Cellular automata was devised by the mathematician John von Neumann in order to construct a self-replicating machine (Schiff, 2005). A cellular automaton consists of cells arranged in a compact grid. The state of each cell transitions with time. The mechanism with which cell transitions depending on set rules. Cells may be shaped in the form of squares, hexagons, cubes and the likes. Elementary CA is a simple 1D CA that has one of two likely states (0 or 1). Here, the cells are in a straight line. The most popular example of a cellular automaton is the "Game of Life" introduced by Conway in the '70s (Allouche, Courbage, & Skordev, 2000). The reason for CA being applicable is that they are "mathematical systems constructed from many identical components, each simple, but together capable of complex behavior" (Wolfram, 1984). An essential characteristic of CA is the parallel computation it offers. In particular, this is beneficial for computationally intensive tasks that are performed in security. A CA can have one or more dimensions. The state of each cell is modified according to time and depends on the previous state of the cell as well as the neighboring cells. In a 1D CA, there are r cells on either side of the cell. The neighborhood in 1D CAs comprises of r cells on either side of the cell. For two-dimensional CAs the neighborhood can be defined by either 5 cells that comprises the four immediate non-diagonal neighbors and the cell itself, or 9 cells that comprises of eight neighbors and the cell itself. Also, there are various rules and update mechanisms that govern the next state of the cells. All the cells change their configuration simultaneously and using the same update rule. The update rule determines the values used in the update mechanism.

Secret Sharing Schemes Based on Cellular Automata

Del Rey et al. (2005) introduced the use of a "delay discrete dynamical system memory cellular automata" to share a secret. They considered a kth order linear memory CA (LMCA) to share secrets to n shareholders such that k consecutive shares are required to reconstruct the secret. Their scheme is proved to be ideal and perfect for the size of the share, and the size of the secret is equal, and no secret is divulged if $k - 1$ or fewer shares are known. A SS scheme based on Boolean functions for digital images to enhance reconstructed secret image using CA was proposed in Ref. (del Rey, et al., 2009).

Eslami et al. proposed a verifiable (n, n)-threshold SS scheme using 2D CA (Eslami et al., 2010) which has a complexity of O(n) in contrast to the complexity of Shamir based SS schemes which a complexity of O($n \log^2 n$). This scheme requires the presence of all the shares to reconstruct the secret successfully. Later, Eslami and Ahmadabadi (2010) developed a scheme in which one-dimensional CA was used for a (k, n)-threshold SS scheme to share t secrets.

Tassa (2007) proposed a threshold SS scheme that was hierarchical and used the Birkhoff interpolation for the reconstruction of the secret. However, this scheme is unable to share multiple secrets. Eslami et al. (2015) then proposed to use CA to devise a new hierarchical threshold secret sharing scheme that enabled the sharing of multiple secrets.

In 2016, Lu et al. (2016) proposed a threshold SS scheme that used linear memory CA and the Chinese Remainder Theorem. A VSS scheme that shares multiple secrets was proposed by Li et al. (2017). SS schemes that use 3D CA have not been research on at length.

SS have a wide range of applications of which multiparty computation and securing devices involved in any distributed computing environment (Boyle, Gilboa, Ishai, Lin & Tessaro, 2018) are the most practical applications.

The Proposed Verifiable 3D Cellular Automata Based Secret Sharing Scheme

The verifiable (k, n)-threshold SS scheme discussed in this section uses 3D CA.

Motivation

CA encourages parallel computations and has proved to be easier to implement from the hardware point of view. Also, earlier SS schemes were based on 1D-CA and 3D-CA has not been used in a VSS scheme. Hence, it is desirable to use a more complex 3D-CA for SS. Adding a layer of verifiability also ensures that corrupt shareholders or dealers cannot hamper the SS or secret reconstruction process which is very vital.

Bilinear or Multilinear mapping is generally used for SS schemes that are linear in nature. Hence, they cannot be used in CA based SS scheme.

Access Structure

It should be noted that the access structure of this scheme is different from the traditional access structures of a (k, n)-threshold SS scheme.

Assumptions

1. Previously (Koikara et al., 2017) it was assumed that the dealer, $\mathcal{D}$, is trusted. Here, any such assumptions are not made.
2. A secure cryptographic pseudo-random number generator should do all random number generations.

The proposed scheme uses three-dimensional CA (3D-CA) that can be represented as a cube. Unlike one-dimensional memory CA, the 3D memory CA are distinct dynamic systems that comprise a finite 3D block of cells. Each block consists of $n = d^3$ cells, where d is the length of each dimension. Each of the cells takes a state: 0 or 1.

Each cell at time t is represented as $c_{x,yz}^{(t)}$. With time the CA evolves depending on an updating mechanism. The previous states of neighboring cells influence the new state of each cell.

Each 3D cell is surrounded by six different cells called neighbors of the current cell. Hence, the neighborhood of cells that affects the state of a cell is in the left (L), right (R), above (A), below (B), in-page (I) and out-page (O) directions. The form of the updating mechanism is given in Equation 3.

$$c_{x,y,z}^{(t+1)} = f\left(L_{x,y,z}^{(t)}, R_{x,y,z}^{(t)}, A_{x,y,z}^{(t)}, B_{x,y,z}^{(t)}, I_{x,y,z}^{(t)}, O_{x,y,z}^{(t)}\right) \tag{3}$$

To simplify the discussion later, let $c_{x,y,z}^{(t+1)} = f\left(F_{x,y,z}^{(t)}\right)$. Terms are considered similar to the one introduced in [19]. Let the configuration of the CA at time t be given by $M^{(t)} = \left(L_{x,y,z}^{(t)}, R_{x,y,z}^{(t)}, A_{x,y,z}^{(t)}, B_{x,y,z}^{(t)}, I_{x,y,z}^{(t)}, O_{x,y,z}^{(t)}\right)$. The initial value of the CA is $M^{(0)}$. The total number of possible configurations is 2^n. As the states of each cell depend on the previous states of neighboring cells, the boundary conditions have to be considered. The purpose of the boundary conditions is to maintain the dynamics of the CA, such that operations for the state of the cells on the edge of the CA are well defined. Additive boundary conditions are applied on the boundary cells. In additive boundary conditions, the cell to the left of the leftmost cell is assigned as any random cell in that row and the cell to the right of the rightmost cell is any random cell in that row. Similarly the cell above the topmost cell is any random cell in that column and the cell below the bottommost cell is any random cell in that column. However, for SS, this randomness makes it impossible for the secret reconstruction to be successful. Hence the format of additive boundary conditions is altered such that, the cell to the left of the leftmost cell is the last cell in that row and the cell to the right of the rightmost cell first cell in that row; similarly, the cell above the topmost cell is the last cell in that column and the cell below the bottommost cell is the first cell in that column. This ensures that all the cells in the 3D-CA are updated efficiently.

As discussed earlier, the total number of possible configurations for the 3D-CA is 2^n, where $n = d^3$. Let, $\mathcal{C}$ be the set of all possible configurations of the 3D-CA, then $|\mathcal{C}| = 2^n$. According to time the state of the cells in 3D-CA changes, i.e., there is a change in configuration. This change is a transformation, $\mathcal{T} : \mathcal{C} \rightarrow \mathcal{C}$, i.e., at every discrete time interval, $M^{(t+1)} = \mathcal{T}\left(M^{(t)}\right)$. For our SS scheme to work efficiently, $\mathcal{T}$ should be bijective, i.e., there should exist another 3D-CA with a transformation $\mathcal{T}^{-1}$. Here, $\mathcal{T}^{-1}$ is the inverse of $\mathcal{T}$. The 3D-CA is reversible if $\mathcal{T}^{-1}$ exists and thus results in a successful reconstruction in the reverse direction.

The update mechanism is now defined. The entire working of the 3D-CA depends on the update mechanism applied to each cell. The transition applied to each cell is given in Equation (4), and it depends on the neighborhood.

$$c_{x,y,z}^{(t+1)} = L_{x,y,z}^{(t)} \oplus, R_{x,y,z}^{(t)} \oplus A_{x,y,z}^{(t)} \oplus B_{x,y,z}^{(t)} \oplus I_{x,y,z}^{(t)} \oplus O_{x,y,z}^{(t)}) \tag{4}$$

where, $0 \leq x, y, z \leq d - 1$

In the above equation $\oplus$ represents the Boolean XOR function. Equation (4) can also be written as:

$$c_{x,y,z}^{(t+1)} = f_1\left(F_{x,y,z}^{(t)}\right) \oplus \cdots \oplus f_{k-1}\left(F_{x,y,z}^{(t-k+2)}\right) \oplus c_{x,y,z}^{(t-k+1)} \tag{5}$$

where, f_i is the local transition function, where $i = [0, k-1]$ and $x, y, z = [0, d-1]$.

Verifiability of Proposed Scheme

In this section, the model for the VSS scheme is detailed. The properties of this VSS scheme satisfies the following properties.

1. **Correctness:** The participants of an authorized subset of the access structure recovers the secret successfully.
2. **Verifiability:** A SS scheme is called verifiable if the shares of the shareholders can be verified for consistency. This ensures that even if a dealer is compromised and influences the SS or if an adversary corrupts the shareholders, then the shares can still be verified and proved to be fake shares.
3. **Secrecy:** When the dealer is honest shareholders of an unauthorized subset of the access structure cannot learn anything about the secret during or after the protocol.

This VSS consists of four algorithms.

1. **The setting up algorithm:** The set of shareholders, $S = [S_1, S_n]$ have public and private parameters. Here the shareholders publish their corresponding public keys.
2. **The sharing algorithm:** This algorithm divides the secret S into shares and distributes it to other shareholders.
3. **The verification algorithm:** This algorithm verifies the shares.
4. **The reconstruction algorithm:** This algorithm takes the available shares and reconstructs the secret message.

Verifiable Secret Sharing Scheme

The SS scheme discussed in this section is a (k, n)-threshold scheme that shares a secret S such that S is divided into n parts and is distributed to n participants. During the reconstruction of the secret, it is sufficient to have at least k-consecutive of the shares to reconstruct it. In this scheme, the secret S is the initial configuration of the kth order 3D-CA, i.e., $M^{(0)} = S$. Initially, we require k configurations; hence the rest of the $k-1$ configurations are randomly generated and are of the same size as S.

The setting up algorithm, the sharing algorithm, the verification algorithm and the reconstruction algorithm that comprises this VSS is given in detail as follows.

Setting up algorithm

The following steps are performed by the dealer, $\mathcal{D}$ to construct a kth order 3D-CA:

Step 1: Choose a prime number \(p\) such that this discrete logarithm problem is intractable in the field GF().

Step 2: Given, and, then an integer such that is the discrete logarithm of to the base . A generator for GF() is selected and and are then made public.

Step 3: Computes random integer r_0 such that $0 \leq r \leq \frac{l}{2} - 1$, where l is the bit length of the secret, $\mathcal{S}$.

Step 4: Compute and publish $k - 1$ random numbers, $\left[r_1, r_{k-1} \right]$ such that $r_i = \left[1, 2^{r_0 + 1} - 1 \right]$, where $i = \left[1, k - 1 \right]$. These numbers help to decide the rule numbers that will be used in the updating mechanism. The rule selection is discussed later in this chapter.

Step 5: Construct the reversible k^{th} order 3D-CA with the following updating mechanism.

$$c_{x,y,z}^{(t+1)} = f_{r_1}\left(F_{x,y,z}^{(t)} \right) \oplus \cdots \oplus f_{r_{k-1}}\left(F_{x,y,z}^{(t-k+2)} \right) \oplus c_{x,y,z}^{(t-k+1)} \qquad (6)$$

where, $\oplus$ represents the XOR function. Here, f_{r_i} is the local transition function, $0 \leq i \leq k - 1$ and $0 \leq x, y, z \leq d - 1$. Here, the authors assume that $c_{x,y,z}^{(t-k+1)} = f_{r_k} F_{x,y,z}^{(t-k+1)}$. This will ensure the reversibility of this equation and hence the secret message will be safely reconstructed in the recovery module.

Step 6: Let the initial configuration $M^{(0)}$ be the secret message. As the threshold for the minimum number of shares is k, the rest of the $k - 1$ initial configurations $M^{(1)}, M^{(2)}, \cdots, M^{(k-1)}$ are assigned pseudo-random numbers.

Secret Sharing Algorithm

In the sharing phase the dealer, $\mathcal{D}$, constructs the various shares that have to be distributed to the participants. $\mathcal{D}$ constructs the various shares that have to be distributed to the participants. $\mathcal{D}$ performs the following steps:

Step 1: Computes a random integer s, $s \geq k$.

Step 1: **Step 2:** Using the initial configurations $M^{(0)}, \cdots, M^{(1)}, \cdots, M^{(k-1)}$, $\mathcal{D}$ computes the $\left(n + s - 1 \right)^{th}$ order of the 3D-CA. Hence, we obtain a set of configurations.

$$\left\{ M^{(0)}, \cdots, M^{(k-1)}, M^{(k)}, \cdots, M^{(s)}, \cdots, M^{(n+s-1)} \right\}$$

Step 3: The last n configurations are the computed shares, i.e., $S_1 = M^{(m)}, S_2 = M^{(m+1)}, \cdots, S_n = M^{(m+s-1)}$.

Step 4: Compute $G_i \equiv g^{S_i} \left(\text{mod} \, p \right)$, where $i = \left[1, n \right]$.

Step 5: Publishes $\left[G_1, G_n \right]$.

Because of the discrete logarithm problem in GF(p), publishing the $\left[G_1, G_n \right]$ values does not hamper the scheme. The shares are still safe. It is this G_i value that permits us to verify the shares of the participants. In order to ensure that even if $\mathcal{D}$ goes rouge the scheme is still secure, the values of $\{r_1, r_{k-1}\}$ are published publicly.

Secret Verification Algorithm

The share is verified by each shareholder, S_i, $i = [1, n]$ as follows:

Step 1: S_i, $i = [1, n]$ can verify if S_j is is valid by calculating $G_j \equiv g^{S_j} \pmod{p}$, $j = [1, n]$, $j \neq i$.
Step 2: If the shares are valid they can be used in the reconstruction algorithm.

In SS, the dealer or a subset of shareholders may get corrupted due to some third party. In the basic SS schemes (Shamir, 1979; Blakley, 1979), the participants are assumed, to be honest. To avoid disruptions caused by malicious participants a VSS scheme was proposed by Feldman (1987). In this scheme, the dealer checks the correctness of the shares during the distribution phase and verifies the shares submitted by participating shareholders during the reconstruction phase. In VSS, shareholders can verify only their own shares. Stadler (1996) proposed a PVSS such that anybody could verify shares. PVSS has large applications

Secret Reconstruction Algorithm

During the recovery phase of a (k, n)-threshold SS scheme, it is sufficient to have at least \(k\)-consecutive shares to reconstruct the secret. The steps required in the recovery phase are as follows.

Step 1: Consecutive shares are represented by $M^{(m+l)}, \cdots, M^{(m+l+k-1)}, 0 \leq l \leq n - k$.
Step 2: Let, $M' = M^{(m+l+k-1)}$, $0 \leq l \leq n - k$. Now, iterating the inverse 3D-CA $m + l + k - 1$ times we obtain the secret $M^{(0)}$.

Solutions and Analysis

The proposed 3D-CA based SS scheme was implemented in C++ language.

In contrast to $O(n \log^2 n)$ complexity of Shamir's SS scheme, the proposed 3D-CA based threshold SS scheme provides a linear computational complexity.

Rules Selection

One of the most important parts of this SS scheme is the updating mechanism. This mechanism depends on the associated rules. To arrive at the appropriate rules, this SS scheme was implemented using all possible combinations of the rules. On evaluating the behavior of the scheme applying those rules, the authors arrived at rule numbers 9, 21, 42 and 45 as yielding the most satisfactory results. As this is a 3D-CA based SS scheme, it is more efficient to restrict the rules to the above-specified rules as the reversibility of the update function needs to be ensured. Hence, in the SS phase, the random numbers $r_i, 1 \leq i \leq k-1$ establish the rules to be selected. This selection is made using the modulus operation. The rules used in this scheme are indicated in Table 1.

Security Analysis

When analyzing a SS scheme there are three essential properties that it has to satisfy. They are correctness, privacy, and k-consistency. Apart from the analysis of the verifiability, efficiency, randomness, and quality of the shares have been done.

Correctness

In SS algorithms correctness refers to the recovery of the secret. The perfect restoration of the secret is very crucial to the success of a SS scheme. The reconstruction algorithm has parameter correctness if and only if it produces a correct reconstruction of the CA. In this case, there is a correct reconstruction if and only if k or more consecutive shares are collected from the participants.

Theorem 1: If $f_k\left(F_{x,y,z}^{(t-k+1)}\right) = c_{x,y,z}^{(t-k+1)}$ then the 3D-CA given in Equation (5) is reversible and its inverse is another 3D-CA given by the following function:

$$c_{x,y,z}^{(t+1)} = \sum_{j=0}^{k-2} f_{k-j-1}\left(F_{x,y,z}^{(t-j)}\right) + c_{x,y,z}^{(t-k+1)} \ (mod\,2) \tag{7}$$

(For ease of explanation $\oplus$ operation has been replaced by mod 2 as they both result in the same output.)

Proof: Let $\left\{M^{(t)}\right\}_{t \geq 0}$ be the evolution of the 3D-CA. Here, $M^{(t)} = \left(c_{0,0,0}^{(t)}, \cdots, c_{d-1,d-1,d-1}^{(t)}\right)$. Also let the evolution of the inverse be, $\bar{M}^{(t)} = \left(\bar{c}_{0,0,0}^{(t)}, \cdots, \bar{c}_{d-1,d-1,d-1}^{(t)}\right)$. To prove the above statement it needs to be shown that, $\bar{M}^{(k+1)} = M^{(t-k+1)}$, when $\bar{M}^{(1)} = M^{(t+1)}, \bar{M}^{(2)} = M^{(t)}, \cdots, \bar{M}^{(k)} = M^{(t-k+2)}$, for every t.

Table 1. Rules for the 3D-CA.

Rule No.	L	R	A	B	I	O
9	0	0	1	0	0	1
21	0	1	0	1	0	1
42	1	0	1	0	1	0
45	1	0	1	1	0	1

Equation (7) gives,

$$\overline{c}_{x,y,z}^{(t+1)} = f_{r_1}\left(\overline{F}_{x,y,z}^{(t)}\right) \oplus f_{k-2}\left(\overline{F}_{x,y,z}^{(k-2)}\right) \oplus \cdots \oplus f_1\left(\overline{F}_{x,y,z}^{(2)}\right) \oplus \overline{c}_{x,y,z}^{(1)} \tag{8}$$

where, $x, y, z = \left[0, d-1\right]$.

Now, $\overline{M}^{(j)} = M^{(t-j+2)}, j = \left[1, k\right]$

Therefore, $\overline{F}_{x,y,z}^{(j)} = F_{x,y,z}^{(t-j+2)}, \; j = \left[1, k\right]$

Equation (7) and (8) gives:

$$\overline{c}_{x,y,z}^{(k+1)} = f_{k-1}\left(F_{x,y,z}^{(t-k+2)}\right) + f_{k-2}\left(F_{x,y,z}^{(t-k+3)}\right) + \cdots + f_1\left(F_{x,y,z}^{(t)}\right) + c_{x,y,z}^{(t+1)}$$

$$= f_{l-1}\left(F_{x,y,z}^{(t-l+2)}\right) + f_{l-2}\left(F_{x,y,z}^{(t-l+3)}\right) + f_1\left(F_{x,y,z}^{(t)}\right) + f_1\left(F_{x,y,z}^{(t)}\right) + \cdots + f_{k-2}\left(F_{x,y,z}^{(t-k+3)}\right) + f_{k-1}\left(F_{x,y,z}^{(t-k+2)}\right) + c_{x,y,z}^{(t-k+1)}$$

$$= c_{x,y,z}^{(t-k+1)} \left(\mathrm{mod}\, 2\right)$$

Hence, $\overline{M}^{(k+1)} = M^{(t-k+1)}, \forall i = \left[0, d-1\right]$. Thus, this proof confirms that the 3D-CA given in Equation (5) is reversible and also that the inverse of that 3D-CA is also a 3D-CA. From this proof, it can be inferred that the scheme discussed in this chapter satisfies the property of correctness.

Privacy

Privacy attributes to the fact that any useful information associated with the shares remains secure. Information with regards to the shares is not revealed to any adversary outside the set of participants. As the access structure is adequately defined, this is not an issue.

Theorem 2: If only one of the configurations, $M^{(t-1)}, 0 \leq i \leq k-1$, is unknown, then the reconstruction of the secret will be impossible.

Proof: Let us show this supposition using the following description.

$$M^{(t-k+1)} = c_{x,y,z}^{(t-k+1)}, 0 \leq x, y, z \leq d-1$$

The above equation does divulge any information about $c_{x,y,z}^{(t+1)}$.

Now,

$$c_{x,y,z}^{(t+1)} = u_{x,y,z} \oplus c_{x,y,z}^{(t-k+1)}$$

where,

$$u_{x,y,z} = f_{r_1}\left(F_{x,y,z}^{(t)}\right) \oplus \cdots \oplus f_{r_{k-1}}\left(F_{x,y,z}^{(t-k+2)}\right)$$

As this is a 3D-CA with d as the length of each dimension, hence there are d^3 equations with $2d^3$ unknown variables. Therefore, it is impossible to solve it, and hence no information on the configurations of the CA can be obtained. This conjecture will be valid if the configurations that are unidentified is one or more than one. Therefore, it is inconceivable to recover the secret if the shares are less than k.

k-Consistency

Each participant presents their share together and not at separate intervals of time. Only then will the 3D-CA reconstruct correctly. This scheme is k-consistent, which means that knowing $k-1$ or fewer shares cannot reveal any information.

Theorem 3: For a kth order 3D-CA. To compute $M^{(t+1)}$ for some $t \geq k$, we require exactly k configurations, $M^{(t)}, M^{(t-1)}, \cdots, M^{(t-k+1)}$.

Proof: Consider that the $(t-1)^{\text{th}}$ configuration of the 3D-CA is unknown where $i = [0, k-1]$. Let $\mathcal{T}_j$ denote the transformation function. We need to determine $M^{(t+1)} = \left(c_{0,0,0}^{(t+1)}, \cdots, c_{d-1,d-1,d-1}^{(t+1)}\right)$. The evolution of the 3D-CA in terms of the transformation function can be written as:

$$M^{(t+1)} = \sum_{j=0, j \neq i}^{k-1} \mathcal{T}_j(M^{(t-j)} + \mathcal{T}_i\left(M^{(t-i)}\right)\left(\bmod 2\right)$$

Let the known elements be signified by W and the unknown elements by U.
where, $W = \left(w_{x,y,z}\right)$ and $U = \left(w_{x,y,z}\right)$, $x, y, z = [0, d-1]$.
Therefore,

$$c_{x,y,z}^{(t+1)} = w_{x,y,z} + u_{x,y,z}\left(\bmod 2\right)$$

This equation forms a system of d^3 equations with $2d^3$ unknown elements. Hence, no information about $M^{(t+1)}$ can be derived, and the proposed scheme is a perfect (k, n)-threshold scheme.

Verifiability

This scheme is publicly verifiable such that anyone who has access to the public parameters can verify the shares. The authenticity of the fact that this scheme is a perfect verifiable (k, n) SS scheme needs to be proved.

Theorem 4: This 3D-CA based (k, n) SS scheme is perfectly verifiable.

Proof: For recovering the secret each share has to satisfy $G_j \equiv g^{S_j} \pmod p$, $j = [1, n]$. The G_j value is obtained from the publicly published parameters. This assumption of the discrete logarithm problem ensures the verifiability of shares and prevents the use of fake shares. Due to the large value of p, the discrete logarithm problem here is a very hard problem. Also, the cooperation of the dealer is not as crucial as the value of $\{r_1, \cdots, r_{k-1}\}$ are publicly known.

Efficiency

The use of 3D-CA ensures much higher efficiency when compared to using one-dimensional CA or 2D CA.

Randomness Analysis

The randomness of the shares is a huge factor to be considered when evaluating a SS scheme. The pseudo-randomness of the shares generated by this VSS is analyzed using the Statistical Test Suite (STS) proposed by the national institute of Standards and Technology (NIST)[44]. Three sets of shares have been evaluated using the NIST test suit. Table 2 shows the result obtained by performing the NIST statistical test on various sets of shares obtained by the scheme described in this chapter. The NIST test suite comprises of 15 tests. Each of the tests that constitute this test suit is designed to assess a particular property that a pseudo-random number should have. The test equates to a success if the randomness probability value (p-value) is larger than 0.01. A sequence is considered random if it passes the test.

Quality of Shares

In an SS scheme, all security issues concerning the shares have to be managed. This determines the quality of the shares. The following properties of this VSS scheme ensure the quality of the shares:

- In the SS algorithm described earlier in this chapter, a set of configurations $\{M^{(0)}, \cdots, M^{(k-1)}, M^{(k)}, \cdots, M^{(s)}, \cdots, M^{(n+s-1)}\}$ is obtained. Of which $M^{(0)}$ is the initial configuration of the secret message and $M^{(1)}$ through $M^{(n+s-1)}$ are the consecutive configurations. Of this, only the last n configurations are the shares that will be distributed among the participants taking part in the SS. Now, this ensures that the dependence of the shares on the original secret is minimal.
- The pseudo-randomness analysis shows that the shares produced have a high randomness factor. This leads to very less similarity in the shares produced by this scheme.

Table 2. The result of the NIST test.

Statistical Test	Set 1		Set 2		Set 3	
	p-value	Result	p-value	Result	p-value	Result
Frequency (mono-bit)	0.4097	Pass	0.3615	Pass	0.3965	Pass
Block-Frequency	0.3214	Pass	0.2537	Pass	0.3558	Pass
Runs Test	0.6911	Pass	0.7385	Pass	0.7481	Pass
Longest Run	0.7259	Pass	0.7155	Pass	0.6727	Pass
Binary Matrix Rank	0.3562	Pass	0.2912	Pass	0.3382	Pass
Fast Fourier Transform	0.7929	Pass	0.7013	Pass	0.7466	Pass
Non-overlapping Templates	0.7099	Pass	0.6927	Pass	0.7113	Pass
Overlapping Templates	0.6258	Pass	0.7279	Pass	0.6865	Pass
Universal Statistical	0.8937	Pass	0.8615	Pass	0.8791	Pass
Linear Complexity	0.4327	Pass	0.6214	Pass	0.5845	Pass
Serial	0.6954	Pass	0.7351	Pass	0.6912	Pass
Approximate Entropy	0.6713	Pass	0.6872	Pass	0.6342	Pass
Cumulative Sums	0.2132	Pass	0.4316	Pass	0.3174	Pass
Random Excursions	0.8954	Pass	0.9148	Pass	0.8961	Pass
Random Excursions Variant	0.9213	Pass	0.9374	Pass	0.9343	Pass

Comparative Analysis

The VSS scheme discussed in this chapter is different from the various proposed CA based SS schemes in the following ways:

1. In Ref. (del Rey et al., 2005) the scheme introduced is based on the structure of one-dimensional CA. Also, it is not verifiable.
2. In Ref. (del Rey et al., 2009) the scheme uses Boolean functions and CA for secret image sharing. Here, CA are used only for the enhancement of reconstructed images.
3. In Ref. (Eslami et al., 2010) a verifiable scheme is proposed. However, this is only for (n, n)-threshold structure. Also, it is not publicly verifiable.
4. In Ref. (Eslami, & Ahmadabadi, 2010) a (k, n)-threshold SS that used the structure proposed in Ref. (Eslami et al., 2010) was made verifiable. However, this uses a one dimensional CA and is not publicly verifiable.
5. In Ref. (Li et al., 2017) the structure used is that of 1-dimensional CA.

Comparisons between this scheme and other CA based schemes, i.e., the schemes of Del Rey et al. (2005), Del Rey et al. (2009), Eslami et al. (2010), Eslami and Ahmadabadi (2010) and Li et al. (2017) are given in Table 3. The terms in which the comparison is carried out is the threshold of the scheme, the verifiability, the existence of proof of security of the scheme and the approach. The results are sum-

Table 3. Comparisons between the proposed scheme and other CA based schemes.

	Del Rey et al. (2005)	Del Rey et al. (2009)	Eslami et al. (2010)	Eslami and Ahmadabadi (2010)	Li et al. (2017)	Our Scheme
Threshold	t, n	$2, n$	t, n	t, n	t, n	t, n
Verifiability	No	No	Privately	Publicly	Privately	Publicly
Proof of security	No	Yes	No	Yes	Yes	Yes
Approach	1D-CA	2D-CA	1D-CA	1D-CA	1D-CA	3D-CA

marized in Table 3. It should be noted that 3D-CA have previously not used for devising a SS scheme. As this scheme enables a threshold of (t, n) it results in fault tolerance.

CONCLUSION

In this chapter, the authors have introduced a publicly verifiable threshold SS scheme based on 3D CA. The security of this scheme is found to be perfect. In this scheme, a secret message is embedded into a 3D-CA, and then various configurations of the 3D-CA are used to develop the shares that are distributed among participants. On satisfying the threshold conditions, the participants can recover the secret from the shares. Various participants and anyone with access to the public parameters can also check on the shares of other participants to make sure that the shares have not tampered. The use of 3D-CA in scheme enables parallel computations, ease of hardware implementations and linear computational complexity in contrast to $\left(n \log^2 n \right)$ complexity of Shamir's SS scheme.

The security analysis of this scheme shows that the shares and the secret are protected unconditionally in the verification process. The quality of the shares is maintained in this scheme. Also, it is impossible to reconstruct the secret if there are shares less than k or if any one of the configurations is unknown. If only one of the configurations is unknown, then reconstruction of the secret is impossible as the access structure of this scheme specifies that a minimum of k consecutive shares is required for reconstructions. Experiments on the use of various rules have shown that the rules used in this scheme are the most efficient. It is also found that the time complexity is much lower than the other schemes.

The NIST test (Rukhin, Soto, Nechvatal, Smid, & Barker, 2001) which is considered the standard to calculate the randomness of a series of bits has been used to analyze the randomness of the pseudo-random shares created. All the 15 tests described by NIST have been passed by our scheme.

For this scheme to be successful a minimum of k consecutive shares is required to reconstruct the secret. The fact that the k shares have to be consecutive may be undesirable in certain situations. Future work has to be done to make sure that any k shares are sufficient to reconstruct the secret. It may be possible to make the proposed scheme hybrid by combining it with a scheme based on Adi Shamir's threshold SS scheme.

Future Research

For the (k, n) SS scheme discussed in this chapter, a minimum of k consecutive shares is required to reconstruct the secret. Hence, the access structure is restricted. The fact that the k shares have to be consecutive though desirable in some situations may be not so elsewhere. Future work has to be done to make sure that any k shares are sufficient to reconstruct the secret. It may be possible to make the proposed scheme hybrid by combining it with a scheme based on Adi Shamir's threshold SS scheme.

The characteristics and mechanism of CA make it applicable for sharing secrets in the form of images and 3D objects (del Rey, 2015; Eslami, & Ahmadabadi, 2010). Research can be done in this area to implement this scheme for secret images and 3D objects. Recently there has been an advent of utilizing deep learning in data hiding (Chaumont, 2018; Zhu, Kaplan, Johnson & Fei-Fei, 2018). The authors believe that similar techniques can be used to improve SS schemes utilizing CA. Machine learning techniques can help significantly reduce or even eliminate issues that arise when sharing complex entities like 3D objects.

ACKNOWLEDGMENT

This study was supported by the BK21 Plus project (SW Human Resource Development Program for Supporting Smart Life) funded by the Ministry of Education, School of Computer Science and Engineering, Kyungpook National University, Korea (21A20131600005).

REFERENCES

Allouche, J. P., Courbage, M., & Skordev, G. (2000). *Notes on cellular automata*. Inst. für Dynamische Systeme.

Asmuth, C., & Bloom, J. (1983). A modular approach to key safeguarding. *IEEE Transactions on Information Theory*, 29(2), 208–210. doi:10.1109/TIT.1983.1056651

Beimel, A. (2011, May). Secret-sharing schemes: a survey. In *International Conference on Coding and Cryptology* (pp. 11-46). Berlin, Germany: Springer. 10.1007/978-3-642-20901-7_2

Benaloh, J., & Leichter, J. (1990, February). Generalized secret sharing and monotone functions. In *Proceedings on Advances in cryptology* (pp. 27–35). Springer-Verlag New York.

Bertilsson, M., & Ingemarsson, I. (1992, December). A construction of practical secret sharing schemes using linear block codes. In *International Workshop on the Theory and Application of Cryptographic Techniques* (pp. 67-79). Berlin, Germany: Springer.

Blakley, G. R. (1979, June). Safeguarding cryptographic keys. In *Proceedings of the national computer conference* (*Vol. 48*, pp. 313-317). Academic Press.

Blundo, C., De Santis, A., Di Crescenzo, G., Gaggia, A. G., & Vaccaro, U. (1994, August). Multi-secret sharing schemes. In *Annual International Cryptology Conference* (pp. 150-163). Berlin, Germany: Springer.

Boneh, D., & Franklin, M. (2001, August). Identity-based encryption from the Weil pairing. In *Annual international cryptology conference* (pp. 213-229). Berlin, Germany: Springer. 10.1007/3-540-44647-8_13

Boyle, E., Gilboa, N., Ishai, Y., Lin, H., & Tessaro, S. (2018). Foundations of homomorphic secret sharing. In *9th Innovations in Theoretical Computer Science Conference (ITCS 2018)*. Schloss Dagstuhl-Leibniz-Zentrum fuer Informatik.

Brickell, E. F. (1989, April). Some ideal secret sharing schemes. In *Workshop on the Theory and Application of of Cryptographic Techniques* (pp. 468-475). Berlin, Germany: Springer.

Capocelli, R. M., De Santis, A., Gargano, L., & Vaccaro, U. (1991, August). On the size of shares for secret sharing schemes. In *Annual International Cryptology Conference* (pp. 101-113). Berlin, Germany: Springer.

Chaumont, M. (2018, January). The emergence of Deep Learning in steganography and steganalysis. Journée" Stéganalyse: Enjeux et Méthodes", labelisée par le GDR ISIS et le pré-GDR sécurité.

Chien, H. Y., Jan, J. K., & Tseng, Y. M. (2000). A practical (t, n) multi-secret sharing scheme. *IEICE Transactions on Fundamentals of Electronics, Communications and Computer Science, 83*(12), 2762–2765.

Chien, H. Y., Jan, J. K., & Tseng, Y. M. (2002). A unified approach to secret sharing schemes with low distribution cost. *Zhongguo Gongcheng Xuekan, 25*(6), 723–733. doi:10.1080/02533839.2002.9670746

Cramer, R., Damgård, I., & Maurer, U. (2000, May). General secure multi-party computation from any linear secret-sharing scheme. In *International Conference on the Theory and Applications of Cryptographic Techniques* (pp. 316-334). Berlin, Germany: Springer. 10.1007/3-540-45539-6_22

Del Rey, A. M. (2015). A multi-secret sharing scheme for 3D solid objects. *Expert Systems with Applications, 42*(4), 2114–2120. doi:10.1016/j.eswa.2014.10.035

Del Rey, A. M., Mateus, J. P., & Sánchez, G. R. (2005). A secret sharing scheme based on cellular automata. *Applied Mathematics and Computation, 170*(2), 1356–1364. doi:10.1016/j.amc.2005.01.026

Del Rey, Á. M., & Sánchez, G. R. (2009, June). A secret sharing scheme for digital images based on cellular automata and boolean functions. In *International Work-Conference on Artificial Neural Networks* (pp. 1200–1207). Berlin, Germany: Springer. doi:10.1007/978-3-642-02478-8_150

Diffie, W., & Hellman, M. E. (1977). Special feature exhaustive cryptanalysis of the NBS data encryption standard. *Computer, 10*(6), 74–84. doi:10.1109/C-M.1977.217750

Eslami, Z., & Ahmadabadi, J. Z. (2010). A verifiable multi-secret sharing scheme based on cellular automata. *Information Sciences, 180*(15), 2889–2894. doi:10.1016/j.ins.2010.04.015

Eslami, Z., Pakniat, N., & Noroozi, M. (2015, October). Hierarchical threshold multi-secret sharing scheme based on Birkhoff interpolation and cellular automata. In *2015 18th CSI International Symposium on Computer Architecture and Digital Systems (CADS)* (pp. 1-6). IEEE. 10.1109/CADS.2015.7377795

Eslami, Z., Razzaghi, S. H., & Ahmadabadi, J. Z. (2010). Secret image sharing based on cellular automata and steganography. *Pattern Recognition, 43*(1), 397–404. doi:10.1016/j.patcog.2009.06.007

Fan, T. Y., Chao, H. C., & Chieu, B. C. (2019). Lossless medical image watermarking method based on significant difference of cellular automata transform coefficient. *Signal Processing Image Communication, 70,* 174–183. doi:10.1016/j.image.2018.09.015

Feldman, P. (1987, October). A practical scheme for non-interactive verifiable secret sharing. In *28th Annual Symposium on Foundations of Computer Science* (pp. 427-438). IEEE. 10.1109/SFCS.1987.4

Goyal, V., & Kumar, A. (2018, August). Non-malleable secret sharing for general access structures. In *Annual International Cryptology Conference* (pp. 501-530). Cham, Switzerland: Springer. 10.1007/978-3-319-96884-1_17

He, J., & Dawson, E. (1994). Multistage secret sharing based on one-way function. *Electronics Letters, 30*(19), 1591–1592. doi:10.1049/el:19941076

Heidarvand, S., & Villar, J. L. (2008, August). Public verifiability from pairings in secret sharing schemes. In *International Workshop on Selected Areas in Cryptography* (pp. 294-308). Berlin, Germany: Springer.

Ito, M., Saito, A., & Nishizeki, T. (1989). Secret sharing scheme realizing general access structure. *Electronics and Communications in Japan (Part III Fundamental Electronic Science), 72*(9), 56–64. doi:10.1002/ecjc.4430720906

Jhanwar, M. P. (2011, May). A practical (non-interactive) publicly verifiable secret sharing scheme. In *International Conference on Information Security Practice and Experience* (pp. 273-287). Berlin, Germany: Springer. 10.1007/978-3-642-21031-0_21

Karchmer, M., & Wigderson, A. (1993, May). On span programs. In *Proceedings of the Eighth Annual Structure in Complexity Theory Conference* (pp. 102-111). IEEE.

Kaya, K., & Selçuk, A. A. (2008, December). A verifiable secret sharing scheme based on the chinese remainder theorem. In *International Conference on Cryptology in India* (pp. 414-425). Berlin, Germany: Springer. 10.1007/978-3-540-89754-5_32

Koikara, R., Kim, P. H., Paul, A., & Yoo, K. Y. (2017). Threshold Secret Sharing based on 3D-Cellular Automata. In *Proceedings of the International Conference on Security and Management (SAM)*. The Steering Committee of the World Congress in Computer Science. Computer Engineering and Applied Computing.

Li, M., Yu, J., & Hao, R. (2017). A cellular automata based verifiable multi-secret sharing scheme without a trusted dealer. *Chinese Journal of Electronics, 26*(2), 313–318. doi:10.1049/cje.2017.01.026

Lu, D., Wang, Y., Zhang, X., & Ji, L. (2016, December). A threshold secret sharing scheme based on lmca and chinese remainder theorem. In *2016 9th International Symposium on Computational Intelligence and Design (ISCID)* (Vol. 2, pp. 439-442). IEEE. 10.1109/ISCID.2016.2109

Menezes, A. J., Okamoto, T., & Vanstone, S. A. (1993). Reducing elliptic curve logarithms to logarithms in a finite field. *IEEE Transactions on Information Theory, 39*(5), 1639–1646. doi:10.1109/18.259647

Mignotte, M. (1982, March). How to share a secret. In *Workshop on Cryptography* (pp. 371-375). Berlin, Germany: Springer.

Rivest, R. L., Shamir, A., & Adleman, L. (1978). A method for obtaining digital signatures and public-key cryptosystems. *Communications of the ACM, 21*(2), 120–126. doi:10.1145/359340.359342

Rukhin, A., Soto, J., Nechvatal, J., Smid, M., & Barker, E. (2001). *A statistical test suite for random and pseudorandom number generators for cryptographic applications.* Mclean, VA: Booz-Allen and Hamilton.

Schiff, J. L. (2005). *Introduction to cellular automata.* Retrieved from http://psoup. math. wisc. edu/ pub/Schiff_CAbook. pdf

Schoenmakers, B. (1999, August). A simple publicly verifiable secret sharing scheme and its application to electronic voting. In *Annual International Cryptology Conference* (pp. 148-164). Berlin, Germany: Springer. 10.1007/3-540-48405-1_10

Shamir, A. (1979). How to share a secret. *Communications of the ACM, 22*(11), 612–613. doi:10.1145/359168.359176

Simmons, G. J. (1991). The geometry of shared secret schemes. *Bulletin of the Institute of Combinatorics and its Applications, 1*, 71-88.

Stadler, M. (1996, May). Publicly verifiable secret sharing. In *International Conference on the Theory and Applications of Cryptographic Techniques* (pp. 190-199). Berlin, Germany: Springer.

Tassa, T. (2007). Hierarchical threshold secret sharing. *Journal of Cryptology, 20*(2), 237–264. doi:10.100700145-006-0334-8

Tian, Y., Peng, C., & Ma, J. (2012). Publicly Verifiable Secret Sharing Schemes Using Bilinear Pairings. *International Journal of Network Security, 14*(3), 142–148.

Tian, Y. L., & Peng, C. (2009). Verifiable secret sharing and its applications based on bilinear pairings. *Computer Engineering, 35*(10), 158–161.

Wolfram, S. (1984). Cellular automata as models of complexity. *Nature, 311*(5985), 419–424. doi:10.1038/311419a0

Wu, T. Y., & Tseng, Y. M. (2011). A pairing-based publicly verifiable secret sharing scheme. *Journal of Systems Science and Complexity, 24*(1), 186–194. doi:10.100711424-011-8408-6

Yu, J., Kong, F., & Hao, R. (2007, July). Publicly verifiable secret sharing with enrollment ability. In *Eighth ACIS International Conference on Software Engineering, Artificial Intelligence, Networking, and Parallel/Distributed Computing* (Vol. 3, pp. 194-199). IEEE. 10.1109/SNPD.2007.256

Zhu, J., Kaplan, R., Johnson, J., & Fei-Fei, L. (2018). Hidden: Hiding data with deep networks. In *Proceedings of the European Conference on Computer Vision (ECCV)* (pp. 657-672). Academic Press.

ADDITIONAL READING

Biggio, B., & Roli, F. (2018). Wild patterns: Ten years after the rise of adversarial machine learning. *Pattern Recognition, 84*, 317–331. doi:10.1016/j.patcog.2018.07.023

Cao, G., Chen, C., & Jiang, M. (2018, November). A Scalable and Flexible Multi-User Semi-Quantum Secret Sharing. In *Proceedings of the 2nd International Conference on Telecommunications and Communication Engineering* (pp. 28-32). ACM. 10.1145/3291842.3291857

Dennunzio, A., Formenti, E., Manzoni, L., Margara, L., & Porreca, A. E. (2019). On the dynamical behaviour of linear higher-order cellular automata and its decidability. *Information Sciences, 486*, 73–87. doi:10.1016/j.ins.2019.02.023

Espejel-Trujillo, A., Iwamoto, M., & Nakano-Miyatake, M. (2018). A proactive secret image sharing scheme with resistance to machine learning based steganalysis. *Multimedia Tools and Applications, 77*(12), 15161–15179. doi:10.100711042-017-5097-8

Kogias, I., Xiang, Y., He, Q., & Adesso, G. (2017). Unconditional security of entanglement-based continuous-variable quantum secret sharing. *Physical Review A., 95*(1), 012315. doi:10.1103/PhysRevA.95.012315

Liu, T., Vaikuntanathan, V., & Wee, H. (2018, April). Towards breaking the exponential barrier for general secret sharing. In *Annual International Conference on the Theory and Applications of Cryptographic Techniques* (pp. 567-596). Springer, Cham. 10.1007/978-3-319-78381-9_21

Papernot, N., McDaniel, P., Sinha, A., & Wellman, M. P. (2018, April). SoK: Security and privacy in machine learning. In *2018 IEEE European Symposium on Security and Privacy (EuroS&P)*(pp. 399-414). IEEE. 10.1109/EuroSP.2018.00035

So, J., Guler, B., Avestimehr, A. S., & Mohassel, P. (2019). CodedPrivateML: A Fast and Privacy-Preserving Framework for Distributed Machine Learning. *arXiv preprint arXiv:1902.00641.*

Zeng, Q. (2018). Efficient Computation and FPGA implementation of Fully Homomorphic Encryption with Cloud Computing Significance.

KEY TERMS AND DEFINITIONS

Access Structure: The structure that consists of authorized subsets of participants that can take part in the SS.

Cryptography: The study of securing information such that they are safe from the hands of third parties.

Key-Management: The management of cryptographic keys that are used in a cryptosystem.

Multiparty Communication: A communication environment that involves two or more parties communicating over a network.

Pseudo-Random: A number that satisfies the tests of a random number but that has been generated using mathematical operations.

Secret Message: The information that has to be safeguarded. This information should not come into the hands of adversaries.

Share: The secret message that has been processed and distributed among participants.

Shareholders: The parties taking part in the SS scheme.

Chapter 14
Big Data Analytics for Intrusion Detection:
An Overview

Luis Filipe Dias
https://orcid.org/0000-0003-2842-6655
Instituto Universitário Militar, Portugal

Miguel Correia
Universidade de Lisboa, Portugal

ABSTRACT

Intrusion detection has become a problem of big data, with a semantic gap between vast security data sources and real knowledge about threats. The use of machine learning (ML) algorithms on big data has already been successfully applied in other domains. Hence, this approach is promising for dealing with cyber security's big data problem. Rather than relying on human analysts to create signatures or classify huge volumes of data, ML can be used. ML allows the implementation of advanced algorithms to extract information from data using behavioral analysis or to find hidden correlations. However, the adversarial setting and the dynamism of the cyber threat landscape stand as difficult challenges when applying ML. The next generation security information and event management (SIEM) systems should provide security monitoring with the means for automation, orchestration and real-time contextual threat awareness. However, recent research shows that further work is needed to fulfill these requirements. This chapter presents a survey on recent work on big data analytics for intrusion detection.

INTRODUCTION

Over the past two decades *network intrusion detection systems* (NIDSs) have been intensively investigated in academia and deployed by industry (Debar et al., 1999). More recently, intrusion detection has become a big data problem because of the growing volume and complexity of data necessary to unveil increasingly sophisticated cyberattacks. The *security information and event management* (SIEM)

DOI: 10.4018/978-1-5225-9611-0.ch014

systems adopted during the last decade show limitations when processing with *big data*, even more in relation to extracting the information it can provide. Therefore, new techniques to handle high volumes of security-relevant data, along with *machine learning* (ML) approaches, are receiving much attention from researchers. This chapter presents an overview of the state-of-the-art regarding this subject.

The Cloud Security Alliance (CSA) suggested that *intrusion detection systems* (IDSs) have been going through three stages of evolution corresponding to three types of security tools (Cárdenas et al., 2013):

- IDS: able to detect well-known attacks efficiently using signatures (misuse detection) and to unveil unknown attacks at the cost of high false alarm rates (anomaly detection);
- SIEM: collect and manage security-relevant data from different devices in a network (e.g., firewalls, IDSs, and authentication servers), providing increased network security visibility by aggregating and filtering alarms, while providing actionable information to security analysts;
- 2nd generation SIEM: the next generation, that should be able to handle and take the best from big data, reducing the time for correlating, consolidating, and contextualizing even more diverse and unstructured security data (e.g., global threat intelligence, blogs, and forums); they should be able to provide long-term storage for correlating historical data as well as for forensic purposes.

The European Agency for Network and Information Security (ENISA) stated that the next generation SIEMs are the most promising domains of application for big data (ENISA, 2015). According to recent surveys from the SANS Institute, most organizations are just starting to evolve from traditional SIEMs to more advanced forms of security analytics and big data processing (Shackleford, 2015, 2016). In fact, the industry developments in the area led Gartner to start publishing market guides for user and entity behavior analytics (UEBA) (Litan, 2015). While recent UEBA technologies target specific security use cases (e.g., insider threats), typical SIEM technologies provide comprehensive rosters of all security events which are also important for compliance requirements. Recent guides from Gartner (Bussa et al., 2016; Kavanagh et al., 2018) state that "Vendors with more mature SIEM technologies are moving swiftly to incorporate big data technology and analytics to better support detection and response", revealing the tendency of moving towards 2nd generation SIEMs.

The focus of this survey is on state-of-the-art techniques that can contribute for such next generation SIEMs, and on the challenges of big data and ML applied to cybersecurity analytics. There are a few related surveys available in the literature, none with this focus. Buczak & Guven (2016) analyze papers that use different ML techniques in the cybersecurity domain; although interesting, most of the experiments of those studies were done with datasets that date back to 1999 and that do not represent the actual cybersecurity landscape. Bhuyan et al. (2014) provide a comprehensive overview of network anomaly detection methods. Zuech et al. (2015) review works considering the problem of big heterogeneous data associated with intrusion detection. While this last work touches topics similar to this chapter, it lacks a comprehensive study on recent techniques that tackle the problem of extracting useful information from such volumes of data.

When selecting the papers to investigate, we prioritized recent work – less than 5 years old – and those that report experiments with real-world data. The rationale is that older approaches and approaches evaluated with synthetic datasets (e.g., KDD99) may be inadequate to detect real/recent attacks. Furthermore, we restricted the focus to papers published in major conferences/journals, with few exceptions.

The studied papers were grouped into four categories: *cluster and classify* (Yen et al., 2013; Gonçalves et al., 2015; Veeramachaneni et al., 2016); *graph models* (Oprea et al., 2015; Nagaraja, 2014; Milajerdi et al., 2019); *real-time log analytics* (Cinque et al., 2017; Du et al., 2017; Mirsky et al., 2018); and *frameworks and context* (Stroeh et al., 2013; Giura & Wang, 2012). The first, consists in detectors based on clustering and classification. These are appealing approaches because of their ability to detect zero-day attacks, i.e., attacks that were previously unknown. The second is about using graph models to represent network flows and events, to extract features which can detect, e.g., botnets (Nagaraja, 2014) and advanced persistent threats (Giura & Wang, 2012). The third group contain proposals to process log streams in real-time, either by using of entropy measurements (Cinque et al., 2017) or by modeling system logs as a natural language sequence (Du et al., 2017). The fourth category explores studies that focus on providing high-level frameworks to address the needs of future security monitoring.

The remainder of this chapter is organized as follows: Section 2 explains basic concepts of big data and ML regarding intrusion detection; Section 3 presents the main challenges; Section 4 presents the state-of-the-art techniques; finally, in Section 5 the researchers draw their conclusions.

BIG DATA AND MACHINE LEARNING

Clearly intrusion detection is facing a big data challenge, whether there is a single source of events or a major architecture that aggregates events from heterogeneous sources (Zuech et al., 2015). To tackle this problem, one must deploy big data handlers, i.e., components that process such data. Furthermore, since handling such high volumes of data is beyond human capabilities, the use of ML to extract useful information from large and multi-dimensional data, seems to be the only way.

This section gives a brief overview of the application of some big data handler technologies and ML techniques in the cybersecurity domain.

Big Data Handlers

Hadoop is an Apache project (White, 2009) that includes open source implementations of the MapReduce distributed programming framework (Dean & Ghemawat, 2004) and of the Google file system (Ghemawat et al., 2003), among other components. In the MapReduce paradigm, the input of a computational job is split into parts that are processed (mapped) by a set of worker nodes; the results of this first processing are themselves processed (reduced) by workers. The Hadoop file-system provides the parallelism for the MapReduce worker nodes to be executed on a large cluster of commodity machines. The runtime system handles scheduling and failures of program executions across the machines.

In the cybersecurity domain, a Hadoop cluster seems to be a suitable option for long-term event storage due to processing, fault tolerance and scalability provided. Hence, it can be used to do analytics to infer trends, create knowledge about old attacks, and feed real-time systems with discovered behavioral signatures, providing a tool for forensic investigations and for contextual awareness. Traditional Hadoop MapReduce does batch processing, so it is unsuitable for data streams processing. It is also not suitable for iterative algorithms that depend on previous computed values (Cloud Security Alliance, 2014). However, some years ago Hadoop evolved to version 2.0 that provides more flexibility, decoupling MapReduce from the filesystem (HDFS), and introducing a resource management layer called YARN. This allowed the appearance of real-time analytics platforms on top of Hadoop 2.0. Apache Spark is the most popular at the moment, as it provides in-memory cluster computing in opposition to disk-based processing (Zaharia et al., 2016; Meng et al., 2016). Spark has shown impressive results when computing machine-learning iterative algorithms, running up to 100x faster than Hadoop MapReduce. More information on big data technologies can be found in (Cloud Security Alliance, 2014).

In what concerns the cybersecurity industry, it is gradually tackling the big data challenges leveraged by SIEMs. Some vendors implemented ElasticSearch (Kononenko et al., 2014) in their software to improve search times. Although it seems to help for faster queries, it does not solve the storage problem. Several vendors are offering tight integration of their SIEMs with big data analytics platforms (e.g., QRadar (Wuest, 2014) or Splunk (Splunk, n.d.)). They provide bi-directional communication, either to collect external big data feeds, or to export old logs. Some companies are exporting older logs from SIEMs (e.g., 1-month old logs) to a Hadoop cluster for longer-term storage, analysis and reporting. However, this option seems costly and has several drawbacks, such as: impact of transferring such big data on normal operations; context in the SIEM is lost; yet another system to manage. The big players in this market are enhancing their new platforms with scalability and big data in mind (Kavanagh et al., 2018). As an example, IBM launched QRadar Data Node which allows to add nodes to the actual SIEM deployment transparently for the end-user. Despite traditional SIEM systems are evolving to more advanced analytics and big data processing, new players with this setup as concept arise, such as Securonix (Securonix, n.d.) or Exabeam (Exabeam, n.d.). The soundest features refereed by these state-of-the-art solutions are: the use of a ML approach for *user and entity behaviour analytics* (UEBA) (Litan, 2015) and big data ready architectures for scalable data collection and processing.

In what concerns academic research, a few works that used Hadoop technologies for cybersecurity are: Gonçalves et al. (2015) implemented an outlier detector using a Hadoop cluster; Lee & Lee (2013) experimented and measured the performance of a DDoS detector using Hadoop technologies; Cheon & Choe (2013) used a Hadoop cluster to do parallel processing with logs collected from several Snort IDS sensors. The results of these studies using Hadoop for IDS, are constrained by the fact that MapReduce is not suited to real-time processing, and often the evaluation is inconclusive. Clearly more research and experimentation are needed in this area. Some big data platforms that combine several Hadoop tools along with Spark, visualization and ML tools, are emerging and can help to easily deploy an environment for cybersecurity research. For instance, Apache Spot (Apache Spot, n.d.) and Apache Metron (Apache Metron, n.d.) are fully dedicated to cybersecurity, although more generic platforms such as Elastic Stack (ELK, n.d.) (previously ELK Stack) or MapR Hadoop distribution (MapR, n.d.) can also be valuable in this field.

ML Approaches

Samuel (1959), a pioneer of ML, defined it as a "field of study that gives computers the ability to learn without being explicitly programmed". ML is often concerned with classification and prediction based on previously learned training data without a specific analytic solution (ideal target function) to the problem; instead, it searches for an approximation to that ideal solution (optimization of a hypothesis function). Typically, the more data you give to a ML classification algorithm, the more accurate it becomes in providing correct outputs. Data mining is a related field of study that uses techniques similar related to those of ML, but often with different purposes. Data mining is usually carried out in a specific situation, on a particular dataset, with a goal in mind, and the result has to be comprehensible for humans. Both systems search through data to look for patterns. However, ML uses data to adjust program actions accordingly.

Next an introduction to the most popular ML categories (supervised and unsupervised learning) is given. Furthermore, some considerations on feature engineering and model evaluation are provided.

Supervised Learning

ML typically involves a dataset that is used for training, i.e., for preparing the ML scheme for later operation. Supervised learning is characterized by the use of a training dataset containing labeled data. The labelling is often done by humans, but the size of the labeled data tends to be small and limited, whereas unlabeled, real-world, data can be much larger or even unlimited.

Classification is a common form of supervised learning. Classification is the act of mapping input data to classes (or labels). Classification has been much used in the security domain for spam detection, and is particularly relevant in this chapter as it is at the core of most forms of malicious activity detection that are based on ML. The input of a classification algorithm is a set of discriminating features (e.g., count of words that tend to appear in spam e-mail), which are used to predict the class that the input item shall be assigned to (e.g., the e-mail is spam or ham, i.e., not spam). The system outputs if the class of the item (e.g., the e-mail is likely to be spam or ham). To accomplish this, the classifier has to be trained with large datasets of both spam and ham e-mails. Some example classification algorithms include: artificial neural networks (ANNs), decision trees, support vector machines, and nave Bayes.

Regression is a second form of supervised learning. The main difference between classification and regression is that classification is concerned with assigning items to classes, whereas regression outputs (predicts) numeric values. Exampled of regression algorithms are: linear regression, polynomial regression, radial basis functions, MARS, and multi-linear interpolation.

Unsupervised Learning

Unsupervised learning aim to find hidden structures on input data. This class of algorithms are characterized by not requiring labeled data. In this case, the only condition for the input data is the presence of representative features that can be further used for knowledge extraction.

Clustering is the most popular method of unsupervised learning. As a simple example, consider that a cyberattack has a behavioral signature (e.g., a combination of steps dispersed in various security logs). First, one selects the distinctive features that security experts would look upon to find indicators of compromise (e.g., volume of uploaded traffic, number of unpopular domains contacted, etc.). Second, the features are extracted from the logs according to a time-window and an entity (e.g., five minutes of logs belonging to the same user or IP), creating a vector of extracted features for each entity. Third, the computed vectors are given as input to a clustering algorithm. Finally, the clustering algorithm groups different entities – i.e., returns clusters – according to their behavioral signature. Often, larger clusters contain entities that have normal behavior, and the smaller clusters contain outliers.

Typical algorithms for unsupervised learning include K-means clustering, gaussian mixture modelling, spectral clustering, hierarchical clustering, principal component analysis, and independent component analysis.

Feature Selection

Feature engineering is an important aspect of ML. Feature engineering is the process of defining a set of features that allow improving the predictive power (performance) of a ML algorithm to solve a certain problem. The rationale is that well-chosen features can improve the results of a classifier, or any other supervised on unsupervised scheme. Intuitively, features like "presence of the word pill" or "presence of the word money" are better to predict if an e-mail is span that the feature "text font used".

According to Domingos (2012) "some machine learning projects succeed and some fail. What makes the difference? Easily the most important factor is the features used". If features are independent from each other and each of the feature correlates well with the class, learning is easy. On the other hand, if the class is a complex function of the features, learning can be impossible. All features should be relevant for the decision process. Domingos also says that feature engineering is the most difficult part when doing a ML project. This happens because it is domain-specific, while learning models are general purpose and mastered enough.

Model Evaluation and Tuning

Tuning and evaluating a ML model is a research topic per se. The two processes require a dataset that is used for that purpose. A common solution consists in breaking that dataset in two parts: one that is used for training, the other for tuning and evaluation. However, if the training dataset is not representative of the other (or of real-world data), the predictive power may be low. A related problem overfitting: the model may be excellent in predicting with the training data, but be too specific, providing bad results with real-world data.

Cross-validation works better because it does not depend on that splitting of the dataset in two. k-fold cross-validation consists in breaking the dataset in k parts, and iteratively train the model with 1 part and test it with the other $k - 1$. A common value is $k = 10$. The result is the average of the k iterations. The cross-validation error provides a good estimation of the model error on new data.

Evaluation of ML models is usually based on a set of metrics. For classifiers, or specifically for intrusion detection, metrics are based on the notions of true positive (TP) and true negative (TN). A TP means that a hit (a detection) is indeed a hit, whereas a TN means a no hit is indeed a not hit. False positives (FP) and false negatives (FN) mean wrong positives and negatives, respectively. Common metrics are accuracy (overall performance of the model), precision (how good the positive predictions are), recall or sensitivity (coverage of the positive sample), false positive rate, and false negative rate. There are many others.

CYBERSECURITY CHALLENGES

The ability to process and correlate high volumes of data is a prerequisite for security analytics solutions. This capacity then allows doing analytical queries, long-term forensic analysis of the data, automated and rapid response, reports, flexible dashboard views and, ultimately, contextual threat awareness. Another requirement is diversity of sources of data, as this is a requirement for performing advanced correlations and support contextual awareness. ML plays a crucial role in helping find correlations that we do not know about and to discover trends and behavioral patterns. Rather than searching attack evidence after being attacked, the predictive capability can be leveraged with ML, allowing to stop threats based on current and past behavior. Furthermore, obtaining more data on which to perform root cause and forensics analysis after an attack happens, should feed and improve an active learning system (Gonçalves et al., 2015; Veeramachaneni et al., 2016).

This section discusses the most challenging problems and difficulties of deploying ML techniques in the cybersecurity domain. In other domains, such as product recommendation, natural language translation or fraud detection, ML plays a fundamental role. That is not yet the case in cybersecurity, except for spam detection. A ML spam detection method was initially proposed by Graham (2002) using Bayesian filtering trained with large datasets of both spam and ham.

Despite extensive research, both academic and industrial, anomaly intrusion detection based on ML is not widely deployed. Apparently, the reason is that most approaches do not fulfil operational requirements such as accuracy. Actually, the great majority of actual IDS deployments use almost exclusively traditional misuse-based detection. However, in the last few years, ML is being used as a buzzword by several security companies. Some examples of ML used by the cybersecurity industry are: Cylance (Cylance, n.d.) claims to be the next-generation anti-virus using ML techniques; WEBROOT (WEBROOT, n.d.) focus on cloud-based threat intelligence services; Lancope's StealthWatch (Lancope, n.d.) infers suspicious movements from Netflow data; DARKTRACE (DARKTRACE, n.d.) claims to leverage artificial intelligence to detect threats that others miss; IBM adapted their Watson project (IBM, n.d.) to be used in cybersecurity, aiming to learn cybersecurity language and process unstructured data from blogs, articles, videos, reports, and alerts, besides other data. ML is also a core capability in the recent product category that Gartner called UEBA (Bussa et al., 2016), which perform behavior analytics to systems, devices, applications, etc. UEBA solutions are still divided on the type of data (e.g., security devices logs, network packets) they ingest and analyze, thus, in general, these solutions are seen as a complement to SIEMs. In fact, most are being integrated in major SIEMs.

Next, we point out the main challenges of ML applied to cybersecurity.

Attack Evolution

The cybersecurity landscape is extremely dynamic with new threats appearing every day. The democratization of cyber-threats increases the global impact along with organized cyber-crime which leverages highly sophisticated techniques. Furthermore, with the growth of technologies and concepts like software as a service (SaaS), cloud infrastructures, or bring your own device (BYOD), enterprise borders are not well-defined anymore. There is an evident need to collect every single data-point that can be security relevant and apply ML to extract information from disparate sources.

Most approaches of ML focus on using outlier detection to find novel attacks. This is commonly accepted as the best way to tackle the problem of attack evolution. As Sommer & Paxson (2010) refers, this approach has to be carefully considered since it raises several problems: high rates of false alarms; attack-free data for the training process is hard to get; attacker can gradually teach the system to accept malicious activity (as Klein & Peter (2015) and W. Xu & Evans (2016) showed). According to (Sommer & Paxson, 2010), the "strength of machine learning tools is finding activity that is similar to something previously seen", although not being necessary to detail that activity up front (as in misuse detection). Furthermore, newer attacks can be significantly different from old ones (both technically and modus operandi). This is a crucial aspect since the feature selection process using an old dataset can generate a feature set that may be different from the one needed to detect future attacks.

In summary, the adversarial setting changes how researchers have to approach the network intrusion detection problem. This adversarial setting seems to be the root cause for the difficulty (at least in the next few years) in removing human experts from the loop of an intrusion detection system.

Heterogeneous Data Sources

At the early days of intrusion detection, security analysts observed logs in order to detect malicious activity or abnormal behaviors, which is something hard to do manually. Moreover, looking for events individually in each security device or software (e.g., firewall, IDS, anti-virus) gives only a narrow vision and does not provide global security awareness. Looking to individual data sources is also not enough to respond fast in case of a breach or to detect multi-step attacks, even less to predict future attacks.

SIEMs aggregate security related logs coming from a myriad of devices (e.g., that have different security functions, or the same function but different vendor). They structure that data in formats that support correlation, generation of alerts, and visualization by the analyst. SIEMs have performance issues due to big data volumes and the need to parse, structure and store that data in databases. This is especially true with large enterprise networks where current SIEM technologies sometimes cannot parse this overwhelming quantity of data into actionable information. Moreover, the parsing and normalization phase compose themselves a big challenge in what concerns timestamp normalization, crucial in global networks and fundamental before performing data correlation.

Nevertheless, as IT environments grow and are increasingly complex, it is commonly accepted that collecting data from every security-relevant source, both traditional (e.g., firewall, database access, web access) and non-traditional (e.g., social media, blog posts, external threat feeds, domain registration) is necessary for a security system that can predict and detect new attacks. The more data we have, the more information we should extract.

Big Data

According to ENISA (ENISA, 2015), "one of the advantages of NoSQL databases, is that they can store such data in a format that is scalable and at the same time allow to create queries and understand the data better. In reality big data offers as added value not only the correlation between unstructured data, but also SIEM scalability". In short, most definitions of big data analytics present it as a set of tools and techniques to store and process large datasets efficiently for that purpose, i.e., for analytics. Big data analytics handles very large datasets (Volume), provides extremely fast insertion (Velocity), manipulates multiple data types (Variety), provides complex data analysis capabilities and requires distributed parallel processing.

In the cyberspace domain, the increasing volume of security log data that enterprises are keeping, be it for compliance or incident response reasons, do not allow SIEM platforms to properly handle such volumes of data (at least in the desired time window). According to Nassar et al. (2013), even one single security event source such as network traffic data, can become a big data challenge. As an example, consider performing deep packet inspection on 1Gbps traffic. Hence, according to Zuech et al. (2015), correlating security events across multiple heterogeneous data sources, where each can pose its own big data challenges is much more complex than performing intrusion detection on a single homogeneous big data source.

Another example, reported in (Cárdenas et al., 2013), comes from HP that at the time of report generated "1 trillion events per day or roughly 12 million events per second". This is clearly a big data problem, that required a large effort just to store that data. The company concluded that they "must move to a scenario where more data leads to better analytics and more actionable information."

At the 2012 RSA conference, Zions Bancorporation showed how Hadoop and analytics can power better security intelligence. They announced that a query to their traditional SIEMs (1 month of data) could take up to an hour. In their new Hadoop system, running queries with the Apache Hive data warehouse software Apache Hive (n.d.), they got the same results in about one minute. Although this happened some years ago, it is still a reality in several enterprises running traditional SIEMs.

In the cybersecurity domain, big data handlers are necessary. They have to exist either by means of new technologies (e.g., Hadoop), data reduction techniques (e.g., raw packet data transformed into Netflow) and dimensionality reduction (e.g., obtaining a set of uncorrelated principal variables). Li et al. (2012) recommended cloud-based enterprise security monitoring (ESM) as a natural solution to handle the big data problem. ESM has the SIEM as core component, enhanced with business context information to provide intelligence for actions and decision making. Their approach envisions a cross boundary information security management and the fusion of enterprise-wide security data, willing to achieve global correlation and intelligence. It is known that there are companies that decided to adopt a managed SIEM off premises, mainly to avoid scalability issues. However, this is a sensitive decision regarding privacy and business-wise.

Privacy and Integrity

As one collect sources of both structured and unstructured data that can be security relevant, privacy (both in the sense of confidentiality and protection of personal data) and integrity concerns arises. This leads to the problem of big data for security versus securing big data (Cárdenas et al., 2013). This is part of any big data problem in general. The trustworthiness of each source has to be assured to protect against tampering and adversarial ML techniques. In other hand, one has to restrict access to big data analytic solutions, so that it does not allow users to invade others privacy. CSA provided generic guidance on how to protect big data (Cloud Security Alliance, 2013).

Dataset Limitations

Intrusion detection can be considered to be a binomial classification problem with two classes: normal or suspicious. ML classification algorithms must be trained with examples of both classes, as this is essential for detection performance. However, considering that we are looking for novel attacks, one cannot train the system with data about these attacks. Unlike other areas of research, there is a significant lack of assessment tools for evaluating IDS. The most used datasets (KDD19, DARPA98), are over 15 years old, thus with very limited interest for current research. On recent surveys on ML applied to cybersecurity (e.g., (Azad & Jha, 2013), (Buczak & Guven, 2016)), it was verified that even recent studies still use the old datasets, which is disappointing. As it was described earlier, feature selection process using an old dataset generates features set that is inadequate to detect actual attacks (new techniques and modus operandi).

Real-world or simulated data are alternatives to the old datasets. However, most organizations are hesitant or legally constrained to disclose such data that can contain sensitive information (e.g., vulnerabilities, privacy concerns, etc.). Furthermore, those datasets can be unreliable or suffer from high anonymization. The problem with lab simulated traffic is the possible unrealistic properties which can result in inaccurate evaluations.

An alternative to generate close to real-world datasets can be done using Honeypots or Honeynets. As an example, Nagaraja (2014) built a Honeynet to get ground truth for specifically injected malware. Although building a honeynet can be costly, it seems a good approach for specific purpose testing (e.g., test accuracy on detecting known botnets).

Finally, very recently new datasets have been appearing, mostly created by the Canadian Institute for Cybersecurity from University of New Brunswick (Canadian Institute for Cybersecurity, n.d.). They have been producing several datasets, real and synthetic, to be used for intrusion detection evaluation. Turcotte et al. (2018) also provided a new dataset containing host and network events from The Los Alamos National Laboratory enterprise network.

Detection Performance

IDS detection performance is of extreme importance because of the costs that a misclassification can represent. In the cybersecurity domain, a false positive lead to an analyst spending time to examine an incident that does not represent malicious activity. If those false alarms happen frequently, the analyst will end up lacking confidence in the system. On the other hand, if we are in the presence of a false negative and the alert is not triggered, the incident can be very disruptive and damage the organization. For better understanding the problem, in the case of spam detector, the false positives can be costly and should be avoided at the cost of having some false negatives with a fairly low cost. Although new variations of spam can easily bypass the system, it seems a necessary trade-off. Again, in IDS, if we are seeking to find novel attacks, this trade-off does not seem appropriate.

Semantic Gap

To get actionable information from a ML-based intrusion detection solution is a considerable challenge. The fact that abnormal does not necessarily means malicious, implies that the system must provide distinctive information so that the analyst can easily understand what the cause and impact of an incident is (contextual information), or at least, what does it mean (e.g., connection burst, unpopular domain contacted, etc.). Typically, outlier detection approaches just report what diverges from normal, whether it is malicious or not. Furthermore, things get more complicated in a scenario where network traffic is extremely unpredictable, varying vastly at different times of day and with new technologies (such as new software or hardware).

Real-Time/Streaming Capabilities

To detect and prevent attacks at an early stage, one must be able to perform close to real-time intrusion detection. The idea is that even if the event count is large, events have to be processed in a short window of time. Specific types of attributes may need to be applied during processing (e.g., universal time stamping). Furthermore, security data analytics platforms should allow for fast contextualization (sorting data into consistent fields and formats for analysis) and fast metadata extraction during processing (Stroeh et al., 2013).

RECENT STUDIES

This section gives an overview of the state-of-the-art in cybersecurity analytics research, with a focus on big data handling and the use of ML. When selecting the papers to investigate, the recent ones (less than five years) and those that made experiments with real-world data were the priority. The rationale for choosing recent papers is that older solutions may be inadequate to detect actual attacks. Furthermore, we restricted our attention mostly to papers published in selective conferences/journals.

The studied papers were grouped in four categories: *cluster and classify* (Yen et al., 2013; Gonçalves et al., 2015; Veeramachaneni et al., 2016), *graph models* (Oprea et al., 2015; Nagaraja, 2014; Milajerdi et al., 2019), *real-time log analytics* (Cinque et al., 2017; Du et al., 2017; Mirsky et al., 2018) and *Frameworks and context* (Stroeh et al., 2013; Giura & Wang, 2012). The first, focuses in generic outlier detection methods; the second on the use of graph models for specific attacks (botnets, advanced persistent threats – APTs, and failure prediction); the third, contains proposals to process log streams in real-time; the last, explores methods for normalization and event aggregation to achieve contextual awareness. *Table 1* presents a summary of the papers that were analyzed.

Cluster and Classify

This group of works includes outlier detectors based on clustering algorithms. Beehive (Yen et al., 2013) uses only the clustering model. The other two (Gonçalves et al., 2015; Veeramachaneni et al., 2016) perform both clustering and classification: event data is given as input to the clustering algorithm; the clusters are then labeled by humans and the classification model is trained with the labeled examples (e.g., normal, malicious).

Beehive: Large-Scale Log Analysis for Detecting Suspicious Activity in Enterprise Networks

Yen et al. (2013) proposed one of the first systems exploring the challenges of big data security analytics for real-world log data. It was tested using two weeks of EMC real logs, with an average of 1.4 billion messages per day (about one terabyte of security logs). Clearly a big data problem.

Beehive uses several different logs: web proxy logs (outbound connections), DHCP logs (for IP to machine correlation), Windows domain controller logs (authentication attempts), antivirus logs (scan results), and VPN server logs (remote connections). Those raw logs were stored at a commercial SIEM. Even so, logs were noisy because of different timestamps (even from different time zones), out of order arrival, different identifiers (IP, usernames, hostnames). The goal was to detect threats in two different scenarios: the first involves a host that is infected or at imminent risk (e.g., contacting C&C servers[1], exfiltrating data, malware); the second concerns policy violations (e.g., peer-to-peer sharing, adult content). To overcome these problems, the Beehive approach considers three layers:

Table 1. Summary of the analyzed papers.

Paper	Published	Year	Approach	Dataset	Achievements
Cluster and Classify					
Beehive (Yen et al., 2013)	ACSAC	2013	- Clustering: K-means after PCA; - Unique/rare pattern ⇒ outlier	Webproxy; DHCP; AV;VPN.	Generic outlier detector.
Big Data analytics(...) (Gonçalves et al., 2015)	Trustcom	2015	- Integrate threat intelligence features; - Clustering (Expectation-Maximization); - Classification (Naive Bayes); - Analyst must check if labels are correct, if needed he can correct, improving classifier accuracy.	DHCP; 802.1x; FW.	Classify after clustering to automate the process.
AI2 (Veeramachaneni et al., 2016)	BigData Sec.	2016	- Oriented to web applications. - Ensemble of unsupervised-learning methods: density-based, matrix-decomposition, neural networks; mix individual scores to get a rank; - Top ranked events are labeled by analysts to seed supervised model.	FW; WebServer.	Ensemble of unsupervised models. Rank alerts.
Graph Models					
(...)Mining Large-Scale Log Data (Oprea et al., 2015)	DSN	2015	- Method: use belief propagation to unveil suspicious hosts/domains (C&C like); - Classify suspects using linear regression.	DNS; Webproxy.	Detection of DGA domains. Unveil malicious and unknown domains.
Botyacc (Nagaraja, 2014)	ESORICS	2014	- Detection of P2P botnets; - Collect Netflow ->graph-model - edge partition; - Markov diffusion process - Random walks; - Infer comparing to Honeynet ground truth.	Netflow; SFlow.	Aprox.97% accuracy to unveil known botnets. FAR (0.1%)
HOLMES (Milajerdi et al., 2019)	S&P	2018	- Map audit logs to APT stage; - Leverage MITRE ATT&CK ;	Windows ETW; Linux auditdw.	Real-time APT detection; Highlevel graph with attack steps.
Real-Time Log Analytics					
Entropy-Based(...) (Cinque et al., 2017)	ICDSN	2017	- Anomaly detector; - Measure log entropy and find deviations from - Baseline.	Logs of an Air Traffic Control System.	New technique for real-time processing; Can be adapted to process other data types.
DeepLog(Du et al., 2017)	CCS	2017	- Anomaly detector; - Model logs as natural language; - Deep Neural Network model using LSTM to learn log patterns and find deviations	HDFS; OpenStack; Emulated: VAST 2011;	General purpose framework for online log anomaly detection; Extensive evaluation with promising results.
Kitsune(Mirsky et al., 2018)	NDSS	2018	- Anomaly detector NIDS; neural networks; - Ensemble AutoEncoders; - Online feature extraction framework.	IP camera network; IoT network.	General purpose framework for online log anomaly detection.
Frameworks and Context					
Correlation of Security Events(...) (Stroeh et al., 2013)	JISA	2013	- Collect snort events ->Normalize (ext. IDMEF); - Group events from same attack and generate meta-events; - Classify (SVM, Bayesian networks, Decision tree) meta events ->Attack or false positive	DARPA99 Scan of the month.	Bridge Semantic gap by aggregating Snort events into real alerts.
(...) (Giura & Wang, 2012)	ASE	2012	- Framework proposal. - Use all recorded events (not only security alerts). - All logs have potential to be useful. - Define planes (physical, user, network, application). - Map events to targets (CEO, servers) - Contexts construction (correlate planes) ->Alert	—	Guidelines for a scalable intrusion detection framework

- Parse, filter and normalize log data – First define how to normalize the timestamps of all log entries to UTC. Second, define how to bind IP addresses to hosts (using DHCP logs). Finally, normalize these attributes of every log entry.
- Feature extraction from the normalized data – Features were selected by security experts, observing known malware and policy violations behavior. Features where grouped in four types:

Destination-based (e.g., new destinations, unpopular destinations), Host-based (new user-agent string), Policy-based (e.g., blocked domain, challenged domain) and traffic-based (e.g., connection spikes or bursts). Daily, for each host, a feature vector is created.

- Perform clustering to identify outliers

The authors of Beehive used real data, so there was no ground-truth, i.e., no information about which attacks were caught in the dataset. To tackle this problem of lack of ground-truth, they applied an unsupervised learning approach (K-means clustering). Hosts that behave similarly (e.g., all hosts in a department, all users with same role) are represented within large clusters, while outliers (with unique behavioral patterns) should appear as smaller clusters (few hosts). They also applied Principal Component Analysis to remove dependencies between features.

In what concerns evaluation and ability to detect security incidents, the Beehive project uncovered 784 security incidents (25% malware related, 39% policy violation, 35% automated unknown software) whereas the enterprise existing security tools only detected 8 of these incidents. It is also noteworthy to refer that by applying techniques such as custom white-listing (popular domains removal), they reduce the data to be processed by 74%.

Beehive represents a remarkable step in outlier detection methods in the context we consider. However, some limitations are remarked to better perceive future work direction: the need for manual analysis to classify the meaning of the unveiled outliers; the evaluation of the system not providing exact information about detection performance (e.g., false positive rate); the analytics is done in a daily basis using processed data from the previous day. The batch processing took more than five hours just for feature extraction of 160GB (after reduction) of logs corresponding to one day.

Big Data Analytics for Detecting Host Misbehavior in Large Logs

Gonçalves et al. (2015) present an approach that "combines data mining and both supervised and unsupervised ML in order to make the detection process as automatic as possible, without having to instruct the system about how entities misbehave". In this case the real-world data was obtained at a major telecommunication company. They considered logs from DHCP (IP to host binding), authentication servers (how often user log in and sessions flows) and perimeter firewalls (security alerts, actions, ports, source and destination).

At first a normalization is performed to clean and combine logs (with similar techniques to Beehive). Next is the feature selection and extraction phase. Finally, the system performs clustering to group entities with similar behavior and then the security analyst must manually classify them as behaving normally or misbehaving. Afterwards, the normal period of execution begins. The overall process is conducted using logs within a time period (e.g., 1 day of logs).

The clustering algorithm (Expectation-Maximization) outputs clusters of similar behaving entities to be classified according to the previously trained classification model. The analyst should always review and confirm classifier output such that the classification model gets updated and more accurate.

Regarding feature selection, they remark that it was a long process to look for features that are potentially able to separate good from bad behavior (e.g., number of sessions, number of admin login tries, unpopular domains). In total they used 34 individual features. It is noteworthy that they also used external feeds, namely threat intelligence from AlienVault (bad reputation IPs), Internet Storm Center (malicious subnets), Sitevet list of worse Autonomous Systems, and CleanTalk (spam activity). To be able to process big data, the authors performed feature extraction using Hadoop MapReduce.

A distinctive improvement in relation to Beehive, is the use of a classification mechanism to minimize the effort of manually labeling clusters. They used Naive Bayes "as it converges quicker than other models". Their approach requires intensive human labor at a first phase to create the classification model (manually labeling a training set), afterwards the analyst has only to monitor and check if results are wrong or not and update the model accordingly (over time the detection performance should increase).

The most relevant limitations of this system are the same as Beehive's. However, there were improvements regarding semi-automatic cluster labeling and the implementation of feature extraction using MapReduce, which potentially can reduce human intervention and processing times. The Hadoop MapReduce framework is intended to execute the jobs in batch; this fact constrains using their scheme for blocking attacks.

AI2: Training a Big Data Machine to Defend

Veeramachaneni et al. (2016) developed a system that follows the same basic ideas of (Yen et al., 2013; Gonçalves et al., 2015). However, there are some distinctive aspects. The chosen feature set is focused on finding web application attacks (e.g., account takeover or new account fraud). During the unsupervised-learning phase, they fuse together three different methods (density-based, matrix decomposition, and ANNs) by projecting individual scores into probabilities. The system tags the events with a rank as a function of the computed probabilities, so that the analyst can prioritize actions. If an event is highly scored by all algorithms it will be considered, highly ranked and shown to the analyst as such.

Regarding the data sources, they used three months of real logs (3.6 billion log lines) from a webscale platform, providing web and firewall logs. To tackle the big data problem of feature extraction, they divided this process in two: activity tracking and activity aggregation. In short, as the system absorbs the generated log stream, it identifies the entities (e.g., IP, user) in each log line and updates the corresponding activity records (designed for efficient feature extraction) which are stored in a temporal window (one minute). To improve performance, they overlap time-scopes and maintain different time-windows (minute, hourly, daily, weekly). Finally, the feature extraction process can be done in any time interval (limited to 24 hours) just by computing on the aggregated activity records. They selected the features (24 in total), which seem to represent indicators an expert would use to investigate an attack to the web platform (e.g., logins on the last 24 hours, time from login to checkout, location, etc.).

They made a simulation of the system using 3 months of logs, claiming that their "results show that the system learns to defend against unseen attacks" getting more accurate over-time along with analysts' feedback. The detection rate shows an increasing trend improving 3.4x and reducing false positives by more than 5x when compared to state-of-the-art unsupervised anomaly detector.

As in the previous systems, automation is hard to achieve. The need for qualified human analysts is fundamental for adequate learning process. However, this research brought new insights on outlier detection mechanism applied to web application. Furthermore, it introduced a ranking mechanism for prioritization of outlier events, with improved confidence and accuracy based on an outlier detection ensemble (to compensate individual model bias). Although performance evaluation is not detailed in their study, the authors believe this choice can have high impact in performance.

Graph Models

The studies in this section, use graphs to represent network flows and events to extract features which can unveil APTs (Oprea et al., 2015; Milajerdi et al., 2019) and botnets (Nagaraja, 2014).

Detection of Early-Stage Enterprise Infection by Mining Large-Scale Log Data

Oprea et al. (2015) proposed a framework to detect early-stage APTs based on belief propagation (Yedidia et al., 2003) from graph theory. An APT is a multi-stage attack that targets a specific organization, often involves sophisticated malware, and adapts to the target environment while maintaining a low profile. The authors leveraged the following common infection patterns to unveil APTs: visits to several domains in a short period (redirection techniques to hide the attacker); connections to C&C servers; use of HTTP(S) to circumvent firewalls; and use of domains related to an attack, sharing location/IP space, same hosts, same time access. The goal was to unveil suspicious communications by internal hosts (indicator of an APT).

The authors used DNS and web proxy logs. A communication graph, either based on DNS or Webproxy logs, is built by modeling domains and hosts as graph vertices, and connections as graph edges. Since they only look to outbound requests, the resulting representation is a bipartite graph having hosts (one side) contacting domains (other side). To keep the graph manageable, they applied a reduction technique that consists in restricting the graph to what they call rare domains and to the hosts contacting them. Rare domains are those never seen before and contacted by a small number of hosts. To further reduce data, they removed popular domains and used domain folding to speed up data processing.

In this framework, belief propagation is used to unveil communities of domains that are likely part of campaigns and have similar features. They start by seeding the algorithm with known malicious domains or hosts, either obtained by security operation center (SOC) hints from previous incidents or by previously computed suspicious domains (C&C-like behavior). The algorithm iteratively computes scores to obtain other rare domains contacted by compromised hosts. The score computation is performed based on the similarity with C&C like behavior or with other suspicious domains from previous iterations (sum of weighted features). Finally, they use a supervised model to classify the domains as suspicious or not suspicious given a threshold. The algorithm outputs suspicious domains and respective hosts connections (with suspiciousness level).

The features set they choose aims to characterize C&C like outbound connections. They extracted the timestamps (to infer periodic communications), hostname, destination domain, user-agent (UA) string (infer rare UA), and web-referrer (infer automated connections).

The approach was evaluated on two different datasets. The first contained two months (1.15TB) of DNS records from the Los Alamos National Lab containing 20 independent and simulated APT-like infections. Their technique achieved 98.33% true positive rate with low false positive rate. The second dataset contained two months of web proxy logs (38.41TB) collected from a large enterprise. They confirmed that 289 of 375 detected domains were malicious and that 98 domains were new discoveries (not recognized by state-of-the-art products). Another remarkable achievement is that they were able to unveil domains generated by malware (using a domain generation algorithm, DGA, to hide the attacker's infrastructure) even before registration (allowing preventive measures).

Some limitations of this approach are that attackers can escape detection by: randomizing C&C connection timings; using standard UA strings; communicating directly to IPs instead of domains. However, these limitations are also a problem to the attackers: randomizing connections would make campaign orchestration harder; UA strings are typically used by malware to send information; using IPs unveils their infrastructure.

Overall, this approach is a complement to existing tools and can be used as a feed to correlate with other sources.

Botyacc: Unified P2P Botnet Detection Using Behavioral and Graph Analysis

Nagaraja (2014) proposed a novel technique to detect peer-to-peer (P2P) botnets. Botmasters started using P2P communications to create resilience and anonymity by decentralizing command throughout the network. The paper's approach consists in leveraging the design characteristic of P2P communication by using Markovian diffusion processes over network flows represented in a graph model. The P2P botnet graph design is distinguishable from those of other communications in network. Finding patterns in connectivity (who talks to whom) and traffic flows (who talks like whom) is the key idea.

The system architecture is composed by four components: monitor, the component which collects flows either being vantage points (e.g., routers with Netflow) or hosts (sflows); aggregator, that receives and collects flows from monitors, and computes an algorithm to separate bot candidates from legitimate traffic; honeynet, to create ground-truth for specifically injected malware and to train the inference mechanism; inference mechanism, which uses as input the traffic traces from both the aggregator and the honeynet to unveil the botnet.

An overview of the approach is the following. The communication graph is given by $G = (V,E)$ where V is the set of hosts and E is the set of flows. Consider the subgraph $Gb = (H,M)$ where H is the set of bots (infected hosts) and M is the set of botnet flows. Notice that $Gb \subseteq G$, and $H \subseteq V$, and $M \subseteq E$. This is an edge-partitioning problem from a graph-theoretic view. Each edge $e \in E(G)$, models a traffic flow represented by a k-dimensional vector. The inference algorithm is a stochastic diffusion process over similar edges. To infer edges similarity, random walks on graphs are performed. The novelty of this walk is that the choice of the next step (outgoing edge) is based on its similarity with the previous (incoming edge), hence, the walk has a bias towards similar flows. To infer similarity, the algorithm computes the Euclidean distance where each flow is represented by a vector of scalar elements defining Cartesian coordinates.

The evaluation of the approach was done using real-world dataset from a university gateway. The captured traffic (corresponding to one month) was injected with popular P2P botnets (Zeus, Spyeye and Miner). The malware traffic flows were obtained using a testbed with 25 servers in a test network, which was connected to the internet. The detection rates ranged from 95% to 99% with very low false positive rate ($\approx 0.1\%$).

This approach represents a different method with interesting results. It seems to be suitable to find known P2P botnets, but accuracy on novel ones is hard to assess.

HOLMES: Real-Time APT Detection Through Correlation of Suspicious Information Flows

Milajerdi et al. (2019) proposed HOLMES, a system with the goal of detecting activities that are part of APT campaigns. Their system collects audit data from hosts (e.g., Linux auditd or Windows ETW data) and other alerts available in the enterprise (e.g., from IDSs) to produce a detection signal. At a high-level, the techniques they developed leverage the correlation between suspicious information flows (e.g., files, processes) that arise during an attack campaign. The system design enables the generation of alerts semantically close to activity steps of APT attackers: the kill chain. The cyber kill chain models APT lifecycle phases: from early reconnaissance to the goal of data exfiltration.

For example, the internal reconnaissance step depends on successful initial compromise and establishment of a foothold. Both lateral movement and exfiltration phases use data gathered during the reconnaissance phase. Correlating APT steps from low-level events and information flow originates the emerging kill chain used by a particular APT actor. To bridge the semantic gap between low-level system-call events and high-level kill chain stages, the authors leveraged the use of MITREs ATT&CK framework[2] (MITRE, n.d.; Strom et al., 2018) to map audit logs to APT stages. MITREs ATT&CK framework describes close to 200 behavioral patterns – tactics, techniques, and procedures (TTPs) – observed in the wild, which can be captured on audit data.

To assist analyst interpretation, HOLMES enables the construction of a high-level scenario graph (HSG) which refer to TTPs. The edges of the graph represent the information flow among TTPs and their entities. The HSG summarizes the attacker's actions in real-time.

The authors evaluated the system using a dataset provided by the DARPA Transparent Computing program, corresponding to streams of audit data of 7 computers (Windows and Linux based) with injected attacks. They published the audit data streams into the Kafka stream processing server and performed real-time analysis and detection by using a previous developed system called SLEUTH (Hossain et al., 2017). Attacks constituted less than 0.001% of the audit data volume. HOLMES was able to distinguish between APT campaigns injected in the dataset and benign activities.

The main limitation of HOLMES is that it assumes the auditing system and the OS kernel are reliable, as well as that the initial attack must originate outside the enterprise, using means such as remote network access. Furthermore, the evaluation was done with a limited number of audit log sources.

Real-Time Log Analytics

This section refers three recent works that provide new methods to capture security-relevant information from logs in real-time. The first (Cinque et al., 2017) uses entropy measurements to infer deviations from the baseline; the second is inspired in natural language processing and interprets logs as elements of a sequence that follows grammar rules (Du et al., 2017); the third (Mirsky et al., 2018) uses an ensemble of ANNs (autoencoders) to differentiate between normal and abnormal traffic patterns.

Entropy-Based Security Analytics: Measurements from a Critical Information System

Cinque et al. (2017) proposed a method to find abnormal behavior within textual, heterogeneous, runtime log streams. They used an entropy-based approach, which has no assumptions on the structure of underlying log entries. The goal is to detect anomalies (i.e., unexpected activity) that should be followed up by analysts, by monitoring entropy for deviations above certain thresholds.

Their technique comprises two main tasks named log entropy sampling and collector. Sampling is a periodic task that computes log entropy of new entries within a predefined time window. The entropy is calculated based on the count of terms in logs, i.e., of sequences of characters separated by a whitespace. The collector acquires the most recent log entropy observations for all logs of the system. It stores the observations in vectors (one vector per log source) where each position of the vector corresponds to a log stream entropy observation.

They evaluated the system measuring logs from a real-world Air Traffic Control information system. To overcome the big data problem, they deployed Apache Storm (Apache Storm, n.d.) as data analytics framework. Experiments showed that entropy-based methods can be a valuable complement to security analytics solutions.

Deeplog: Anomaly Detection and Diagnosis from System Logs through Deep Learning

Du et al. (2017) proposed a deep neural network model that uses long short-term memory (LSTM) to model a log as a natural language sequence. The key insight is that log entries are the result of structured code. Hence, logs can be seen as a sequence of events of a structured language.

In short, as a log entry arrives it is parsed into a log key (e.g., type of event) and a parameter value vector (e.g., event content). An entry is labeled as an anomaly if either its log keys or its parameter values vector is predicted as being abnormal. In a first phase, DeepLog has to learn what good behavior is, being trained with log data from normal execution. After this initial training, it can detect anomalies (i.e., log patterns deviated from normal) over incoming log streams. In addition, the authors proposed a technique to incrementally update the model in runtime, adapting it to new log patterns over time, although this requires to incorporate user feedback. Moreover, DeepLog allow the analyst to perform root cause analysis, by constructing workflows from the underlying system logs.

Although DeepLog is an innovative method, at the training stage it assumes having good behavior logs, which is something hard to assure.

Kitsune: An Ensemble of Autoencoders for Online Network Intrusion Detection

Mirsky et al. (2018) propose what they call a plug-and-play NIDS. This NIDS can learn to detect attacks on the local network, without supervision and online, in an efficient manner. The authors point out that Kitsune aims to overcome the shortcomings of typical approaches using ANNs as NIDS. Some of these shortcomings are: the need for a labeled dataset; the fact that most supervised learning approaches are limited to known attacks and need a strong CPU to train a model; run the newly trained models is only possible after transferring updates to organizations NIDS. In light of these challenges, Kitsune aims to be a lightweight NIDS based on an ANN, online, using unsupervised learning. It is designed to run on network routers in real-time.

In sum, the Kitsune framework is composed by a packet capturer and parser (e.g., meta information of the packet), a feature extractor (e.g., statistics of the channel), and a feature mapper to map features into a bigger set to be processed by the anomaly detector. Kitsunes core algorithm for anomaly detection, KitNET, uses an ensemble of small ANNs – called autoencoders – to differentiate between normal and abnormal traffic patterns. The feature extraction framework efficiently tracks the patterns of every network channel in an online fashion. To accomplish this, the framework uses damped incremental statistics maintained in an hash table.

To evaluate Kitsune, they made experiments on an operational IP camera surveillance network and IoT network deploying several attacks. They achieved good results running Kitsune on a simple Raspberry PI.

As in the previous studies, if the network is already contaminated, Kitsune is arguably inefficient.

Frameworks and Context

This last group includes two studies that focus on providing high-level frameworks to address the future needs of security analytics.

Using Large Scale Distributed Computing to Unveil Advanced Persistent Threats

Giura & Wang (2012) propose a framework for detecting APTs and a generalized method that can be implemented in any organization. They introduced a conceptual attack model, which they named attack pyramid, starting from the notion of attack tree. The attack goal is at the top of the pyramid, while the lateral planes represent environments where the attack can occur. The environments (planes) are as follows: physical, network, user, application, other. From the base to the top of the pyramid, it is represented the attack time-line evolving the following stages: reconnaissance, delivery, exploitation, operation, data collection and exfiltration (goal). The unfolded attack pyramid version, gives the possible paths (and vulnerable elements), naturally traversing multiple planes, towards the goal.

To determine long-term events across planes and infer if they are part of a coherent attack is a hard task: an APT is not detected by observing a specific event; it has to be unveiled by event correlation. Hence, they tackle the problem by exploring new large-scale distributed systems as a processing platform, allowing to cover more attack paths and more security-relevant sources. A prototype of multiprocessing implementation with MapReduce is presented. The idea is to correlate in parallel all the relevant events across all the pyramid planes into contexts. They recommend collecting data in all planes such as "physical" location of hardware or users, "users" importance (e.g., admins, CFO, etc.), security and "network" devices logs, "application" logs (web-server, critical end-points).

In summary, the method consists in profiling potential APT targets (servers, important employees, data center location) and group collected events into contexts (set of events corresponding to a target). For each target there is an attack pyramid. Different pyramids can share one or more planes and each plane is defined by a set of events. The big data ready large-scale distributed computing should Map events to targets and construct contexts, then Reduce to target and alert (detection mechanisms).

Apparently, the proposed system was not implemented, and only preliminary results are presented in the paper.

An Approach to the Correlation of Security Events based on Machine Learning Techniques

Stroeh et al. (2013) proposed a ML method to tackle the excess of false positives of an IDS. They do not use network traffic or other sources; they solely use IDS logs (e.g., Snort).

Their approach has two major steps. The first step is to normalize the incoming events (from the IDS) according to an extended version of the Intrusion Detection Message Exchange Format (IDMEF). After normalization, events from the same attack are aggregated into meta-events. The second step consists in classifying meta-events into attacks (alerts) or false positives.

The alerts aggregate events that represent an action (e.g., failed login), a condition (e.g., port unreachable) or suspiciousness (deduction from previous two). Furthermore, the alerts belong to some class of attack (e.g., DoS, probing, remote access, etc.). Each alert can be aggregated into high-level objects named meta-alerts. The meta-alert as a bit-array field where each bit of that field, represents an alert-type, and the more alert-type count the more likely to have an attack. The internal product of two arrays is used to infer the similarity between two meta-alerts. Hence, this field is essential for the classification process using supervised models (SVM, Bayesian networks and decision tree). They choose different models to infer which one was more accurate and concluded that Bayesian networks had the best results.

To conclude, it is noteworthy that they evaluated their approach using the DARPA99 dataset and data from the Scan-of-the-month Honeynet. They achieved data to information ratios in the order of 2,1% and 50% respectively.

CONCLUSION

Both the cybersecurity industry and academic research have been engaging the big data challenge faced by security analytics and intrusion detection. Major SIEM vendors are evolving to distributed computing technologies and are integrating behavioral analytics (using ML) in their solutions. These new capabilities materialize the emergence of a new generation SIEMs, that the CSA designated 2nd generation SIEMs.

ML algorithms are being used to deal with big data in several domains, but in cybersecurity there is a sense that there is much more to be done. In the cybersecurity domain, the use of ML is being more successful on specific use cases (e.g., high value assets, track privileged users) in opposition to more generic goals (e.g., generic outlier detector), which may lead to high rates of false alarms. When applying ML to cybersecurity, the greatest challenge is the fact that we are dealing with human adversaries that are to some extent unpredictable. One of the consequences of this adversarial setting is the evolution of attacks, which does not allow to obtain the necessary ground-truth to a fully automated system that can predict new attacks accurately.

Security experts are still necessary in the intrusion detection cycle. A stand-alone and fully automated solution seems hard to achieve. Even so, handling such high volume of data produced in the security domain, is surely beyond human capabilities, and the use of ML to extract useful information from large and multi-dimensional data, seems to be the best complement to achieve a close to real-time contextual threat awareness.

ACKNOWLEDGMENT

This research was supported by national funds through Fundação para a Ciência e a Tecnologia (FCT) with reference UID/CEC/50021/2019 (INESC-ID), by the Portuguese Army (CINAMIL), and by the European Commission under grant agreement number 830892 (SPARTA).

REFERENCES

Apache Hive. (n.d.). Retrieved from https://hive.apache.org/

Apache Metron. (n.d.). Retrieved from http://metron.apache.org/

Apache Spot. (n.d.). Retrieved from http://spot.incubator.apache.org/

Apache Storm. (n.d.). Retrieved from http://storm.apache.org/

Azad, C., & Jha, V. K. (2013). Data mining in intrusion detection: A comparative study of methods, types and data sets. *International Journal of Information Technology and Computer Science*, *5*(8), 75–90. doi:10.5815/ijitcs.2013.08.08

Bhuyan, M., Bhattacharyya, D., & Kalita, J. (2014). Network anomaly detection: Methods, systems and tools. *IEEE Communications Surveys and Tutorials*, *16*(1), 303–336. doi:10.1109/SURV.2013.052213.00046

Buczak, A., & Guven, E. (2016). A survey of data mining and machine learning methods for cyber security intrusion detection. *IEEE Communications Surveys and Tutorials*, *18*(2), 1153–1176. doi:10.1109/COMST.2015.2494502

Bussa, T., Litan, A., & Phillips, T. (2016). *Market guide for user and entity behavior analytics*. Gartner.

Canadian Institute for Cybersecurity. (n.d.). Retrieved from http://www.unb.ca/research/iscx/dataset/index.html

Cárdenas, A., Manadhata, P., & Rajan, S. (2013). *Big data analytics for security intelligence*. Cloud Security Alliance.

Cheon, J., & Choe, T.-Y. (2013). Distributed processing of snort alert log using Hadoop. *IACSIT International Journal of Engineering and Technology*, *5*, 2685–2690.

Cinque, M., Corte, R. D., & Pecchia, A. (2017). Entropy-based security analytics: Measurements from a critical information system. In *2017 47th Annual IEEE/IFIP International Conference on Dependable Systems and Networks (DSN)* (pp. 379–390). IEEE. doi:10.1109/DSN.2017.39

Cloud Security Alliance. (2013). *Expanded top ten big data security and privacy challenges*. Academic Press.

Cloud Security Alliance. (2014). *Big data taxonomy*. Academic Press.

Cylance. (n.d.). Retrieved from https://www.cylance.com/

Darktrace. (n.d.). Retrieved from https://www.darktrace.com

Dean, J., & Ghemawat, S. (2004). MapReduce: simplified data processing on large clusters. In *Proceedings of the 6th USENIX Symposium on Operating Systems Design and Implementation* (pp. 137–150). USENIX.

Debar, H., Dacier, M., & Wespi, A. (1999). Towards a taxonomy of intrusion detection systems. *Computer Networks*, *31*(8), 805–822. doi:10.1016/S1389-1286(98)00017-6

Domingos, P. (2012). A few useful things to know about machine learning. *Communications of the ACM*, *55*(10), 78–87. doi:10.1145/2347736.2347755

Du, M., Li, F., Zheng, G., & Srikumar, V. (2017). *Deeplog: Anomaly detection and diagnosis from system logs through deep learning.* Academic Press.

ELK. (n.d.). Retrieved from https://www.elastic.co/

ENISA. (2015). *Big data security - good practices and recommendations on the security of big data systems.* Academic Press.

Exabeam. (n.d.). Retrieved from https://www.exabeam.com/

Ghemawat, S., Gobioff, H., & Leung, S.-T. (2003). The Google file system. *Operating Systems Review*, *37*(5), 29. doi:10.1145/1165389.945450

Giura, P., & Wang, W. (2012). Using large scale distributed computing to unveil advanced persistent threats. *Science Journal*, *1*, 93–105.

Gonçalves, D., Bota, J., & Correia, M. (2015). Big data analytics for detecting host misbehavior in large logs. In *Proceedings of the 14th IEEE International Conference on Trust, Security and Privacy in Computing and Communications.* IEEE. 10.1109/Trustcom.2015.380

Graham, P. (2002). *A plan for spam.* Retrieved from http://www.paulgraham.com/spam.html

Hossain, M. N., Milajerdi, S. M., Wang, J., Eshete, B., Gjomemo, R., Sekar, R., . . . Venkatakrishnan, V. (2017). Sleuth: Real-time attack scenario reconstruction from cots audit data. In *Proc. USENIX Secur.* (pp. 487–504). USENIX.

IBM. (n.d.). *Cognitive security with Watson.* Retrieved from https://www.ibm.com/security/artificial-intelligence

Kavanagh, K. M., Sadowski, G., & Bussa, T. (2018). *Magic quadrant for security information and event management.* Academic Press.

Klein, B., & Peter, R. (2015). *Defeating machine learning.* Black Hat Briefings.

Kononenko, O., Baysal, O., Holmes, R., & Godfrey, M. W. (2014). Mining modern repositories with ElasticSearch. *Proceedings of the 11th IEEE Working Conference on Mining Software Repositories.*

Lancope. (n.d.). Retrieved from https://www.lancope.com

Lee, Y., & Lee, Y. (2013). Toward scalable internet traffic measurement and analysis with Hadoop. *Computer Communication Review*, *43*(1), 5–13. doi:10.1145/2427036.2427038

Li, Y., Liu, Y., & Zhang, H. (2012). Cross-boundary enterprise security monitoring. In *Proceedings of the IEEE International Conference on Computational Problem-Solving* (pp. 127–136). IEEE.

Litan, A. (2015). *Market guide for user and entity behavior analytics.* Gartner.

MapR. (n.d.). Retrieved from https://www.mapr.com

Meng, X., Bradley, J., Yavuz, B., Sparks, E., Venkataraman, S., Liu, D., & ... Talwaker, A. (2016). MLlib: Machine learning in apache spark. *Journal of Machine Learning Research, 17*, 1235–1241.

Milajerdi, S. M., Gjomemo, R., Eshete, B., Sekar, R., & Venkatakrishnan, V. (2019). Holmes: Realtime apt detection through correlation of suspicious information flows. In *Proceedings of the 40th IEEE Symposium on Security and Privacy (S&P).* IEEE.

Mirsky, Y., Doitshman, T., Elovici, Y., & Shabtai, A. (2018). Kitsune: An ensemble of autoencoders for online network intrusion detection. *Proceedings of the Network and Distributed System Security Symposium (NDSS) 2018.* doi:10.14722/ndss.2018.23204

MITRE. (n.d.). *Adversarial tactics, techniques and common knowledge.* Retrieved from https://attack.mitre.org/

Nagaraja, S. (2014). Botyacc: Unified p2p botnet detection using behavioural analysis and graph analysis. In *European Symposium on Research in Computer Security* (pp. 439–456). Academic Press.

Nassar, M., al Bouna, B., & Malluhi, Q. (2013). Secure outsourcing of network flow data analysis. In *Proceedings of the 2013 IEEE International Congress on Big Data* (pp. 431–432). IEEE. 10.1109/BigData.Congress.2013.71

Oprea, A., Li, Z., Yen, T.-F., Chin, S. H., & Alrwais, S. (2015). Detection of early-stage enterprise infection by mining large-scale log data. In *Proceedings of the 45th Annual IEEE/IFIP International Conference on Dependable Systems and Networks* (pp. 45–56). IEEE. 10.1109/DSN.2015.14

Samuel, A. L. (1959). Some studies in machine learning using the game of checkers. *IBM Journal of Research and Development, 3*(3), 210–229. doi:10.1147/rd.33.0210

Securonix. (n.d.). Retrieved from https://www.securonix.com/

Shackleford, D. (2015). *Analytics and Intelligence Survey.* Paper SANS Institute – InfoSec Reading Room.

Shackleford, D. (2016). *Security Analytics Survey.* Paper SANS Institute – InfoSec Reading Room.

Sommer, R., & Paxson, V. (2010). Outside the closed world: On using machine learning for network intrusion detection. In *Proceedings of the 30th IEEE Symposium on Security and Privacy* (pp. 305–316). IEEE. 10.1109/SP.2010.25

Splunk. (n.d.). Retrieved from https://www.splunk.com

Stroeh, K., Madeira, E. R. M., & Goldenstein, S. K. (2013). An approach to the correlation of security events based on machine learning techniques. *Journal of Internet Services and Applications, 4*(1), 7. doi:10.1186/1869-0238-4-7

Strom, B. E., Applebaum, A., Miller, D. P., Nickels, K. C., Pennington, A. G., & Thomas, C. B. (2018). *MITRE ATT&CK: Design and philosophy.* Academic Press.

Turcotte, M. J. M., Kent, A. D., & Hash, C. (2018). Unified host and network data set. Data Science for Cyber-Security, 3(1), 1–22. doi:10.1142/9781786345646_001

Veeramachaneni, K., Arnaldo, I., Cuesta-Infante, A., Korrapati, V., Bassias, C., & Li, K. (2016). AI2: Training a big data machine to defend. In *Proceedings of the 2nd IEEE International Conference on Big Data Security on Cloud.* IEEE.

Webroot. (n.d.). Retrieved from http://www.webroot.com/

White, T. (2009). *Hadoop: The Definitive Guide.* O'Reilly.

Wuest, B. (2014). *Integrating QRadar with Hadoop.* White Paper from IBM.

Xu, W., Qi, Y., & Evans, D. (2016). Automatically evading classifiers. In *Proceedings of the 2016 Network and Distributed Systems Symposium.* Academic Press. 10.14722/ndss.2016.23115

Yedidia, J. S., Freeman, W. T., & Weiss, Y. (2003). Understanding belief propagation and its generalizations. *Exploring Artificial Intelligence in the New Millennium, 8,* 236–239.

Yen, T.-F., Oprea, A., Onarlioglu, K., Leetham, T., Robertson, W., Juels, A., & Kirda, E. (2013). Beehive: large-scale log analysis for detecting suspicious activity in enterprise networks. In *Proceedings of the 29th ACM Annual Computer Security Applications Conference.* ACM. 10.1145/2523649.2523670

Zaharia, M., Xin, R. S., Wendell, P., Das, T., Armbrust, M., Dave, A., & ... . (2016). Apache spark: A unified engine for big data processing. *Communications of the ACM, 59*(11), 56–65. doi:10.1145/2934664

Zuech, R., Khoshgofthaar, T., & Wald, R. (2015). Intrusion detection and big heterogeneous data: a survey. *Journal of Big Data,* 90–107.

KEY TERMS AND DEFINITIONS

Anomaly Detection: Finds deviations from normal. Rare events or observations raise suspicions when differ significantly from most of the data.

Big Data: Traditional technologies of data processing, have difficulties to handle in tolerable time a large dataset.

Clustering: Aims to group data automatically according to their degree of similarity.

Log Analysis: It seeks to extract knowledge about threats or malfunctions, from records generated by a device.

Security Analytics: Is an approach to cybersecurity focused on the analysis of data.

SIEM: A software solution that allows to collect, manage and correlate security events generated by several network devices.

Stream Processing: Given a data set (a stream), an operation is applied to all elements of the stream.

ENDNOTES

[1]   Botnet command and control servers.

[2]   The name of the framework is indeed ATT&CK but it comes from adversarial tactics, techniques, and common knowledge.

Chapter 15

Big Data Analytics With Machine Learning and Deep Learning Methods for Detection of Anomalies in Network Traffic

Valliammal Narayan
Avinashilingam Institute for Home Science and Higher Education for Women, India

Shanmugapriya D.
Avinashilingam Institute for Home Science and Higher Education for Women, India

ABSTRACT

Information is vital for any organization to communicate through any network. The growth of internet utilization and the web users increased the cyber threats. Cyber-attacks in the network change the traffic flow of each system. Anomaly detection techniques have been developed for different types of cyber-attack or anomaly strategies. Conventional ADS protect information transferred through the network or cyber attackers. The stable prevention of anomalies by machine and deep-learning algorithms are applied for cyber-security. Big data solutions handle voluminous data in a short span of time. Big data management is the organization and manipulation of huge volumes of structured data, semi-structured data and unstructured data, but it does not handle a data imbalance problem during the training process. Big data-based machine and deep-learning algorithms for anomaly detection involve the classification of decision boundary between normal traffic flow and anomaly traffic flow. The performance of anomaly detection is efficiently increased by different algorithms.

DOI: 10.4018/978-1-5225-9611-0.ch015

INTRODUCTION

Over the past decades, the significance of cyber-security has increased and developed as a general branch of an individual life that is associated with a computer or a mobile phone. When a person submits his/ her information via online, it becomes susceptible to cyber-attacks or cyber-crimes like hijacking or unauthorized access, injection of virus, malware, etc. As a result, authorized access via web services is offered by cyber-security. This chapter summarizes the significance of cyber-security, how it can be developed and the considered key points during the selection of a cyber-security service provider.

The cyber world is expanding rapidly day by day and more and more people are getting connected to this world, resulting in generation of a large amount of data called Big Data. Big data is large in both quantity and quality and can be efficiently used to analyze certain patterns and behaviour anomalies which can help us prevent or be prepared for the thread or any upcoming attack. This proactive and analytical approach will help us greatly reduce the rate of Cyber Crimes and also get the knowledge out of that data which was not previously observable. Big Data analytics using machine learning techniques have a major and evolving role to play in cyber security (M.D. Anto Praveena, 2017) as in Figure 1 The cyber security problems can now impact every aspect of modern society, from hospitals, banks, and telecoms to governments and individuals.

The battle against cyber security breaches is fought along the four dimensions of Prevention, Preparation, Detection, and Response. Over the last decade, the security industry seems to have largely given up on Prevention, but that is a topic for another day. It is in the dimensions of Preparation and Detection

Figure 1. Overview of the Big Data Analytics for Cyber Security

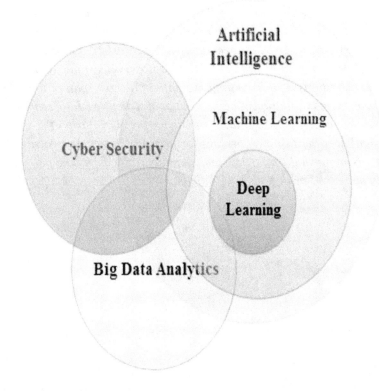

that Big Data Analytics capabilities are being used to identify anomalous patterns and to connect the dots across diverse systems and data sets. The data may be categorized into transaction and interaction data, entity data, systems operations data, reference data, and activity logs data. Big Data analytics using artificial intelligence techniques will self-learn normal patterns by observing a data flows under normal operations (Sebestyen.G, 2017).

CYBER SECURITY

Several aspects of human survival rely on the computer networks including interactions, transportation, administration, economics, medication and academic. Cyber-security, also known as computer security or Information Technology (IT) security involves the prevention of those systems from thievery or damage to their components or electronic data. There are different cyber-security standards or techniques available to protect the cyber environment of a user or organization. The major goal is reducing the threats by preventing or mitigating the cyber attacks from unintended or unauthorized access (Craigen, 2014). Due to this, authorized access and a secure data transmission are provided to the user.

Principles of Cyber-Security

The core principles of cyber-security are:

- SECRECY: The secrecy level of sensitive data is unchanged and shared only with authorized users.
- Reliability: Data should maintain its reliability and not be changed from its original state.
- Accessibility: Systems and data should be accessible to those who want it.

Cyber-Security Techniques

- Access Control and password security
- Authentication of data
- Malware scanners
- Firewalls
- Anti-virus software

ANOMALY DETECTION IN CYBER SECURITY

Anomaly detection considers that a hijacker can acquire access to his/her required targets and is powerful in infringing a given security policy. While unwanted activities occur during the data transmission without any interference, anomaly or intrusion detection takes place to offer warning information that something went mistaken and to respond in a suitable manner. The existence of a security policy that declares which activities are assumed malicious and must be protected is an indispensable for an anomaly/ intrusion detection system. Infringes may only be identified while activities are compared against given rules (Ahmed, 2014b).

Mostly, Anomaly Detection Systems (ADS) are designed for detecting anomalies or intrusions against a target network satisfying the following requirements:

- Accuracy
- Performance
- Completeness
- Fault tolerance
- Scalability

WHY ANOMALY DETECTION FOR CYBER SECURITY IS IMPORTANT?

The increasing amount and complexity of cyber security risks including aiming phishing scams, information thievery and other web susceptibilities insist that people remain attention about protecting their computers and data. A typical vulnerable system linked to the network can be compromised in moments (Balabine, 2018). Each and every day, thousands of spoiled web pages are being exposed and billions of files have been involved in information infringes. New attack models are launched endlessly. Below Figure 2 shows the top 20 countries with appropriate percentage levels of cyber-crime.

Figure 2. Cyber-Crime: Top 20 Countries

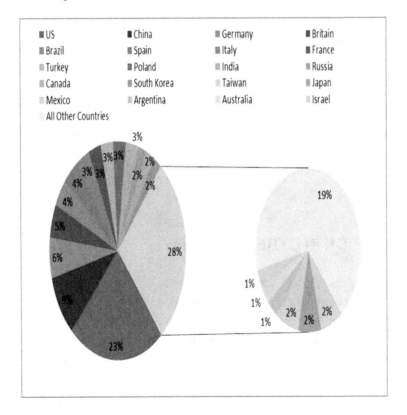

Anomaly Detection Methods

In a networked atmosphere, information security has been a foremost concern for network manager and security personnel who has the complete responsibility for network security, since the networks are under risk by adversaries. Creation of new information from previous information becomes more crucial when data from multiple sources are integrated. An anomaly may get access to significant information and they may share or steal the information, causing harm to the network and applications operating on the database. Several methods and techniques have been considered for securing the data from one place to another (Deljac, 2015). Some methods include:

- **Authentication:** Technology that requires user authentication before using the system or network. There are different levels of authentication like verifying the user with one-factor authentication (user id and password), two-factor authentication (security token) or three-factor authentication (fingerprint).
- **Packet Inspection:** It analyzes the data of a bundle as it passes an investigation point, hunting down convention rebelliousness, infections, spam, oddities or characterized criteria for choosing whether the parcel may pass or in the event that it requires to be directed to an alternate goal or for the utilization of gathering the measurable data.
- **Signature Detection:** It screens the packets in the system and contrasts them and pre-designed and pre-decided assault designs.

Fundamental Methodology of ADS

- **Parameterization***:* Information is pre-processed to get pre-established formats such that it is suitable or along with the targeted system's behaviour.
- **Training phase:** A model is constructed based on the normal or abnormal behaviour of a system. Depending on the considered type of anomaly detection, different ways of training are chosen. It can be both automatic and manual.
- **Detection phase:** Once the model for the system is constructed, it is compared with the observed traffic. If the observed variance exceeds from a fixed threshold, then a warning will be triggered.

Anomaly Detection in Cyber Security

In networks used for cyber-security, the traffic is dominated by periodical data flows. Normally, the data acquisition, pre-processing, storage and visualization are achieved in a periodical way and thus the traffic related to these activities adopts the similar periodicity. Moreover, the order of the activities is somehow stable. This quasi-stable state may change if a malicious code tries to penetrate in the system or if few types of physical malfunction occurred and the system reacts with some countermeasures. These both cases may be classified as anomalies (Ahmed, 2015). According to these observations, an anomaly discriminator is defined as an important change in the pattern of the packets transmitted on the network. The pattern may be detected through the following characteristics:

- Frequencies of different types of packets
- Order of different types of packets

- Lengths of different packet types
- Delays between different packets

In the training phase, the program may recognize the types of packets transferred via the network, their periodicity, the typical length and the order of the packets by using a network sniffer component. Occasionally, these data are a-priori recognized by the physical system's designer or by the control systems developer. Likewise, in some industrial networks, the traffic pattern is set in the configuration phase and it is firmly forced via a MAC protocol. Any change in this pattern is called as an anomaly.

In less restricted networks, few pattern characteristics can still be identified and converted into anomaly detection rules. In a training phase, a sniffer program may decide all the package types transmitted through the network, their length interval and recurrence frequency. Any major variation from normal values is considered as a candidate for an anomaly. Sporadic packets do not have a normal repetition time, but even in this case, a minimum frequency may be estimated from the physical phenomena or component that initiated it. For example, in a CAN network (i.e., car), the frequency of packets transmitted by the rotation sensor located on the engine cannot exceed the maximum rotation frequency of that engine. Multiple detection points should be established in a regular way, in different points of the network structure.

The cyber security breaches include external attacks and internal attacks. The reason for abnormality might be a pernicious action or some sort of interruption as shown in Figure 3. This abnormal behaviour found in the dataset is interesting to the analyst and this is the most important feature for anomaly detection. In this system, to detect the anomaly by solely monitor its cyber system footprint in network. Thus, we focus on monitoring applications network behaviour and aim to detect unexplained changes any time they occur.

Figure 3. Anomaly Detection in cyber Security

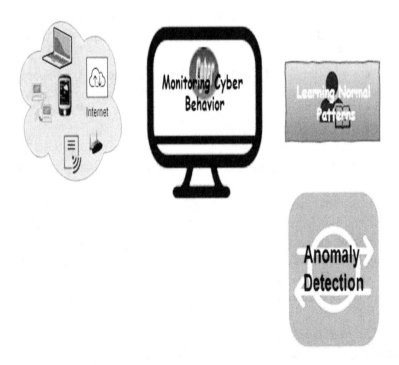

Motivation for Anomaly Detection

The aim of anomaly detection technique is their probable to detect previously unseen anomalies events. The security breaks are exceptionally basic now in the general public and associations neglect to take viable measures. Today digital assaults are regular in the general population managing an account area, wellbeing associations, protection, and administration division, so associations are have to give preparing and rules, approach changes, venturing up mindfulness programs. So our point is to plan for successful answers for maintain a strategic distance from the digital lawbreakers, infections, malware, etc.

Types of Anomalies

An anomaly may be classified into the following types:

- **Point Anomaly:** When specific information is varied from the normal pattern of the data, it may be known as a point anomaly. For instance, if a normal car fuel usage is six litres per day but if it becomes sixty litres in any random day, then it is a point anomaly. Example of this anomaly is Remote-to-User (R2U) and User-to-Root (U2R) since these are condition specific and sophisticated.
- **Contextual Anomaly:** When information acts anomalously in a specific context, it is known as a contextual or conditional anomaly. For instance, expenses on a credit card during festivals are normally higher than during the remaining days. Though it may be high, it may not be anomalous since high expenditures are contextually normal in nature. Conversely, an equally high expense during a non-festive day could be believed as a contextual anomaly. Probe attacks are considered as a contextual anomaly since these are based on the particular intention for attaining information and exploration.
- **Collective Anomaly:** When a collection of similar information acts anomalously with respect to the entire data, the group of information is called a collective anomaly as shown in Figure 4. For instance, in an individual Electro Cardiogram (ECG) output, the existence of low values for a long duration indicates an outlying phenomenon corresponding to an abnormal premature contraction, whereas one low value by itself is not considered as anomalous. The Denial-of-Service (DoS) attacks are categorized under collective anomaly. In DoS attack, many connection requests to a web server is a collective anomaly; however, a single request is legitimate.

General Framework for ADS

Figure 5 shows the general framework for ADS or network anomaly detection. The input data requires processing since the data or packets are different types. For instance, the IP addresses are hierarchical whereas the protocols are categorical and port numbers are statistical in nature. Data processing techniques are performed based on the anomaly detection techniques which are classified into two types, namely supervised and unsupervised. To evaluate the output, either scores or labels are used.

The following are the challenges addressed in anomaly detection techniques:

Figure 4. Types of Anomaly

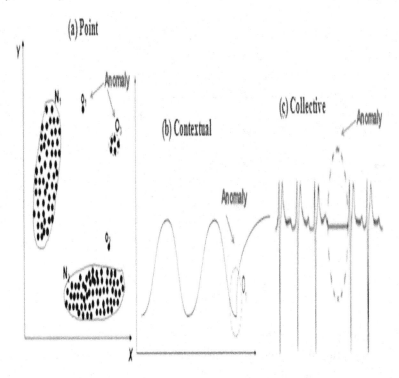

Figure 5. General Framework for ADS

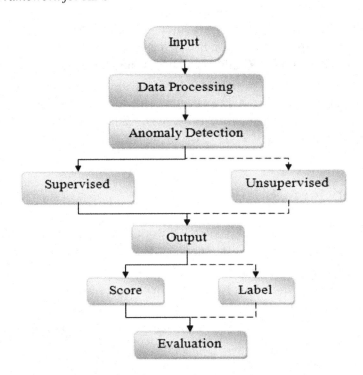

- A lack of generally applicable anomaly detection technique; for instance, an anomaly detection technique in a wired network may be of modest utilization in a wireless network.
- The information contains noise which tends to be a genuine anomaly and therefore is complex for segregation.
- A lack of widely accessible labelled dataset to be used for anomaly detection.
- As normal characteristics are frequently evolving and may not be normal, existing anomaly detection techniques may not be practical in the prospect [8]. A need for novel and more sophisticated techniques has been increased since the impostors are alert of the general techniques.

Classification of Anomaly Detection Techniques

Figure 6 illustrates the taxonomy of anomaly detection techniques. The detection of anomalies includes:

- Classification-based techniques
- Statistical-based techniques
- Clustering-based techniques
- Information theory techniques

Figure 6. Taxonomy of Anomaly Detection Techniques

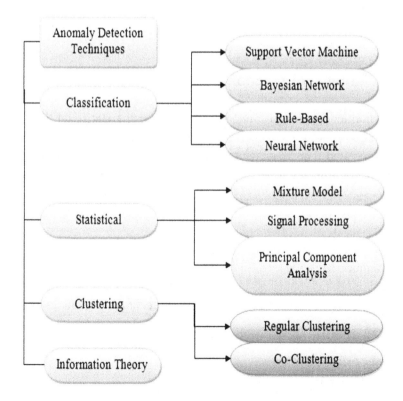

Classification-based Anomaly Detection

These techniques rely on expert's general information of the network attacks behaviours. When a network expert provides characteristics information to the detection system, an attack with a known pattern is identified as soon as it is established. This is only dependent on the attack's signature as a system which is able to detect an attack solely if its signature has been provided prior by a network expert. This concludes a system which can identify only what it knows is susceptible to new attacks which are always emerging in different versions and more surreptitiously established. Even if a novel attack's signature is generated and incorporated in the system, the primary loss is unique and the restore process is particularly high-priced.

Classification-based techniques rely on the normal traffic activities that construct the knowledge base and consider the activities diverge from baseline characteristics as anomalous. The benefit lies in their ability to identify the attacks which are fully new, considering that they reveal sufficient divergences from the normal characteristics. Also, when normal attack not incorporated in the knowledge base is assumed as an attack, there will be unintentional false alarms. As a result, training is needed for anomaly detection techniques for constructing normal activity characteristics which are time-consuming and also depends on the availability of fully normal traffic database. Besides, it is very complex for maintaining a normal characteristic up-to-date due to modern dynamic network atmospheres (A. Meshram, 2017). Four major clustering-based techniques are:

- Support Vector Machine (SVM)
- Bayesian Network
- Neural Network
- Rule-Based

Statistical-Based Anomaly Detection

Some anomaly detection techniques have been designed by using statistical theories. For instance, a chi-square theory is used for detecting an anomaly. Based on this technique, a profile of normal events in a given system is generated. The fundamental concept of this technique is detecting a large departure of events from a normal as anomalous and intrusions. The anomaly is detected based on the following three major features:

- Type of request
- Length of request
- Payload distribution

Three main types of statistical-based anomaly detection techniques include:

- Mixture Model
- Signal processing technique
- Principal Component Analysis (PCA)

Information-theory-based Anomaly Detection

Information-theoretic measures such as entropy, conditional entropy, relative entropy, information gain and information cost are also used for detecting anomalies by describing the characteristics of a given dataset. According to these measures, suitable anomaly detection models have been constructed. Supervised anomaly detection techniques need a training dataset followed by test data for evaluating the accuracy of a model. In this case, information-theoretic measures are initially used for computing whether a model is suitable for testing the new dataset.

Clustering-based Anomaly Detection

Typically, clustering is an unsupervised learning algorithm that does not need pre-labelled data for extracting the rules to combine similar information. This technique is mainly classified as regular and co-clustering. The major difference between these two clustering is the processing of rows and columns. Regular clustering technique such as k-means is used to cluster the data considering the rows of the dataset whereas the co-clustering considers both rows and columns of the dataset simultaneously for creating clusters (Ahmed, 2014a). The following three key statements are prepared while clustering-based techniques are used for detecting anomalies:

- **Statement 1:** Since clusters of only normal data are created, some following new data that do not robust with existing clusters of normal data are considered as anomalies. For instance, noise is considered as anomalous as density-based clustering algorithms do not contain noise inside the clusters.
- **Statement 2:** While a cluster has both normal and anomalous information, it has been discovered that the normal information lies near to the closest clusters centroid, but anomalies are far away from the centroids. Under this statement, anomalous events are identified by using a distance score.
- **Statement 3:** In a clustering with clusters of different sizes, a smaller and sparser may be considered as anomalous whereas a thicker is normal. Instances belonging to the clusters of sizes or densities below than a threshold are considered as anomalous.

Two main types of clustering-based anomaly detection techniques follow:

- **Regular Clustering:** This is the simplest technique to detect anomalous information. Mostly, k-means clustering is used for generating the normal and anomalous clusters. After generating the clusters, these are analyzed by using the above-mentioned statements. In Syarif et al. [21], different clustering algorithms were investigated while they have been applied for detecting anomalies through the network.
- **Co-clustering:** It is used to generate the clusters of both rows and columns simultaneously. Initially, a clustering criterion is defined and then it is optimized. It simultaneously discovers the subsets of rows and columns of a data matrix by using a particular criterion. The advantages of this technique over regular clustering are the following:
  - The simultaneous combination of both rows and columns may provide a more compressed representation and it maintains information enclosed in the original data.

- ○ It may be assumed as a dimensionality reduction technique and it is most suitable to create novel features.
- A considerable reduction in computational complexity. Such as, k-means clustering algorithm has a computational complexity as $O(mnk)$ where m is the number of rows, n is the number of columns and k refers to the number of clusters. However, the co-clustering algorithm has a computational complexity as $O(mkl + nkl)$ wherein l refers to the number of column clusters.

The comparison of these techniques shown in Table 1 is evaluated based on the following criteria:

- Computational complexity: Linear, quadratic and exceptional
- Preference of attack detection: DoS, Probe, R2U and U2R
- Output: Label and score

From this comparison in Table 1, the anomaly detection techniques which only have the labelled output are more efficient than the score-based outputs. In this analysis, clustering and information theory-based techniques are improved than the classification and statistical-based techniques. When the priority of attack detection is concerned, the classification and clustering-based techniques are more involved in identifying the DoS attacks. The reasons behind why clustering and classification-based techniques have the quadratic complexity are:

- Clustering techniques have need of pair wise distance computation.
- Classification techniques require quadratic optimization for separating two or more classes.

The information theory based techniques have exponential complexity due to the computation of the measurements such as entropy, relative uncertainty, etc. As well, these techniques require dual optimization to minimize the subset size and simultaneously reduce the complexity in the dataset. From this analysis, it is concluded that these techniques cannot be applied to data streams which are evolving and need to be mined in a single iteration. Above all, these anomaly detection techniques are used for monitoring a single system or network by carrying out local analysis for attacks. Hybrid techniques based on big data analytics are very essential which consist of different sensors for collecting data.

Table 1. Comparison of Anomaly Detection Techniques

Technique	Output	Attack Priority	Complexity
Classification-based	Label, score	DoS	Quadratic
Statistical-based	Label, score	R2U, U2R	Linear
Clustering-based	Label	DoS	Quadratic
Information Theory-based	Label	Neutral	Exponential

BIG DATA ANALYTICS

The term Big Data is characterized for the informational collections that are extremely expansive or complex that customary informational index handling application programming is deficient or can't manage these intricate or substantial informational indexes. The significant contrast between custom and huge information is as far as volume, velocity, and variation. For better understanding, these are outlined as in Figure 7.

Big Data analysis need to store efficient data and to query large data sets, thus the techniques which make complete data sets instead of sampling are focused. These implications are in areas like machine learning, deep learning etc.

Data Availability

Today data is generated and stored in various sectors. That data may be video, image, audio and text files. Data availability in different sectors are listed as follows,

- Banking
- Social Networks & Smart phones
- Communication & Media
- Legacy Documents

Figure 7. Five V's of Big Data

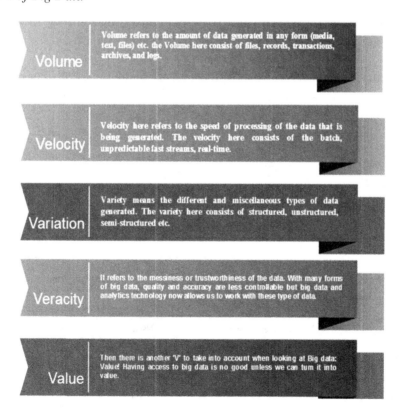

- Education
- Resource Industries

Security Analysis for Big Data

The security of Big Data has also become one of the most challenging factors. As the data sets are increasing dramatically the storage and analysis also increases and because of that security should be increased as an unauthorized person can also download the data of a particular person and can harm him. Different surveillance tools and trackers are used to track the attacker but as the data is increasing the security also should increased. Overall, collection, storage, analysis and usage of personal data are now part of our everyday life at all levels of security. A solution for this problem can be data hiding. In this, the data can be hiding in the form of a pattern which only the analyst can decode. These data sets should also not be recognizable by the data collector otherwise the data can be leaked to the unauthorized party. But it is a difficult for large number of data sets. Big Data Analytics in cyber security includes the capacity to accumulate a huge measure of computerized data to investigate, picture and draw knowledge that can make it conceivable to foresee and stop digital assaults. The focus is on learning the cyber attack patterns both known and unknown so that the data can be more authenticated and secure. Theft of information, disruption of services, and unauthorized disclosures are believed to be the most serious cyber security threats. To reduce these risks the detection of anomaly and different attacks are taken into concerned. The big data sources are to be taken into considerations so that the security analysis can be more secure. Table 2 shows the sources of big data.

The focus is on learning the cyber attack patterns both known and unknown so that the data can be more authenticated and secure. Some examples of how to make big data secure are given as follows which can increase the efficiency of data. These are used for detecting and analyzing abnormal patterns related to server manipulations.

- **Network Traffic**: Detecting and analyzing the network traffic for the suspicious sources and destinations and unauthorized accesses of third party users with abnormal traffic patterns.

Table 2. Big data sources for security analysis

S.NO	Types of Data	Data sources
1	System-Based Data	IP Locations, Keyboard typing/Mouse click stream patterns etc
2	Mobile-Based Data	GPS Locations, Network Locations etc
3	Travel Data	Travel patterns, Sources, Destinations etc
4	Credential Data	User name & Password
5	OTP	One Time Passwords which are used for online access
6	Digital Certificates	Used for the authentication
7	Biometric Identification Data	Fingerprints, Iris, Speech Recognitions
8	Social Media Data	Face book, Google Drive, Twitter etc
9	Human Resource data	Organizational role and privilege of the user.

- **Network Sources**: Detecting and predicting abnormal user patterns from the sources the data is transmitting.
- **User Credentials**: Detecting anomalies with respect to a user, or a group of users of their transmission or access time.
- **Network Servers**: A Network Server is a computer system which is used as a central repository or data and various programs that are shared within a network.

Big Data Analytics Layers

Big data analytics has the following four layers for superior performance,

- **Data Layer:** This layer has RDBMS based structured data, Semi-structured and unstructured based data. NoSQL databases are used to store the unstructured data. For instance, MongoDB and Cassandra are the NoSQL databases. Streaming data from the web world, social media domain, data from IoT sensors and operational systems are the examples to unstructured and semi-structured data. Software tools such as HBase, Hive, HBase, Spark and Storm are also sitting at this layer. Hadoop and Map Reduce also support this layer.
- **Analytics Layer:** Analytics layer has the environment to implement the dynamic data analytics and deploy the real time values. It has building models developing environment and modify the local data in regular interval. This also improves the performance of the analytical engine.
- **Integration Layer:** This layer integrates the end user applications and analytical engine. This includes usually a rules engine and an API for dynamic data analytics.
- **Decision Layer:** This layer is where the end product hits the market. It includes applications of end user such as mobile app, desktop applications, interactive web applications and business intelligence software. This is the layer where people interact with the system. Each and every layer described above is associated with different sets of end users in real time and enables a crucial phase of real time data analytics implementation.

Types of Data Analytics Approaches

- **Descriptive Analytics**: Descriptive analytics can be said to be the starting stage of data processing which does a summarization of historical data to get out useful information.
- **Diagnostic Analytics**: Diagnostic analytics is type of advanced analytics which gets to the root of the notion why certain thing happened with techniques like drill down, data discovery etc.
- **Predictive Analytics:** This analytics procedure is used to determine or predict the future events on the basis of previous behaviors, by the techniques of data mining, modeling etc.
- **Prescriptive Analytics**: This analytics approach deals with finding of best course of action to take after certain situation. This in layman's terms is the remedy to take in consideration after certain situations.

Big Data Analytics Procedure

- **Collection of data from many sources:** In this step, the collection of data takes places from different sources. This collected data has variety of nature, some might be structured some might be unstructured. This collected data also needs to be stored for further processing.
- **Maintaining the data consistency**: In this step, the different nature data is taken and then pre-processing (the process of transforming raw data into understandable format) is done on it to make that data even. Different techniques of data pre-processing are shown in Table 3.
- **Perform Correlation**: In this process after the data is entered into the data warehouse the correlation and dependencies of one data set is checked with other data set to possibly find out that to which extent those sets fluctuate together.
- **Positive Correlation:** If the correlation between the data sets comes out to be positive then we can get the extent of those data sets decrease or increase in parallel i.e. they are directly proportional to each other.
- **Negative Correlation:** If the correlation between the data sets comes out to be negative then we can make out to the extent to which one data set increases as other decreases i.e. they are inversely proportional to each other.

The Role of Big Data Analytics in Cyber Security

In this modern era, cyber security has come into the big data analytics. The emergence of big data not only modifies the human lifestyle and effort, but also inherently modifies the research mode. Due to the rapid development of information technology, i.e., networking, the applications of big data have become an essential part in human's life. Conversely, as increasingly valuable information can be acquired, security issues fix huge awareness. The cyber security or network security has huge challenges due to the complexity of increased networks. Commonly, big data cannot be solved by conventional techniques in a specific time due to the complexity of network traffic and attack patterns; therefore novel techniques must be provided to deal with big data, namely machine learning and deep learning algorithms.

Generally, big data analytics can incorporate methods and techniques, hardware and software to gather, handle and analyze a large-scale structured and unstructured data in real-time. Nowadays, big data analytics provides a number of solutions in different ways and few of them are follows:

- It offers end-to-end visibility.
- It permits self-organization among network functions and entities.
- It allows evaluation of long-term dynamics of the network

Table 3. Data pre-processing

Data Cleaning	It is the process of filling out unavailable information, removing noise from data and deleting unwanted value.
Data Integration	Data is taken and put together with different representation to resolve the conflicts within the data sets.
Data Transformation	The data is normalized i.e. the redundancy from the data is removed and is generalized
Data Reduction	After the data is pre-processed it is then reduce so that it can be integrate into the data warehousing where the analytical process will take place on this data

- It constructs faster and proactive network.
- It facilitates energy efficient network functions.
- It enables a unified performance evaluation.

BIG DATA AND MACHINE LEARNING IN CYBER SECURITY

Machine learning algorithms can gather, analyze and process the information. In case of cyber security, these algorithms help for analyzing previous cyber-attacks efficiently and providing respective defence responses. Primarily, this approach enables an automated cyber defence system with a minimum-skilled cyber security power. When distributed by Google, 50-70% of emails on Gmail are spam. With the aid of these algorithms, Google makes it feasible to block those superfluous communications with the highest accuracy. Likewise, Apple takes benefit of these algorithms for protecting its user's private information and confidentiality [9].

With the use of machine learning algorithms, ADS can be automated and even deployed in real-time to detect malfunctions before any harm is achieved. For instance, a well-trained machine learning model will have the ability for detecting an abnormal traffic pattern on the network and removing these links as occurs. In addition to this, it also has the capability to detect the new samples of anomaly that may evade human generated signatures and maybe quarantine these samples before they may even execute. Also, a machine learning model trained on the common operating system of a given endpoint can able to detect when the endpoint itself is engaging in odd activities, maybe at the request of a malicious insider trying to thieve or destroy the susceptible information. Most of the machine learning algorithms in cyber security acts as warning or alerting system. They frequently require an individual in the loop for making the final decision with sufficient accuracy (Lee.B, 2018).

The rapid growth of internet usage includes a huge amount of data transmitting on the web or internet. It is not possible to analyze big data directly for individuals. The detection of events which have malicious activities becomes more challenging with increasing amount of data or traffic flow on the network. So, cyber security domain wants to strengthen their infrastructure by using machine learning algorithms. Therefore, combined these algorithms with big data analytics helps to increase the ability to perform previously impractical computations. Big data and machine learning are two modules which are balancing each other. Machine learning and data analytics will include significance to both government administrations and private organizations in supporting them battle cyber threats. Meanwhile, they must construct defense system that can tolerate more and more sophisticated cyber-attacks. Therefore, with increasing number of cyber-attacks from intruders, advances in big data and machine learning algorithms are more essential than ever. The classification of machine learning algorithms for cyber security applications is shown in following figure.

The advantages and disadvantages of using machine learning algorithms using big data for cyber security are summarized in Table 4.

ML and Big Data Analytics Methods for Cyber Security

This section describes a machine learning (ML) and big data analytics (BDA) methods for cyber security in support of anomaly detection. As cyber threats continue to evolve, combining BDA and ML capabilities as part of a more powerful approach to cyber security. Cyber assaults are expanding at a fast pace

Figure 8. Classification of machine Learning Algorithms for Cyber Security

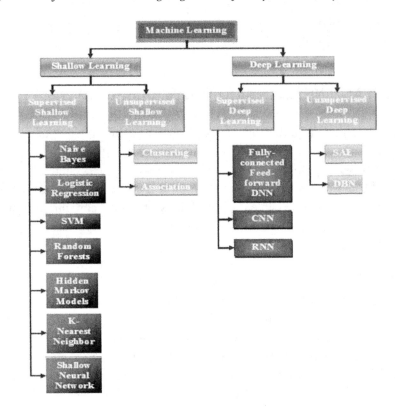

and are currently methodically focused towards defenceless nations. The developing number of online clients and their information is further compounding the circumstance (Alexandra L Heureux, 2017). What's more, there is an interconnection between advanced utilization and the clients in basic business parts, for example, keeping the money, which is offering ascend to cyber wrongdoings like never before previously.

Datasets

The cyber security data sets for BDA and ML are given below:

- Packet Level Data
- Net flow Data
- Public Data Sets

Packet Level Data

Protocols are used for transmission of packet through network. The network packets are transmitted and received at the physical interface.

- Packets are captured by API in computers called as pcap.

Table 4. Comparison of Machine Learning Algorithms with Big Data Analytics in Anomaly Detection.

Methods	Merits	Demerits
SVM	Insensitivity to input data dimension. High training rate and decision rate. Better learning ability for small data samples.	Inadequate to binary classifiers which cannot provide additional data about detected attack type. Longer training time.
DT	High detection accuracy. Operates better with large-scale datasets.	Computationally demanding to construct the trees.
LR	Linear models can be updated simply by means of new data. It is easy to understand and explain how decisions are made. It can be regularized for avoiding over fitting problem. More robust.	Its performance is poor when there are multiple or non-linear decision boundaries. Inflexible to obtain more complex patterns and high time consumption.
NB	It can integrate both prior knowledge and data. It can determine probabilistic relationships among the variables of interest.	It is not consider as a better classifier while the prior knowledge is inaccurate. Inflexible to manage continuous features.
RF	They can able to deal with unbalanced and missing data. Runtime is quite fast. Better performance on several problems including non-linear. Less computation cost for training process.	They may over-fit data that are specifically includes noise. No interpretability. Need to select the number of trees.
K-means	It is the most popular since its easiness. Flexible to pre-processed data and meaningful features.	The user should specify the number of clusters. It generates poor clusters if the true underlying clusters in the data are not spherical.

- For Linux it is Libpcap and for windows it is WinPCap.
- Ethernet port have payload called as IP payload

Major Steps in ML Net Flow Data

It is introduced as a router feature by Cisco. Version 5 defines unidirectional flow of packets.

- The packet attributes: ingress interface, source IP address, destination IP address, IP protocol, source port, destination port and type of services.
- Net flow includes compressed and preprocessed packets.

ML is a data analysis method that automates building of an analytical model using algorithms that learn from data which can be easily automated, and find insights in the data without being explicit programming as to where to look. Machine Language is a computer program that learns from experience with respect to some class of task and performance measure. ML has three phases such as training, validation, and testing. To decide which best model of the alternatives is, the selection should be based on the performance of the model against validation data and not on the accuracy on test data set. The following steps are performed:

- Identify the features from training data.

- Identify the subset of attributes necessary for classification.
- Learn model using training data.
- Use trained model to classify unknown data and predict result accurately.

ML/BDA Framework

In this system, the idea is to deploy a platform that aggregates and manages big data, and to combine this with a machine learning algorithm that analyzes this data to uncover hidden patterns and detect anomalies. As cyber security methodologies advance to ensure against programmers, programmers are growing progressively complex systems to sidestep these assurances. Utilizing machine figuring out how to computerize their assaults, programmers are making breaks increasingly more hard to identify. Malignant performing artists can utilize machine figuring out how to robotize the determination of the exploited people most defenceless against their dangers. They can likewise utilize machine figuring out how to discover feeble purposes of digital protection frameworks or to grow new advancements that sidestep security programming. Here, the fundamental element for machine learning is big data analytics. Machine learning analyzes this information to find patterns, correlations, and anomalies within the big data. It means processing massive amounts of security data and distilling it into something more readable for security teams (Hirak Kashyap, 2014). So, the simple detection of security events isn't useful unless it's understandable to human beings. When machine learning technology processes and organizes data, security teams are able to assess anomalies within the vast amount of data as in Figure 9.

BDA and ML are part of a single architecture, a powerful duo that together can protect against even the most complex anomalies. A solid cyber security stage requires inbuilt information the board stage that gathers and sorts out huge information, in the mix with machine learning calculations that examine this information, react to assaults, and counteract against new assaults. Without big data analytics and machine learning, it would be impossible for security professionals to gather and organize the heaps of security events and to interpret all potential attacks. While security experts will dependably have an imperative task to carry out in choosing the proper behaviour on these occasions, the job of machine learning is to distil the lot of information into data. Using machine learning for automate anomaly detection and response to produce quick and robust cyber defense system. There are three main types of ML/BDA approaches:

- Unsupervised
- Semi-supervised
- Supervised

Computational Complexity of ML and BDA Methods

Factors that determine performance of ML and BDA methods in cyber security are as below:

- Accuracy
- Time for training a model
- Time for classifying unknown
- Instance of trained model
- Readability of final solution

Figure 9. ML/BDA framework for anomaly detection in cyber security system

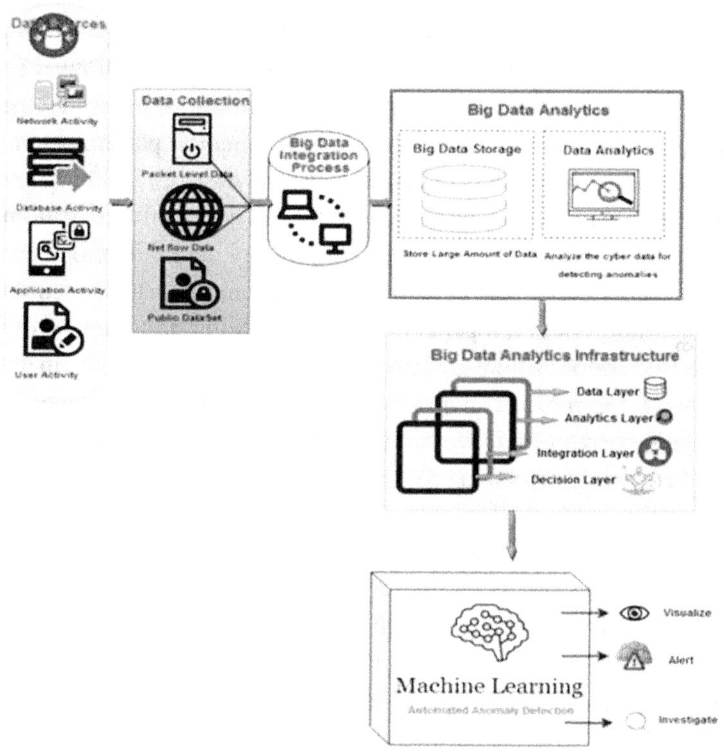

If one were to compare the accuracy of several ML/BDA methods, those methods should be trained on exactly the same training data and tested on exactly the same testing data. Unfortunately, even in the studies that used the same data set, when they compared their results with the best methods from the big data, they did so in an imperfect fashion. It used a subset of the big data set, but not necessarily the same subset that the other method used. So, the accuracy of these outcomes is not equivalent. The time for training a model is an important factor due to ever changing cyber-attack types and features. Indeed, even abnormality indicators should be prepared as often as possible, maybe gradually, with crisp anomaly signature refreshes.

Time for classifying a new instance is an important factor that reflects the reaction time and the packet processing power of the intrusion detection system. Understand ability or readability of the classification model is a means to help the administrators examine the model features easily in order to patch their systems more quickly. This information (such as packet type, port number, or some other high level network packet feature that reflects the cyber-attack footpath) will be available through the feature vectors that are tagged by the classifier as an anomaly category.

There are some peculiarities of the cyber problem that make ML and BDA methods more difficult to use. They are especially related to how often the model needs to be retrained. A fertile area of research would be to investigate the methods of fast incremental learning that could be used for daily updates of models for anomaly detection. In order to stay ahead, cyber defence systems need to deploy deep learning algorithms that are just as or even more powerful and complex.

BIG DATA AND DEEP LEARNING IN CYBER SECURITY

Large-scale organizations such as Google, Microsoft and Amazon are analyzing a huge amount of data for business analysis and decisions, forcing conventional and advanced technology. Likewise, social media organizations such as Facebook, Twitter and YouTube have billions of users that frequently generate an extremely high quality of data. Mining and extracting consequential patterns from huge input data for decision-making and prediction is at the core of big data analytics (C. L. Philip Chen, 2016). Big data analytics poses distinctive challenges for machine learning and data analysis including highly distributed input sources, noisy and poor quality data, high dimensionality data reduction, scalability, imbalanced input data, inadequate supervised/labeled data, unsupervised and uncategorized data, parallel and distributed computing, integration of heterogeneous data, innovating novel models for big data analysis, etc. As a result, big data and deep learning are two high-focus of cyber security in upcoming years. Deep learning algorithms known Deep Neural Network (DNN) can extract high-level and complex abstractions as data representations by means of a hierarchical learning process. Complex deliberations are scholarly at a given dimension dependent on to some degree simpler reflections detailed in the learning of tremendous measure of unsupervised information, making it a valuable device for big data analytics where raw data is mostly unlabeled and uncategorized.

Deep learning algorithms are one promising opportunity of research into an automated removal of complex data representations at high levels of abstraction. Such algorithms build a layered, hierarchical architecture of learning and representing data where higher-level features are defined in terms of lower-level features. The hierarchical learning architecture of deep learning algorithm is encouraged by artificial intelligence emulating the deep, layered learning process of the main sensorial regions of the neocortex in the human mind which naturally removes highlights and reflections from the basic information. Deep learning algorithms are relatively valuable for extracting the meaningful representations and patterns from big data while dealing with learning from huge number of unsupervised data and normally learn data representations in a greedy layer-wise manner (Anna L, 2016).

Once the hierarchical data abstractions are learnt from unsupervised data with deep learning, several traditional discriminative models can be trained with the help of comparatively smaller number of supervised or labeled data points where the labeled data is usually discovered via human or expert input. Mainly, deep learning algorithms have better performance to extract non-local and global relationships and patterns in the data compared to the shallow learning manner. When there are other helpful features of deep learning based representations of data, the most specific features of the learnt abstract representations by deep learning and big data analytics comprise:

- Comparatively uncomplicated linear models may perform efficiently with the knowledge attained from the more complex and more abstract data representations.
- Improved automation of data representation and extraction from unsupervised data may facilitate its broad application to different data types such as image, textual, audio, etc.
- Relational and semantic knowledge may be acquired at higher-levels of abstraction and representation of the raw data.

The advantages and disadvantages (Maryam M Najafabadi, 2015) of using deep learning algorithms using big data for cyber security are summarized in Table 5.

In the broader field of machine learning, the recent years have witnessed proliferation of deep neural networks, with unprecedented results across various application domains (Bilal Jan, 2017). Deep learning is subset of machine discovering that accomplishes great execution and adaptability by figuring out how to speak to the information as settled progression of ideas inside layers of neural system. Deep learning is the element of artificial neural networks and related machine learning algorithms that contain more than one hidden layer.

Deep learning is a piece of a more extensive group of machine learning strategies dependent on learning portrayals of information. One of the guarantees of profound learning is supplanting carefully assembled highlights with proficient calculations for unsupervised or semi-directed element learning and progressive element extraction. Profound learning beats the customary machine learning as the size of information increments as shown in Figure 10. In recent years, deep learning-based anomaly detection algorithms have become increasingly popular and have been applied for diverse set of tasks. Therefore, the following figure has shown that deep learning completely surpasses traditional methods.

Motivation for DL/BDA Anomaly Detection System in Cyber Security

Performance of traditional algorithms in detecting anomalies is sub-optimal on complex cyber security data sets. As the volume of dataset increases, it becomes nearly impossible for the traditional methods to scale such large scale data. Deep anomaly detection techniques learn hierarchical discriminative features from data. This automatic feature learning capability reduces the need of feature engineering process in machine leaning system. Therefore, this lack of well defined challenges is resolved by DL/ BDA algorithms in cyber security.

DL/BDA Framework

In order to protect legitimate users from anomaly, machine learning based efficient anomaly detection methods are developed. In the classical machine learning methods, the process of anomaly detection is usually divided into two stages: *feature extraction and classification/clustering*. The performance of

Table 5. Comparison of Deep Learning Algorithms with Big Data Analytics in Anomaly Detection.

Methods	Merits	Demerits
DBN	Supervised learning method with unlabelled data iteratively for significant feature or attribute representations	High computational cost due to extensive initialization process by huge number of parameter.
CNN	Robust supervised deep learning with high competitive performance Scalability is increased and the training time complexity is reduced with new features of CNN. Automatically learn features from security raw data	High computational cost. Challenge: Implementation on resource-constrained systems to support on-board security systems.
RNN	Better performance using sequential data	Key disadvantage: the problem of diminishing or exploding gradients.

Figure 10. Performance Comparisons of Deep learning Vs Traditional Algorithms

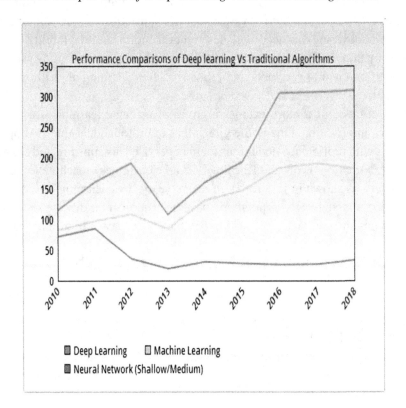

traditional detection approaches critically depend on the extracted features and the methods for classification/clustering. The challenge associated in anomaly detection problems is the sheer scale of data, for instance considering data as bytes a certain sequence classification problem could be of the order of two million time steps. Furthermore the anomaly is very adaptive in nature, wherein the attackers would use advanced techniques to hide the anomaly behavior. Deep learning techniques address these challenges effectively and detect anomaly in greater approach.

The substantial advances are made by deep learning methods then compared to many machine learning problems. In recent years a number of new deep learning based anomaly detection techniques with greatly reduced computational requirements have been developed. Based on training objectives employed and availability of labels, deep learning-based anomaly detection techniques can be categorized into supervised, unsupervised, hybrid, and one-class neural network. For each category of techniques are described as follows,

- Supervised deep anomaly detection
- Semi-supervised deep anomaly detection
- Unsupervised deep anomaly detection
- One class neural network (OC-NN).
- Hybrid Models

Deep learning procedures can be utilized to extricate the inconsistencies of digital security in enormous informational index effectively. Profound learning joins propel in figuring force and extraordinary sorts of neural systems to learn confounded examples in a lot of information [17]. Figure 11 shows the generalization of DL system with big data analytics model when applied in cyber security for anomaly detection.

Big data technologies help enhance cyber security by improving the maintenance, storage, and analysis of security data. Anomaly occurs in the cyber space. Big Data analytics grants positive aspects of handle and process the large amount of data in efficient way. In response, DL needs to reinvent itself for big data analytics.

Output of DL/BDA Techniques

A critical aspect for anomaly detection methods is the way in which the anomalies are identified. In general, the outputs produced by anomaly detection techniques classified as follows,

- **Anomaly Score:** Anomaly score describes the level of outliers for each data point. The data instances may be ranked according to anomalous score, and a domain specific threshold (commonly known as decision score) will be selected by subject matter expert to identify the anomalies.

Figure 11. DL/BDA framework for anomaly detection in cyber security system.

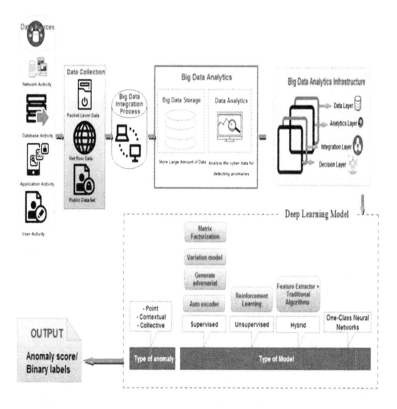

- **Binary Labels:** Instead of assigning scores, some techniques may assign a category label as normal or anomalous to each data in-stance. Unsupervised anomaly detection techniques using auto encoders measure the magnitude of residual vector (i,e reconstruction error) for obtaining anomaly scores, later on the reconstruction errors are either ranked or threshold by domain experts to label data instances.

ANOMALY DETECTION DATASETS AND ISSUES

Few openly available network traffic datasets for anomaly detection are mainly based on the modern operating systems and hardware. On the other hand, various researches committed to the improvement of benchmark anomaly detection evaluation datasets are presently being undertaken (Chen X-W, 2015). Some of the datasets are listed in below:

- PREDICT: Protected Repository for the Defence of Infrastructure against Cyber Threats (PREDICT) is a US-based commune of creators of security-relevant network functions data and consists of researchers of networking and data security. This dataset is useful for developers and evaluators by providing frequently updated network data related to the cyber-security research.
- CAIDA: It offers fundamental confined network traces, yet it is not labelled and requires multiple-attack scenarios (Ozlem Yavanoglu, 2017).
- Internet Traffic Archive: It is a repository to support common access to traces of network traffic and is supported by ACM SIGCOMM. Nonetheless, it undergoes from deep anonymization, re-quires the required packet information which is not labeled and has no multiple-attack scenarios (M. Bhuyan, 2014).
- DEFCON: It is entirely conflicting from real network traffic and consists mostly of anomaly traffic and commonly used for the alert correlation technique.
- ADFA Intrusion Detection Datasets: It encloses both Linux and Windows that are designed for the evaluation by a system call-based host-based ADS.
- NSL-KDD: It is a dataset suggested to solve few inherent issues of the KDD dataset stated in testing intrusion detection systems.
- KYOTO: It has traffic data from Kyoto University's Honeypots.
- ISCX 2012: It is designed by Information Security Centre of Excellence at University of New Brunswick. It includes seven days captured traffic with overall 2450324 flows with DoS attacks (Donghwoon Kwon, 2017).
- ICS Attack: Oak Ridge National Laboratories (ORNL) have generated three datasets which con-sist of measurements relevant to electronic transmission system normal, disturbance, control and cyber attack characteristics.

PERFORMANCE METRICS

Typically, the analysis of ADS performance using the various machine and deep learning algorithms with big data analytics is carried out based on the confusion matrix that defines the relationship between the actual data and predicted data of anomalies. During the detection process, each predicted data will belong to one of the four following possible outcomes that evaluate the accuracy of each algorithm:

- True Positive (TP) is actual positive data which are exactly detected as positives.
- True Negative (TN) is the actual negative data which are detected exactly as negatives.
- False Positive (FP) is known negative data which are wrongly predicted as positives.
- False Negative (FN) is known positive data which are wrongly predicted as negatives.

Likewise, the Receiver Operating Curve (ROC) also used for analyzing the efficiency of anomaly detection algorithms. Usually, ROC is the variation between accuracy on positive data and inaccuracy on negative data. As well, Area Under the Curve (AUC) performance differs between 0 and 1; the worst performance is indicated by 0 and the best performance is indicated by 1. The primary metrics used for anomaly detection are listed in Table 6.

The complexities of conventional anomaly detection techniques are addressed. To overcome such complexities, machine and deep learning with big data analytics to handle the numerous amounts of data while detecting the anomalies through the network. From Table 3 and 4, the advantages and disadvantages including their effectiveness of both machine and deep learning with big data analytics for cyber-security are discussed, respectively. It is concluded that big data deep learning algorithms achieve higher performance than the big data machine learning algorithms since these do not have the capability of solving the data imbalance issue due to high-dimensional large-scale datasets. As well, deep learning

Table 6. Primary Metrics for Anomaly Detection.

Metric	Formula
Accuracy	$\dfrac{TP + TN}{TP + FP + FN + TN}$
Recall/Sensitivity	$\dfrac{TP}{TP + FN}$
Specificity	$\dfrac{TN}{TN + FP}$
Precision	$\dfrac{TP}{TP + FP}$
F-measure	$2 \times \dfrac{Precision \times Recall}{Precision + Recall}$
G-Mean	$\sqrt{Sensitivity * Specificity}$
AUC	$\dfrac{1 + TP - FP}{2}$

algorithms simplify the big data analytics process by automatically extracting the complex data representations from numerous amounts of unsupervised and un-categorized raw data.

CONCLUSION AND FUTURE SCOPE

With the advancement of the Internet, attacks are changing quickly and the cyber security circumstance isn't hopeful. Since machine learning techniques can gradually achieve human-like learning, it is becoming tightly associated with big data analytics.

Datasets for cyber security are very important for training and testing systems. The ML and DL methods do not work without representative data, and obtaining such a dataset is difficult and time-consuming. However, there are many problems with the existing public dataset, such as uneven data, outdated content and the like. Big Data analytics has become the greatest assets in the current scenario to handling this kind of difficult task. It has powerful techniques to make large set of data retrieval, management and storage in a great way. Deep Learning is an area of Machine Learning which applies neuron like mathematical structures for learning tasks.

A great deal of attention has been given to machine learning over the past several years. Nowadays, new deep learning techniques are emerging with improved functionality. Many computer applications actively utilize such deep learning algorithms and report enhanced performance through them. In this chapter, we present an overview of machine and deep learning methodologies, including big data analytics relevant to anomaly detection in cyber security. From this analysis, Deep learning is discovered and proves the best technique with state-of-the-art performances.

In the future, the vision of cyber-security involves the technologies which may be implemented along with the advanced hybrid algorithms applied by the security experts. These suggest near-term detections based on novel innovations and a number of logical evolutionary patterns. Generally, this logical evolution is a bottom-up process wherein the features are detected across a specific application and then verified for synergistic impacts. Moreover, quantum computing will establish to increase the computing speed directly as twice as conventional computing speed. Further, dynamic networks will apply to support higher levels of automation, self-healing, reconfigurability and performance. More significantly, the new cyber-security experts will be trained to explain cross domain crises and problems. Novel tools will support them.

REFERENCES

Ahmed, M., & Mahmood, A. N. (2014). Clustering based semantic data summarization technique: a new approach. *2014 IEEE 9th Conference on Industrial Electronics and Applications (ICIEA),* 1780-1785. 10.1109/ICIEA.2014.6931456

Ahmed, M., & Mahmood, A. N. (2014a). Network traffic analysis based on collective anomaly detection. *2014 IEEE 9th Conference on Industrial electronics and applications (ICIEA),* 1141-1146. 10.1109/ICIEA.2014.6931337

Ahmed, M., & Mahmood, A. N. (2014b). Network traffic pattern analysis using improved information theoretic co-clustering based collective anomaly detection. In *International Conference on Security and Privacy in Communication Systems*, (pp. 204-219). Cham, Switzerland: Springer.

Ahmed, M., & Mahmood, A. N. (2015). Novel approach for network traffic pattern analysis using clustering-based collective anomaly detection. *Annals of Data Science, 2*(1), 111–130. doi:10.100740745-015-0035-y

Balabine, I., & Velednitsky, A. (2018). *Method and system for confident anomaly detection in computer traffic.* Google Patents.

Bhuyan, M., Bhattacharyya, D., & Kalita, J. (2014). Network anomaly detection: Methods, systems and tools. IEEE Commun. Surv. Tuts., 16(1), 303–336.

Buczak, A. L., & Guven, E. (2016). A Survey of Data Mining and Machine Learning Methods for Cyber Security Intrusion Detection. IEEE Communications Surveys & Tutorials, 18(2).

Chen, C. L. P. (2016). Big Data Challenges, Techniques, Technologies, and Applications and How Deep Learning can be Used. *Proceedings of IEEE 20th international conference on Computer supported cooperative work in design.*

Chen, X.-W., Lin, X. (2014). Big data deep learning: challenges and perspectives. *IEEE Access, 2,* 514–525.

Craigen, D., Diakun-Thibault, N., & Purse, R. (2014). Defining cyber security. *Technology Innovation Management Review, 4*(10).

Deljac, Ž., Randić, M., & Krčelić, G. (2015). Early detection of network element outages based on customer trouble calls. *Decision Support Systems, 73,* 57–73. doi:10.1016/j.dss.2015.02.014

Jan, B., Farman, H., Khan, M., Imran, M., Islam, I. U., Ahmad, A., … Jeon, G. (2017). Deep learning in big data Analytics: A comparative study. *Computers and Electrical Engineering.*

Najafabadi, M. M., Villanustre, F., Khoshgoftaar, T. M., Seliya, N., Wald, R., & Muharemagic, E. (2015). Deep learning applications and challenges in big data analytics *Journal of Big Data 2*(1), 1. doi:10.118640537-014-0007-7

Kashyap, H., Ahmed, H. A., Hoque, N., Roy, S., & Bhattacharyya, D. K. (2014). Big Data Analytics in Bioinformatics: A Machine Learning Perspective, *Journal of Latex Class Files, 13*(9). Retrieved from https://data-flair.training/blogs/deep-learning-vs-machine-learning/

Kwon, D., Kim, H., Kim, J., Suh, S. C., Kim, I., & Kim, K. J. (2017, September). A survey of deep learning-based network anomaly detection. *Cluster Computing,* 1–13.

L'heureux, A., Grolinger, K., Elyamany, H. F., & Capretz, M. M. (2017). Machine learning with big data: Challenges and approaches. (Vol. 5). IEEE.

Lee, B., Amaresh, S., Green, C., & Engels, D. (2018). Comparative Study of Deep Learning Models for Network Intrusion Detection. *SMU Data Science Review, 1*(1), 8.

Meshram, A., & Haas, C. (2017). *Anomaly detection in industrial networks using machine learning: a roadmap.* In *Machine Learning for Cyber Physical Systems.* Berlin, Germany: Springer. doi:10.1007/978-3-662-53806-7_8

Praveena, M. A., & Bharathi, B. (2017, February). A survey paper on big data analytics. In *2017 International Conference on Information Communication and Embedded Systems (ICICES)*(pp. 1-9). IEEE.

Sebestyen, G., & Hangan, A. (2017). Anomaly detection techniques in cyber-physical systems. *Acta Universitatis Sapientiae Informatica, 9*(2), 101–118.

Wang, J., & Paschalidis, I. C. (2017). Botnet detection based on anomaly and community detection. *IEEE Transactions on Control of Network Systems 4*(2), 392-404.

Yavanoglu, O., & Aydos, M. (2017). A review on cyber security datasets for machine learning algorithms. *IEEE International Conference on Big Data.* 10.1109/BigData.2017.8258167

Chapter 16
A Secure Protocol for High-Dimensional Big Data Providing Data Privacy

Anitha J.
Dayananda Sagar Academy of Technology and Management, India

Prasad S. P.
Dayananda Sagar Academy of Technology and Management, India

ABSTRACT

Due to recent technological development, a huge amount of data generated by social networking, sensor networks, internet, etc., adds more challenges when performing data storage and processing tasks. During PPDP, the collected data may contain sensitive information about the data owner. Directly releasing this for further processing may violate the privacy of the data owner, hence data modification is needed so that it does not disclose any personal information. The existing techniques of data anonymization have a fixed scheme with a small number of dimensions. There are various types of attacks on the privacy of data like linkage attack, homogeneity attack, and background knowledge attack. To provide an effective technique in big data to maintain data privacy and prevent linkage attacks, this paper proposes a privacy preserving protocol, UNION, for a multi-party data provider. Experiments show that this technique provides a better data utility to handle high dimensional data, and scalability with respect to the data size compared with existing anonymization techniques.

INTRODUCTION

The term big data is defined as a new generation of technologies and architectures, designed to economically extract value from very large volumes of a wide variety of data, by enabling high-velocity capture, discovery, and/or analysis. Based on this definition, the properties of big data are reflected as volume, velocity, variety, veracity and value. Volume refers to the amount of data generated. With the emergence of social networking, there is dramatic increase in the size of the data. The rate at which new data are generated is often characterized as velocity. A big data may contain text, audio, image, or video

DOI: 10.4018/978-1-5225-9611-0.ch016

etc. This diversity of data is denoted by variety. Veracity refers to the data that are generated uncertain in nature. It is hard to know which information is accurate and which is out of date. Finally the Value of data is valuable for society or not.

The life cycle of the big data has various phases like data generation, data storage and data processing. In data generation phase, large, diverse and complex data are generated by human and machine. Usually, the data generated is large, diverse and complex. Therefore, it is hard for traditional systems to handle them. The data generated are normally associated with a specific domain such as business, Internet, research, etc. Data storage phase refers to storing and managing large data sets. A data storage system consists of two parts namely hardware infrastructure and data management. Hardware infrastructure is utilizing information and communications technology (ICT) resources for various tasks. Data management refers to the set of software deployed on top of hardware infrastructure to manage and query large scale data sets. It should also provide several interfaces to interact with and analyze stored data. In data processing phase, various computations and transformations takes place on data set.

Data processing phase is the process of data collection, data transmission, pre-processing and data extraction. Data collection is needed because data may be coming from different diverse sources i.e., sites that contains text, images and videos. In data transmission phase, after collecting raw data from a specific data production environment, a high speed transmission mechanism to transmit data into a proper storage for various types of analytic applications. The pre-processing phase aims at removing meaningless and redundant parts of the data so that more storage space could be saved. Finally in data extraction phase only useful information are retrieved from data sets.

The excessive data and domain specific analytical methods are used by many application to derive meaningful information. Although different fields in data analytics require different data characteristics, few of these fields may leverage similar underlying technology to inspect, transform and model data to extract value from it. Emerging data analytics research can be classified into the following six technical areas: structured data analytics, text analytics, multimedia analytics, web analytics, network analytics, and mobile analytics (Xu et al., 2014).

Data generation can be classified into active data generation and passive data generation. Active data generation means that the data owner is willing to provide the data to a third party, while passive data generation refers to the situations that the data are generated by data owner's online activity (e.g., browsing) and the data owner may not even be aware of that the data are being collected by a third party. The major challenge for data owner is that how can he protect his data from any third party who may be willing to collect them. The data owner wants to hide his personal and sensitive information as much as possible and is concerned about how much control he could have over the information.

The data processing phase includes Privacy Preserving Data Publishing (PPDP). During PPDP, the collected data may contain sensitive information about the data owner. Directly releasing the information for further processing may violate the privacy of the data owner, hence data modification is needed in such a way that it does not disclose any personal information about the owner. On the other hand, the modified data should still be useful, not to violate the original purpose of data publishing. The privacy and utility of data are inversely related to each other. Intrusion Detection Scheme (IDS) schemes have been implemented in wired and semi-wired networks. These systems look for certain misbehavior patterns in the network which would give a whiff of a malicious act and thereby trigger attack mitigating mechanism. Many studies have been conducted to modify the data before publishing or storing them for further processing.

There are two different models of data publishing: the trusted and untrusted models. In case of trusted model, the data publisher is trustworthy and record owners are willing to provide their personal information to the data publisher; however, the trust is not transitive to the data recipient. Whereas in case of untrusted models, the data publisher is not trusted and may attempt to identify sensitive information from record owners.

The most basic form of PPDP the data holder which has a table of the form D(Explicit Identifier, Quasi Identifier, Sensitive Attributes, Non-Sensitive Attributes), where Explicit Identifier is a set of attributes, such as name and social security number (SSN), containing information that explicitly identifies record owners; Quasi Identifier is a set of The attributes that cannot uniquely identify a record by themselves but if linked with some external dataset may be able to re-identify the records. Sensitive Attributes consist of sensitive person-specific information such as disease, salary, and disability status; and Non-Sensitive Attributes are attributes which if disclosed will not violate the privacy of the user. All attributes other than identifier, quasi-identifier and sensitive attributes are classified as non-sensitive attributes.

The privacy protection of data can be defined as the access to the published data should not enable the attackers to know any extra information about any victim targeted even though having the background knowledge obtained from the other sources of information. According to Dwork, absolute privacy protection is highly impossible due to presence of background knowledge. Based on the concept of attacks on the data, the privacy protection models are categorized as two types. The first category considers that when an attacker is able to link a record owner to a record in a published data table, to a sensitive attribute in a published data table, or to the published data table itself. The attacks can be either through record linkage, attribute linkage, and table linkage. In all these linkage attacks, the attacker knows the quasi identifier of the victims. The second category considers that the published table should provide the attacker with little additional information beyond the background knowledge. If the attacker analyzes the variation between the prior and posterior beliefs, then it is probabilistic attack.

Anonymization is generally means as unknown i.e., it makes the objects indifferent from other objects. Anonymization of data refers to the Privacy Preserving Data Publishing approach that seeks to hide the identity and/or the sensitive data of record owners, assuming that sensitive data must be retained for data analysis. The data are anonymized by removing the identifiers and modifying the quasi-identifiers before publishing or storing for further processing. As a result of anonymization, identity of the data owner and sensitive values are hidden from the adversaries. How much data should be anonymized mainly depends on how much privacy need to preserve in that data. Before publishing, the original table is modified according to the specified privacy requirements.

The objectives of the proposed protocol can be stated as:

1. To provide an effective technique in big data to maintain data privacy i.e., no party is able to learn unnecessary information about other parties.
2. To introduce a new data processing protocol that is scalable with respect to high dimensional data.
3. To provide a new anonymization technique to prevent the data leakage while linking multiple data sets.
4. To impose high privacy protection.
5. To reduce the runtime regardless of the number of parties.

DATA ANONYMIZATION

Data anonymization is an information sanitization whose intent is to provide privacy protection. It is the process of either encrypting or removing personally identifiable information from data sets, so that the people whom the data describe remain anonymous. The data privacy technique, seeks to protect private or sensitive data by deleting or encrypting personally identifiable information from a database. Data anonymization is done for the purpose of protecting an individual's or companies private activities while maintaining the integrity of the data gathered and shared.

Data anonymization and encryption are related topics and are both useful techniques from privacy and security breaches, but they are not the same thing. Data anonymization is the process of transforming data so that it can be processed in a useful way, while preventing that data from being linked to individual identities of people, objects, or organizations. Encryption involves transforming data to render it unreadable to those who don't have the key to decrypt it. Encryption can be a useful tool for doing anonymization particularly when hiding identifying information in a set of data. However, encryption while useful is neither necessary nor sufficient for doing anonymization. Data can be successfully anonymized without encryption and encrypted data is not necessarily anonymized.

To preserve the privacy, one of the following anonymization operations is applied to the data.

- **Generalization**: Generalization works by replacing the value of specific QID attributes with less specific description. In this operation some values are replaced by a parent value in the taxonomy of an attribute. The types of generalization techniques include full domain generalization, sub tree generalization, multidimensional generalization, sibling generalization, and cell generalization. There are different types of generalization techniques which are often used by different researchers.
  - **Full Domain Generalization**: Full domain generalization is also known as global generalization. Full domain generalization generalizes all values in an attribute to the same level of the tree structure.
  - **Subtree Generalization**: Sub tree generalization generalizes either all child or none at any node other than leaf node.
  - **Sibling Generalization**: Sibling generalization follows similar generalization technique as Subtree generalization. The only difference between these two is that in Sibling generalization may leave some siblings ungeneralized.
  - **Local Generalization**: Local generalization is also known as cell generation. All of the above generalization techniques are examples of Global generalization to some extent. Local Generalization differs from Global generalization in such a way that in this generalization attribute values can be generalized to different levels.
- **Suppression**: In suppression, some values are replaced with a special character or symbols (e.g., ``*''), which indicates that a replaced value is not disclosed.
- **Anatomization**: Instead of modifying the quasi-identifier or sensitive attributes, anatomization works by de-associating the relationship between QID and SA. The data on QID and SA are released in two separate tables, one table contains quasi-identifier and the other table contains sensitive attributes. Both tables contain one common attribute which is often called GroupID.
- **Permutation**: In permutation, the relationship between quasi-identifier and numerically sensitive attribute is de-associated by partitioning a set of records into groups and shuffling their sensitive values within each group.

- **Perturbation**: In perturbation, the original data values are replaced by some synthetic data values, so that the statistical information computed from modified data does not differ significantly from the statistical information computed from the original data. Some examples include adding noise, swapping data, and generating synthetic data.

Data Anonymization Techniques

K-Anonymity

This model was developed because of the possibility of indirect identification of records from public database. This is because combinations of record attributes can be used to exactly identify individual records. A data set complies with K anonymity protection if each individual's record stored in the released table cannot be distinguished from at least K-1 individual records. Let Release Table RT have attributes of A1, A2…A be a table and QI, be the quasi identifier associated with it. The RT is said to be K-anonymity if and only if each sequence of values in the RT appears with at least K occurrences in RT [QI]. This method protects the data against identity disclosure.

Drawbacks of K-Anonymity:

- Unsorted matching attack against K-anonymity i.e., tuple position within the table reveals the sensitive attribute
- Complementary release attack against K-anonymity
- Temporal attack against K-anonymity
- Homogeneity attack
- Background Knowledge attack

L-Diversity

Information about an individual could not be published without revealing the sensitive attribute of the table. In case of K-anonymity, the data was not protected because of the homogeneity and background knowledge. L-diversity techniques describes that there are at least L- well represented values for the sensitive attribute would have the same frequency. The adversary needs (L-1) damaging pieces of background knowledge to eliminate (L-1) possible sensitive values and infer a positive disclosure. The advantages of this method are it no longer requires knowledge of full distribution of SA and NSA, it does not require the publisher to have as much information as the adversary has and removes the drawbacks of K anonymity.

Drawbacks of L-diversity:

- L-diversity may be difficulty and unnecessary to achieve it.
- L-diversity is insufficient to prevent attribute disclosure, skweness attack and similarity attack.

T-Closeness

It has been proposed to describe the distribution of sensitive attribute with equivalence class. An equivalence class is said to have t-closeness if the distance between the distribution of the sensitive attribute in the class and the distribution of the attributes in the whole table is no more than threshold t.

This technique is useful when it is important to keep the data as close as possible to the original one to that end, a further constraint is placed on the equivalence class, namely that not only at least l different values should exist within each equivalence class, but also that each value is represented as many times as necessary to mirror the initial distribution of each attribute.

Slicing

The generalization technique loses significant amount of information particularly for high dimensional data. The bucketization technique does not prevent membership. Slicing was a popular data anonymization technique which could be formalized by comparing with generalization and bucketization. In Slicing the data set is partition into both horizontally and vertically. The vertical partition is done by grouping attribute into columns contains a subset of attributes that are highly correlated. The horizontal partition is done by grouping tuples into buckets, within each bucket; the values in each column are randomly sorted to break the linkage between different columns. This technique provides the protection against membership disclosure attack.

Attacks on Different Privacy Models

For getting access to private data, attackers try to attack privacy models in various ways. Privacy models can be differentiated in two separate classes according to ways of attack on them. First category of models is consisting of Linkage attacks where attackers try to build up a link between data table of different records which are already published or sensitive data and owner of records. We can name them as record linkage, table linkage and attribute linkage respectively. Usually, in all of these attacks attacker knows the Quasi Identifier of the owner. In second category attackers have an intention to gain more information along with available Back ground knowledge in the published record. This can be classified as a probabilistic attack if the difference between attackers prior and post beliefs are found. Different types of attacks on privacy models are given below.

Record Linkage

In record linkage attackers try to match a value with values at a table and try to and out message or storage related to that value. This message is usually called group message. In this attack, there is a probability to identify a victims record perfectly with help of additional information or knowledge.

Attribute Linkage

Attack that is performed with help of linking an attribute of record is considered as Attribute linkage. Through this process, an attacker may not get all the records but he/she might get some sensitive information regarding Victims' associated group.

Table Linkage

In table linkage attackers are able to and out all types of information stored in a table related to the victim. Both record linkage and attribute linkage are combined in table linkage.

Probabilistic Linkage

This type of attack is not directly linked with the record, attribute or table of a record. Except these, probabilistic type attack mainly deals with attackers' belief on sensitive data of a record which is already published and analyzed by the attackers. This type of attack briefly can create a difference between prior belief and posterior beliefs of data to an attacker.

Threats to Privacy

Publishing a private data may suffer from different types of privacy threats. During the publishing of private data especially microdata the published data may suffer from following types of disclosure threats.

Membership Disclosure

Membership information can reveal the identity of an entity from the published data. Therefore, it is crucial to avert an attacker from knowing whether a particular persons' data is in the published table. This is more necessary especially when data is collected from a wide range of population based on some sensitive criteria. And this particular threat to published data is known as Membership disclosure.

Identity Disclosure

Another threat to published data is Identity disclosure. In practice, most of the time a single person is related to a particular record in the published data. If a persons identity is exposed then his corresponding private information will not be private anymore. Identity disclosure can be protected by protecting membership disclosure only when the membership information is unknown to the attacker. If the attacker is certain about the membership of an individual in a published record then protecting membership disclosure may not be applicable or it may be insufficient in protecting identity disclosure.

Attribute Disclosure

Another threat to published data is attribute disclosure. It may occur if the published data helps in exposing the value of a sensitive attribute of a particular person more than it would possible from the unpublished data. Attribute disclosure is closely related to identity disclosure and membership disclosure. If the identity of a person is exposed then the value of the sensitive attribute related to him/her is also exposed. However, exposing of an attribute value can happen whether the identity is exposed or not especially when the value of the sensitive attribute is identical in each of the matching records.

BACKGROUND

Latanya Sweeney (2002), "K-Anonymity: A Model For Protecting Privacy", in this paper a formal protection model named k-anonymity is introduced. A dataset complies with k-anonymity protection if each individual's record stored in the released dataset cannot be distinguished from at least k-1 individuals whose data also appears in the dataset. This protection guarantees that the probability of identifying an individual based on the released data in the dataset does not exceed 1/k. For every combination of QID values in anonymized table, there are atleast k records that share those values so that individual cannot be uniquely identified by linking records.

The term data refers to person-specific information that is conceptually organized as a table of rows (or records or tuple) and columns (or fields). *Quasi-identifier (QID)* is a set of features whose associated values may be useful for linking with another data set to re-identify the entity that is the subject of the data. While releasing private tables for research purpose identifiers are removed from the table to de-identify the person but still by matching quasi-identifiers from private table with public table one can easily identify the person. Therefore k-Anonymization is used to make at least k tuple similar by using generalization or suppression. Generalization is process of substituting attribute values with semantically consistent but less precise values. Suppression refers to removing a certain attribute value and replacing occurrences of the value with a special value "*", indicating that any value can be placed instead.

Even when sufficient care is taken to identify the QID, k-anonymity still is vulnerable to attacks. Some of the attacks are unsorted matching attack, complementary release attack and temporal attack. The attackers can be able discover the sensitive values if there is lack of diversity in storing the sensitive attributes. k-anonymity does not guarantee privacy against attacks using the background knowledge and it cannot prevent the attribute disclosure.

Machanavajjhala et al. (2007) "*l*-diversity: Privacy Beyond k- Anonymity", in this paper proposed a new techniques of anonymization which overcomes the drawbacks of k-anonymity like an attacker can discover the values of sensitive attribute and no guarantee of privacy against attackers using background knowledge. This proposes a technique called *l*-diversity in which an equivalence class is said to have *l*-diversity if there are atleast *l* – "well represented" values for the sensitive attributes. They gave a number of interpretations of the term "well-represented" in this principle:

1. **Distinct *l*-Diversity**: The simplest understanding of "well represented" would be to guarantee there are at any rate *l*- distinct values for the delicate trait in every equivalence class. An equivalence class may have one value seem significantly more frequently than different values, enabling a foe to conclude that an element in the equivalence class is likely to have that value.

2. **Entropy *l*-Diversity:** Entropy diversity degree can be defined as:

$$D(E) = -\sum S \in S\ p(E,s) \log p(E,s)$$

where $p(E, s)$ is the fraction of tuples in the equivalence class E with sensitive attribute level s.

A table is said to have entropy *l*-diversity if for each equivalence class E, Entropy(E) $\geq$ log l. Entropy l - diversity is solid than distinct *l*-diversity.

3. **Recursive** (c, *l*)**-Diversity:** Diversity degree of the table T can be defined as:

$$D(T) = \min(D(Ei))$$

where Ei denotes the i-th equivalence class which obtained by anonymizing T.

Recursive (c, *l*)-diversity makes beyond any doubt that the most continuous value does not show up too frequently, and the less regular values don't show up too rarely.

The important limitation of *l* -diversity are: a) *l* -diversity may be difficult and unnecessary to achieve.

4. **L-diversity** is insufficient to prevent attribute disclosure. The Attacks on *l* -diversity are Skweness Attack and Similarity Attack.

Yang Xu et al. (2014) "A Survey of PPDP Using Generalization & Suppression", in this paper k-anonymity has been proposed for privacy preservation data processing which prevent linkage attack by means of anonymization operation such as generalization and suppression. Generalization is that replacing specific value of quasi identifier with more general value. Suppression is the ultimate state of generalization operation which uses special symbolic character to replace its authentic value.

Girish Agarwal et al. (2013) "Privacy Preserving For High Dimensional Data Using Anonymization Techniques", in this paper introduced a data anonymization technique called slicing to improve the current state of art. Slicing partition the data set into vertically and horizontally. The vertical partitioning is done by grouping attributes into columns based on the correlations among the attributes. Each column contains a subset of attributes that are highly correlated. Horizontal partitioning is done by grouping tuples into buckets. Slicing preserves the utility because it groups highly correlated attributes together and preserves the correlations between such attributes.

Snehal M Nargundi and Rashmi Phalnikar, (2012) "K-Anonymization Using Multidimensional Suppression For Data De-Identification", in this paper a new approach which will make use of suppression based k-anonymization method to allow the data publisher to de-identify datasets and only certain attributes from record are suppressed based on values of other attributes. The main advantage of this approach is it does not require taxonomy tree for anonymization process.

Freny Presswala, Amit Thakkar, and Nirav Bhatt, (2015) "Survey On Anonymization In Privacy Preserving Data Mining", in this paper classification of privacy preservation data mining are discussed. The anonymization models like k-anonymity, *l*- diversity and t-closeness are discussed along with various limitations and attacks on each of them.

C. Gentry (2009) "A Fully Homomorphic Encryption Scheme'', a noval encryption scheme called Fully Homomorphic encryption is introduced. One way to protect the data is to encrypt the data and store them on cloud and allow the cloud to perform computations over encrypted data. Fully homomorphic encryption is the type of encryption which allows functions to be computed on encrypted data. Given only the encryption of a message, one can obtain an encryption of a function of that message by computing directly on the encryption. Homomorphic encryption provides full privacy but it comes at the cost of computational complexity and sometimes very hard to implement with existing technologies.

Today's globally networked society places great demands on the dissemination and sharing of information. While in the past released information was mostly in tabular and statistical form, many situations call for the release of specific data (microdata). In order to protect the anonymity of the entities (called respondents) to which information refers, data holders often remove or encrypt explicit identifiers such as names, addresses, and phone numbers. Un-identifying data, however, provides no guarantee of anonymity. Released information often contains other data, such as race, birth date, sex and ZIP code that can be linked to publicly available information to re-identify respondents and inferring information that was not intended for disclosure. It address the problem of releasing microdata while safeguarding the anonymity of respondents to which the data refer. The approach is based on the definition of k-anonymity. A table provides k-anonymity if attempts to link explicitly identifying information to its content map the information to at least k entities. We illustrate how k-anonymity can be provided without compromising the integrity of the information released by using generalization and suppression techniques. We introduce the concept of minimal generalization that captures the property of the release process not distorting the data more than needed to achieve k-anonymity, and present an algorithm for the computation of such a generalization. We also discuss possible preference policies to choose among different minimal generalizations.

PROPOSED SYSTEM

The data privacy in the era of big data is mainly reflected in digging data under the premise of not exposing sensitive information of the user. Existing privacy preserving techniques are focusing on anonymization of data which have a fixed scheme with a small number of dimensions. So there is a need of new anonymization technique for dealing with high dimensional data. There are various types of attacks on the privacy of data like linkage attack, homogeneity attack and background knowledge attack. The anonymization techniques like generalization has following issues: There is huge amount of information loss particularly for high dimensional data and there is a significant decrease in the data utility of the generalized data. The existing anonymization techniques are insufficient to prevent the attribute disclosure. So, there is a need of a privacy model to overcome the above mentions issues.

This paper presents a novel technique called UNION which concentrates on two major issues like data privacy and data utility in data publishing. As the data privacy concern increases, the utility of the data from the published data get decreases. Many authors concluded that data privacy and utility are inversely proportional to each other. This protocol helps for integrating the distributed person specific data while preserving both privacy and information utility. The main idea is to slice the given dataset vertically into set of columns and each column is distributed into multiple parties. Because of splitting the data set into vertical columns, it makes very easier to handle the high dimensional data. Splitting preserver's better data utility than the generalization.

Consider the Table 1 which has the raw data. This raw data is vertically sliced and distributed between three data providers P1, P2 and P3 which provide the data during integrating the data. These data providers own the different set of attributes about the same individuals and P2 owns the Class Attribute. The Figure 1 shows the data distribution among the various data providers.

Figure 1. Privacy preserving data distribution among data providers

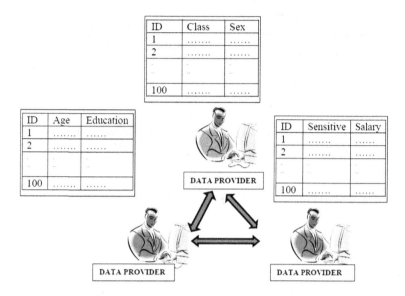

Table 1. Raw data owned by different data providers

UID	Data Provider P1		Data Provider P2		Data Provider P3	
	Age	**Education**	**Class**	**Sex**	**Sen**	**Salary**
1	54	11th	Yes	Male	S2	15K
2	27	Master	Yes	Female	S1	35K
3	39	7th	No	Male	S2	5K
4	67	Doctorate	No	Female	S1	95K
5	29	Bachelor	Yes	Male	S2	29K

The data being integrated is in the form of a relational table that is vertically partitioned into sub tables and each of which is owned by one separate data provider. Each party Pi owns a table which has UID, explicit identifier (EID), quasi identifier (QID), sensitive attribute (SA) and class which is a categorical target class attribute for classification analysis.

Now implement the anonymization technique of generalization to make the uniform distribution supposition that each value in a generalized interval is equally possible, as no additional distribution assumptions can be made. It contains generalizing the range which will substitute attribute value with more semantically consistent but minimum precise value. When using generalization, the original values are replaced by the more general ones of it. The Table 2 show the generalized data set values.

Table 2. Generalized data set values

UID	Data Provider P1		Data Provider P2		Data Provider P3	
	Age	Education	Class	Sex	Sen	Salary
1	1-99	Secondary	Yes	Any_Sex	S2	(10-70)K
2	1-99	University	Yes	Any_Sex	S1	(10-70)K
3	1-99	Secondary	No	Any_Sex	S2	(10-70)K
4	1-99	University	No	Any_Sex	S1	(70-100)K
5	1-99	University	Yes	Any_Sex	S2	(10-70)K

UNION: A SECURE PROTOCOL FOR HIGH DIMENSIONAL

Solution Overview

This paper introduces a protocol, named UNION, for integrating distributed person specific data among multiple parties while preserving both privacy and information utility on the final published integrated data. The main idea is to perform initially data anonymization by generalizing all raw data records to a topmost level of hierarchical general state value, and then performing a sequence of specializations to choose the specialization with the highest score to maintain the highest possible information utility. The specialization process will be carried until there is no new specialization score. Our solution consists of two main protocols:

Distributed Score Specialization (DSS)

Since Class attribute is only owned by one party, this protocol enables all parties to securely determine at each specialization step the best value for specialization.

Hierarchal Data Mashup (HDM)

This protocol presents a distributed hierarchical approach for integrating high dimensional data from multiple data providers, while preserving the data quality for the data mining tasks.

Multi Party Protocol for Distributed Score Specialization

In distributed environment, different *QID* attributes are owned by different parties and the *Class* attribute is owned by only one party. The secure protocol compute the scores and determine the best specialisation while ensuring no extra information is leaked to the parties. Protocol 1 in Table 3 explains how the data providers can securely determine the winner candidate for specialization. A table *T* is constructed from the leaf partitions of the specialization tree. Let *Pc,* the party that owns the *Class* attribute, can be independently computed its score of valid specialization values. On the other hand, other party that has a

Table 3. DSS algorithm

Distributed Specialization Score (DSS)
Let Pcls be the party that owns the Class attribute. We assume that each party already received from Pcls the class values encrypted under the data providers's distributed public key: 1. Following Construction 6.1, Pcls directly computes the score for each valid specialization of every attribute in ∪QID it owns. 2. For each valid specialization v → child(v) of every attribute in ∪QID owned by Pk:$1 \leq k \leq p$ (except Pcls), Pk does the following: (a) Choose a party randomly and then together execute to compute E(T [v]). (b) For each c ∈ child(v), it randomly chooses another party and then together execute to compute E(T [c]). (c) Homomorphically compute the score of specialization over v. (d) Request one of the parties to partially decrypt Score(v), and then uses its own share of the secret key to fully decrypt the ciphertext and obtain Score(v). 3. All parties engage in a secure circuit evaluation process to determine which party has the specialization value with the highest score.

valid specialization value must utilize the other parties to achieve that. The perception is to get different parties to compute different parts of the each score, and then the party owning the specialization value put together for computing the total score. The idea is for party Pi to blind the class ciphertexts using a random number, decrypt it using its secret decryption key, and then send them to party Pj who in turn decrypts, counts the equivalent classes, and then calculates the entropy.

Using the same random number to blind each class ciphertext, ensures the decrypted data is protected but the other party can still count and compute the entropy. We assume that at the beginning of the protocol, all parties agreed on a parameter d for converting decimal values to integers to be able to encrypt them. Observe that in Equation S, we needed to multiply by modules values of 10 to convert it to an integer while maintaining the scale between all computed scores.

To prove that privacy is preserving, we can show that the data is protected throughout the protocol execution. While encrypted, all ciphertexts are exchanged between the parties are protected under the CPA-security scheme. The attacker cannot decrypt items, as the decryption key is (2, n) shared between all data owners, requiring a collusion with another party, which contradicts our non-colluding semi-honest adversarial model. While Decrypting data, the party Pj receives a set of class attribute ciphertexts from party Pi in order to decrypt received one and to compute the entropy. Decrypting the ciphertexts makes the party Pj to count the equivalent class values. However, since the decrypted data is blinded with a random number, Pj cannot determine the exact class values of the data due to the the hardness of computing discrete logarithms. However, using different exponential random numbers for blinding the different set of class values prevents the party Pj from comparing two different set of blinded class values it has received from two separate requests. Leaking of the partial information about a score to each assisting party, since entropies are computed by assisting parties in clear text. We assume that this leakage of information is tolerable and very neglible since assisting party Pj can determine neither to which attribute the computed entropy belongs, nor what the underlying class values are.

Multi Party Protocol for Hierarchal Data Mashup (HDM).

Given the distributed data splitted tables Tl, ..., Tp , the taxonomy trees of generalized values of for *uQID,* thresholds values and constant C, the goal is to generate an integrated and anonymous data for data mining. To ensure that no party learns unnecessary and unkown extra information about other parties' data during the mashup process, we propose a hierarchal approach for specializing the data called Hierarchal Data Mashup (HDM).

The general idea of this approach is to initially generalize all the QID of the data sets using data anonymization technique and assign all records to go under the splitting process to partition, and then apply a topdown specialization process obtained from the taxonomy trees to specialize the records and assign then to disjoint child partitions until no further partitions can be created. The partition si a data structure which has two components like Hierarchical Cut and the Unique record identifer UID for partioned records. The Table 4 explains the algorithm for HDM:

The records R can be assigned to a partition *Pt* if for each attribute *A* belongs to the UID of the record. Assume that R.A can be generalized to *Pt.HCut.A,* where *R.A* and *Part.HCut.A* are the values in R and *Part.HCut* that correspond to attribute *A,* respectively. To determine which valid value to specialize on, all parties jointly run this Protocol. In general, a specialization involves generating a child partition for each child value in *child(v).* The cut of a taxonomy tree to which *v* belongs is pushed downwards, and *v* is replaced in the hierarchy cuts of the newly generated partitions by its children values *child(v).* The party that owns the winner value preforms the actual specialization. A specialization is said to be valid if after the child partitions are created, each leaf partitions as a whole in the partitioning tree still satisfies privacy constraints. The specialization process completes when there are no more valid specialization is available. The integrated data from all the distributed one for the final release can be constructed from the hierarchy cut of the leaf partitions, where each hierarchy cut is duplicated for the number of times that the records are assigned to the partition. once a specialization on a value becomes *invalid,* further specializations on *child(v)* will always be invalid. This property significantly reduces the partitioning space, while guaranteeing that the output is suboptimal. The step by step procedure to implement this protocol is shown as in Figure 2: Overall Procedure of the Protocol.

EXPERIMENTAL RESULTS

Experiments were carried out on adult data set taken from UC Irvine Machine Learning Repository - UCI Machine Learning. The data set contains 48842 instances with 14 attributes both categorical and integer. The data contains sensitive and non-sensitive (quasi identifier) attributes. The data was cleansed and formatted and made into sets of 40000, 80000, 160000, 320000 and 640000 with random replication. The Comparison and Analysis of Anonymization Techniques for Preserving Privacy in Big Data 251

Table 4. HDM Algorithm

Input: Principle party Pi, assisting party Pj, potential specialization value x
Output: Encrypted entropy of T (x)
1.Pi chooses random integer r from Z∗, and then for each ciphertext cls ∈ T [x].Class, q
where T [v].Class denotes the set of ciphertexts from the encrypted Class attribute that corresponds to the group of records generalized to v, it performs the following:
(a)Blind cls by exponentiating in r: cls.r = clsr.
(b)Partially decrypt clsr using its own share of the secret key.
2.Pi sends the set of partially decrypted ciphertexts to Pj through a secure channel.
3.Using its own share of the secret key, Pj decrypts the set of ciphertexts and obtains a set of blinded class values.
4.Pj computes the entropy E(T [x]).
5.Pj computes the integer value E(T [x]) × 10^d, encrypts it using the distributed public

Figure 2. Overall procedure of the protocol

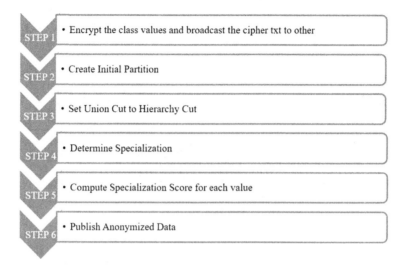

experiments are conducted on a machine with Intel ® Core TM i5-2120 CPU @ 3.30 GHZ, 4 GB RAM, Window 7, JAVA –JDK 8.0. The objective of the experiment is to find out performance metrics such as execution time, data utility and privacy of the various privacy preservation models applied to big data.

Execution Time

The execution time – the time taken by the algorithm to perform the task by various models with different data size. Rather than releasing an anonymous mashup data for classification analysis, each data provider could release a *classifier* of its data. To determine the usefulness of our approach with respect to classification analysis, author utilize C4.5 classifier to compare the classification error of the mashup data with the classification error of the classifier of each party. Authors used 30,160 records (213) to build (train) the classifiers, and 15,062 records (113) for testing. The classification error for each individual party, as well as for the mashup data. The classification error is measured with respect to the anonymity threshold K, where K linearly increases from 40 and 200. Authors approach is robust with respect to L, since it was found out that increasing the prior knowledge of the adversary does not impact the data quality. The classification error for *P1* is 17%, *P2* is 17.5% and *P3* is 18.4%. On the other hand, the mashup classification error decreases from 18.8% to 16.3% as K increases from 40 to 200. Except when $K = 40$, we observe that all data providers benefits from participating in mashup process, where the maximum benefit is as much as 2.1% and the minimum benefit is as low as 0.6%.

Scalability

Authors measure the scalability of Union with respect to the number of attributes and the number of records in three distributed settings: 3 parties, 4 parties and 5 parties.

Attribute Scalability: The runtime from 3 to 13 attributes, for $L = 3$, $K = 40$, $C = 100\%$ and 45,222 records. It was observed that the runtime grows sublinearly when the number of attributes linearly in-

Figure 3. Execution time

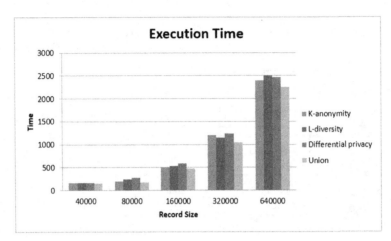

creases, regardless of the number of parties in the setting. We also observe that runtime decreases as the number of parties increases, due to the load reduction on each individual party.

Record Scalability: The runtime from 200,000 to 1,000,000, for $L = 3$, $K = 40$, $C = 100\%$ and 13 attributes. We observe that it takes up to 195 minutes to run union on a dataset with 1,000,000 records in a 3-party setting. This is mainly due to the fact that we perform a modular exponentiation operation every time a cipher text is blinded in Sub Protocol. However, it was also observed that the runtime is still scalable with respect to the linear increase in the number of records, regardless of the number of parties in the setting. The runtime decreases as the number of parties increases. The Figure 3: Execution Time shows the comparison of the execution time of different algorithms taken to execute based on the number of records.

Data Utility and Complexity

Data utility is measured by the accuracy of the queries MIN, MAX, COUNT on the original data and the transformed data after applying the privacy preserving techniques as shown in the Table 5.

Table 5. Data utility and complexity of data models

Sl. No	Models	Data Utility	Complexity
1	k-anonymity	Low	Very Low
2	l-diversity	High	Low
3	t-closeness	High	Very high
4	Differential privacy	Medium	High
5	Slicing	Medium	High

CONCLUSION AND FURTHER WORK

In this paper, we present a secure protocol for data integration in a distributed setting. The protocol is privacy preserving, while the output is a mash up data for data mining. We empirically show that the mash up data contains higher information utility, and that the protocol is scalable with respect to the number of records as well as the number of attributes in the mash up data. For future work, we plan to address the privacy-preserving data mash up problem in a malicious adversarial model with public verifiability.

REFERENCES

Agarwal, G., & Patil, P. (2013, June). Privacy preserving for high dimensional data using anonymization techniques. *Int. Journal of Advanced Research in CS.*

Benjamin, C. M., Fung, M., Wang, K., Chen, R., & Yu, P. S. (2010). Privacy-preserving data publishing: A survey of recent developments. *ACM Comput. Surv.*, 42(4), 1-53.

Dagher, G. C., Iqbal, F., Arafati, M., & Fung, B. C. (2015, December). Fusion: Privacy preserving distributed protocol for high-dimensional data mashup. In *IEEE International Conference on Parallel and Distributed Systems* (pp. 760-769). IEEE.

Gantz, J., & Reinsel, D. (2011). Extracting Value from Chaos. *Proc. IDC IView.*

Gentry, C. (2009). *A Fully Homomorphic Encryption Scheme* (Ph.D. dissertation). Dept. Comput. Sci., Stanford Univ., Stanford, CA.

Machanavajjhala, A., Kifer, D., Gehrke, J., & Venkitasubramaniam, M. (2007). L-diversity: Privacy beyond k-anonymity. *TKDD, 1*(1).

Mehmood, A., Natgunanathan, I., Xiang, Y., Hua, G., & Guo, S. (2016). *Protection of big data privacy, Theoretical Foundations For Big Data Applications Opportunities.* Academic Press.

Nargundi, S. M, ., & Phalnikar, R. (2012). k-Anonymization using Multidimensional Suppression for Data De-identification. *International Journal of Computers and Applications, 975, 8887.*

Presswala, F., *Thakkar, A., & Bhatt, N.* (2015). *Survey on Anonymization in Privacy Preserving Data Mining. IJIERE.*

Sweeney, L. (2002). K-anonymity: A model for protecting privacy. *Int. J. Uncertainty, Fuzziness Knowl. Based Syst., 10*(5), 557-570.

Xu, Y., Ma, T., Tang, M., & Tian, W. (2014). A survey of privacy preservation data publishing using generalization and suppression. *Int. Journal Applied Mathematics & Information Sciences*, 1103-1116.

Chapter 17
A Review of Machine Learning Methods Applied for Handling Zero-Day Attacks in the Cloud Environment

Swathy Akshaya M.
Avinashilingam Institute for Home Science and Higher Education for Women, India

Padmavathi Ganapathi
Avinashilingam Institute for Home Science and Higher Education for Women, India

ABSTRACT

Cloud computing is an emerging technological paradigm that provides a flexible, scalable, and reliable infrastructure and services for organizations. Services of cloud computing is based on sharing; thus, it is open for attacker to attack on its security. The main thing that grabs the organizations to adapt the cloud computing technology is cost reduction through optimized and efficient computing, but there are various vulnerabilities and threats in cloud computing that affect its security. Providing security in such a system is a major concern as it uses public network to transmit data to a remote server. Therefore, the biggest problem of cloud computing system is its security. The objective of the chapter is to review Machine learning methods that are applied to handle zero-day attacks in a cloud environment.

INTRODUCTION

Cloud Computing (CC) is an international collection of hardware and software from thousands of computer network. It permits digital information to be shared and distributed at very less cost and very fast to use. Cloud Computing has become popular in organizations and individual users. Cloud Computing is the foremost technology which has been emerging in all fields of network applications.

Cloud Computing and web services run on a network structure and they are open to network type attacks. Security issues such as data loss, phishing and botnet pose serious threats to organization's data and software. It has become a serious challenge to contain security threats and vulnerabilities. Of all

DOI: 10.4018/978-1-5225-9611-0.ch017

the security threats Zero-Day attacks are the most vulnerable and complex one. Zero-Day Attack (ZDA) could not be easily detected. Zero-Day attack may be from outside or inside. Managing Zero-Day attack is a challenging task.

Cyber Security Ventures recently predicted that there will be one new zero-day exploit per day by 2021. Zero-day attacks are purposively created and developed by many companies and they are sold for profits. For instance, Trend Micro and Zerodium offer up to $500,000 for zero-day attacks.

The number of zero-day exploits detected keeps increasing at an alarming rate. The well-known WannaCry Ransomware attack that hit the majority of the world in May 2017 is an example of the worst-case scenario that could happen due to a Zero-day attack. Zero-Day attacks are difficult to detect as they are not known. Zero-Day attacks usually exploit vulnerabilities that unknown to public including network defenders.

Cloud Environment Attacks

Cloud Computing: A New Vector for Cyber Attacks - Cloud computing technology provides a shared pool of computing resources over the internet at any time for little to no cost. Using cloud computing, many individuals and businesses have already improved the efficiency of their operations while reducing IT costs (Ammar, Gupta, et.al, 2013). While cloud computing models are full of advantages compared to on-site models, they're still susceptible to both inside and outside attacks. Therefore, cloud developers need to take security measures to protect their users' sensitive data from cyber-attacks are shown in table. 1.

Attack Vectors for Cloud Computing

The main goals of cyber-attacks against cloud computing are getting access to user data and preventing access to cloud services. Both can cause serious harm to cloud users and shatter confidence in the security of cloud services. When arranging attacks in the cloud, hackers usually intrude into communications between cloud users and services or applications by:

- Exploiting vulnerabilities in cloud computing.
- Stealing users' credentials somewhere outside the cloud.
- Using prior legitimate access to the cloud after cracking a user's passwords.
- Acting as a malicious insider.

ATTACKS ON CLOUD

There are many ways to attack cloud computing services, and hackers are constantly working on developing more sophisticated ones. However, becoming aware of at least the most common will help cloud developers design more secure solutions. Here's a list of most common types of cyber-attacks performed against cloud users which are shown in figure 1.

Table 1. Cloud Computing Overview

Cloud computing	
Definition	• Delivery method for providing data and computing resources over the network on demand
Core Attributes	• On-demand service • Broad network access • Resource pooling • Rapid elasticity • Measured service
Use cases	• Software as a Service • Platform as a Service • Infrastructure as a Service
Advantages	• Cost saving compared to maintaining physical infrastructure or on-premise solutions • Availability and ease of use • Performance and stability • All updates and patches are applied automatically by the vendor
Disadvantages	• Privacy considerations – your data in the hands of another company • Security considerations – security of your data depends on another company • Availability considerations – cloud computing depends on internet access, virtualization can work without it • Potentially high costs – in some cases, cloud computing can be more expensive than virtualization
Summary	• Used to save costs on computing resources and infrastructure • Convenient subscription-based model, where vendor handles all the issues and client just uses service as needed

Figure 1 Cloud Attack Classifications

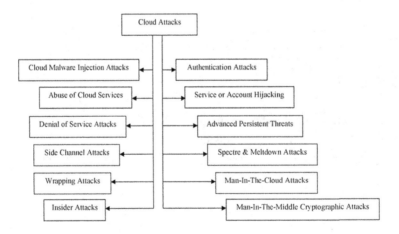

Cloud Malware Injection Attacks

Malware injection attacks are done to take control of a user's information in the cloud. For this purpose, hackers add an infected service implementation module to a SaaS or PaaS solution or a virtual machine instance to an IaaS solution. If the cloud system is successfully deceived, it will redirect the cloud user's requests to the hacker's module or instance, initiating the execution of malicious code. Then the attacker can begin their malicious activity such as manipulating or stealing data or eavesdropping. The most common forms of malware injection attacks are

Abuse of Cloud Services

Hackers can use cheap cloud services to arrange DoS and brute force attacks on target users, companies, and even other cloud providers. For instance, security experts Bryan and Anderson arranged a DoS attack by exploiting capacities of Amazon's EC2 cloud infrastructure in 2010. As a result, they managed to make their client unavailable on the internet by spending only $6 to rent virtual services.

Denial of Service Attacks

DoS attacks are designed to overload a system and make services unavailable to its users. These attacks are especially dangerous for cloud computing systems, as many users may suffer as the result of flooding even a single cloud server. In case of high workload, cloud systems begin to provide more computational power by involving more virtual machines and service instances. While trying to prevent a cyber-attack, the cloud system actually makes it more devastating. Finally, the cloud system slows down and legitimate users lose any availability to access their cloud services. In the cloud environment, DDoS attacks may be even more dangerous if hackers use more zombie machines to attack a large number of systems.

Side Channel Attacks

A side channel attack is arranged by hackers when they place a malicious virtual machine on the same host as the target virtual machine. During a side channel attack, hackers target system implementations of cryptographic algorithms. However, this type of threat can be avoided with a secure system design.

Wrapping Attacks

A wrapping attack is an example of a man-in-the-middle attack in the cloud environment. Cloud computing is vulnerable to wrapping attacks because cloud users typically connect to services via a web browser. An XML signature is used to protect users' credentials from unauthorized access, but this signature doesn't secure the positions in the document. Thus, XML signature element wrapping allows attackers to manipulate an XML document. For example, vulnerabilitywas found in the SOAP interface of Amazon Elastic Cloud Computing (EC2) in 2009. This weakness allowed attackers to modify an eavesdropped message as a result of a successful signature wrapping attack.

Man-In-The-Cloud Attacks

During this type of attack, hackers intercept and reconfigure cloud services by exploiting vulnerabilities in the synchronization token system so that during the next synchronization with the cloud, the synchronization token will be replaced with a new one that provides access to the attackers. Users may never know that their accounts have been hacked, as an attacker can put back the original synchronization tokens at any time. Moreover, there's a risk that compromised accounts will never be recovered.

Insider Attacks

An insider attack is initiated by a legitimate user who is purposefully violating the security policy. In a cloud environment, an attacker can be a cloud provider, administrator or an employee of a client company with extensive privileges. To prevent malicious activity of this type, cloud developers should design secure architectures with different levels of access to cloud services.

Account or Service Hijacking

Account or service hijacking is achieved after gaining access to a user's credentials. There are various techniques for achieving this, from fishing to spyware to cookie poisoning. Once a cloud account has been hacked, attackers can obtain a user's personal information or corporate data and compromise cloud computing services. For instance, an employee of Sales force, a SaaS vendor, became the victim of a phishing scam which led to the exposure of all of the company's client accounts in 2007.

Advanced Persistent Threats (APTs)

APTs are attacks that let hackers continuously steal sensitive data stored in the cloud or exploit cloud services without being noticed by legitimate users. The duration of these attacks allows hackers to adapt to security measures against them. Once unauthorized access is established, hackers can move through data center networks and use network traffic for their malicious activity.

Spectre and Meltdown Attacks

These two types of cyber-attacks have already become a new threat to cloud computing. With the help of malicious JavaScript code, adversaries can read encrypted data from memory by exploiting a design weakness in most modern processors. Both, Spectre and Meltdown break the isolation between applications and the operating system, letting attackers read information from the kernel. This is a real headache for cloud developers, as not all cloud users install the latest security patches.

Authentication Attacks

Authentication is a weak point in cloud computing services which is frequently targeted by an attacker. Today most of the services still use simple username and password type of knowledge based authentication, but some exception are financial institutions which are using various forms of secondary authentication (such as shared secret questions, site keys, virtual keyboards, etc.) that make it more difficult for popular phishing attacks. Some authentication attacks are:

- **Brute Force Attacks**: In this type of attack, all possible combinations of password apply to break the password. The brute force attack is generally applied to crack the encrypted passwords where the passwords are saved in the form of encrypted text.
- **Dictionary Attack**: This type of Attack is relatively faster than brute force attack. Unlike checking all possibilities using brute force attack, the dictionary attack tries to match the password with most occurring words or words of daily life usage.

- **Shoulder Surfing:** Shoulder Surfing is an alternative name of "spying" in which the attackers pies the user's movements to get the password. In this type of attack the attacker observes the user; how he enters the password i.e. what keys of keyboard the user has pressed.
- **Replay Attacks:** The replay attacks are also known as the reflection attacks. It is a way to attack challenge response user authentication mechanism.
- **Phishing Attacks**: It is a web based attack in which the attacker redirects the user to the fake website to get passwords/ Pin Codes of the user.
- **Key Loggers**: The key loggers are the software program which monitors the user activities by recording each and every key pressed by the user.

Man-In-The-Middle Cryptographic Attacks

A man in the middle attack is one in which the attacker intercepts messages in a public key exchange and then retransmits them, substituting his own public key for the requested one, so that the two original parties still appear to be communicating with each other. In the process, the two original parties appear to communicate normally. The message sender does not recognize that the receiver is an unknown attacker trying to access or modify the message before retransmitting to the receiver. Thus, the attacker controls the entire communication. Some type of MIM attacks are:

- **Address Resolution Protocol Communication (ARP)**: In the normal ARP communication, the host PC will send a packet which has the source and destination IP address inside the packet and will broadcast it to all the devices connected to the network. The device which has the target IP address will only send the ARP reply with its MAC address in it and then communication takes place. The ARP protocol is not a secured protocol and the ARP cache doesn't have a foolproof mechanism which results in a big problem.
- **ARP Cache Poisoning**: In ARP cache poisoning, the attacker would be sniffing onto the network by controlling the network switch to monitor the network traffic and spoof the ARP packets between the host and the destination PC and perform the MIM attack.
- **DNS Spoofing**: The target, in this case, will be provided with fake information which would lead to loss of credentials. This is a kind of online MIM attack where the attacker has created a fake bank website, so when the user visits the bank website it will be redirected to the website created by the attacker and then the attacker will gain all the credentials.
- **Session Hijacking**: In this once the session is established between the host PC and the web server the attacker can obtain certain parts of the session establishment which is done by capturing the cookies that were used for the session establishment.

Countermeasures for Cloud Attacks

- As customers lose control over their data as soon as they move that to cloud, Customers must make sure that the data stored in cloud is encrypted and if possible should retain the keys with them only.

- Detect the side-channel attack during the placement phase only. This can be done by collecting logs for new machines starting and stopping and feed them to a SIEM solution. High number of new machines being spawned and shut down within a defined time interval could be an indicator of an attacker perform the co-residency check.
- Instead of simple username and password authentication check, multifactor authentication must be implemented.
- Hiring a CCSP (Certified Cloud Security Professional) to manage the cloud.
- Check for the integrity of data by implementing encryption /decryption for the data over wire.
- Implement Firewalls, IPS and other ACL filters at perimeter. Apply black holing and sink holing.
- Implement a combination of Virtual Firewall and Randomized Encryption/Decryption. Placement can be protected by enabling virtual firewalls at VM level which restricts traffic between VM and to protect against side-channel attack, implement randomized encryption and decryption thus making the process more complex to break.

Vulnerability - Key Cloud Computing Vulnerabilities

Cloud technology is still being actively developed, and thus it has much vulnerability that can be exploited by cybercriminals or malicious insiders (Sitalakshmi & Mamoun, 2018). The key cloud computing vulnerabilities that raise security concerns among cloud users are depicted in figure 2.

Figure 2 Cloud Vulnerabilities and Solutions

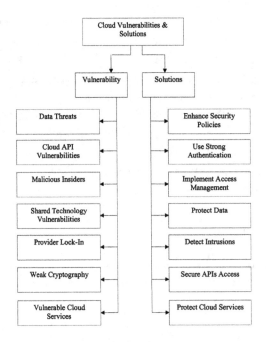

Cloud Vulnerabilities

Data Threats

Cloud users store various types of data in cloud environments, and a lot of that data contains sensitive information about users or business activities. However, this data is susceptible to loss, breach, or damage as the result of human actions, application vulnerabilities, and unforeseen emergencies. It's obvious that a cloud service provider can't prevent all data threats, but cloud developers should apply modern encryption algorithms to ensure the integrity of data in transit from the user to the cloud.

Cloud API vulnerabilities

Application programming interfaces (APIs) allow users to interact with cloud-based services. However, vulnerabilities in APIs may significantly impact the security of cloud orchestration, management, provisioning, and monitoring. Cloud developers need to implement strong controls over APIs.

Malicious Insiders

Legitimate cloud users who act maliciously have many ways to arrange attacks or leak data in cloud environments. This threat can be minimized by cloud developers, however, by implementing identity and access management (IAM) technologies.

Shared Technology Vulnerabilities

Cloud computing involves the use of shared technologies such as virtualization and cloud orchestration. Thus, by exploiting vulnerabilities in any part of these technologies, attackers can cause significant damage to many cloud users. Weaknesses in a hypervisor can allow hackers to gain control over virtual machines or even the host itself. In the case of a virtual machine escape, hackers can gain unrestricted access to the host through shared resources. So it's necessary to pay attention to the security of the cloud provider that entrust with cloud solution.

Provider Lock-In

Most modern cloud service providers make their clients dependent on their services with high switching costs. Many cloud users feel locked in when providers aren't able to provide all the services they need. Make sure that the solution has tools to help users easily migrate from other providers, such as the ability to import data in various formats.

Weak Cryptography

Though cloud providers use cryptographic algorithms to protect data in storage, they usually use limited sources of entropy (such as the time) to automatically generate random numbers for data encryption. For instance, Linux-based virtual machines generate random keys only from the exact millisecond. This may not be enough for strong data encryption; however, as attackers also use sophisticated decoding mechanisms to hack information. Cloud developers should think about how to secure data before it moves to the cloud.

Vulnerable Cloud Services

While cloud computing platforms are designed as distributed systems of cloud services, these services have little protection against each other. An attacker can exploit vulnerabilities in any one cloud service to gain unauthorized access to data of legitimate users. For instance, the OpenStack cloud platform had more than 150 known weaknesses in its cloud services in 2016. Creating a strong architecture can isolate a user's operations in the cloud.

To Ensure the Security of Cloud-Based Vulnerability Solutions

The dynamic nature of cloud services breaks the traditional security model used for on-site software. It's obvious that a cloud service provider is unable to ensure total security in the cloud. Part of the responsibility also lies with cloud users. While the best way to protect user data in the cloud is by providing a layered security approach, cloud service providers should implement industry best practices to ensure the utmost level of cloud security (Jordan & Mitchell, 2015). There are some seven key points on how cloud developers can ensure the security of their cloud-based vulnerability solutions.

Enhance Security Policies

By providing cloud services, software vendors should limit the scope of their responsibility for protecting user data and operations in the cloud in their security policies. Inform the clients about what to do to ensure cloud security as well as what security measures they need to take on their side.

Use Strong Authentication

Stealing passwords is the most common way to access users' data and services in the cloud. Thus, cloud developers should implement strong authentication and identity management. Establish multi-factor authentication. There are various tools that require both static passwords and dynamic passwords. The latter confirms a user's credentials by providing a one-time password on a mobile phone or using biometric schemes or hardware tokens.

Implement Access Management

To increase the security of services, cloud developers should let cloud users assign role-based permissions to different administrators so that users only have the capabilities assigned to them. Moreover, cloud orchestration should enable privileged users to establish the scope of other users' permissions according to their duties within the company.

Protect Data

Data in the cloud environment needs to be encrypted at all stages of its transfer and storage:

- At the source (on the user's side)
- In transit (during its transfer from the user to the cloud server)
- At rest (when stored in the cloud database)

Data needs to be encrypted even before it goes to the cloud. Modern data encryption and tokenization technologies are an effective defense against account hijacking. Moreover, it's important to prove end-to-end encryption for protecting data in transit against man-in-the-middle attacks. Using strong encryption algorithms that contain salt and hashes can effectively deflect cyber-attacks. Data stored in the cloud is also vulnerable to unintentional damage, so ensure its recovery by providing a data backup service.

Detect Intrusions

Provide cloud-based solution with a fully managed intrusion detection system that can detect and inform about the malicious use of cloud services by intruders. Use an intrusion detection system that provides network monitoring and notifies about the abnormal behavior of insiders.

Secure APIs Access

Cloud developers should be sure that clients can access the application only through secure APIs. This might require limiting the range of IP addresses or providing access only through corporate networks or VPNs. However, this approach can be difficult to implement for public-facing applications. Implement security protection via an API using special scripts, templates, and recipes.

Protect Cloud Services

Limiting access to cloud services is necessary to prevent attackers from gaining unauthorized access to a user's operations and data through weaknesses in cloud services. When designing cloud service architecture, minimize event handler permissions to only those necessary for executing specific operations. Moreover, restrict security decisions to only those cloud services that are trusted by users to manage their data security.

Zero-day Attack

Zero-day vulnerability is a computer-software vulnerability that is unknown to those who would be interested in mitigating the vulnerability. Until the vulnerability is mitigated, hackers can exploit it to adversely affect computer programs, data, additional computers or a network. The security infection in the software is susceptible to malware infection remains unknown and unfixed by the vendor which is further exploited by the malicious cyber criminals even before the vendor becomes aware of it (Louridas & Ebert, 2016). This type of exploit is called zero day attack which is further explained in figure 3.

Figure 3 Zero-day Terms

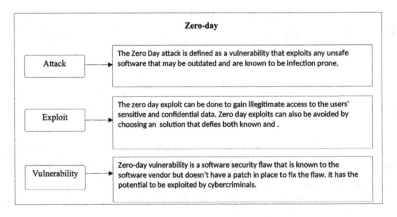

Terminology of Zero-Day

Zero-day attacks require extra security safeguards to ensure the framework; the customary protections are feeble against them.

- **Zero-day Vulnerability:** Zero-day vulnerability is one for which no fix is promptly accessible and seller could conceivably know. The nonattendance of a fix for multi day helplessness introduces a zero-day risk to sellers and clients.
- **Zero-day Exploit:** A zero-day exploit is a type with bit of programming, piece of information or arrangement of directions that exploits zero-day weakness.
- **Zero-day Attack:** A zero-day attack is one that abuses zero-day helplessness.
- **Obfuscation:** Refers to procedures that safeguard the program's semantics and usefulness while, in the meantime, make it harder to comprehend or peruse the program's structure.
- **Packing:** In packing, malignant code is covered up by more than one layer of pressure or encryption.
- **Polymorphic worm:** A worm which changes its format with every contamination. The payload is scrambled and utilizes diverse key for every contamination.
- **Metamorphic worm:** A worm that makes semantically proportionate totally extraordinary variants of code at every instant.
- **Alarm:** An alarm created by finder proposing that a framework is or being assaulted.
- **True Positive**: Number of accurately distinguished noxious code.
- **False Positive:** Number of mistakenly distinguished amiable code as vindictive code. Finder creates caution when there is no real assault.
- **False Negative:** Number of inaccurately dismissed pernicious code. Finder neglects to recognize real assault and no caution are created while the framework is under assault.
- **Noise**: Data or impedance that can trigger a false positive.

Zero-Day Vulnerability Lifecycle

Amontip et. al. groups defenselessness life-cycle into five classifications and addresses different components, for example, accessibility of patches and endeavor code that add to the likelihood of Zero-day assault (Mamoun, Sitalakshmi, et. al, 2011). Figure 4 describes the lifecycle of zero-day.

- **Zero-Day Assault (ZDA)**: The defenselessness is found by a dark cap and isn't pitched. The dark cap works unobtrusively on an adventure code.
- **Pseudo Zero-Day Assault (PZDA)**: This is like ZDA, it results from mercy with respect to framework directors not having any significant bearing a specific fix despite the fact that the fix was discharged by merchant sometime prior.
- **Potential for Pseudo Zero-Day Assault (PPZDA)**: This is like PZDA. Notwithstanding, helplessness has not been assaulted, yet has a high probability of being misused in spite of the accessibility of a fix.
- **Potential for Assault (POA)**: Vulnerabilities and their subtleties are uncovered and computerized exploit code or projects are known. The merchants are not yet ready to create patches for wide conveyance and in this way, the defenselessness of this sort progress toward becoming ZDA after the flare-up of assault.
- **Latent**: In this, exploit codes have not yet been created or accessible.

Examples of Zero-Day

The following are the some examples of zero-day exploits.

2017 Zero-Day Exploits

- <u>CVE-2017-8759- SOAP WSDL Parser Code Injection</u> Recently detected a malicious Microsoft Office RTF document leveraging CVE-2017-8759, SOAP WSDL parser code injection vulnerability. This vulnerability allows a malicious actor to inject arbitrary code during the parsing of SOAP WSDL definition contents.
- <u>CVE-2017-0261- EPS "restore" Use-After-Free</u> Detected a "restore" use-after-free vulnerability in Encapsulated PostScript (EPS) of Microsoft Office- CVE-2017-0261- being used to deliver SHRIME malware from a group known as Turla, and NETWIRE malware from an unknown financially motivated actor.

Figure 4 Zero-Day Vulnerability Lifecycle

- **CVE-2017-0262-Type Confusion in EPS** Observed APT28 using a type confusion vulnerability in Encapsulated PostScript (EPS) of Microsoft Office-CVE-2017-0262- to deliver a GAMEFISH payload.

2016 Zero-Day Exploits

- **CVE-2016-4117 Flash Zero-Day Exploited in the Wild** Detected an attack exploiting a previously unknown vulnerability in Adobe Flash Player (CVE-2016-4117) and helped facilitate release of a patch just four days later.
- **CVE-2016-0167 Microsoft Windows Zero-Day Local Privilege Escalation** Identified more than 100 organizations in North America that fell victim to a campaign exploiting previously unknown elevation of privilege vulnerability (CVE-2016-0167) in Microsoft Windows.
- **CVE-2016-1019 Security Advisory for Adobe Flash Player** A critical vulnerability (CVE-2016-1019) exists in Adobe Flash Player 21.0.0.197 and earlier versions for Windows, Macintosh, Linux and Chrome OS. Successful exploitation could cause a crash and potentially allow an attacker to take control of the affected system.

2015 Zero-Day Exploits

- **Adobe Flash Zero-Day: CVE-2015-3113** APT3 threat group sent spear-phishing emails with links to compromised web servers.
- **CVE-2015-2424** Microsoft Office Zero-Day CVE-2015-2424 leveraged by Tsar Team.
- **CVE-2015-1701** Adobe & Windows Zero-Day exploits likely leveraged by Russia's APT28 in highly targeted attack.

Essentials of Zero-Day Vulnerabilities

- Keep the software up-to-date to help protect against zero-day vulnerability.
- Check for a solution when zero-day vulnerability is announced. Most software vendors work quickly to patch security vulnerability.
- Don't underestimate the threat. Cybercriminals will seek to exploit security holes and gain access to devices and personal information. They can use information for a range of cybercrimes including identity theft, bank fraud, and ransomware.
- Always use reliable security software to keep devices safe and secure.

Different Zero-Day Attack handling Mechanisms

The following section deals with different handling mechanisms for zero-day attack shown in the figure 5.

Techniques

The startling idea of zero-day attacks is a genuine concern, particularly on the grounds that they might be utilized in focused assaults and in the proliferation of vindictive code (Payam, Timo, et.al, 2016). The figure 6 describes the steps involved in zero-day exploits.

Figure 5 Zero-Day Handling Mechanisms

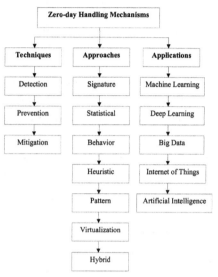

Figure 6 Steps for Zero-Day Exploit

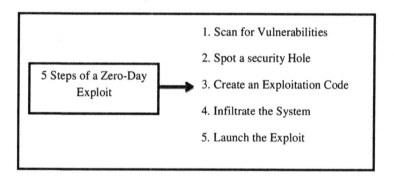

Detection

Any association associated with the web has one regular danger of zero-day assaults. The reasons for these assaults are, detecting private data, observing target's activities, robbery of business data and framework interruption. This segment broke down the examination endeavors done in course of safeguard against zero-day abuse. The essential objective of safeguard systems is to recognize the endeavor as close as conceivable to the season of abuse, to dispense with or limit the harm caused by the assault. The examination network has comprehensively ordered the guard procedures against zero-day misuses as measurable based, signature-based, conduct based, and half and half methods.

- **Statistical-based**: Statistical-based assault discovery procedures keep up the log of past adventures that are presently known. With this authentic log, assault profile is made to create new parameters for new assaults recognition. This strategy decides the ordinary exercises and distinguishes the exercises which are to be blocked. As the log is refreshed by verifiable exercises, the more drawn out any framework using this method, the more precise it is at learning or deciding typical exercises. Measurable based procedures manufacture assault profiles from authentic information, which are static in nature; in this manner they are not ready to receive the dynamic conduct of system condition. In this way, these systems can't be utilized for identification of malware progressively.

- **Signature-based**: For discovery of polymorphic worms, signature-based procedures are utilized to distinguish their new portrayals on each new contamination. There are essentially 3 classes of mark based location systems: content-based marks, semantic based marks and helplessness driven marks. These strategies are commonly utilized by infection programming merchants who will accumulate a library of various malware marks. These libraries are always being refreshed for recently distinguished marks of recently misused vulnerabilities. Mark based systems are frequently utilized in infection programming bundles to protect against malevolent payloads from malware to worms.

- **Behavior-based**: These systems depend on the capacity to foresee the stream of system traffic. They will likely foresee the future conduct of system framework so as to oppose the peculiar conduct. The expectation of future conduct is finished by machine learning approach through the present and past collaborations with the web server, server or injured individual machine. Conduct based strategies decide the basic attributes of worms which don't require the examination of payload byte designs Intrusion location and interruption counteractive action marks incorporate these safeguard systems. These marks need two fundamental characteristics first; they ought to have a high discovery rate. Second, they ought to create couple of false alarms. The objective of any strategies utilized by an association ought to be to recognize continuously the presence of a zero-day misuse and avoid harm and multiplication of the zero-day abuse.

- **Hybrid-based**: Hybrid-based methods join heuristics with different blends of the three past systems which are measurable based, signature-based, and conduct based procedures. Utilizing a half breed show system will defeat a shortcoming in any single strategy.

Prevention

Zero-Day vulnerabilities can be powerless to Zero-Day assaults with grievous outcomes to business. This sounds a bit of overwhelming however can take proactive and receptive safety efforts. Zero-day defenselessness will open the framework to the likelihood of a moment assault that could have lamentable outcomes and grave monetary results. Subsequently, it's vital to be aware of this probability and act if and when powerlessness appears. A few stages to prevent zero-day attacks are shown in figure 7.

Figure 7 Steps to prevent Zero-day Attacks

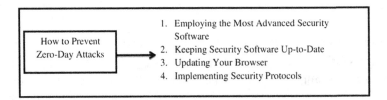

Employing the Most Advanced Security Software

Basic security programming is essentially insufficient in the present online atmosphere, where programmers utilize the most exceptional methods for framework hacking. Programming that just ensures against realized dangers is no counterpart for the programmer who grows better approaches to assault, since Zero-Day assaults are, by definition, assaults not yet known.

Keeping Security Software Up-to-Date

As new techniques for hacking wind up known, security programming is refreshed to forestall such hacks. Just with normal, convenient programming updates can adequately shield the system from a zero-day abuse.

Implementing Security Protocols

For a system to be completely prepared to follow up on zero-day helplessness, all organization work forces must be prepared on the accepted procedures for security. Create and actualize a succession of safety efforts and show your workforce when and how to sanction these measures.

Use refreshed programs

Programs are most loved focuses for Zero-Day assaults. Updates to programs are regularly programmed, yet ensure programs are altogether refreshed as they frequently contain patches to vulnerabilities. Check for explicit program refresh guidelines.

Establish security best practices

Ensure you set a case of individual online security best practices and have every one of your representatives do likewise.

Mitigation

Zero-day misuses are not kidding security escape clauses that are abused around the same time they are uncovered. They are relevantly named "multi day" in light of the fact that the system chairmen have zero days to fix the security blemish, which could have just been abused. Here are five of the prescribed procedures on the best way to alleviate zero-day assaults. The following figure 8 deals with defence against zero-day attacks.

Limit the Use of Email Attachments

- Networks where clients are probably going to accidentally take part in sending or accepting vindictive email connections are frequently inclined to hacking.
- To guarantee they work in safe client situations, organizations should survey their arrangements and firmly limit email connections by sifting them through.

Figure 8 Defend Against Zero-Day Attacks

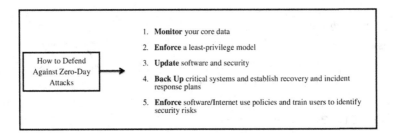

- Hackers will in general cover up malevolent code in connections, which can trade off the system's security when opened by a clueless client.
- Only connections with the concurred expansions should then be allowed in the system. This will wipe out any zero-day abuses, since connections that neglect to meet the concurred criteria are rejected on landing.
- Furthermore, deactivating HTML messages is likewise a vital system in barrier against zero-day assaults. To convey dangers and assaults on an organization's system, programmers can cover up vindictive code in HTML messages before sending them out.
- In this way expanding the dangers of zero-day abuses. It is prudent, hence, to inactivate HTML to relieve such dangers.

Pay special mind to Anomalous Activity

- Any unpredictable action on your processing foundation should raise a warning.
- For precedent, controlling how your framework interfaces or speaks with different frameworks inside the system can help in confining any harm that may happen on account of zero-day misuses.
- Based on the organization's necessities, there ought to be decides that expound on how and which frameworks can interface and the degree to which different parts of the framework can be gotten to.
- This keeps any contaminations from spreading inside the system in the event that it goes under assault.

Filter through Outbound Traffic

- Hackers and different aggressors will in general introduce bot projects and Trojans on active exchanges or associations with catch and change directions to a remote framework for various strategies.
- Installing firewalls and outbound intermediaries will help in distinguishing and blocking such associations.
- Companies should set up borders that permit explicit inbound traffic and deny and obstruct any outbound associations on the switch as a matter of course.

- For precedent, the movement sign on the switch in connection to inbound and outbound traffic over some undefined time frame ought to be adequate in figuring out what traffic ought to be allowed and what ought to be refused.

Set up Robust Preventive Security Procedures

- Limiting authoritative benefits to a solitary client can help in keeping remote programmers from completely picking up control of the framework. For instance, it is fitting to kill JavaScript to shield clients from the expansive outcomes of the web-established ANI misuses.
- In expansion to leading helplessness examines all the time, it is imperative to utilize boycotting programming to bolt out any pernicious exercises and whitelist destinations that represent no dangers.
- Furthermore, appropriate client training, content sifting of ANI documents, and utilizing refreshed antivirus programming are other preventive techniques that can help in relieving zero-day abuses.

Create Disaster Recovery Measures

- Since zero-day abuses happen quickly, it is important to build up thorough techniques that can be pursued to recuperate from harms at whatever point the assault happens or moderate the threats once they are detected.

Approaches

- **Signature:** This method matches the signatures of already known attacks that are stored into the database to detect the attacks in the computer system.
- **Statistical:** This approach detects the abnormal behavior or attacks in the computer networks by comparing the new traffic with the already created profiles.
- **Behavior:** This technique detects faulty behavior when malicious codes are executed, improved version of heuristic-based technique.Malicious behavior is revealed not only in executable files, but also in document files, such as PDF, DOC, and HWP. This technique determines characteristics of malicious behaviorbased on file, registry, network, process, etc.
- **Heuristic:** This technique determines specific behavior of malicious codes, so this can check new and variant codes by analyzing abnormal behavior not signatures.
- **Pattern:** After defining the specific pattern of existing malicious codes as their characteristics, malicious codes are detected and blocked by matching defined pattern with a pattern of incoming codes.
- **Virtualization:** This approach is closely related to dynamic heuristic-based technique. Malicious codes are analyzed in virtual system.
- **Hybrid:** Combines various methods mentioned above.

Applications

- **Machine Learning:** Machine Learning (ML) is a method of data analysis that automates analytical model building. ML is a category of algorithm that allows software applications to become more accurate in predicting outcomes without being explicitly programmed. The basic premise of machine learning is to build algorithms that can receive input data and use statistical analysis to predict an output while updating outputs as new data becomes available.
- **Deep Learning:** Deep learning is a collection of algorithms used in machine learning, used to model high-level abstractions in data through the use of model architectures, which are composed of multiple nonlinear transformations. It is part of a broad family of methods used for machine learning that are based on learning representations of data.
- **Artificial Intelligence**: A branch of computer science dealing with the simulation of intelligent behavior in computers and has the capability of a machine to imitate intelligent human behavior.
- **Big Data:** Big data is an evolving term that describes a large volume of structured, semi-structured and unstructured data that has the potential to be mined for information and used in machine learning projects and other advanced analytics applications.
- **Internet of Things:** The internet of things, or IoT, is a system of interrelated computing devices, mechanical and digital machines, objects, animals or people that are provided with unique identifiers (UIDs) and the ability to transfer data over a network without requiring human-to-human or human-to-computer interaction.

MACHINE LEARNING

Machine learning (ML) is an application of artificial intelligence (AI) that provides systems the ability to automatically learn and improve from experience without being explicitly programmed. The primary aim is to allow the computers learn automatically without human intervention or assistance and adjust actions accordingly (Pierre, Julio, et.al, 2018). The figure 9 accounts ML advantages and disadvantages.

Figure 9 ML Advantages & Disadvantages

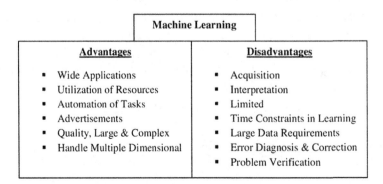

Requirements for ML

- Data preparation capabilities
- Algorithms – basic and advanced
- Automation and iterative processes
- Scalability
- Ensemble modeling

Process of ML

- Identifies relevant datasets and prepares them for analysis.
- Choose the type of machine learning algorithms to use.
- Builds an analytical model based on the chosen algorithm.
- Trains the model on test data sets, revising it as needed.
- Runs the model to generate scores and other findings.

Machine Learning Methods

- **Supervised Machine Learning** can apply what has been learned in the past to new data using labeled examples to predict future events (Prakash, Lei, et.al, 2013). Starting from the analysis of a known training dataset, the learning algorithm produces an inferred function to make predictions about the output values. The system is able to provide targets for any new input after sufficient training. The learning algorithm can also compare its output with the correct, intended output and find errors in order to modify the model accordingly.
- **Unsupervised Machine Learning** is used when the information used to train is neither classified nor labeled. Unsupervised learning studies how systems can infer a function to describe a hidden structure from unlabeled data. The system doesn't figure out the right output, but it explores the data and can draw inferences from datasets to describe hidden structures from unlabeled data.
- **Semi-Supervised Machine Learning** fall somewhere in between supervised and unsupervised learning, since they use both labeled and unlabeled data for training – typically a small amount of labeled data and a large amount of unlabeled data. The systems that use this method are able to considerably improve learning accuracy. Usually, semi-supervised learning is chosen when the acquired labeled data requires skilled and relevant resources in order to train it / learn from it. Otherwise, acquiring unlabeled data generally doesn't require additional resources.
- **Reinforcement Machine Learning** is a learning method that interacts with its environment by producing actions and discovers errors or rewards. Trial and error search and delayed reward are the most relevant characteristics of reinforcement learning. This method allows machines and software agents to automatically determine the ideal behavior within a specific context in order to maximize its performance. Simple reward feedback is required for the agent to learn which action is best; this is known as the reinforcement signal.

Machine learning enables analysis of massive quantities of data. While it generally delivers faster, more accurate results in order to identify profitable opportunities or dangerous risks, it may also require additional time and resources to train it properly (Sahoo, Liu & Hoi, 2017). Combining machine learning with AI and cognitive technologies can make it even more effective in processing large volumes of information.

Machine Learning Algorithms

Basically, there are two ways to categorize Machine Learning algorithms which are shown in figure 10 (Sharma, Kalita & Borah, 2016).

- The first is a grouping of ML algorithms by the learning style.
- The second is a grouping of ML algorithms by a similarity in form or function.

Risks in Machine Learning

Machine learning models come with risks which include large false positives due to bad learning algorithms that the hackers can exploit (Sitalakshmi & Mamoun, 2018). Another unwanted guest to the model is the contaminated or compromised data from a recently hacked host (Umesh, Chanchala & Suyash, 2016).

- Hacker can use fake biometric fingerprints, Iris and facial characteristics to impersonate a legitimate user.
- Hacker can fool a machine learning model into classifying malicious training samples as legitimate at test or execution time.
- This can cause the model to behave significantly and widely different than the expected outputs.
- **Perform Ethical Hacking:** An ethical hacker is a trusted security professional who breaks into a system to discover machine learning vulnerabilities overlooked by a firewall, an intrusion detection system or any other security tools. In a simple scenario of gaining access, the ethical

Figure 10 Machine Learning Algorithms

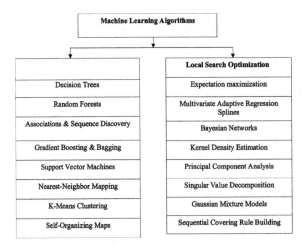

hacker uses a fake finger reconstructed from the fingerprint left behind by a legitimate user on a dirty device. Once in the system, the ethical hacker sneaks into a fingerprint database, retrieves a biometric template belonging to another legitimate user and then reconstructs a fake finger. To combat these risks, the device reader must be free of dirt, grease and moisture after each use and the database should be encrypted.

- **Encrypt Security Logs:** A system administrator has super user privileges to analyze machine learning log files. The reasons for doing it include checking for compliance with security policies, troubleshooting the system and conducting forensics. Encrypting log files is one way of protecting log files from being hacked. Encryption keys needed to change log contents are not revealed to the malicious hacker. If this hacker tries to delete a log file on hacking activities, the administrator should get an immediate loud-sounding alert on the always-on desktop computer.

- **Clean Out Training Data:** A machine learning model behaves well when it is fed by good training data. The model developer must know where the data comes from. The data must be clean and free of biases, anomalies and poisoned data. It must be avoided if the source host has been attacked. Bad data can cause the model to behave differently and ultimately shut down the system. When using multiple learning tools to assess data for a particular task, the model developer should restructure all data into a common format.

- **Apply Devops To Model Lifecycle:** Hackers can take advantage of false positives from a machine learning platform. One way of combating this and other risks in machine learning is to apply DevOps to the learning model lifecycle. DevOps lets the development and training, quality assurance and production teams collaborate with one another.

- **Implement a Security Policy:** A security policy should be implemented on the course of actions to take for machine learning risk management. In a simple scenario, the policy should consist of five sections: purpose, scope, background, actions and constraints. The scope section puts a fence around what's to be covered: machine learning model type, training data and data mining algorithm -- regression, clustering or neural networks. The background section looks at the reasons behind the policy, the actions section covers how the risks can be combated using DevOps and the constraints section considers machine learning limitations, and availability of test data.

MLM Applied in Zero-Day Attack

There are wide varieties of machine learning applications available, the following table. 2 illustrates the machine learning models applied so far in zero-day attack Vishal, Kyungroul, et.al, 2017).

CONCLUSION

Cloud computing technology is extremely popular among users due to its many advantages. However, this technology also introduces vulnerabilities that can become new vectors for cyber-attacks. With the rapid increase in the adoption of cloud computing by many organizations, security issues arise. Overall, zero-day attack prevention and detection are extremely difficult problems, but there's no denying the high demand for solutions in these areas. As cloud computing is on the rise, and especially due to its enormous attraction to organized criminals. This chapter deals with various aspects of zero-day attack. It provides a detailed account of machine learning aspects related to zero-day attack.

Table 2. MLM Applied in Zero-Day Attack

Author Names	Title	ML Approach	Problem	Outcome
Pierre Parrend, Julio Navarro, Fabio Guigou, Aline Deruyverand Pierre Collet - 2018	Foundations and Applications of Artificial Intelligence for Zero-day and Multi-Step Attack Detection	Statistical approaches include rule-based and outlier-detection-based solutions. Machine learning includes the detection of behavioural anomalies and event sequence tracking	Zero-day attacks that are not publicly disclosed	Eases the characterisation of novel complex threats and matching Artificial Intelligence-based Counter-measures
Sitalakshmi Venkatraman and Mamoun Alazab - 2018	Use of Data Visualisation for Zero-Day Malware Detection	Hybrid method of feature based and image-based visualisation	Similarity mining to Identify and classify malware accurately	Efficient and accurate in identifying malware visually
Vishal Sharma, Kyungroul Lee, Soonhyun Kwon, Jiyoon Kim, Hyungjoon Park, Kangbin Yim, and Sun-Young Lee - 2017	A Consensus Framework for Reliability and Mitigation of Zero-Day Attacks in IoT	Context behavior- Reliability and consensus	Mitigation of zero-day attacks in IoT networks	Mitigate the zero-day attacks in IoT network without compromising its performance
Payam Vahdani Amoli, Timo Hamalainen, Gil David, Mikhail Zolotukhin, Mahsa Mirzamohammad - 2016	Unsupervised Network Intrusion Detection Systems for Zero-Day Fast-Spreading Attacks and Botnets	Unsupervised machine-learning algorithms	To detect fast spreading, known and zero-day intrusion	A-NIDS increases the detection rate of zero-day and complex attacks
Umesh Kumar Singh, Chanchala Joshi, Suyash Kumar Singh - 2016	ZDAR System: Defending Against the Unknown	Supervised classification & unsupervised classification -ZDAR (Zero-Day Attack Remedy) system	To sense network traffic that detects anomalous behavior of network in order to identify the presence of zero-day exploit	This method is effective and efficient in detecting zero day attacks than the typical statistical based anomaly detection techniques
Ammar Almomani, B. B. Gupta, Tat-Chee Wan, Altyeb Altaher, Selvakumar Manickam - 2013	Phishing Dynamic Evolving Neural Fuzzy Framework for Online Detection "Zero-day" Phishing Email	Phishing dynamic evolving neural fuzzy framework (PDENF), hybrid (supervised/ unsupervised) learning approach	To detect a new zero-day phishing emails	To increase the level of accuracy and increase the performance of classification and prediction of phishing email values
Prakash Mandayam Comar, Lei Liu, Sabyasachi Saha, Pang-Ning Tan, Antonio Nucci - 2013	Combining Supervised and Unsupervised Learning for Zero-Day Malware Detection	Tree-based Feature Transformation, SVM	To detect known and newly emerging malware at a high precision	Identify flows of existing and novel malwares with very high precision
Mamoun Alazab, Sitalakshmi Venkatraman, Paul Watters, and Moutaz Alazab - 2011	Zero-day Malware Detection based on Supervised Learning Algorithms of API call Signatures	Supervised Learning Algorithms, The Sequential Minimal Optimization (SMO) Algorithm, Artificial Neural Networks (ANN) Algorithm, J48 Algorithm, K-Nearest Neighbors (kNN) Algorithm	To detect and classify zero-day malware with high levels of accuracy and efficiency based on the frequency of Windows API calls	Data mining algorithm over the other for accurately detecting zero-day malware

REFERENCES

Alazab, M., Venkatraman, S., Watters, P., & Alazab, M. (2011). Zero-day Malware Detection based on Supervised Learning Algorithms of API call Signatures. In *Proceedings of the Ninth Australasian Data Mining Conference* (vol. 121, pp. 171-182). Australian Computer Society.

Almomani, A., Gupta, B. B., Wan, T., Altaher, A., & Manickam, S. (2013). *Phishing dynamic evolving neural fuzzy framework for online detection zero-day phishing email.* Academic Press.

Amoli, P. V., Hamalainen, T., David, G., Zolotukhin, M., & Mirzamohammad, M. (2016). Unsupervised Network Intrusion Detection Systems for Zero-Day Fast-Spreading Attacks and Botnets. JDCTA, 10(2), 1-13.

Buczak, A. L., & Guven, E. (2016). A survey of data mining and machine learning methods for cyber security intrusion detection. *IEEE Communications Surveys & Tutorials, 18*(2).

Comar, P. M., Liu, L., Saha, S., Tan, P., & Nucci, A. (2013). Combining Supervised and Unsupervised Learning for Zero-Day Malware Detection. In 2013 Proceedings IEEE INFOCOM (pp. 2022-2030). IEEE.

Jordan, M. I., & Mitchell, T. M. (2015). Machine learning: Trends, perspectives, and prospects. *Science, 349*(6245), 255-260.

Parrend, P., Navarro, J., Guigou, F., Deruyver, A., & Collet, P. (2018). Foundations and Applications of Artificial Intelligence for Zero-day and Multi-Step Attack Detection. EURASIP Journal on Information Security, 2018(1), 4.

Sahoo, D., Liu, C., & Hoi, S. C. H. (2017). Malicious URL detection using machine learning. *Survey (London, UK).*

Sharma, V., Lee, K., Kwon, S., Kim, J., Park, H., Yim, K., & Lee, S. Y. (2017). A Consensus Framework for Reliability and Mitigation of Zero-Day Attacks in IoT. *Security and Communication Networks.*

Sharma, R. K., Kalita, H. K., & Borah, P. (2016). Analysis of machine learning techniques based intrusion detection systems. In *Proceedings of 3rd International Conference on Advanced Computing, Networking and Informatics* (pp. 485-493). New Delhi, India: Springer.

Singh, U. K., Joshi, C., & Singh, S. K. (2016). ZDAR System: Defending against the Unknown. *International Journal of Computer Science and Mobile Computing, 5*(12), 143-149.

Venkatraman, S., & Alazab, M. (2018). Use of Data Visualisation for Zero-Day Malware Detection. *Security and Communication Networks.*

Chapter 18
Adoption of Machine Learning With Adaptive Approach for Securing CPS

Rama Mercy Sam Sigamani
Avinashilingam Institute for Home Science and Higher Education for Women, India

ABSTRACT

The cyber physical system safety and security is the major concern on the incorporated components with interface standards, communication protocols, physical operational characteristics, and real-time sensing. The seamless integration of computational and distributed physical components with intelligent mechanisms increases the adaptability, autonomy, efficiency, functionality, reliability, safety, and usability of cyber-physical systems. In IoT-enabled cyber physical systems, cyber security is an essential challenge due to IoT devices in industrial control systems. Computational intelligence algorithms have been proposed to detect and mitigate the cyber-attacks in cyber physical systems, smart grids, power systems. The various machine learning approaches towards securing CPS is observed based on the performance metrics like detection accuracy, average classification rate, false negative rate, false positive rate, processing time per packet. A unique feature of CPS is considered through structural adaptation which facilitates a self-healing CPS.

INTRODUCTION

Cyber Physical Systems (CPS)

CPSs are frameworks that connect the physical world (e.g., through sensors or actuators) with the virtual universe of data handling. They are formed from differing constituent parts that team up to make some worldwide conduct. These constituents will incorporate programming frameworks, correspondences innovation, and sensors/actuators that communicate with this present reality, frequently including installed advances.

An average CPS as shown in Figure 1 may:

DOI: 10.4018/978-1-5225-9611-0.ch018

Figure 1 CPS SYSTTEM

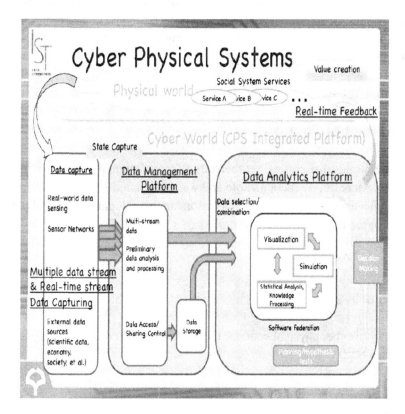

- Monitor and control physical and hierarchical or business forms
- Be an extensive scale framework with various - and notwithstanding clashing - objectives crossing distinctive application spaces
- Require incorporation of various specialized orders and diverse application spaces
- Require a high level of constancy
- Involve generous client contribution/communication
- Continuously screen and advance its own execution
- Adapt and advance continually accordingly changes in nature, through constant (re)configuration, sending or (de)commissioning
- Require progressive choice frameworks with a high level of self-sufficiency on neighborhood, territorial, national, and worldwide dimension
- Be circulated and interconnected frameworks of frameworks

Example Application Domains

CPSs can be conveyed in a wide range of settings and application territories. Here are a few precedents:

- Improving productivity and security in homes and workplaces
- Supporting old individuals living alone.

- Monitoring security and developments of travelers in an open transport framework, or of vehicles on a street arrange.
- Optimizing crop yield and decreasing pesticide/compost use, by utilizing CPSs to distinguish and convey them just where they are required.

Figure 2 shows the CPS and embedded systems.

CPS and the Internet of Things

IoT and CPS share numerous difficulties, yet there are a few refinements as shown in Figure 3 IoT has a solid accentuation on interestingly recognizable and web associated gadgets and installed frameworks. CPS building has a solid accentuation on the connection among calculation and the physical world (e.g., between complex programming and equipment parts of a framework).

Cps Security

CPS Security Objectives

In assuring the security of cyber physical systems, there are several security objectives to achieve. They are

Figure 2 CPS AND EMBEDDED SYSTEMS

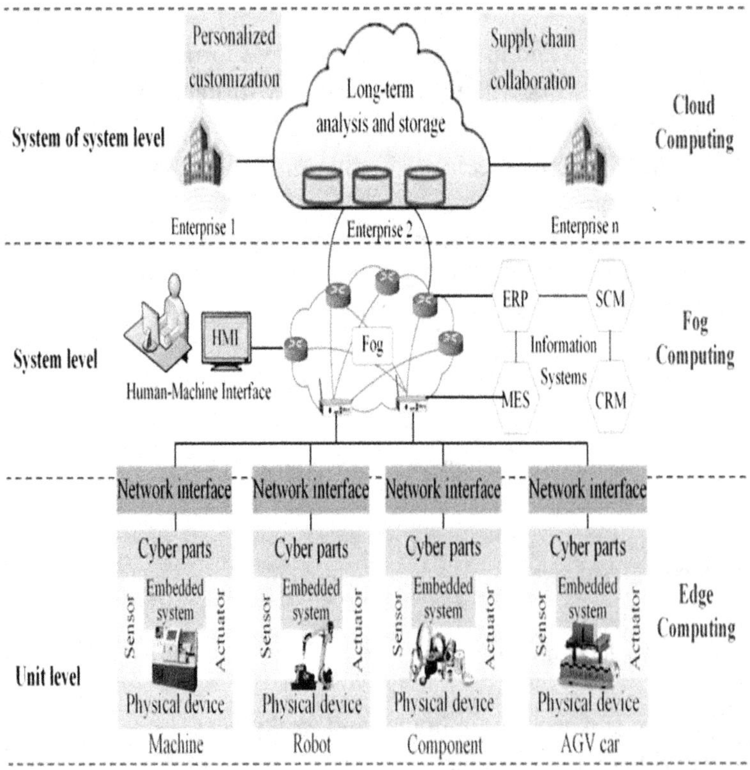

Figure 3 CPS – IOT

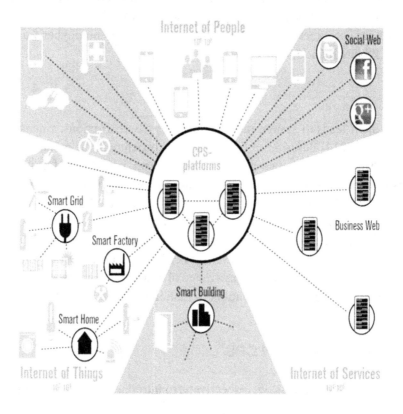

Confidentiality

Confidentiality means that cyber physical systems should have the capacity to prevent the disclosure to unauthorized individuals or systems. To realize confidentiality, a cyber-physical system should protect the communication channels between sensors and controllers and between the controllers and actuators from eavesdropping.

Integrity

Integrity refers to data or resources cannot be modified without authorization (Alom et al., 2015). To ensure the integrity, cyber physical systems should have the capacity to achieve the physical goals by preserving, detecting, or blocking deception attacks on the information attacks on the information sent and received by the sensors and actuators or controllers (Griffor et al., 2017). Ensuring data integrity requires the ability to detect any changes introduced (maliciously or otherwise) in the massage being communicated (Manadhata et al., 2011). Omar Al Ibrahim, et al., in Louridas et al. (2016) present some thoughts to utilize the physical unclonable functions technology to build secure coupling between cyber and physical substrates based on intrinsic physical material to achieve integrity of CPS.

Availability High availability of cyber physical system aims to always provide service by preventing computing, controls, communication corruptions due to hardware failures, system upgrades, power outages or denial-of-service attacks. Sazia Parvin, et al., proposes a multicyber framework to improve the availability of CPS based on Markov model.

Reliability

An unreliable CPS often leads to system malfunctions, service disruptions, financial losses and even human life. Leon Wu, (2014) describes a framework for benchmarking reliability of cyber physical systems. Leon Wu (2014) describe a data-centric runtime monitoring system for improving the reliability of these types of cyber physical systems, which employs automated online evaluation, working in parallel with cyber physical system to continuously conduct automated evaluation at multiple stages in the system workflow and provide real-time feedback for reliability improvement. Robert Mitchell, et al. (n.d.) analyze the effect of intrusion detection and response on the reliability of cyber physical systems and develop a probability model based on stochastic Petri nets to describe the behavior of the CPS in the presence of both malicious nodes exhibiting a range of attacker behaviors, and an intrusion detection and response system for detecting and responding to malicious events at runtime.

IMPORTANCE OF SECURITY IN CPS

CPS solutions can be stratified discussion, respectively, to introduce the solution of each layer as shown in Figure 4

Sensing Layer Security

The sensor of the sensing layer acquires the external entity information, which is constructed by these wireless sensors into the wireless sensor network. The sensor layer needs to consider the safety of the sensor network. The perceived layer of node computing, storage capacity is weak, cannot use complex encryption algorithm, so the need to design lightweight password algorithms and protocols. In order to prevent the node from being controlled, steal or tampered with, it is necessary to perform node authentication and data integrity verification. Through the expansion of the spectrum, the message priority and other security means to prevent the perception of the frequency interference. Using intrusion detection and intrusion recovery mechanism as a passive attack security measures to improve the robustness of the system.

Network Layer Security

The network layer consists of a large number of heterogeneous networks, different networks to resist security threats in different ways, so the design of the network layer security structure need to consider the network layer compatibility and consistency. Network layer security tasks include network layer identity authentication, network resource access control, data transmission confidentiality and integrity, remote access security, routing system security. The security structure of the network layer has two layers: point-to-point security sub-layer and end-to-end security sublayer. Among them, the point-to-point security

Figure 4 CPS Layers

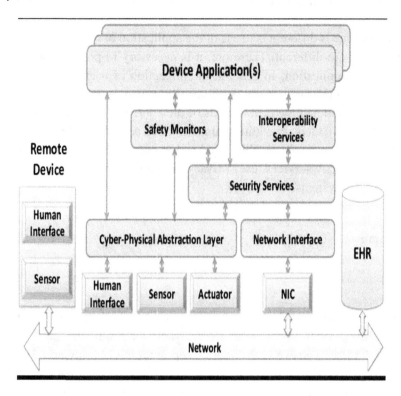

sub-layer guarantees the security of the data in hop-by-hop transmission. The corresponding security mechanism includes mutual authentication between nodes, hop-by-hop encryption, and cross-network authentication and so on. The end-to-terminal layer primarily implements end-to-end confidentiality and protects network availability. The corresponding security mechanisms include end-to-end authentication and secret key negotiation, secret key management and cryptographic algorithm selection, denial of service and distributed denial of service attack detection and defense, hierarchical architecture, broadcast radius limit, port interception and so on.

Collaborative Solution Security

The task of the collaborative processing layer is to collect useful data and then analyze and process the data. Therefore, the security task of this layer is to identify and delete the malicious information in the data source, collect the effective information and keep it on the basis of security. In addition, the collaborative processing layer of the synergy of the information obtained can have different sources, there may be different receivers, so in order to ensure the confidentiality and integrity of the data, the recipient and the sender need to be certified, and the information content and information sources are separated to protect the privacy of users. The security measures of the collaborative processing are as follows: virus detection, good confidence in data sources, access control box disaster recovery, secure multi-party computing and secure cloud computing, and efficient data mining for encrypted data.

Application Control Layer Security

The application layer service is different because of the application of CPS system, and the corresponding security requirements are different. Therefore, it is necessary to provide targeted security service according to the specific application. In general, the protection of user privacy is the most common security services, such as in the medical system, the need to protect the patient's personal privacy, the patient's personal information and medical records of the contents of the need to be separated to prevent user privacy theft by outsiders. In addition, unauthorized access is prohibited, and can be secured by computer security measures to ensure this. Application control layer security measures are mainly differentiated database security services, user privacy protection mechanism, access control, security software, patches, upgrade systems.

ATTACKS ON CPS

Cyber Attack

The Internet in today's society may be a key a part of human life. We tend to use internet at home, in the office and on mobile devices anywhere and everywhere we go. It's become important to be connected to internet 24/7, to keep an eye on business, keep in bit with family and friends, and to stay up to date on news around the world. Being connected doesn't only concern with the advancement in life or business, it comes with variety of potential danger like got taken valuable knowledge, lost privacy or identity, device infected by malware. Security for any legitimate network is under threat of attack. A number of the researchers have defined these cyber attacks as cyber war (Feizollah et al., 2013) and supply some initial guidelines for future defense of cyber house. The process in the main issues with the understanding of their own network, nature of the attacker, motive of the attacker, methodology of attack, security weakness of the network to mitigate future attacks. to grasp the character of a cyber attack, it's vital to model attack earlier to form network more secure, which may be customized depending on the organization's needs (Khan et al., 2010).

A cyber attack is deliberate exploitation of pc systems, technology-dependent enterprises and networks. Cyber attacks use malicious code to alter computer code, logic or information, resulting in disruptive consequences that may compromise information and result in cybercrimes, like information and identity theft. Cyber attack is also known as a network attack (CNA). Cyber attacks occurred targeting banks and broadcasting firms in South Korea on March 20. The malware concerned in these attacks brought down multiple websites and interrupted bank transactions by overwriting the Master Boot Record (MBR) and every one the logical drives on the infected servers rendering them unusable. it was reported that thirty two thousand computers had been damaged and also the actual quantity of the financial damage has not yet been calculated. A lot of serious is that we tend to area unit likely to have greater damages in case of occurring additional attacks, since exact analysis of cause isn't done however. APT(Advanced Persistent Threat), that is becoming a big issue due to this attack, isn't a brand new way of attacking, but a kind of keyword standing for a trend of recent cyber attacks.

Moreover, cyber security measured with regards to access, integration of information, security, storage and transfer of information through electronic or different modes (Khan et al., 2010). Cyber security indicates three important factors. The methods of protecting information Technology (IT), the information itself, the information being processed and transmitted together with physical and virtual setup, the level of protection obtained by applying such measures and also the professional aspects associated (Kurakin et al., 2016).

Physical Attack

Physical attacks are inevitable threats in sensor networks. Physical attacks are relatively simple to launch and fatal in destruction. Within the simplest case, the Xun Wang, Sriram Chellappan, Wenjun Gu and Dong Yuan are with The Department of computer science and Engineering. A better attacker will detect and destroy sensors with concealment by moving across the sensor network. In any case, the end results of physical attacks are often quite fatal. The backbone of the network (the sensors themselves) is destroyed. Destruction of sensors may additionally lead to the violation of the important network paradigms. a large spectrum of impacts might result because of physical attacks and once left unaddressed, physical attacks have the potential to render the complete sensing element network mission useless. Our focus in this paper is Search-based Physical Attacks. We define search-based physical attacks as those who seek for sensors, and so physically destroy them.

The searching process is executed by means of detecting electronic, magnetic, heat signals emitted by the sensors. Once sensors are identified, the attacker physically destroys the sensors. This method is opposed to a rather blind or brute force destruction of sensors in the field (using bombs, grenades, tanks etc) that will cause casualties to the deployment field, that the attacker might want to preserve (airports, oil fields, battlefields etc. of interest to the attacker). The salient options of search based mostly physical attacks return from the power to search for and then destroy sensors. This improves the potency of the attack method, because the wrongdoer will identify and destroy important sensors (cluster-heads, knowledge aggregators etc.). The search-based wrongdoer will cause physical destruction of the sensors whereas causing minimum casualties to the field of deployment.

The small type issue of sensors, coupled with the unattended and distributed nature of their deployment exposes detector networks to a special category of attacks that might lead to the physical destruction of sensors. We tend to denote Physical Attacks as those who lead to the physical destruction of sensors, thereby rendering them for good nonoperational. During this paper we tend to model and study a representative category of physical attacks, particularly Search-Based physical attacks to know their behavior and impacts.

Our performance information clearly shows that search-based physical attacks dramatically reduce accumulative coverage, further highlighting the importance of our work. we tend to observe that the attacker parameters, namely attacker's detection ranges, accuracy and movement speed, and the sensor network parameters such as the frequencies of sensors' beacons and frequency of cluster-head rotation have vital impacts on attack effectiveness. we tend to also observe that using a hierarchical sensor network has a mixed impact on maintaining AC under attacks; on one hand, the compromised cluster-heads (in hierarchical networks) cause decrease in AC significantly; on the other hand but, the existence of cluster-heads with cluster-head rotation will mislead the attacker and create its movements less efficient. We tend to also observe that the impacts of the attacker and sensor network parameters to attack effectiveness move with each other to affect AC. Physical attacks are patent and potent threats to future detector networks. We tend to believe that viability of future detector networks is conditional their ability to resist physical attacks.

Cyber and Physical Attack

Cyber Physical Systems refer to systems that have an interaction between computers, communication channels and physical devices to solve a real world problem. Towards industry 4.0 revolution, Cyber Physical Systems presently become one among the main targets of hackers and any injury to them lead to high losses to a nation. Consistent with valid resources, many cases reported involved security breaches on Cyber Physical Systems. Understanding basic and theoretical concept of security in the digital world was discussed worldwide. Yet, security cases in relevance the cyber physical system area unit still remaining less explored. In addition, limited tools were introduced to beat security issues in Cyber Physical System. To boost understanding and introduce heaps additional security solutions for the cyber physical system, the study on this matter is highly on demand.

The world accepted that Cyber Physical Systems (CPSs) connect computers, communication devices, sensors and actuators of the physical substratum, either in heterogeneous, open, systems of systems or hybrid. Systems become additional interconnected, thereby additional advanced (Tonge et al., 2013). Computer networks currently have joined water, food, transportation, and energy because the important resource for the perform of the nationals" economy. Application of cps will be seen in several styles of industries. The common sector is oil and gas, the power grid producing, defense and public infrastructures are fully relying on the advancement of cps. Therefore, cyber physical systems security has become a matter for societal, infrastructures and economic to ever y country in the world because of the tremendous number of electronic devices that are interconnected via networks communication (Alfayyadh et al., 2010). Latest reports have shown that cyber-attacks are aimed to destroy nations systems that used for country development. CPS starts with by not simply disrupt a single enterprise or damage an isolated machine; however a target to damage infrastructures via modern dynamics threats (Biggio et al., 2014). Those forms of attacks are able to offer destruction to important infrastructures system that used in sectors such as defense, finance, health, and the public (Biggio et al., 2014). To accomplish their goals criminals, activists, or terrorists are mostly searching for new and innovative techniques and targets, thus cyber physical systems currently one of the necessary targets for the hackers (Biggio et al., 2014). Increased security risk awareness and appropriately security relevant information management offer an equally important role within the trusted infrastructure maintenance. Figure 5 shows the CPS system.

Attacks Classification

Currently, in the middle of an emergence of Cyber Physical Systems (CPS) in almost all aspects of our life, CPS are manifold and include all kinds of unmanned or remote controlled vehicles, robotized manufacturing plants, critical infrastructure such as electrical power grid and nuclear power plants, smart homes, smart cities, and many more. Based on our experience with computer and network security, CPS will become targets of adversary attacks. Attacks on CPS are neither science fiction nor the matter of the distant future. Multiple attacks on various CPS have been already performed. Currently, the most famous attack is Stuxnet. Stuxnet is considered to be the first professionally crafted attack against CPS. This attack has reportedly damaged over 1000 centrifuges at an Iranian uranium enrichment plant (Feizollah et al., 2013). Multiple further examples of attacks on various CPS have been reported or shown in the research literature. These include attacks on modern car electronics (Khan et al., 2010), attacks on remotely controlled UAVs via GPS spoofing (Kurakin et al., 2016), or even attacks which use CPS as a carrier to infect the maintenance computer (Tonge et al., 2013). There is a broad consensus among researchers

Figure 5 CPS and its diagram

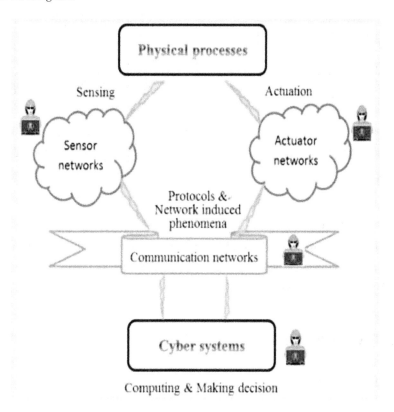

that adversary goals of attacks on CPS might differ from the goals of attacks on cyber systems. For instance, many attacks on CPS would try to compromise the system's safety or physical integrity instead of data privacy usually considered in cyber-security. However, technical aspects have even more severe implications on the CPS security. Figure.5. depicts various attacks which can be performed at targets located at different system layers. It is clear that attacks will affect the attacked targets. Additionally, due to the high degree of the dependencies and interdependencies between CPS elements at different layers, secondary effects can occur at CPS elements which have not been directly attacked. These induced effects can occur at elements located in different layers or even belonging to different (cyber or physical) domains. Such cross-layer and cross-domain attacks on CPS are very intricate and barely understood so far. Below, we will use qualifier "cross-domain" as a synonym for both cross-domain and cross-layer. Figure 6 shows the layer specific attacks.

Surveying known attacks on CPS, one can notice that a significant portion exhibits cross-domain effects. This makes it extremely important to consider such attacks alongside with the conventional cyber-attacks. In order to do this, we first should be able to describe not only the single-domain but also cross-domain attacks.

Attack Categorization: The most significant feature of the proposed taxonomy is the clear distinction between Influenced Element and Victim Element. As both these dimensions are independent from each other, elements of these dimensions can belong to cyber or physical domain regardless of the

Figure 6. Layer specific attacks on CPS

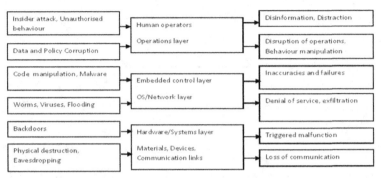

domain affiliation of each other. Therefore, the description of cross-domain attacks becomes possible. Furthermore, based on the domain of these elements, we can define following four attack categories: Cyber-to-Cyber (C2C), Cyber-to-Physical (C2P), Physical-to-Physical (P2P), and Physical-to-Cyber (P2C). These derivatives can be used to characterize attacks.

MACHINE LEARNING AND DEEP LEARNING

Fortunately, Machine Learning can aid in solving the most common tasks including regression, prediction, and classification. In the era of an extremely large amount of data and cyber security talent shortage, ML seems to be an only solution as in Figure 7.

This chapter is an introduction written to give the practical technical understanding of the current advances and future directions of ML research applied to cyber security.

Machine Learning Terminology

- **AI (Artificial Intelligence)**: A broad concept. A Science of making things smart or, in other words, human tasks performed by machines (e.g., Visual Recognition, NLP, etc.). The main point is that AI is not exactly Machine Learning or smart things. It can be a classic program installed in your robot cleaner like edge detection. Roughly speaking, AI is a thing that somehow carries out human tasks.
- **ML (Machine Learning)**: An Approach (just one of many approaches) to AI that uses a system that is capable of learning from experience. It is intended not only for AI goals (e.g., copying human behavior) but it can also reduce the efforts and/or time spent for both simple and difficult tasks like stock price prediction. In other words, ML is a system that can recognize patterns by using examples rather than by programming them. If your system learns constantly, makes decisions based on data rather than algorithms, and change its behavior, it's Machine Learning.
- **DL (Deep Learning)**: A set of Techniques for implementing Machine Learning that recognize patterns of patterns – like image recognition. The systems identify primarily object edges, a structure, an object type, and then an object itself. The point is that Deep Learning is not exactly Deep

Figure 7. Machine learning methods

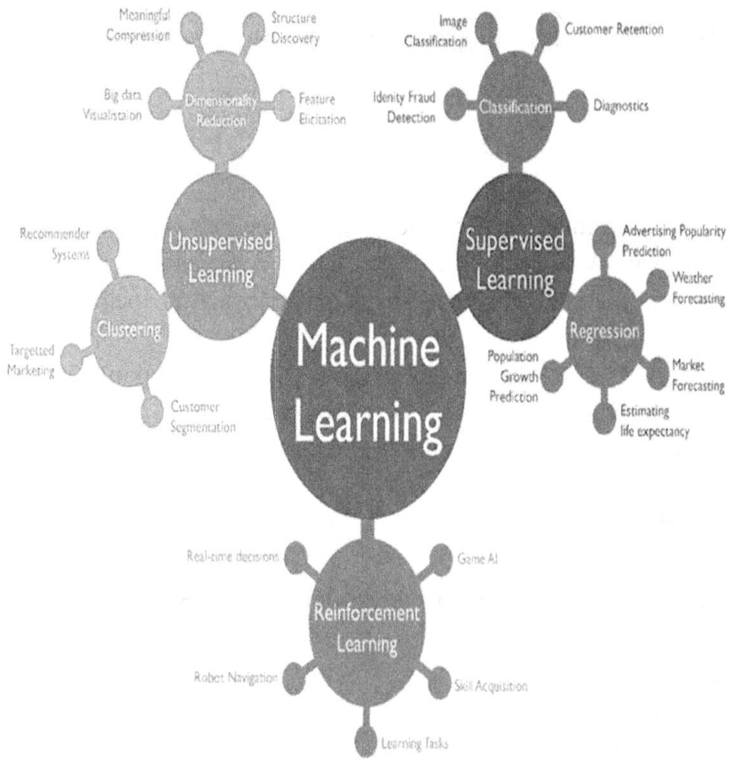

Neural Networks. There are other algorithms, which were improved to learn patterns of patterns, such as Deep Q Learning in Reinforcement task.

The definitions show that cyber security field refers mostly to Machine Learning (not to AI). And a large part of the tasks are not human-related. Machine learning means solving certain tasks with the use of an approach and particular methods based on data you have.

Most of the tasks are subclasses of the most common ones, which are described below:

- **Regression (or Prediction)**: A task of predicting the next value based on the previous values.
- **Classification**: A task of separating things into different categories.
- **Clustering**: Similar to classification but the classes are unknown, grouping things by their similarity.
- **Association Rule Learning (or Recommendation):** A task of recommending something based on the previous experience.
- **Dimensionality Reduction**: Or generalization, a task of searching common and most important features in multiple examples.
- **Generative Models**: A task of creating something based on the previous knowledge of the distribution.

There are different approaches in addition to these tasks.

Machine Learning Tasks and Cyber Security

Let's see examples of different methods that can be used to solve Machine Learning tasks and how they are related to cyber security tasks.

Regression

Regression (or prediction) is simple. The knowledge about the existing data is utilized to have an idea of the new data. Take an example of house prices prediction. In cybersecurity, it can be applied to fraud detection. The features (e.g., the total amount of suspicious transaction, location, etc.) determine a probability of fraudulent actions.

As for the technical aspects of regression, all methods can be divided into two large categories: Machine Learning and Deep Learning. The same is used for other tasks.

For each task, there are examples of ML and DL methods.

Deep Learning for Regression

For regression tasks, the following Deep Learning models can be used:

- Artificial Neural Network (ANN)
- Recurrent Neural Network (RNN)
- Neural Turing Machines (NTM)
- Differentiable Neural Computer (DNC)

Machine Learning for Classification

- Logistic Regression (LR)
- K-Nearest Neighbors (K-NN)
- Support Vector Machine (SVM)
- KernelSVM
- NaiveBayes
- DecisionTreeClassification
- Random Forest Classification

It's considered that methods like SVM and random forests work best. Keep in mind that there are no one-size-fits-all rules, and they probably won't operate properly for your task.

Deep Learning for Classification

- Artificial Neural Network
- Convolutional Neural Networks

Deep Learning methods work better if you have more data. But they consume more resources especially if you are planning to use it in production and re-train systems periodically.

Machine Learning for Clustering

- K-nearest neighbours (KNN)
- K-means
- Mixture model(LDA)
- DBSCn
- Bayesian
- GaussianMixtureModel
- Agglomerative
- Mean-shift

Deep Learning for Clustering

- Self-organized Maps (SOM) or Kohonen Networks

Association Rule Learning (Recommendation Systems)

Netflix and Sound Cloud recommend films or songs according to your movies or music preferences. In cyber security, this principle can be used primarily for incident response. If a company faces a wave of incidents and offers various types of responses, a system learns a type of response for a particular incident (e.g., mark it as a false positive, change a risk value, run the investigation). Risk management solutions can also have a benefit if they automatically assign risk values for new vulnerabilities or mis-configurations built on their description.

There are algorithms used for solving recommendation tasks.

Machine Learning for Association Rule Learning

- Apriori
- Euclat
- FP-Growth

Deep Learning for Association Rule Learning

- Deep Restricted Boltzmann Machine (RBM)
- Deep Belief Network (DBN)
- Stacked Auto encoder

The latest recommendation systems are based on restricted Boltzmann machines and their updated versions, such as promising deep belief networks.

Dimensionality Reduction

Dimensionality reduction or generalization is not as popular as classification, but necessary if you deal with complex systems with unlabeled data and many potential features. You can't apply clustering because typical methods restrict the number of features or they don't work. Dimensionality reduction can help handle it and cut unnecessary features. Like clustering, dimensionality reduction is usually one of the tasks in a more complex model. As to cyber security tasks, dimensionality reduction is common for face detection solutions — the ones you use in your iPhone.

Machine Learning for Dimensionality Reduction

- Principal Component Analysis (PCA)
- Singular-value decomposition (SVD)
- T-distributed Stochastic Neighbor Embedding (T-SNE)
- Linear Discriminant Analysis (LDA)
- Latent Semantic Analysis (LSA)
- Factor Analysis (FA)
- Independent Component Analysis (ICA)
- Non-negative Matrix Factorization (NMF)

Generative Models

The task of generative models differs from the above-mentioned ones. While those tasks deal with the existing information and associated decisions, generative models are designed to simulate the actual data (not decisions) based on the previous decisions.

The simple task of offensive cyber security is to generate a list of input parameters to test a particular application for Injection vulnerabilities.

Alternatively, you can have a vulnerability scanning tool for web applications. One of its modules is testing files for unauthorized access. These tests are able to mutate existing filenames to identify the new ones. For example, if a crawler detected a file called login.php, it's better to check the existence of any backup or test its copies by trying names like login_1.php, login_backup.php, login.php.2017.

Cyber Security Tasks and Machine Learning

Instead of looking at ML tasks and trying to apply them to cyber security, let's look at the common cyber security tasks and Machine Learning opportunities. There are three dimensions (Why, What, and How).

The first dimension is a goal, or a task (e.g., detects threats, predict attacks, etc.). According to Gartner's PPDR model, all security tasks can be divided into five categories:

1. Prediction;
2. Prevention;
3. Detection;
4. Response;
5. Monitoring.

Machine Learning for Network Protection

Network protection is not a single area but a set of different solutions that focus on a protocol such as Ethernet, wireless, SCADA, or even virtual networks like SDNs.

Network protection refers to well-known Intrusion Detection System (IDS) solutions. Some of them used a kind of ML years ago and mostly dealt with signature-based approaches.

ML in network security implies new solutions called Network Traffic Analytics (NTA) aimed at in-depth analysis of all the traffic at each layer and detects attacks and anomalies.

Now-a-days the construct of machine learning is used in many applications and may be a core construct for intelligent systems (Ge et al., 2017) as in Figure 8.

Machine learning tasks are generally classified depending on the nature of the learning "signal" or "feedback" available to a learning system.

- Supervised learning
- Unsupervised learning
- Semi-supervised Learning
- Reinforcement learning
- Multitask Learning
- Ensemble Learning
- Neural Network Learning

Figure 8 Machine Learning Types

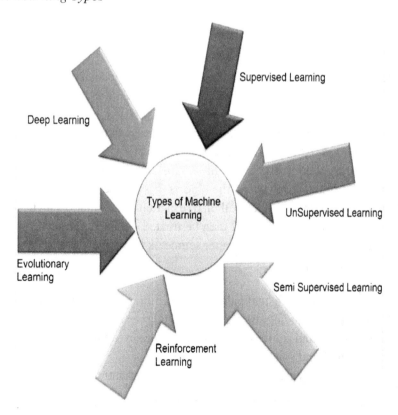

- Instance-Based Learning

Supervised Learning

It is the machine learning task of inferring a function from labeled training data. The training data consists of a set of training examples. A supervised learning algorithm analyzes the training data and produces an inferred function that can be utilized for mapping fresh examples. To work out on a given problem of supervised learning, one has to carry out the following steps:

1. Decide the kind of training examples. The user should decide what kind of data is to be used as a training set.
2. Collect a training set. The training set needs to be envoy of the real-world use of the function. Thus, a set of input objects is collected and corresponding outputs are also collected.
3. Decide the input feature depiction of the learned function. The accuracy of the learned function relies sturdily on how the input object is represented. Normally, the input object is altered into a feature vector that contains a number of features that are descriptive of the object. The number of features should not be too large.
4. Decide the structure of the learned function and corresponding learning algorithm.
5. Complete the design. Run the learning algorithm on the gathered training set. Some supervised learning algorithms need the user to find out certain control parameters.
6. Assess the accuracy of the learned function. After parameter adjustment and learning, the performance of the resulting function should be measured on a test set that is separate from the training set.

Unsupervised Learning

It is the machine learning task of inferring a perform to depict concealed structure from "unlabeled" information. Since the examples specified to the learner are unlabeled, there's no assessment of the accuracy of the structure that's output by the relevant algorithm which is a way of characteristic unsupervised learning from supervised learning and reinforcement learning. A central case of unsupervised learning is that the problem of density estimation in statistics [19].

Unsupervised learning used information that has no historical labels and therefore the goal is to explore the data and realize similarities between the objects. It's the technique of discovering labels from the info itself. Unsupervised learning works well on transactional information such as identify segments of consumers with similar attributes who will then be treated similarly in marketing campaigns. Or it will find the main attributes that separate customer segments from one another.

Other unsupervised learning problems are:

- Given detailed observations of distant galaxies, determine which features or combinations of features are most important in distinguishing between galaxies.
- Given a mixture of two sound sources for example, a person talking over some music, separate the two which is called the blind source separation problem.
- Given a video, isolate a moving object and categorize in relation to other moving objects which have been seen.

Typical unsupervised task is clustering where a set of inputs is divided into groups, unlike in classification; the groups are not known before. Popular unsupervised techniques include self-organizing maps, nearest-neighbor mapping, k-means clustering and singular value decomposition. These algorithms are also used to segment text topics, recommend items and identify data outliers.

Semi-Supervised Learning

In many practical learning domains such as text processing, video indexing, bioinformatics, there is large supply of unlabeled data but limited labeled data which can be expensive to generate .So semi supervised learning is used for the same applications as supervised learning but it uses both labeled and unlabeled data for training. There is a desired prediction problem but the model must learn the structures to organize the data as well as make predictions.

Semi-supervised learning is useful when the cost associated with labeling is too high to allow for a fully labeled training process. This type of learning can be used with methods such as classification, regression and prediction. Early examples of this include identifying a person's face on a web cam. Example algorithms are extensions to other flexible methods that make assumptions about how to model the unlabelled data.

DEEP LEARNING

Deep learning is a rising area of machine learning (ML) analysis. It contains multiple hidden layers of artificial neural networks. The deep learning methodology applies nonlinear transformations and model abstractions of high level in massive databases. The recent advancements in deep learning architectures inside numerous fields have already provided important contributions in AI.

A Deep Neural Network (DNN) is defined to be an artificial Neural Network (ANN) with a minimum of one hidden layers of units between the input and output layers. The additional layers provide it additional levels of abstraction, so enhancing its modeling capability. The foremost popular sorts of Deep Learning models are referred to as Convolutional Neural Nets (CNN), or just ConvNets. These space type of feed-forward artificial neural network, extensively utilized in laptop vision, wherever the individual neurons are covered in such the way that they reply to overlapping regions within the visual view. In recent times, CNN shave also been with success applied to automatic speech recognition (ASR). Deep Belief Network sand Convolutional Deep Belief Networks are another popular deep learning architectures in use.

Reinforcement Learning

A computer program interacts with a vibrant environment in which it must perform a certain goal. The program is provided feedback in terms of rewards and punishments as it navigates its problem space.

It is often used for robotics, gaming and navigation. It is the learning technique which interacts with a dynamic environment in which it must perform a certain goal without a teacher explicitly telling it whether it has come close to its goal. With reinforcement learning, the algorithm discovers through trial and error which actions yield the greatest rewards. So in the chess playing, reinforcement learning learns to play a game by playing against an opponent which performs trial and error actions to win.

Multitask Learning

Multitask learning has a simple goal of helping other learners to perform better. When multitask learning algorithms are applied on a task, it remembers the procedure how it solved the problem or how it reaches to the particular conclusion. The algorithm then uses these steps to find the solution of other similar problem or task. This helping of one algorithm to another can also be termed as inductive transfer mechanism. If the learners share their experience with each other, the learners can learn concurrently rather than individually and can be much faster [23].

Ensemble Learning

When various individual learners are combined to form only one learner then that particular type of learning is called ensemble learning. The individual learner may be Naïve Bayes, decision tree, neural network, etc. Ensemble learning is a hot topic since 1990s. It has been observed that, a collection of learners is almost always better at doing a particular job rather than individual learners. Two popular Ensemble learning techniques are given below (Jordan et al., 2015):

1. **Boosting**: Boosting is a technique in ensemble learning which is used to decrease bias and variance. Boosting creates a collection of weak learners and converts them to one strong learner. A weak learner is a classifier which is barely correlated with true classification. On the other hand, a strong learner is a type of classifier which is strongly correlated with true classification (Papernot et al., 2016).
2. **Bagging**: Bagging or bootstrap aggregating is applied where the accuracy and stability of a machine learning algorithm needs to be increased. It is applicable in classification and regression. Bagging also decreases variance and helps in handling over fitting (Papernot et al., 2016).

Neural Network Learning

The neural network (or artificial neural network or ANN) is derived from the biological concept of neurons. A neuron is a cell like structure in a brain. To understand neural network, one must understand how a neuron works. A neuron has mainly four parts .They are dendrites, nucleus, soma and axon.

The dendrites receive electrical signals. Soma processes the electrical signal. The output of the process is carried by the axon to the dendrite terminals where the output is sent to next neuron. The nucleus is the heart of the neuron. The inter-connection of neuron is called neural network where electrical impulses travel around the brain.

An artificial neural network behaves the same way. It works on three layers. The input layer takes input (much like dendrites). The hidden layer processes the input (like soma and axon). Finally, the output layer sends the calculated output (like dendrite terminals) (Abdelhamid et al., 2014) as in Figure 9.

Instance-Based Learning

In instance-based learning, the learner learns a particular type of pattern. It tries to apply the same pattern to the newly fed data. Hence the name instance based. It is a type of lazy learner which waits for the test data to arrive and then act on it together with training data. The complexity of the learning algorithm

Figure 9. Neural network

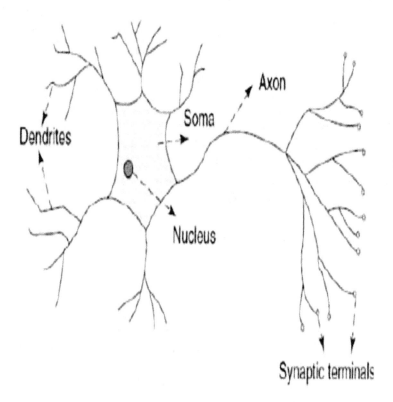

increases with the size of the data. Given below is a well-known example of instance-based learning which k-nearest neighbor is (Papernot et al., 2016).

1. **K-Nearest Neighbor**: In k-nearest neighbor (or KNN), the training data (which is well-labeled) is fed into the learner. When the test data is introduced to the learner, it compares both the data. K most correlated data is taken from training set. The majority of k is taken which serves as the new class for the test data (Papernot et al., 2016).

MACHINE LEARNING ON CYBER ATTACK

ML algorithms and techniques were originally designed for stationary environments in which both the training and test data were assumed to be generated from the same distribution (Griffor et al., 2017). Increasingly, these algorithms are now being used as online learners, where they are periodically retrained for decision making in security oriented systems. Examples include fraud detection, spam filtering, and even network intrusion detection systems. In these applications, the purpose of the ML models is to prevent access from unauthorized users.

ML algorithms can be susceptible to an adept and sophisticated adversary in both the retraining and decision-making phases. Research in this area has been termed Adversarial Machine Learning and has been defined by Huang et al. as "the design of machine learning algorithms that can resist sophisticated attacks, and the study of the capabilities and limitations of attackers" (Louridas et al., 2016).

Attack Surface

The attack surface of any system is the set of points or vectors where the system is vulnerable to attack. Papernot et al. (2016) presents the attack surface of a ML system as a data processing pipeline. The four sections of their pipeline consist of an input physical domain, digital representation, ML model, and the output physical domain. The input physical domain is where input features are collected from the physical world. This could come from physical I/O hardware such as cameras or infrared sensors. This input is then processed into a digital representation, such as a JPEG image, into the system. The digital representation can then be used by the ML model to produce an output. The output can then be transferred to the output physical domain.

Threat Model

An early attempt to categorize adversarial machine learning attacks was done by Barreno et al. In their paper, they explored the security of ML and developed a taxonomy based on a three-axis model of the attack space. The first axis labeled as influence, describes the capabilities of the attacker as either causative or exploratory. Causative attacks modify the training process via influence over the training data, whereas exploratory attacks use other methods such as probing that do not affect the training data but rather attempt to gather information about the learning model. The second axis of their model is labeled as security violation and defines the goal of the adversary as either an integrity attack where the machine learner allows false negatives (intrusions into the system), or as an availability attack where the learner is subjected to a denial of service event by allowing false positives (blocking legitimate data).

The third axis, labeled as specificity, refers to the precision of the attacker's intention as either targeted or indiscriminate. An attacker with a targeted intention is attempting to degrade the machine learner's performance for a small set of data points or a particular data point. An indiscriminate attack would cause the machine learner to fail in a broader set of data. The taxonomy developed by Barreno et al. has been further developed in subsequent work and later incorporated into a framework for security evaluation. Biggio et al. (2014) provided the framework used to evaluate the security of pattern classifier algorithms in three real world examples of spam filtering, biometric authentication, and network intrusion detection.

Later the same research group evaluated the security of support vector machines using the framework in the application examples of malware detection in PDF files and image recognition of handwritten digits. The framework is also used by Mozaffari et al. to evaluate the security of six different types of ML algorithms (decision tree, rule based, naïve bayes, nearest neighbor, artificial neural network, and support vector machine) in healthcare applications. Through the use of the framework, the ML algorithms can be evaluated on the attack methods described in the next section.

Papernot et al. (2016) contributed a threat model taxonomy that represented the complexity of ML attacks. Their model showed that the complexity of an attack increased as the adversary's knowledge of the model decreased and as the adversary's goals became more targeted. The least complex attack in their taxonomy would come from an adversary that had complete knowledge of the ML model and whose goal was to reduce the confidence in the model's output. The most complex attack would come from an adversary that only had sample input and output data with a goal of forcing a specific output from a specific input.

MACHINE LEARNING SECURITY FOR CPS

In this section, security vulnerabilities of ML are considered from a CPSs view. The attack surface will be described and possible methods of attacking CPSs through their ML model are discussed. Additionally, scenarios are presented discussing how CPSs such as autonomous vehicles and drones might be attacked via these methods.

CPS Attack Surface

The attack surface of embedded systems categorized based on the layers of the system are the hardware, firmware/operating system, and application layers. Hardware layer attacks could occur both during and post production by various methods including hardware backdoors, hardware trojans, eavesdropping, fault injection, and hardware modification. Firmware and operating system layer attacks could occur by the attacker installing malicious versions of the system's firmware or drivers through updates or by attacking vulnerabilities or bugs in the underlying operating system.

Attacks to the application layer occur as attacks to the software programs or applications that the embedded system executes. Some examples include viruses, worms, software trojans, and buffer overflow attacks. As previously discussed, CPSs such as drones or autonomous vehicles are embedded systems and systems like these can also have a ML component. However, ML security is not well represented in the attack surface categorized by Papp et al. The ML component is not part of the hardware of a cyber-physical system though it can be directly influenced by the hardware or sensors. Nor is it part of the firmware or operating system, even though it can also be influenced by both the firmware and operating system. Some might consider the ML model as part of the application layer as it is generally responsible for a particular function of the system such as image identification.

However, a ML component does not fit well as a normal software application. In general, a software application or program is thought of as a group of instructions that are executed in logical steps to perform a particular task. These instructions are written by a programmer and do not change unless the program is modified by the developer. Therefore, no matter what input data the application processes, a predetermined result will be produced based on the static nature of the program instructions. This is not the case with a ML algorithm as they are not programmed but rather trained to produce an output. In the case of an online learning method such as reinforcement learning, the program output could gradually change over time.

Since ML does not fit well in the application layer, it is suggested that that the classification developed by Papp et al. be extended to cover attacks that target ML. It is proposed that a ML attack layer be added to the classification. This layer will only contain attacks (i.e., evasion and data poisoning) that are targeting the ML model of an embedded system. The extended target level categorization is presented. It is worth noting that the attack surface by Papernot et al. depicted in section 2 is contained in the ML layer. The only exception would be a possible overlap with respect to the hardware layer and the physical input and output domains described by Papernot et al.

The main difference is that these systems will operate in the physical world on a day to day basis and will have to react to real world situations. As such, these systems are likely to be online or reinforcement learners. Recently, the Israeli company Mobileye announced that it will be testing the reinforcement learning approach on roads with BMW. In this section, we briefly describe some possible attack methods.

Sensor Driver Attack

For this attack, we must assume that the attacker has some level of knowledge of the interface between the firmware drivers of the CPS and their interaction with the ML model. In this attack, an adversary would install a malicious version of a sensor's firmware driver. The malicious driver could then feed the ML model malicious or distorted data. In an online learner, this could affect the training of the model over time to produce incorrect outputs.

An example of this form of attack could be the camera firmware used for image detection. If corrupted, the driver could introduce noise into the data fed to the machine learner. This could result in images being misclassified. Or if used in an online learning situation the training of the classifier could cause the model to degrade over time. Interestingly enough this type of attack could be classified as an exploratory attack in the first case and as a causative attack in the latter case.

Adversarial Data Attack

This is an exploratory form of attack that would require no modification to the CPS whatsoever. In this method, adversarial data could be crafted and presented to the CPS via sensors in order to fool the ML model. This involve external manipulation of sensors of a CPS. Several of these sensor related attacks are detailed in work done by Petit et al. (n.d.) on automated vehicle sensors. In this work, simple laser pointers or LEDs were used to degrade the performance of cameras used for autonomous vehicles.

Additionally, fake echoes were created in the LiDAR sensors by using two transceivers. Given that previous research has shown that transferability exists between models, it's easy to see how an adversary could take the necessary steps to create and train their own model for use with camera or LiDAR sensors, then use their model and possibly some of the methods in craft adversarial examples. The adversary could then use these examples on the ML model employed by the CPS.

External Poisoning Attacks

As previously mentioned, in a poisoning attack the adversary is attempting to influence the training data of the machine learner. If we consider that CPSs like autonomous vehicles or drones are trained in an online fashion then they will be susceptible to poisoning attacks in day to day operation. A case could be surmised where an adversary devised a method to fool a camera on an automated vehicle to always think that a stop sign or impediment existed on a particular street. Over time, the existence of the projected stop sign or impediment would affect the training of the autonomous vehicle. This could result in a slower approach by the vehicle to the particular location or possibly the vehicle may reroute itself to avoid the location.

Logic Corruption Attack

This attack is very similar to other classic software or firmware attacks where malicious code is inserted into a running program. However, it must be mentioned, as it is the strongest form of attack on a ML system. In this case, the adversary would have complete control of the ML model and be able to directly manipulate the outputs, alter the feature set, or modify the underlying algorithm which could result in a change in the behavior or training of the model. It is assumed that the attacker would have a high level of knowledge about the system and access through a HW communications port in order to perform this attack. This form of attack would be causative in nature as it directly makes internal modifications to the ML model.

Need for CPS Intelligence

The incorporation of intelligence will make the CPS to be able to execute complex tasks in dynamic environments and under unforeseen conditions. To address this uncertainty of physical world, machine learning provides solutions in a statistic manner, which would always try to make optimal decisions in terms of performance such as prediction accuracy, efficiency, robustness, and other specific metrics. Among many types of machine learning methods, classification and clustering would have wide applications in CPS to identify patterns among the collected sensor data, such as anomaly detection for protecting system safety, behavior recognition for understanding surrounding environment, prediction for system optimization and planning, to name a few. In this thesis, we will propose a wide range of learning algorithms ranging from feature representation, classification and anomaly detection, and show that they can improve the learning performance for many real-life applications.

Machine Learning Algorithms in CPS

The first important part of intelligent CPS considered in this thesis is the development of advanced machine learning algorithms which is the study of how to automatically learn from past observations to make accurate predictions and decisions. The incorporation of machine learning algorithms will bring intelligence into various kinds of systems and enable them to handle uncertainty in the interaction of physical world. In below, we will briefly discuss the motivations of different types of machine learning problems in the context of CPS applications:

Feature Representation in CPS

The wide use of high-resolution sensors leads to high-dimensional data sets in many CPS. The learning performance will be reduced when the dimensionality increases for limited labeled data, which is usually referred to as the \curse of dimensionality" issue. Instead of using all features, it is better to select those most important features to reduce redundancy and irrelevancy among data, thereby improving the learning performance and reducing the computational burden as well. Most existing feature selection methods consider the dependency and relevancy among features as the rule, and their theoretical analysis is missing. An optimal feature selection rule is needed to select those features with maximum discriminative capacity for discrimination.

Machine Learning Usage In Cyber Security

Machine learning (ML) is not something new that security domain has to adapt or utilize. It has been used and is being used in various areas of cyber security. Different machine learning methods have been successfully deployed to address wide-ranging problems in computer security. Following sections highlight some applications of machine learning in cyber security such as spam detection, network intrusion detection systems and malware detection.

Spam Detection

Traditional approach of detecting spam is usage of rules also known as knowledge engineering. In this method, mails are categorized as spam- or genuine-based set of rules that are created manually either by the user. For example, a set of rules can be:

- If the subject line of an email contains words 'lottery', its spam.
- Any email from a certain address or from a pattern of addresses is spam. However, this approach is not completely effective, as a manual rule doesn't scale because of active spammers evading any manual rules. Using machine learning approach, there is no need specifying rules explicitly; instead, a decent amount of data pre-classified as spam and not spam is being used. Once a machine learning model with good generalization capabilities is learned, it can handle previously unseen spam emails and take decisions accordingly.

Network Intrusion Detection

Network intrusion detection (NID) systems are used to identify malicious network activity leading to confidentiality, integrity or availability violation of the systems in a network. Many intrusion detection systems are specifically based on machine learning techniques due to their adaptability to new and unknown attacks.

Malware Detection

Over the last few years, traditional anti-malware companies have stiff competition from new generation of endpoint security vendors that major on machine learning as a method of threat detection. Using machine learning, machines are taught how to detect threats, and, with this knowledge, the machine can detect new threats that have never been seen before. This is a huge advantage over signature-based detection which relies on recognizing malware that it has already seen.

Machine Learning and Security Information and Event Management (Siem) Solution

Security information and event management (SIEM) solutions have started leveraging machine learning into its latest versions, to make it quicker and easier to maximize the value machine data can deliver to organizations. Certain vendors are enabling companies to use predictive analytics to help improve IT, security and business operations.

Table 1. ML and Dl algorithm classification ranges

Method	Classification Accuracy %
C4.5	80%
ANN	92%
b-Clustering	95%
Intelligible SVM	93.4%
Hybrid model of hierarchical clustering	86%
SVM with RBF	80%
ANN	79%
ANN	85%
LDA-SVM and FFNN	72%
Self-organized Maps (SOM) –clustering	75%
K-means clustering	83%
Convolutional Neural Networks	95%

CONCLUSION

There is a range of different components in a system where each has particular communication input-output and its own set tasks, which provide particular challenges associated with controlling or predicting the behavior of such systems. This chapter emphasizes on securing CPSs is a hard problem, even with the recognition that the goal is not absolute security. The cross study of computing, communication, controlling and other disciplines brought a broad application prospects and more benefits to CPS, but it also brings a lot of new difficulties, such as designing of connection between different components. Thus, the better understanding of the conception and meaning of CPS, provide guidance to integrate better mechanisms with the CPS design ideas. The security objectives to be fulfilled based on possible challenges in CPS, attacks and its countermeasures are discussed based on adoption of machine learning and deep learning thus providing an intelligent CPS.

REFERENCES

Abdelhamid, N., Ayesh, A., & Thabtah, F. (2014). Phishing detection based associative classification data mining. *Expert Systems with Applications*, *41*(13), 5948–5959. doi:10.1016/j.eswa.2014.03.019

Alfayyadh, B., Ponting, J., Alzomai, M., & Jøsang, A. (2010). Vulnerabilities in personal firewalls caused by poor security usability. *IEEE Int'l Conf. on Infor. Theor. and Infor. Security*, 682–688.

Alom, M. Z., Bontupalli, V., & Taha, T. M. (2015). Intrusion detection using deep belief networks. *IEEE National Aerospace and Electronics Conference (NAECON)*.

Biggio, Fumera, & Roli. (2014). Security evaluation of pattern classifiers under attack. *IEEE Transactions on Knowledge and Data Engineering, 26*(4), 984-996.

Biggio, B. (2014). *Security evaluation of support vector machines in adversarial environments. In Support Vector Machines Applications* (pp. 105–153). Springer.

Biggio. (n.d.). Evasion attacks against machine learning at test time. *Joint European Conference on Machine Learning and Knowledge Discovery in Databases*, 387-402. doi:10.1109/ICITIS.2010.5689490

Feizollah. (2013). A study of machine learning classifiers for anomaly-based mobile botnet detection. *Malaysian Journal of Computer Science*.

Friedberg, I., McLaughlin, K., Smith, P., Laverty, D., & Sezer, S. (2017). STPA-SafeSec: Safety and security analysis for cyber-physical systems. *J. Inf. Secur. Appl.*, *34*, 183–196.

Gardiner, J., & Nagaraja, S. (2016). On the Security of Machine Learning in Malware C8C Detection. *ACM Computing Surveys*, *49*(3), 1–39. doi:10.1145/3003816

Ge. (2017). Analysis of Cyber-Physical Security Issues via Uncertainty Approaches. In *Advanced Computational Methods in Life Systems Modeling and simulation*. Springer.

Giani, A., Bitar, E., Garcia, M., McQueen, M., Khargonekar, P., & Poolla, K. (2013). Smart grid data integrity attacks. *IEEE Transactions on Smart Grid*, *4*(3), 1244–1253.

Hink, R. C. B. (2014). *Machine learning for power systems disturbance and cyber-physical attacks discrimination*. IEEE ISRCS.

Hug, G., & Giampapa, J. A. (2012). Vulnerability assessment of ac state estimation with respect to false data injection cyber-attacks. *IEEE Transactions on Smart Grid*, *3*(3), 1362–1370.

Jordan, M. I., & Mitchell, T. M. (2015). Machine learning: Trends, perspectives, and prospects. *Science*, *349*(6245), 255–260. doi:10.1126cience.aaa8415 PMID:26185243

Khan, Baharudin, Lee, & Khan. (2010). A review of machine learning algorithms for text documents classification. *Journal of Advances in Information Technology*.

Kurakin, A., Goodfellow, I., & Bengio, S. (2016). *Adversarial examples in the physical world*. arXiv preprint arXiv: 1607.02533

Louridas, P., & Ebert, C. (2016). Machine Learning. *IEEE Software*, *33*(5), 110–115. doi:10.1109/MS.2016.114

Manadhata, P. K., & Wing, J. M. (2011). An attack surface metric. *Software Engineering, IEEE Transactions on*, *37*(3), 371–386. doi:10.1109/TSE.2010.60

Mitchell, R., & Chen, I.-R. (n.d.). *Effect of intrusion detection and response on reliability of cyber physical systems*. Retrieved from: http://people.cs.vt.edu/~irchen/ps/Mitchell-TR13a.pdf

Mozaffari-Kermani, M., Sur-Kolay, S., Raghunathan, A., & Jha, N. K. (2015). Systematic poisoning attacks on and defenses for machine learning in healthcare. *IEEE Journal of Biomedical and Health Informatics*, *19*(6), 1893–1905. doi:10.1109/JBHI.2014.2344095 PMID:25095272

Nelson, B. (2012). Query strategies for evading convex inducing classifiers. *Journal of Machine Learning Research*, *13*(May), 1293–1332.

NIST Special Publication 1500-201. (2017). NIST Framework for Cyber-Physical System: volume 1. Overview.

Papernot, N., McDaniel, P., Goodfellow, I., Jha, S., Celik, Z. B., & Swami, A. (2016). *Practical black-box attacks against deep learning systems using adversarial examples.* arXiv preprint arXiv:1602.02697

Papernot, N., McDaniel, P., Jha, S., Fredrikson, M., Celik, Z. B., & Swami, A. (2016). The limitations of deep learning in adversarial settings. In *Security and Privacy (EuroS&P), 2016 IEEE European Symposium on* (pp. 372-387). IEEE. 10.1109/EuroSP.2016.36

Papernot, N., McDaniel, P., Sinha, A., & Wellman, M. (2016). *Towards the Science of Security and Privacy in Machine Learning.* arXiv preprint arXiv:1611.03814

Pascanu, R., Stokes, J. W., Sanossian, H., Marinescu, M., & Thomas, A. (2015). Malware classification with recurrent networks. *IEEE International Conference on Acoustics, Speech and Signal Processing (ICASSP).*

Pasqualetti. (2013). Attacks detection and identification in cyber-physical security systems. *IEEE TAC, 58*(11).

Petit, J., Stottelaar, B., Feiri, M., & Kargl, F. (n.d.). *Remote attacks on automated vehicle sensors: experiments on camera and LiDAR.* Retrieved from: https://pdfs.semanticscholar.org/e06f/ef73f5bad-0489bb033f490d41a046f61878a.pdf

Sabaliauskaite. (2013). Intelligent checkers to improve attack detection in cyber-physical systems. *IEEE CyberC.*

Szegedy, C. (2014). *Intriguing properties of neural networks.* arXiv preprint arXiv: 1312.6199

Tao, L., Golikov, S., Gai, K., & Qiu, M. (2015). A reusable software component for integrated syntax and semantic validation for services computing. *9th Int'l IEEE Symposium on Service-Oriented System Engineering,* 127–132. 10.1109/SOSE.2015.10

Taylor. (2017). Security Challenges and methods for protecting critical infrastructure cyber-physical systems. *IEEE MoWNeT.*

Tonge, A., Kasture, S., & Chaudhari, S. (2013). Cyber security: Challenges for society-literature review. *IOSR Journal of Computer Engineering, 2*(12), 67–75. doi:10.9790/0661-1226775

Wang, J. (2017). *Detecting time synchronization attacks in cyber-physical security systems with machine learning techniques.* IEEE ICDCS.

Wu, L. L. (2014). *Improving system reliability for cyber-physical systems.* Columbia University. Retrieved from: https://www.researchgate.net/profile/Roger_Anderson20/publication/329044383_Leon_Wu_PhD_Thesis_Improving_System_Reliability_for_CyberPhysical_Systems_2014/links/5bf30f83299bf1124fde5df9/Leon-Wu-PhD-Thesis-Improving-System-Reliability-for-CyberPhysical-Systems-2014.pdf

Chapter 19
Variable Selection Method for Regression Models Using Computational Intelligence Techniques

Dhamodharavadhani S.
Periyar University, India

Rathipriya R.
Periyar University, India

ABSTRACT

Regression model (RM) is an important tool for modeling and analyzing data. It is one of the popular predictive modeling techniques which explore the relationship between a dependent (target) and independent (predictor) variables. The variable selection method is used to form a good and effective regression model. Many variable selection methods existing for regression model such as filter method, wrapper method, embedded methods, forward selection method, Backward Elimination methods, stepwise methods, and so on. In this chapter, computational intelligence-based variable selection method is discussed with respect to the regression model in cybersecurity. Generally, these regression models depend on the set of (predictor) variables. Therefore, variable selection methods are used to select the best subset of predictors from the entire set of variables. Genetic algorithm-based quick-reduct method is proposed to extract optimal predictor subset from the given data to form an optimal regression model.

DOI: 10.4018/978-1-5225-9611-0.ch019

INTRODUCTION

Describe Variable selection method plays a vital role to select the best subset of predictors. Variable selection method is the process of selection a subset of relevant predictors for fitting the model. In Regression model, variable selection is used to select the best subset of predictors to build the best regression model. Because redundant predictors are occurs in model that changes the behavior of effective predictors and also degree of freedom is misrepresented (Abraham A, 2003). There are many existing in the literature for regression model. Basically, three methods are used to select the variables for regression model. They are graphical represented in figure 1

The figure 2 describes the workflow of variable selection method. Generation Procedure implements a search method. This is used to generate subset of variables (Bjorvand, 1997). Evaluation Procedure is used to halt the process when an optimal subset is reached. Stopping Criterion is tested every iteration to determine whether the variable selection process should continue or not. If stopping condition has been satisfied, then the loop has been terminated. Validation procedure is used to validate the subset of variables (C. B. Lucasius, 1992).

Filter Methods

Filter feature selection methods apply a statistical measure to allocate a value to each feature. The features are ranked based on the value and also selected or removed from the dataset. The methods are frequently univariate and reflect the feature independently, or with regard to the dependent variable.

Figure 1. Variable selection methods

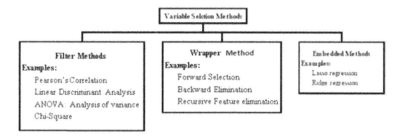

Figure 2. Workflow of variable selection method

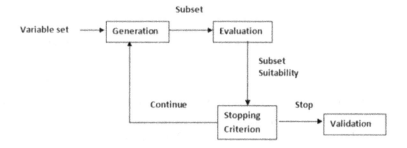

Wrapper Methods

A wrapper method is used to selection of a set of features as a search problem. sometimes different combinations are prepared, evaluated and compared to other combinations. A predictive model us used to evaluate a combination of features and assign a value based on model accuracy.

Embedded Methods

Embedded methods study which features best donate to the accuracy of the model. The most common type of embedded feature selection methods are regularization methods. Regularization methods are also called penalization methods that introduce additional constraints into the optimization of a predictive algorithm (such as a regression algorithm) that bias the model toward lower complexity (fewer coefficients) (Airong Cai, 2009) (Bruce Ratner, 2010).

Feature selection is the method of reducing data dimension while doing predictive analysis. Various kinds of feature selection techniques are used in machine learning problem. The feature selection techniques simplify the machine learning models in order to make it easier to interpret by the researchers. Also, this technique reduces the problem of overfitting by enhancing the generalization in the model. Hence, it helps in better understanding of data, improves prediction performance, reducing the computational time as well as space which is required to run the algorithm (Airong Cai, 2009) (Bruce Ratner, 2010).

In this chapter, computational intelligence based variable selection method is introduced for regression model. It identify the optimal subset of predictors to build the effective regression model for better predicting accuracy.

Objective of Chapter

1. To select the best optimal predictor subset to fitting the regression model from the given dataset.
2. GA Based Variable Selection Method proposed for selecting optimal subset of predictors

Outline of this Chapter

The outline of this chapter is organized as follows: Section 2 describes the literature survey. In section 3, methods and materials required for the proposed work are discussed. In session 4, presents the proposed GA based Variable Selection Algorithm for regression model and experimental results are discussed and analyzed. Section 5 concludes the proposed work.

Background

Rough sets (Pawlak, 1982, 1991, 1997) can handle uncertainty and vagueness, discovering patterns in inconsistent data. Rough sets have been a useful feature selection method in pattern recognition (Chouchoulas and Shen, 2001) (Abraham A, 2003) (Bjorvand, 1997).

The rough set approach to feature selection is to select a subset of features (or attributes), which can predict the decision concepts as well as the original feature set. The optimal criterion for rough set feature selection is to find shortest or minimal reducts while obtaining high quality classifiers based on the selected features (Swiniarski and Skowron, 2003) (C. B. Lucasius, 1992).

Bir Bhanu, Yingqiang Lin proposed Genetic algorithm-based feature selection for target detection in SAR images. A genetic algorithm (GA) approach is presented to select a set of features to discriminate the targets from the natural clutter false alarms in SAR images (Dash, M, 1997).

Yi Hong, Sam Kwong, Yuchou Chang proposed Unsupervised feature selection using clustering ensembles and population based incremental learning algorithm unsupervised feature selection algorithm is to search for a subset of all features such that the clustering algorithm trained on this feature subset can achieve the most similar clustering solution to the one obtained by an ensemble learning algorithm (De Castro, 2002).

Amit Saxena and John Wang proposed Dimensionality Reduction with Unsupervised Feature Selection and Applying Non-Euclidean Norms for Classification Accuracy an unsupervised approach to select a subset of features is applied. GA is used to select stochastically reduced number of features with Sammon Error as the fitness function. Different subsets of features are obtained.

C.Velayutham and K.Thangavel proposed Unsupervised Quick Reduct Algorithm Using Rough Set Theory which is applied in unsupervised dataset for reducting a noisy and irrelevant attributes (C.Velayutham, 2011).

C.Velayutham and K.Thangavel proposed unsupervised feature selection based on the measures of degree of dependency using rough set theory in digital mammogram image classification (C.Velayutham, 2011).

Nasrin Sheikhi, Amirmasoud Rahmani proposed An Unsupervised Feature Selection Method Based On Genetic Algorithm. In this method we introduce a new kind of features that we called multi term features. Multi-term feature is the combination of terms with different length. So we design a genetic algorithm to find the multi term features that have maximum discriminating power.

C.Velayutham and K.Thangavel proposed a novel entropy based unsupervised Feature Selection algorithm using rough set theory (C.Velayutham, 2012).

Wu jian, proposed Unsupervised Intrusion Feature Selection based on Genetic Algorithm and FCM, A novel feature selection based on genetic algorithm (GA) and fuzzy c-means clustering (FCM) for unsupervised intrusion detection is proposed. A novel feature selection based on genetic algorithm (GA) and fuzzy c-means clustering (FCM) for unsupervised intrusion detection is proposed. A novel feature selection based on genetic algorithm (GA) and fuzzy c-means clustering (FCM) for unsupervised intrusion detection is proposed.

Pirooz Shamsinejadbabki, Mohammad Saraee proposed A new unsupervised feature selection method for text clustering based on genetic algorithms (Pirooz Shamsinejadbabki,2012).

Majid Mahrooghy, Nicolas H. Younan proposed algorithm using Genetic Algorithm Filter for Feature Selection Technique for Satellite Precipitation Estimation (Mahrooghy, 2012).

Bruce Ratner (2010) variable selection in regression to identifying the best subset among many variables to include in a model is arguably the hardest part of model building. The purpose of this article is two-fold: (1) to re-examine the scope of the literature addressing the weaknesses of variable selection methods and (2) to re-enliven a possible solution to defining a better-performing regression model (Bruce Ratner, 2010).

Airong Cai(2009) The proposed algorithm performs well in simulation studies with 60 to 300 predictors. As a by-product of the proposed procedure, we are able to study the behavior of variable selection criteria when the number of predictors is large. Such a study has not been possible with traditional search algorithms.

From this study, variable selection methods are necessary for regression model to identifying the best subset of predictors from the entire set of variables. And also Computational Intelligence based variable selection method is effective method. In this chapter, Genetic Algorithm based quick reduct method is proposed to extract optimal predictor subset from the given data to form optimal regression model.

METHODS AND MATERIALS

Computational intelligence Algorithms: An Overview

Present your perspective on the issues, controversies, problems, etc., as they relate to theme and arguments supporting your position. Compare and contrast with what has been, or is currently being done as it relates to the chapter's specific topic and the main theme of the book. Computational Intelligence is a general term referring to computing inspired by nature. The idea is to mimic the complex a phenomenon occurring in the nature as computational processes in order to enhance how is performed from a problem solving point of view. Characteristic for man-designed computing inspired by nature is the metaphorical use of concepts, principles and mechanisms underlying natural systems (R. Eberhart, 1995).

Computational Intelligence Algorithms

Computational intelligence technique provides two major categories. They are shown in figure3.

Evolutionary Algorithm

Evolutionary algorithms are adaptive methods which may be used to solve search and optimization problems based on the genetic processes of biological organisms. In many generations natural populations evolve according to the principles of natural selection and 'survival of the fittest'. By mimicking this process evolutionary algorithms are able to 'evolve' solutions to real world problems if they have been suitably encoded (Abraham A, 2003).

Figure 3. Computational intelligence algorithms

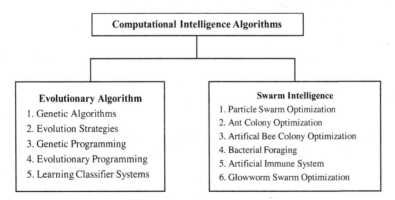

Usually grouped under the term evolutionary algorithms or evolutionary computation we find the domains of genetic algorithms, evolution strategies, genetic programming evolutionary programming, and learning classifier systems. These methods are share a common conceptual base of simulating the evolution of individual structures via processes of selection, mutation, and reproduction.

Swarm Intelligence

Swarm intelligence is aimed at collective behavior of intelligent agents in decentralized systems. Most of the basic ideas are derived from the real swarms in the nature, which includes ant colonies, bird flocking, honeybees, bacteria and microorganisms etc. Swarm models are population-based and the population is initialized with a population of potential solutions. These individuals are then manipulated (optimized) over many several iterations using several heuristics inspired from the social behavior of insects in an effort to find the optimal solution (El-Gallad, 2001).

The major advantages of using Computational Intelligence methods are: Scalability, Adaptability, Collective Robustness and Simplicity

Regression Model

Regression model is an effective predictive modeling method. It based on the relationship between a dependent (Target) variables and independent variables (predictor).This model is used for prediction based on relationship between the variables. If the independent variable (predictor) is changed, then changes occur in dependent variable. This two variables are related each other. It shows the important of relationship between dependent variable and independent variable and specifics the strength of multiple independent variables on a dependent variable. Regression model are also finding the effective variables based on the different measures. These are very useful to selecting the best set of variables to be used for building the best predictive models (Airong et. al, 2009).

Various techniques are existing for build the regression model. These techniques are depends on the three measures. They are (Airong et. al, 2009)

- Number of independent variables
- Type of dependent variables
- Shape of regression line

Three common types of Regression Model are used as shown below

- Simple Linear Regression Model
- Multiple Linear Regression Model
- Logistic Regression Model

Simple Linear Regression Model

Simple Linear Regression Model is used to predict a measureable response variable Y based on the only one predictor variable X. To build a regression model based on the relationship between the X and Y variables (Airong Cai, 2009).

The General equation of $y = \alpha + \beta * x + \varepsilon$ (1)

y = Response, outcome, or dependent variable
x = Predictor, explanatory, or independent variable
α = Intercept
β = Slope of the line
ε = Error term

Multiple Linear Regression model is used to predict a measureable response variable Y based on the more than one predictor variables X1, X2..... .

The general form of this model is (Bruce Ratner, 2010):

$$y = \beta_0 + \beta_1 x_1 + \beta_2 x_2 + ... + \beta_k x_k + \varepsilon \qquad (2)$$

y = Response, outcome, or dependent variable
$x_1, x_2 ... x_k$ = Predictor, explanatory, or independent variable
$\beta_0, \beta_1 ... \beta_k$ = Regression weight or Beta Coefficient
ε = Error

Logistic Regression Model

Logistic Regression is a classification model. It is used to predict the binary / categorical (1 / 0, Yes / No, True / False) response variable given a set of predictor variables. It predicts the likelihood occurrence of variables by fitting a model based on logit function (Bruce Ratner, 2010)

$$Log = \left(\frac{P}{1-P}\right) y = \beta_0 + \beta_1 x_1 + \beta_2 x_2 + ... + \beta_k x_k \qquad (3)$$

Where P = probability

y = Response, outcome, or dependent variable
$x_1, x_2 ... x_k$ = Predictor, explanatory, or independent variable
$\beta_0, \beta_1 ... \beta_k$ = Regression weight or Beta Coefficient

Genetic Algorithm (GA) Concepts

The GA is a stochastic global search method that mimics the metaphor of natural biological evolution. GAs operates on a population of potential solutions applying the principle of survival of the fittest to produce (hopefully) better and better approximations to a solution. At each generation a new set of approximations is created by the process of selecting individuals according to their level of fitness in the problem domain and breeding them together using operators borrowed from natural genetics. This process leads to the evolution of populations of individuals that are better suited to their environment than the individuals that they were created from, just as in natural adaptation. Individuals or current approximations are encoded as strings, chromosomes composed over some alphabet(s) so that the genotypes (chromosome values) are uniquely mapped onto the decision variable (phenotypic) domain (Han, J, 2004).

Once the individuals have been assigned a fitness value they can be chosen from the population with a probability according to their relative fitness and recombined to produce the next generation. Genetic operators manipulate the characters (genes) of the chromosomes directly using the assumption that certain individual's gene codes on average produce fitter individuals. The recombination operator is used to exchange genetic information between pairs or larger groups of individuals (J. Kennedy, 1995).

Selection

Selection is the process of determining the number of times or a trial a particular individual is chosen for reproduction and thus the number of offspring that an individual will produce (J. Borges, 1999). The selection of individuals can be viewed as two separate processes:

1)   Determination of the number of trials an individual can expect to receive, and
2)   Conversion of the expected number of trials into a discrete number of offspring.

The first part is concerned with the transformation of raw fitness values into a real valued expectation of an individual's probability to reproduce and is dealt with in the previous subsection as fitness assignment (J. Sadri, 2006). The second part is the probabilistic selection of individuals for reproduction based on the fitness of individuals relative to one another and is sometimes known as sampling. The remainder of this subsection will review some of the more popular selection methods in current usage.

Single Point Cross-Over

The simplest recombination operator is that of single-point crossover.
Consider the two parent binary strings:

P1 = 1 0 0 1 0 1 1 0, and
P2 = 1 0 1 1 1 0 0 0.

If an integer position, i is selected uniformly at random between 1 and the string length l, minus one [1, l-1] and the genetic information exchanged between the individuals about this point then two new offspring strings are produced (Krishnanand, K.N, 2009). The two offspring below are produced when the crossover point i = 5 is selected,

O1 = 1 0 0 1 0 0 0 0, and
O2 = 1 0 1 1 1 1 1 0.

Mutation

This crossover operation is not necessarily performed on all strings in the population. Instead it is applied with a probability Px when the pairs are chosen for breeding (Komorowski, J, 1999). A further genetic operator called mutation. Then we applied to the new chromosomes again with a set probability Pm. Mutation causes the individual genetic representation to be changed according to some probabilistic rule. In the binary string representation mutation will cause a single bit to change its state0 $\Rightarrow$ 1 or 1 $\Rightarrow$ 0. So, for example, mutating the fourth bit of O1 leads to the new string

O1m = 1 0 0 0 0 0 0 0.

Mutation is generally considered to be a background operator that ensures that the probability of searching a particular subspace of the problem space is never zero. This has the effect of tending to inhibit the possibility of converging to a local optimum rather than the global optimum (Kennedy, 1997).

After recombination and mutation the individual strings are then if necessary decoded the objective function evaluated a fitness value assigned to each individual and individuals selected for mating according to their fitness and so the process continues through subsequent generations. In this way, the average performance of individuals in a population is expected to increase as good individuals are preserved and bred with one another and the less fittest individuals die out. The GA is terminated when some criteria are satisfied. e.g. a certain number of generations a mean deviation in the population or when a particular point in the search space is encountered (M. Dorigo, 2005).

Genetic Algorithm based Variable Selection Algorithm

1.   Initialize the Population.
2.   2. Evaluate the fitness of the Population using equation()

$$\alpha * \delta R(D) + \beta * \frac{|C| - |R|}{|C|}$$

3.   For t=1 to max_iteration

```
Select p(t)
Crossover p(t)
Mutation p(t)
 Reinsertion p(t)
 Evaluate the fitness of p(t)
 End
```

4.   Return the maximum fitness individuals as the reduct

Find the Fitness function value using fitness function1

$$\alpha * \delta R(D) + \beta * \frac{|C| - |R|}{|C|} \qquad (4)$$

take random value α and β

Find the Fitness function value using fitness function2

$$\cos t\left(R\right) = \left[\frac{{}^3{}_C\left(D\right) - {}^3{}_R\left(D\right)}{{}^3{}_C\left(D\right)}\right] + \left[\frac{|R|}{|C|}\right] \qquad (5)$$

take random value α and β, similarly calculated all possible attributes (M. Fatih Tasgetiren, 2007).

New Fitness Values

Select the best three individuals. After selection, the selected individuals are inserted into the old population by replacing three worst individuals from it. Again, the above process is repeated until the max iteration is reached (M. F. Bramlette, 1991).

Selection p(t)

Selection is the process of determining the number of times or trials a particular individual is chosen for reproduction and thus the number of offspring that an individual will produce

Crossover p(t) (Single-Point Crossover)

When selection process is completed, single point crossover method is used to new individuals. Select the individual with maximum fitness value for next iteration.

Mutation p(t)

For every iteration, best individuals are selected using RWS. These individuals are undergoes the crossover and mutation. Using reinsert operator, 10% of the best individuals are reinserted into the old population. Again, the calculate the fitness function new population. The above process is proceed until if reached maximum iterations (Passino, K.M, 2002).

Fitness Function

The fitness function is used to provide a measure of how individuals have performed in the problem domain. In the case of a minimization problem the most fittest individuals will have the lowest numerical value of the associated objective function (Pawlak, Z, 1982). This raw measure of fitness is usually only used as an intermediate stage in determining the relative performance of individuals in a GA. Genetic algorithm used two different types of fitness functions.

They are,

Fitness Function 1

$$\alpha * \delta R(D) + \beta * \frac{|C| - |R|}{|C|} \tag{6}$$

where $\delta R(D)$ is the classification quality of condition attributes set R relative to decision D |R| is the length of the total number of features . α and β are two parameters that correspond to the importance of classification quality and subset length with $\alpha \in [0,1]$ and $\beta = 1-\alpha$. Setting a high α value assures that the best positions at least a real rough set reduct. The goal then is to maximize fitness values (R. Eberhart, 1995).

Fitness Function 2

$$\text{cost}(R) = \left[\frac{^3{}_C(D) - {}^3{}_R(D)}{^3{}_C(D)} \right] + \left[\frac{|R|}{|C|} \right] \tag{7}$$

where $\delta R(D)$ is the classification quality of condition attributes set R relative to decision D |R| is the length of the total number of features. The cost function attempts to maximize the rough set dependency (δ) whilst minimizing the subset cardinality (S. K. Madria, 1999) (Smith, M. G, 2003).

Experimental Results and Analysis

Dataset Description

In this chapter, to show the performance and effectiveness of the proposed feature selection algorithms, an empirical study is conducted on two datasets namely MSNBC and MSWEB.

- The MSWEB dataset is taken from the UCI KDD archive http://kdd.ics.uci.edu/databases/msweb/msweb.html) (Zhang, M., 2004)
- It records the logs within www.microsoft.com that users visited in one-week time frame during February 1998.
- After data preprocessing of web log data, the preprocessed data consist of 32711 sessions and 285 pages.
- Only root pages were considered in the page view of a session.
- This preprocessing step resulted in total of 17 categories namely

Table 1. Dataset description

DATASETS	ROWS (User Session)	COLUMNS (Pageview)
Msweb	2531	17
Msnbc	3386	17

```
"library", "developer", "home", "finance", "repository", "gallery", "cata-
log", "mail", "ads", "education", "magazine", "support", "ms", "technology",
"search", "country", "business", "entertainment", "news", "feedback".
```

- The MSNBC data set from the UCI dataset repository (http://kdd.ics.uci.edu/) that consists of Internet Information Server (IIS) logs for msnbc.com and news- related portions of msn.com for the entire day of September 28, 1999 (Pacific Standard Time).
- Each sequence in the dataset corresponds to page views of a user during that twenty-four hour period.
- It consists of 17 page view categories, namely,

```
"front page",  " news", "tech", "local", "opinion", "on-air",    "misc",
"weather", "health", "living", "business", "sports",    "summary", "bbs" (bul-
letin board service), "travel",    "msn-news" and "msnsports"
```

Table 2 shows the performance of the proposed variable selection using GA. It records the information such as number of variables selecting for each dataset. In order to identify the best predictor subset, entropy measure is used to evaluate the quality of the variable subset.

Table 3 shows variable selecting for predictors in GA based variable Selection method.

Table 4 and 5 shows that maximum fitness value for the GA based variable selection method which means that performance of this method is better.

Table 2. Total No. of variables selecting in GA-QR

DATASETS	US-GA-QR
MSWEB	9
MSNBC	6

Table 3. Variable selecting for predictors GA-QR

DATASETS	GA-QR
MSWEB	2,3,6,7,8,9,13,14,16
MSNBC	1,4,7,11,14,17

Table 4. Maximum fitness value using fitness function 1

DATASETS	GA-QR
MSWEB	0.7822
MSNBC	0.9294

Table 5. Maximum fitness value using fitness function 2

DATASETS	GA-QR
MSWEB	0.7709
MSNBC	0.9941

A table 6 and 7 show that entropy value for the GA based variable selection method which means that performance of this method is better.

From this study, it has been observed that GA-QR variable selection method is efficient in identifying the optimal subset of variables. GA-QR method is used to build the regression model. The detail description of regression model building is given in the subsequent section.

Analysis and Discussion of Regression Model

In this chapter two methods of model fitting were used for fitting multinomial logistic regression model to establish the variables that are related with web page usage. The two methods are used to build the regression model. The model1 GA-QR based variable selection method and model2 full variables are fitting the model (without variable selection method). A comparison of the models to determine the best method of model fitting was also conducted using AIC, Residual deviance and R-squared.

Table 6. Best entropy value in GA-QR fitness function 1

DATASETS	GA-QR
MSWEB	0.9995
MSNBC	0.9997

Table 7. Best entropy value in GA-QR fitness function 2

DATASETS	GA-QR
MSWEB	0.9993
MSNBC	0.9941

Multinomial Logistic Regression Model with GA-QR

Multinomial logistic regression is used to model nominal outcome variables, in which the log odds of the outcomes are modeled as a linear combination of the predictor variables. This section describes the multinomial logistic regression model with Genetic Algorithm based Ouick Reduct (GA-QR). GA-QR acted as a variable selection method to identify optimal subset of predictors for MSNBC dataset

Selection of Dependent and Independent Variables

.The variables used in the multinomial logistic regression model1 and model2 are summarized in the table 8 and 9.
  Model1

Formula: y~x1+x4+x7+x11+x14+x17 (8)

Mode12 Formula:y=x1+x2+x3+x4+x5+x6+x7+x8+x9+x10+x11+x12+x13+x14+x15+x16+x17
(9)

Table 10 summarized the variables of model1. The absolute value of the z-score tells you how many standard deviations you are away from the mean. If a z-score is equal to 0, it is on the mean. If a Z-Score is equal to +1, it is 1 Standard Deviation above the mean. If a z-score is equal to +2, it is 2 Standard Deviations above the mean. In the model, all predictor variables are equal to 0 and intercept is also -0.7146, therefore the model on the mean standard deviation.

The p-value for each term tests the null hypothesis that the coefficient is equal to zero means no effect. A low p-value (< 0.05) indicates to reject the null hypothesis. High p-value (> 0.05) indicates to best fit to model.

These are the logistic coefficients relative to the reference category. For example, under 'misc', the 0.98 suggests that for one unit increase in 'misc' score, the logit coefficient for 'class 2' relative to 'class1' will go down by that amount, 0.98. In other words, the user visiting 'misc' page time increases one unit; they have chances grouped the class 1 is highly compared to class2.

Table 8. Variables used model 1 (with variable selection)

Parameters	Variables (web pages)	Dependent (Response) / Independent (predictors)
Y	Class	Dependent
X1	Front page	Independent
X4	Local	Independent
X7	Misc	Independent
X11	Business	Independent
X14	Bbs	Independent
X17	Msnsports	Independent

Table 9. Variables used model2 (without variable selection)

Parameters	Variables (web pages)	Dependent (Response) / Independent (predictors)
Y	Class	Dependent
X1	Front page	Dependent
X2	News	Independent
X3	Tech	Independent
X4	Local	Independent
X5	Opinion	Independent
X6	On-air	Independent
X7	Misc	Independent
X8	Weather	Independent
X9	Health	Independent
X10	Living	Independent
X11	Business	Independent
X12	Sports	Independent
X13	Summary	Independent
X14	Bbs(bulletin board service)	Independent
X15	Travel	Independent
X16	msn-news	Independent
X17	Msnsports	Independent

Table 10. Variables in the equation (model 1 with variable selection)

Variables	Z score	p-Value	coef
X1	0.2896918	0.7720521	19.048277
X4	0.05778239	0.9539220	1.983923
X7	-0.002081131	0.9983395	0.98142
X11	-0.01546310	0.9876627	9.532704
X14	0.007155408	0.9942909	1.0846955
X17	0.1741106	0.8617785	3.227405
Intercept	-0.7146272	0.9748394	1.346133

The table 11 shows coefficient values for model1 based on class (response class). All other variables are constant in class2, if front page visiting increases one unit and also 19.048 times likely to stay in the class2 as compared to the class1 response variable. The coefficient however is significant.

All other variables are constant in class3, if front page visiting increases one unit and also 1.213 times likely to stay in the class2 as compared to the class3 response variable. The coefficient, however is significant

Table 11. Coefficients value for model 1 (variable selection) with class

Independent variable	Dependent variable	
	2 (1)	3(2)
X1	19.048 (10.173)	1.213 (12.764)
X4	1.984 (11.856)	1.306 (11.494)
X7	0.981(9.012)	1.194 (8.518)
X11	0.095 (152.003)	22,021.380 (160.987)
X14	1.085 (11.362)	0.972 (11.422)
X17	322,740,484.000 (112.528)	0.00000 (117.929)
Constant	0.000 (276.683)	0.000 (290.026)
AIC	28.001	28.001

Table 12 and 13 describes predicted probability of model. In model1, predicted probability for class1 is 2.162816 and predicted probability of class2 is 4.403364 based on class3. In model2, predicted probability for class1 is 0.0170616 and predicted probability of class2 is 0.7015274 based on class3

Table 14 shows the comparison of the methods of model fitting. Based on the Residual Deviance measures is goodness fit of a model. The value of the deviance is higher number it always indicates bad fit. The model 1 (with variable selection) residual deviance value is 0.00 and model 2 (without variable selection) value is 3.11. Comparing the two models deviance value model 1 is smaller than the model 2, therefore model 1 is best fit.

Based on the Akaike's Information Criterion (AIC) measure which takes into consideration the log-likelihood value and the number of variables retained in the model with variable selection method produced the best model (AIC = 28.0012 compared to 72.00003 for the model2).

In regression model R-squared (R2) represents the correlation coefficient between the response variable and predictor variables. R2 value is between ranges 0 to 1 (positive) it indicates best regression model. R2 value is closer to -1 (Negative) it indicates not a good fitting model. In above table model1 R2 value is 0.9351 and model2 is 0.006. It shows model1 is better than the model2.

Table 12. Predicted probability of model 1 (with variable selection)

Variables	Mean
X1	31.75
X4	50.16071
X7	41.91071
X11	21.71429
X14	151.2143
X17	6.321429
pred.prob.1	2.162816
pred.prob.2	4.403364
pred.prob	3

Table 13. Prediction probability of model 2 (without variable selection)

Variables	Mean
X1	31.75
X2	124.5536
X3	28.55357
X4	50.16071
X5	42.41071
X6	64.125
X7	41.91071
X8	26.39286
X9	6.125
X10	148.75
X11	21.71429
X12	58.42857
X13	5.446429
X14	151.2143
X15	4.517857
X16	4.178571
X17	6.321429
pred.prob.1	0.0170616
pred.prob.2	0.7015274
pred.prob	3

Table 14. Comparison of the two models

Model	Residual Deviance	AIC	R-Squared
Model1(with variable selection)	0.001195493	28.0012	0.9351
Model2 (without variable selection)	3.116591e-05	72.00003	0.006

In general, the most commonly used metrics for measuring regression model quality and for comparing models are R2, Adjusted R2, AIC and Cp as shown figure 4.

Regression Model in Cyber Security

For the past one decade, there is a rapid growth of the internet usage which in due increases the number of computer attacks and threats. The occurrence of cyber-attack activities has given rise to the need to prevent these attacks activities from damaging the computer system. Cyber-attacks threaten physical, economic, social and political security very miserably. Simply, it exploits the computer system and network without knowledge of the internet user. Regression Model is a commonly used technique to predict the cyber-attack / cyber threat from the set of variables or factors such as vulnerability, infusion

Figure 4. Regression model accuracy metrics: R-square, AIC, BIC, Cp

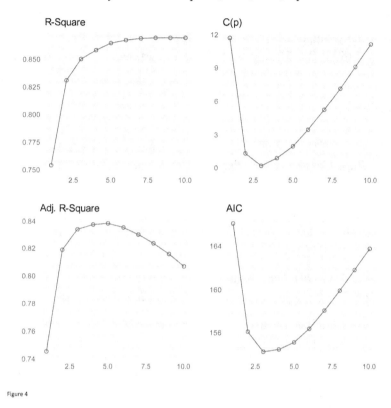

Figure 4

and social data, and network traffic. The discussed regressions models may be used to predict the impact of threat based on the significant factors that influence cyber security. Thus, the prediction of possibility of threat may be used to enhance the power of cyber security.

CONCLUSION

In this chapter, Genetic Algorithm Based variable selection method is introduced to extract the optimal predictor subset (i.e. subset of web pages of a website) from the web usage data. The empirical study was conducted for comparing the regression model using variable selection with the regression model without variable selection. It has been observed that regression model using optimal predictor subset (AIC 28.0012) outperforms normal regression model (AIC 72.00003). Therefore GA based variable selection method is better for fitting the regression model to predict the cyber- attack in advance from the significant factors.

ACKNOWLEDGMENT

This chapter is financially supported by the UGC- Special Assistance Programme (SAP) DRS-II (Ref. No.F.5-6/2018/DRS-II (SAP-II)), 26 July 2018 in the Department of Computer Science.

REFERENCES

Abraham, A., & Ramos, V. (2003). Web Usage Mining Using Artificial Ant Colony Clustering and Genetic Programming. *IEEE Congress on Evolutionary Computation (CEC2003)*, A1384-1391. 10.1109/CEC.2003.1299832

Bjorvand, A. T., & Komorowski, J. (1997). Practical applications of genetic algorithms for efficient reduct computation. *Proceedings of the 15th IMACS World Congress on Scientific Computation, Modelling and Applied Mathematics*, 4, 601–606.

Borges, J., & Levene, M. (1999). Data mining of user navigation patterns. *Proceedings of the WEB-KDD'99 Workshop on Web Usage Analysis and User Profiling*, 31–36.

Bramlette, M. F. (1991). Initialization, Mutation and Selection Methods in Genetic Algorithms for Function Optimization, *Proc ICGA 4*, 100-107.

Cai, A., Tsay, R. S., & Chen, R. (2009, September). Variable Selection in Linear Regression With Many Predictors. *Journal of Computational and Graphical Statistics*, 18(3), 573–591. doi:10.1198/jcgs.2009.06164

Dash, M., & Liu, H. (1997). Feature Selection for Classification. *Intelligent Data Analysis*, 1(3), 131–156. doi:10.3233/IDA-1997-1302

De Castro, L. N., & Timmis, J. I. (2002). *Artificial Immune Systems: A New Computational Intelligence Approach*. Springer-Verlag.

Dorigo, M., & Blum, C. (2005). Ant colony optimization theory A survey. *Theoretical Computer Science, 344*(2–3), 243–278.

Eberhart, R., & Kennedy, J. (1995). A New Optimizer Using Particles Swarm Theory. *Proc. Sixth International Symposium on Micro Machine and Human Science IEEE Service Center*, 39-43. 10.1109/MHS.1995.494215

El-Gallad, A. I., El-Hawary, M., Sallam, A. A., & Kalas, A. (2001). A Swarm intelligence for hybrid cost dispatch problem. *Canadian Conference on Electrical and Computer Engineering, 2*, 753-757.

Han, J., Hu, X., & Lin, T. Y. (2004, June). Feature Subset Selection Based on Relative Dependency between Attributes. *Rough Sets and Current Trends in Computing: 4th International Conference, RSCTC 2004*, 176–185. 10.1007/978-3-540-25929-9_20

Kennedy, J., & Eberhart, R. C. (1997). A discrete binary version of the particle swarm Algorithm. *IEEE Conference on Systems, Man, and Cybernetics*, 4104-4108.

Kennedy, J., & Eberhart, R. (1995). Particle Swarm Optimization. *IEEE Conference on Neural Networks*, 1942-1948.

Komorowski, J., Pawlak, Z., & Polkowski, L. (1999). Skowron, A Rough Sets Perspective on Data and Knowledge. In W. Klosgrn, & J. Zylkon (Eds.), *The Handbook of Data Mining and Knowledge Discovery* (pp. 134–149). New York, NY: Oxford University Press.

Krishnanand, K. N., & Ghose, D. (2009). Glowworm Swarm Optimization for Searching Higher Dimensional Spaces. In C. P. Lim, & S. Dehuri (Eds.), Innovations in Swarm Intelligence. Berlin, Germany: Springer-Verlag. doi:10.1007/978-3-642-04225-6_4

Lucasius, C. B., & Kateman, G. (1992). Towards Solving Subset Selection Problems with the Aid of the Genetic Algorithm. In R. Männer, & B. Manderick (Eds.), *Parallel Problem Solving from Nature 2* (pp. 239–247). Amsterdam, The Netherlands: North-Holland.

Madria, S. K., Bhowmick, S. S., Ng, W. K., & Lim, E. P. (1999). Research issues in web data Mining. *Proceedings of First International Conference of Data Warehousing and Knowledge Discovery, DaWaK'99*, 301-312.

Mahrooghy, M., Younan, N. H., Anantharaj, V., & Aanstoos, J. (2012). Enhancement of Satellite Precipitation Estimation via Unsupervised Dimensionality Reduction. *IEEE Transactions on Geoscience and Remote Sensing*.

Passino, K. M. (2002, June). Biomimicry of Bacterial Foraging for Distributed Optimization and Control. *IEEE Control Systems Magazine*, 52–67.

Pawlak, Z. (1982). Rough Sets. *International Journal of Information and Computer Sciences, 11*(5), 341–356. doi:10.1007/BF01001956

Ratner, B. (2010, March). Variable selection methods in regression: Ignorable problem, outing notable solution. *Journal of Targeting, Measurement and Analysis for Marketing, 18*(1), 65–75. doi:10.1057/jt.2009.26

Sadri, J., & Suen, C. Y. (2006). A Genetic Binary Particle Swarm Optimization Model. *IEEE Congress on Evolutionary Computation*, 656-663. 10.1109/CEC.2006.1688373

Shamsinejadbabki, P., & Saraee, M. (2012). A New Unsupervised Feature Selection Method for Text Clustering Based on Genetic Algorithms. *Journal of Intelligent Information Systems, 38*, 1-16.

Smith, M. G., & Bull, L. (2003). Feature construction and selection using genetic programming and a genetic algorithm. *Proceedings of the 6th European Conference on Genetic Programming, 229*–237. 10.1007/3-540-36599-0_21

Tasgetiren, M. F., & Yiang, Y.-C. (2007). A Binary Particle Swarm Optimization Algorithm for Lot Sizing Problem. *Journal of Economic and Social Research, 5*, 1-20.

Velayutham, C., & Thangavel, K. (2011). Unsupervised quick reduct algorithm using rough set theory. *Journal of Electronic Science and Technology, 9*, 193–201.

Velayutham, C., & Thangavel, K. (2011). Unsupervised feature selection based on the measures of degree of dependency using rough set theory in digital mammogram image classification. *Proceedings of the 3rd International Conference on Advanced Computing – IcoAC*. 10.1109/ICoAC.2011.6165167

Velayutham, C., & Thangavel, K. (2012, March). A novel entropy based unsupervised Feature Selection algorithm using rough set theory, *IEEE-International Conference On Advances In Engineering, Science And Management (ICAESM -2012)*.

Zhang, M., & Yao, J. T. (2004, June). A Rough Sets Based Approach to Feature Selection. *Proceedings of the 23rd International Conference of NAFIPS*, 434–439. 10.1109/NAFIPS.2004.1336322

KEY TERMS AND DEFINITIONS

Genetic Algorithm (GA): It is an evolutionary algorithm used for solving various optimization problems.

Particle Swarm Optimization (PSO): Commonly used swarm intelligence algorithm devised based on the bird flocking behavior.

Swarm Intelligence: It refers to the peculiar group behavior followed by any of the biological systems.

Compilation of References

Abdelhamid, N., Ayesh, A., & Thabtah, F. (2014). Phishing detection based associative classification data mining. *Expert Systems with Applications, 41*(13), 5948–5959. doi:10.1016/j.eswa.2014.03.019

Abraham, A., & Ramos, V. (2003). Web Usage Mining Using Artificial Ant Colony Clustering and Genetic Programming. *IEEE Congress on Evolutionary Computation (CEC2003)*, A1384-1391. 10.1109/CEC.2003.1299832

Abu-Nimeh, S., Nappa, D., Wang, X., & Nair, S. (2007). A comparison of machine learning techniques for phishing detection. *APWG eCrime Researchers Summit.* 10.1145/1299015.1299021

Advanced Persistent Threat. (2019). Retrieved from https://www.hackread.com/hackers-abusing-google-app-engine-to-spread-pdf-malware/

Agarwal, G., & Patil, P. (2013, June). Privacy preserving for high dimensional data using anonymization techniques. *Int. Journal of Advanced Research in CS.*

Aggarwal, C., & Yu, P. (May 2001). Outlier detection for high dimensional data. In *Proc. of the 2001 ACM SIGMOD international conference on Management of data* (pp. 37-46). Santa Barbara, CA: ACM.

Ahmed, M., & Mahmood, A. N. (2014). Clustering based semantic data summarization technique: a new approach. *2014 IEEE 9th Conference on Industrial Electronics and Applications (ICIEA)*, 1780-1785. 10.1109/ICIEA.2014.6931456

Ahmed, M., & Mahmood, A. N. (2014a). Network traffic analysis based on collective anomaly detection. *2014 IEEE 9th Conference on Industrial electronics and applications (ICIEA)*, 1141-1146. 10.1109/ICIEA.2014.6931337

Ahmed, M., & Mahmood, A. N. (2014b). Network traffic pattern analysis using improved information theoretic co-clustering based collective anomaly detection. In *International Conference on Security and Privacy in Communication Systems*, (pp. 204-219). Cham, Switzerland: Springer.

Ahmed, M., Mahmood, A., & Hu, J. (2016, January). A survey of network anomaly detection techniques. *Journal of Network and Computer Applications, 60*, 19-31.

Ahmed, H. M., Hassan, N. F., & Fahad, A. (2017). Designing a smartphone honeypot system using performance counters. *Karbala International Journal of Modern Science, 3*(1), 46–52. doi:10.1016/j.kijoms.2017.02.004

Ahmed, M., & Mahmood, A. N. (2015). Novel approach for network traffic pattern analysis using clustering-based collective anomaly detection. *Annals of Data Science, 2*(1), 111–130. doi:10.100740745-015-0035-y

Alain, G., & Bengio, Y. (2012). *What regularized auto-encoders learn from the data generating distribution.* Technical Report.

Alazab, M., Venkatraman, S., Watters, P., & Alazab, M. (2011). Zero-day Malware Detection based on Supervised Learning Algorithms of API call Signatures. In *Proceedings of the Ninth Australasian Data Mining Conference* (vol. 121, pp. 171-182). Australian Computer Society.

Aldwairi, M., Khamayseh, Y., & Al-Masri, M. (2015). Application of artificial bee colony for intrusion detection systems. *Security and Communication Networks, 8*(16), 2730–2740. doi:10.1002ec.588

Alfayyadh, B., Ponting, J., Alzomai, M., & Jøsang, A. (2010). Vulnerabilities in personal firewalls caused by poor security usability. *IEEE Int'l Conf. on Infor. Theor. and Infor. Security*, 682–688.

Alippi, C. (2014). Intelligence for Embedded Systems. Springer-Verlag.

Ali, W. (2017). Phishing website detection based on supervised machine learning with wrapper features selection. *International Journal of Advanced Computer Science and Applications, 8*(9), 72–78. doi:10.14569/IJACSA.2017.080910

Al-Jarrah, O. Y., Al-Hammdi, Y., Yoo, P. D., Muhaidat, S., & Al-Qutayri, M. (2018). Semi-supervised multi-layered clustering model for intrusion detection. *Digital Communications and Networks, 4*(4), 277–286. doi:10.1016/j.dcan.2017.09.009

Al-Jarrah, O. Y., Yoo, P. D., Muhaidat, S., Karagiannidis, G. K., & Taha, K. (2015). Efficient machine learning for big data: A review. *Big Data Research, 2*(3), 87–93. doi:10.1016/j.bdr.2015.04.001

Allouche, J. P., Courbage, M., & Skordev, G. (2000). *Notes on cellular automata*. Inst. für Dynamische Systeme.

Almomani, A., Gupta, B. B., Wan, T., Altaher, A., & Manickam, S. (2013). *Phishing dynamic evolving neural fuzzy framework for online detection zero-day phishing email*. Academic Press.

Almseidin, M., Alzubi, M., Kovacs, S., & Alkasassbeh, M. (2018). Evaluation of Machine Learning Algorithms for Intrusion Detection System. In *IEEE 15th International Symposium on Intelligent Systems and Informatics* (pp.1-12). IEEE.

Alom, M. Z., Bontupalli, V., & Taha, T. M. (2015). Intrusion detection using deep belief networks. *IEEE National Aerospace and Electronics Conference (NAECON)*.

Alotaibi, F., Furelli, S., Stengeli, I., & Papadakii, M. (2016). A Survey of Cyber-Security Awareness in Saudi Arabia. *11th International Conference for Internet Technology and Secured Transactions (ICITST-2016)*. 10.1109/ICITST.2016.7856687

Alsaidi Altaher, M., & Mohd Ismail, T. (2010). A Comparison of Some Thresholding Selection Methods for Wavelet Regression. *World Academy of Science, Engineering and Technology, 4*, 105–111.

Alshehri, S., Mishra, S., & Raj, R. K. (2016). Using Access Control to Mitigate Insider Threats to Healthcare Systems. In *2016 IEEE International Conference on Healthcare Informatics (ICHI)* (pp. 55–60). Chicago, IL: IEEE. 10.1109/ICHI.2016.11

Alshinina, A. R., & Elleithy, M. K. (2018). A highly accurate deep learning based approach for developing wireless sensor network middleware. *IEEE Access: Practical Innovations, Open Solutions, 6*, 29885–29898. doi:10.1109/ACCESS.2018.2844255

Altaher, A. (2016). An improved Android malware detection scheme based on an evolving hybrid neuro-fuzzy classifier (EHNFC) and permission-based features. *Neural Computing & Applications, 28*(12), 4147–4157. doi:10.100700521-016-2708-7

Amardeep, R., & Swamy, K. T. (2017). Training Feed forward Neural Network with Back propogation Algorithm. *International Journal of Engineering And Computer Science, 6*(1), 19860–19866.

Ambre, A., & Shekokar, N. (2015). Insider Threat Detection Using Log Analysis and Event Correlation. *Procedia Computer Science, 45*, 436–445. doi:10.1016/j.procs.2015.03.175

Amin, M. R. (2016) Behavioral malware detection ap- proaches for Android. *IEEE International Conference on Communications (ICC)*.

Amoli, P. V., Hamalainen, T., David, G., Zolotukhin, M., & Mirzamohammad, M. (2016). Unsupervised Network Intrusion Detection Systems for Zero-Day Fast-Spreading Attacks and Botnets. JDCTA, 10(2), 1-13.

Amor, N. B., Benferhat, S., & Elouedi, Z. (2004). Naive bayes vs decision trees in intrusion detection systems. In *Proceedings of the 2004 ACM symposium on Applied computing* (pp. 420-424). ACM. 10.1145/967900.967989

Amudha, P., Karthik, S., & Sivakumari, S. (2015). A hybrid swarm intelligence algorithm for intrusion detection using significant features. *The Scientific World Journal*, 2015. PMID:26221625

Analyzing Web Traffic ECML/PKDD. (2007). *Discovery Challenge*. Retrieved from http://www.lirmm.fr/pkdd2007-challenge/

Anbuchelian, S., & Lokesh, S., & Baskaran, M. (2016). Improving security in wireless sensor network using trust and metaheuristic algorithms. *International Conference on Computer and Information Sciences*, 233-241. 10.1109/ICCOINS.2016.7783220

Andrea, I., Chrysostomou, C., & Hadjichristofi, G. (2015, February). Internet of Things: Security vulnerabilities and challenges. In *Proc. IEEE Symposium on Computers and Commun*, (pp. 180–187). Larnaca, Cyprus: IEEE. 10.1109/ISCC.2015.7405513

Android Malware. (2008). Retrieved from https://forensics.spreitzenbarth.de/android-malware/

Android OS. (2008). Retrieved from https://en.wikipedia.org/wiki/Android_(operating_system)

Anti-Phishing Working Group. (n.d.). *Phishing and Fraud solutions*. Available at http://www.antiphishing.org

Anyanwu, L. O., Keengwe, J., & Arome, G. A. (2010). Scalable Intrusion Detection with Recurrent Neural Networks. *IEEE 2010 Seventh International Conference on Information Technology: New Generations*, 919–923.

Apache Hive. (n.d.). Retrieved from https://hive.apache.org/

Apache Metron. (n.d.). Retrieved from http://metron.apache.org/

Apache Spot. (n.d.). Retrieved from http://spot.incubator.apache.org/

Apache Storm. (n.d.). Retrieved from http://storm.apache.org/

AppA. (2008). Retrieved from https://play.google.com/store/

Applications of Deep Learning. (2016). Retrieved from https://machinelearningmastery.com/inspirational-applications-deep-learning/

Apruzzese, G., & Colajanni, M. (2018). On the Effectiveness of Machine and Deep Learning for Cyber Security. *2018 10th International Conference on Cyber Conflict*, 371-390.

Apruzzese, G., Colajanni, M., Ferretti, L., Guido, A., & Marchetti, M. (2018). On the effectiveness of machine and deep learning for cyber security. In T. Minárik, R. Jakschis, & L. Lindstrom (Eds.), *International Conference on Cyber Conflict* (pp. 371-390), Tallinn, Estonia: Academic Press. 10.23919/CYCON.2018.8405026

Araújo, N., de Oliveira, R., Shinoda, A. A., & Bhargava, B. (2010). Identifying important characteristics in the KDD99 intrusion detection dataset by feature selection using a hybrid approach. In *2010 IEEE 17th International Conference on Telecommunications (ICT)*, (pp. 552-558). IEEE. 10.1109/ICTEL.2010.5478852

Asmuth, C., & Bloom, J. (1983). A modular approach to key safeguarding. *IEEE Transactions on Information Theory*, 29(2), 208–210. doi:10.1109/TIT.1983.1056651

Aung, Y. Y., & Min, M. M. (2018). An analysis of k-means algorithm based network intrusion detection system. *Advances in Science. Technology and Engineering Systems Journal*, 3(1), 496–501. doi:10.25046/aj030160

Azad, C., & Jha, V. K. (2013). Data mining in intrusion detection: A comparative study of methods, types and data sets. *International Journal of Information Technology and Computer Science*, 5(8), 75–90. doi:10.5815/ijitcs.2013.08.08

Bache, K., & Lichman, M. (2013). *UCI Machine Learning Repository*. Irvine, CA: University of California, School of Information and Computer Science. Retrieved from http://archive. ics. uci. edu/ml

Bae, C., Yeh, W.-C., Mohd, A. M. S., Chung, Y. Y., & Hsieh, T.-J. (2012). A novel anomaly-network intrusion detection system using ABC algorithms. *International Journal of Innovative Computing, Information, & Control*, 8(12), 8231–8248.

Bahrampour, S., Ramakrishnan, N., Schott, L., & Shah, M. (2015). Comparative study of caffe, neon, theano, and torch for deep learning. CoRR, vol. abs/1511.06435

Balabine, I., & Velednitsky, A. (2018). *Method and system for confident anomaly detection in computer traffic*. Google Patents.

Bankovic, Z., Vallejo, J. C., Fraga, D., & Moya, J. M. (2014, December). *Detecting Bad-Mouthing Attacks on Reputation Systems Using Self-Organising Maps*. Researchgate.net.

Baracaldo, N., & Joshi, J. (2013). An adaptive risk management and access control framework to mitigate insider threats. *Computers & Security*, 39, 237–254. doi:10.1016/j.cose.2013.08.001

Barnett, V., & Lewis, T. (1994, February). Outliers in Statistical Data (3rd ed.). Hoboken, NJ: John Wiley & Sons.

Barona López, L., Valdivieso Caraguay, L., Maestre Vidal, J., Sotelo Monge, M., & García Villalba, L. (2017, January). *Towards Incidence Management in 5G Based on Situational Awareness*. Academic Press.

Baskaran B & Ralescu A (2016), A Study of Android Malware Detection Techniques and Machine Learning, *MAICS2016*, 15-23.

Basnet, R., Mukkamala, S., & Sung, A. H. (2008). Detection of phishing attacks: A machine learning approach. In B. Prasad (Ed.), Soft Computing Applications in Industry (pp. 373-383). Berlin, Germany: Springer-Verlag.

Beimel, A. (2011, May). Secret-sharing schemes: a survey. In *International Conference on Coding and Cryptology* (pp. 11-46). Berlin, Germany: Springer. 10.1007/978-3-642-20901-7_2

Benaicha, S. E., Saoudi, L., Bouhouita Guermeche, S. E., & Lounis, O. (2014). Intrusion detection system using genetic algorithm. *Science and Information Conference (SAI)*, 564-568.

Benaloh, J., & Leichter, J. (1990, February). Generalized secret sharing and monotone functions. In *Proceedings on Advances in cryptology* (pp. 27–35). Springer-Verlag New York.

Bengio, Y., Courville, A., & Vincent, P. (2013). Representation Learning: A Review and New Perspectives. *IEEE Transactions on Pattern Analysis and Machine Intelligence*, 35(8), 1798–1828. doi:10.1109/TPAMI.2013.50 PMID:23787338

Beni, G., & Wang, J. (1993). Swarm intelligence in cellular robotic systems. In *Robots and Biological Systems: Towards a New Bionics?* (pp. 703–712). Berlin, Germany: Springer. doi:10.1007/978-3-642-58069-7_38

Benjamin, C. M., Fung, M., Wang, K., Chen, R., & Yu, P. S. (2010). Privacy-preserving data publishing: A survey of recent developments. *ACM Comput. Surv.*, 42(4), 1-53.

Bertilsson, M., & Ingemarsson, I. (1992, December). A construction of practical secret sharing schemes using linear block codes. In *International Workshop on the Theory and Application of Cryptographic Techniques* (pp. 67-79). Berlin, Germany: Springer.

Bhamare, D., Salman, T., Samaka, M., Erbad, A., & Jain, R. (2016). Feasibility of Supervised Machine Learning for Cloud Security. In *2016 International Conference on Information Science and Security (ICISS),* (pp. 1- 5). Academic Press.

Bhattacharya, A., & Goswami, R. T. (2017). DMDAM: data mining based detection of android malware. *Proceedings of the first international conference on intelligent computing and communication,* 187–194. 10.1007/978-981-10-2035-3_20

Bhuyan, M., Bhattacharyya, D., & Kalita, J. (2014). Network anomaly detection: Methods, systems and tools. IEEE Commun. Surv. Tuts., 16(1), 303–336.

Bhuyan, M., Bhattacharyya, D., & Kalita, J. (2014). Network Anomaly Detection: Methods, Systems and Tools. IEEE Communications Surveys & Tutorials, 16(1), 303-336.

Bhuyan, M., Bhattacharyya, D., & Kalita, J. (2014, June). Network Anomaly Detection: Methods, Systems and Tools. *IEEE Communications Surveys & Tutorials, 16*(1), 303-336.

Bhuyan, M. H., Bhattacharyya, D. K., & Jugal, K. (2015). An empirical evaluation of information metrics for low-rate and high-rate DDoS attack detection. *Pattern Recognition Letters*, *51*, 1–7. doi:10.1016/j.patrec.2014.07.019

Bhuyan, M. H., Dhruba, K. B., & Jugal, K. K. (2015). *Towards Generating Real- life Datasets for Network Intrusion Detection. IJ Network Security.*

Bhuyan, M., Bhattacharyya, D., & Kalita, J. (2014). Network anomaly detection: Methods, systems and tools. *IEEE Communications Surveys and Tutorials*, *16*(1), 303–336. doi:10.1109/SURV.2013.052213.00046

Biggio, Fumera, & Roli. (2014). Security evaluation of pattern classifiers under attack. *IEEE Transactions on Knowledge and Data Engineering, 26*(4), 984-996.

Biggio. (n.d.). Evasion attacks against machine learning at test time. *Joint European Conference on Machine Learning and Knowledge Discovery in Databases*, 387-402. doi:10.1109/ICITIS.2010.5689490

Biggio, B. (2014). *Security evaluation of support vector machines in adversarial environments. In Support Vector Machines Applications* (pp. 105–153). Springer.

Bishop, C. M. (2006). *Pattern recognition and machine learning.* Springer.

Biswas, S. K. (2018). Intrusion Detection Using Machine Learning: A Comparison Study. *International Journal of Pure and Applied Mathematics*, *118*(19), 101–114.

Bjorvand, A. T., & Komorowski, J. (1997). Practical applications of genetic algorithms for efficient reduct computation. *Proceedings of the 15th IMACS World Congress on Scientific Computation, Modelling and Applied Mathematics*, 4, 601–606.

Blakley, G. R. (1979, June). Safeguarding cryptographic keys. In *Proceedings of the national computer conference* (*Vol. 48*, pp. 313-317). Academic Press.

Blasing, T., Schmidt, A.-D., Batyuk, L., Albayrak, S., & Camtepe, S. A. (2010), An android application sandbox system for suspicious software detection. *5th international conference on Malicious and unwanted software (MALWARE),* 55–62.

Blundo, C., De Santis, A., Di Crescenzo, G., Gaggia, A. G., & Vaccaro, U. (1994, August). Multi-secret sharing schemes. In *Annual International Cryptology Conference* (pp. 150-163). Berlin, Germany: Springer.

Boneh, D., & Franklin, M. (2001, August). Identity-based encryption from the Weil pairing. In *Annual international cryptology conference* (pp. 213-229). Berlin, Germany: Springer. 10.1007/3-540-44647-8_13

Borges, J., & Levene, M. (1999). Data mining of user navigation patterns. *Proceedings of the WEBKDD'99 Workshop on Web Usage Analysis and User Profiling*, 31–36.

Boriah, S., Chandola, V., & Kumar, V. (2008, April). Similarity Measures for Categorical Data: A Comparative Evaluation. In *International SIAM Conference of Data Mining*, (pp. 243-254). Atlanta, GA: Academic Press. 10.1137/1.9781611972788.22

Bouachir, O., Abrassart, A., Garcia, F., Larrieu, N. (2014, May). A Mobility Model For UAV Ad hoc Network. *International Conference on Unmanned Aircraft Systems,* 383-388.

Boukhtouta, A., Mokhov, S. A., Lakhdari, N.-E., Debbabi, M., & Paquet, J. (2016). Network malware classifcation comparison using DPI and fow packet headers. *J Computer Virol Hacking Tech, 12*(2), 69–100. doi:10.100711416-015-0247-x

Bouzida, Y., & Cuppens, F. (2006, September). Neural networks vs. decision trees for intrusion detection. In *IEEE/IST Workshop on Monitoring, Attack Detection and Mitigation (MonAM)* (pp. 81-88). IEEE.

Boyle, E., Gilboa, N., Ishai, Y., Lin, H., & Tessaro, S. (2018). Foundations of homomorphic secret sharing. In *9th Innovations in Theoretical Computer Science Conference (ITCS 2018)*. Schloss Dagstuhl-Leibniz-Zentrum fuer Informatik.

Bramlette, M. F. (1991). Initialization, Mutation and Selection Methods in Genetic Algorithms for Function Optimization, *Proc ICGA 4,* 100-107.

Brickell, E. F. (1989, April). Some ideal secret sharing schemes. In *Workshop on the Theory and Application of of Cryptographic Techniques* (pp. 468-475). Berlin, Germany: Springer.

Brun, O., Yin, Y., & Gelenbe, E. (2018). *Deep learning with dense random neural network for detecting attacks against IoT-connected home environments.* Science Direct.

Buczak, A. L., & Guven, E. (2016). A survey of data mining and machine learning methods for cyber security intrusion detection. *IEEE Communications Surveys & Tutorials, 18*(2).

Buczak, A. L., & Guven, E. (2016). A Survey of Data Mining and Machine Learning Methods for Cyber Security Intrusion Detection. IEEE Communications Surveys & Tutorials, 18(2).

Buczak, A. L., & Guven, E. (2016). A survey of data mining and machine learning methods for cyber security intrusion detection. *IEEE Communications Surveys and Tutorials, 18*(2), 1153–1176. doi:10.1109/COMST.2015.2494502

Buczak, A., & Guven, E. (2015). A survey of data mining and machine learning methods for cyber security intrusion detection, *IEEE Communications Surveys and Tutorials.*

Bussa, T., Litan, A., & Phillips, T. (2016). *Market guide for user and entity behavior analytics.* Gartner.

Buster Sandbox Analyzer. (2011). Retrieved from http://bsa.isoftware.nl/

Cai, A., Tsay, R. S., & Chen, R. (2009, September). Variable Selection in Linear Regression With Many Predictors. *Journal of Computational and Graphical Statistics, 18*(3), 573–591. doi:10.1198/jcgs.2009.06164

Canadian Institute for Cybersecurity. (n.d.). Retrieved from http://www.unb.ca/research/iscx/dataset/index.html

Capocelli, R. M., De Santis, A., Gargano, L., & Vaccaro, U. (1991, August). On the size of shares for secret sharing schemes. In *Annual International Cryptology Conference* (pp. 101-113). Berlin, Germany: Springer.

Cárdenas, A., Manadhata, P., & Rajan, S. (2013). *Big data analytics for security intelligence.* Cloud Security Alliance.

Carlini, N., & Wagner, D. (2017). Towards evaluating the robustness of neural networks. *IEEE Symposium on Security and Privacy (SP)*, 39–57. 10.1109/SP.2017.49

Cavelty, M. D. (2010). Cyber-security. *The Routledge Handbook of New Security Studies*, 154-162. Retrieved from https://www.researchgate.net/profile/Myriam_Dunn_Cavelty/publication/281631032_Cyber-security/links/55f1426408ae199d47c243b1/Cyber-security.pdf

Cha, S. (2007, January). Comprehensive Survey on Distance/Similarity Measures between Probability Density Functions. *International Journal of Mathematical Models and Methods in Applied Sciences, 1*(4), 300-307.

Chandola, V., Banerjee, A., & Kumar, V. (2009, July). Anomaly Detection: A Survey. *ACM Computing Surveys, 41*(3).

Chang, S. G., & Bin Yu, M. V. (2000). Adaptive Wavelet Thresholding for Image Denoising and Compression. *IEEE International transactions on Image Processing*, 1532 -1546.

Chapelle, O., Scholkopf, B., & Zien, A. (2009). Semi-supervised learning (O. Chapelle et al., Eds.; 2006) [book review]. IEEE Transactions on Neural Networks, 20(3), 542-542.

Chaudhary, A., Tiwari, V. N., & Kumar, A. (2014). Design an anomaly based fuzzy intrusion detection system for packet dropping attack in mobile ad hoc networks. *IEEE International Conference on Advance Computing (IACC)*, 256-261. 10.1109/IAdCC.2014.6779330

Chauhana, S., Arorab, A. S., & Kaula, A. (2010). A survey of emerging biometric modalities. *Procedia Computer Science, 2*, 213–218. doi:10.1016/j.procs.2010.11.027

Chaumont, M. (2018, January). The emergence of Deep Learning in steganography and steganalysis. Journée" Stéganalyse: Enjeux et Méthodes", labelisée par le GDR ISIS et le pré-GDR sécurité.

Chellapilla, K., & Simard, P. Y. (2005). Using Machine Learning to Break Visual Human Interaction Proofs (HIPs). In Advances in neural information processing systems (pp. 265–272). Academic Press.

Chen, C. L. P. (2016). Big Data Challenges, Techniques, Technologies, and Applications and How Deep Learning can be Used. *Proceedings of IEEE 20th international conference on Computer supported cooperative work in design.*

Chen, X.-W., Lin, X. (2014). Big data deep learning: challenges and perspectives. *IEEE Access, 2,* 514–525.

Chen, M., Xu, Z., Winberger, K., & Sha, F. (2012). *Marginalized denoising autoencoders for domain adaptation*. ICML.

Cheon, J., & Choe, T.-Y. (2013). Distributed processing of snort alert log using Hadoop. *IACSIT International Journal of Engineering and Technology, 5*, 2685–2690.

Chetlur, S., Woolley, C., Vandermersch, P., Cohen, J., Tran, J., Catanzaro, B., & Shelhamer, E. (2014). *DNN: Efficient Primitives for Deep Learning*. ArXiv e-prints.

Chhikara, PPatel, K. A. (2013). Enhancing network security using Ant Colony Optimization. *Global Journal of Computer Science and Technology Network. Web & Security, 13*(4), 1–5.

Chien, H. Y., Jan, J. K., & Tseng, Y. M. (2000). A practical (t, n) multi-secret sharing scheme. *IEICE Transactions on Fundamentals of Electronics, Communications and Computer Science, 83*(12), 2762–2765.

Chien, H. Y., Jan, J. K., & Tseng, Y. M. (2002). A unified approach to secret sharing schemes with low distribution cost. *Zhongguo Gongcheng Xuekan, 25*(6), 723–733. doi:10.1080/02533839.2002.9670746

Cho, D., & Bui, T. D. (2014). Fast image enhancement in compressed wavelet domain. *Signal Processing, 98*, 295–307. doi:10.1016/j.sigpro.2013.11.007

Chowdhury, S. (2017). Botnet detection using graph-based feature clustering. *Journal of Big Data,* 1-13.

Cinque, M., Corte, R. D., & Pecchia, A. (2017). Entropy-based security analytics: Measurements from a critical information system. In *2017 47th Annual IEEE/IFIP International Conference on Dependable Systems and Networks (DSN)* (pp. 379–390). IEEE. doi:10.1109/DSN.2017.39

Ciresan, D., Meier, U. & Schmidhuber, J. (2012). Multi-column deep neural networks for image classification. *IEEE Conference on Computer Vision and Pattern Recognition,* 3642–3649. doi:. doi:10.1109/cvpr.2012.6248110

Clark. (2009). *History of Mobile Apps.* Retrieved from http://www.uky.edu/~jclark/mas490apps/History%20of%20Mobile%20Apps.pdf

Cloud Security Alliance. (2013). *Expanded top ten big data security and privacy challenges.* Academic Press.

Cloud Security Alliance. (2014). *Big data taxonomy.* Academic Press.

Cohen, A., Nissim, N., & Elovici, Y. (2018). Novel set of general descriptive features for enhanced detection of malicious emails using machine learning methods. *Expert Systems with Applications, 110,* 143–169. doi:10.1016/j.eswa.2018.05.031

Coleman, C., Narayanan, D., Kang, D., Zhao, T., Zhang, J., Nardi, L., … Zaharia, M. (2017). Dawnbench: An end-to-end deep learning benchmark and competition. *NIPS ML Systems Workshop.*

Colorossi, J. L. (2015). Cyber Security. In *Security Supervision and Management* (pp. 501–525). Elsevier. doi:10.1016/B978-0-12-800113-4.00038-9

Comar, P. M., Liu, L., Saha, S., Tan, P., & Nucci, A. (2013). Combining Supervised and Unsupervised Learning for Zero-Day Malware Detection. In *2013 Proceedings IEEE INFOCOM* (pp. 2022-2030). IEEE.

Coronoa, I., Giacinto, G., & Roli, F. (2013, August). Adversarial attacks against intrusion detection systems: Taxonomy, solutions and open issues. *Information Sciences, 239,* 201-225.

Cortes, C., & Vapnik, V. (1995). Support-vector networks. *Machine Learning, 20*(3), 273–297. doi:10.1007/BF00994018

Craigen, D., Diakun-Thibault, N., & Purse, R. (2014). Defining cyber security. *Technology Innovation Management Review, 4*(10).

Cramer, R., Damgård, I., & Maurer, U. (2000, May). General secure multi-party computation from any linear secret-sharing scheme. In *International Conference on the Theory and Applications of Cryptographic Techniques* (pp. 316-334). Berlin, Germany: Springer. 10.1007/3-540-45539-6_22

Cranor, L. F., Egelman, S., Hong, J., & Zhang, Y. (2006). *Phinding phish: An evaluation of anti-phishing toolbars.* Technical Report CMU-CyLab-06-018. CMU.

Cylance. (n.d.). Retrieved from https://www.cylance.com/

Dagher, G. C., Iqbal, F., Arafati, M., & Fung, B. C. (2015, December). Fusion: Privacy preserving distributed protocol for high-dimensional data mashup. In *IEEE International Conference on Parallel and Distributed Systems* (pp. 760-769). IEEE.

Dali, Z., Hao, J., Ying, Y., Wu, D., & Weiyi, C. (2017). Deep Flow: deep learning-based malware detection by mining Android application for abnormal usage of sensitive data. In *2017 IEEE symposium on computers and communications (ISCC),* (pp. 438–443). IEEE.

Darktrace. (n.d.). Retrieved from https://www.darktrace.com

DARPA Intrusion Detection Evaluation Dataset. (1998). Retrieved from https://www.ll.mit.edu/r-d/datasets/1998-darpa-intrusion-detection-evaluation-dataset

Dash, M., & Liu, H. (1997). Feature Selection for Classification. *Intelligent Data Analysis, 1*(3), 131–156. doi:10.3233/IDA-1997-1302

Data Mining with Open Source Machine Learning. (n.d.). Available from www.cs.waikato.ac.nz/ml/weka/

Dataset. (2010). *ISOT Research lab.* Retrieved from https://www.uvic.ca/engineering/ece/isot/datasets/

David, O. E., & Netanyahu, S. N. (2015). Deepsign: Deep learning for automatic malware signature generation and classification. In *International Joint Conference on Neural Networks* (pp. 1-8). Killarney, Ireland: Academic Press.

David, L. D. (1995). Denoising by soft-thresholding. *IEEE Transactions on Information Theory, 41*(3), 613–627. doi:10.1109/18.382009

De Castro, L. N., & Timmis, J. I. (2002). *Artificial Immune Systems: A New Computational Intelligence Approach.* Springer-Verlag.

Dean, J., & Ghemawat, S. (2004). MapReduce: simplified data processing on large clusters. In *Proceedings of the 6th USENIX Symposium on Operating Systems Design and Implementation* (pp. 137–150). USENIX.

Debar, H. (2000). An introduction to intrusion-detection systems. *Proceedings of Connect, 2000.*

Debar, H., Dacier, M., & Wespi, A. (1999). Towards a taxonomy of intrusion detection systems. *Computer Networks, 31*(8), 805–822. doi:10.1016/S1389-1286(98)00017-6

Deep Learning. (2009). Retrieved from https://en.wikipedia.org/wiki/Deep_learning

Deepa, T. P. (2014). *Survey on need for cyber security in India.* doi:10.13140/2.1.4555.7768

Del Rey, A. M. (2015). A multi-secret sharing scheme for 3D solid objects. *Expert Systems with Applications, 42*(4), 2114–2120. doi:10.1016/j.eswa.2014.10.035

Del Rey, A. M., Mateus, J. P., & Sánchez, G. R. (2005). A secret sharing scheme based on cellular automata. *Applied Mathematics and Computation, 170*(2), 1356–1364. doi:10.1016/j.amc.2005.01.026

Del Rey, Á. M., & Sánchez, G. R. (2009, June). A secret sharing scheme for digital images based on cellular automata and boolean functions. In *International Work-Conference on Artificial Neural Networks* (pp. 1200–1207). Berlin, Germany: Springer. doi:10.1007/978-3-642-02478-8_150

Deljac, Ž., Randić, M., & Krčelić, G. (2015). Early detection of network element outages based on customer trouble calls. *Decision Support Systems, 73*, 57–73. doi:10.1016/j.dss.2015.02.014

Demirel, H., & Anbarjafari, G. (2011). Image resolution enhancement by using discrete and stationary wavelet decomposition. *IEEE Transactions on Image Processing, 20*(5), 1458–1460. doi:10.1109/TIP.2010.2087767 PMID:20959267

Deng, L. (2014). A tutorial survey of architectures, algorithms, and applications for deep learning. *APSIPA Trans. Signal Inf. Process., 3*(e2), 1–29.

Denning, D. E. (1987). An intrusion-detection model. *IEEE Transactions on Software Engineering, SE-13*(2), 222–232. doi:10.1109/TSE.1987.232894

Diamantidis, N. A., Karlis, D., & Giakoumakis, E. A. (2000). Unsupervised stratification of cross-validation for accuracy estimation. *Artificial Intelligence, 116*(1-2), 1–16. doi:10.1016/S0004-3702(99)00094-6

Diffie, W., & Hellman, M. E. (1977). Special feature exhaustive cryptanalysis of the NBS data encryption standard. *Computer, 10*(6), 74–84. doi:10.1109/C-M.1977.217750

Diro, A. A., & Chilamkurti, N. (2017). Distributed attack detection scheme using deep learning approach for Internet of Things. *Future Generation Computer Systems, 82*, 761–768. doi:10.1016/j.future.2017.08.043

Divya, K., Thangavel, K., & Sasirekha, K. (2016). Fingerprint image enhancement using DWT domain with adaptive gamma parameter. *The International Journal of Scientific Research in Science Engineering and Technology, 2*(4), 2395–1990.

Djioua, M., & Plamondon, R. (2009, October). Studying the variability of handwriting patterns using the Kinematic Theory. *Human Movement Science, 28*(5), 588-601.

Do Hoon Kim, T. L., Jung, S. O. D., In, H. P., & Lee, H. J. (2007, August). Cyber threat trend analysis model using HMM. In *Proceedings of the Third International Symposium on Information Assurance and Security* (pp. 177-182). Academic Press.

Dokas, P., Ertoz, L., Kumar, V., Lazarevic, A., Srivastava, J., & Tan, P. N. (2002, November). Data mining for network intrusion detection. In *Proc. NSF Workshop on Next Generation Data Mining* (pp. 21-30). Academic Press.

Dollah, R. F. M., Faizal, M. A., Arif, F., Mas'ud, M. Z., & Xin, L. K. (2018). Machine learning for http botnet detection using classifier algorithms. *Journal of Telecommunication, Electronic and Computer Engineering, 10*(1-7), 27-30.

Domingos, P. M. (2012). A few useful things to know about machine learning. *Communications of the ACM, 55*(10), 78–87.

Dorigo, M., & Blum, C. (2005). Ant colony optimization theory A survey. *Theoretical Computer Science, 344*(2–3), 243–278.

Druzhkov, P., & Kustikova, V. (2016). A survey of deep learning methods and software tools for image classification and object detection. *Pattern Recognition and Image Analysis, 26*(1), 9–15. doi:10.1134/S1054661816010065

Du, M., Li, F., Zheng, G., & Srikumar, V. (2017). *Deeplog: Anomaly detection and diagnosis from system logs through deep learning.* Academic Press.

Dua, S., & Du, X. (2016). *Data mining and machine learning in cybersecurity.* Auerbach Publications. doi:10.1201/b10867

Dynamic Malware Detection. (2014). Retrieved from https://www.iit.cnr.it/sites/default/files/dynamic-malware-detection.pdf

Eberhart, R., & Kennedy, J. (1995). A New Optimizer Using Particles Swarm Theory. *Proc. Sixth International Symposium on Micro Machine and Human Science IEEE Service Center*, 39-43. 10.1109/MHS.1995.494215

Eberhart, R., & Shi, Y. (2011). *Computational Intelligence: Concepts to Implementations.* Elsevier Morgan Kaufmann Publications.

Edgeworth, F. (1887). On discordant observations. *Philosophical Magazine, 23*(5).

Eesa, A. S., Orman, Z., & Brifcani, A. M. A. (2015). A new feature selection model based on ID3 and Bees algorithm for intrusion detection system. *Turkish Journal of Electrical Engineering and Computer Sciences, 23*(2), 615–622. doi:10.3906/elk-1302-53

El-Gallad, A. I., El-Hawary, M., Sallam, A. A., & Kalas, A. (2001). A Swarm intelligence for hybrid cost dispatch problem. *Canadian Conference on Electrical and Computer Engineering, 2,* 753-757.

ELK. (n.d.). Retrieved from https://www.elastic.co/

El-leithy, I. M., Salama, G. I., & Mahmoud, T. A. (2017). Fingerprint representation and matching for secure smartcard authentication. *International Journal of Biometrics, 9*(2), 81–95. doi:10.1504/IJBM.2017.085671

Elmendili, F., Maqran, N., Idrissi, Y. E. B. E., & Chaoui, H. (2017). A security approach based on honeypots: Protecting online social network from malicious profiles. *Advances in Science. Technology and Engineering Systems Journal*, *2*(3), 198–204. doi:10.25046/aj020326

Elrawy, M. F., Awad, A. I., & Hamed, H. F. A. (2018). *Intrusion detection systems for IoT-based smart environments*. Springer.

Endler, D. (1998, December). Intrusion detection. Applying machine learning to Solaris audit data. In *Proceedings of the 14th Annual Computer Security Applications Conference, 1998* (pp. 268-279). IEEE.

Endsley, M. (1988, January). Design and evaluation for situation awareness enhancement. In *Proc. of the 32nd Annual Meeting on Human Factors Society*, (pp. 97–101). Santa Monica, CA: Academic Press.

ENISA. (2015). *Big data security - good practices and recommendations on the security of big data systems*. Academic Press.

Eslami, Z., Pakniat, N., & Noroozi, M. (2015, October). Hierarchical threshold multi-secret sharing scheme based on Birkhoff interpolation and cellular automata. In *2015 18th CSI International Symposium on Computer Architecture and Digital Systems (CADS)* (pp. 1-6). IEEE. 10.1109/CADS.2015.7377795

Eslami, Z., & Ahmadabadi, J. Z. (2010). A verifiable multi-secret sharing scheme based on cellular automata. *Information Sciences*, *180*(15), 2889–2894. doi:10.1016/j.ins.2010.04.015

Eslami, Z., Razzaghi, S. H., & Ahmadabadi, J. Z. (2010). Secret image sharing based on cellular automata and steganography. *Pattern Recognition*, *43*(1), 397–404. doi:10.1016/j.patcog.2009.06.007

Exabeam. (n.d.). Retrieved from https://www.exabeam.com/

Fan, T. Y., Chao, H. C., & Chieu, B. C. (2019). Lossless medical image watermarking method based on significant difference of cellular automata transform coefficient. *Signal Processing Image Communication*, *70*, 174–183. doi:10.1016/j.image.2018.09.015

Farid, D. M., & Rahman, M. Z. (2008). Learning Intrusion Detection Based on Adaptive Bayesian Algorithm. IEEE.

Faruki, P., Bharmal, A., & Laxmi, V. (2015, May). Android Security: A Survey of Issues, Malware Penetration, and Defenses. *IEEE Communications Surveys & Tutorials, 17*(2), 998-1022.

Features of Android OS. (2008). Retrieved from https://en.wikipedia.org/wiki/List_of_features_in_Android

Feizollah. (2013). A study of machine learning classifiers for anomaly-based mobile botnet detection. *Malaysian Journal of Computer Science*.

Feldman, P. (1987, October). A practical scheme for non-interactive verifiable secret sharing. In *28th Annual Symposium on Foundations of Computer Science* (pp. 427-438). IEEE. 10.1109/SFCS.1987.4

Ferreira, E. W. T., Carrijo, G. A., de Oliveira, R., & de Souza Araujo, N. V. (2011). Intrusion Detection System with Wavelet and Neural Artificial Network Approach for Networks Computers. *IEEE Latin America Transactions, 9*(5), 832-837.

Ford, V., & Siraj, A. (2013, December). Clustering of smart meter data for disaggregation. *Proceedings of IEEE Global Conference on Signal and Information Processing*. 10.1109/GlobalSIP.2013.6736926

Ford, V., & Siraj, A. (2014). Applications of machine learning in cyber security. In *International Conference on Computer Applications in Industry and Engineering* (pp. 1-7). Academic Press.

Foss, A., Markatou, M., Ray, B., & Heching, A. (2016, July). A semiparametric method for clustering mixed data. *Machine Learning*, 1-40. doi:10.100710994-016-5575-7

Freitas, A. A. (2003). A survey of evolutionary algorithms for data mining and knowledge discovery. In *Advances in evolutionary computing* (pp. 819–845). Berlin, Germany: Springer. doi:10.1007/978-3-642-18965-4_33

Friedberg, I., McLaughlin, K., Smith, P., Laverty, D., & Sezer, S. (2017). STPA-SafeSec: Safety and security analysis for cyber-physical systems. *J. Inf. Secur. Appl.*, *34*, 183–196.

Gaietto, J. T. (2018). *Three emerging cyber security trends to focus on in 2018*. Retrieved from https://www.housingwire.com/blogs/1-rewired/post/43827-three-emerging-cybersecurity-trends-to-focus-on-in-2018

Galllagher, B., & Eliassırad, T. (2009). *Classification of http attacks: a study on the ECML/PKDD 2007 discovery challenge. Lawrence Livermore National Laboratory*. Livermore, CA: LLNL.

Gan, G., Ma, C., & Wu, J. (2007, July). Data Clustering: Theory, Algorithms, and Applications. SIAM, 20.

Gandomi, A. H., Yang, X. S., & Alavi, A. H. (2013). Cuckoo search algorithm: A metaheuristic approach to solve structural optimization problems. *Engineering with Computers*, *29*(1), 17–35. doi:10.100700366-011-0241-y

Gantz, J., & Reinsel, D. (2011). Extracting Value from Chaos. *Proc. IDC IView*.

Gan, X. S., Duanmu, J. S., Wang, J. F., & Cong, W. (2013). Anomaly intrusion detection based on PLS feature extraction and core vector machine. *Knowledge-Based Systems*, *40*, 1–6. doi:10.1016/j.knosys.2012.09.004

Gao, N., Gao, L., Gao, Q., & Wang, H. (2014). An Intrusion Detection Model Based on Deep Belief Networks. *Second International Conference on Advanced Cloud and Big Data,* 247–252.

García-Teodoro, P., Díaz-Verdejo, J., Maciá-Fernández, G., & Vázquez, E. (2009). Anomaly-based network intrusion detection: Techniques, systems and challenges. *Computers & Security*, *28*(1–2), 18–28. doi:10.1016/j.cose.2008.08.003

Gardiner, J., & Nagaraja, S. (2016). On the Security of Machine Learning in Malware C8C Detection. *ACM Computing Surveys*, *49*(3), 1–39. doi:10.1145/3003816

Garg, S., Singh, A. K., Sarje, A. K., & Peddoju, S. K. (2013). *Behaviour Analysis of Machine Learning Algorithms for detecting P2P Botnets*. IEEE. doi:10.1109/ICACT.2013.6710523

Gavrilut, D., Cimpoesu, M., Anton, D., & Ciortuz, L. (2009). Malware detection using machine learning. In *Proceedings of the International Multiconference on Computer Science and Information Technology* (pp. 735–741). Mragowo, Poland: Academic Press.

Ge. (2017). Analysis of Cyber-Physical Security Issues via Uncertainty Approaches. In *Advanced Computational Methods in Life Systems Modeling and simulation*. Springer.

Gentry, C. (2009). *A Fully Homomorphic Encryption Scheme* (Ph.D. dissertation). Dept. Comput. Sci., Stanford Univ., Stanford, CA.

Gharbi, M., Chaurasia, G., Paris, S., & Durand, F. (2016). Deep joint demosaicking and denoising. ACM Transactions on Graphics, 35(6).

Ghemawat, S., Gobioff, H., & Leung, S.-T. (2003). The Google file system. *Operating Systems Review*, *37*(5), 29. doi:10.1145/1165389.945450

Gholipour Goodarzi, B., Jazayeri, H., & Fateri, S. (2014). Intrusion detection system in computer network using hybrid algorithms (SVM and ABC). *Journal of Advances in Computer Research*, *5*(4), 43–52.

Ghourabi, A., Abbes, T., & Bouhoula, A. (2013). Automatic analysis of web service honeypot data using machine learning techniques. In *International Joint Conference CISIS'12-ICEUTE´12-SOCO´12 Special Sessions* (pp. 1-11). Berlin, Germany: Springer-Verlag. 10.1007/978-3-642-33018-6_1

Giani, A., Bitar, E., Garcia, M., McQueen, M., Khargonekar, P., & Poolla, K. (2013). Smart grid data integrity attacks. *IEEE Transactions on Smart Grid, 4*(3), 1244–1253.

Giménez, C. T., Villegas, A. P., & Marañón, G. Á. (2010). *HTTP dataset CSIC.* Retrieved from http://www.isi.csic.es/dataset/

Giura, P., & Wang, W. (2012). Using large scale distributed computing to unveil advanced persistent threats. *Science Journal, 1*, 93–105.

Glenn, M., & Lambert, I. I. (2017). *Security Analytics: Using deep learning to detect cyber attacks.* University of North Florida.

Goldstein, M., & Uchida, S. (2016, April). A Comparative Evaluation of Unsupervised Anomaly Detection Algorithms for Multivariate Data. *PLoS One.* doi:10.1371/journal.pone.0152173

Golovko, V., Kroshchanka, A., & Treadwell, D. (2016). The nature of unsupervised learning in deep neural networks: A new understanding and novel approach. *Optical Memory and Neural Networks*, 127–141.

Gonçalves, D., Bota, J., & Correia, M. (2015). Big data analytics for detecting host misbehavior in large logs. In *Proceedings of the 14th IEEE International Conference on Trust, Security and Privacy in Computing and Communications.* IEEE. 10.1109/Trustcom.2015.380

Gondara, L. (2016). *Medical image denoising using convolutional denoising autoencoders. Data Mining Workshops.* ICDMW.

Goyal, V., & Kumar, A. (2018, August). Non-malleable secret sharing for general access structures. In *Annual International Cryptology Conference* (pp. 501-530). Cham, Switzerland: Springer. 10.1007/978-3-319-96884-1_17

Goyal, P., Doll´ar, P., Girshick, R., Noordhuis, P., Wesolowski, L., Kyrola, A., Tulloch, A., Jia, Y., & He, K.,(2017). *Accurate, Large Minibatch SGD: Training ImageNet in 1 Hour.* ArXiv e-prints.

Graham, P. (2002). *A plan for spam.* Retrieved from http://www.paulgraham.com/spam.html

Graves, A., Abdel-rahman, M., & Hinton, G. (2013). Speech Recognition with Deep recurrent neural networks. *IEEE International Conference on Acoustics, Speech and Signal Processing*, 26-31. 10.1109/ICASSP.2013.6638947

Grosan, C., Abraham, A., & Chis, M. (2006). Swarm intelligence in data mining. In *Swarm Intelligence in Data Mining* (pp. 1–20). Berlin, Germany: Springer. doi:10.1007/978-3-540-34956-3_1

Grubbs, F. (1969, February). Procedures for Detecting Outlying Observations in Samples. *Technometrics, 11*(1), 1-21.

Guerrero-Higueras, Á. M., DeCastro-García, N., & Matellán, V. (2018). Detection of Cyber-attacks to indoor real time localization systems for autonomous robots. *Robotics and Autonomous Systems, 99*, 75–83. doi:10.1016/j.robot.2017.10.006

Gutierrez, M., & Kiekintveld, C. (2017). Adapting with honeypot Configurations to detect evolving exploits. In *Conference on Autonomous Agents and MultiAgent Systems* (pp. 1565-1567). Sao Paulo, Brazil: Academic Press.

Habibi, J., Midi, D., Mudgerikar, A., & Bertino, E. (2017). Heimdall: Mitigating the Internet of Insecure Things. *IEEE Internet of Things Journal, 4*(4), 968–978. doi:10.1109/JIOT.2017.2704093

Haddadi, F., Le Cong, D., Porter, L., & Zincir-Heywood, A. N. (2015, May). On the effectiveness of different botnet detection approaches. In ISPEC (pp. 121–135). Cham, Switzerland: Springer.

Hajimirzaei, B., & Navimipour, N. J. (2019). Intrusion detection for cloud computing using neural networks and artificial bee colony optimization algorithm. *ICT Express*, *5*(1), 56–59. doi:10.1016/j.icte.2018.01.014

Han, J., Hu, X., & Lin, T. Y. (2004, June). Feature Subset Selection Based on Relative Dependency between Attributes. *Rough Sets and Current Trends in Computing: 4th International Conference, RSCTC 2004*, 176–185. 10.1007/978-3-540-25929-9_20

Han, J., Kamber, M., & Pei, J. (2011, July). Data Mining: Concepts and Techniques. Elsevier.

Han, J., Pei, J., & Kamber, M. (2012). Data mining: concepts and techniques. Amsterdam, The Netherlands: Elsevier.

Haneef, F., & Singh, S. (2017). Selection technique for intrusion detection system based on IWD and ACO. *International Journal of Advanced Research in Computer Science*, *8*(9), 270–275. doi:10.26483/ijarcs.v8i9.4857

Hardy, W., & Chen, L., Hou, S., & Ye, Y. (2015). *A Deep Learning Framework for Intelligent Malware Detection*. Springer.

Hardy, W., Chen, L., Hou, S., Ye, Y., & Li, X. (2016). DL 4 MD: A deep learning framework for intelligent malware detection. In *Int'l Conf. Data Mining* (pp. 61-67). CSREA Press.

Hassanpour, R., Dogdu, E., Choupani, R., Goker, O., & Nazli, N. (2018). Phishing E-mail Detection By Using Deep Learning Algorithms. *ACMSE Conference*, New York. NY. 10.1145/3190645.3190719

Hawkings, D. (1980). *Identification of Outliers*. Monographs on Applied Probability and Statistics. doi:10.1007/978-94-015-3994-4

Haykin, S. (2005). Neural Networks (2nd ed.). Prentice Hall of India.

He, X., Dai, H., Ning, P., & Dutta, R. (2015, December). Dynamic IDS Configuration in the Presence of Intruder Type Uncertainty. In *Proc. IEEE Global Communications Conference* (pp. 1-6). San Diego, CA: IEEE.

Heidarvand, S., & Villar, J. L. (2008, August). Public verifiability from pairings in secret sharing schemes. In *International Workshop on Selected Areas in Cryptography* (pp. 294-308). Berlin, Germany: Springer.

He, J., & Dawson, E. (1994). Multistage secret sharing based on one-way function. *Electronics Letters*, *30*(19), 1591–1592. doi:10.1049/el:19941076

He, K., Zhang, X., Ren, S., & Sun, J. (2016). Deep residual learning for image recognition. *Proceedings of the IEEE conference on computer vision and pattern recognition*, 770–778.

Hersey. (2017). *Smart Phones*. Retrieved from https://en.wikipedia.org/wiki/Smartphone

Hink, R. C. B. (2014). *Machine learning for power systems disturbance and cyber-physical attacks discrimination*. IEEE ISRCS.

Hinton, G. E., Osindero, S., & Teh, Y.-W. (2006). A fast learning algorithm for deep belief nets. *Neural Computation*, *18*(7), 1527–1554. doi:10.1162/neco.2006.18.7.1527 PMID:16764513

Hoang, X. D., & Nguyen, Q. C. (2018). Botnet detection based on machine learning techniques using DNS query data. *Future Internet*, *10*(43), 1–11.

Hodashinsky, I. A., & Mech, M. A. (2018). Constructing a fuzzy network intrusion classifier based on differential evolution and harmonic search. *International Journal of Computer Networks & Communications*, *10*(2), 85–91. doi:10.5121/ijcnc.2018.10208

Holte, R. (1993, April). Very simple classification rules perform well on most commonly used datasets. *Machine Learning, 11*(1), 63-90.

Hoque, M. S., Mukit, M., Bikas, M., & Naser, A. (2012). *An implementation of intrusion detection system using genetic algorithm.* arXiv preprint arXiv:1204.1336

Hoque, N., Dhruba, K. B., & Jugal, K. K. (2016). A novel measure for low-rate and high-rate DDoS attack detection using multivariate data analysis, In *8th International Conference on Communication Systems and Networks (COMSNETS).* IEEE.

Hossain, M. N., Milajerdi, S. M., Wang, J., Eshete, B., Gjomemo, R., Sekar, R., . . . Venkatakrishnan, V. (2017). Sleuth: Real-time attack scenario reconstruction from cots audit data. In *Proc. USENIX Secur.* (pp. 487–504). USENIX.

How Do APIs Work. (2016). Retrieved from https://blogs.mulesoft.com/biz/tech-ramblings-biz/what-are-apis-how-do-apis-work/

Huang, W., & Stokes, J. W. (2016, July). MtNet: a multi-task neural network for dynamic malware classification. In *International Conference on Detection of Intrusions and Malware, and Vulnerability Assessment* (pp. 399-418). Cham, Switzerland: Springer. 10.1007/978-3-319-40667-1_20

Huang, K., Ye, Y., & Jiang, Q. (2009). Ismcs: an intelligent instruction sequence based malware categorization system. In *ASID'09: Proceedings of the 3rd international conference on Anti-Counterfeiting, security, and identification in communication,* (pp. 509–512). Piscataway, NJ: IEEE Press. 10.1109/ICASID.2009.5276989

Hug, G., & Giampapa, J. A. (2012). Vulnerability assessment of ac state estimation with respect to false data injection cyber-attacks. *IEEE Transactions on Smart Grid, 3*(3), 1362–1370.

IBM. (n.d.). *Cognitive security with Watson.* Retrieved from https://www.ibm.com/security/artificial-intelligence

Introduction to Pattern Recognition System. (2012). Retrieved from http://shodhganga.inflibnet.ac.in/bitstream/10603/25143/7/07_chapter%201.pdf

Introduction to Smart Phones. (2008). Retrieved from https://www.telstra.com.au/content/dam/tcom/seniors/pdf/beginners-intro-smartphones.pdf

Ioffe, S., & Szegedy, C. (2015). *Batch Normalization: Accelerating Deep Network Training by Reducing Internal Covariate Shift.* ArXiv e-prints.

ISOT Dataset Overview. (2011). Retrieved from https://www.uvic.ca/engineering/ece/isot/assets/docs/isot-datase.pdf

Ito, M., Saito, A., & Nishizeki, T. (1989). Secret sharing scheme realizing general access structure. *Electronics and Communications in Japan (Part III Fundamental Electronic Science), 72*(9), 56–64. doi:10.1002/ecjc.4430720906

Jain, A. K., Ross, A., & Nandakumar, K. (2011). Introduction. In Introduction to Biometrics. Springer.

Jain, A., Ross, A. A., & Prabhakar, S. (2004). An introduction to biometric recognition. *IEEE Transactions on Circuits and Systems for Video Technology, 14*(1), 4–20. doi:10.1109/TCSVT.2003.818349

Jan, B., Farman, H., Khan, M., Imran, M., Islam, I. U., Ahmad, A., … Jeon, G. (2017). Deep learning in big data Analytics: A comparative study. *Computers and Electrical Engineering.*

Javaid, A., Niyaz, Q., Sun, W., & Alam M. (2014). *A Deep Learning Approach for Network Intrusion Detection System.* Science Direct.

Jhanwar, M. P. (2011, May). A practical (non-interactive) publicly verifiable secret sharing scheme. In *International Conference on Information Security Practice and Experience* (pp. 273-287). Berlin, Germany: Springer. 10.1007/978-3-642-21031-0_21

Jogalekar, P., & Woodside, M. (2000, June). Evaluating the scalability of distributed systems. *IEEE Transactions on Parallel and Distributed Systems, 11*(6), 589-603.

Jordan, M. I., & Mitchell, T. M. (2015). Machine learning: Trends, perspectives, and prospects. *Science, 349*(6245), 255-260.

Jordan, M. I., & Mitchell, T. M. (2015). Machine learning: Trends, perspectives, and prospects. *Science, 349*(6245), 255–260. doi:10.1126cience.aaa8415 PMID:26185243

Joshi, S. A., & Pimprale, V. S. (2013). Network Intrusion Detection System (NIDS) based on data mining. *International Journal of Engineering Science and Innovative Technology, 2*(1), 95–98.

Jung, W., Kim, S., & Choi, S. (2015). *Deep Learning for Zero-day Flash Malware Detection.* IEEE.

Juvekar, C. (2018, August). *More Efficient Security for Cloud-Based Machine Learning.* Retrieved from http://0-search.proquest.com.cisne.sim.ucm.es/docview/2090233415?accountid=14514

Kang, M. J., & Kang, J.-W. (2016). Intrusion detection system using deep neural network for in-vehicle network security. *PLoS ONE, 11*(6).

Kang, M.-J., & Kang, J.-W. (2017). Intrusion Detection System Using Deep Neural Network for In-Vehicle Network Security. *PLOS One,* 1-17. doi:.Pone.0155781 doi:10.1371/journal

Kantardzic, M. (2011). *Data mining: concepts, models, methods, and algorithms.* Hoboken, NJ: John Wiley & Sons. doi:10.1002/9781118029145

Karchmer, M., & Wigderson, A. (1993, May). On span programs. In *Proceedings of the Eighth Annual Structure in Complexity Theory Conference* (pp. 102-111). IEEE.

Kashyap, H., Ahmed, H. A., Hoque, N., Roy, S., & Bhattacharyya, D. K. (2014). Big Data Analytics in Bioinformatics: A Machine Learning Perspective, *Journal of Latex Class Files, 13*(9). Retrieved from https://data-flair.training/blogs/deep-learning-vs-machine-learning/

Kasun, L. L. C., Zhou, H., Huang, G. B., & Vong, C. M. (2013). Representational learning with extreme learning machine for big data. *IEEE Intelligent Systems, 28*(6), 31–34.

Kato, K., Vitaly, K. (2014). An Intelligent DDoS Attack Detection System Using Packet Analysis and Support Vector Machine. *IJICR,* 478-485.

Kaur, A., Pal, S., & Singh, A. P. (2018). Hybridization of k-means and firefly algorithm for intrusion detection system. *International Journal of System Assurance Engineering and Management, 9*(4), 901–910. doi:10.100713198-017-0683-8

Kavanagh, K. M., Sadowski, G., & Bussa, T. (2018). *Magic quadrant for security information and event management.* Academic Press.

Kaya, K., & Selçuk, A. A. (2008, December). A verifiable secret sharing scheme based on the chinese remainder theorem. In *International Conference on Cryptology in India* (pp. 414-425). Berlin, Germany: Springer. 10.1007/978-3-540-89754-5_32

Kelly, M., Hand, D., & Adams, N. (1999, August). The impact of changing populations on classifier performance. In *5th ACM SIGKDD international conference on Knowledge discovery and data mining* (pp. 36-371). San Diego, CA: ACM.

Kennedy, J., & Eberhart, R. C. (1997). A discrete binary version of the particle swarm Algorithm. *IEEE Conference on Systems, Man, and Cybernetics*, 4104-4108.

Kennedy, J., & Eberhart, R. (1995). Particle Swarm Optimization. *IEEE Conference on Neural Networks*, 1942-1948.

Khalil, T. (2017). IoT security against DDoS attacks using machine learning algorithms. *International Journal of Scientific and Research Publications*, *7*(6), 739–741.

Khan, Baharudin, Lee, & Khan. (2010). A review of machine learning algorithms for text documents classification. *Journal of Advances in Information Technology*.

Khan, M. K., & Zhang, J. (2008). Multimodal face and fingerprint biometrics authentication on space-limited tokens. *Neurocomputing*, *71*(13), 3026–3031. doi:10.1016/j.neucom.2007.12.017

Khanna, U., & Singh, P. (2017). *Hybrid Approach of KNN+ Euclidean Distance to Detect Intrusion within Cloud Based Systems*. Retrieved from http://www.irjaes.com/pdf/V2N3Y17-IRJAES/IRJAES-V2N2P325Y17.pdf

Kira, K., & Rendell, L. A. (1992, July). The feature selection problem: Traditional methods and a new algorithm. In AAA (vol. 2, pp. 129-134). Academic Press.

Klein, B., & Peter, R. (2015). *Defeating machine learning*. Black Hat Briefings.

Kohavi, R., & Quinlan, J. R. (2002, January). Data mining tasks and methods: Classification: decision-tree discovery. In Handbook of data mining and knowledge discovery (pp. 267-276). Oxford, UK: Oxford University Press.

Koikara, R., Kim, P. H., Paul, A., & Yoo, K. Y. (2017). Threshold Secret Sharing based on 3D-Cellular Automata. In *Proceedings of the International Conference on Security and Management (SAM)*. The Steering Committee of the World Congress in Computer Science. Computer Engineering and Applied Computing.

Komorowski, J., Pawlak, Z., & Polkowski, L. (1999). Skowron, A Rough Sets Perspective on Data and Knowledge. In W. Klosgrn, & J. Zylkon (Eds.), *The Handbook of Data Mining and Knowledge Discovery* (pp. 134–149). New York, NY: Oxford University Press.

Kononenko, O., Baysal, O., Holmes, R., & Godfrey, M. W. (2014). Mining modern repositories with ElasticSearch. *Proceedings of the 11th IEEE Working Conference on Mining Software Repositories*.

Kotenko, I., Saenko, I., & Branitskiy, A. (2018). *Framework for Mobile Internet of Things Security Monitoring Based on Big Data Processing and Machine Learning*. IEEE. doi:10.1109/ACCESS.2018.2881998

Kotsiantis, S. B., Zaharakis, I., & Pintelas, P. (2007). Supervised machine learning: A review of classification techniques. *Emerging Artificial Intelligence Applications in Computer Engineering*, *160*, 3-24.

Kozik, R., Choras, M., Renk, R., & Hołubowicz, W. (2015). A Proposal of Algorithm for Web Applications Cyber Attack Detection. In *IFIP International Conference on Computer Information Systems and Industrial Management* (pp. 680-687). Berlin, Germany: Springer.

Kozik, R., & Choraś, M. (2014). Machine learning techniques for cyber attacks detection. In R. S. Choraś (Ed.), *Image Processing and Communications Challenges 5* (pp. 391–398). Springer International Publishing. doi:10.1007/978-3-319-01622-1_44

Kozik, R., Choraś, M., Ficco, M., & Palmieri, F. (2018). A scalable distributed machine learning approach for attack detection in edge computing environments. *Journal of Parallel and Distributed Computing*, *119*, 18–26. doi:10.1016/j.jpdc.2018.03.006

Kreuk, F., Barak, A., Aviv, S., Baruch, M., Pinkas, B., & Keshet, J. (2018). Deceiving End-to-End Deep Learning Malware Detectors using Adversarial Examples. In *Conference on Neural Information Processing Systems* (pp. 1-6), Montreal, Canada: Academic Press.

Kriegel, H., Kröger, P., & Zimek, A. (2010). Outlier Detection Techniques. *16th ACM SIGKDD Conference on Knowledge Discovery and Data Mining*, Washington, DC.

Krishnanand, K. N., & Ghose, D. (2009). Glowworm Swarm Optimization for Searching Higher Dimensional Spaces. In C. P. Lim, & S. Dehuri (Eds.), Innovations in Swarm Intelligence. Berlin, Germany: Springer-Verlag. doi:10.1007/978-3-642-04225-6_4

Krizhevsky, A., Sutskever, I., & Hinton, G. (2012). ImageNet Classification with Deep Convolutional Neural Networks. NIPS 2012: Neural Information Processing Systems, Lake Tahoe, NV.

Krizhevsky, A., & Hinton, G. (2009). *Learning multiple layers of features from tiny images*. University of Toronto.

Kumar, K. P., & Prasad, B, B. R. (2015). Investigating open issues in swarm intelligence for mitigating security threats in MANET. *Iranian Journal of Electrical and Computer Engineering*, *5*(5), 1194–1201.

Kumarnath, J., & Batri, K. (2018). A BAT algorithm based enhancement of physical layer security in a multi domain-elastic optical network. *International Journal of Pure and Applied Mathematics*, *119*(15), 2519–2525.

Kurakin, A., Goodfellow, I., & Bengio, S. (2016). *Adversarial examples in the physical world*. arXiv preprint arXiv: 1607.02533

Kwon, D., Kim, H., Kim, J., Suh, S. C., Kim, I., & Kim, K. J. (2017). A survey of deep learning-based network anomaly detection. In Cluster Computing (pp 1-13). Springer Science+Business Media.

Kwon, D., Kim, H., Kim, J., Suh, S. C., Kim, I., & Kim, K. J. (2017, September). A survey of deep learning-based network anomaly detection. *Cluster Computing*, 1–13.

L'heureux, A., Grolinger, K., Elyamany, H. F., & Capretz, M. M. (2017). Machine learning with big data: Challenges and approaches. (Vol. 5). IEEE.

Lab, L. (2015). *Deep Learning Tutorial*. Available at http: //deeplearning.net /tutorial / deeplearning.pdf

Laftah Al-Yaseen, W., Ali Othman, Z., & Ahmad Nazri, M. Z. (2015). Hybrid Modified-Means with C4. 5 for Intrusion Detection Systems in Multiagent Systems. *The Scientific World Journal*, *2015*, 1–14. doi:10.1155/2015/294761 PMID:26161437

Lancope. (n.d.). Retrieved from https://www.lancope.com

Laskov, P., Düssel, P., Schäfer, C., & Rieck, K. (2005, September). Learning Intrusion Detection: Supervised or Unsupervised? In *Proc. of the 13th International Conference on Image Analysis and Processing*, (pp. 50-57). Cagliari, Italy: Academic Press.

LeCun, Y., Bengio, Y., & Hinton, G. (2015). Deep learning. *Nature, 521*(7553), 436.

LeCun, Y., Bengio, Y., & Hinton, G. (2015). Deep learning. *Nature, 521*(7553), 436–444. doi:10.1038/nature14539 PMID:26017442

Lecun, Y., Bottou, L., Bengio, Y., & Haffner, P. (1998). Gradient-based learning applied to document recognition. *Proceedings of the IEEE*, *86*(11), 2278–2324. doi:10.1109/5.726791

Lee, B., Amaresh, S., Green, C., & Engels, D. (2018). Comparative Study of Deep Learning Models for Network Intrusion Detection. *SMU Data Science Review, 1*(1), 8.

Lee, C.-H., Su, Y.-Y., Lin, Y.-C., & Lee, S.-J. (2017). Machine learning based network intrusion detection. *2nd IEEE International Conference on Computational Intelligence and Applications.* doi:10.1109/CIAPP.2017.8167184

Lee, Y., & Lee, Y. (2013). Toward scalable internet traffic measurement and analysis with Hadoop. *Computer Communication Review, 43*(1), 5–13. doi:10.1145/2427036.2427038

Lefkimmiatis, S. (2016). *Non-local color image denoising with convolutional neural networks.* arXiv:1611.06757

Lekies. (2015). *Dangers of Scripting.* Retrieved from https://www.usenix.org/system/files/conference/cset17/cset17-paper-gagnon.pdf

Li, H. (2014). Deep Learning for Image Denoising. *International Journal of Signal Processing, Image Processing and Pattern Recognition*, 171-180.

Li, J., Zhou, Y., & Lamont, L. (2013). Communication Architectures and Protocols for Networking Unmanned Aerial Vehicles. *Globecom 2013 Workshop - Wireless Networking and Control for Unmanned Autonomous Vehicles, 13,* 1415-1420.

Li, Y., & Wang, Y. (2012). A misuse intrusion detection model based on hybrid classifier algorithm. *International Journal of Digital Content Technology and its Applications, 6*(5).

Liao, H.-J., Richard Lin, C.-H., Lin, Y.-C., & Tung, K.-Y. (2013). Intrusion detection system: A comprehensive review. *Journal of Network and Computer Applications, 36*(1), 16–24. doi:10.1016/j.jnca.2012.09.004

Li, M., Yu, J., & Hao, R. (2017). A cellular automata based verifiable multi-secret sharing scheme without a trusted dealer. *Chinese Journal of Electronics, 26*(2), 313–318. doi:10.1049/cje.2017.01.026

Lin, Z., Chen, G., Guo, W., & Liu, Y. (2008). PSO-BPNN-based prediction of network security situation. In *International Conference on Innovative Computing Information and Control* (pp. 1-5). Dalian, Liaoning, China. IEEE.

Linda, O., Manic, M., Vollmer, T., & Wright, J. (2011, April). Fuzzy logic based anomaly detection for embedded network security cyber sensor. In *2011 IEEE Symposium on Computational Intelligence in Cyber Security (CICS),* (pp. 202-209). IEEE. 10.1109/CICYBS.2011.5949392

Li, S.-H., Kao, Y.-C., Zhang, Z.-C., Chuang, Y.-P., & Yen, D. C. (2015). A network behavior-based botnet detection mechanism using PSO and k-means. *ACM Transactions on Management Information Systems, 6*(1), 1–30. doi:10.1145/2676869

Litan, A. (2015). *Market guide for user and entity behavior analytics.* Gartner.

Liu, Y. Z. Y., Li, H., & Chen, X. (2016). A hybrid malware detecting scheme for mobile Android applications. IEEE.

Liu, Q., Li, P., & Zhao, W. (2018). *A Survey on Security Threats and defensive techniques of Machine Learning: A Data-Driven View.* IEEE.

Liu, Q., Li, P., Zhao, W., Cai, W., Yu, S., & Leung, C. M. V. (2018). A survey on security threats and defensive techniques of machine learning: A data driven view. IEEE. *IEEE Access: Practical Innovations, Open Solutions, 6,* 12103–12117. doi:10.1109/ACCESS.2018.2805680

Liu, X., Zhao, M., Li, S., Zhang, F., & Trappe, W. (2017, June). A security framework for the Internet of Things in the future Internet architecture. *Future Internet, 9*(3), 1–28. doi:10.3390/fi9030027

Li, X., Lu, R., Liang, X., Shen, X., Chen, J., & Lin, X. (2011, November). Smart community: An Internet of Things application. *IEEE Communications Magazine, 49*(11), 68–75. doi:10.1109/MCOM.2011.6069711

Li, X., & Yin, M. (2015). Modified cuckoo search algorithm with self-adaptive parameter method. *Information Sciences, 298*, 80–97. doi:10.1016/j.ins.2014.11.042

Li, Y. (2015). Detection, Classification and Characterization of Android Malware Using API Data Dependency. In *International Conference on Security and Privacy in Communication Systems*. Springer International Publishing. 10.1007/978-3-319-28865-9_2

Li, Y., Ma, R., & Jiao, R. (2013). *A hybrid malicious code detection method based on deep learning*. Springer.

Li, Y., Liu, Y., & Zhang, H. (2012). Cross-boundary enterprise security monitoring. In *Proceedings of the IEEE International Conference on Computational Problem-Solving* (pp. 127–136). IEEE.

Lobo, L. M. R. J., & Chavan, S. B. (2012). Use of genetic algorithm in network security. International Journal of Computers and Applications, 53(8), 1–7. doi:10.5120/8438-2221 doi:10.5120/8438-2221

Lobo, S. (2018). *Six artificial intelligence cyber security tools you need to know*. Retrieved from https://hub.packtpub.com/6-artificial-intelligence-cybersecurity-tools-you-need-to-know/

Lore, K. G., Akintayo, A., & Sarkar, S. (2016). Llnet: A deep autoencoder approach to natural lowlight image enhancement. *Pattern Recognition*, 1–13.

Louridas, P., & Ebert, C. (2016). Machine Learning. *IEEE Software, 33*(5), 110–115. doi:10.1109/MS.2016.114

Lu, D., Wang, Y., Zhang, X., & Ji, L. (2016, December). A threshold secret sharing scheme based on lmca and chinese remainder theorem. In *2016 9th International Symposium on Computational Intelligence and Design (ISCID)* (Vol. 2, pp. 439-442). IEEE. 10.1109/ISCID.2016.2109

Lucasius, C. B., & Kateman, G. (1992). Towards Solving Subset Selection Problems with the Aid of the Genetic Algorithm. In R. Männer, & B. Manderick (Eds.), *Parallel Problem Solving from Nature 2* (pp. 239–247). Amsterdam, The Netherlands: North-Holland.

Machanavajjhala, A., Kifer, D., Gehrke, J., & Venkitasubramaniam, M. (2007). L-diversity: Privacy beyond k-anonymity. *TKDD, 1*(1).

Madria, S. K., Bhowmick, S. S., Ng, W. K., & Lim, E. P. (1999). Research issues in web data Mining. *Proceedings of First International Conference of Data Warehousing and Knowledge Discovery, DaWaK'99*, 301-312.

Madry, A., Makelov, A., Schmidt, L., Tsipras, D., & Vladu, A. (2017). *Towards deep learning models resistant to adversarial attacks*. arXiv preprint arXiv:1706.06083

Maestre Vidal, J., Sandoval Orozco, A., & García Villalba, L. (2016, November). Online masquerade detection resistant to mimicry. *Expert Systems with Applications, 61*, 162-180.

Maestre Vidal, J., Sandoval Orozco, A., & García Villalba, L. (2017, November). Alert Correlation Framework for Malware Detection by Anomaly-based Packet Payload Analysis. *Journal of Network and Computer Applications, 29*, 11–22. doi:10.1016/j.jnca.2017.08.010

Maestre Vidal, J., Sandoval Orozco, A., & García Villalba, L. (2018). Adaptive Artificial Immune Networks for Mitigating DoS flooding Attacks. *Swarm and Evolutionary Computation, 38*, 94–108. doi:10.1016/j.swevo.2017.07.002

Maestre Vidal, J., Sotelo Monge, M., & García Villabla, L. (2018). A Novel Pattern Recognition System for Detecting Android Malware by Analyzing Suspicious Boot Sequences. *Knowledge-Based Systems, 150*, 198–217. doi:10.1016/j.knosys.2018.03.018

Mahalakshmi, S., & Vadivel, R. (2018). Particle Swarm Optimization algorithm (PSO) used for security enhancement in MANET. *International Journal of Advanced Research in Computer Science, 9*(2), 233–241. doi:10.26483/ijarcs.v9i2.5643

Mahrooghy, M., Younan, N. H., Anantharaj, V., & Aanstoos, J. (2012). Enhancement of Satellite Precipitation Estimation via Unsupervised Dimensionality Reduction. *IEEE Transactions on Geoscience and Remote Sensing.*

Maimo, L. F., Angel, L. P. G., Clemente, F. G. J., Pérez, M. G., & Pérez, G. M. (2018). A self-adaptive deep learning-based system for anomaly detection in 5G networks. In Special on Cyber-Physical-Social Computing and Networking (pp. 7700 – 7712). Academic Press.

Malicious Code. (2009). Retrieved from https://www.veracode.com/security/rise-malicious-mobile-applications

Malicious Mobile Apps. (2009). Retrieved from https://searchsecurity.techtarget.com/securityschool/How-best-to-find-and-fend-off-malicious-mobile-apps

Malware Detection. (2013). Retrieved from https://www.researchgate.net/publication/258820759_Malware_detection_by_behavioural_sequential_patterns

Malware Identification. (2009). Retrieved from https://www.consumer.ftc.gov/articles/0011-malware

Malware. (2006). Retrieved from https://en.wikipedia.org/wiki/Malware

Manadhata, P. K., & Wing, J. M. (2011). An attack surface metric. *Software Engineering, IEEE Transactions on, 37*(3), 371–386. doi:10.1109/TSE.2010.60

MapR. (n.d.). Retrieved from https://www.mapr.com

Marsland, S. (2011). *Machine learning: an algorithmic perspective.* Chapman and Hall. Retrieved from http://dspace.fue.edu.eg/xmlui/bitstream/handle/123456789/3667/10501.pdf?sequence=1

Mehmood, A., Natgunanathan, I., Xiang, Y., Hua, G., & Guo, S. (2016). *Protection of big data privacy, Theoretical Foundations For Big Data Applications Opportunities.* Academic Press.

Menezes, A. J., Okamoto, T., & Vanstone, S. A. (1993). Reducing elliptic curve logarithms to logarithms in a finite field. *IEEE Transactions on Information Theory, 39*(5), 1639–1646. doi:10.1109/18.259647

Meng, X., Bradley, J., Yavuz, B., Sparks, E., Venkataraman, S., Liu, D., & ... Talwaker, A. (2016). MLlib: Machine learning in apache spark. *Journal of Machine Learning Research, 17*, 1235–1241.

Meshram, A., & Haas, C. (2017). *Anomaly detection in industrial networks using machine learning: a roadmap.* In *Machine Learning for Cyber Physical Systems.* Berlin, Germany: Springer. doi:10.1007/978-3-662-53806-7_8

Michalski, R. S., Carbonell, J. G., & Mitchell, T. M. (Eds.). (2013). *Machine learning: An artificial intelligence approach.* Springer Science & Business Media.

Mignotte, M. (1982, March). How to share a secret. In *Workshop on Cryptography* (pp. 371-375). Berlin, Germany: Springer.

Milajerdi, S. M., Gjomemo, R., Eshete, B., Sekar, R., & Venkatakrishnan, V. (2019). Holmes: Realtime apt detection through correlation of suspicious information flows. In *Proceedings of the 40th IEEE Symposium on Security and Privacy (S&P).* IEEE.

Milenkoski, A., Vieira, M., Kounev, S., Avritzer, A., & Payne, B. (2015, September). Evaluating Computer Intrusion Detection Systems: A Survey of Common Practices. *ACM Computing Surveys, 48*(12), 1-41.

Ming, J., Xin, Z., Lan, P., Wu, D., Liu, P., & Mao, B. (2016). Impeding behavior-based malware analysis via replacement attacks to malware specifications. *J Computer Virol Hacking Tech, 13*(3), 193–207. doi:10.100711416-016-0281-3

Minku, L., White, A., & Yao, X. (2010, May). The impact of diversity on online ensemble learning in the presence of concept drift. *IEEE Transactions on Knowledge and Data Engineering, 22*(5), 731-742.

Mirsky, Y., Doitshman, T., Elovici, Y., & Shabtai, A. (2018). Kitsune: An ensemble of autoencoders for online network intrusion detection. *Proceedings of the Network and Distributed System Security Symposium (NDSS) 2018.* doi:10.14722/ndss.2018.23204

Mitchell, R., & Chen, I.-R. (n.d.). *Effect of intrusion detection and response on reliability of cyber physical systems.* Retrieved from: http://people.cs.vt.edu/~irchen/ps/Mitchell-TR13a.pdf

MITRE. (n.d.). *Adversarial tactics, techniques and common knowledge.* Retrieved from https://attack.mitre.org/

Mobile App. (2008. Retrieved from https://en.wikipedia.org/wiki/Mobile_app

Mobile Malware Detection. (2015). Retrieved from https://www.ijcsmc.com/docs/papers/December2015/V4I12201556.pdf

Mobile Security Threats. (2010). Retrieved from https://www.google.com/search?q=10+high+risk+mobile+malware+apps&spell=1&sa=X&ved=0ahUKEwils4OV36PgAhUKY48KHaT9BuUQBQgrKAA&biw=1536&bih=754

Mohaisen A., Alrawi O., & Mohaisen M. (2015). *AMAL: high-fidelity, behavior-based automated malware analysis and classification.* Academic Press.

Mohammadi, M., Al-Fuqaha, A., Sorour, S., & Guizani, M. (2018). Deep Learning for IoT Big Data and Streaming Analytics: A Survey. *IEEE Communications Surveys and Tutorials, 20*(4), 2923–2960. doi:10.1109/COMST.2018.2844341

Mohideen, S. K., Perumal, S., Krishnan, N., Sathik, M., & Kumar, T. (2008). Image denoising multi-wavelet and threshold. *IEEE International conference on Computing, Communication and Networking*, 1-5.

Mozaffari-Kermani, M., Sur-Kolay, S., Raghunathan, A., & Jha, N. K. (2015). Systematic poisoning attacks on and defenses for machine learning in healthcare. *IEEE Journal of Biomedical and Health Informatics, 19*(6), 1893–1905. doi:10.1109/JBHI.2014.2344095 PMID:25095272

Mrabet, Z. E., Kaabouch, N., Ghazi, H. E., & Ghazi, H. E. (2018). Cyber-security in smart grid: Survey and challenges. *Computers & Electrical Engineering, 67*, 469–482. doi:10.1016/j.compeleceng.2018.01.015

Murphree, J. (2016). *Machine learning anomaly detection in large systems.* Anaheim, CA: IEEE Autotestcon. doi:10.1109/AUTEST.2016.7589589

Nagaraja, S. (2014). Botyacc: Unified p2p botnet detection using behavioural analysis and graph analysis. In *European Symposium on Research in Computer Security* (pp. 439–456). Academic Press.

Najafabadi, M. M., Villanustre, F., Khoshgoftaar, T. M., Seliya, N., Wald, R., & Muharemagic, E. (2015). Deep learning applications and challenges in big data analytics *Journal of Big Data 2*(1), 1. doi:10.118640537-014-0007-7

Nallakannu, S. M., & Thiagarajan, R. (2016). PSO-based optimal peer selection approach for highly secure and trusted P2P system. *Security and Communication Networks, 9*(13), 2186–2199.

Nargundi, S. M, ., & Phalnikar, R. (2012). k-Anonymization using Multidimensional Suppression for Data De-identification. *International Journal of Computers and Applications, 975, 8887.*

Nasrabadi, N. M. (2007). Pattern recognition and machine learning. *Journal of Electronic Imaging, 16*(4), 049901. doi:10.1117/1.2819119

Nassar, M., al Bouna, B., & Malluhi, Q. (2013). Secure outsourcing of network flow data analysis. In *Proceedings of the 2013 IEEE International Congress on Big Data* (pp. 431–432). IEEE. 10.1109/BigData.Congress.2013.71

Navarro-Lara, J., Deruyver, A., & Parrend, P. (2016). Morwilog: An ACO-based System for Outlining Multi-Step Attacks. In *IEEE Symposium Series on Computational Intelligence* (pp. 1-9). Athens, Greece: IEEE. 10.1109/SSCI.2016.7849902

Nazeer, M. I., Mallah, G. A., Bhatra, N. R., & Memon, R. A. (2018). Implication of genetic algorithm in cryptography to enhance security. *International Journal of Advanced Computer Science and Applications*, *9*(6), 375–379. doi:10.14569/IJACSA.2018.090651

Neethu, B. (2013). Adaptive Intrusion Detection Using Machine Learning. *International Journal of Computer Science and Network Security*, *13*(3), 118.

Nelson, B. (2012). Query strategies for evading convex inducing classifiers. *Journal of Machine Learning Research*, *13*(May), 1293–1332.

Nguyen, H. T., & Franke, K. (2012). Adaptive Intrusion Detection System via online machine learning. In *12th International Conference on Hybrid Intelligent Systems*. IEEE.

Nguyen, H. A., & Choi, D. (2008, October). Application of data mining to network intrusion detection: classifier selection model. In *Asia-Pacific Network Operations and Management Symposium* (pp. 399-408). Berlin, Germany: Springer. 10.1007/978-3-540-88623-5_41

Nikolopoulos, S.D., & Polenakis, I. (2016) A graph-based model for malware detection and classification using system-call groups. *J Comput Virol Hacking Tech, 13,* 29–46.

NIST Special Publication 1500-201. (2017). NIST Framework for Cyber-Physical System: volume 1. Overview.

Norouzi, M., Souri, A., & Samad Zamini, M. (2016). A data mining classification approach for behavioral malware detection. *J Comput Netw Commun, 2016,* 9.

O'Reilly, C., Gluhak, A., Imran, M., & Rajasegarar, S. (2014). Anomaly Detection in Wireless Sensor Networks in a Non-Stationary Environment. *IEEE Communications Surveys and Tutorials*, *16*(3), 1413–1432. doi:10.1109/SURV.2013.112813.00168

Ognawala, S., Amato, R. N., Pretschner, A., & Kulkarni, P. (2018). Automatically assessing vulnerabilities discovered by compositional analysis. In *International Workshop on Machine Learning and Software Engineering in Symbiosis* (pp. 16-25). New York, NY: Academic Press. 10.1145/3243127.3243130

Ojugo, A. AEboka, A. OOkonta, O. EYoro, R. E., & Aghware, F. O. (2012). Genetic Algorithm Rule-Based Intrusion Detection System (GAIDS). *Journal of Emerging Trends in Computing and Information Sciences*, *3*(8), 1182–1194.

Ong, P. (2014). Adaptive cuckoo search algorithm for unconstrained optimization. *The Scientific World Journal*, 2014. PMID:25298971

Oprea, A., Li, Z., Yen, T.-F., Chin, S. H., & Alrwais, S. (2015). Detection of early-stage enterprise infection by mining large-scale log data. In *Proceedings of the 45th Annual IEEE/IFIP International Conference on Dependable Systems and Networks* (pp. 45–56). IEEE. 10.1109/DSN.2015.14

Othman, S. A., & Stambouli, T. B. (2016). Undecimated discrete wavelet transform for touchless 2D fingerprint identification. *International Journal of Biometrics*, *8*(3-4), 202–215. doi:10.1504/IJBM.2016.082595

Othman, S. M., Fadl, M. B. A., Alsohybe, N. T., & Al Hashida, A. Y. (2018). Intrusion detection model using machine learning algorithm on Big Data environment. *Journal of Big Data*, *5*(34).

Owezarski, P. (2014). Unsupervised classification and characterization of honeypot attacks. In *International Conference on Network and Service Management* (pp. 1-10). Rio de Janeiro, Brazil: Academic Press. 10.1109/CNSM.2014.7014136

Ozcelik, I., & Brooks, R. (2015, February). Deceiving entropy based DoS detection. *Computers & Security, 48*(1), 234-245.

Panda, M., & Patra, M. R. (2007). Network intrusion detection using naive Bayes. *International Journal of Computer Science and Network Security, 7*(12), 258-263.

Papernot, N., McDaniel, P., Goodfellow, I., Jha, S., Celik, Z. B., & Swami, A. (2016). *Practical black-box attacks against deep learning systems using adversarial examples.* arXiv preprint arXiv:1602.02697

Papernot, N., McDaniel, P., Jha, S., Fredrikson, M., Celik, Z. B., & Swami, A. (2016). The limitations of deep learning in adversarial settings. In *Security and Privacy (EuroS&P), 2016 IEEE European Symposium on* (pp. 372-387). IEEE. 10.1109/EuroSP.2016.36

Papernot, N., McDaniel, P., Sinha, A., & Wellman, M. (2016). *Towards the Science of Security and Privacy in Machine Learning.* arXiv preprint arXiv:1611.03814

Parrend, P., Navarro, J., Guigou, F., Deruyver, A., & Collet, P. (2018). Foundations and Applications of Artificial Intelligence for Zero-day and Multi-Step Attack Detection. EURASIP Journal on Information Security, 2018(1), 4.

Pascanu, R., Stokes, J. W., Sanossian, H., Marinescu, M., & Thomas, A. (2015). Malware classification with recurrent networks. *IEEE International Conference on Acoustics, Speech and Signal Processing (ICASSP).*

Pascanu, R., Stokes, J. W., Sanossian, H., Marinescu, M., & Thomas, A. (2015). Malware classification with Recurrent networks. *IEEE International Conference on Acoustics, Speech and Signal Processing (ICASSP).*

Pasqualetti. (2013). Attacks detection and identification in cyber-physical security systems. *IEEE TAC, 58*(11).

Passino, K. M. (2002, June). Biomimicry of Bacterial Foraging for Distributed Optimization and Control. *IEEE Control Systems Magazine*, 52–67.

Pattern Recognition. (2016). Retrieved from https://en.wikipedia.org/wiki/Pattern_recognition

Pattern Recognition: An Overview. (2012). Retrieved from http://article.sapub.org/pdf/10.5923.j.ajis.20120201.04.pdf

Pavani, K., & Damodaram, A. (2014). Anomaly detection system for routing attacks in mobile ad hoc networks. *International Journal of Network Security, 6*, 13–24.

Pawlak, Z. (1982). Rough Sets. *International Journal of Information and Computer Sciences, 11*(5), 341–356. doi:10.1007/BF01001956

Pei, Z., & Song, J. (2008). Application of Immune Algorithm to Generate Fuzzy-detector in Intrusion detection. *Fourth International Conference on Natural Computation (ICNC), 5*, 183-186. 10.1109/ICNC.2008.840

Peng, K., & Leung, V., Zheng, LWang, S., Huang, C., & Lin, T. (2018). Intrusion Detection System Based on Decision Tree over Big Data in Fog Environment. *Wireless Communications and Mobile Computing*, 1–10.

Peng, K., Leung, V. C., & Huang, Q. (2018). Clustering approach based on mini batch K-means for intrusion detection system over Big Data. *IEEE Access: Practical Innovations, Open Solutions.*

Pengyuan, P. (2017). Studies on the Network Anomaly Intrusion Detection of a Fish Swarm Optimization Algorithm Based on Neural Network. *Revista de la Facultad de Ingeniería U.C.V., 32*(13), 585-589.

Petit, J., Stottelaar, B., Feiri, M., & Kargl, F. (n.d.). *Remote attacks on automated vehicle sensors: experiments on camera and LiDAR.* Retrieved from: https://pdfs.semanticscholar.org/e06f/ef73f5bad0489bb033f490d41a046f61878a.pdf

Polakis, I., Diamantaris, M., Petsas, T., Maggi, F., & Ioannidis, S. (2015, July). Powerslave: Analyzing the Energy Consumption of Mobile Antivirus Software. In *12th International Conference on Detection of Intrusions and Malware, and Vulnerability Assessment*, (pp. 165-184). Milan, Italy: Academic Press. 10.1007/978-3-319-20550-2_9

Police, E. (2016). *The Internet Organised Crime Threat Assessment (iOCTA)*. Retrieved from https://www.europol.europa.eu/activities-services/main-reports/internet-organised-crime-threat-assessment-iocta-2016

Prabha, S., & Yadav, R. (2018). Differential evolution for mobile ad-hoc networks: A review. *International Journal on Computer Science and Engineering, 6*(6), 1459–1467.

Praveena, M. A., & Bharathi, B. (2017, February). A survey paper on big data analytics. In *2017 International Conference on Information Communication and Embedded Systems (ICICES)*(pp. 1-9). IEEE.

Presswala, F., *Thakkar, A., & Bhatt, N.* (2015). *Survey on Anonymization in Privacy Preserving Data Mining. IJIERE.*

Protection from Malware. (2009). Retrieved from https://www.consumer.ftc.gov/media/video-0056-protect-your-computer-malware

Rahouti, M., *Kaiqi, X., & Ghani, N. (2018). Bitcoin Concepts, Threats, and Machine-Learning Security Solutions*. IEEE.

Ramasamy, S., & Eswaramoorthy, K. (2017). Ant colony optimization based handoff scheme and verifiable secret sharing security with M-M scheme for VoIP. *International Journal of Intelligent Engineering and Systems, 10*(5), 267–277. doi:10.22266/ijies2017.1031.29

Rashedul & Rofiqul. (2010). *Mobile Applications*. Retrieved from http://www.ijens.org/107506-0909%20ijet-ijens.pdf

Ratner, B. (2010, March). Variable selection methods in regression: Ignorable problem, outing notable solution. *Journal of Targeting, Measurement and Analysis for Marketing, 18*(1), 65–75. doi:10.1057/jt.2009.26

Refaeilzadeh, P., Tang, L., & Liu, H. (2009). Cross-validation. In *Encyclopedia of database systems* (pp. 532–538). Boston, MA: Springer.

Revett, K., Gorunescu, F., Gorunescu, M., Ene, M., Magalhaes, S. T., & Santos, H. M. D. (2007). A machine learning approach to keystroke dynamics based user authentication. *International Journal of Electronic Security and Digital Forensics, 1*(1), 55. doi:10.1504/IJESDF.2007.013592

Rifai, S., Vincent, P., Muller, X., Glorot, X., & Bengio, Y. (2011). Contractive auto-encoders: explicit invariance during feature extraction. In *Proceedings of ICML*, (pp. 833–840). Academic Press.

Rifai, S., Bengio, Y., Dauphin, Y., & Vincent, P. (2012). *A generative process for sampling contractive auto-encoders*. ICML.

Rivest, R. L., Shamir, A., & Adleman, L. (1978). A method for obtaining digital signatures and public-key cryptosystems. *Communications of the ACM, 21*(2), 120–126. doi:10.1145/359340.359342

Rukhin, A., Soto, J., Nechvatal, J., Smid, M., & Barker, E. (2001). *A statistical test suite for random and pseudorandom number generators for cryptographic applications*. Mclean, VA: Booz-Allen and Hamilton.

Saad, S., Traore, I., Ghorbani, A. A., Sayed, B., Zhao, D., Lu, W., Felix, J., & Hakimian, P. (2011). Detecting P2P botnets through network behaviour analysis and machine learning. In *Proceedings of 9th Annual Conference on Privacy, Security and Trust (PST2011)*. Montreal, Quebec, Canada: Academic Press.

Saad, S., Traore, I., Ghorbani, A., Sayed, B., Zhao, D., Lu, W., ... Hakimian, P. (2011). Detecting P2P botnets through network behavior analysis and machine learning. In *Proceedings of 9th Annual International Conference on Privacy, Security and Trust (PST2011)*. Montreal, Quebec, Canada: Academic Press.

Sabaliauskaite. (2013). Intelligent checkers to improve attack detection in cyber-physical systems. *IEEE CyberC.*

Sabhnani, M., & Serpen, G. (2003). *Application of Machine Learning Algorithms to KDD Intrusion Detection Dataset within Misuse Detection Context.* MLMTA.

Sadri, J., & Suen, C. Y. (2006). A Genetic Binary Particle Swarm Optimization Model. *IEEE Congress on Evolutionary Computation,* 656-663. 10.1109/CEC.2006.1688373

Safa, N. S., Maple, C., Watson, T., & Von Solms, R. (2018). Motivation and opportunity based model to reduce information security insider threats in organisations. *Journal of Information Security and Applications, 40,* 247–257. doi:10.1016/j.jisa.2017.11.001

Sahoo, D., Liu, C., & Hoi, S. C. H. (2017). Malicious URL detection using machine learning. *Survey (London, UK).*

Salama & Bach. (2013). *Smart Phones.* Retrieved from https://www.researchgate.net/publication/256703317_Introduction_of_6th_Generation_Smart_Phone_combining_the_features_of_both_Apple_and_Android_smart_phone

Samuel, A. L. (1959). Some studies in machine learning using the game of checkers. *IBM Journal of Research and Development, 3*(3), 210–229. doi:10.1147/rd.33.0210

Sasirekha, K., & Thangavel, K. (2014). A Comparative Analysis on Fingerprint Binarization Techniques. *International Journal of Computational Intelligence and Informatics, 4*(3).

Sasirekha, K., & Thangavel, K. (2014). A Novel Wavelet based Thresholding for Denoising Fingerprint Image. In *IEEE International Conference on Electronics, Communication and Computational Engineering,* (pp. 119-124). IEEE. 10.1109/ICECCE.2014.7086644

Sasirekha, K., & Thangavel, K. (2016). *A Novel Feature Extraction Algorithm from Fingerprint Image in Wavelet Domain. Springer.*

Savage, D., Zhang, X., Yu, X., Chou, P., & Wang, Q. (2014, October). Anomaly detection in online social networks. *Social Networks, 39,* 62-70.

Schiff, J. L. (2005). *Introduction to cellular automata.* Retrieved from http://psoup.math.wisc.edu/pub/Schiff_CAbook.pdf

Schmidhuber, J. (2015). Deep learning in neural networks: An overview. *Neural Networks, 61,* 85–117. doi:10.1016/j.neunet.2014.09.003 PMID:25462637

Schoenmakers, B. (1999, August). A simple publicly verifiable secret sharing scheme and its application to electronic voting. In *Annual International Cryptology Conference* (pp. 148-164). Berlin, Germany: Springer. 10.1007/3-540-48405-1_10

Schubert, E., Weiler, M., & Zimek, A. (2015). Outlier Detection and Trend Detection: Two Sides of the Same Coin. *IEEE International Conference on Data Mining Workshop,* (pp. 40-46). Atlantic City, NJ: IEEE. 10.1109/ICDMW.2015.79

Schubert, E., Wojdanowski, R., Zimek, A., & Kriegel, H. (2012). On Evaluation of Outlier Rankings and Outlier Scores. In 12th SIAM International Conference on Data Mining (SDM), (pp. 1047-1058). Anaheim, CA: Academic Press.

Scope of Buster Sandbox Analyzer. (2011). Retrieved from https://www.securityartwork.es/2012/12/12/buster-sandbox-analyzer/

Sebestyen, G., & Hangan, A. (2017). Anomaly detection techniques in cyber-physical systems. *Acta Universitatis Sapientiae Informatica, 9*(2), 101–118.

Sebopelo, R., Isong, B., & Gasela, N. (2019). Identification of compromised nodes in MANETs using machine learning technique. *International Journal of Computer Network and Information Security, 1*(1), 1–10. doi:10.5815/ijcnis.2019.01.01

Securonix. (n.d.). Retrieved from https://www.securonix.com/

Sedjelmaci, H., Senouci, S. M., & Ansari, N. (2017). Intrusion Detection and Ejection Framework Against Lethal Attacks in UAV-Aided Networks: A Bayesian Game-Theoretic Methodology. *IEEE Transactions on Intelligent Transportation Systems, 18*(5), 1143–1153. doi:10.1109/TITS.2016.2600370

Sedjelmaci, H., Senouci, S. M., & Ansari, N. (2018). A Hierarchical Detection and Response System to Enhance Security Against Lethal Cyber-Attacks in UAV Networks, IEEE Transactions on Systems, Man, and Cybernetics. *Systems, 48*(9), 1594–1606.

Sekeh, M. A., & Bin Maarof, M. A. (2009). Fuzzy Intrusion Detection System via Data Mining Technique with Sequences of System Calls. *Fifth International Conference on Information Assurance and Security (IAS '09), 1*, 154-157. 10.1109/IAS.2009.32

Shackleford, D. (2015). *Analytics and Intelligence Survey.* Paper SANS Institute – InfoSec Reading Room.

Shackleford, D. (2016). *Security Analytics Survey.* Paper SANS Institute – InfoSec Reading Room.

Shafiq, M., Yu, X., Kashif Bashir, A., Chaudrhry, H., & Wang, D. (2018). A machine learning approach for feature selection traffic classification using security analysis. *The Journal of Supercomputing, 74*(10), 4867–4892. doi:10.100711227-018-2263-3

Shamir, A. (1979). How to share a secret. *Communications of the ACM, 22*(11), 612–613. doi:10.1145/359168.359176

Shams, S., Platania, R., Lee, K., & Park, S. J. (2017). Evaluation of deep learning frameworks over different hpc architectures. *IEEE 37th International Conference on Distributed Computing Systems (ICDCS),* 1389–1396.

Shamsinejadbabki, P., & Saraee, M. (2012). A New Unsupervised Feature Selection Method for Text Clustering Based on Genetic Algorithms. *Journal of Intelligent Information Systems, 38,* 1-16.

Sharma, R. K., Kalita, H. K., & Borah, P. (2016). Analysis of machine learning techniques based intrusion detection systems. In *Proceedings of 3rd International Conference on Advanced Computing, Networking and Informatics* (pp. 485-493). New Delhi, India: Springer.

Sharma, V., Lee, K., Kwon, S., Kim, J., Park, H., Yim, K., & Lee, S. Y. (2017). A Consensus Framework for Reliability and Mitigation of Zero-Day Attacks in IoT. *Security and Communication Networks.*

Sheen, S., Anitha, R., & Natarajan, V. (2015). Android based malware detection using a multi feature collaborative decision fusion approach. *Neurocomputing, 151*(2), 905–912. doi:10.1016/j.neucom.2014.10.004

Shelke, M. P. K., Sontakke, M. S., & Gawande, A. D. (2012). Intrusion detection system for cloud computing. *International Journal of Scientific & Technology Research, 1*(4), 67–71.

Sheng, Z., Yang, S., Yu, Y., Vasilakos, A., Mccann, J., & Leung, K. (2013, December). A survey on the IETF protocol suite for the Internet of Things: Standards, challenges, and opportunities. *IEEE Wireless Communications, 20*(6), 91–98. doi:10.1109/MWC.2013.6704479

Shen, X. J., Wang, L., & Han, D. J. (2016). Application of artificial bee colony optimized BP neural network in intrusion detection. *Computer Engineering, 42*(2), 190–194.

Shepard, D. P., Bhatti, J. A., Humphreys, T. E., & Fansler, A. A. (2012). Evaluation of smart grid and civilian UAV vulnerability to GPS spoofing attacks. *Proc. ION GNSS Meeting,* 1–15.

Shrivastava, A., Baghel, M., & Gupta, H. (2013). A Novel Hybrid Feature Selection and Intrusion Detection Based on PCNN and Support Vector Machine. *International Journal of Computer Technology and Applications., 4*(6), 922–927.

Shrivastava, N., & Richariya, V. (2012). Ant colony optimization with classification algorithms used for intrusion detection. *International Journal of Computational Engineering & Management, 15*(1), 54–63.

Shu, G., & Lee, D. (2007). Testing Security Properties of Protocol Implementations – a Machine Learning Based Approach. *Proceedings of 27th International Conference on Distributed Computing Systems (ICDCS'07).* 10.1109/ICDCS.2007.147

Siddiqui, M., Wang, M. C., & Lee, J. (2008). A survey of data mining techniques for malware detection using fle features. In *Proceedings of the 46th annual southeast regional conference on xx.* ACM. 10.1145/1593105.1593239

Simmons, G. J. (1991). The geometry of shared secret schemes. *Bulletin of the Institute of Combinatorics and its Applications, 1*, 71-88.

Singh, U. K., Joshi, C., & Singh, S. K. (2016). ZDAR System: Defending against the Unknown. *International Journal of Computer Science and Mobile Computing, 5*(12), 143-149.

Singh, R., & Om, H. (2017). Newborn face recognition using deep convolutional neural network. *Multimedia Tools and Applications*, 1–11.

Smith, M. G., & Bull, L. (2003). Feature construction and selection using genetic programming and a genetic algorithm. *Proceedings of the 6th European Conference on Genetic Programming,* 229–237. 10.1007/3-540-36599-0_21

Sokolova, M., & Lapalme, G. (2009). A systematic analysis of performance measures for classification tasks. *Information Processing & Management, 45*(4), 427–437. doi:10.1016/j.ipm.2009.03.002

Sommer, R., & Paxson, V. (2010). Outside the closed world: On using machine learning for network intrusion detection. In *Proceedings of the 30th IEEE Symposium on Security and Privacy* (pp. 305–316). IEEE. 10.1109/SP.2010.25

Song, X., Wu, M., Jermaine, C., & Ranka, S. (2007, May). Conditional Anomaly Detection. *IEEE Transactions on Knowledge and Data Engineering, 19*(5), 631-645.

Sotelo Monge, M., Maestre Vidal, J., & García Villalba, L. (2017). Entropy-Based Economic Denial of Sustainability Detection. *Entropy (Basel, Switzerland)*, 2.

Sotelo Monge, M., Maestre Vidal, J., & García Villalba, L. (2017). Reasoning and Knowledge Acquisition Framework for 5G Network Analytics. *Sensors (Basel)*, 17. PMID:29065473

Sowah, A. R., Ofori-Amanfo, K. B., Mills, G. A., & Koumadi, M. K. (2019). Detection and prevention of man-in-the-middle spoofing attacks in MANETs using predictive techniques in Artificial Neural Networks (ANN). *Journal of Computer Networks and Communications*, 1-14.

Splunk. (n.d.). Retrieved from https://www.splunk.com

Srinivas, M. & Sung, A. H. (2013). *Detecting Denial of Service Attacks Using Support Vector Machines.* IEEE.

Srinivasan, H., Srihari, S. N., & Beal, J. M. (2006). Machine learning for signature verification. In P. Kalra, & S. Peleg (Eds.), Computer Vision, Graphics and Image Processing (pp. 761-775). Berlin, Germany: Springer-Verlag.

Srivastava, N., Hinton, G., Krizhevsky, A., Sutskever, I., & Salakhutdinov, R. (2014). Dropout: A Simple Way to Prevent Neural Networks From Over fitting. *Journal of Machine Learning Research, 15*(1), 1929-1958.

Stadler, M. (1996, May). Publicly verifiable secret sharing. In *International Conference on the Theory and Applications of Cryptographic Techniques* (pp. 190-199). Berlin, Germany: Springer.

Stark, J. A. (2000). Adaptive image contrast enhancement using generalizations of histogram equalization. *IEEE Transactions on Image Processing, 9*(5), 889–896. doi:10.1109/83.841534 PMID:18255459

Stiennon, R. (2016). *Chief Research Analyst*. IT-Harvest, National Fintech Cybersecurity Summit.

Stroeh, K*., Madeira, E. R. M., & Goldenstein, S. K. (2013). An approach to the correlation of security events based on machine learning techniques.* Springer Open Journal.

Stroeh, K., Madeira, E. R. M., & Goldenstein, S. K. (2013). An approach to the correlation of security events based on machine learning techniques. *Journal of Internet Services and Applications, 4*(1), 7. doi:10.1186/1869-0238-4-7

Strom, B. E., Applebaum, A., Miller, D. P., Nickels, K. C., Pennington, A. G., & Thomas, C. B. (2018). *MITRE ATT&CK: Design and philosophy.* Academic Press.

Study of Malware. (2009). Retrieved from https://pdfs.semanticscholar.org/4265/8775f329f2544c268c23c0375f60845 b2ac6.pdf

Subbulakshmi, T., Shalinie, S. M., & Ramamoorthi, A. (2010). Detection and Classification of DDoS Attacks using Machine Learning Algorithms. *European Journal of Scientific Research, 47*(3), 334 – 346.

Sweeney, L. (2002). K-anonymity: A model for protecting privacy. *Int. J. Uncertainty, Fuzziness Knowl. Based Syst., 10*(5), 557-570.

Swersky, K., Ranzato, M., Buchman, D., Marlin, B., & de Freitas, N. (2011). On score matching for energy based models: Generalizing autoencoders and simplifying deep learning. In *International Conference on Machine Learning ICML-11,* (p. 1201). Academic Press.

Szegedy, C. (2014). *Intriguing properties of neural networks.* arXiv preprint arXiv: 1312.6199

Szegedy, C., Zaremba, W., Sutskever, I., Bruna, J., Erhan, D., Goodfellow, I., & Fergus, R. (2013). *Intriguing properties of neural networks.* arXiv preprint arXiv:1312.6199

Takeuchi, J., & Yamanishi, K. (2006, April). A unifying framework for detecting outliers and change points from time series. *IEEE Transactions on Knowledge and Data Engineering, 18*(4), 482-492.

Talreja, V., Valenti, M. C., & Nasrabadi, M. N. (2017). Multibiometric secure system based on deep learning. In *IEEE Global Conference on Signal and Information Processing* (pp. 298-302). West Virginia University. 10.1109/Global-SIP.2017.8308652

Tamada, H., Okamoto, K., Nakamura, M., Monden, A., & Matsumoto, K. (2007). Design and Evaluation of Dynamic Software Birthmarks based on API calls. Nara Institute of Science and Technology, Technical Report.

Tang, T. A., Mhamdi, L., McLernon, D., Zaidi, S. A. R., & Ghogho, M. (2016). Deep Learning Approach for Network Intrusion Detection in Software Defined Networking. IEEE.

Tao, L., Golikov, S., Gai, K., & Qiu, M. (2015). A reusable software component for integrated syntax and semantic validation for services computing. *9th Int'l IEEE Symposium on Service-Oriented System Engineering*, 127–132. 10.1109/SOSE.2015.10

Tasgetiren, M. F., & Yiang, Y.-C. (2007). A Binary Particle Swarm Optimization Algorithm for Lot Sizing Problem. *Journal of Economic and Social Research, 5,* 1-20.

Tassa, T. (2007). Hierarchical threshold secret sharing. *Journal of Cryptology, 20*(2), 237–264. doi:10.100700145-006-0334-8

Taylor. (2017). Security Challenges and methods for protecting critical infrastructure cyber-physical systems. *IEEE MoWNeT.*

Tchakoucht, T. A., & Ezziyyani, M. (2018). Building a fast intrusion detection system for high-speed-networks: Probe and DoS attacks detection. *Procedia Computer Science*, *127*, 521–530. doi:10.1016/j.procs.2018.01.151

Thangavel, K., & Sasirekha, K. (2016). *Denoising Iris Image Using a Novel Wavelet Based Threshold*. Digital Connectivity–Social Impact. doi:10.1007/978-981-10-3274-5_5

The fingerprint database FVC2004. (n.d.). Retrieved from http://bias.csr.unibo.it/fvc2004/download.asp

The ORL Database of Faces. (n.d.). Retrieved from http://www.cl.cam.ac.uk/research/dtg/attarchive/facedatabase.html

Tian, Y. L., & Peng, C. (2009). Verifiable secret sharing and its applications based on bilinear pairings. *Computer Engineering*, *35*(10), 158–161.

Tian, Y., Peng, C., & Ma, J. (2012). Publicly Verifiable Secret Sharing Schemes Using Bilinear Pairings. *International Journal of Network Security*, *14*(3), 142–148.

Tonge, A., Kasture, S., & Chaudhari, S. (2013). Cyber security: Challenges for society-literature review. *IOSR Journal of Computer Engineering*, *2*(12), 67–75. doi:10.9790/0661-1226775

Torrano-Gimenez, C., Perez-Villegas, A., & Alvarez, G. (2009, July). An Anomaly-based Web Application Firewall, In *Proc. of International Conference on Security and Cryptography (SECRYPT 2009)* (pp. 23-28). INSTICC Press.

Tsai, D. Y., Matsuyama, E., & Chen, H. M. (2013). Improving image quality in medical images using a combined method of undecimated wavelet transform and wavelet coefficient mapping. *International Journal of Biomedical Imaging*, *2013*, 1–11. doi:10.1155/2013/797924 PMID:24382951

Tsang, I. W., Kwok, J. T., & Cheung, P. M. (2005). Core vector machines: Fast SVM training on very large data sets. *Journal of Machine Learning Research*, *6*(Apr), 363–392.

Turcotte, M. J. M., Kent, A. D., & Hash, C. (2018). Unified host and network data set. Data Science for Cyber-Security, 3(1), 1–22. doi:10.1142/9781786345646_001

UCI Machine Learning Archive. (2009). Available from http://www.kdd.ics.uci.edu/databases/kddcup99/task.html

Uma, M., & Padmavathi, G. (2013). *A Survey on Various Cyber Attacks and Their Classification*. Academic Press.

Uma, M., & Padmavathi, G. (2013). A Survey on Various Cyber Attacks and their Classification. *IJ Network Security*, *15*(5), 390-396.

Vanitha, N., & Padmavathi, G. (2017). A Study on Various Cyber-Attacks and their Classification in UAV Assisted Vehicular Ad-Hoc Networks. *Springer Nature*, *844*, 124-132.

Vanitha, N., & Padmavathi, G. (2018). A Comparative Study on Communication Architecture of Unmanned Aerial Vehicles and Security Analysis of False Data Dissemination Attacks. In *International Conference on Current Trends towards Converging Technologies (ICCTCT)*. IEEE.

Vardhini, K., & Sitamahalakshmi, T. (2017). Enhanced Intrusion Detection System Using Data Reduction: An Ant Colony Optimization Approach. International. *Journal of Applied Engineering Research*, *12*(9), 1844–1847.

Veeramachaneni, K., Arnaldo, I., Cuesta-Infante, A., Korrapati, V., Bassias, C., & Li, K. (2016). AI2: Training a big data machine to defend. In *Proceedings of the 2nd IEEE International Conference on Big Data Security on Cloud*. IEEE.

Velayutham, C., & Thangavel, K. (2011). Unsupervised feature selection based on the measures of degree of dependency using rough set theory in digital mammogram image classification. *Proceedings of the 3rd International Conference on Advanced Computing – IcoAC*. 10.1109/ICoAC.2011.6165167

Velayutham, C., & Thangavel, K. (2012, March). A novel entropy based unsupervised Feature Selection algorithm using rough set theory, *IEEE-International Conference On Advances In Engineering, Science And Management (ICAESM -2012)*.

Velayutham, C., & Thangavel, K. (2011). Unsupervised quick reduct algorithm using rough set theory. *Journal of Electronic Science and Technology, 9*, 193–201.

Venkatraman, S., & Alazab, M. (2018). Use of Data Visualisation for Zero-Day Malware Detection. *Security and Communication Networks*.

Vincent, P. (2011). A connection between score matching and denoising autoencoders. *Neural Computation, 23*(7), 1661–1674. doi:10.1162/NECO_a_00142 PMID:21492012

Vincent, P., Larochelle, H., Bengio, Y., & Manzagol, P. A. (2008). *Extracting and composing robust features with denoising autoencoders*. ICML. doi:10.1145/1390156.1390294

Wang, J., & Paschalidis, I. C. (2017). Botnet detection based on anomaly and community detection. *IEEE Transactions on Control of Network Systems 4*(2), 392-404.

Wang, J., & Paschalidis, I. C. (2017). Botnet detection based on anomaly and community detection. *IEEE Transactions on Control of Network Systems*.

Wang, F., Cheng, J., & Yu, Y. (2015). *A Hybrid Spectral Clustering and Deep Neural Network Ensemble Algorithm for Intrusion Detection in Sensor Networks*. Science Direct.

Wang, G. (2016). A perspective on deep imaging. *IEEE Access: Practical Innovations, Open Solutions, 4*, 8914–8924. doi:10.1109/ACCESS.2016.2624938

Wang, J. (2017). *Detecting time synchronization attacks in cyber-physical security systems with machine learning techniques*. IEEE ICDCS.

Wang, L. (Ed.). (2005). *Support vector machines: theory and applications* (Vol. 177). Springer Science & Business Media.

Wang, Y., Chen, Q., & Zhang, B. (1999). Image enhancement based on equal area dualistic sub-image histogram equalization method. *IEEE Transactions on Consumer Electronics, 45*(1), 68–75. doi:10.1109/30.754419

Wang, Z. (2018). Deep learning-based intrusion detection with adversaries. *IEEE Access. Challenges and Opportunities of Big Data Against Cyber Crime, 6*, 38367–38384.

Wang, Z., Bovik, A., Sheikh, H., & Simoncelli, E. (2004). Image quality assessment: From error visibility to structural similarity. *IEEE Transactions on Image Processing, 13*(6). PMID:15376593

Webroot. (n.d.). Retrieved from http://www.webroot.com/

Wei, S., Ge, L., Yu, W., & Chen, G. (2014). Simulation Study of Unmanned Aerial Vehicle Communication Networks Addressing Bandwidth Disruptions. In *Sensors and Systems for Space Applications VII* (Vol. 9085). Academic Press.

Wei, W., Liu, L., Truex, S., Yu, L., Gursoy, E., & Wu, Y. (2018). *Demystifying Adversarial Behaviors in Deep Learning*. Georgia Institute of Technology, School of Computer Science.

Weller-Fahy, D., Borghetti, B., & Sodemann, A. (2014, March). A Survey of Distance and Similarity Measures Used Within Network Intrusion Anomaly Detection. IEEE Communications Surveys & Tutorials, 17(1), 70-91.

Weng, L. (2017). *An Overview of Deep Learning for Curious People*. Retrieved from https://lilianweng.github.io/lil-log/2017/06/21/an-overview-of-deep-learning.html

White, T. (2009). *Hadoop: The Definitive Guide*. O'Reilly.

Wijesinghe, U., Udaya, T., & Vijay, V. (2015). An enhanced model for network flow based botnet detection. *Proceedings of the 38th Australasian Computer Science Conference (ACSC 2015)*, 27.

Witten, I. H., Frank, E., Hall, M. A., & Pal, C. J. (2016). *Data Mining: Practical machine learning tools and techniques.* Burlington, MA: Morgan Kaufmann.

Wolfram, S. (1984). Cellular automata as models of complexity. *Nature, 311*(5985), 419–424. doi:10.1038/311419a0

Woon, I., Tan, G. W., & Low, R. (2005). A protection motivation theory approach to home wireless security. *ICIS 2005 Proceedings*, 31.

World Internet, . (2010, May). *World internet users and 2016 population stats.* World Internet.

Wu, L. L. (2014). *Improving system reliability for cyber-physical systems.* Columbia University. Retrieved from: https://www.researchgate.net/profile/Roger_Anderson20/publication/329044383_Leon_Wu_PhD_Thesis_Improving_System_Reliability_for_CyberPhysical_Systems_2014/links/5bf30f83299bf1124fde5df9/Leon-Wu-PhD-Thesis-Improving-System-Reliability-for-CyberPhysical-Systems-2014.pdf

Wu, Y., Liu, L., Pu, C., & Wei, W. (2018). GIT DLBench: A Benchmark Suite for Deep Learning Frameworks: Characterizing Performance, Accuracy and Adversarial Robustness. Georgia Institute of Technology, School of Computer Science, Tech. Rep.

Wuechner, T., Cislak, A., Ochoa, M., & Pretschner, A. (2017). Leveraging compression-based graph mining for behavior-based malware detection. *IEEE Trans Dependable Secur Comput.*

Wuest, B. (2014). *Integrating QRadar with Hadoop.* White Paper from IBM.

Wu, M., Miller, R. C., & Garnkel, S. L. (2006). Do security toolbars actually prevent phishing attacks? *Proceedings of the SIGCHI conference on Human Factors in computing systems.* 10.1145/1124772.1124863

Wu, S., Wang, P., Li, X., & Zhang, Y. (2016). Effective detection of android malware based on the usage of data fow APIs and machine learning. *Information and Software Technology, 75*, 17–25. doi:10.1016/j.infsof.2016.03.004

Wu, T. Y., & Tseng, Y. M. (2011). A pairing-based publicly verifiable secret sharing scheme. *Journal of Systems Science and Complexity, 24*(1), 186–194. doi:10.100711424-011-8408-6

Wu, T.-X., Lian, X.-C., & Lu, B. L. (2012). Multi-view gender classification using symmetry of facial images. *Neural Computing & Applications, 21*(4), 661–669. doi:10.100700521-011-0647-x

Xiang, C. (2018). Network intrusion detection by using particle swarm optimization and neural network. *Journal of Networking Technology, 9*(1), 22–30.

Xiao, L., Li, Y., Han, G., Liu, G., & Zhuang, W. (2016, December). PHY-layer spoofing detection with reinforcement learning in wireless networks. *IEEE Transactions on Vehicular Technology, 65*(12), 10037–10047. doi:10.1109/TVT.2016.2524258

Xiao, L., Li, Y., Huang, X., & Du, X. J. (2017, October). Cloud-based malware detection game for mobile devices with offloading. *IEEE Transactions on Mobile Computing, 16*(10), 2742–2750. doi:10.1109/TMC.2017.2687918

Xie, J., & Xu, L. (2012). Image denoising and inpainting with deep neural networks. In *International Conference on Neural Information Processing Systems*, (pp. 341-349). Academic Press.

Xie, M., Jiankun, H., & Jill, S. (2014). Evaluating host-based anomaly detection systems: Application of the one-class svm algorithm to adfa-ld. In *11th International Conference on Fuzzy Systems and Knowledge Discovery.* IEEE.

Xin, Y., Kong, L., Liu, Z., Chen, Y., Li, Y., Zhu, H., & Wang, C. (2018). Machine learning and deep learning methods for cybersecurity. *IEEE Access: Practical Innovations, Open Solutions, 6,* 35365–35381. doi:10.1109/ACCESS.2018.2836950

Xu, P., Shi, S., & Chu, X. (2017). *Performance Evaluation of Deep Learning Tools in Docker Containers.* ArXiv e-prints.

Xu, W., Qi, Y., & Evans, D. (2016). Automatically evading classifiers. In *Proceedings of the 2016 Network and Distributed Systems Symposium.* Academic Press. 10.14722/ndss.2016.23115

Xu, Y., Ma, T., Tang, M., & Tian, W. (2014). A survey of privacy preservation data publishing using generalization and suppression. *Int. Journal Applied Mathematics & Information Sciences,* 1103-1116.

Yang, X. S., & Deb, S. (2009, December). Cuckoo search via Lévy flights. In *World Congress on Nature & Biologically Inspired Computing, 2009. NaBIC 2009* (pp. 210-214). IEEE.

Yao, Y., Marcialis, G. L., Pontil, M., Frasconi, P., & Roli, F. (2003). Combining flat and structured representations for fingerprint classification with recursive neural networks and support vector machines. *Pattern Recognition, 36*(2), 397–406. doi:10.1016/S0031-3203(02)00039-0

Yavanoglu, O., & Aydos, M. (2017, December). A review on cyber security datasets for machine learning algorithms. In *2017 IEEE International Conference on Big Data (Big Data)* (pp. 2186-2193). IEEE. 10.1109/BigData.2017.8258167

Yavanoglu, O., & Aydos, M. (2017, December). A review on cyber security datasets for machine learning algorithms. In *2017 IEEE International Conference on Big Data* (pp. 2186-2193). IEEE.

Ye, Y., Li, T., Jiang, Q., & Wang, Y. (2010). CIMDS: Adapting postprocessing techniques of associative classification for malware detection. *IEEE Transactions on Systems, Man, and Cybernetics, Part C (Applications and Reviews), 40*(3), 298–307.

Ye, Y., Squartini, S., & Piazza, F. (2013, September). Online sequential extreme learning machine in nonstationary environments. *Neurocomputing, 116,* 94–101.

Yedidia, J. S., Freeman, W. T., & Weiss, Y. (2003). Understanding belief propagation and its generalizations. *Exploring Artificial Intelligence in the New Millennium, 8,* 236–239.

Yen, T.-F., Oprea, A., Onarlioglu, K., Leetham, T., Robertson, W., Juels, A., & Kirda, E. (2013). Beehive: large-scale log analysis for detecting suspicious activity in enterprise networks. In *Proceedings of the 29th ACM Annual Computer Security Applications Conference.* ACM. 10.1145/2523649.2523670

Yin, C., Zhu, Y., Fei, J., & He, X. (2017). A deep learning approach for intrusion detection using recurrent neural networks. *IEEE Access: Practical Innovations, Open Solutions, 5,* 21954–21961. doi:10.1109/ACCESS.2017.2762418

Yi, P., Guan, Y., Zou, F., Yao, Y., Wang, W., & Zhu, T. (2018). Web phishing Detection Using a Deep Learning Framework. *Wireless Communications and Mobile Computing, 2018,* 1–9. doi:10.1155/2018/4678746

Yosinski, J., Clune, J., Bengio, Y., & Lipson, H. (2014). How transferable are features in deep neural networks? *Advances in Neural Information Processing Systems,* 3320–3328.

Yousefi-Azar, M., Varadharajan, V., Hamey, L., & Tupakula, U. (2017, May). Autoencoder-based feature learning for cyber security applications. In *2017 International joint conference on neural networks (IJCNN)* (pp. 3854-3861). IEEE. 10.1109/IJCNN.2017.7966342

Yu, J., Kong, F., & Hao, R. (2007, July). Publicly verifiable secret sharing with enrollment ability. In *Eighth ACIS International Conference on Software Engineering, Artificial Intelligence, Networking, and Parallel/Distributed Computing* (Vol. 3, pp. 194-199). IEEE. 10.1109/SNPD.2007.256

Yuan, Z., Lu, Y., Wang, Z., & Xue, Y. (2014). *Droid-sec: Deep learning in android malware detection.* ACM.

Yuan, Z., Lu, Y., & Xue, Y. (2016). Droid detector: Android malware characterization and detection using deep learning. *Tsinghua Science and Technology, 21*(1), 114–123. doi:10.1109/TST.2016.7399288

Yu, W., Jiang, X., & Xiong, B. (2009). Data preparation for sample-based face detection. *International Journal of Computer Applications in Technology, 35*(1), 10–22. doi:10.1504/IJCAT.2009.024591

Zaharia, M., Xin, R. S., Wendell, P., Das, T., Armbrust, M., Dave, A., & ... . (2016). Apache spark: A unified engine for big data processing. *Communications of the ACM, 59*(11), 56–65. doi:10.1145/2934664

Zait, M., & Messatfa, H. (1997, November). A comparative study of clustering methods. *Future Generation Computer Systems, 13*(1), 149-159.

Zamani, M., & Mahnush, M. (2013). *Machine learning techniques for intrusion detection.* arXiv preprint arXiv:1312.2177

Zekri, M., El Kafhali, S., Aboutabit, N., & Saadi, Y. (2017). DDoS attack detection using machine learning techniques in cloud computing environments. In *International Conference of Cloud Computing Technologies and Applications* (pp. 1-8). Rabat, Morocco: Academic Press. 10.1109/CloudTech.2017.8284731

Zhang. (2015). *Pattern Recognition Techniques.* Retrieved from https://fredfeng.github.io/papers/demobile14.pdf

Zhang, C., Patras, P., & Haddadi, H. (2019). Deep learning in mobile and wireless networking: A survey. *IEEE Communications Surveys and Tutorials, 1.* doi:10.1109/COMST.2019.2904897

Zhang, M., & Yao, J. T. (2004, June). A Rough Sets Based Approach to Feature Selection. *Proceedings of the 23rd International Conference of NAFIPS,* 434–439. 10.1109/NAFIPS.2004.1336322

Zhang, T., & Zhu, Q. (2018). Distributed privacy-preserving collaborative intrusion detection systems for VANETs. IEEE Transactions on Signal and Information Processing over. *Networks, 4*(1), 148–161.

Zheng, Lui, & Sun. (2013). Droid analytics: a signature based analytic system to collect, extract, analyze and associate android malware. *Trust, Security and Privacy in Computing and Communications (TrustCom), 2013 12th IEEE International Conference,* 163–171.

Zhicheng Yan, H. Z. (2016). Automatic Photo Adjustment Using Deep Neural Networks. *ACM Transactions on Graphics, 35*(2).

Zhu, J., Kaplan, R., Johnson, J., & Fei-Fei, L. (2018). Hidden: Hiding data with deep networks. In *Proceedings of the European Conference on Computer Vision (ECCV)* (pp. 657-672). Academic Press.

Zhu, X. H. (2017). Application of artificial neural network based on artificial fish swarm algorithm in network intrusion detection. *Modern Electronic Technology, 40*(1), 80-82.

Zhu, J. Y., Park, T., Isola, P., & Efros, A. A. (2017). Unpaired image-to-image translation using cycle-consistent adversarial networks. In *Proceedings of the IEEE international conference on computer vision* (pp. 2223-2232). IEEE. 10.1109/ICCV.2017.244

Zimek, A., Campello, R., & Sander, J. (2013, June). Ensembles for unsupervised outlier detection: challenges and research questions. *ACM SIGKDD Explorations Newsletter, 15*(1), 11-22.

Zimmermann, A. (2014, December). The Data Problem in Data Mining. *ACM SIGKDD Explorations Newsletter, 16*(2), 38-45.

Zuech, R., Khoshgofthaar, T., & Wald, R. (2015). Intrusion detection and big heterogeneous data: a survey. *Journal of Big Data*, 90–107.

About the Contributors

Padmavathi Ganapathi is the Professor in Computer Science having 31 years of teaching experience with 17 years of research experience and one year of Industrial experience. Has more than 200 significant publications at National and International level. Her areas of interest include Cyber Security, Real Time Communication, Wireless Communication, Network Security and Cryptography. She is the life member of CSI, ISTE, ISCA, WSEAS, AACE, ACRS and UWA. Executed many research projects funded by AICTE, UGC, DRDO and DST worth more than 2 crores. Presently she is the course co-ordinator for UGC-SWAYAM-MOOC on Cyber security.

D. Shanmugapriya received a B.Sc degree in Computer Science and Computer Applications (1999), a M.Sc degree in Computer Science (2001), a Ph.D degree in Computer Science (2013), from Avinashilingam Institute for Home Science and Higher Education for Women, Coimbatore, Tamil Nadu, India, and a M.Phil Degree in Computer Science (2003) from Manonmanium Sundaranar University, Tamil Nadu. She is currently the Head and an Assistant professor in the Department of Information Technology at Avinashilingam Institute for Home Science and Higher Education for Women, Coimbatore, Tamil Nadu, India, with 19 years of teaching and Research experience. She has more than 25 research papers in reputed journals and conference proceedings. She was the co-principal Investigator for the projects sanctioned by DRDO and UGC. Her research interests include Cyber Security, Biometrics and Image Processing.

* * *

Swathy Akshaya M. is currently a PhD Research Scholar in Computer Science registered at Avinashilingam Institute for Home Science and Higher Education for Women, Coimbatore, Tamil Nadu, India. She received her M. Sc (CS) degree and BCA Degree from Sri G.V.G Visalakshi College for Women, Udumalpet, Tamilnadu. Broadly her field of Research Interest includes Cloud Computing and Cyber Security.

Vaishnavi A. is pursuing her post graduate in the Department of Computer Science, School of Engineering and Technology, Pondicherry University. Her Area of interest includes Cyber security, Computer Network, etc.

Tanu Choudhary is a student pursuing B.tech with specialization in Cyber Security and Forensics from Manav Rachna International Institute of Research and Studies.

Miguel Correia is an Associate Professor with Habilitation at Instituto Superior Tcnico (IST) of Universidade de Lisboa (ULisboa), in Lisboa, Portugal. He is a Senior Researcher at INESC-ID in the Distributed Systems Group (GSD). He has a PhD in Computer Science from the Universidade de Lisboa Faculdade de Cincias. He has been involved in several international and national research projects related to cybersecurity, including the SafeCloud, PCAS, TCLOUDS, ReSIST, CRUTIAL, and MAFTIA European projects. He has more than 150 publications and is Senior Member of the IEEE.

T. T. Dhivyaprabha has completed M.Sc., M.Phil. in Bharathiar University. She has four years of teaching experience. She has completed Ph.D. (Computer Science) programme in the Department of Computer Science, Avinashilingam Institute for Home Science and Higher Education for Women, Coimbatore. Her areas of interest include Computational Intelligence and Image Processing.

Luis Dias is an Army Major, specialized in Information Assurance. He holds a Master degree in Computers and Telecommunications Engineering from Portuguese Military Academy. Before starting his Ph.D., he conducted incident response at higher tier at the Army Security Operations Center. He has several industry certifications and is a member of GIAC advisory board. His Ph.D. investigation focus is on big data analytics for Intrusion Detection.

Sailesh Iyer is working as Associate Professor, R. B Institute of Management Studies, Ahmedabad. His research interests are Data Analytics, Information Security and Image Processing.

Anitha J. is working as a Professor in the Department of Computer Science, Dayananda Sagar Academy of Technology & Management Bangalore.

Sasirekha K. is a research Scholar in the Department of Computer Science, Periyar University.

Thangavel K. is Professor and Head of the Department of Computer Science at Periyar University, Salem.

Rosemary Koikara received her M.Tech. Degree in Computer Science and Engineering from Christ University, Bengaluru, India. She is pursuing her Ph.D. degree in Information Security in the School of Computer Science and Engineering, Kyungpook National University, Daegu, South Korea. She has co-authored and authored more than 15 papers in her area of research.

Marimuthu Krishnaveni is an Assistant Professor of the Department of Computer Science, Avinashilingam University for Women, Coimbatore. She has six years of experience working as a researcher in Naval Research Board, Defence Research Development Organisation, Ministry of Defence. She was been a consultant for a Military-related application project. She has published several papers in her research specialization with an overall count of about 90 both nationally and internationally. She focuses on research and experimental processes with the use of digital technologies such as: MATLAB, Computer Science, Biological computation, along with machine intelligence and real-time physical computation. She also acts as a resource person and holds national and international funded research projects which come under University Grants Commission (India) and Department of Science and Technology and DRDO-NPOL. She is a recipient of awards such as best young teacher award IASTE 2017,best NSS Programme officer award, NYLP 2016,Goverment of India.

Thangavel M. is an Assistant Professor working in the Department of Information Technology at Thiagarajar college of Engineering, Madurai. He presently holds four and a half years of Teaching and Research experience in Thiagarajar college of Engineering, Madurai and two years of Teaching and Research experience in Madras Institute of Technology, Anna University - Chennai. He graduated as a B.E. Computer Science and Engineering from M.A.M College of Engineering, Trichy (Anna University - Chennai) and as an M.E. Computer Science and Engineering from J.J. College of Engineering and Technology, Trichy (Anna University - Chennai) and Pursuing his PhD from Madras Institute of Technology, Chennai under Anna University - Chennai. He is a Gold Medalist in UG and Anna University - First Rank Holder with Gold Medal in PG. His specialization is Cloud Computing, and Information Security. His Areas of Interest include DNA Cryptography, Ethical Hacking, Compiler Design, Computer Networks, Data Structures and High-Performance Computing. He has published five articles in International Journals, eight book chapters in International Publishers, 14 in the proceedings of International Conferences, and three in the proceedings of national conferences /seminars. He has attended 38 Workshops/FDPs/Conferences in various Higher Learning Institutes like IIT, Anna University. He has organized 21 Workshops/FDPs/Contests/Industry-based courses in the past five years. He has been a delegate for Cyber Week 2017, organized by Tel Aviv University, Israel. He has been recognized by IIT Bombay; SAP CSR as SAP Award of Excellence with cash reward of Rs.5000/- for the best Participation in IITBombayX: FDPICT001x Use of ICT in Education for Online and Blended Learning. He shows interest in student counseling, in motivating for better placements, and in helping them design value-based life-style.

Jorge Maestre Vidal is Senior Specialist in Cyber Defence at Indra and former researcher in the Department of Software Engineering and Artificial Intelligence (DISIA) of the Faculty of Computer Science and Engineering at the Complutense University of Madrid (UCM), Spain. He holds PhD in Computer Science since 2018. His academic experience includes teaching and direction of final degrees projects. He participated in projects funded by private organizations (Banco Santander, Safelayer Secure Communications S.A., etc.) and public institutions (NATO, EDA, FP7, Horizon 2020, 5G-PPP Security WG, Plan Nacional de I+D+i, Spanish Ministry of Defense, etc.). His main research interests are Artificial Intelligence, Information Security, and the emerging Communication Technologies.

Sergio Mauricio Martínez Monterrubio received a Computer Science degree in 1998 and a Master in International Business Administration in 2003, both at the Universidad Nacional Autonoma de Mexico, UNAM. His computer science thesis obtained the National Prize for thesis convened by the ANFECA in 1999 (Mexico). Sergio received a Ph.D. in Computer Science in 2016 from the Instituto Tecnologico y de Estudios Superiores de Monterrey, ITESM (Mexico). He is making a postdoctoral research in the

Department of Software Engineering and Artificial Intelligence at the Universidad Complutense de Madrid (UCM) in the GAIA Group (Group of Artificial Intelligence Applications) located in the Computer Sciences Faculty and Engineering at the UCM Campus. His professional experience includes working in companies as McAffe, Oracle, Entrust Technologies, Colgate Palmolive, ABC Medical Center, and Continental Automotive Systems. In Continental, he was assigned a year to the enterprise administration of the e-mail system in Frankfurt, Germany. His main research interests are data mining, big data, knowledge acquisition and machine learning and its applications in cyber security.

S. Rama Mercy is working as Assistant Professor in Computer Science Department, Avinashilingam Institute for Home Science and Higher Education for Women, Coimbatore. Her areas of interest include data mining, network security, Cyber Physical System security, and artificial intelligence.

Valliammal N. is the Assistant Professor (SS) in the Department of Computer Science in Avinashilingam Institute for Home Science and Higher Education for Women. She has more than 20 Years of teaching Experience. Her research interests include Cyber Security, IoT, and Big Data Analytics. She has more than 16 publications at International and National level. She is a Life member of one of the professional organizations in Indian Science Congress Association and CSI. She has acted as a reviewer of IJCNC and IJCSEA.

Vanitha N. received her Master of Computer Applications from the Avinashilingam Institute for Home Science and Higher Education for Women, Coimbatore, in 2008. In 2008 she was hired as a Software programmer in LMW group, Coimbatore. Since 2011, she has been working as an Assistant Professor in the Computer science department at Dr. N. G. P. Arts and Science College, Coimbatore. In 2013, she received her Master of Philosophy in Computer Science at Dr. N. G. P. Arts and Science College, Coimbatore. She is pursuing Doctor of Philosophy in Computer Science (Part Time), under the guidance of Dr. G. Padmavathi, Professor, Department of Computer Science at the Avinashilingam Institute for Home Science and Higher Education for Women, Coimbatore. She writes and presents widely on UAV Networks, Cyber Security, Machine, and Deep Learning.

M. Newlin Rajkumar completed his Bachelor of Engineering in EEE in 2001 in India and Master of Science by Research (M.S) in Electrical and Control Engineering from National Chiao Tung University, Taiwan, in 2007. During his studies in Taiwan, he was a recipient of International Student Scholarship from the Ministry of Education, Taiwan. He received an Academic Excellency award and was recognized as One of the Outstanding International Alumni Students, and was honored by the President of the University. He has guided 140 M.E/M,Tech students and 40 U.G students. He has published many papers in reputed International Journals, Participated and presented his papers in various International and National Conferences. He has Chaired and organized several Conferences and in many events. He has pursued his Ph.D with Specialization in Cloud Computing in Anna University, India. His areas of interest includes Cloud Computing, Big Data Analytics, IoT, Network Security, and Networking. He has more than 11 years of teaching experience. He is working as Assistant Professor in the Department of Computer Science and Engineering, Anna University Regional Campus, Coimbatore.

Amudha P. has graduated her B.E in Computer Science and Engineering, and has an M.Tech degree in Information Technology. She obtained her Ph.D in Information and Communication Engineering from Anna University. She has 18 years of teaching experience and 10 years of research experience in the field of Computer science. Her research interests include Data mining, Machine Learning, Information Security, and Swarm Intelligence. She has published many papers in the National/International journals and conferences. She is a life member of ISTE, and an associate member of CSI and IAENG.

Priyadharshini P. is studying ME computer science and information security. Areas of interest are security and cyber security.

Shanthi Bala P. is working as an Assistant Professor in the Department of Computer Science, Pondicherry University, Puducherry.

Anand Paul is working in the School of Computer Science and Engineering, Kyungpook National University, South Korea, as an Associate Professor, and he got his Ph.D. degree from the Electrical Engineering Department at National Cheng Kung University, Taiwan, R.O.C. in 2010. His research interests include Big Data Analytics/IoT, Machine Learning. He was track chair for ACM SAC Human-Computer interaction 2014-2018.

Rathipriya R. is an Assistant Professor in the Dept. of Computer Science at Periyar University, India. Her research interest is Bio-Inspired Optimization techniques.

Sridaran R. is a Ph.D in Computer Science from Madurai Kamaraj University. He has published 50+ research papers in leading journals, and has chaired many conferences. He has also guided a number of research scholars in the areas of Cloud Computing & Security, IoT, e-learning, and Block Chain. He has gotten more than 25 years of academic experience with leading educational institutions at senior academic administration levels. He is currently the Dean of Faculty of Computer Applications, Marwadi University Rajkot. He has initiated the formation of Computer Society of India, Rajkot Chapter, as a founder Chairman.

Vijayabhasker R. is presently working as Assistant Professor in the Department of ECE, Anna University Regional Campus, Coimbatore, Tamilnadu, India. His area of Specialization is Power Electronics and Drives.

Dhamodharavadhani S. is pursuing Ph. D (Computer Science) in Periyar University, Salem, Tamil Nadu. Her research interests are climate data analysis, Regression model, and Big data.

Sivakumari S. has graduated her B.E in Electronics and Communication Engineering, and M.E in Applied Electronics. She obtained her Ph.D in data mining area. She has more than 25 years of teaching experience and 15 years of research experience in the field of Computer science. Her research interests include data mining, machine Learning, pattern recognition, and computational Intelligence. She has published many papers in the National/International journals and conferences. She is a life member of ISTE, and associate member of CSI and IAENG.

Prasad S. P. has been working as an Assistant Professor in a department of Information Science for more than 10 years, and is pursuing PhD and research work for more than three years.

Barani Shaju is a part-time Research scholar in Department of Computer Science at Avinashilingam University, Coimbatore. Her domain of work can be sheltered under the umbrella of Data science, Analytics, and Cyber Security. She works as Technology Specialist at Robert Bosch Engineering and Business Solutions at Keeranatham, Coimbatore. Her core technical strengths are on JEE frameworks, Perl, Python with Data science library and database – Oracle, MySQL.

R. Shanmugavalli has obtained her Masters in Computer Science from Vivekanandha College of Arts and Sciences for Women, Tamil Nadu, India. She is pursuing Ph.D. from Avinashilingam Institute for Home Science and Higher Education for Women, Coimbatore. Her research interest includes Computer Networks.

Marco Antonio Sotelo Monge holds a Ph.D. in Computer Science from Universidad Complutense de Madrid (2018), where he has worked as a researcher at the Department of Artificial Intelligence and Software Engineering. His main research areas include 5G networks, Information Security, SDN/NFV, and Artificial Intelligence; and the outcomes of his research activity have been disseminated in specialized scientific journals and international conferences. Marco Antonio has professional experience in the areas of Information Technology and Quality Assurance in Education, activities that have combined with teaching since 2007 in Peru, and in Spain since 2016. In the past few years, he has participated in the European research projects SELFNET (H2020-ICT-2014-2/671672) and RAMSES (H2020-FCT-04-2015/700326), funded by the Horizon 2020 Programme of the European Commission. In addition, he contributed in the publication of the first White Paper entitled "5G PPP Phase 1 Security Landscape" released by the 5P PPP Security Working Group in June 2017. An excellence scholarship awarded by the Peruvian Ministry of Education in 2013 enabled him to conduct international postgraduate studies in Spain, where he developed his research career afterwards.

Parthasarathy Subashini received a B.Sc (Mathematics) degree from Gobi Arts College, Bharathiar University, TamilNadu, India, in 1990 and M.CA degree from the same in 1993. She has also received qualified degree of M.Phil and Ph.D respectively in Computer Science in 1998 and 2009 from Avinashilingam University for Women, Tamil Nadu, India. From 1994 to 2007, she worked in the Computer Science Department of Avinashilingam University, where she is currently a Professor. She has also held a few short-term appointments at several institutions around the state. Professor Subashini's research has spanned a large number of disciplines like Image analysis, Pattern recognition, Neural networks, and Computational Intelligence. Concurrently, she contributed to several fields of mathematics, especially Nature-inspired computing. She has authored or co-authored one book, four book chapters, one monograph, and 145 papers, including IEEE and Springer, in various international and national journals and conferences. Professor Subashini has mentored more than 100 post-graduate students and guided several doctoral students. She has held positions as reviewer and chairperson for different peer reviewed journals. Under her supervision, she has 10 research projects worth more than 1.4 crores from various funding agencies like Defence Research and Development Organization, Department of Science and Technology, SERB, and University Grants Commission. She has visited Singapore, Malaysia, Dubai, France, Switzerland, Italy, Canada, Germany, Spain, Czech Republic, Rome, Morocco, USA, and China for various knowledge-sharing events. As a member of IEEE, IEEE Computational Intelligence Society, and IEEE Computer Society of India, she extended her contribution as IEEE Chair for Women in Computing under IEEE Computer Society of India Council in 2015-2016.

Abiramie Shree T. G. R. pursued Bachelor Degree in Information Technology at National Engineering College, Kovilpatti. She did her UG project on Big Data with the help of Hadoop. She is now pursuing Master Degree in Computer Science and Information Security, which is a specialization course in security at Thiagarajar College of Engineering, Madurai. She is very much interested in the security-related domain. She is doing her PG project on Blockchain technology. She made a book chapter proposal on Review on machine learning and deep learning for cyber security.

P. Thiyagarajan is working as Assistant Professor and Head in Department of Computer Science, Central University of Tamil Nadu, Thiruvarur - 05.

V. Venkatesa Kumarr has completed his Bachelor of Engineering in ECE in 2001 and Master of Engineering in CSE in 2006. He has pursued his Ph.D with Specialization in Cloud Computing in Anna University, India, in 2013. His areas of interest include Cloud Computing, Big Data Analytics, IoT, Network Security, and Networking. He has 11 years of teaching and Industrial experience. He is working as Assistant Professor in the Department of Computer Science and Engineering, Anna University Regional Campus, Coimbatore.

Charu Virmani is working as a Professor in Department of Computer Science and Engineering at Manav Rachna International Institute of Research and Studies, Faridabad, Haryana. She holds B.E in Information Technology, M.Tech in Computer Science from M.D.U., Rohtak & Ph.D in Computer Engineering from YMCA University of Science and Technology, Faridabad. She has 13 years of teaching experience. She published 28 Research Papers in National, International conferences and Journals. She has attended and organized many workshops, Guest Lectures, seminars, national and International conferences. She has delivered workshops on cyber security, social network mining, and design thinking. She is also associated with professional societies like ACM and CSI. Her guided project, 'CAR PARKING SYSTEM' got first prize in FIA in the year 2014 and appreciated by Dr. APJ Abdul Kalam during the 61st General Body meeting and concluding ceremony of Diamond Jubilee celebration of FIA. She is the spokesperson for an Industrial-Academia collaboration with a Japan-based organisation. She is a reviewer for high indexed journals (IGI,TSII to name a few). Dr. Charu's research interests are cyber security, data mining, big data, machine learning, Artificial Intelligence.

Eun-Jun Yoon received the Ph.D. degree in computer engineering from Kyungpook National University, South Korea, in 2006. He is currently a Professor with the Department of Cyber Security, Kyungil University, South Korea. He has authored 125 conference proceedings and 100 journal publications. His research interests are cryptography, authentication technologies, smart card security, multimedia security, network security, mobile communications security, and steganography.

Index

A

access structure 268-269, 273, 279, 283-284, 288
ad hoc security 5, 16
ADS-B 222, 241
AIC 425, 428-430
ANN 9, 120, 223, 229, 233, 241, 306, 402-403
anomalies 55, 60, 62, 89, 92, 101, 139, 193-200, 211, 306, 314-315, 317-318, 320, 322, 324, 333, 336, 338, 340, 400
anomaly detection 5, 16, 33, 43, 55, 59, 101, 119, 137, 148-149, 156-157, 187, 198-201, 203, 210, 220, 224, 290, 306-307, 313-314, 316-320, 322-325, 330, 333-334, 336-341, 408
anomaly recognition 192, 198-200, 202-210
anonymization 26, 298, 344, 346-349, 351-355, 357
API calls 57, 113, 116, 178, 183-184, 187
Artificial Intelligence 2, 16, 23-24, 26-27, 30, 38-39, 48, 64-66, 68, 71, 81, 95-96, 129-130, 141, 155, 179, 244, 262, 295, 316, 335, 379
Attack handling Mechanisms 373
autoencoder 57, 242, 245-247, 249-254, 257-258, 262
autonomous 27-28, 84, 86, 144, 155, 216, 229, 302, 406-407

B

benign 114, 122, 184, 187, 305
big data 2, 51, 68, 77, 80-82, 93, 129, 179, 289-292, 296-297, 299, 301-302, 306-308, 313-316, 325-330, 333-335, 338-341, 344-345, 353, 357-358
big data analytics 68, 289, 292, 296, 301, 314-316, 325-330, 333, 335, 338-341

C

centralized 139, 155, 216-220, 223-224
cloud computing 2, 129, 152, 194, 361-362, 364-365, 367-369, 382, 390
clustering 4, 29, 56, 65, 70, 74, 89-90, 143-144, 156-157, 165, 177, 201, 291, 293, 299, 301, 313, 324-325, 336-337, 398-399, 402, 408, 416
CNN 5, 12, 74, 231, 241, 402
CPS 385-391, 393-395, 406-408, 410
CPS Intelligence 408
CPS Security Objectives 387
Cryptography 23, 71, 132, 272, 288, 368
cyber attack 44-45, 47-49, 54, 223, 327, 391, 404
cyber-attacks 1-2, 32, 38, 47, 66, 91, 101, 134, 217, 221, 223, 225, 314-315, 330, 362, 365, 370, 382, 385, 393-394, 429
Cyber Crime 65-67, 72, 76-77
cybersecurity 43-44, 47-48, 52-55, 57, 60-62, 68-69, 91-92, 95, 97-98, 130, 145, 192-193, 290-292, 294-295, 297-299, 308, 313, 397, 413
cyber security 1-3, 5-7, 9, 12, 16-17, 22-26, 30, 32, 34, 37-39, 42-44, 47-48, 54-55, 60, 62, 64-71, 77, 80-81, 86, 95, 97-98, 101, 103, 121-122, 125-126, 217, 289, 315-319, 327, 329-331, 333-336, 338, 341, 362, 385, 391, 395-399, 409, 429-430
cyber threats 24, 38, 42, 44, 47, 60, 129-130, 136, 223, 314, 330

D

Data Mashup 355-357
data mining 35, 51, 54, 69, 76, 155, 292, 301, 352, 355-356, 360, 390

Recommended Reference Books

ISBN: 978-1-5225-8876-4
© 2019; 141 pp.
List Price: $135

ISBN: 978-1-5225-8100-0
© 2019; 321 pp.
List Price: $235

ISBN: 978-1-5225-7847-5
© 2019; 306 pp.
List Price: $195

ISBN: 978-1-5225-6313-6
© 2019; 349 pp.
List Price: $215

ISBN: 978-1-5225-7628-0
© 2019; 281 pp.
List Price: $220

ISBN: 978-1-5225-5855-2
© 2019; 337 pp.
List Price: $185

Ensure Quality Research is Introduced to the Academic Community

Become an IGI Global Reviewer for Authored Book Projects

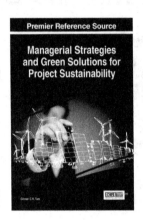

The overall success of an authored book project is dependent on quality and timely reviews.

In this competitive age of scholarly publishing, constructive and timely feedback significantly expedites the turnaround time of manuscripts from submission to acceptance, allowing the publication and discovery of forward-thinking research at a much more expeditious rate. Several IGI Global authored book projects are currently seeking highly-qualified experts in the field to fill vacancies on their respective editorial review boards:

Applications and Inquiries may be sent to:
development@igi-global.com

Applicants must have a doctorate (or an equivalent degree) as well as publishing and reviewing experience. Reviewers are asked to complete the open-ended evaluation questions with as much detail as possible in a timely, collegial, and constructive manner. All reviewers' tenures run for one-year terms on the editorial review boards and are expected to complete at least three reviews per term. Upon successful completion of this term, reviewers can be considered for an additional term.

If you have a colleague that may be interested in this opportunity, we encourage you to share this information with them.

IGI Global Proudly Partners With eContent Pro International

Receive a 25% Discount on all Editorial Services

Editorial Services

IGI Global expects all final manuscripts submitted for publication to be in their final form. This means they must be reviewed, revised, and professionally copy edited prior to their final submission. Not only does this support with accelerating the publication process, but it also ensures that the highest quality scholarly work can be disseminated.

English Language Copy Editing

Let eContent Pro International's expert copy editors perform edits on your manuscript to resolve spelling, punctuaion, grammar, syntax, flow, formatting issues and more.

Scientific and Scholarly Editing

Allow colleagues in your research area to examine the content of your manuscript and provide you with valuable feedback and suggestions before submission.

Figure, Table, Chart & Equation Conversions

Do you have poor quality figures? Do you need visual elements in your manuscript created or converted? A design expert can help!

Translation

Need your documjent translated into English? eContent Pro International's expert translators are fluent in English and more than 40 different languages.

Hear What Your Colleagues are Saying About Editorial Services Supported by IGI Global

"The service was very fast, very thorough, and very helpful in ensuring our chapter meets the criteria and requirements of the book's editors. I was quite impressed and happy with your service."

– Prof. Tom Brinthaupt,
Middle Tennessee State University, USA

"I found the work actually spectacular. The editing, formatting, and other checks were very thorough. The turnaround time was great as well. I will definitely use eContent Pro in the future."

– Nickanor Amwata, Lecturer,
University of Kurdistan Hawler, Iraq

"I was impressed that it was done timely, and wherever the content was not clear for the reader, the paper was improved with better readability for the audience."

– Prof. James Chilembwe,
Mzuzu University, Malawi

Email: customerservice@econtentpro.com

www.igi-global.com/editorial-service-partners

Publisher of Peer-Reviewed, Timely, and
Innovative Academic Research Since 1988

IGI Global's Transformative Open Access (OA) Model:
How to Turn Your University Library's Database Acquisitions Into a Source of OA Funding

In response to the OA movement and well in advance of Plan S, IGI Global, early last year, unveiled their OA Fee Waiver (Offset Model) Initiative.

Under this initiative, librarians who invest in IGI Global's InfoSci-Books (5,300+ reference books) and/or InfoSci-Journals (185+ scholarly journals) databases will be able to subsidize their patron's OA article processing charges (APC) when their work is submitted and accepted (after the peer review process) into an IGI Global journal.*

How Does it Work?

1. When a library subscribes or perpetually purchases IGI Global's InfoSci-Databases including InfoSci-Books (5,300+ e-books), InfoSci-Journals (185+ e-journals), and/or their discipline/subject-focused subsets, IGI Global will match the library's investment with a fund of equal value to go toward subsidizing the OA article processing charges (APCs) for their patrons.

   Researchers: Be sure to recommend the InfoSci-Books and InfoSci-Journals to take advantage of this initiative.

2. When a student, faculty, or staff member submits a paper and it is accepted (following the peer review) into one of IGI Global's 185+ scholarly journals, the author will have the option to have their paper published under a traditional publishing model or as OA.

3. When the author chooses to have their paper published under OA, IGI Global will notify them of the OA Fee Waiver (Offset Model) Initiative. If the author decides they would like to take advantage of this initiative, IGI Global will deduct the US$ 1,500 APC from the created fund.

4. This fund will be offered on an annual basis and will renew as the subscription is renewed for each year thereafter. IGI Global will manage the fund and award the APC waivers unless the librarian has a preference as to how the funds should be managed.

Hear From the Experts on This Initiative:

"I'm very happy to have been able to make one of my recent research contributions, 'Visualizing the Social Media Conversations of a National Information Technology Professional Association' featured in the *International Journal of Human Capital and Information Technology Professionals*, freely available along with having access to the valuable resources found within IGI Global's InfoSci-Journals database."

– Prof. Stuart Palmer,
Deakin University, Australia

For More Information, Visit:

www.igi-global.com/publish/contributor-resources/open-access or
contact IGI Global's Database Team at eresources@igi-global.com.

Printed in the United States
By Bookmasters